Regional Concept:
The Anglo-American Leaders

Regional Concept:
The Anglo-American Leaders

Robert E. Dickinson

Routledge & Kegan Paul
London, Henley and Boston

First published in 1976
by Routledge & Kegan Paul Ltd
76 Carter Lane, London EC4V 5EL,
Reading Road, Henley-on-Thames, Oxon RG9 1EN,
and 9 Park Street, Boston, Mass. 02108, USA
Set in 10/11pt Linotype Times
and printed in Great Britain by
Willmer Brothers Limited, Birkenhead
ISBN 0 7100 8272 X

We sometimes hear of the New Geography but . . . it is more profitable to consider the present position of geography as the outcome of the thought and labours of an unbroken chain of workers, continuously modified by the growth of knowledge, yet old in aim, old even in the expression of the ideas that we are apt to consider most modern.

Hugh Robert Mill

Contents

Preface   xiii

Acknowledgments   xix

1   The background   1
    The Meaning of Geography
    The Development of Modern Geographical Thought
    The Modes of Geographical Analysis
    The Generations of Modern Geographers

PART ONE   THE UNITED KINGDOM

2   A Review   11
    Victorian Antecedents
    Modern Beginnings
    Chairs of Geography in British Universities (H. J. Fleure)
    Recent Growth Trends
    Main Centres
    The Commonwealth
    Changing Viewpoints

3   Patrick Geddes, 1854–1932   27

4   Halford J. Mackinder, 1861–1947   35

5   Andrew J. Herbertson, 1865–1915   43

6   The Second Generation   55
        Herbert John Fleure, 1877–1969
        Percy Maude Roxby, 1880–1947

7   The Third Generation   69
        L. Dudley Stamp: The Man and His Work (R. O. Buchanan)
        Henry Clifford Darby (P. J. Perry)
        Commentary

8   Founders of the Main Centres   87
    I   Edinburgh
        John Murray, 1841–1914 (R. N. Rudmose Brown)
        Marion I. Newbigin, 1869–1934
        George G. Chisholm, 1850–1930 (A. G. Ogilvie)
        Alan G. Ogilvie, 1887–1933 (T. W. Freeman)
    II Cambridge
        Frank Debenham, 1883–1965 (J. A. Steers)
    III London
        Lionel W. Lyde, 1883–1948
                (C. Daryll Forde and Alice Garnett)
        John Frederick Unstead, 1876–1965 (E. W. Gilbert)
        Eva G. R. Taylor, 1879–1966 (G. R. Crone)
        Ll. Rodwell Jones, 1880–1947 (S. W. Wooldridge)
        C. B. Fawcett, 1883–1952 (R. O. Buchanan)
        James Fairgrieve, 1870–1952 (H. J. Fleure)
    IV The Commonwealth Leader: Thomas Griffith Taylor
        Thomas Griffith Taylor, 1880–1963 (J. K. Rose)
        A Personal Appreciation (R. E. Priestley)

9   The Royal Geographical Society   119
        Retrospect, 1830–1930 (H. R. Mill)
        Trends since 1930
        Douglas Freshfield, 1845–1934 (T. G. Longstaff)
        Hugh Robert Mill, 1861–1950 (R. N. Rudmose Brown)

10 Inter-War Trends   135
        The General Trend
        Classifications of Regions of the World
        The Role of Physical Geography:
                J. A. Steers and S. W. Wooldridge

11 Post-War Trends   163
        Models and Paradigms (R. J. Chorley and P. Haggett)
        Organism and Ecosystem as Geographical Models
                (D. R. Stoddart)
        Research in Human Spatial Systems (M. Chisholm)
        Trends in Physical Geography (E. H. Brown)

PART TWO   AMERICA

12   A Review   183
     The Beginnings
     Changing Concepts
     The Major Contributors
     The Main Centres

13   William Morris Davis, 1850–1934   193

14   Mark Jefferson, 1863–1949   209
     A Memorial (I. Bowman)

15   Albert Perry Brigham, 1889–1929 (R. E. Dodge)   218

16   J. Russell Smith, 1874–1966   224
     A Memorial (Dorothy Orchard)

17   The Chicago Sequence   231
     Rollin D. Salisbury, 1858–1922 (S. S. Visher)
     Harlan H. Barrows, 1877–1960
         (C. C. Colby and G. F. White)
     J. Paul Goode, 1862–1933 (W. H. Haas and H. B. Ward)
     Wellington Downing Jones. 1886–1957 (C. C. Colby)
     Charles C. Colby, 1884–1965 (C. D. Harris)
     Robert S. Platt, 1891–1964 (R. Hartshorne)
     Derwent Stainthorpe Whittlesey, 1890–1956 (E. A. Ackerman)

18   Ellen Churchill Semple, 1863–1932 (C. C. Colby)   260

19   Ellsworth Huntington, 1876–1947   269
     A Memorial (S. S. Visher)
     An Appraisal (O. H. K. Spate)

20   The Second Generation   276
     Robert DeCourcy Ward, 1867–1931 (W. M. Davis)
     Curtis Fletcher Marbut, 1863–1935 (H. L. Shantz)
     Charles Warren Thornthwaite, 1899–1963 (J. B. Leighly)
     Douglas W. Johnson, 1878–1944 (J. K. Wright)
     Wallace W. Atwood, 1872–1949 (S. Van Valkenburg)
     Oliver Edwin Baker, 1883–1949 (S. S. Visher and C. Y. Hu)
     Vernor Clifford Finch, 1883–1959 (R. Hartshorne)

21   The American Geographical Society   293
     Isaiah Bowman, 1878–1950 (J. K. Wright)
     John Kirtland Wright, 1891–1969 (M. J. Bowden)

22   Carl Ortwin Sauer, 1889–1975   314
     Environmentalism
     The Reaction: Landscape and Ecology
     The Views of Sauer
     The Chorographic School of Geographers (c. 1930)

23   The Third Generation   327
        Kirk Bryan, 1888–1950 (D. Whittlesey)
        Ralph Hall Brown, 1898–1948 (S. D. Dodge)
        George Babcock Cressey, 1896–1963 (T. Herman)
        John Ewing Orchard, 1893–1962 (O. P. Starkey)
        Preston E. James, 1899–
        John B. Leighly, 1895–
        Glenn Thomas Trewartha, 1896–

24   Post-War Trends in the USA   345
        General Trends
        Field Studies
        Regional Geography
        Regional Science or Quantitative Geographical Analysis
        The Analysis of Spatial Systems
        The Geographical Tradition
        Geographical Education

Conclusion   378

Notes   384

Subject Index   393

Name Index   396

Illustrations

PLATES

1   Patrick Geddes   *Between pages 170 and 171*
2   Halford J. Mackinder
3   Andrew J. Herbertson
4   Herbert John Fleure
5   Percy Maude Roxby
6   L. Dudley Stamp
7   Marion I. Newbigin
8   Alan G. Ogilvie
9   Hugh Robert Mill
10 William Morris Davis
11 Mark Jefferson
12 J. Russell Smith
13 Harlan H. Barrows
14 Wellington Downing Jones
15 Charles C. Colby
16 Wallace W. Atwood
17 Isaiah Bowman
18 Carl Ortwin Sauer

FIGURE

1   The Dimensions of Environment   369

TABLES

1   The Geddes Scheme of Regional Survey   33
2   Leading Departments by Quality of Graduate Faculty   190
3   Leading Departments by Graduate Programmes   191
4   Leading Departments in 1957, 1964 and 1969   191
5   Ph.Ds in Geography in the USA, 1964–6   192
6   The Divisions of the Biosphere   370

Preface

This book is an appraisal of contributions to what has been regarded throughout the development of modern geography over the last 150 years as the core of its field of study. Carl Troll, one of the foremost scholars in Germany and a former president of the International Geographical Union, expressed this view, based upon a phenomenal body of his own research throughout a long career (he died in 1975), in the following words:[1]

> It is in the spirit of the times that over the last three decades there has been a strong trend in geographical study toward a new kind of synthesis. This aims at the evaluation of the spatial interconnections of the forms of the earth's surface in terms of regional integration rather than in reference to any one set of phenomena. The concern of geography, in other words, is not the mechanics of glacial movement, or particular floristic distributions, or the range of particular items of international trade. It seeks to understand the areal interrelation of physical and human spatially-arranged phenomena in terms of the concept of the region.

Stated in 1950, these words refer to the period since about 1920 when the specialized study of geography was first established in universities in both Britain and America. My own summation of this regional concept was expressed in *The Makers of Modern Geography* (1969) as follows: 'The modes of the areal association of phenomena on the earth in terms of localization, and explanation as to origin, composition and spread.' I have since devoted a book to the history, theory and practice of the same concept, entitled *Regional Ecology: The Study of Man's Environment* (1970).

The key word is defined in both standard English dictionaries. The *Oxford English Dictionary* reads: 'A whole formed by the composition or juncture of parts, a framework or system of conjoined parts, a complex structure.' Webster's *Third New International*/American/*Dictionary* reads: 'A structure of many parts united into a functioning whole: a complex structure; especially a large geographic region.' The word so defined is 'compages'. This was used by Derwent Whittlesey in America twenty years ago as the focal concept of regionalism, in order to avoid completely the popular and academic ambiguities of the word 'region'. It is remarkable that this word has not been accepted by Whittlesey's successors, but such conceptually is the precise meaning of the regional concept.

This is the yardstick of relevance in the present book. It is essential at the outset that the intending reader should realize this, since geography, like other fields of study, offers a wide umbrella under which shelter many disciplines concerned with the earth's surface, each with its own goals and historical record, which I have no intention of pursuing. The French geographer C. Vallaux pointed out fifty years ago that the regional concept is the 'autonomous' field of geography. 'Ancillary' fields are drawn upon in so far as they contribute to an understanding of it. This, incidentally, was also one of the most famous aphorisms of Carl Ritter in Germany 150 years ago. New ancillaries include what is currently called 'regional science', as well as geomorphology (a history of which is in progress in Britain in three volumes), plant ecology, atmospheric physics, soil science, and palynology (pollen grain analysis). These rapidly developing fields, each today with highly sophisticated techniques, are needed by, but are subsidiary to, the goals and purpose of the regional concept.

In preparing this book I have drawn heavily upon the writings and appraisals of men who have been leaders of this field of scholarship. Let me state at once, however, that although I draw on obituary notices, death is not a prerequisite for appraisal in these pages. Modern geography, as a university discipline, has developed over the past fifty years. Many of the outstanding leaders are still with us, approaching or in retirement, and it would be quite absurd (as one British reader suggested) to omit their works as leaders. I have lived through this period. After training through the 1920s, I found leadership and guidance in the USA during a session (1931–2) at Chicago and Berkeley. The theory of regions received little systematic attention in Britain at that time, but today the tables are turned. Many American geographers of the present generation—thankfully not all—have discarded the achievements and signposts of their leaders of the last generation, whereas in Britain, particularly in the field of the study of man, attention is being given to the logic and techniques of the regional concept. This will become clear as the reader peruses these pages.

The book is based on a wide reading of the literature for nearly fifty years, and it would be impossible to attempt a bibliography. My assessment, however, will be found in *The Makers of Modern Geography*, to which this book is a sequel, and in *Regional Ecology*. Long verbatim extracts are taken from appraisals by those scholars who were at the time best able to make them. Unnamed sources in the extracts must of necessity stand. I have, however, given the dates of publication of all books, and added where necessary for clarification a personal footnote. Footnotes and other references are deliberately kept to a minimum.

I am grateful to Walter Freeman of Manchester, England, and Preston E. James of Syracuse, NY, for reading the script and making many helpful suggestions and to an anonymous publisher's referee for a very thorough critique of the script, which has resulted in some modification of its arrangement and content. One point, above all, this referee made clear to me. My concern is not with an evaluation of the work of all those who can call themselves geographers. Its standard of relevance is the regional concept and that is the reason for its title. It is my measure of appraisal of the work of contributors, for, as is evidenced throughout its history, this has been the constant and distinctive purpose of geography. Its field of enquiry is of outstanding importance not only in the advancement of knowledge, but also in its relevance to current affairs.

The name of Richard Hartshorne occurs infrequently in these pages, but his thoughts, in both repercussion and parallel, lie behind the whole book. His name should certainly stand as a preeminent leader of the third generation. This omission of direct reference is deliberate, for I have sought throughout my career to make an independent evaluation of what geographers have done and are doing. But I wish now to put it clearly on record that Hartshorne's writings have had a profound and fruitful impact upon current geographic thought, especially in America. I refer, of course, not only to his substantive studies, which in themselves are notable, but also to *The Nature of Geography* (1939) and particularly *Perspective on the Nature of Geography* (1960), which is both shorter and sharper, and to his work on political geography. This is a word of tribute which I prefer to make in the Preface rather than in the text.

Hartshorne supports unequivocally the regional concept as the focus of geographical enquiry. He writes in *Perspective* that 'geography is concerned to provide accurate, orderly, and rational description and interpretation of the variable character of the earth's surface'. This he formulates as a more precise variant of 'the science of areal differentiation' of the earth surface of Sauer and 'the science of the earth surface in terms of its regional differences, i.e. as a complex of continents, lands, districts, and localities' of Hettner, the German scholar. Hettner, following the conceptual framework of von Richthofen, calls this 'the chorological study of the earth surface', meaning 'the existence together and interrelation among the different realms of reality and their varied manifestations'. This is the meaning of the regional concept, the development of which is the purpose of this book (see Postscript on p. xviii).

I must state at the outset the main conclusion drawn from the assessment in *The Makers of Geography* as to what the regional concept is and what it is not. This has been thoroughly discussed in my *Regional Ecology*, and I merely wish to reiterate its main conclusions. This concept is not exclusively concerned with the origins of lakes, coral reefs, or volcanoes; nor with the measurement and chronological development of slopes and terraces. It is, moreover, not exclusively concerned with analysis of the economics of location of industrial plants or commercial establishments, or the exhaustive analysis of the occupational structure of a town; nor with the history of ownership, use, or management of patches of land; nor with the characteristics of use or people in buildings or blocks. It is concerned with the data of such studies in so far as they serve its distinctive ends. These ends are the modes of spatial association of earthbound phenomena, their modes of clustering, and especially their impact on the range and associations of natural, biotic and human phenomena. It searches, in other words, for methods of description of, and processes involved in, the spatial associations of phenomena over the earth's surface. In the realm of human uses of land, it seeks to identify areas with common characteristics that are relevant to human development—existing conditions, current trends, and potentialities, an emphasis that clearly distinguishes it from the objectives of 'regional science' or 'area development' or land management, or resource development. It searches at the local and fundamental level for the smallest unit areas and foci of spatial cohesion—of land, work, economy or social traits.

I have been criticized (in Britain) for an excessive concentration on what is customarily called 'human geography'; and neglect of 'physical geography'. This is due to a misinterpretation of the pur-

pose of the chorological study of the earth, which has been a continuing term and theme in Germany for 100 years. Such critics
would have these fields vaguely defined in the Strabonic tradition
in order to give full latitude to their intellectual pursuits. Unbridled
scope for a single discipline I categorically refuse to accept, unless
an all-embracing 'faculty of geographical sciences' be established,
as is the case in the University of Moscow. Departments in the
Western world become increasingly specialized and expertly narrowed. The criticism noted above is, in fact, entirely misdirected.
Some two-thirds to three-quarters of the face of the earth are
nature's domain, and only about a quarter is man's domain. My
own work has been in the latter area, but the chorological synthesis
of local and worldwide variations of nature's domain also needs
such investigation, not merely the sophisticated analysis of isolated
systematic fragments such as geomorphology or palynology. A
recent contribution in English in this direction without question is
Pierre Dansereau's *Biogeography: An Ecological Perspective* (1957).
Attention is also drawn to A. G. Isachenko, *Principles of Landscape
Science and Physical—Geographic Regionalization* (1973), translated from the original Russian by R. J. Zatorski and edited by a
young American, John S. Massey. There is of course, a fundamental
difference between nature's arrangement of the earth's surface
(chorological), and the actual or potential impact and uses by man
(ecological). The latter is the perspective from the standpoint of
human ecology, and this is one of the most urgent academic and
social problems of environment for expert investigation. It is
amazing how little attention has been given to the discovery and
description of areal differences of human occupance in any part of
the world, although such demands were made in Germany by Penck
fifty years ago, and in Britain by Stamp, and in the USA by Bowman
in the 1930s.

These limitations of the regional concept do not imply criticism
of the scholarly work of colleagues sheltering under the same
academic umbrella. They imply a rigorous standard of measurement and assessment of a concept in the scientific world as well as
in current human affairs, which are matters of the greatest social
significance. The demands of optimum use of land and the arrangement of the human habitat in a world confronted with what the
clichés describe as 'population explosion' and 'environmental
dereliction' must be based on the facts and trends of spatial arrangement and cohesion of human activities. This is the core of the
regional concept, that has been the stimulus to many scholars of

international distinction over the past hundred years. The book is not a discussion of a field of departmentalized study, but an appraisal of the meaning and development of a concept in the light of its outstanding leaders.

Postscript

Having acknowledged the contribution of Hartshorne, it is appropriate to raise several critical comments on his work. His exposition has three main defects. First, he grossly underrates the study of the man-made landscape, as first expounded by J. Brunhes and O. Schlüter and vigorously pursued ever since in France and Germany. Second, he completely ignores the French contribution to geographic thought, as founded by Paul Vidal de la Blache. Third, as a consequence, his emphasis lies on the geographic distribution of associated groups of phenomena, and he fails to confront his readers with the problems and procedures of composite regional study. Regional study, in this last sense, changing in approach, is evidenced by the numerous volumes of the German *Forschungen zu deutschen Landeskunde* and the exhaustive French regional monographs. It involves a threefold burden—scientific, humanistic and literary (writing and cartography). It is best exemplified by Jean Gottmann, a French-trained geographer, long time resident in the United States and now professor in the University of Oxford. His massive books on *Megalopolis* and *Virginia* have drawn wide attention. Hartshorne sowed the seeds of systematic, compartmental, specialization, which has been dominant in Britain and America over the past generation, and the true challenge of the regional concept has been misunderstood and neglected.

P. E. James's *All Possible Worlds* (1972) and E. W. Gilbert's *British Pioneers in Geography* (1972), each dealing with aspects of the same theme, were published after the completion of this manuscript.

ROBERT E. DICKINSON

Acknowledgments

The author and publishers wish to thank the following for permission to reproduce copyright material: the American Geographical Society (extract from the epilogue to *Geography in the Making* by J. K. Wright; the following essays from the *Geographical Review*: 'Mark Jefferson: a memorial' by I. Bowman; 'Douglas W. Johnson' by J. K. Wright; and 'Derwent Stainthorpe Whittlesey' by E. A. Ackerman); the American Geographical Society and Mrs Dorothy Orchard ('J. Russell Smith: a memorial' by D. Orchard); the American Geographical Society and Dr Samuel Van Valkenburg ('Wallace W. Atwood' by S. Van Valkenburg); Associated Book Publishers (two extracts from *Models in Geography* by R. J. Chorley and P. Haggett); the Association of American Geographers (the following essays from *Annals*: 'Principles of geographical description' by W. D. Davis; 'Oliver Edwin Baker' by S. S. Visher and C. Y. Hu; 'Harlan H. Barrows' by C. C. Colby and G. F. White; 'Albert Perry Brigham' by R. E. Dodge; 'Ralph Hall Brown' by S. D. Dodge; 'Kirk Bryan' by D. Whittlesey; 'Charles C. Colby' by C. D. Harris; 'George Babcock Cressey' by T. Herman; 'Robert DeCourcy Ward' by W. M. Davis; 'Robert DeCourcy Ward: an appraisal' by C. F. Brooks; 'Vernor Clifford Finch' by R. Hartshorne; 'J. Paul Goode' by W. H. Haas and H. B. Ward; 'Ellsworth Huntington: a memorial' by S. S. Visher; 'Wellington Downing Jones' by C. C. Colby; 'Curtis Fletcher Marbut' by H. L. Shantz; 'John Ewing Orchard' by O. P. Starkey; 'Robert S. Platt' by R. Hartshorne; 'Rollin D. Salisbury' by S. S. Visher; 'Ellen Churchill Semple' by C. C. Colby; 'Thomas Griffith Taylor' by J. K. Rose; 'Charles Warren Thornthwaite' by J. B. Leighly; and 'John Kirtland Wright' by M. J. Bowden); Professor E. H. Brown (the paper 'Physical geography in Great Britain in the post-1945 era'); Columbia University Press ('Isaiah Bowman' by J. K. Wright in National Academy of Sciences, *Biographical Memoirs*, vol. 33); Professor J. W. Darbyshire (letter p. 66); Eastern Michigan University (*Mark Jefferson: Geographer* by G. J. Martin); the Geographical Association (the following essays from *Geography*: 'Chairs of geography in British universities' by H. J. Fleure; 'Classifications of the regions of the world'; 'James Fairgrieve' by H. J. Fleure; 'Lionel W. Lyde' by C. Daryll Ford and A. Garnett; 'Hugh Robert Mill' and 'John Murray' by R. N. Rudmose Brown; 'Physiogeography: some reflections and trends' by J. A. Steers and S. W. Wooldridge); *Geographische Zeitschrift* and Franz Steiner Verlag, Wiesbaden (extract from 'Henry Clifford Darby' by P. J. Perry); the Institute of British Geographers (extract from the memorial volume *Dudley Stamp: The Man and his Work* by R. O. Buchanan); Professor John Leighly (letter on p. 338); Manchester University Press (extract from *The Geographer's Craft* by T. W. Freeman); Professor R. L. Morrill (extract from a letter, p. 357); National Academy of Sciences (extract from *The Science of Geography*, Publication 1277, *Ad Hoc* Committee on Geography, National Academy of Sciences—National Research Council, Washington DC, 1965); Ronald Press (extract from *Biography: An Ecological Perspective* by P. Dansereau, Copyright © 1957, The Ronald Press Company, New York); the Royal Geographical Society (the following essays from *Geographical Journal*: 'Douglas Freshfield' by T. G. Longstaff; 'Thomas Griffith Taylor: a personal appreciation' by R. E. Priestley; 'Retrospect' by H. R. Mill; 'Ll. Rodwell Jones' by S. W. Wooldridge; 'John Frederick Unstead' by E. W. Gilbert); the Royal Geographical Society and Professor R. O. Buchanan ('C. B. Fawcett' by R. O. Buchanan); the Royal Geographical Society and G. R. Crone Esq. ('Eva G. R. Taylor' by G. R. Crone); the Royal Geographical Society and Professor J. A. Steers ('Frank Debenham' by J. A. Steers); the Royal Scottish Geographical Society (the following essays from the *Scottish Geographical Magazine*: 'Marion Isabel Newbigin' (Anon.) and 'George G. Chisholm' by A. G. Ogilvie); Social Science Research Council (extract from *Research in Human Geography*, edited by M. D. I. Chisholm); University of California Press (extract from *Land and Life: A Selection from the Writings of Carl Ortwin Sauer*, edited by John Leighly, originally published by the University of California Press; reprinted by permission of the Regents of the University of California).

Acknowledgments are also due to the following for permission to reproduce illustrations: Mrs J. Geddes (Plate 1); The Royal Geographical Society (Plates 2, 7 and 9); the School of Geography, University of Oxford (Plate 3); the *Hull Daily Mail* (Plate 4); the

Acknowledgments

University of Liverpool (Plate 5); Bassano Ltd (Plate 6); the Royal Scottish Geographical Society (Plate 8); the American Geographical Society (Plates 10, 11, 12, 15, 16, 17 and 18); Professor G. F. White (Plate 13); Professor N. Ginsberg (Plate 14). Ronald Press (Figure 1 and Table 6); *Sociological Review* (Table 1); American Council of Education (Tables 2, 3 and 4); and *Orbis Geographicus* (Table 5).

1

The Background

THE MEANING OF GEOGRAPHY

The word geography is of Greek origin, and its roots, as a descriptive pursuit and as a mathematical science, are to be found in the works of the great scholars of classical Greece. The word is derived from the Greek word *ge*, meaning the earth, and *grapho,* meaning I write. It literally means, therefore, writing about, or description of, the earth. Its practitioners since the days of the Greek poet Homer have written about the lands and peoples of the inhabited world—the Greek *oecumene*—and speculated about lands and peoples beyond the range of human knowledge. Geography is thus one of the oldest fields of human curiosity and knowledge. As a discipline, it is, like many others, a relative newcomer. Contrary to popular belief, however, its modern development reaches back over 300 years. It is with the modern growth that I shall be concerned in these pages. Preparatory to doing so I shall portray the background during the nineteenth century in respect to the spread of exploration, the development of map-making, and the general development of philosophical thinking.

Geography has often been referred to as the mother of sciences. Fields of knowledge developed in the nineteenth century and gradually hived off. No longer can geography claim to be, as it was named for centuries, 'the science of the earth's surface'. Indeed, aspects of physical geography, such as geomorphology, climatology, plant geography, are now able to stand alone. The position of geography in relation to the social sciences has been given much attention in this century. Environmentalism, ecology, chorology and regional science are synonyms that have been associated with geography in recent years. The field is vast and attracts increasingly more students with diverse interests and qualifications—geologists, meteorologists, botanists, economic historians, social scientists and others. As knowledge and know-how increase, and the narrowly

1

specialized scientific approach becomes more sophisticated, the diversity of interest and competence increases. Historians are confronted with exactly the same problem. It is frankly one that must be accepted as a scientific trend and need of our time. It presents the challenge to look forward rather than to consolidate gains. Certain fields of enquiry need to be released from the parent of geography. The scope, concepts and procedures of the core of geography, the field of problems to which it can uniquely contribute among other scholastic contributions, need to be redefined in terms of distinctive problems. It is time for a thorough stocktaking and a reformulation of the conceptual framework. This is not a question of defining watertight compartments or of what has been called 'arid definition'. It is a question of clarifying content, objectives and expertise. Physical and social scientists want to know what the geographer contributes distinctively to the realm of knowledge.

Geography long claimed as its field the description of all terrestrial phenomena, and there are still those who reproach geographers with the claim of being 'kings of [terrestrial!] space'. This view was still maintained around 1900. Its development over the last 200 years has witnessed the narrowing of this field through the expansion of knowledge and the growth of new daughter sciences, which formerly lay within its sphere. These developments came partly as a result of the scientific progress after the middle of the eighteenth century in science and the humanities. Also, knowledge of the character and distribution of physical and human phenomena throughout the world was greatly increased through the work of scientific explorers. The greatest of these were naturalists such as Alexander von Humboldt; Robert Brown, the botanist who travelled extensively in Australia and collected some 4,000 new species of plants; Charles Darwin, who travelled the world in the *Beagle* (1831–6); Thomas Huxley, the distinguished zoologist; Sir Joseph Hooker, who accompanied Ross to the Antarctic and travelled in northern India (1847–51); and Alfred Russel Wallace, who carried out epoch-making work on the flora and fauna of the Malay Archipelago.

The improvement in cartographic methods, the initiation and, in many civilized countries, the completion of national topographical surveys, the production of maps based on general surveys of the unexplored continental interiors, improvements in astronomical observations and methods of land measurement, and the collection of data under the auspices of governments and learned societies—all these developments resulted in a vast accumulation of facts bearing on all aspects of science, which formed the raw material of the astounding scientific progress of what has been called 'the wonderful century'. There has been amazing progress in the collection of data of the surface of the earth in the twentieth century, in the lifetime indeed of the present writer. The whole of the earth is now mapped—on the ground, from manned aircraft and from satellites. Census reports in states and small units within them are available through national and international agencies. Fieldwork from pole to pole and over the world's oceans has added a mass of data about the location and variations of physical and human phenomena over the earth.

THE DEVELOPMENT OF
MODERN GEOGRAPHICAL THOUGHT

During the first half of the nineteenth century empiricism was the keynote to scientific progress, for two main reasons. First, this is the initial stage in the systematization of new facts, in advance of the deduction of general laws. Secondly, the old idea of the origin of the earth, known as catastrophism, as opposed to the developing view of uniformitarianism, was still generally held. This was reflected in the predominance of the old cosmogony (as opposed to the evolutionary concept) which, based upon the evident adaptation of all forms of life to environment, argued that divine design was responsible for the apparently perfect order and harmony on the earth.

The theory of evolution, preached by Kant and brought to fruition by Darwin and others, breathed new life into the scientific spirit, and in particular it resulted in the introduction of causal as opposed to teleological interpretation into the earth sciences and the humanities. The early twentieth century was characterized by the more critical study of human relations with environment, for it became recognized that man is not a creature of his environment, but, through conscious endeavour, according to his stage of development and social heritage, adjusts himself to it. The interpretation of his adjustment, wrote the geographer Vidal de la Blache, has its core in the small area with a distinct type of environment.

Chorography, to use Ptolemy's term, was still current in geographical parlance at the end of last century. It is still evident in the German term for the smallest geographical unit (*chore* derived from the Greek word *choros*). It is concerned with the explanatory description of the regional (or geographical) variations of the earth's surface. In this sense, as philosophically defined by A. Hettner, the German scholar, geography is a chorological science—that is, it is the regional science. Chorography implies description. But, as von Richthofen asserted eighty years ago, we must seek for areal coincidences and try to explain them. In this sense, the objectives can be described as chorological. This term was first suggested by the German critic F. Marthe in 1877 and was formally incorporated into the conceptual framework of geography by von Richthofen in 1883.

In a century of widening horizons, culminating in the 1860s, it was natural that there should be a prodigious increase in the accumulation of facts about and interpretation of the relations between nature and man. Explorers of all kinds were expanding the realm of knowledge about lands and peoples. Widely dispersed and incredibly long and difficult routes were taken by explorers through uninhabited grassland, desert and forest. It was not until the latter half of the century that the front of close agricultural settlement expanded in America and Australia and, to a more limited extent, in South America and South Africa. It was not until this time that geography as an organized body of knowledge began to take shape, alongside allied disciplines in the natural and social sciences. Indeed, the first major interest of geographical societies founded at this time was to promote exploration and advance the use of the statistics that were being amassed by the new generation of census-takers.

Geography, as the mother of sciences of the earth, after drawing materials and ideas in abundance from explorers and academicians, found it necessary, when emerging as a distinct study around 1900, more rigorously to define its field. The promotion of geography in the last decade of the nineteenth century owed most to geologists and ethnographers. Its range was so catholic that all concerned with lands and peoples—geologists, oceanographers, botanists and ethnographers—either considered themselves 'geographers' or were enlisted, as specialists, by the growing new breed of young geographers. These latter, after the days of Humboldt and Ritter—who in effect were among the great scholars of the pre-evolutionary epoch in the first half of the century—had to put their new house in order so as to establish its position in the realm of knowledge. This was begun in Germany, where speculation on the scope and problems of geography was a subject of concern from the middle of the eighteenth century until our own day, a period of 200 years.

The task for the latter half of the twentieth century is to narrow the scope of geography and clarify its objectives. Its development in the nineteenth century was associated with the collection of data from all quarters of the earth by specialists. As an organized field of modern knowledge, with its roots in the seventeenth and eighteenth

4

centuries, the development of geography is almost exclusively associated with Germany. The claims of Alexander von Humboldt and Carl Ritter, however, were so eclectic and so out of tune with the evolutionary ideas of the 1860s, that for two or three decades thereafter the subject fell into disrepute. In the last decades of the nineteenth century and the early twentieth century, however, geography was firmly established in the universities. The field was adumbrated by some of its greatest fieldworkers: von Richthofen, Friedrich Ratzel, William Morris Davis, Vidal de la Blache, Alfred Hettner and Halford Mackinder. The work of all these men overlapped into the twentieth century. The first generation of university geographers in Europe as well as in America thus dates from the last two decades of the nineteenth century. The field has experienced a prodigious growth in the twentieth century both as an educational medium and as a research discipline.

THE MODES OF GEOGRAPHICAL ANALYSIS

Changes in thought over the past 100 years are reflected in the procedures of geographical analysis in a formidable number of such studies of local areas, continental areas and the world as a whole over the past 100 years. These I have called the environmental approach, the systematic approach, the survey approach, the landscape approach, the ecological approach and the scientific approach. These are basically chronological phases, but they merge into each other, and, as always in human thought and scientific work, the old modes linger and die hard, or are slowly modified.

The environmental approach arose from the Darwinian interpretation of nature and (as developed later by students of man) human societies. Its vocabulary includes 'environmental determinism', and 'controls and influences' of nature over man. It supposed and sought for an almost mechanistic chain of direct cause from particular physical conditions of the human environment to the characteristics and activities of human societies. It continued and prevailed in the Anglo-American world between the wars and was basic to teaching procedures in schools. The approach dies hard and educators are still searching for alternative methods to the study of the human environment.

The systematic approach was concerned with the analysis of the distribution and exploration of *one* set of geographical variables. Such study ranged from a local area to a worldwide pattern. It embraced, as examples, plants, volcanoes, the cross-section of human hair or skin-colour.

The survey approach was associated in Britain with the philosophy and teaching of Patrick Geddes. Instead of being guided by a nature-man approach, it advocated that in any area occupied by man there were three interconnected and interacting elements, like the feet of a tripod—Place, Work and Folk. This approach served as a springboard in research and teaching. It made a profound impact in Britain between the wars, but had a negligible direct influence in America.

There is a close parallel over the same period of time between Geddes's survey approach and the approach in France of what came to be called 'possibilism'. This was a reaction against environmentalism and, in the study of any area, argued that, given a particular natural environment, the occupying people would adjust themselves to it according to their heritage and technology. British geographers referred to this as 'adjustment', but they still clung to the idea that the study of human societies should be limited to the evaluation of relations to the physical earth. It is interesting that this is the main view that Preston James has frequently adumbrated over the past fifty years in America.

The landscape approach came into vogue at the opening of this century. It is now generally accepted in Europe as a basic field of enquiry of geographical research. It seeks to understand the areal variations of the earth's surface in terms of visible associations of phenomena of land, vegetation and the human impact on the natural earth. It is an approach which made a deep impact in Germany and France in the second quarter of this century. It was clarified and given direction by Carl Sauer in America in the mid-1920s. But in both Britain and America it made a negligible, or entirely superficial, impact between the wars. The demands of its scholarship were misunderstood, minimized or even derided. There has been a strong shift towards the study of landscape, however, in Britain over the past twenty-five years, and economic historians have been among its spectacular contributors. In the USA, on the other hand, such study was rejected as unrewarding and since the war very few studies of landscape have appeared. Here a more allegedly 'scientific' approach has virtually reigned supreme.

This scientific approach seeks to develop methods of quantitative analysis and social behaviour to explain what are often described as 'geographical' variables. It is predominantly mathematical in emphasis. It seeks to understand spatial variables and the organization of space. It belittles the geographical analysis of small areas and seeks to arrive ultimately at scientifically accurate generalizations about the modes of human occupance of the earth's surface. Small wonder that it has not made a single contribution to the composite analysis of the land and man's impact upon it in small areas.

The ecological approach is concerned with the earth's surface as the environment of man. It seeks to understand the variations of the earth's natural surface in terms of the modes and potentialities of human occupance. It is concerned, therefore, *not* with the analysis of individual spatial variables, such as the differential distribution of motor-cars, but with the interrelated *composites* of areally distributed phenomena selected and interpreted in the light of man's exploitation and adjustment to the natural environment, and to the man-made environment which he creates. Its beginnings, like that of the ecology of plants and animals, were apparent about fifty years ago. It was especially marked on the Continent in the 1920s, but between the wars made a very small, and usually very obtuse, impact (breaking away from the various forms of environmental determinism) in Britain and America. It is still not clearly embedded in the conceptual procedure of Anglo-Americans. Geography in Britain forges ahead from its traditional roots. In America the majority are dedicated to 'regional science' and have sacrificed their birthright for a mess of potage under the banner of the analysis of geographical variables.

THE GENERATIONS OF MODERN GEOGRAPHERS

The development of thought and of geographical analysis is evidenced in the work of the outstanding makers and their lesser contemporaries. I have traced this progress in continental Europe in *The Makers of Modern Geography*. Here I shall confine attention to the Anglo-American contributors.

Britain had its founders in Halford J. Mackinder, Andrew J. Herbertson and Hugh Robert Mill. These men were professionally active from about the 1880s to the 1920s. A second generation, when honours schools of geography came into being in many British universities, was led by Herbert J. Fleure, Percy M. Roxby and George Chisholm. A third generation, most of whom are in retirement, emerged directly or indirectly from these masters. They had their outstanding contributor in Dudley Stamp, who was knighted by the Queen for his contribution to 'the use of the land'. A fourth generation includes the younger scholars in their forties who have twenty to thirty years of active leadership before them. I shall not refer to their individual work or emphasis, but will confine my comments to selected current trends of which they collectively are the leaders.

In America, geography found its modern roots in the work and stimulus of William Morris Davis, Mark Jefferson, R. D. Salisbury, Ellen C. Semple and J. Russell Smith between the 1880s and 1920s. A second generation was active in the second quarter of this century when, as in Britain, geography was established in the universities. There were many contributors, but quite outstanding were Isaiah Bowman, Ellsworth Huntington and Carl Sauer, the last of whom still engaged in active research and publication until his death in 1975. A third generation, growing from the second but reaching seniority in the third quarter of the century, yields a long list of contributors. Among these, special note should be made of the pupils of Sauer, notably F. Kniffen and S. Dicken; and Glenn T. Trewartha, R. Hartshorne and Preston James, the last of whom came under the spell of Atwood at Harvard. A fourth generation embraces again the younger scholars, such as Brian Berry in the USA (exactly parallel in age and approach to Peter Haggett in Britain).

Part One

THE UNITED KINGDOM

2

A Review

VICTORIAN ANTECEDENTS

This is no place to recapitulate the remarkable advances of human knowledge in the 'wonderful years' that followed the publication of Darwin's *Origin of Species* in 1859. But these affected dramatically the springboard of geographical study. The change in outlook and interpretation of nature and man is reflected in several books that had wide circulation for several decades. Mary Somerville's *Physical Geography* was first published in 1848 and belonged essentially in its ideology to the pre-evolutionary era of the first half of the century. It was the main work in this field in Britain, passing through several editions, with changes in substance appropriate to the rapid march of knowledge in the natural sciences. The last edition appeared in 1877, edited by H. W. Bates, the Secretary of the Royal Geographical Society. It held its pre-eminence until the publication of H. R. Mill's *Realm of Nature: An Outline of Physiography* in 1892.

Mill's compendious tome, written still in the tradition and purpose of Humboldt's *Cosmos*, was preceded in 1877 by T. H. Huxley's *Physiography: An Introduction to the Study of Nature*. This book was based on talks which Huxley gave to schoolchildren from the London area in 1869. He tells us that he used the term 'physiography' to mean the surface features of the earth in preference to the commonly-used term 'physical geography', to which he objected as an '*omnium gatherum* of scraps of all sorts of undigested and unconnected information'. He began his presentation by reference to the children's first-hand observations of the River Thames, and ended with the earth as a member of the solar system.

Physical geography was claimed by geologists. In fact, geologists such as A. Geikie at Edinburgh and Boyd Dawkins at Manchester were the main advocates for introducing it into the university curriculum. Physical geography, however, in the general usage of

B

the time, still included man, as in 'The races of man' in Mill's *Realm of Nature,* although there was no clear conception of what a 'geography of man' should embrace apart from 'distributions'. Ethnographers, like Deniker and Haddon (and W. Z. Ripley in America!), were much occupied in writing about the distribution of racial types of men and their classification, though the first generation of geographers in the universities were quite unclear as to their distinct purpose and problems in the realm of nature, man and area.

The attitude of scholars in this Victorian era to a 'geography of man' can best be evaluated from the notions of the relation between (physical) geography and history as envisaged by the great historians, for they gave the matter much thought. The essays of the German geographer Carl Ritter were published in English in the 1860s in both London and New York. They were mainly pre-evolutionary in concept and teleological in viewpoint, and it is probably for this reason that they wielded little influence on historians. It remains a fact, however, that Ritter adumbrated goals of geographical enquiry that were far ahead of his time and they had a negligible impact on scholars of man. The works of the historians of this period included J. R. Green's *History of the English People* (1877–80), E. A. Freeman's *Historical Geography of Europe* (1881), and C. Lucas's *Historical Geography of the British Colonies* (1888), published in the year following Mackinder's appointment at Oxford. William Hughes of King's College, London, published in 1862 a *Geography of British History* with the subtitle 'A geographical description of the British Islands at successive periods from the earliest times to the present day'. H. B. George of Oxford set out his views in *Relations of Geography and History* in 1901. Thomas Arnold, the Regius Professor of History at Oxford at mid-century, had, says J. N. L. Baker, 'without doubt, the greatest influence on geography' and 'he, like Hakluyt before him [at Oxford] and like Mackinder after him, claimed to preach a new geography'.[1]

All these historians were primarily concerned with the geographical location of historical events, far less with the cause-effect relations of nature and man, though there were extremists among their numbers, like H. T. Buckle. This historian, pursuing the thought of Herbert Spencer and Charles Darwin, wrote in a two-volume *History of Civilization in England* (1857–61) that the history of man was 'in accordance with certain fixed and universal laws' of nature. These natural and physical agents are what he called climate, food, soil and 'the general aspects of nature'. He continued

12

that 'to one of these four classes may be referred all the external phenomena by which man has been permanently affected'.

Against this background of Victorian scholarship one can better evaluate the great contribution to historical geography in Mackinder's *Britain and the British Seas,* a classic that was published in 1902. And it is surely worth noting in conclusion that Mackinder was trained as an undergraduate in history and turned subsequently to what he described at a meeting of the Royal Geographical Society in 1887 as the 'new geography'. The question is, as James puts it, 'What's new?'

MODERN BEGINNINGS

Geography in education—teaching about the physical environment and man's role in it—at the end of the nineteenth century was mainly a matter of memorizing rather than learning. I recall at the age of twelve having private tuition so as to cram for a public school entrance examination (which I failed) and one of my assignments was to learn by heart all the capes and bays of the British Isles, working in a clockwise direction from Land's End. This explains the great importance of T. H. Huxley's lectures in the Kensington Museum for children on the personal observation of the work of nature as a starting point for understanding the wider physical world—what he called physiography. Even though there was a stimulus to the study of nature, in accordance with the new concepts of evolution there was no genuine understanding of the scope of the life of mankind on the earth, and, therefore, how to present it in education. Yet this was a great era of exciting exploration and discovery, and the accumulation of scientific data about the lands, peoples and seas of the world. John Scott Keltie's report to the Royal Geographical Society in 1884, concerning the teaching of geography on the Continent, led to appointments in Oxford and Cambridge. Mackinder when at Oxford in the 1890s played a great part, together with his young colleague A. J. Herbertson, and H. R. Mill, then the librarian of the Royal Geographical Society, in the promotion of geography in schools and in the foundation of an association of teachers of geography in schools.

Following on Keltie's report and recommendations, courses in geography were introduced at Oxford and Cambridge, and later at London, Manchester and Edinburgh. There were no degrees in the subject, only some kind of diploma. This was the state of affairs in 1893, the year in which the Geographical Association was founded, primarily under the guidance of B. B. Dickinson from the public school of Rugby. The first concern of this small organization was to collect lantern slides for use in schoolteaching for exchange among schoolmasters, who, at this time, were virtually all teachers in public schools. They were soon obliged to turn their attention to examinations in geography. They suggested that 'physical geography' should be the basis. It should be reiterated here that at this time physical geography was still envisaged, as it was by Humboldt, as embracing mankind. This is evident in the content of the textbooks on physical geography that appeared in both Britain and the USA around 1900. The most distinguished of them all in Britain was H. R. Mill's *Realm of Nature,* which followed almost exactly the same procedure as Humboldt's *Cosmos.* The place of a geography of man had still to be worked out in the following years. The same procedure is found in school and college texts in both Britain and America, certainly throughout the first quarter of this century, and it is a procedure that dies hard indeed among students of the earth sciences.

Geography owed its growth not only to the support of the Royal Geographical Society, but also to certain geologists and 'ethnographers'. In both Britain and the USA, almost all the first university geographers were trained experts in geology.

In 1899 the building of the school of geography at Oxford was organized under Mackinder. As assistants he had A. J. Herbertson, H. N. Dickson and G. B. Grundy, who offered courses on 'physical' and 'ancient' geography. Herbertson became the general secretary of the Geographical Association in 1900, succeeding B. B. Dickinson, and began forthwith the publication of a magazine for teachers, the *Geographical Teacher.* The membership of the association increased from 500 in 1905 to 1,000 in the 1910s and to 4,500 in the mid-1920s. It is now not far short of 10,000.

Geography grew in the universities from the beginnings just noted. Lionel Lyde, a classics scholar, became the first Professor of Geography in University College, London, in 1903, although George Chisholm had been doing extension teaching at Birkbeck College since 1895. Mackinder was appointed to Oxford in 1887, becoming lecturer in geography at the London School of Economics in 1895, the year of its foundation. He was appointed director of the school in 1903. In 1908 he left this post to become reader in geography and received the status of professor in 1923. He retired from academic life in 1925, though he long continued as a prominent public servant on various royal commissions. At

Cambridge the first appointment, supported, as at Oxford, by the Royal Geographical Society, was made in 1888. A Board of Studies in Geography was formed in 1903; its subsequent developments are discussed in a later chapter. J. MacFarlane (a graduate of Edinburgh) was appointed at Manchester in 1903, though he moved to Aberdeen in 1918. H. N. Dickson, a climatologist (also a graduate of Edinburgh), left Oxford to become a lecturer at Reading in 1904. P. M. Roxby left Oxford for Liverpool in the same year. H. J. Fleure was transferred from zoology to geography at Aberystwyth in 1907. G. G. Chisholm, lecturing at Birkbeck College since 1895, was appointed head of a new department at Edinburgh in 1908. J. F. Unstead followed Chisholm at Birkbeck in 1909 (after a year of service by Lyde), and became Professor of Geography in 1922 until an early retirement in 1930. R. N. Rudmose Brown was appointed to Sheffield in 1908. Though these men and others following them held posts as geographers, there was only one chair, held by Lyde at University College, London. Herbertson's distinction was tardily recognized at Oxford by his appointment to a personal chair. H. O. Beckit became the new head following the death of his chief and carried the title of Reader. Roxby was promoted to a new endowed chair in 1916 at Liverpool and Fleure was appointed to a combined chair of geography and anthropology at Aberystwyth in 1917. Immediately the first specialized honours degrees in geography were established by both these two men. Similar honours degrees were established within several years in other universities.

With the death of Herbertson, H. J. Fleure became the general secretary of the Geographical Association, which remained the primary forum, at its annual meetings and field courses, of teachers both in schools and universities until the establishment of the professional Institute of British Geographers in 1933. Fleure established a series of biennial Herbertson Memorial Lectures. In 1926 the name of the journal was changed to *Geography*. In 1947 Dr Alice Garnett became secretary and D. L. Linton editor of the journal. The Geographical Association has served the interests of the school for over seventy years. The Institute is the professional parallel of the Association of American Geographers, although the British group came into being thirty years after its American counterpart.

CHAIRS OF GEOGRAPHY IN BRITISH
UNIVERSITIES, *by H. J. Fleure*[2]

1903—University of London, University College. L. W. Lyde was appointed Professor of Economic Geography. Captain Maconochie had held a professorship of geography during 1833–6 and was the first Professor of Geography in the UK. C. B. Fawcett became Professor of Economic Geography in 1928; his title was changed to 'Professor of Economic and Regional Geography' in 1931 and to 'Professor of Geography' in 1944. H. C. Darby became Professor of Geography in 1949. Honours courses in geography for the degrees of B.A. and B.Sc. were instituted in 1919. Courses in geography for the degree of B.Sc. (Econ.) were instituted in 1912.

1917—University of Liverpool. P. M. Roxby was appointed John Rankin Professor of Geography and honours courses in geography for the degree of B.A. were instituted. Roxby had been an assistant lecturer in the subject from 1905 and a lecturer from 1908. He resigned in 1944; H. C. Darby was professor from 1945 to 1949 and Wilfred Smith from 1950 to 1955. R. W. Steel became professor in 1957. B.Sc. honours degrees were instituted in the session 1953–4.

1917—University College of Wales, Aberystwyth. H. J. Fleure was appointed Gregynog Professor of Geography and Anthropology. He had been lecturer in charge of the subject since 1907. Honours courses for the degrees of B.A. and B.Sc. were instituted in 1918. C. D. Forde became professor in 1930 and E. G. Bowen in 1946.

1922—University of London, London School of Economics. Sir H. J. Mackinder was appointed Professor of Geography. The subject had been taught for the B.Sc. (Econ.) and for the Academic Diploma in Geography by an independent reader since 1900, and an honours school in the faculty of arts was instituted in 1918 jointly with King's College. In 1925 L. Rodwell Jones succeeded Mackinder as professor and was himself succeeded in 1945 by L. Dudley Stamp. In 1949 Stamp was translated to the chair of social geography (a new chair) and R. O. Buchanan became Professor of Geography. In 1958 when Stamp retired, the chair of social geography was not filled, and M. J. Wise was appointed to a new chair of geography. Buchanan retired in 1961 and was succeeded in the chair of geography by Emrys Jones.

1922—University of London, Birkbeck College. J. F. Unstead was appointed Professor of Geography. He had been lecturer and head of department since 1920. Eva G. R. Taylor became professor in 1930, S. W. Wooldridge in 1944 and W. G. East in 1947.

1927—University of Exeter (then University College of the South-West). W. Stanley Lewis was appointed to the Reardon Smith Chair of Geography. He had been lecturer and head of department since 1920, following W. W. Jervis. P. W. Clayden had lectured in geography at an earlier period. Honours courses were instituted for University of London degrees in the faculties of arts, science and economics in 1922. Arthur Davies became professor in 1948.

1930—University of Manchester. H. J. Fleure was appointed Professor of Geography. A lectureship in political and commercial geography was established in 1892, held first by H. Yule Oldham and later by A. J. Herbertson (1894–6). J. McFarlane was lecturer in economic and political geography (1903–8) and lecturer in geography (1908–19). A. G. Ogilvie and W. H. Barker were readers and heads of the department from 1919 to 1920 and from 1922 to 1929 respectively. Honours courses in the faculty of arts were instituted under W. H. Barker in 1923. W. Fitzgerald was professor from 1944 to 1949. P. R. Crowe became professor in 1953.

1931—University of Cambridge. F. Debenham was appointed Professor of Geography. F. H. H. Guillemard (lecturer, 1888), H. Yule Oldham (lecturer, then reader, 1889–1908), P. Lake (reader and head of department, 1919–27) and F. Debenham (1927–31) had previously had charge of the subject. Examinations in geography for the ordinary B.A. degree and for the diploma in geography were established in 1903; honours courses were instituted in 1919. J. A. Steers became professor in 1949.

1931—University of Sheffield. R. N. Rudmose Brown was appointed Professor of Geography. He had been lecturer and head of department since 1908. Honours courses in the faculty of science were instituted in 1924, in arts in 1926 and in economic and social studies in 1961. D. L. Linton was professor from 1945 to 1958 and C. A. Fisher became professor in 1959.

1931—University of Edinburgh. A. G. Ogilvie was appointed Professor of Geography. G. G. Chisholm (1908–29) and A. G. Ogilvie (1929–31) had previously been lecturers and heads of department. Honours courses in the faculty of arts were instituted in 1930 and a postgraduate diploma (post-M.A.) course was established in 1958. J. W. Watson became professor in 1954.

1932—University of Oxford. K. Mason was appointed as first statutory Professor of Geography; the chair was attached to

Hertford College. H. J. Mackinder had had charge of the subject, as reader in geography, between 1887 and 1905. A school of geography, with three members of staff, was established in 1899, the first in Britain. The offices of reader in geography and director of the school were held by A. J. Herbertson (1905–15) and by H. O. Beckit (1919–31). A. J. Herbertson also held the personal title of professor from 1910 until his death in 1915. The honours school of geography was established in 1932. E. W. Gilbert became the second statutory Professor of Geography in 1953.

1933—University of Bristol. W. W. Jervis was appointed Professor of Geography. He had been lecturer and head of department since 1924 and reader since 1926. Honours courses for the degree of B.A. were instituted in 1924 and for the degree of B.Sc. in 1932. R. F. E. W. Peel became professor in 1957.

1943—University of Reading. A. A. Miller was appointed Professor of Geography. He had been independent lecturer since 1936 and joint lecturer in charge between 1926 and 1936. H. N. Dickson had been Professor of Geography from 1907 to 1920. Sir H. J. Mackinder had lectured in geography when he was Principal of University College, Reading; he resigned in 1903. Honours courses were instituted in the faculty of arts in 1926 and in the faculty of science in 1929.

1943—University of Durham, King's College, Newcastle-upon-Tyne. G. H. J. Daysh was appointed Professor of Geography. He had been lecturer in charge of the department, which was founded in 1928, since 1930 and reader from 1939. Honours courses for the degrees of B.A. and B.Sc. were instituted in 1930.

1944—University of Leeds. A. V. Williamson was appointed Professor of Geography; he had been head of the department since 1928. Ll. Rodwell Jones was assistant lecturer in geography in the department of economics, 1912–19, and C. B. Fawcett was head of the department of geography, 1919–28. The department was founded in 1919 with an honours school in the faculty of arts; an honours school in the faculty of science was added in 1954. R. F. E. W. Peel was professor from 1953 to 1957 and R. E. Dickinson became professor in 1958.

1945—Queen's University of Belfast. E. Estyn Evans was appointed Professor of Geography. He had been independent lecturer since the foundation of the department in 1928 and was made reader in 1944. Honours courses for the degree of B.A. were instituted in 1931 and for the degree of B.Sc. in 1935.

1947—University of Glasgow. A. Stevens was appointed Professor of Geography. He had been lecturer and head of department since 1918. The department was founded in 1909 and previous heads of department were H. G. Lyons and J. D. Falconer. Honours courses for the degree of B.Sc. were instituted in 1912 and for the degree of M.A. in 1947. R. Miller became professor in 1953.

1947—University of London, King's College. S. W. Wooldridge was appointed Professor of Geography. He had been lecturer in charge of the subject in 1925–44. W. Hughes had been Professor of Geography 1863–76 and H. G. Seeley was Professor of Geography 1876–96 and of Geography and Geology 1896–1909. T. F. Sibly succeeded to the headship of the department of geology in 1908 and W. T. Gordon became Professor of Geology and administrative head of the department of geography when joint work with the London School of Economics began in 1918. The present department was founded in 1920 and honours courses for the degrees of B.A. and B.Sc. were instituted in 1921.

1948—University of London, Bedford College. Gordon Manley was appointed Professor of Geography. Miss B. Hosgood had been lecturer, then reader (1923), and head of the department since its foundation in 1919 when honours courses for the degree of B.A. were instituted. Honours courses for the degree of B.Sc. were begun in 1925.

1948—University of Birmingham. R. H. Kinvig was appointed Professor of Geography. He had been reader and head of department since its institution in 1924. Honours courses in the faculty of arts were instituted in 1926, in the faculty of science in 1938 and in the faculty of commerce and social science in 1946. D. L. Linton became professor in 1958.

1949—University of Nottingham. K. C. Edwards was appointed Professor of Geography. He had been independent lecturer in geography since 1934, and reader and head of department since 1939. Honours courses were instituted in the University College of Nottingham for University of London B.A. and B.Sc. degrees in 1924 when Professor Swinnerton was made head of the department in addition to his previous responsibility as Professor of Geology. Honours courses were included in the faculty of law and social science in 1958.

1950—University College of North Staffordshire. S. H. Beaver was appointed Professor of Geography. The department was set up when the University College was founded and honours courses for the degree of B.A. in the groups humanities, social studies and science were instituted at the same time.

1951—University of Aberdeen. A. C. O'Dell was appointed

Professor of Geography. He had been lecturer and head of department since 1945. The department was founded in 1919 with J. MacFarlane as lecturer, later reader, and head of department. Honours courses for the degrees of M.A. and B.Sc. were instituted in 1922.

1954—University of Southampton. F. J. Monkhouse was appointed Professor of Geography. The department was founded in 1913 in the University College of Southampton and its successive heads of department have been C. B. Fawcett (1913–20), W. H. Barker (1920–2), O. H. T. Rishbeth (1922–38) and Miss F. Miller (1938–54). Honours courses were instituted for University of London B.A. and B.Sc. degrees about 1918.

1954—University College of Swansea, University of Wales. W. G. V. Balchin was appointed Professor of Geography. Geography had been taught in the college from its foundation in 1920, first in the department of geology by A. E. Trueman and S. W. Rider. The first full lecturer in charge of geography in a newly named department of geology and geography was D. Trevor Williams (1931–46), followed by B. H. Farmer (1946–8) and J. Oliver (1948–54). Honours courses for the degrees of B.A. and B.Sc. were instituted along with the creation of a separate department of geography in 1954.

1954—University of Hull. H. King was appointed Professor of Geography; he had been head of department since 1928. Honours courses for University of London B.A. and B.Sc. degrees were instituted in the University College of Hull in 1928; and for the B.A. and B.Sc. degrees of the University of Hull in 1954. H. R. Wilkinson became professor in 1958.

1954—University of Leicester. N. Pye was appointed Professor of Geography. P. W. Bryan had been appointed lecturer in the University College of Leicester in 1922 and was made professor in 1953. Honours courses for the University of London degrees of B.A. and B.Sc. were instituted in 1922 and 1925 respectively. Honours courses for the degree of B.A. in the social sciences began in 1957.

1956—University of Durham, Durham Colleges. W. B. Fisher became professor. G. Manley (1928–38) and L. Slater (1938–47) successively held the position of lecturer, the latter also as reader (1947–53) in charge of the subject. W. B. Fisher was appointed reader in 1953. The department was founded in 1928 and the honours school was instituted in the faculty of arts in 1930 and in the faculty of science in 1934.

1961—University of London, Queen Mary College. The personal

title of Professor of Geography was given to A. E. Smailes in 1955 but his chair of geography was established in 1961. He had been reader since 1953. P. R. Crowe held a readership created in 1947 until 1953. Before 1947, geology and geography were in a combined department under H. G. Smith. Honours courses for the degrees of B.A. and B.Sc. were instituted in 1921.

The University of St Andrews has lecturers in geography who are heads of departments respectively at St Salvator's College, St Andrews (Kathleen M. McIver), and at Queen's College, Dundee (S. J. Jones). Honours courses in geography for the degree of M.A. were instituted at St Salvator's College in 1949 and at Queen's College in 1956, and in the latter college in the faculty of social science in 1961.

RECENT GROWTH TRENDS[3]

There has been a remarkable growth in geography of both research and teaching since the 1930s. The enrolment of the Institute of British Geographers when founded in 1933 was 39, but had soared to 1,255 by 1969. The membership of the Geographical Association, which embraces both university and schoolteachers (with the latter in large majority) grew from 3,000 in 1950 to 8,500 in 1968. There were some 500 staff members in departments in British universities in 1969, whereas the total was certainly not in excess of 50 in the early 1930s. The number of students at postgraduate level in Britain increased from 273 in 1959–60 to 571 in 1966–7. The total number of degrees in geography awarded in 1959–60 was 704 and in 1966–7 reached 1,184. Studentships (research grants of various kinds) reached 114 in 1969. Such is the record of growth, with a much accelerated tempo in the last decade.

There are now 37 departments of geography in all British universities and many others in colleges of various categories. The university departments have an average of about 15 staff members. Many now have two chairs, one usually in human geography, and the other in physical geography (normally geomorphology).[1]

A still more recent and comprehensive report by S. Gregory and J. W. House has been published in *Area* for 1973. It concerns students for higher degrees from 1967 to 1971. Information came from 37 university departments of geography for research degrees

(Ph.D., M.A. and M.Sc.) *completed* during these five calendar years. The total was 397, three-quarters of whom were British. Two facts stand out. First, a considerable proportion (nearly a third) moved directly to posts overseas. Second, half the Ph.D.s, and a quarter of other research degrees, were in physical geography, and half in geomorphology. Urban geography *alone* stands out from the other branches of human geography.

Masters degrees embraced 254 awards from 13 departments. Nearly half came from London. Fields of study embraced physical geography (a quarter) and 42 per cent in what is described as 'planning' (meaning urban, applied and resources). The graduates moved into high school teaching, further research, or 'planning'. Nearly a quarter took posts overseas.

This record of status may be compared with the USA.[4] It should be recalled that America has four times the population of Britain, and that it is much easier to study for a higher degree there. The number of departments in 1967–8 was 351 (ten times the British number). There were 120 graduate programmes (many, I suspect, on paper only). Higher degrees awarded in 1967 were: masters 463, doctorates 79, bachelors 2,163. A projection for 1977 puts the total doctorates at 427 among 45 departments (11 of these being classed as 'distinguished' or 'strong').

In order to reach a fair Anglo-American comparison, we must divide the British figures by five. This gives about 80 doctorates a year, which is roughly the same as in the USA, with a tenth of its places of university study. Such is the difference in attainment between the two countries. Britain has evidently a surplus of expertise. America has a shortage of numbers and quality. The physical specialists are few and weak in America, strong in Britain, for geography in America is generally regarded as a 'behavioural' or 'social science'.

MAIN CENTRES

What is the comparative status of departments of geography as seats of scholarship and teaching? This is an invidious, but necessary, exercise. As we shall later learn, such evaluations have been made on several occasions in the USA by highly reputable authorities using methods that are as objective as such appraisals can be. These American ratings are based on the listing of the number of higher degrees awarded, and on a subjective choice by well-informed persons on the relative scholarly standing of departments as seats of higher learning. It is impossible singlehanded to attempt a similar appraisal for Britain, though it needs to be done for the guidance of the increasing number of students at all levels. However, I have adopted a simple and direct procedure of assessment by working though the index of names and standing of university geographers in the *Orbis Geographicus*.[5] (It should be noted, however, that this directory excludes those who carry higher degrees, who are in business or government of some kind.) I include the masters degrees, though these vary very much in meaning from one university to another. Included are all the Ph.Ds, D. Phils (Oxford) and B. Litts (Oxford). Names of several outstanding younger scholars are for some reason omitted from the Orbis Geographicus.

According to this directory, in the early 1960s there were 151 persons who held doctorates, the overwhelming majority of which had been awarded during the preceding twenty years. Out of this total, 63 were conferred by the University of London. There is no consistent specification of the college in London in which the candidates studied, but the School of Economics (together with King's College) is the dominant centre. This aggregate is followed by the University of Cambridge, which has 18 awards, but with the addition of the missing names would undoubtedly rise to 20. Oxford follows with 8 B.Litts and 5 D.Phils, ranging (unlike the others) over a period of fifty years. A full record received from the London Joint School (London School of Economics and King's) reveals the award of 127 Ph.Ds and three D.Scs (the higher doctorate) during the period 1924–71. The latter were awarded to S. W. Wooldridge, Hilda Ormsby and L. Dudley Stamp. About one third of the Ph.Ds were awarded to foreign students, mainly from India, Pakistan and West Africa.

The holders of masters degrees, M.A. and M.Sc., total 229. The breakdown by universities has some interesting features. Cambridge, with 60, had by far the biggest number. The whole of the University of London, however, totalled only 37, which is under half of the doctorate awards. Oxford comes next with 26, the University of Wales fourth with 17, Liverpool with 15 and Edinburgh with 10. The remaining universities conferred only several masters degrees each. This basis alone, disregarding the merits of the faculty as productive researchers, gives a basis of assessment of the relative strength of the main centres.

THE COMMONWEALTH

There has been a remarkable growth of geography in the universities of the Commonwealth since the end of the Second World War.

As a springboard it may be noted that the number of departments in British universities is today 37, and the total listing of geographers given in *Orbis Geographicus 1968–72* (the source of the data that follow), reached nearly 500. By way of comparison, Australia has 14 departments and 175 geographers; Canada, 37 departments and 199 geographers; India, 44 departments and 129 geographers; Pakistan, 6 departments and 25 geographers; the Union of South Africa (though no longer a Commonwealth member, it should definitely be included here), 10 departments and 37 geographers; New Zealand, 10 departments and 52 geographers. This list includes a few colleges of education and two or more departments in one university (as at Canberra).

Almost all of these geographers received their degrees in British universities, and particularly noticeable is the large contribution of the University of London (especially the School of Economics and King's College) to the Indian quota. This is truly a Commonwealth diffusion, and it embraces many other Commonwealth countries, from Trinidad through West Africa to Hong Kong. There has, moreover, been a remarkable upsurge of new departments in the 1960s, especially in Canada. There was a wave of new departments immediately after the war (1945–56) but very few were founded in the interwar period. These older departments should be noted, for they are the senior members of a worldwide fraternity. Australia's first department in the University of Sydney was founded in 1920 under the leadership of Griffith Taylor. Canada had its earliest department at Toronto, founded in 1935, again under the headship of Taylor, after he had spent a few years at the University of Chicago. Five departments were founded immediately after the war, at McGill (Montreal) in 1945, Western Ontario in 1946, University of Montreal (French) in 1947, Laval, Quebec (French) in 1946 and Carleton in 1950. Especially significant was the foundation at Laval, since it was launched and frequently visited by R. Blanchard from France, who during his sojourn carried out quite remarkable geographical work on French Canada. Today the institute at Laval is one of the most prestigious in the university and its researches are closely associated with sub-Arctic (Nordic) studies. It retains close associations with French geographers, without, however, as in other affairs, losing its own identity. McGill also started at this time under the leadership of G. H. T. Kimble, who shortly moved to the directorship of the American Geographical Society for a short time, and thence to the University of Indiana. He was followed by K. F. Hare, a Wooldridge man from London, who moved for a short period to his Alma Mater, but returned to

Canada, first as President of the University of British Columbia, and then to the academic fold of the University of Toronto as Professor of Climatology. Special mention should be made of the three departments in French Canada with a very strong French connection (Laval, Montreal, Sherbrooke), but with, however, a weak association with their English-speaking colleagues to whom they could offer so much as a bridgehead with metropolitan France.

The Union of South Africa has several of the oldest departments in the Commonwealth. These are at the universities of the Orange Free State, Witwatersrand, Natal, Pretoria and Stellenbosch: all have roots in the early 1920s. A department in the University of Cape Town was founded in 1936. India had its first department at the University of Benares in 1946, Pakistan at the University of the Punjab (Lahore) in 1944 and at Dacca in 1947. New Zealand is a flourishing seat of geography with distinguished leaders. The oldest department was founded at the University of Canterbury, Christchurch, in 1937, but immediately after the war new departments were founded at Auckland, Otago and Wellington. The University of Tasmania also made its addition.

There are today nearly 100 departments of geography in colleges and universities throughout the Commonwealth, excluding the UK. These include the older dominions and range from Jamaica and Trinidad through Africa and Southern Asia to Fiji. Though primarily concerned with basic teaching, their common interests are cared for by the Commonwealth Geographical Bureau. It is also notable that the first Commonwealth Conference, held in Ghana in September 1970, had as its theme 'Geography and economic development in West Africa'.

CHANGING VIEWPOINTS

There have undoubtedly been big changes of viewpoint in the field of geography in Britain over the past fifty years, but it is difficult to pin them down to specific leading statements. The main trends, which are typical of the pragmatic approach of British scholarship, should be found most clearly evident in the work and discourses of leading exponents. The first university geographers had to put their house in some kind of order and there were a number of published statements around 1900. The most stimulating and indicative of scope and trends were two lectures delivered before the Royal Geographical Society, the first by H. J. Mackinder on the 'scope and method of geography' in 1887, and the second by the

American W. M. Davis on 'a scheme of geography' in 1903. Thereafter, in the 1930s there were three particularly noteworthy statements, by H. R. Mill, H. J. Mackinder and P. M. Roxby, the last being exclusively concerned with the field of human geography. The exposition of Sauer in 1925 did not make the slightest impact and R. Hartshorne's *Nature of Geography,* published in 1939, caused some attention, though this was delayed by the war years when most geographers were otherwise occupied in action, Intelligence or civil defence. However, during the interwar years the vague notions of adjustment and possibilism in respect to man's environment held the field, and the idea of land-man relationships predominated over concern with places and their spatial arrangement across the earth's surface. The conceptual framework was normally considered to be outside the dignity of a serious scholar and it was positively indecent to subject a learned research presentation to a methodological diagnosis.

In these years, three viewpoints were prevalent. The first sought to clarify the 'modes of adjustment' of human activities to the physical environment; environmental determinism on the Davis model died hard, in both school and university. The second examined the operation of natural processes in the formation of landscape features, and was, and remains, closely affiliated to geology. A third, which gradually asserted itself in the 1930s, was the delineation of physical and economic entities on the earth's surface (Unstead and Wooldridge, Chapter 10). There is also clear and refreshing evidence that Frank Debenham, and his colleagues at Cambridge, were concerned with the significance of place— geography as 'philosophy of place', the character of places and their associations as landscape elements of the earth's surface (see Chapter 8). Unfortunately this group pursued their studies in academic seclusion and published little. The gist of their teaching in the classroom is indicated by the series of books edited by Frank Debenham in the early 1950s.

Since the war the dominant trend has been towards a more scientific approach in the physical, biotic and human fields, in terms of natural and human processes, although one frequently gets the impression that the emphasis is given to understanding the process and its working rather than its spatial impact over the earth's surface on a local or worldwide scale. These new viewpoints are suggested in Chapter 11 by excerpts from the writings of their leading younger exponents.

3

Patrick Geddes, 1854-1932

The founder of geography as a university study was Halford J. Mackinder. But the source of many of the ideas of the relationship between man and environment was Patrick Geddes, and his ideas demand attention as a background to the modern growth of geography in Britain. Contemporaries who owed a great deal to him were A. J. Herbertson, H. R. Mill, J. Scott Keltie and G. G. Chisholm. Herbert J. Fleure was also among this group and he became the leading geographer in Britain in the first half of this century so that it is appropriate to include a brief appraisal of the work of Geddes.

Patrick Geddes, 'a pioneer of the study of society as a framework of regional survey', was one of the most dynamic and resourceful figures of his generation and made a profound impact on the thinking of his day. Many are the links between Geddes's ideas and the conceptual framework of the French scholars Frédéric Le Play and Élisée Reclus. He also greatly influenced the foremost British town planners, Raymond Unwin and Patrick Abercrombie in particular, and several young men who became leading geographers—H. J. Mackinder, H. J. Fleure, P. M. Roxby and C. B. Fawcett. All these men were strongly influenced by both Le Play (who died in 1882, before their time) and Geddes (who first met E. Demolins in 1883 in Paris). All met and worked with Geddes and came under his spell and shared his attitude to social problems. Geddes has his greatest living disciple in Lewis Mumford, an American social philosopher. Mumford's major works reveal again and again the basic ideas of Geddes: 'Geddes gave me the framework of my thinking: my task has been to put flesh on his abstract skeleton.' The present writer, as a student of C. B. Fawcett and in close contact with Roxby's school at Liverpool from 1922 to 1925, was nurtured on Geddes and Demolins, and as an undergraduate was introduced to the works of P. Kropotkin, H. G. Wells, Frédéric Le Play and Graham Wallas. The same was true, I believe, of the schools of geography established at the time by Roxby and Fleure. It is therefore important in the development of modern geography to appreciate the work of Geddes and its repercussions.

Geddes was by training a biologist. He was a student under the great T. H. Huxley—another thread of continuity—and there is not the slightest doubt that Geddes's notions of 'physiography' and of 'regional survey' were derived from the ideas of his master. In the early 1880s he carried out biological work of various kinds in France (where he met Demolins, the social geographer, and Flahault, the botanist), Mexico (where apparently he cultivated the practice of devising 'thinking machines' during a long spell of eye trouble when he was confined to a dark room) and Naples. He returned to Scotland to become demonstrator in botany in the University of Edinburgh and stayed there for nine years. He was invited to the chair of botany at the University of Dundee, where he remained until his retirement, although the university placed no limits on his absence provided that he appeared for a few months of lecturing at regular intervals.

While in Edinburgh he purchased an old tower building in 1892 and established in it the first geographical museum, with a *camera obscura* on the top floor reflecting the city and its environs, and exhibitions of Scotland, Europe and the world on the floors beneath. It began with the local area and, working outwardly to a world view, exhibited the conditions of life in terms of Place, Work and Folk. He also initiated the idea of summer courses for mature scholars, and among his helpers were A. J. Herbertson, J. Arthur Thomson, the biologist and his lifelong collaborator, Victor Branford, banker and social philosopher, Élisée Reclus, a geographer already in advanced years and a political exile from France, and Peter Kropotkin, a social philosopher from Russia. The Outlook Tower was a museum in which the idea of 'regional survey' was put into action and Geddes himself guided visitors from 1895 to 1914. Amongst other material, the exhibits included maps, diagrams, graphs and photographs. Their arrangement was prepared with the help of A. J. Herbertson, who was Geddes's assistant at Dundee before going to Oxford under Mackinder. Help was also given there by Pierre Reclus, the son of Élisée Reclus. The Outlook Tower was described at that time as 'the world's first sociological laboratory'. It was, without question, as anyone who has visited it will testify, the first geographical museum. (It has been repaired since 1945 under the supervision of Geddes's son Arthur, a geographer in the University of Edinburgh, now retired.) This exhibit had tremendous repercussions on the teaching of geography, nature study, civics and town planning. In 1900 Geddes organized at the Paris Exhibition an international school for scholars, and established a temporary Outlook Tower for a period of five months. In 1902 he was eagerly promoting the idea of a National Institute of Geography. This would have been a geographical museum on the same lines, for which he sought to raise funds for the erection of a globe, 80 feet in diameter, designed by Élisée Reclus. This was what he described as one of his 'magnificent failures'.

During the 1900s Geddes transferred his activities to London. His zeal for social reform, and particularly the reconstruction of cities, became a lifelong interest for which he was an indefatigable enthusiast. In 1904 he was asked by the Carnegie Foundation to prepare a diagnosis and plan for the rebuilding of the birthplace of Andrew Carnegie at Dunfermline. His report, entitled *City Development: A Study of Parks, Gardens and Cultural Institutions,* published in 1904, is one of the pioneer works in town planning, in which one can see an association with the ideas of Ebenezer Howard. The plan was far too expensive for the funds made available and was another failure, but a magnificent effort of composition and social vision. In London, Victor Branford, inspired by Geddes, founded the Sociological Society. This was located in a building named Le Play House, and that in itself indicates the extent to which Geddes built his ideas on those of the great French sociologist. In its rooms and in the pages of the *Sociological Review,* Geddes developed his ideas of the interrelations of Place, Work and Folk, ideas that were basic to the social studies of Le Play. 'Regional survey' served as the framework for such study. This embraced the organization and interrelations of the fields of knowledge of society. The notion of the 'valley section' was an idealized regional segment in which the main social types of human societies through history were portrayed. The council of the Sociological Society included a galaxy of intellectual stars—Hobhouse, Hobson, Westermarck, Graham Wallas and Mackinder, with James Bryce as its first president!

In his town planning work, Geddes insisted always on a regional survey before action. He was invited by the Minister of Health to organize a Cities and Town Planning Conference in London in 1910. It was held in the Royal Academy and although the exhibition lacked glamour, Geddes was always on the spot to talk to visitors and show them around. The exhibits of the survey in the Outlook Tower in Edinburgh were shifted to London. Raymond Unwin, Patrick Abercrombie and H. V. Lanchester, three of Britain's future leading planners, were involved as friends and participants in this exhibition. In the following few years, it was transferred to Dublin, then Belfast, and finally to Edinburgh. The citizens of Dublin formed a housing and planning association to promote a survey of the city. In 1914 there was a prolonged exhibition, a school of civics was founded, and the citizens became keenly interested in rebuilding their city. The team of lecturers in Dublin at this conference included Victor Branford, H. J. Fleure, Mabel Barker and several architects. A competition was held for the replanning of Dublin and it was won by Patrick Abercrombie of Liverpool, though it was not published until 1925.

It was at a summer course in Edinburgh in 1914 that Geddes established the Regional Survey Association. In 1913 he organized a collection of city surveys at the International Exhibition at Ghent. In 1914 he sailed for India. The ship carrying the Cities Exhibition was torpedoed and sunk. Geddes's wife and friends speedily despatched substitute exhibits for the Exhibition at Madras. Geddes spent the best part of the next ten years in India, returning each year to carry out his brief duties at Dundee. He resigned the latter post, however, to become Professor of Civics and Sociology in the University of Bombay. Geddes was much in demand to survey and reconstruct Indian cities. The high mark of his work was his report on Indore, whither he was invited by its maharaja to replan the capital city. While there (for one year) he also organized the great annual festival 'procession'—the Diwali—designing it as a great masque of civic renovation.[1] During this period, in his journeys between Britain and India, he also became involved in the planning of the new university in Jerusalem.

Geddes made three visits to the USA, the first in 1898, when he gave lectures on the evolution of sex (one of his early fields of professional concern as a biologist), and the last in 1923, when Mumford served as his secretary and made his travel arrangements. Geddes left a heritage of town planning ideas in New York, together with Ebenezer Howard's garden city and green belt ideas. Lewis Mumford carried the torch, and Benton Mackaye's *New Exploration*, published in 1924, was an early reflection of Geddes's thinking. The progressive group of Lewis Mumford, Clarence Stein, Henry Wright and Catherine Bauer Wooster, carried on the ideas of city and regional planning, out of which there emerged in the USA in the 1920s the neighbourhood concept and the green belt (dormitory) town.

Geddes and Branford were much concerned with the social problems of the First World War and its aftermath. They held a three-week conference in the University of London in July 1915, before

Geddes returned to India. Many distinguished lecturers participated, including Gilbert Slater, Raymond Unwin and H. V. Lanchester, and the geographers H. J. Mackinder and H. J. Fleure. Geddes started a series of books to deal with these problems, with the title The Making of the Future. The first volumes to appear were joint works: *Ideas at War* (with G. Slater) and *The Coming Polity* (with V. Branford) (both 1917). Soon after there appeared three important books by the leading geographers of the time. Halford Mackinder's *Democratic Ideals and Reality* (1919), in terms of its international impact, may be regarded as one of the most influential books of the first half of the century. C. B. Fawcett's *Provinces of England* (1919) presented an argument and plan for the establishment of major regions of government in England. Both these books remain so cogent that they were reprinted in 1944 and 1959 respectively. H. J. Fleure's *Human Geography in Western Europe* (1918) had a strong anthropological bias. These works indicate the close association of Geddes with the geographical viewpoint at this time.

Returning from India, Geddes resumed at the age of seventy his long interest in universities by building the Collège des Écossais at Montpellier, which was opened in 1925. Associated with the university, this college housed about twenty students, some of them drawn from India, who were able to live and work with the master. It was at this time that Geddes, in collaboration with J. A. Thomson, completed a work on *Outlines of General Biology*, published in 1931. Geddes was knighted in 1932, having declined the honour on a previous occasion. He died shortly afterwards at Montpellier.

Geddes's ideas are of particular significance for the development of the regional concept. He adopted the Le Play formula of Place, Work and Folk. He believed that a concrete understanding of society must be based on studies within the framework of distinct geographical areas, country or city, with the aid of notebook and camera, for just as the biologist must reach his generalizations through first-hand experience with nature, so must the sociologist work through the medium of observation, record and analysis. He envisaged all aspects of the study of an area, both those of a social nature and those relating to physical environment—in brief, the framework and substance of 'regional survey', focusing upon Place, Work and Folk; or Environment, Function and Organization; or Geography, Economics and Anthropology. 'Here is the content of social science.'

These ideas Geddes summed up in his famous Valley Section. This includes the environment of the fisherman with his net on the coast; the gardener with his spade; the peasant with his plough on the better soils of the lower levels; the poorer peasant or crofter growing oats and potatoes on poorer land; the shepherd and the hunter on the moorland and in the forest; and, finally, on the timbered or mineralized uplands, the woodman and the miner, identified by their typical implements, the axe and the pick. This is the key diagram, the constructive formula, of the 'regional survey'. These are the 'six human pieces on the chessboard of nature', the 'prime movers of civilization', who play through history the drama of war and peace. From this general background of occupational types there emerge in more complex societies the engineer, boatman, soldier, merchant and priest. Out of this complex emerges the city as a higher unity.

The simple trilogy is elaborated by Geddes in one of his well-known expressive cartograms (see Table 1). The sequence is reversed in city study as: Polity (Folk), Culture (Work) and Art (Place). The highest social grouping is the 'polity', or school of thought, which through its 'culture' affects and strives to improve the environment and finds expression in 'art'. The Geddes conception of regional survey (together with his interpretation of the disciplinary structure of social science, or, as he called it, sociology) was put forward in many published papers. These appeared in the *Sociological Review* in the 1910s and 1920s and in the *Sociological Papers* that preceded the *Review*. (One of the earliest papers, 'Civics as applied sociology', appeared in *Sociological Papers* for 1905–6.) The cartogram shown here as Table 1 was used by Geddes in many variations in what he liked to call 'the game of nine squares'.

This cartogram may be explained as follows. Regional structure contains three interacting conditions, *Place* or land (including location, relief, climate, vegetation and natural resources); *Work* or economics; and *Folk* or people and their cultural heritage. Place affects the occupations (place—*Work*), and the people (place—*Folk*). Folk affect the modes of settlement (folk—*Place*) and the occupations (folk—*Work*). *Work* affects the occupations (work—*Folk*) and the environment (land uses) (work—*Place*). Place, work and folk have their own distinctive characters and are likened by Geddes to geography, economics and anthropology, with the other interacting aspects as auxiliary fields.

Let us clarify the scheme further by repeating the words of Geddes:[2]

Now, from the original triad, Place, Work, Folk, arise new combinations and new ideas. 'Place-Work' is thus mining, forestry or fishing: work that can be done only in certain places. Similarly 'place-Folk' are Eskimos, nomads, or Vikings:

32

people definitely shaped by their environment. But there is constant action and reaction, for if Holland made the Dutch, it is no less true that the Dutch made Holland. Here is a beginning of simple but scientific sociology in a nutshell; yet how the sociologists do scoff even as I steal this real treasure from under their sceptical noses!

This scheme of regional study was widely used between the wars in teaching by geographers, and by regional and city planners in their diagnostic surveys preparatory to planned action.[3]

TABLE 1 *The Geddes Scheme of Regional Survey, Showing the Interaction of Place, Folk and Work*

PLACE	place WORK (natural) advantages	place FOLK (natives)
work PLACE (pasture, fields, mine, workshop)	WORK	work FOLK (industrial)
folk PLACE (village, home, etc.)	folk WORK (occupation)	FOLK

The Le Play Society in London endeavoured to put into practice the teaching of the Le Play School as elaborated by Geddes. It organized many surveys in Great Britain and on the Continent, several of which are published. These surveys were undertaken by groups who visited selected areas, with the guidance of authoritative leaders, most of whom were geographers.

From Geddes there emerged a host of new concepts and terms, many of which have entered our vocabulary and have been further developed. The rebuilding of the human habitat on the basis of regional analysis he referred to as geotechnics. His nearest contemporary counterpart, Constantin Doxiades of Greece, describes this as *ekistics*. He coined the terms paleotechnic (nineteenth century) and neotechnic (twentieth century) and biotechnic, to which Mumford has added eotechnic (the first phase of human muscle, wood, wind and water). The term conurbation, covered in his famous work on *Cities and Evolution* (1915), refined by the later work of

33

C. B. Fawcett, is now officially accepted by the Registrar-General in the Census of Britain. The notion of regional survey found repercussion in the idea of regionalism in political reconstruction and is reflected in Mackinder's *Democratic Ideals and Reality* and Fawcett's *Provinces of England*. The six stages of growth of the city are referred to by Geddes as eopolis (village economy), polis, metropolis, megalopolis, tyrannopolis and necropolis. This idea has been further developed by Lewis Mumford in America.

The spirit of the regional survey was adopted in city and regional planning schemes between the two world wars as an essential preliminary to proposals for future development. Unfortunately this approach resulted in a widely dispersed assembly of facts without a focus on central practical problems. Such a change in outlook, however, has pervaded planning work since the Second World War. The method of regional survey as an educational medium was expounded by Geddes's disciple, Mabel Barker, and was adopted in schools, particularly in the teaching of geography in school and university. It was adopted in the field studies of the Le Play Society in areas of undisturbed peasant societies, so that people with diverse backgrounds—botanists, geologists, anthropologists, geographers, social workers—could work together in their own way, with their own interest, but in the same area. The Le Play Society broke away from the Sociological Society and finally concluded its activities in 1960.

Regional survey served an invaluable educational purpose. It proved in the long run, however, to be of doubtful utility to either planners or social scientists. It deliberately sought to organize the whole content of an area around different disciplines. It opened wide the doors to a broad range of studies with no common ground except the area (region) of investigation. It had no focus of enquiry. Social betterment, so ardently desired by Geddes, needs research into specific social and economic aspects of spatial structure that are relevant to physical planning. Similarly, what is essential in the study of a particular area is the selection of distinct and clearly defined problems either as the ends of particular disciplines, or as a means of human betterment. It is undoubtedly true that regional survey is invaluable as an educational medium. This, however, has been one of the main deterrents to the conceptual growth of the regional concept.

4

Halford J. Mackinder, 1861-1947

Halford Mackinder obtained first class honours in natural science at Oxford in 1883 and served in that year also as president of the Oxford Union. He then read modern history, in which he graduated in 1884. Subsequently he read for the Bar and was called to the Inner Temple in 1886. He participated in launching the Oxford University Extension Movement, which sought to take university teaching beyond the precincts of the campus by means of travelling lecturers. Mackinder was one of the pioneers in this field, taking as his theme 'the new geography'. He gave 600 popular lectures of this kind in a few years in cities all over the land. In 1887 he was asked by the Royal Geographical Society, which was then considering the introduction of geography to the universities, to address the society. At the age of twenty-six, he addressed the society on 'the scope and methods of geography'. The society decided on an appointment at Oxford and Mackinder accepted it. He remained there from 1887 to 1905, but it was not until 1900 that a separate department of geography was established, and then only with a diploma in the subject.

Meanwhile, out of the Oxford University Extension Movement, Michael Sadler engineered in 1892 the beginnings of a new college at Reading, and invited Mackinder to be its principal. Mackinder held this post until 1903 but was not in continuous residence. He was also involved in the beginnings of the London School of Economics in 1895, where he became in that year a lecturer in economic geography. In the summer of 1898 he was climbing in the Alps and in 1899 made the first ascent of Mount Kenya.

Mackinder's association with the London School of Economics lasted from 1895 to 1925. For some years his post there was a part-time one and it was not until 1902 that he received full-time status. (The Board of Studies for Geography at that time included a majority of geologists plus three geographers, Mackinder, Keltie and Chisholm.) In 1903 Mackinder became the second director of the school, a post he held for four years. He resigned his post at Reading and held the readership at Oxford until 1905. For many years (1906–14), at the request of Lord Haldane, Mackinder gave courses on geography for Army officers. He resigned as director of the London School of Economics in October 1908, devoting his time to professional work as reader in economic geography there, and to his parliamentary interests. He did not accept the title of professor until 1923, two years before he left academic life.

The rest of Mackinder's life, after 1925, was devoted to service to the government. He put up for Parliament in 1900 and in 1909, but was defeated on both occasions. In 1910 he was elected for a division of Glasgow, which he then represented until 1922. He carried out various special missions as an MP and was knighted in 1921. He was Chairman of the Imperial Shipping Committee from 1920 to 1945 and Chairman of the Imperial Economic Committee until 1931. He died in 1947 at the age of eighty-six.

Mackinder's dynamic personality, his ability to give simple expression to complex ideas and his power of broad generalization (especially with a background of effective wall maps) made him a brilliant lecturer. He was responsible for such terms as 'nodality' and 'man-power', and the application to public affairs of such concepts as 'social momentum' and 'the going concern'—in which we suspect a reflection of the ideas of his friends the Webbs, Graham Wallas and others. His thinking was permeated by visualization, both on the map and in the mind, of the world's regional complexes as combinations of varied physical and human elements.

He regarded geography as a bridge across the great gap (deplored in our day by C. P. Snow and others) between the humanities and the natural sciences, between history and geology. He applied these concepts above all to the interpretation of world political affairs and formulated in 1904 a concept of the 'geographical pivot of history', and a theory of 'the natural seats of power', a few weeks before the beginning of the Russo-Japanese War. Out of this grew the idea of the 'pivot area' or the 'Heartland' in the 'World Island'. This concept and its geostrategic implications may soberly be assessed today as one of the most influential in world affairs in the twentieth century. He repeated the same view in 1943, a few years before his death. He emphasized at this later date, during the Second World War, the danger of the Heartland falling in its entirety under the control of the Soviet Union and Russia's ability then to strike out to the peripheral lands to east, south and west of the 'World Island'. Mackinder's 'regional concept' also pervaded his interpretation of countries, particularly the British Isles. His concept of 'Metropolitan England', as the area of the south-east that is dominated by association with London, was expressed sixty years ago. It is one of the dominant realities of our day, one to which we are still seeking means of adjustment in terms of regional and national planning. The thinking of Mackinder was a generation ahead of his time.

There is ample evidence in the statements of Mackinder that, in his early formative years, he was familiar with some of the work of his German contemporaries. He established a distinctive brand of British geography that was parallel in some respects to the ideas of his Continental colleagues. He was closer to the thinking of Patrick Geddes than that of foreign scholars, and his view of geography was far more mature and balanced than Davis's 'influences of physical environment on human activities' or Mill's 'mobile distributions', both men being essentially natural scientists who viewed man on the earth as dependent upon his physical environment. From the maturity of his views one suspects that he was influenced by his close association with distinguished contemporaries in other fields of history and social philosophy.

The professional works of Mackinder include two books of outstanding significance. The first is his *Britain and the British Seas*, published in 1902. This work stands as a classic in modern British literature, shows a more mature and sounder approach to a regional interpretation than Vidal de la Blache's *Tableau* or Ratzel's *Deutschland*. It is a remarkable essay in regional synthesis. It is here, to select one theme, that we read of his unique interpretation at that time of Metropolitan England: 'The metropolis in its largest meaning includes all the counties for whose inhabitants London is "Town", whose men do habitual business there, whose women buy there, whose morning paper is printed there, whose standard of thought is determined there.'

This was without question the best work in a series of high-standard 'regional geographies' that Mackinder edited in the 1900s. These included the work of the German geographer J. Partsch on *Central Europe* (1903) and of the American geologist I. C. Russell on *North America* (1904).

Mackinder's second great work is *Democratic Ideals and Reality*, published in 1919. He formulated in this book an interpretation of world power-politics with an eye to the establishment of a sound 'strategy of peace'. Here he developed the concept of the Heartland (Russia) of the World Island (the Old World of Eur-Asia and Africa). If the Heartland were under the control of one land-power, this power could (as history had revealed, notably in the struggles between Russia and Britain in the last 100 years or more) threaten the peripheral lands, that were accessible to and outflanked the life-lines of British sea-power. This geostrategic interpretation is expressed in the zones of conflict in central Europe, Scandinavia and the Straits, as in the Middle East, northern India and Manchuria. These strategic trends were dominant in the First World War and in the Second World War. Russia has since consolidated its power and now threatens its peripheries. Sea-power was held until twenty-five years ago by the USA, Britain and their allies. The American policy of containment is a continuation of this geostrategic situation. Korea, Formosa, Southern Vietnam and the uneasy zones of the Middle East and the Soviet satellites, lie in the zone of contact and potential conflict between land-power and sea-power. This grand interpretation has had its repercussions in thought and strategy, directly and indirectly, on American policy in the post-war generation. We are ever mindful of Mackinder's famous dictum: 'Who rules East Europe commands the Heartland: Who rules the Heartland commands the World Island: Who rules the World Island commands the World.'

This work, *Democratic Ideals and Reality,* fell into obscurity between the wars, but it was reprinted in the USA as a paperback during the Second World War in 1942, for it had the same cogency in the 1945 geostrategic situation as in 1914. The book is one of the most pregnant and provocative works of the first half of the century. It is based on a geographic interpretation that has been analysed and reinterpreted in a host of ways since its publication.

It should be emphasized that over the past twenty-five years the Soviet Union has become a strong naval power. For the first time in history she commands the seas fringing the periphery of the World Island. Soviet vessels also navigate under various pretexts the Indian Ocean and the Atlantic. Many Soviet writers refer in geostrategic terms to the World Ocean. This is the new world reality that will shape the course of world strategy and economic aid over the next generation.

If a great book is to be judged by repercussions in thought and action, this is indeed one of them.[1]

The views of Mackinder on the scope of 'the new geography' must now be considered. These were expressed in two important addresses: the first was delivered, by invitation, before the Royal Geographical Society in 1887, in his twenty-seventh year; the second, was the presidential address given at the age of thirty-four before the geographical section of the British Association for the Advancement of Science.

The address to the Royal Geographical Society in 1887 was entitled 'On the scope and methods of geography'. It begins with the question, 'What is geography?' The answer is contained in the following crisp sentence: it is 'the science whose main function is to trace the interaction of man in society and so much of his environment as varies locally'. He also gives an alternative in a footnote: 'the science which traces the arrangement of things on the earth's surface'. The 'varying environment', he continues, is 'the function of physical geography'. The following are further quotations from the same address:

Geography is like a tree which early divides into two great branches, whose twigs may nonetheless be inextricably inter-woven . . . we insist on the teaching of geography as a whole.

True physical geography aims at giving us a causal description of the distribution of the features of the earth's surface. The data must be regrouped on a topographical basis.

Physiography asks of a given feature, 'Why is it?' Physical geography, 'What is there?' Political geography, 'How does it act on man in society, and how does he react on it?' Geology asks, 'What riddle of the past does it help to solve?' Physiography is common ground to the geologist and the geographer. The first four subjects are the realm of the geographer. The questions come in sequence.

The true distinction between geology and geography seems to me to lie in this: the geologist looks at the present that he may interpret the past; the geographer looks at the past that he may interpret the present.

Geography must be a continuous argument, and the test of whether a given point is to be included or not must be this: Is it pertinent to the main line of argument?

The main line of geographical argument Mackinder then defines as follows:

We presuppose a knowledge of physiography. Successive chapters in a regional study postulate what has gone before. The sequence of argument is unbroken.

An environment is a natural region. The smaller the area included, the greater tends to be the number of conditions

39

uniform or nearly uniform throughout the area. Thus we have
environments of different orders. . . . So with communities . . .
communities are of different [geographical] orders—races,
nations, provinces, towns . . .

Man alters his environment, and the action of that environment
on his posterity is changed in consequence.

The relative importance of physical features varies from age
to age according to the state of knowledge and of material
civilization.

I believe that on lines such as I have sketched a geography may
be worked out which shall satisfy at once the practical requirements of the statesman and the merchants, the theoretical
requirements of the historian and the scientist, and the
intellectual requirements of the teacher.

This exposition launched geography as a university study,
beginning with the support of the Royal Geographical Society at
Oxford and Cambridge. Its main tenets in reference to the role
of man in society have been guideposts in research and teaching
for nearly fifty years.

Mackinder's presidential address to the geographical section
(section E) of the British Association for the Advancement of
Science in 1895 includes the following statements:

The facts of geography are capable of two kinds of treatment.
The chapter-headings may be such as 'Rivers', 'Mountains',
'Cities', or such as 'Ireland', 'Italy', Australia'. In other words,
we may consider the phenomena of a given type of all parts of
the globe, or we may discuss in a given part of the globe the
phenomena of all types. In the former case, our book should
as a whole observe the order of what has been called the
geographical argument; in the latter case each chapter, the
discussion of each country, should exhibit that order complete.
For historical reasons . . . we English have fallen into a bad
habit of describing the former treatment as 'physical geography',
and the latter as 'geography'. The Germans are more reasonable
when they contrast *Allgemeine Erdkunde* with *Länderkunde*,
but chorography, our nearest English equivalent to *Länderkunde,*
is a clumsy expression. An alternative would be to speak of
'special geography', thereby implying a correlative to 'general
geography', which is a precise rendering of *Allgemeine Erdkunde.*
By whatever name we call it, however, it is clear that the treat-

ment by regions is a more thorough test of the logic of the geographical argument than is the treatment by types of phenomena.

The geographical argument begins in its first chapter, he continues, with geomorphology. This he describes as

the half artistic, half genetic consideration of the form of the lithosphere. The second chapter might be called geophysiology; it postulates a knowledge of geomorphology, and may be divided into two sections—oceanography and climatology. At the head of the third and last chapter is the word 'biogeography', the geography of organic communities and their environments. It has three sections, phytogeography, or the geography of plants; zoogeography, or the geography of animals; and anthropogeo-graphy, or the geography of man. This chapter postulates all that has preceded, and within the chapter itself each later section presupposes whatever has gone before. To each later section and chapter there is an appendix dealing with the reaction of the newly-introduced element on the elements which have been considered earlier. Finally, there is a supplement to the whole volume, devoted to the history of geography, or the development of geographical concepts and nomenclature.

In defining the nature of anthropogeography Mackinder empha-sizes the study of the physical *qua* geographical conditions and the fact that 'races', which have 'a great variety of initiative', are 'the product, in the main, of [their] past history'. Further, 'in each age, certain elements of this initiative are selected for success, chiefly by geographical conditions'. 'Human genius' sometimes sets 'geographical limitation at defiance'. 'Temporary effects contrary to nature may be within human possibilities, but in the long run nature reasserts her supremacy.' The facts of human geography, like other fields of geography, are 'the resultant for the moment of the conflict of two elements, the dynamic and the genetic':

Geographical advantages of past times permitted a distribution and a movement of men which, by inertia, still tend to maintain themselves even in the face of new geographical disadvantages. Economic or commercial geography should probably be regarded as the basic division of the treatment. The streams of com-modities over the face of the earth, considered as an element in human environments, present many analogies to the currents of the ocean or the winds of the air. Strategical opportunities, also, have a constant action on communities, in the shape of tempting or threatening possibilities. Political geography becomes reasonable when the facts are regarded as the resultant, in large measure, of genetic or historical elements, and of such dynamic elements as the economic and strategic.

The following comments may be made on this discourse, that reflects the attitude of the time and certainly affected the subsequent trends of geographical work in Britain. First, it is assumed that the facts of the physical inorganic environment as given by nature are the geographical conditions or the geographical environment. Second, the measurement of the influences of these environmental conditions on man is the problem of 'anthropogeography', with the introduction of a variety of counterchecks reflected by the terms 'dynamic' and 'genetic'. Though no acknowledgment is made, this view is remarkably parallel to the pronouncement of von Richthofen in 1883 (see my volume *The Makers of Modern Geography*). Third, it is assumed that there is an automatic chain of cause and effect, a cumulation of the 'chapters' of geography, with man on top, that subsumes, in sequence, all that has gone before. It would, therefore, be unthinkable for an anthropogeographer not to have a very firm foundation in geomorphology, which is the *sine qua non* for all other geographies.

At a much later date, 1931, Mackinder raised his voice in criticism of the 'greedy and misguided claims of the geomorphologist'. Thereby he set himself in the camp lined up against the views of W. M. Davis[2]:

Geomorphology as it has now developed, has internal coherence and a consistent philosophy, and in their hunger for these joys many of our geographers, it seems to me, have blinded themselves to the fact that, as geomorphologists, they are not in the centre but on the margin of geography.

5

Andrew J. Herbertson, 1865-1915

Andrew John Herbertson was a Scot, born in Galashiels in 1865. He entered the University of Edinburgh in 1886 and studied physics, mathematics and geology. He did not qualify and never took an undergraduate degree. Like Geddes, who probably encouraged this attitude, he scorned examinations and believed in the search for knowledge as an end in itself. It was not until 1895 that he was awarded a doctorate degree at the University of Freiburg-in-Breisgau for a thesis on the distribution of the world's rainfall. This in itself means that Herbertson was thoroughly familiar with the developments of geography at that time in Germany. He also made contact with the school of Vidal de la Blache in Paris, and was (as a botanist) especially impressed by Flahault's work at Montpellier—pioneer studies of plant association. During the 1890s he followed an almost peripatetic career, holding posts briefly at Dundee, Manchester and Edinburgh, and pursued research (based on scholarships) on hygrometric measurements at observatories on Ben Nevis and at Fort William.

He took a first post in 1891 as a botanist under Patrick Geddes at Dundee. From that time onwards, Geddes (and, through him, Le Play) exercised an abiding influence on Herbertson's attitude and work. He also served some years with Alexander Buchan in the preparation of world maps of meteorological data in the cartographic establishment of Bartholomew in Edinburgh. This joint work appeared in the *Atlas of Meteorology* in 1899. These maps formed the basis of the Oxford Wall Map series and were also used as a framework for working out 'major natural regions'. Geddes ran short summer schools at Edinburgh. At one of these Herbertson met his future wife, Dorothy, and they were married in 1893. They lived near Geddes's Outlook Tower and Herbertson assisted in organizing the exhibits in the tower. Mrs Herbertson wrote a biography of Le Play, although it was not published until 1950.

43

c

It is evident that Geddes exercised a strong and abiding influence on both the Herbertsons.

Mackinder went to Oxford in 1887 and in 1899 an independent school of geography was established with Mackinder as its head. Mackinder needed an assistant, and when Herbertson was about to be lured to New York, Mackinder offered him a post at Oxford. Herbertson accepted the offer and in 1899 became lecturer in regional geography at Oxford. Here he remained until his premature death in 1915.

Herbertson drew to his school at Oxford many hundreds of students. These included R. N. Rudmose Brown, J. L. Myres (the Oxford classical scholar and great friend of geography) and J. F. Unstead. Several American geographers also participated in the summer school in 1908, their names being A. P. Brigham, W. M. Davis, C. R. Dryer, N. Fenneman and D. W. Johnson. Oxford offered a diploma in geography, beginning in 1900, long before an honours degree was established in 1930. The persons who were awarded diplomas under Herbertson included C. B. Fawcett, the present writer's first teacher (1922–5) and chief for twenty years (1928–47); O. J. R. Howarth, a close collaborator with Herbertson in the *Oxford Survey of the British Empire* (1914), and author with the present writer of *The Making of Geography*; O. H. T. Rishbeth, subsequently head of the department at Southampton; Eva G. R. Taylor, a life-time colleague of J. F. Unstead and for many years his successor at Birkbeck College, London; O. G. S. Crawford, the distinguished archaeologist; Nora MacMunn, who remained on the staff at Oxford and later wrote a book on Europe on lines set by Herbertson; and W. G. Kendrew, the Oxford climatologist. Several other geographers attended these courses and we note especially P. M. Roxby—who always spoke of Herbertson as 'his master'— A. G. Ogilvie, and H. J. Fleure, who had long talks with Herbertson shortly before his death in 1915. These men all became leaders of British geography.

Herbertson wrote many books for use in schools. *Man and His Work: An Introduction to Human Geography* was first published in 1899 and reached its eighth edition in 1963. It reveals the strong influence of the approach of Le Play. (The same, indeed, is true of Marion Newbigin's *Man and His Conquest of Nature,* published in 1912. Both of these books were studied in high school by the present writer during the First World War.) His *Senior Geography,* published in 1907, was a text based on 'natural regions' instead of political units. This book again was used as a standard text by the writer in high school. In 1900 Herbertson became the secretary of the Geographical Association. He established and edited its journal, *Geographical Teacher,* in 1901.

Herbertson acknowledged the assistance of the German scholar, Supan, in his early study of the world distribution of rainfall. A scheme of the major natural regions of the world was first published in 1905. The further development of this concept, described as the 'higher units', was published in an obscure Continental journal (*Scientia*) in 1913 (reprinted in a memorial volume in *Geography* in 1965). Herbertson urged in the 1900s that systematic hydrographic surveys should be undertaken as a means of checking and surveying the water resources of Britain. He served on a royal commission on inland waterways and urged that areas be defined in terms of their levels of economic development. In 1914 Oxford University Press produced the *Oxford Survey of the British Empire* in six volumes, edited by Herbertson and O. J. R. Howarth. Just before Herbertson's death the Oxford Wall Map series was published. He and his students had spent many years in the preparation of these base maps, which are still in general use and were the bases of Herbertson's scheme of natural regions. All these achievements reveal a deep concern with the use of geography for practical purposes. Indeed, Herbertson referred to 'applied geography' as far back as 1898.

Special attention must now be given to Herbertson's central conception of the 'natural region'. This was expressed in the 'higher units' noted above. It has been a fundamental springboard in the development of the regional concept in Britain.

Geography, for Herbertson, was conceived as the study of orders or hierarchies of natural and man-made environments. These he named provisionally localities, districts, regions, groups of regions or countries, in growing order of complexity and magnitude. The close parallel will be observed here with the concept and nomenclature of A. Hettner in Germany. The presentation of Herbertson's article is concerned with the 'higher units' in this hierarchy, defined on a generic basis from selected worldwide criteria. He wrote as follows:[1]

In classifying these higher units we may arbitrarily select this or that element as characteristic, as Linnaeus selected the stamens when classifying flowering plants; or we may adopt a 'natural system' and take into account all of their forms and qualities. We may divide the world into structural regions, orographical regions, hydrographical regions, climatic regions, biological regions and

anthropological regions. Such divisions are invaluable for the
student of these subjects. They are also invaluable and necessary
for the geographer. He must examine them carefully before
attempting to determine the natural geographical regions. As the
structural, climatic, biological and other divisions are in many
cases almost congruent, it is possible to make a very satisfactory
natural classification for geographical purposes by laying stress
on two or three of them.

In practice it is best to choose (1) relief, as indicative of structure
and of the processes which have modelled the surface forms of
the skeleton; and (2) vegetation as the expression of quality, quality
of climate and quality of soil, for through vegetation animal life
in general and human life in particular are most closely bound
to the non-vital elements.

In modern works on geomorphology much stress is rightly laid
on the history of land forms, and attempts are made to classify
them genetically. This is a great gain and has led to a precision
and delicacy of observation hitherto unknown. The power of seeing
and interpreting land forms is necessary in a geographer who has
to recognize and interpret the more complex unit of which the
land is but the skeleton. For our present purpose it is sufficient to
group the various types of regional skeleton into varieties of plain,
tableland, scarpland, folded mountain and denuded highlands,
which have been modelled by different denuding agents. In
classifying land forms climate as well as structure has to be taken
into account.

We have also to examine the surface covering of these land
forms. The chief types of vegetation can be grouped into five
classes: forest, park, grass or herb, scrub and desert. Here again
climate has to be considered, and its part is greater than that of
the soil in determining the major divisions. It is only in sub-divisions,
in areas over which climatic conditions are fairly uniform, that
soil has to be placed first.

Of the different climatic elements rainfall and temperature are
the most obviously significant. If either is deficient there is dearth
of vegetation, if both are excessive there is luxuriance.

Relief and structure, temperature and rainfall, soil and vegetation
have all to be taken into account in classifying natural regions.
For instance, the contrast between mountain and plain is a
contrast between climatic and vegetative diversity and uniformity,
as well as a contrast between a varied and a uniform surface relief.
Yet the more each of these is examined the more difficult it
becomes to think of mountain or plain as having one and only

one characteristic, and the more one feels that every element in each is essential and must not be left out of account.... The classification adopted is broadly one of belts of temperature divided meridionally by areas of different rainfall, annual and occasional, and broken into regular and irregular areas by the great mountain masses which rise up to different elevation and as regions apart. Their very diverse conditions of surface, climate and vegetation, closely crowded together, differentiate them from any extensive plains at their base, even if many plants of their lower valleys are the same as those in the plains.

In all branches of human studies the environment must be taken into consideration, and the discovery of any better way of examining and classifying environments must be of great importance. The question, however, may be asked: What is the role of man in a geographical region? He is too often considered a thing apart, or at best an active agent in a passive medium. If he is treated in this way the treatment is incomplete. We are surely long past the days of quarrelling about whether a man is dominated by heredity or by environment. He is influenced by both; he is, as it were, a part of both. We are accustomed nowadays to look at him as but a fleeting aspect of a changing whole, a little of whose past we can review and still less of whose future we can foresee. We have not yet grown to look at him as but a small part of a complex whole whose control of him we can but slightly trace.

If the geographical region is a macro-organism then men are its nerve cells. In some of the huge regional creatures this collection of human units is more or less amorphous, a scattered mass of undifferentiated nerve cells, an unimportant part of the whole. In others he is well organized and specialized as an essential part of it, having set his mark all over its surface, in fact he is a sort of a higher nervous system in it. But he is no more, though no less, to be considered apart from the rest of these leviathans than the nervous system is to be considered apart from the rest of the organism of which it is an essential element. For purposes of investigation it is often necessary to consider one element alone; but for the full understanding of the organism, or of the macro-organism, the nervous system, or the human society, cannot be separated from it.

Analogies must never be pushed too far. The life history or cycle of these natural regions is not exactly the same as that of any cell, or organism. Its material and physical birth and growth and decay are of quite a different character, and while a study of the life cycles of simpler forms throws light on that of the larger and more complex ones, it is quite insufficient to summarize the latter merely in terms of the former. They must be studied as they are themselves.

That such regional leviathans exist and that we each are a part of one is the theme of this paper. The personality of such leviathans, like the personality of men, is another question.

Herbertson gave much thought to the role of heredity and heritage in the adjustment of human societies to the natural environment, as shown in the following extracts from an important article he wrote shortly before his death, an article which reflects clearly the thought of his time and his projections and programmes of study of man's role on the earth. It reveals clearly a departure from the naïve assumptions of environmental determination of social Darwinism: [2]

It is germane to our subject to consider for a moment the question of heredity and environment. These fascinating problems have also been mishandled by those who explain everything by race, and by those for whom all is determined by environment.
Mr and Mrs Whetham, sound eugenists, pour scorn on the simple faith of many social reformers and politicians, who cite diminished death rates and other statistical evidence of the value of improved material conditions of life. The eugenists reply, 'True, but you are merely preserving the unfit who breed most quickly, and it is by the elimination of the unfit that progress is obtained.' It is obvious that no matter how fit any organism is, unless it lives in optimum conditions, it cannot achieve the best results.
The quarrel is endless until we realize that for society, as distinct from the individual man, heredity and environment have not the simple meanings we often give them. The inheritance of a society is transmitted in a much more complex way than by continuity of germ plasm. Convection and radiation as well as conduction are as it were at work. There is not merely the transference of tradition from father and mother to child, not merely that from dead men, whose works live after them, to living men.
Environment, too, is not merely the physical circumstances among which we live, important though those are. It, too, is found to be more complex and more subtle the more we examine it. *There is a mental and spiritual environment as well as a material one.* It is almost impossible to group precisely the ideas of a community into those which are the outcome of environmental

contact, and those which are due to social inheritance.

Environment is not constant, but changes, even physically, for example, when a new drainage or irrigation or railway system is constructed. Social tradition is not constant. In fact, heredity and environment are very convenient ideas for analysis. Abstract either element from the whole—and it is less than the whole—and the whole cannot be understood.

It is no doubt difficult for us accustomed to these dissections to understand that the living whole, while made up parts with different structures and functions, is no longer the living whole when it is so dissected, but something dead and incomplete. *The separation of the whole into man and his environment is such a murderous act.* There are no men apart from their environment.

There is a whole for which we have no name, unless it is a *country,* of which men are a part. We cannot consider men apart from the rest of the country, nor an inhabited country apart from its inhabitants without abstracting an essential part of the whole. It is like studying a human being without his nervous system, and his nervous system apart from the rest of him. It may be a useful form of analysis at a particular stage of our investigation, but it is inadequate and misleading until we have once more considered the complete man.

So it is with a country, a region, a district—whatsoever name we care to give it. In its present form and activities man is an essential element of it, and *man cannot be considered apart from the rest of it* without limiting our study to something less than the whole. The analogy with an individual man is no doubt useful. There are specialists skilled in the knowledge of healthy and diseased conditions of the bones, the muscles, the digestive system, the eye, the brain, and so on; but the wise physician must know something of all of these, and as a rule his conception of the whole man is more complete and truer than that of the specialist. So with the higher natural whole or region, tinker, tailor, soldier, sailor and the thousand and one necessary specialists do not replace the wise man who knows the countryside thoroughly, and thinks of it and loves it naturally as a whole.

When we take such a complex whole as a valley or a countryside, we find *the present conditioned by the past.* The structure and surface forms of the land bear evidences of a long history, and we can speak of *inheritance from the past,* as definite and apparently as inevitable as in the case of the skeleton inherited by the individual man. When we look at its surface-covering of soil and plants and the animals living in and around them, we also find elements which have been inherited, some apparently unalterable, others capable of modification. Even the human beings themselves have the same mixture of fixed and variable characters, for nothing is more impressive than the persistence of the same stocks in most countrysides which are without minerals or manufactures to attract outsiders. Excluding the consideration of such industrial areas for the moment, we find in most others a very large element which is relatively stable and fixed—the rocks, the soil these make, the climate, the general character of plants and animals including the human inhabitants. There are also variable elements. Leaving out of account secular changes of land forms and of climate, there are minor adjustments of plants and animals to each other, and to modifications in the surface conditions due to flood, droughts, etc., and even to the minor variations of seasons, and there are also the more conscious efforts of man to alter the conditions as far as they can be changed for his advantage.

Nowhere is there unchanging permanence, nowhere is there unrestricted change.

A number of common thoughtless phrases obscure the truth. We are assured that progress is through the struggle for existence and that the strongest is victor. The people who have to struggle the hardest for existence, such as the Eskimo, have little time for anything else. We hear of man's conquest of nature—a misleading phrase, man's disciplining of himself would be nearer the truth: the so-called conquest of nature is due to a more intimate knowledge of nature's ways, and the use of certain natural forces to overcome certain natural obstacles. The man who uses natural products without payment, who takes the goods the gods provide without any return, is the hunter and fisher, the wanderer on the face of the earth, whose hand is against every other man's, who fights and sleeps and feasts and starves alternately. He tries to use nature without return. He is parasitic on the countryside, and in some regions of the world a limited number of such parasites can be supported.

Human progress has been bound up with more and more intimate association of man and the earth, man giving more and more of himself. Far from geography becoming less important as society becomes more complex, it becomes more important. The geographical divisions are the real divisions which form a whole, and all other groups are incomplete. The more important the human element becomes in a region, the more important

the region becomes geographically. It grows more complex,
it becomes a higher type. . . .

The resources of many regions are very varied, and some of
these resources may be more important in one stage of development
than in another. The changes from bison hunting grounds to
bonanza farms, from poor rural to busy mining industrial districts
in many coalfields, are obvious. The character of the region
changes. Its structure and climate have not altered, but they are
bound up with man in a new way and we rightly class the district
in a different category. A migration of men may modify a district
as well as the district may modify the immigrants.

The remarkable development of means of transport (of ideas
and aspirations as well as of men and materials) is sometimes
said to have annihilated space and time. It has not annihilated
space, it has not altered the soil or the seasons, but it has allowed
man to bring in and use more easily materials for improving the
soil, to make more of the favourable seasons and to guard against
the disasters of unfavourable seasons. It allows a more intimate
union of man and space. It allows man to use one part of space
to better advantage and to supplement its deficiencies from other
parts of space which have also been more intimately understood
and utilized by their inhabitants.

Information and even ideas can be transmitted almost
instantaneously. But the movement of ideas is not dependent on
cables or wireless apparatus alone. There must be the society fit
to receive them as well as the society capable of producing them.
These are not instantaneously shaped. Only within very narrow
limits can we hurry growth, and all our efforts for higher education
show that we strive to lengthen rather than to shorten the most
actively growing period.

Before road and railways, telegraphs and telephones, newspapers
and books penetrated everywhere, *each district was more or less
self-supporting and isolated;* each person living in it was an
intimate part of it. It had its good years and bad years, its joys
and its sorrows, in which all shared; but these were little affected
by the world beyond and rarely stirred by outside events, hardly
by great ones such as the catastrophe of some war or the ferment
of some religious inspiration.

Each district as it becomes less self-supporting does not
become less important to itself, but it has to consider more than
its own needs. It has to take into account the conditions of the
world around it and decide what it is best fitted for. It may have
to look far beyond its neighbouring districts even to the other side

51

C*

of the world. The agricultural depression of England was the first outcome of the expansion of railways across the American prairies. The agricultural regeneration which is now going on in England is based on a better knowledge of other districts and their needs and capacities for serving them. The farmers are developing a regional consciousness. As they come to grasp this for their own region they will begin to grasp it for others.

The new regional consciousness differs from the old one when each region was almost independent of the outer world, because it is bound to take the outer world into consideration. No doubt each region must consider and decide how far it should become self-supporting, or how far it should produce the most of the best and seek other things in accessible markets. In either case the best results will depend in the long run on the conscious activity of each individual, knowing his neighbourhood and its needs, and sure of his part in it.

There will be people who know intimately every square yard of some part of the land and how to keep it in a healthy condition capable of yielding good returns year after year. This intimate union must be personal and local. Production for the best results must be individualized. On the other hand matters of collection and distribution are more communal than individual. They must be communized. The proportion of men needed for this service, however, will always be smaller than that of the producers, but this question and that of the distribution of human activities within a region are too large to be discussed in the present article; and so is the obvious application of these ideas to many current political problems.

This has been written to make it clear that for the understanding of history, or economics, or politics, or any study of mankind, it is necessary (1) to realize that the wholes which are greater than the individual are geographical, (2) to grasp the idea of a region and the need for a feeling of regional consciousness. It is not enough to know where certain mountains and rivers are, where towns or boundaries are or have been, not enough to know in what parts of the world wheat or cotton or rubber can be had, not enough to distinguish between protectorates and colonies, or to appreciate the situation of naval stations and fortified camps. A regional consciousness is not obtained in this way. The region must be recognized as a whole, composed of different parts, each with its own character and role. Its essential elements may not alter, but in the course of human history its surface has changed and man has been incorporated in it in very different ways.

It is necessary to understand the permanent elements, the phases of development the region has passed through, and something of its potentialities. It is not merely a passive environment, a theatre of human action of which we must know the stage properties. It is something alive, active, not merely letting man act on it, but vigorously reacting on man.

No one who has read any description of the retreat from Moscow can ever think of environment as passive, but neither can anyone who has understood the huertas of Spain or the terraced vineyards of the Rhine.

The historian must be able to recognize a natural region when he sees one, to know its present characters, to distinguish between those which are permanent and those which are relatively transient, and to trace the sequence of changes of the latter. The economist must evaluate the wealth of the district, not merely actual but also potential. The statesman must so measure the forces of the present transition period, for all periods are times of transition, that he can guide the changes to a finer issue.

This involves no purely materialistic interpretation of history or of geography. The geographer is no more confined to materialistic considerations than the historian. There is a *genius loci* as well as a *Zeitgeist—a spirit of a place as well as of a time*. No social psychology is worth much that is not also regional psychology, and no regional psychology is possible without a loving familiarity with the region. The regional psychology is not the same at all periods of the region's history— though no doubt we can speak of the spirit of the mountains, the fascination of the desert, and so on. The spirit of a place changes with the spirit of the time; it alters with man's relation to the region. The historian has to reckon with both changes in his great cycle, the geographer has to consider both in trying to understand the present regional consciousness.

It is not safe therefore to argue from the present regional psychology to the past without historical knowledge of the region. It is not safe to apply conclusions from the social psychology of one region to those of another, without understanding the differences in their regional characters.

For all the problems of man the two studies of history and geography, of heredity and environment, are essential. They cannot be separated with impunity. They have both to become more discerning and catholic. No simple chronicle suffices for the historian, no superficial geographical inventory suffices for the geographer—and economists, statesmen and everyone concerned in more than his own individual life has to become regionally conscious, to know intimately his own region and its history, and, through the sympathetic understanding of this, to appreciate other regions and their histories, and their relations to his own region and to each other.

Herbertson wrote specifically of both natural or physical and mental or spiritual environments, to use his own terms. He envisaged them as 'living wholes' of different orders, from a local to a worldwide scale: *'The separation of the whole into man and his environment is a murderous act.* There are no men apart from their environment.'

The term *compages,* as defined by the Oxford and Webster dictionaries (see p. xiv), is precisely what Herbertson was discussing. It was adopted by Derwent Whittlesey at Harvard about twenty years ago with the approval of his colleagues (Chapter 2 on the 'Regional concept' in *American Geography,* edited by P. E. James and W. D. Jones, 1954). In spite of its recognized usage in the English language, however, it has found no acceptance by either British or American scholars. But they continue to devise their own more sophisticated labels for the same regional concept. Currently, with emphasis on functional interrelatedness of spatially connected phenomena, one might speak, as I do, of spatial syndromes. I stand after fifty years irrevocably by this concept as first broadly adumbrated by Herbertson. It is for this reason that I have finally chosen the title of this book and have evaluated its contributions. The diligent and able quantitative analysts of particular geochronological processes, or particular geographic variables (under the banner of 'regional science'), must eventually reassemble their data and search for the character and processes in the formation of spatial interconnections if they are to enhance the geographical tradition.[3]

6

The Second Generation

This chronological group of scholars embraces those who passed the formative years of their careers in varied fields in the two decades before the First World War, and became shortly thereafter, in the early 1920s (beginning in a few cases before the war), professors and heads of the first honours schools of geography that were established in the universities. They alone were responsible for the content and examination for the new field of study. They numbered about one dozen. Outstanding seats of geographical scholarship, with Victorian antecedents, alike in support and productive work, were at Oxford, Cambridge, Edinburgh and London. Two men, however, located at the University of Wales at Aberystwyth and the University of Liverpool, had the most notable impact on geographical scholarship and turned out the most sought-after stream of young disciples, virtually all taking up university posts immediately after the award of first class honours bachelors degrees in geography. The leaders to whom I refer are Herbert John Fleure (who later moved to Manchester) and Percy Maude Roxby. This chapter is devoted to the work of these two scholars, each of whom produced what can genuinely be called a school of thought.

HERBERT JOHN FLEURE, 1877–1969

Herbert John Fleure was born in Guernsey in the Channel Islands in 1877. Owing to a long illness, he studied privately for several years in his teens and, even at this stage, became deeply interested in the Darwinian view of evolution. He went as an undergraduate to the University of Wales at Aberystwyth in 1897. He studied zoology and then continued research at Zurich, Switzerland, from January 1903 to July 1904. He received a doctorate in science at Aberystwyth in 1904 for zoological researches, and a first post at Aberystwyth as assistant lecturer, combining teaching in zoology, geology and botany, an obviously heavy load. Even at that time he was especially interested in geography, and in 1907 took over the teaching of that subject as well as zoology and geology. For the next three years he was in charge of these three subjects, assisted for a short time by Gladys Wrigley, before she moved to a long and distinguished career as editor of the *Geographical Review* in New York (retiring in 1950). Fleure was appointed Professor of Zoology in 1910 and remained in this position until 1917, though he still handled the teaching of geography. In 1917 he accepted an endowed chair of geography and anthropology. In the same year, at the invitation of Halford Mackinder, he followed Herbertson as secretary of the Geographical Association, which at that time was the only association of geographers outside the Royal Geographical Society. In 1930 he was invited to the new chair of geography at Manchester University where he remained until his retirement in 1944.

Fleure travelled rather widely in a professional capacity. It is noticeable, however, that he carried out no personal field studies abroad of any magnitude. Most of his fieldwork (mainly anthropological) was undertaken in Great Britain. He travelled to Cairo and Palestine (1925), South Africa (1929) and visited the Continent many times in various capacities. Fleure's students entered various professional fields. A volume of essays dedicated to him and published in 1930 was somewhere described as 'a classifier's nightmare'. This, from the standpoint of the advancement of geography, is both the strength and the weakness of Fleure's approach to geography. Fleure became a Fellow of the Royal Society in 1936 (as a natural scientist, not as a geographer) and received honorary degrees at Bowdoin, USA (1945) and Edinburgh (1950). In 1938 he received the Charles P. Daly Medal of the American Geographical Society and in 1946 the Victoria Medal of the Royal Geographical Society. After retirement Fleure lived in London. He died in 1969.

The scholastic contributions of Fleure are numerous and significant in various unexplored fields. He said that four major works influenced his thinking most: *Das Antlitz der Erde* by E. Suess; *Die Alpen im Eiszeitalter* by A. Penck and E. Bruckner; *Tableau de la géographie de la France* by Vidal de la Blache, and *China: Ergebnisse eigener Reisen* by F. von Richthofen. All these, be it noted, were works published around the turn of the century. This is highly significant to an appraisal of the Fleure school and to the subsequent developments of geography in Britain.

As Fleure was a native of the Channel Islands and an early student of zoology, it is not surprising to find that his earliest publications, around 1900, dealt with these islands and medical matters. For the latter he received the doctorate degree in 1904. Furthermore, as a confirmed francophile, his interests were drawn to the myths of the Breton people. He soon got to work on related questions in Wales and wrote an article on the human geography of Cardiganshire on the same lines in 1911. At this time his interest had shifted from zoology to the races and languages of man in both the Channel Islands and in Wales. One of his most important articles was on the idea of human regions, published in the *Annales de géographie* in 1917, and in English translation in the *Scottish Geographical Magazine* in 1919. Here it was that he conceived of human communities as living in environments that might be thought of as regions of effort, of difficulty, of lasting difficulty, of debilitation and of increment. Fleure seemed to pay little attention to statistical matters, except in handling calipers for anthropological measurements. But his idea of human regions, directly, and, I believe, for the most part indirectly, have had deep parallels in the measurement of levels of living and their actual geographical occurrence. We suspect that lying behind this were the ideas of Le Play, which either reached him directly (through reading his work) or through Geddes and Herbertson, both of whom were much influenced in their thinking by the French sociologist. A book on the human geography of western Europe appeared in The Making of the Future series put out by Patrick Geddes and Victor Branford. It revealed the strong and often obscure though stimulating racial bias that was to play such an important part in Fleure's researches in the next two decades. Stature and the shape of heads seemed to play a primary role in the heritage of peoples.

Fleure was actively concerned with the understanding and reshaping of the world after the First World War. His anthropological work in England and Wales appeared in book form in 1923. His deep interest in cultural heritage and origins is evident in the best-known of his scholastic works, the nine-volume *Corridors of Time* (1927–36), written in collaboration with the late H. J. E. Peake.

It is of interest and importance to pay attention to Fleure's mature ideas, at the age of seventy-five, about the future of research in the field of geography. In a memorial lecture to Herbertson, he spoke of the lines on which he would develop the ideas of the master. Turning to problems of physical anthropology in relation to the physical environment, he said: 'If man and environment are to be studied together a great advance of science may be hoped for as more facts of climate become known, facts beyond the data of temperature, pressure and rainfall.'[1] Such facts are the 'quality of radiation', the origin of skin pigmentation, and hair texture in relation to climatic conditions. He also points to unsolved questions of the relation between climatic elements and sex and fertility. He also considers the relations between climatic elements and the biological processes of soil development, such as the formation or destruction of humus. 'These few examples'—and they are indeed stimulating examples—'are intended to show how the study of natural regions based on climate and vegetation may be developed and may help research into what is probably one of the two most urgent problems of humanity.' One of these is soil conservation. The other is the Malthusian problem of population increase.

By pursuing such enquiries, Fleure claims to be following the thought of Herbertson, and seeks 'to liberate our subject from an artificial limitation then [nearly fifty years ago!] approved even by some geographers.' These 'limiters' as he describes them (and it seems to be implied that they are still around), would have us confine our attention as geographers to 'picturing the actual world as it exists in the present':

> The important work is to see how the present world has come to be what it is. Only in this way shall we get beyond gazetteer description into the region of understanding of the present world. That in this field of study we meet historians and anthropologists starting from standpoints and using disciplines differing from ours, is a gain to all. None of us is able or lives long enough with intellectual initiative to look all around, so we supplement one another, and if there is some overlap, that is all to the good. Let us build out on Herbertson's substructures and have no fear of losing our subject's identity. The historians and anthropologists need geographers' help as also we need theirs.

This approach is little concerned with description or regional characterization as an end, but with processes and origins. It has its parallels in the USA, especially in the school of Sauer as it developed in the decades after his arrival at Berkeley. Sauer's studies on human origins in America and on the origin and spread of plants and animals, and other studies on human diets and nutrition, point in the same direction. We are in agreement with the need for appraisal of cultural and biological processes. But we are bound to raise the question: To what end? Fleure insists on the evaluation of man-land relationships in the case just quoted, specifically climatic relationships. But such evaluation may end in the mapping of distributions and this, in itself, though an invaluable technique, is peripheral to the essential geographical concern with land and the life of people upon it in their areal variations.

Two concluding comments may be made in assessing the significance of Fleure's contribution to the regional concept. First, Fleure made outstanding contributions to the advancement of anthropology, both physical and cultural. Second, he gave to geography in Britain a deep concern for pre-history and the evaluation of the cultural heritage. This is evident from the work and appointments of those now in senior posts who studied under him. It is also evident in the approach to cultural anthropology of the distinguished works of O. G. S. Crawford (who had early training under Herbertson) and Cyril Fox. It should be pointed out that this eclectic approach, in which various scholars pursue common ends and in so doing are in need of each other's expertise, is precisely the same as Carl Sauer's attitude to be discussed later. It is averse to the attempt to narrow the field. This explains the dislike of many British geographers for what they apparently regard as a 'dictatorial' approach. There are others, however, who clearly find provocative questions and problems from both sources.

Fleure adhered to a strong humanistic tradition. Right through the 1930s, geographers were apparently unable to wean themselves from the Darwinian notion of environmentalism. The study of the physical earth remained the basis of the human superstructure. The younger generation today realizes at last that the regional system needs a new approach and that, as such, a discipline needs to be formulated with clearer and more limited objectives and procedures both historical and quantitative.

The standing of Fleure, as outlined above, has been strongly corroborated by E. G. Bowen, one of the earliest students of Fleure, and for many years his successor in the chair of geography and anthropology at the University of Wales in Aberystwyth. He writes in a letter (May 1972):

> I think you have shown at least by implication that Roxby was a geographer, and Fleure an anthropologist. This is perfectly true, and I would be willing to go even further than your text implies in the case of Fleure.
>
> The significant point is that Fleure felt that the scientific revolution of the mid-nineteenth century (Darwin/Huxley) had shattered completely the conventional view of the Universe, especially its unity deriving from the Creator Himself—a Creator who had arranged for the divine creation of man as a *separate* being. Darwin, on the contrary, had shown that man

was a part of nature, and Fleure sought to emphasize thereby that a new unity could in this way replace the old. Likewise, as Darwin had taught, all living things were adapted to their environments, and man himself was no exception. Herein we see all that Fleure meant by 'geography'. The above emphasizes his interest in man as a terrestrial animal (Anthropology), and his adaption to his environment (Geography), and this evoked 'a sympathetic understanding of other peoples' (through studying their environment and cultural evolution), (*Corridors of Time*), and his work for world peace, etc.

There resulted, therefore, an anomalous situation, wherein this distinguished French-speaking francophile—the admirer of Paul Vidal de la Blache (and all of them in Paris) never produced a single regional study on the French model. Compare his chapter on Wales with that of Roxby's on East Anglia in Ogilvie's *Regional Essays*. Roxby makes a real regional study of East Anglia, as you point out, but Fleure failed to see in Wales the true *Pays de Galles*—all he saw was a lot of little Welshmen, with different-shaped heads and different styles of speech, without any unity of any kind. All this was cloaked under the traditional French regional headings, relief, climate etc.—a series of facts gathered under a list of systematic groupings—but failing in this case completely to convey 'the spirit of the place', as the French regional geographers had done.

PERCY MAUDE ROXBY, 1880–1947

Percy Maude Roxby was the son of a rector of Buckden in the heart of rural Huntingdonshire in England. He graduated at Oxford in 1903 in history and afterwards studied geography under Herbertson. In 1904 he was recommended by Herbertson to the University of Liverpool to teach geography. He remained there for forty years, a pillar of strength to the university and the organizer and inspirer of an honours school of geography with exacting scholastic standards of dedication and excellence. He was granted a travelling fellowship to China, India and the USA in 1912–13. His interest in the Far East dominated the rest of his life. In 1945 when he resigned from the chair he went to China with his wife for the fourth time as chief representative of the British Council, dying there in 1947.

Roxby's views are clearly illuminated not only in his own publications, but also in those of his students. Limiting comment here to his own work, it is not surprising to find that his starting point is the rural countryside of his home base, his work then spreading by choice and application, as in his life, to China.

His first articles were on the agricultural geography of England and particularly of East Anglia. He was dedicated to the work of the agricultural economists at the end of the eighteenth century, who wrote volumes for Arthur Young on agricultural practices and prospects in the counties of England, and used in particular the work of William Marshall on Norfolk. (Roxby was my examiner for the doctorate on 'The urban settlements of East Anglia' in 1931. He brought along to the oral examination his copy of Marshall on Norfolk, to which he made repeated reference.) The culmination of his work is to be found in the short, but mature, essay on East Anglia in the composite volume *Great Britain*, edited by A. G. Ogilvie in 1928.

From the days of his first travelling fellowship in 1912–13, Roxby had a continued interest in China. His two essays on 'The Far Eastern question in its geographical setting', published in 1913 in the *Geographical Teacher*, are classics. A series of articles appeared during the ensuing three decades.

If a man is to be designated as a leader in terms of his scholarship and ability to motivate students in training and subsequent pursuit, and in terms, therefore, of his undefinable though real charismatic quality, Roxby without question ranks as one of the most influential thinkers and teachers in the geographical tradition in Britain. Yet, one is left with the conclusion that he inculcated a mode of approach in the study of human affairs rather than acting as a springboard for research objectives.

The views of Roxby are in a strong French tradition, and most satisfactorily reflect the thought of the interwar period. To this I can personally testify, since it was only because I lacked matriculation Latin in 1922 that I was not admitted to Liverpool but was guaranteed entry to Leeds (under C. B. Fawcett), regardless of whether I should pass or fail Latin in the examinations preceding the 1922–3 session. In this period of the mid-1920s my schoolfellows studied under Roxby and I diligently read, with books of notes, the works he prescribed for the undergraduate honours degree in geography. These included, as I now recall, W. Z. Ripley's *Races of Europe* (1900), W. J. Sollas's *Ancient Hunters* (1911), J. L. Myres's *Dawn of History* (1911), J. Deniker's *Races of Man* (1899), de Préville's *Les Sociétés africaines* (1894) and E. Demolins's *Comment la route crée le type social* (1901–3). It was not until 1967 that I destroyed the bulky notes on each of these volumes, testimony of the truth of that labour during the summer vacations of 1923 and 1924. The works of Vidal de la Blache and Brunhes were the basis of this superstructure that had a predominantly humanistic bias, although well grounded in study of the physical environment. It should be emphasized (for American readers) that this *undergraduate* curriculum, as in all other British universities (and most of them to this day), included a substantial thesis that was the major concern of the third year of study, a tradition that in general continues unchanged.

There is a feature of the work of Roxby that has completely escaped the attention of commentators. Roxby was described by his colleague H. J. Fleure as an 'expositer'. This was evident in the work of his students. They compiled, selected, arranged and presented 'geographical studies' of remote areas which they had never visited, the materials for which were gleaned from printed sources and the available maps. Wilfred Smith eventually published his thesis on coal and iron in China. Ethel Simkins published her work on the agricultural geography of the Deccan Plateau of southern India. Walter Fitzgerald worked on the historical geography of 'early Ireland'. And one of Roxby's best students in 1925 prepared a large dissertation for the undergraduate honours course on Szechwan, the most south-westerly and least-known province of China.

This expository approach is of value as a first exercise in research. I recall the late Professor E. G. R. Taylor (University of London), some forty years ago, assigning to several junior colleagues the task of compiling and arranging a geographical portrayal of a remote area of the earth, using *exclusively* the reports of explorers in the *Geographical Journal* and whatever maps were available. This is an invaluable exercise of exposition in the training of a geographer. It was Roxby's method.

Roxby's ideas on the field of human geography and the regional concept are summarized in his 1930 presidential address to the geography section of the British Association for the Advancement of Science. Human geography, he states, embraces:

(a) the adjustment of human groups to their physical environment, including the analysis of their regional experience, and (b) interregional relations as conditioned by the several adjustments and geographical orientation of the groups living within the respective regions. The term 'adjustment' I take to cover not only the 'control' which the physical environment exerts on their activities, but the use which they make and can make of it. Human geography is the study of an interaction rather than of a control. The adjustment has distinct but usually closely related aspects which form the main branches of human geography.

In Roxby's view, the four principal aspects of human geography are racial, social, economic and political. Racial geography treats of the distribution of racial types, and their mental and physical traits relative to the environments in which they are found, and in so far as they affect the human response in different environments. In the light of what can be gleaned from anthropology, the geographer should study 'the relative aptitude and adaptability, climatic and otherwise, of various racial groups for developing them [regions] and the extent and manner in which co-operation between different groups may, in certain cases, be secured for this end'. Economic geography includes the geography of production and consumption, exchange and transport. Social geography is defined as 'the analysis of the regional distribution and interrelation of different forms of social organization arising out of particular modes of life, which themselves represent a direct response—although we may concede to M. Febvre not necessarily the only possible response—to distinctive types of physical environment'. The function of political geography is 'to study and appraise the significance of political and administrative units in relation to all the major geographical groupings, whether physical, ethnographic, social and economic, which affect mankind'. Finally, 'historical geography is human geography in its evolutionary aspects. It is concerned with the evolution of the relations of human groups to their physical environment and with the development of inter-regional relations as conditioned by geographical circumstances.'

The development of the concept of the 'natural region' in France and Germany in the late nineteenth and early twentieth centuries is discussed in *The Makers of Modern Geography*. In Britain, the teaching of Herbertson was unquestionably imparted to Roxby in his year of study under the master at Oxford, and was an indelible frame for his historical training. Roxby's first formal published statement is to be found in a short article in the *Geographical Teacher* for 1913–14. He referred to William Marshall's *Rural Economy of the West of England* (1793). Marshall had written: '*Natural* not *fortuitous* lines are requisite to be traced: *agricultural* not *political distinctions* are to be regarded.' He further commented: 'A *natural district* is marked by a uniformity of soil and surface, whether by such uniformity a marsh, a vale, an extent of upland, a range of chalky heights, or a stretch of barren mountain

be produced.' An agricultural district, he went on to say, shows
uniformity or similarity of practice—grazing, sheep-farming, arable
management or mixed cultivation or some particular product—
dairy-produce, fruit-liquor (cider apples).[2]

On the basis of this definition Marshall gave the first accurate
delimitation of minor units within one of the major divisions of the
British Isles—East Anglia.

Two comments are needed on this. Marshall's 'natural regions',
or soil units, had been mapped in one of the reports prepared by
the Board of Agriculture, at the instigation of Arthur Young, 150
years (and more) ago. These county reports presented the condition of agriculture at the end of the eighteenth century as a means
to the betterment of production. As a framework for their presentation it was evident that the physical conditions provided the essential base for assessing the conditions of agricultural economy, and
practicable modes for its improvement. The main determinant and
indicator of these conditions was seen to be soil. Thus for each
county report there was a sub-division into what we should now
call homogeneous agricultural units based primarily upon the condition of the soil. These soil units were defined by the agricultural
experts because they had a narrowly and clearly defined objective,
namely the location and limits of various agricultural practices.

A second point of interest is that in the late 1890s H. R. Mill
suggested a method of geographical description for a small area
(however defined as to limits). He pleaded for geographical reports
on each of the one-inch Ordnance Survey maps, comparable to the
geological descriptions of individual sheets put out by the Geological
Survey. He demonstrated his procedure for a small area in the
south-west of Sussex. Each monograph was to consist of an orderly
schematic arrangement of sets of phenomena in the area.

Mill's model[3] was arranged as follows: geographical position;
areas of main geological formation ('upon which are based the
"natural regions"'); dangers to navigation off the coast (from the
Admiralty Chart); rivers; roads and railroads; climate; woodland
and agriculture; population (by parishes, of which there were eighty-
three complete, plus twenty-six 'other' [partial] parishes); and
industries. The plan did not materialize, but it was adopted by
Mackinder at Oxford, and later by Herbertson and the heads of
other departments of geography. Students were allotted a topographic sheet for 'geographical description'. Three of these early
studies were published. They involved the tracing of data from
the map, and probably the preparation of population and crop
maps. But there was little creative effort involved in the delimitation

of natural areal combinations. In other words, the area was factually fragmented into topics and there was little cartographic or descriptive effort involved in synthesizing and interpreting the data.

Roxby argued in the same article that Britain should be divided into physical units in terms of criteria relevant to agriculture (relief, geology, climate). These could serve as a base for the analysis of agricultural development since the Agrarian Revolution, and current agricultural possibilities and population trends. Such a work was later undertaken by L. D. Stamp in the 1930s, but the reports of the latter were based on counties, albeit many of them using the soil divisions of the county reports of the end of the eighteenth century (noted above) as a framework of reference for the development of the existing agricultural patterns.

A changed and matured interpretation was evident some twenty years later. In 1926 Roxby asserted that the natural 'region' was a 'true synthesis of different but related kinds of spatial facts', both physical and human, and that 'the nature of human response depended on its *intrinsic* conditions as well as on its *external* space-relations. Such natural units are exemplified by the *pays* of France.' He writes that, other things being equal, a 'natural region' of the *pays* class will tend to develop the type of rural economy most appropriate to its particular size and climatic conditions; a physical unit tends to become an economic unit and, the more developed the means of communication, the more pronounced is regional specialization.

External influences, such as the impact of a large city on agricultural production, may offset these local adjustments, but even so the intrinsic physical conditions will always make themselves apparent. Roxby applied this concept to a subdivision of Central Europe:[4]

> It is the comprehensive study of the region and of interregional
> relations which gives unity and distinctiveness to geographical
> investigation, and the region as so conceived may be compared
> to an organism, at least as implying a complex unity made up
> of a particular integration of different elements, physical,
> biological and human.

The major natural regions (geographical regions according to Unstead!) combine 'a distinctive association of intrinsic conditions with a definite set of space relations', and the lower categories of regions should be marked by the prevalence of a particular character or relations; the smaller the unit, the narrower the basis of differentiation.

To this organic analogy, that persisted so long, we reply, with C. Vallaux in France (1925), that 'what strikes us above all today is the poetic and metaphoric character of the concept, the limitation of its point of view and the positive errors to which it leads'. This applies to the above definition of a geographical region as well as to its analogy to an organism. But the concept in some form persisted through the 1920s and 1930s. Sauer wrote in 1925 of the landscape unit having 'organic quality'. But Roxby continued to define areas as physical entities and then to assert that they were *ipso facto* human entities. This completes a circle and shuts the door on the investigation of the degree to which the concept is valid.

These statements of *natural* and *geographical* regions are declarations of faith. The problem is to devise ways and means of measuring the degrees of coincidence of terrestrial distributions, without recource to mystical, aesthetic or biological analogies. Moreover, this is largely a problem of selecting areal criteria that are determinants or resultants of a whole range of dependent areal variables, and that can therefore be used for defining homogeneous regional associations. This is the essence of all geographical research that could well dispense entirely with the shades of Darwinism. There is no necessary coincidence, either on the local or continental scales, between human land-patterns or distributions and the framework of physical divisions. Nor can such physical divisions be systematically defined on the basis of one or two elements.

It is fitting to conclude this appraisal of Roxby with a personal tribute from one of his first students, J. W. Darbyshire, a schoolfellow of the writer, who entered the University of Liverpool in the early 1920s to study for an honours degree in geography under Roxby. Darbyshire was a near-contemporary of several 'disciples', some of whom I have already named, now dead or retired, who achieved distinction as university teachers. Now retired after a long career as head of an outstanding school, he writes as follows: [5]

P. M. Roxby's approach to geography was similar to, and sprang from, his approach to living. He was a charmingly uncomplicated person whose integrity, self-discipline, sensitivity and humility shone through his mastery of the English language and his comprehensive and profound knowledge of his subject. Deeply, but unostentatiously religious and idealistic, he was originally a historian who became primarily a human geographer.

For him, human geography involved a study of racial, historical, social, economic, political and general cultural factors and values. As defined in his Presidential address to Section E of the British Association at Bristol in 1930 he regarded it as 'a valuable mental discipline' and 'a vital element in training for national and international citizenship'. It called for 'an exact sense of proportion in appraising the value of many factors and more specifically developing the great quality of sympathetic understanding'. However, it was more than 'an educational instrument': through the programme of constructive work which it advocates', it can 'contribute to the realization of the ideal of unity in diversity . . . the only possible ideal for the life of humanity on a planet, which . . . will always retain its infinite variety'.

Geography as a whole he regarded as a study of change and momentum, of the interaction between man and his environment, an environment that was both physical and human. He visualized man evolving as a part of nature and learning to live increasingly in harmony with nature, rather than in antagonism to it, or in terms of its conquest. In general, he felt that appraisal of the values of many of the factors involved in such study could best be achieved in a regional setting in which synthesis followed careful analysis. Consequently, he gave a great deal of thought to the study of regional geography, which provided the framework for much of his own work and that of his students. Between his regions, whether major or minor, he also looked for transition zones and 'space relationships'.

The meticulous care which he took with his appraisal of values and conclusions severely curtailed the volume of Roxby's publications. Of necessity also, these were limited because of the pastoral care he lavished on his students, to whom he gave most generously of his time. Another limiting factor was his strong sense of duty as a citizen: to Merseyside and its university, to his country and to the world at large, particularly China. Through his magnetic personality, academic brilliance and unselfish attitude, he fostered the study of geography by personal contact as well as through his lectures both in and outside the university.

It is no exaggeration to assert that the relationship between 'P.M.' and those students who knew him well (and there were many!) was one of genuine affection. For the students, this was tinged with a sense of awe and reverence, a relationship with a master whose example as a man, whose understanding as a mentor and whose genius as a teacher left an indelible impression. P. M. Roxby's many disciples have carried on his pioneering work far beyond Merseyside, where the school of

The United Kingdom

geography he founded goes from strength to strength. Our geographical heritage has been abundantly enriched by his labours; the unselfish and strenuous endeavours of a great and good man to promote harmony and sympathetic understanding through the study of geography have been greatly rewarded.

7

The Third Generation

The 'third generation' refers here to those senior geographers in Britain today who are near or have entered retirement. They have careers that began in the mid-1920s and several were students of, and much influenced by, Fleure or Roxby or their contemporaries. Several are deceased and others have not enjoyed the same scholastic prominence. Among the leaders of this generation are H. C. Darby, E. E. Evans, L. Dudley Stamp, T. W. Freeman, A. A. Miller, S. W. Wooldridge and W. Smith. This chapter is confined to the work of L. D. Stamp and H. C. Darby as conspicuous examples of outstanding contributions over a period of nearly forty years to the furtherance of the regional concept. Stamp trained as a geologist, Darby as an economic historian. Both have been concerned with man's use of land in Britain, the first from the standpoint of agriculture and its potentialities, the second from the standpoint of modes of agricultural practice in the past and notably in early medieval times. Both have been conspicuous leaders in academic and public service. Their work and views are essential to understanding the advancement of the regional concept in the interwar period.

L. DUDLEY STAMP: THE MAN AND HIS WORK
by R. O. Buchanan[1]

Laurence Dudley Stamp was born on 9 March 1898, the youngest child of a well-established middle-class family in Catford, southeast London. He was in fact very largely self-taught, but performed so brilliantly at school in 1913 that he was admitted as a student at King's College, London, though he was only fifteen years old. In the following four years he completed the full honours courses in geology and in botany. In 1917, at the end of the university session, he enlisted, but obtained special leave to sit the honours examination in geology, emerging with first class honours. Soon afterwards he was commissioned into the Royal Engineers and arrived in France in 1918. There he was able to do a surprising amount of geological investigation, on the results of which he qualified for his M.Sc. while still in the army and published his first paper immediately after.

On demobilization he was appointed as a research scholar in his old department of geology in King's College, London. Over the next two years, a stream of papers testified to his interest in the geology of Britain, Belgium and north-east France. His publications based on these researches earned him his D.Sc. at the early age of twenty-three. During these two years, however, he had in addition been registered as an external student for the newly instituted B.A. honours degree in geography of the University of London. In 1921 he sat the first examination held for the degree and added another first class honours result to the one he already held in geology.

At the end of 1921 he accepted an appointment in Burma as an oil geologist to a commercial company, an appointment he was to hold until May 1923, when he returned to England to be married before taking up his new appointment as Professor of Geology and Geography in the University of Rangoon. Major work on the vegetation of Burma and continued geological investigations were supplemented by efforts to lay the foundations for the adequate teaching of geography in the University of Rangoon and in the schools of India, Burma and Ceylon.

Three years of intense activity while occupying the chair in Rangoon were followed in 1926 by his appointment to a readership at the London School of Economics. There his chief was Professor Ll. Rodwell Jones, whom he succeeded in the chair in 1945. In 1949 he was translated to the newly instituted chair of social geography, from which he retired in 1958, on reaching the age of sixty.

With Stamp's return to England in 1926, his geological interests retreated somewhat into the background, and it was as geographer that he made his place in the academic world. His major contributions may be summarized as lying in two main fields: first, education in geography, especially through the medium of textbooks, and, second, the development of land-use studies.

Without any doubt it was *The World* that made the widest and most important impact of all his numerous textbooks. It was first published in 1927 under the title *The World: A General Geography for Indian Schools*. This was quickly followed by *The*

*World: A general geography, South African Edition; The World:
A General Geography, Australian Edition; and The World:
A General Geography for British Schools.* These separate
versions of what was essentially the same book exploited for
the first time the advantage of combining general world geography
with an extended treatment of the 'home area', thus suiting the
work to the special local needs of schools as well as to their
common general needs. The British version had run to sixteen
editions by 1960. No other single British author, not even
Herbertson, has had such a widespread and deep influence on
pupils at the formative ages in their study of geography, and no
one can estimate how many geographers had their interest first
aroused by his attractive school texts.

Textbooks were one contribution to geographical education,
a widespread, general, but somewhat impersonal contribution. In
Britain itself, Stamp made a more personal, but perhaps equally
important, impact by his work for the Le Play Society and the
Geographical Association. Following the lead given by Le Play
himself and Patrick Geddes, the Le Play Society found its role
in the organizing of field-study trips to various parts of Europe.
The members of the groups participating in these study trips
were predominantly teachers, and the demonstrating and
inculcating of sound methods of conducting field studies were
no less important than the results of the studies themselves.
Stamp was only one of a number of distinguished men who
led these parties, but his services were given more frequently
and over a longer period than appears to have been the case with
any other leader. All told, he led seven Le Play study groups,
beginning with Finland in 1930 and ending with Corsica
in 1957. . . .

It needed the academic foresight of a Stamp to perceive the
value, to the subject of geography and to the national planning
of the land of Britain, of a systematic survey of the whole
country based on a single scheme of land-use classification.
It was in 1930 that he addressed himself to the task. By the end
of 1931, every county of England had been organized and the
actual work of surveying was in progress. By the end of 1932,
all the counties of Scotland and Wales had been added and
the preliminary work was finished.

The actual surveying was done by university and college
geographers, and schoolteachers working alone or supervising
groups of their students. Field by field, the existing use of every
acre of the country at the time of the mapping was entered on

the sheets of the six-inch (1:10,560) Ordnance Survey map, and Stamp himself made sample checks of the completed field surveys in every county of Britain. As the field sheets were completed, they were sent to headquarters in London, where a small team of geographer-cartographers produced the necessary drawings for publication in colour on the one-inch (1:63,360) scale, following the sheet lines of the current Ordnance Survey Popular Edition. The magnitude of the task, both in the field and in the drawing-office, is sufficiently indicated by the fact that the six-inch map, as it then existed, comprised some 11,000 sheets. Naturally, the rate of progress in the field surveying varied greatly from county to county, but the rate of publication of the finished work varied also with the state of the finances. The first two sheets came off the press early in 1933, the last not till after the Second World War. The completed one-inch map, itself a generalization, was further generalized by reduction to the ten-mile (1:625,000) scale, on which the whole country was covered in two sheets.

The Land-Use Survey map presents a picture of the actual use of the land of Britain in the 1930s. This was a time when the depression-induced financial plight of British agriculture was reflected in the swiftest and most drastic change in the geography of its agriculture that the country had experienced since the enclosures of the early nineteenth century. For that very reason it has a unique value as a historical record and also as a kind of base level against which the subsequent striking changes may be evaluated. The map itself was supplemented and the work of the survey rounded off by the publication of a complete series of county monographs, each based on the map but drawing on historical, economic, climatic, relief and soil data as aids to the interpretation of the map and the understanding of the agricultural geography of the time. Stamp edited every volume and wrote several of them himself. Quality inevitably varied, but some of the volumes were of outstanding excellence, and the complete series together with the maps constitutes a quite remarkable addition to the geographical literature of the country. Further, just as the one-inch map was generalized to the ten-mile scale, so Stamp distilled the essence of the county reports into *The Land of Britain: Its Use and Misuse,* a massive tome which was published in 1948. Perhaps the main significance of this book from our present point of view is that it demonstrates the trend of Stamp's thinking, based on the record of how the land was in fact being used, but concerned progressively with how it should be used. . . .

In the survey lay the genesis of Stamp's conviction of the necessity for physical planning. The beginnings of his interest in planning go back to the later 1930s, but were strongly reinforced by the public service duties to which he was officially called as expert during the Second World War. The first of these public appointments was the vice-chairmanship of Lord Justice Scott's committee on land utilization in rural areas, set up in 1941. In the report of that committee, the hand of Stamp is plainly evident, and it was essentially government acceptance of the general lines of the report that led to the passing of the Town and Country Planning Act of 1947 and the development of the Ministry of Town and Country Planning to give effect to its provisions. Planning of this kind was not entirely new, but the act widened its scope and greatly strengthened the powers available to guide and control the evolution of the face of Britain. In passing it may be noted that this was the first official recognition that the concept of regional planning is a geographical concept and that the trained skill of the geographer is an essential research component if the areal assessments on which plans must be founded are to be adequate.

The Scott committee proved to be only the first of a whole series of demands for the employment of Stamp's expertise in the public service. While it was still sitting, he was in 1942 appointed chief adviser on rural land-use to the Ministry of Agriculture. A natural, indeed almost an inevitable, consequence of the respect he earned in the ministry was his appointment after the war as the official United Kingdom adviser on land-use to the Food and Agriculture Organization of the United Nations. In the meantime, he had been appointed a member of the research committee of the Ministry of Town and Country Planning. This was work very close to his heart and he was active in helping to shape the structure of the planning organization of the ministry and in establishing the central planning team. His next official appointment was to the Royal Commission on Common Land. The commission was set up in 1955, and a clue to the complexity of the problems involved is given by the inability of the commission, despite intense effort, to report before 1958. In addition to Stamp's general contribution to the investigation and the resulting recommendations, he was himself entirely responsible for a very substantial account of the geographical distribution of common land. The labours of the commission were hardly completed when he became a member of the Nature Conservancy and of two of its committees, the Committee for England, of which he became chairman in 1963, and the Scientific Policy Committee. Finally, in 1965, he was appointed to a post for which he was singularly well fitted by virtue of his great knowledge and experience of the land of Britain, the chairmanship of the Natural Resources Advisory Committee of the newly formed Ministry of Land and Natural Resources. . . .

The work of the Land Utilization Survey continued throughout the war and into the post-war years. He nevertheless found time and energy to continue his travels and to write more books. *The Land of Britain* has already been mentioned. No other approached that in magnitude of task, but mention may be made of the book published in 1952 by the American Geographical Society under the title *Land for Tomorrow: The Underdeveloped World*. This book, an expanded version of the Pattern Lectures, delivered by invitation in America, had land-use as its central theme, including both the dangers of inappropriate use of land and the scope for further development in already highly developed countries, such as the United States. His concepts of the implications of land-use were widening and his vision was extending far beyond the confines of Britain. English editions of this book under the titles *Our Underdeveloped World* and *Our Developing World* appeared in 1952 and 1960 respectively.

From 1949, under the auspices of the International Geographical Union, he was concerned with the launching of the World Land Use Survey, of which he became director in 1951. This was a venture different both in kind and in scale from the original survey of Britain, and Stamp's part as director was essentially that of organizer and publisher. The task was to find and encourage investigators who would work to an agreed scheme. The complexity arose from the vast range of possible land uses and human activities in widely separated areas of the world, of differing natural and human conditions, and the further practical difficulties imposed by the lack of large-scale base maps for the field surveying of land-use. Where good air photo cover was available, it could be used to supplement ground mapping, or even as a substitute for it. The land-use map of Cyprus, for example, illustrates the combination of ground investigation and photo interpretation, while the Sudan map was almost entirely dependent on air photo interpretation. In the world land-use studies, as in the original British survey, the completed maps provided the basis for textual analysis....

Stamp's official and semi-official appointments were themselves evidence of official recognition of the stature he had already achieved in his chosen fields, no less than they were sound investments in expected services. That the services to the public weal matched the expectations is attested by the award in 1946 of the CBE and in 1965 of knighthood, both for services to land-use. But long preceding these public honours, and continuing parallel with them, came a succession of academic honours. In 1950, he was president of the Geographical Association and from 1952 to 1956 president of the International Geographical Union. His term of presidency of this latter body included in its last year the Eighteenth International Geographical Congress, held in Rio de Janeiro. His presidential address to the congress on 'Measurement of land resources' dealt with a problem to which he had quite naturally been drawn through his studies of land-use and to which he was later to return in other contexts. In 1956 he was president of the Institute of British Geographers, of which he was also one of the founder members. His presidential address to the institute, 'Geographical agenda: a review of some tasks awaiting geographical attention', ran true to form in being concerned wholly with practical tasks. From 1956 to 1963, he was a vice-president and, from 1963 to 1966, president of the Royal Geographical Society. Finally, throughout his career a succession of awards, national and international, testified to the growing width and depth of his influence.

HENRY CLIFFORD DARBY, *by P. J. Perry*[2]

Born and brought up in Wales, Professor Darby was educated in Neath and at St Catherine's College, Cambridge, already by the late 1920s a college with as strong a geographical tradition as any in the university. In 1932 he was appointed to a university lectureship in geography at Cambridge which he held concurrently with a research fellowship in history at King's College, Cambridge. In 1945 he became professor at Liverpool, in 1952 at London, and in 1966 he returned to the chair of geography at Cambridge and a fellowship at King's College.

It was, then, at Cambridge that the formative years of his academic career were spent, as undergraduate and research student in comparative obscurity, and then as a lecturer and as fellow of one of the most famous of the colleges. During this period he appears to have read unusually widely; for example he attended lectures on medieval Latin literature. The breadth and depth of this reading, his knowledge of classical and modern literature in particular, is apparent in much of his published writing, especially on methodology. His doctoral dissertation 'The role of the Fenland in English history' was completed in 1932 but published as two monographs, *The Medieval Fenland* and *The Draining of the Fens,* only in 1940; meanwhile in 1936 there appeared *An Historical Geography of England before 1800* of which he was both editor and a contributor. As a university lecturer and fellow of a wealthy and prestigious college he was in an academic environment as favourable as any in Britain during the 1930s, and more so than most in terms of financial status and security, time and facilities for research (notably libraries), and contacts with numerous and eminent scholars, few of them geographers but many of them very interested in his work. (In contrast most of the provincial universities, where many of his Cambridge contemporaries began their academic careers, were small, ill-equipped, and understaffed, mainly as a result of their financial weakness.) The importance to Darby of such an environment and the academic contacts which it made possible is hard to assess, but it is readily acknowledged in the work which Darby published at this time. Three of his teachers were particularly important in this respect.

Frank Debenham, Australian, explorer, and the first Professor of Geography at Cambridge, instigated Darby's work on the Fens, and the department which he was building and of which Darby was part during the 1930s was the setting in which *An Historical Geography of England before 1800* 'grew up'. Darby worked under Debenham as an undergraduate, specializing in physical as well as in historical and political geography. To Debenham's teaching and department must be ascribed in part Darby's high estimate of the importance and basic position of geomorphology within geography and his secondary but considerable interest in man-land relationships, in conservation, and in applied geography.

Sir John Clapham, Professor of Economic History and Vice-Provost of King's College, also played an important part in the origins of *An Historical Geography of England before 1800.* In Darby's own words, 'fostered by the encouragement of Dr Clapham, the idea became a concrete plan'. It is because of Clapham's three-volume *Economic History of Modern Britain*

(1926–38), which deals with the nineteenth century, that Darby's book ends at 1800. Clapham also gave Darby considerable personal as well as editorial assistance with the two Fenland monographs. There is a striking similarity in the general character of the work of the two scholars.

Bernard Lord Manning, fellow and bursar of Jesus College and university lecturer in medieval history, 'soundly practical' and 'deeply spiritual', possessed some of the omnicompetence of the 'Renaissance man'. His contact with Cambridge geographers was primarily as an examiner and teacher of historical geography during the 1920s and 1930s, although he did not publish in this field. He was with Debenham and Clapham the instigator of *An Historical Geography of England before 1800,* and to him are dedicated the two Fenland monographs which grew out of work executed under his direction as Darby's research supervisor.

Darby's contribution to geography is best considered under five headings: his work on the Fens; *An Historical Geography of England before 1800*; the Domesday series; numerous papers on his varied secondary interests from Northern Rhodesia to National Parks; and his rather fewer methodological essays.

Darby's two books and several papers on the Fens are of substantive interest to geographers of all kinds, as well as to engineers and social and agricultural historians. They are also of considerable methodological significance. The first, *The Medieval Fenland,* is an example of flexibility and pragmatism, a characteristic of much of Darby's work, the varied methods and approaches employed reflecting the character and problems of the sources. The second, *The Draining of the Fens,* is an evolutionary study, written at a time when instantaneous cross-sections were still apparently the orthodoxy of historical geography, an orthodoxy to which Darby himself had been committed, judging by the aims, if not the results, of his editorial activity of four years earlier. Emphasis on the sources is a second striking characteristic of the two volumes. Moreover the author generally allows the sources to speak for themselves, often at length and with no more than explanatory and augmentatory comment rather than paraphrase or summary. It is this which makes the two monographs simultaneously authoritative and readable. In their concern with man-land relationships and land-use problems in a regional setting they are more obviously the product of contemporary geographical thought; and in their thorough understanding and exposition of the region's physical geography they are very much a product of the Cambridge school of the 1930s.

The impact of the two books is hard to assess. Probably because they were published in 1940, it seems to have been less than their substantive and methodological merits deserved. Generally they received favourable reviews, although one geographer could still be found to criticize their concern with the past rather than the present, and one to be troubled by the abundance of quotation. But the author's view of the nature and methods of historical geography attracted little attention, possibly because the books were published in a series of monographs on economic history rather than as historical geography. Their severest critic was the medieval economic and social historian R. Lennard, who felt that they were inadequate on the peculiar institutions associated with the Fens and their drainage problems (deliberately omitted by Darby as outside the scope of historical geography) and on the local economy. This view was at least arguable at the time and has since become more so as further research on the area has been undertaken, especially by agricultural historians.

This body of work, probably the least known of all that executed by Darby, is, then, of more importance than its localized and specialized, almost obscure, setting would suggest. *The Medieval Fenland* is a work of variety and flexibility written at a time of rather rigid orthodoxy. *The Draining of the Fens* one of the earliest, and still one of the most satisfying, studies of geographical change by an historical geographer.

An Historical Geography of England before 1800, fourteen studies edited (and contributed to) by Darby, has been, and remains, an influential and widely read book among both historians and geographers.[3] It is usually thought of as epitomizing and justifying in intention and execution a concept of historical geography as 'the reconstruction of past geographies'. This is stated in the preface, where, however, it is also pointed out that the chapters were written separately and not all upon the same pattern. The book is self-evidently more of a methodological mixture than was said or implied to be the case by the editor and some reviewers when it was first published. Eight of the fourteen chapters are primarily 'cross-sectional', but three of these also discuss more than a little of their material in evolutionary terms, and the cross-sectionalism of another three results from their concentration on a single source. Curiously, when Darby (on looking back on and revising the 1936 volume in 1960) commented on the importance of sources and problems in determining methodology, it was not with respect to these chapters, but less logically to the evolutionary ones, which in the case of his own contributions drew on a wide variety of sources. A concern with geographical change is to be found in seven of the essays, and two others are essentially studies of the effects of geographical factors upon settlement patterns and processes; the result in one of these, by Professor S. W. Wooldridge, is equally a study of change. The volume thus contains examples of a variety of methods of writing historical geography, in some cases within a single chapter, and at least one view of historical geography, which many historians wished neither to encourage nor to exemplify, as 'the influence of geographical factors upon historical events'. Yet the book is still widely regarded as essentially 'cross-sectional', suggesting that many readers have not progressed beyond the preface in forming their judgments. Geographers, in their reviews, welcomed the book wholeheartedly for its substantive merits and comprehensive appeal, its high standards of geographical, historical and cartographic scholarship, and its non-deterministic outlook. It was accurately foreseen that it would make a great contribution to the status and teaching of historical geography in Britain.

It was in no sense deterministic, no straightforward explanation of history in terms of physical geography, such as had often been put forward earlier in the century. That a very high standard of both historical and geographical scholarship and insight, much of the latter strikingly new to the historians, had been achieved was widely recognized. Historical geography had become academically acceptable. In Sir George Clark's words, 'Historical geography, still a little uncertain of its place among the sciences, has great promise for the future. Mr [*sic*] Darby and his collaborators have shown that it has already won an important place in the study of British history.'

An important consequence of the book was then that the validity and utility, and some of the methods and results, of historico-geographical scholarship became known and largely accepted among a diverse academic audience. At the same time it was apparent that some historical geographers, contributors and others, could no more than partially accept the methodological position and intention of the volume. The limitations of this cross-sectionalism are most apparent in some of the chapters which follow it most closely, notably those by E. G. R. Taylor and W. G. East. Taylor's treatment of Tudor England is unbalanced largely because it concentrates on those permanent or slowly changing elements in the rural scene which are most amenable to her methodological position, and neglects those which were changing rapidly. East's picture of the eighteenth century is likewise too static a view of a century in which industrial, agricultural and transport revolutions were in progress, an approach which cannot be justified merely by pleading that these were nineteenth- rather than eighteenth-century developments to a greater extent than is generally realized. In other chapters, notably that by J. N. L. Baker, change is described but without its causes being much considered, another unsatisfactory solution to a basic and pressing problem in writing historical geography to which Darby himself later returned in his methodological essays. Reviewing the book twenty-four years after its first publication, Darby admitted the necessity of connecting narrative to augment, explain and connect the cross-sections, and some contributors have since produced much more dynamic historical geographies.

The methodological significance of *An Historical Geography of England before 1800* is then that while establishing the scholarly merits of historical geography in the most general sense, it did not justify the narrow view of historical geography set out in its preface. Rather it demonstrated, largely through the frequency with which the authors departed from such an approach, the necessity and desirability of a concern for change among historical geographers. It was, albeit unintentionally, itself a cause of changes in the methods of historical geography, although its unsought success in this respect was no more immediate than that of the Fenland monographs, and it is still often considered to be the successful epitome of the static and instantaneous cross-sectional approach.

Darby's interest in Domesday Book and in medieval England dates back to the early 1930s, perhaps resulting primarily from his close association with Manning, but it has been his main research interest only since the war with the publication since 1952 of five regional volumes of the *Domesday Geography of England*. Now [1967] there remains unpublished only the sixth volume, of editorial summary and synthesis. It is by this great undertaking that Darby is now, in all probability, most widely known, and by which his scholarship is likely to be longest remembered and most often judged, since early and substantial revision and rewriting of so large a subject seems unlikely.

Of major interest to historical geographers and medieval

historians alike, the series has been universally well received.
Its imaginative conception was a revelation to the historians in
particular; its most serious critic, Professor Postan of Cambridge,
admitted that such an approach to Domesday Book, and the
resultant insights, would probably have never occurred to a
medieval economic and social historian such as himself. In this
respect the series has, like the 1936 volume, made evident to
historians just how fruitful and enlightening the analysis of
historical data by geographers can be. Its high level of historical
scholarship coupled with its 'caution, tact and ingenuity' have
been equally widely applauded. . . .

In addition to his work on the three major themes discussed
above, Darby has published a number of papers and reviews on
his other geographical interests, notably the conservation and use
of areas of outstanding interest and beauty such as Britain's
'National Parks' and the New Forest, the history of surveying
techniques, and English agriculture in the eighteenth and
nineteenth centuries. Detailed documentary study characterizes
the last of these as much as any of his work, and concern with
the evolving, man-made landscape connects all three, and some
of the other topics he has treated, Hardy's Wessex and place
names for example. It would almost be possible, from a cursory
reading of this varied output, to conclude that Darby has at
times viewed historical geography as the study of landscape
evolution. Thus in his review article on place name studies he
writes, 'of what relevance are these investigations to the study of
the English landscape', and in his retrospective review of *An
Historical Geography of England before 1800,* he suggests that a
revised version might include 'chapters dealing with the economic
changes that gave successive landscapes a new look'. One other
among these papers deserves mention, that on population in
mid-nineteenth-century Cambridgeshire, a study of changes
in space and time over a period of ten years, and an exercise in
the skilful and imaginative manipulation of a source which has
since been much exploited by British historical geographers.

Darby's methodological papers, of which there are four of
major importance, are characterized by an open-minded and
pragmatic approach to the methods and problems of writing
historical geography. The work of other scholars is examined
with the aim not of testing it against any yardstick of geographical
orthodoxy, but of assessing how effective the approach employed
has been in solving that particular problem, and whether it has
a more general usefulness. In the 1953 paper an interest in the

problems and shortcomings of the cross-sectional approach, dating perhaps from 1936, as far as explanation is concerned is evident, although the advantages of this method are also given recognition. The problem of the validity of narrative writing in geographical scholarship is stated and Darby concludes that this is an acceptable method, although this assertion is placed somewhat ambiguously in a landscape context and his overall position on this issue is not entirely clear. The quintessence of Darby's pragmatism is perhaps to be found in a discussion of the frontiers of geography, somewhat reminiscent of C. O. Sauer, in this same paper: 'These limits are not to be defined by nice methodological arguments or by jugglery with words and definitions. The limits are best set by the nature of a particular problem ... the character of a particular landscape.' Likewise his review article of 1960 strongly favours experiment in the writing of historical geography; it is in this essay also that he himself admits that not all the chapters in *An Historical Geography of England before 1800* are cross-sectional. In 1962 another methodological paper ends with a plea for methodological tolerance and diversity, with little or no emphasis on the correctness of any one of the six methods of writing historical geography which it outlines.

The problem of the 'vital spark' of time and its essential but difficult place in geographical scholarship has been the second major theme of Darby's methodological writing. A dynamic approach is proposed in 1953—'let us not then study a static picture but a process that is continuing'—and in 1960 reviewing his own book he strongly, but not dogmatically, favours Broek's method of alternating cross-section and narrative. In 1963 this matter receives its fullest discussion in an essay contained in a volume primarily by and for historians. (It is in this same essay that the point that geography is concerned with more than the landscape, with society and politics as well for example, is strongly made, more so than in most of his earlier and more specifically geographical essays.) He concludes, as is indicated in earlier papers, that geographical narrative is both unavoidable and intellectually acceptable, and in the last resort no different from that of the historian. To a large extent he sees the difference between history and geography as more one of topics than of principles, a pragmatic position (scarcely a philosophy) very different from that enunciated by Hettner and Hartshorne and often since regarded as the essence of geographical orthodoxy.

How far from orthodoxy Darby has moved, in fact if not in reputation, is evident in some of the other statements of these methodological papers, especially that of 1962. Here he suggests that there is no particular logical order for geographical description; that imaginative (and thus individualistic) description is as necessary as the more usually practised (and commonly very laboured) variety; that the idea of regional synthesis is of very dubious value. Each of these statements is a radical criticism of a formerly or presently accepted norm of geographical scholarship, although they have excited little comment or attention and seem to have done little to alter Darby's orthodox reputation.

To a great extent Darby's methodological writings have been concerned with the technical problems of writing historical geography and have more and more accepted the necessity and validity of studies of geographical change in the form of narrative. Their second major concern has been to plead for diversity, experiment and tolerance in criticizing the methods and substance of historico-geographical scholarship, with the suggestion that in practice the methods of any piece of work are better (and in fact more often) pragmatically than philosophically determined, and that this should also be true of critical judgments and evaluations.

More than any other individual Darby has established the place of historical geography in the British universities, and both directly and through his students has much influenced its methodological development. Flexible and pragmatic in his own work he has moved from orthodox cross-sectionalism to accept, if not in his own recent work to practise, the need for historical geographers to study change; his work has also been characterized by—and very significant in— its close attention to and skilful use of sources. The value and importance of maps and fieldwork he accepts but rarely emphasizes, although he has long enjoyed an enviable reputation among his students as a field teacher. Many now widely accepted and well-known aspects of Darby's scholarship represented a new and radical approach when he first adopted and advocated them; that such radicalism has characterized the greater part of his work does not, however, seem to be widely known, probably because he is now most often thought of as the author of the methodologically conservative (and pragmatic) Domesday volumes and only occasionally as the author of the Fenland monographs, and the methodological papers which most strongly present this radical viewpoint. Seen as a whole Darby's work is now, as it was twenty-five years ago, a sound and subtle synthesis of geography and history, and the

D*

most sustained, successful and stimulating scholarship of
its kind yet achieved by a British geographer.

COMMENTARY

The work of Stamp and Darby reflects that of most of their contemporaries and the students who studied under them. It reveals certain important attitudes in the development of the regional concept in Britain in the interwar years. I would like to emphasize these traits in a few paragraphs.

First, as a geologist, as were many of his contemporaries, Stamp sought to evaluate the 'physical base' as the environmental framework of human activity. Indeed, the term 'physical base' was firmly rooted in the examination syllabuses and teaching of the departments of geography in the University of London. This was often referred to as 'the geographic background'. Thus it appears in the arrangement of the first county monographs of Stamp's land-use studies. When asked how he would handle variations of land-use that were the expression of economic conditions rather than of the 'physical base', a distinguished geomorphologist replied to this writer in 1960, 'Leave them out.' Another geomorphologist in 1941 was examining the fieldwork exercises in one area of some of my own graduating honours students. They had recorded throughout the area the grouping of buildings and outhouses and enclosures of farmsteads, in order to discover if there were any patterns with a marked regional distribution. His comment was, 'These are largely a matter of chance.' He was, in fact, quite wrong, since we found close correlations between farm layout and type of agricultural economy. He showed neither interest nor understanding of this problem of the regional variations of landscape and society. These are hangovers from the 'environmental approach' of the natural scientists.

Second, Stamp, like others of his generation, slowly shifted from this position, and began to examine land-use and agricultural systems and other human data in their regional variations as ends in themselves. He himself turned to many such problems that were relevant to human welfare and planning. His unit of measurement of land potential in peasant agrarian societies and his study of the distribution of 'life and death' are examples. Yet, he never seems to have forsaken the notion of the physical base. This results in some curious contradictions in his work, for his assessment of regional variations of phenomena was of sterling quality in the service of physical planning.

Third, neither Stamp nor Darby shows a definitive and continuous focal concern with the variations and changes through time of the landscape—fields, farms, hedges, walls, hamlets, villages, towns, tracks. With all respect to the scholarship of Darby and his colleagues, the book edited by Darby on the *Historical Geography of England before 1800* was a series of place studies of economic history. Not one essay turned to the landscape scene and its variations as the reflection of the changing historical conditions they so ably presented. Not one of the contributors, in other words, apparently had any real understanding of Jean Brunhes's work on landscape (it was available in English), although this is quoted as a target in Darby's preface. It should be noted, however, that Darby has devoted attention on several occasions to studies in landscape analysis in Britain. Moreover, some of the writers of monographs in Stamp's series turned to the characterization and distribution of farm structures and farming systems. Yet landscape analysis took a back seat. Since the war economic historians have brilliantly grasped the opportunity; some younger geographers have followed their lead. This is a remarkable lag, since Sauer's work on 'the morphology of landscape' (discussed in Part Two) was published as far back as 1925, but seems to have made, from this evidence, no impact whatever on geographic thought in Britain between the wars. In fact, one department of geography did not even have a copy of the monographs in its library in 1960.

Fourth, both Stamp and Darby encouraged the use of a special expertise in regional (man-land) analysis. These skills involved the selection, recognition, classification and mapping of data. Stamp's work embraced the mapping of land-use both in the field and from aerial photographs. This had its parallels, as we shall see, in the USA. Darby's approach demands skills in deciphering and interpreting historical documents, a skill that is equally shared by medieval historians.

Fifth, certain terms (such as 'geographic description', 'totality' or 'holism', 'geographic synthesis', 'cross-section approach', i.e. geographic description in a particular time period), which constantly cropped up between the wars are still used, even by the reporters on Stamp and Darby. They were considered to be very elusive. This is simply due to the lack of clear objectives. There were very few indications between the wars of real clarification of such terms and the problems they raised. Their pseudo-philosophical discourses were intellectual exercises and of little practical value. The British mind is essentially analytical and pragmatic. But there are many signs in the work of Stamp and Darby and their colleagues through four decades of a shift in focus and a considerable advance in the objectives and techniques of regional analysis. This has become sharply marked in the last two decades, as we shall see in the next chapters.

In conclusion, the point of these comments is not a plea for intellectual constraint, but for clarity of objectives. This is necessary not merely in the field of research (which after all is a matter of personal choice), but for undergraduate training in the discipline we seek to advance. Most geographers between the wars limited their concern to human activities that were derived from or related to the physical earth, although some sought escape from this strait-jacket. The environmental approach was spelled out many times by Stamp, but it obviously did not fit with the many regional variants of human activity which he so assiduously pursued in his later years and for which he deservedly gained royal recognition.

8

Founders of the Main Centres

Honours schools in geography, involving two years of specialized study of one subject, together with a substantial thesis in the final year, with variations of approach, were established in virtually all British universities about fifty years ago. The first such bachelors degrees were established by Roxby at Liverpool and Fleure in the University of Wales at Aberystwyth. These were quickly followed by many others and the position ten years ago is summarized in Chapter 2 by Fleure. Since the Second World War ten new universities have been chartered and ten technical colleges have received university status. In nearly all of these institutions there are departments of geography, though the emphasis and degree procedures vary considerably.

All departments annually award bachelors degrees to their students, who are normally in their early twenties. The number has increased greatly in the post-war years. Today an average number of graduates would be about fifty, but in some departments it runs into hundreds. In the year in which I graduated, 1925 (the second year of honours degree awards in the University of Leeds), the number was three, and rather than a specialized disciplinary degree it was a first-rate general education.

From the total listing of university departments, I have selected the main centres according to the numbers of higher degrees awarded, the pre-eminence of distinguished founders, and the contribution to geographical scholarship. Three centres of learning are outstanding: Edinburgh, London and Cambridge. The departments with which Roxby (Liverpool) and Fleure (Wales and Manchester) were associated are also prominent. Finally, two universities founded departments that have continued to grow, reaching high peaks since the Second World War. These two centres are at Manchester beginning in 1892, and Sheffield in 1908. The first has been associated with several leading figures though none of them stayed for a very long period until the appointment of Fleure in 1930. The second had one founder, R. N. Rudmose Brown, who stayed there from 1908 for thirty years. Both of these centres are among the major seats of geographical tuition today. Attention in this chapter will be limited to the leaders of Edinburgh, Cambridge, London and the Commonwealth. I mainly reproduce excerpts from obituaries written by those best equipped to evaluate their work, and conclude with a note on Thomas Griffith Taylor, the Commonwealth leader.

I EDINBURGH

Scholars in Scotland of the natural sciences, particularly in Edinburgh, made a remarkable contribution to the advancement of knowledge in the latter half of the nineteenth century, out of which emerged a department of geography in the university in 1908. The Geikie brothers, Archibald and James, Professors of Geology at the university, were among the earliest protagonists of the work on the agents of erosion on the development of land forms. Archibald's book on the *Scenery of Scotland* appeared as early as 1865 and for his life work he was subsequently knighted. One should also note here the work of the geologist J. W. Gregory at the University of Glasgow, for he also was concerned with the characteristics and origins of the earth's surface features, as illustrated, for example, by his classic work on the nature and origin of fjords. The oceanographic work of the *Challenger* expedition in the 1880s, sponsored by the Royal Society in London, was directed by Sir John Murray in the University of Edinburgh. Two great cartographic establishments had their seats in Edinburgh, W. and A. K. Johnston, founded in 1825, produced a *National Atlas* in 1843, and employed the great German cartographer A. H. Petermann for two years in the preparation of a modified version of the famous German work, Berghaus's *Physical Atlas of Natural Phenomena.* John Bartholomew founded the map firm of that name and he was followed with distinction by his son, J. G. (1860–1920). The latter assisted Murray in the preparation of the *Challenger* reports, and also Dr Buchan in the preparation of the *Meteorological Atlas*, which the firm published in 1899. The peak of the Bartholomew achievement is the *Times Atlas*, first published after the First World War, with a second edition after the Second World War. The Scottish Geographical Society was established in 1885 to promote through its meetings and a journal the diffusion of the findings of exploration and the advancement of geographical knowledge, and for years was directed by Marion Newbigin, a great pioneer of geography in

Britain. Hugh Robert Mill was early associated with Murray but transferred to London and became a pillar of strength to the Royal Geographical Society. We have already noticed the close association of both Geddes and Herbertson with Edinburgh. Out of all this stimulus Mill and Bartholomew urged the university to establish a teaching appointment. This was filled in 1908 by George Chisholm, an economic geographer, and a graduate of the university, and he was followed by Alan Grant Ogilvie, and he in turn by the present senior professor, Wreford Watson, a graduate of the University of Edinburgh. Chisholm, Mill, Geddes and Herbertson pursued undergraduate studies at Edinburgh, as did several men who later became leading geographers, notably MacFarlane and Dickson.

In what follows we shall present appraisals of the work of four of these scholars, Murray, Newbigin, Chisholm and Ogilvie. H. R. Mill is discussed in Chapter 9, where he is placed in the seat of his major geographical work, the Royal Geographical Society.

JOHN MURRAY, 1841–1914,
by R. N. Rudmose Brown[1]

Towards the turn of the century there were several marked influences in Edinburgh that specially contributed to the rise and growth of modern scientific geography and they were very diverse in their nature and outlook. I would dwell for a little on these influences because they made a strong impression on Herbertson and were influences whose weight has often been overlooked. First, there was the pronounced trend towards physical geology exercised by a long line of prominent Scottish geologists. Physical processes rather than stratigraphy occupied the minds of Lyell, Playfair, Murchison, Ramsay, the Geikies, Peach and Horne— perhaps because many of the physical agents can be so profitably studied in Scotland while the stratigraphical side is but poorly illustrated; there was one influence leading direct to geography. Then, too, by the work of a succession of Edinburgh naturalists zoology was becoming a living science. It was reviving from the study of the dead to that of the living. Biology was replacing necrology. Edinburgh was famed in marine zoology and its wider outlook, marine ecology. The work of John Goodsir, Edward Forbes and Wyville Thomson brought about the close association of Edinburgh with the *Challenger* expedition of 1872 when the leadership was entrusted to the last named, then a professor at Edinburgh University.

But another Scottish association of that expedition was largely a matter of chance—and one of the most fortunate chances in the history of science. Herdman recounts how the staff of the *Challenger* had been settled when on the eve of sailing one of the naturalists dropped out and hurriedly the post was offered to a young worker in Tait's laboratory (Tait was then Professor of Natural Philosophy), by name John Murray, a Canadian by birth but of Scottish descent. After the return of the *Challenger,* Murray became the director of the *Challenger* commission, the editor of its results, the author of the narrative and the founder of modern oceanography. His approach was largely a physical one through his studies of the configuration of the ocean basins and the classification of deep-sea deposits. Until the days of this expedition, data on both those subjects were so scanty that no conclusions of value could be made, at least beyond the confines of the North Atlantic. Many of Murray's conclusions have stood the test of time and his classification of deep-sea deposits is essentially the accepted classification today. These interests in the depths and the floor of water areas Murray carried at a later date to the English lakes and lochs of Scotland, where he was associated with another Scottish geographer, H. R. Mill. Murray inspired a whole succession of budding oceanographers, and taught them the discipline of scientific argument and encouraged independence of thought.

No better example of scientific deduction from circumstantial evidence could be found than Murray's argument for the existence, and his drawing with Bartholomew of the outline, of an Antarctic continent in 1886, at a time when the data were scanty and many authorities disbelieved entirely in the existence of such a continent. Murray based his arguments on the few deep soundings available in high southern latitudes, on the apparent continuity of the terrigenous deposit of blue mud, the composition of the few glacial boulders found on the sea floor in iceberg areas, the direction and temperatures of the winds in high latitudes, the prevalent distribution of the pack-ice, the nature of the icebergs, the form of the glaciers, and the diversity of the fauna on opposite sides of the Antarctic area. Subsequent exploration has not merely confirmed Murray's theory of a continent and its structure but almost exactly confirmed his suggested extent and outline.

Murray and the *Challenger* office were at the base of much of the research and teaching in physical geography in the early years of this century and had a wider influence also, inasmuch as oceanography is less analytical than synthetic, and biological as well as physical. So it paved the way for a wider study of the correlation between not merely physical but also organic distributions. Hence came the inspiration to such pioneers as H. N. Dickson, H. R. Mill, E. Heawood, J. Y. Buchanan and to a great extent Herbertson—in his researches on rainfall, in the solid physical basis to his natural regions, in his share in the survey of the English lakes and his other associations with Murray. Another enthusiasm of Murray's led to the high-level observatory on Ben Nevis which functioned from 1883 to 1904. Without Murray's driving power this triumph could never have been accomplished. Many young enthusiasts took their turn at staffing the observatory and so became keen meteorologists and often geographers. Ben Nevis was certainly a strong influence in Herbertson's development as a geographer.

MARION I. NEWBIGIN, 1869–1934[2]

Marion Isabel Newbigin was born at Alnwick in 1869, and died in Edinburgh on 20 July 1934. In November 1902 she was appointed editor of the *Scottish Geographical Magazine,* Sir John Murray having been re-elected president of the Scottish Geographical Society and Professor James Geikie being the honorary editor. The volumes of the *Magazine* issued since that date, their gradual evolution reflecting the progress of the times, and directed by an able and accomplished editor, themselves constitute the proper eulogium of Marion Newbigin.

Marion Newbigin had the distinction of winning honours in two fields. Her early training was obtained in London; her university terms she kept at Aberystwyth and Edinburgh. Her degrees of B.Sc. (1893) and D.Sc. (1898) were conferred by London. These were the days when the universities still maintained much of their medieval attitudes to women. University medievalism, moreover, did not facilitate the pursuit of academic careers by women, however outstanding their ability. Women were not admitted to the medical classes in the University of Edinburgh until 1916, but until that time there was in Edinburgh an extramural school of Medicine for women. As a student here Miss Newbigin came under the influence of J. Arthur Thomson, and when Thomson was transferred to Aberdeen she succeeded him as lecturer on biology and zoology at the Edinburgh school. She disliked lecturing, yet both as regards matter and manner she was a lecturer of that conspicuous ability which seems to become rarer every day.

91

Unusually large audiences welcomed her infrequent appearances on the lecture platform.

Miss Newbigin's original work in zoology appears to have taken two directions. As a biologist she patiently collected a mass of data relating to coloration in animals. She produced several papers on sections of this work, and on its completion published *Colour in Nature* (1899).

Marion Newbigin could not have failed to submit to the influences which at the end of last century emanated from the *Challenger* office and pervaded scientific Edinburgh to a remarkable extent. This gave the second direction to her zoological work. *Life by the Sea-Shore* (1901) is a volume which has a remarkable distribution. With singular appropriateness it was modernized by the director of the Millport Marine Biological Station; but when a book is still in demand after these thirty years of biological vicissitude, can the epithet 'classic' be withheld?

It is in some ways much harder to speak of Miss Newbigin's place as a geographer than as a biologist, in spite of the fact that she was emphatically in the first rank as such. But geography is far from having consolidated a definite position, British geography particularly so. In Germany and France there is a certain and characteristic degree of crystallization, but in this country, and perhaps in all English-speaking countries, there is still a lack of such things as a definite and common technique of the subject, and that natural occupation by research workers of a recognized field of research, to which better organized and more fully developed sciences owe much of their definiteness and prestige. Miss Newbigin was in fact among the parents of modern British geography. Of these some are already gone. The influence of Herbertson upon those who came in contact with him seems to have been profound, yet Herbertson left little bearing the hallmark of such authority. Something similar might be said of the late H. N. Dickson, G. G. Chisholm and H. R. Mill. But unlike Herbertson and Dickson, Marion Newbigin has left, apart from her shorter papers, more than a dozen books, and unlike Chisholm and Mill she covered in them the whole field of geography. Her *Introduction to Physical Geography* (1912) is the stand-by of many students. Her *Plant and Animal Geography* (1936) is a pioneer work in English, as is her *Ordnance Survey Maps* (1913), which has inspired many successors. *Aftermath* (1920) is a remarkable essay in political geography, as *Canada* (1927) is in historical, and *Southern Europe* (1932), her last important volume, is a study in synthetic geography which has no superior in English.[3] Of these books some are small,

all are tentative, essays towards an organization which is not yet achieved. They show Miss Newbigin as the first of the British pioneers in geography who gave complete expression to her ideas. She is the first geographer—without any qualification such as physical, economic, human or other—whom we have produced, and who has consolidated her position.

No geographer of our acquaintance has lavished on his work so much of true scientific method as Marion Newbigin. No one has left work more capable of standing the ordeal of critical study. No one has exerted a better influence on the modern student. Not the least important vehicle of this influence has been the *Scottish Geographical Magazine*. No British geographical organ is more indispensable in the libraries of geographical schools and institutions, and none has given greater encouragement to serious workers in geography. The *Magazine* owes this, and much that it implies, to its late editor. Many of its contributors owe her no less: advice, criticism, even textual improvements in their articles.

GEORGE G. CHISHOLM, 1850–1930,
by A. G. Ogilvie[4]

Born in Edinburgh in 1850, Dr Chisholm was within a few months of completing his eightieth year, though few of his associates realized the fact. He was educated at the high school, and took his M.A. and BSc. degrees at Edinburgh University, which after his retirement from the office of reader in geography bestowed upon him in 1924 the honorary degree of doctor of laws. Of the work of his earlier maturity the *Handbook of Commercial Geography*, first published in 1889, is outstanding. Mr McFarlane of Aberdeen University wrote an appreciation after the appearance of the ninth edition in 1922. In this Mr McFarlane speaks of the author's 'early scientific training, his wide historical knowledge and his interest in political and social as well as economic problems', and says that in the *Handbook* its author demonstrates that geography gives opportunity 'for that rigorous search after truth for truth's sake, for that balanced judgment between conflicting views, and for that precise statement, which are the essence of all real scholarship'.... Upon just what basis of wide and exact geographical knowledge that book was founded may be realized by glancing at the massive tome of *Longman's Gazetteer of the World*, first published in 1895, of which Dr Chisholm was editor....

It was, in part, this extreme conscientiousness, this sense of the need of laying firm foundations before a truly scientific geography could be established, which brought recognition. position and honours to him relatively late.

In 1895, after an earlier life spent mainly in his native land, he went to London, and till 1908 was engaged there in lecturing and writing. In that year he was appointed the first lecturer in geography in Edinburgh University, becoming reader in 1921. In 1910 he became secretary of the Scottish Geographical Society, carrying on the duties simultaneously with his university work, and continuing in the office for two years after his retirement as reader in 1923. His last years were spent in investigating and reflecting on the population question and means of modifying the struggle for existence as it affects subject peoples and groups. He was an excellent German scholar and had a good knowledge of French and Italian.

Apart from literature his interests were wide. A great letter-writer, he carried on correspondence with geographers and economists in almost all parts of the world, giving to his letters the same care and trouble which characterized all his activities. Though never a climber in the technical sense he was an ardent walker.

A notable step in the promotion of geographical study in Scotland was taken when the University of Edinburgh established a lectureship in geography in 1908. This was the first recognition of geography by a Scottish university, and clearly it was a matter of great importance that the services of a man of Chisholm's calibre were obtained as the exponent of the new subject. . . .

The need for university instruction in geography was pressing, if only because of the demand in Scotland for teachers with an adequate training in a subject of great educational value. The rapid realization of this fact is reflected in the numbers of students who followed the course for the M.A. degree, or who came back, as a number of graduate teachers did, to take the class. During three of the pre-war years (1910–11 to 1912–13) there were over 100 students, and altogether about 1,000 men and women had the advantage of hearing these lectures.

The foundation of the bachelor of commerce degree offered a welcome opportunity for imparting knowledge of the principles of geography to those who might make use of it in a business career; and from 1919 this class of student was added to the number of his pupils. In 1919 a postgraduate diploma in geography was established. He contributed courses on 'Economic geography' and on 'Economic ethnography'. The first of these gave ample scope for his notable gift of making trade statistics live, and of tracing the rise of commercial nations as affected by geographical conditions. This course was taken with great advantage by certain honours students of economics. The second course dealt with a subject that Dr Chisholm himself originated, and under a somewhat cumbrous title he found himself free to discuss many questions of first-class importance. Among these he was particularly interested in problems of race and labour, and he carried on an extensive correspondence with scholars all over the world who had similar interests. ... From 1920 to 1923 Dr Chisholm was giving four separate courses of instruction, and on his retirement he made the generous offer to continue his lectures on economic ethnography without emoluments, and he did so for three further sessions.

ALAN G. OGILVIE, 1887–1933,
by T. W. Freeman[5]

A. G. Ogilvie was the only child of Sir Francis and Lady Grant Ogilvie, principal of the Heriot-Watt College in Edinburgh and later at the Royal Scottish Museum and at the South Kensington Museums. Born in Edinburgh in 1887, he was educated mainly in England at Westminster, and at Magdalen College, Oxford, where he graduated in history in 1909; at that time no degree was available in geography. He had, however, already met A. J. Herbertson, who was working in Edinburgh for the Bartholomew map firm. Ogilvie became a postgraduate student at Berlin University, where he met the great Albrecht Penck, then at the height of his powers. In Paris at the Sorbonne he encountered the famed French geographers of the time, Vidal de la Blache and Emmanuel de Martonne. He also met W. M. Davis and attended his lecture course at the Sorbonne. He was a member of the transcontinental excursion across America in 1912, on which he came to know some eighty geographers of varying fame and ability. It was a liberal and in some ways a leisurely introduction to his life work and in February 1912 he became a junior demonstrator in Oxford on the resignation of O. G. S. Crawford, since widely known as an archaeologist. In Oxford, he gave lectures on general and physical geography, assisted with a course on the British Isles, organized the library and helped with fieldwork, much of it done on bicycle tours of the neighbouring countryside.

While resident in Paris, Ogilvie collected a great deal of material on Morocco in the Bibliothèque Nationale, which he presented as a paper to the research division of the Royal Geographical Society in 1912. Warmly commended at the time for this work, Ogilvie had not then visited Morocco but took the view that through map work and various sources one could construct an image of a country. Though he was humorously apologetic about this early work in his mature years, he was firmly of the opinion that intelligent map study can be a substitute for fieldwork, giving at least partial satisfaction: in any case it is hardly possible for a writer, even on a small country, to see every corner of it. The right use of the map was something he carefully considered in all his teaching; in one Edinburgh meeting of the university staff, a distinguished ancient historian spoke of the difficulty of teaching students to discern all there was in any historic manuscript. How similar, Ogilvie commented afterwards, was the problem of teaching students to see all there was in a map and to analyse it effectively. At the same time, he did not favour the 'guess work' sometimes advocated in textbooks. He was deeply interested in the teaching of map work to the pass students of the university, then numerous, and deeply critical of many of the textbooks filled with shallow generalizations (and their writers). His honours students were taught regional geography, which he placed in the final year as the culmination of the course, with the full use of detailed topographical maps and visual aids such as photographs and slides.

Ogilvie was to have toured the world in 1914–15 as an Albert Kahn fellow, two years after P. M. Roxby, but this was not to be. He served in the Royal Field Artillery and in a field service unit, and in 1918 was sent to the geographical section of the General Staff, with which he went to Versailles as a member of the British delegation. Part of his work was to make a survey of southern Macedonia, and in the Balkans he acquired a great deal of experience which was to be the basis of valuable contributions to the Admiralty handbooks on Greece published nearly thirty years later. He conceived the task of the map-makers at the Versailles conference as the delineation of boundaries that would be least likely to make trouble afterwards, but he was fully aware of the dangers that lay ahead and as early as 1935 regarded the possibilities of European war as grave: a visit he paid to Germany in that year did not lessen his fears. The principles underlying the territorial decisions of the peace conference were partially geographical, due largely to the cohesive work of the American 'Enquiry' centred at the house of the Geographical Society in New York: the British government drew its data from a number of different departments, with much overlapping. In seeking to change the political allegiance of people from one State to another, the conference tried to reduce ethnic variety and also to leave the new or altered states with adequate communications, both for ordinary commercial movement and for military purposes. The 1 : 1,000,000 map was the standard base for boundary delimitation, with more detailed work on the 1 : 200,000 maps or those of similar scales. The military value of hill ranges, the military and economic value of railway junctions, and the retention within one state of natural entities such as intermontane basins and valleys were considered. Inevitably the politicians were able to overrule the experts and some of the frontiers were not drawn up on principles that could be called geographical. In fact, many boundaries included large minority groups, such as the Magyars, both in western Rumania, where the boundary through the Danubian plain was so drawn to include a railway, and in the Slovak part of Czechoslovakia, which was provided with good railway links and a foothold on 100 miles of the Danube. In the pamphlet of 1922, Ogilvie considers critically the boundaries of Czechoslovakia, Yugoslavia, Rumania and Bulgaria with Italy, Austria and Hungary as defined in the treaties of Versailles, St Germain, Trianon and Neuilly. His work shows a deep knowledge of military strategy and also of the fundamental regional geography of the time.

In 1919 Ogilvie went to Manchester University, but left after one year to join the staff of the American Geographical Society, where one of his main tasks was to write *The Geography of the Central Andes,* published in 1922 as one of the society's research series. This work was a contribution to the general survey of Hispanic America, and whose partial culmination came in the publication of a complete series of 1 : 1,000,000 maps for which the society had assumed responsibility. In fact, Ogilvie never went to the Andes, and was entirely dependent on maps, photographs and printed sources, so the gift for evoking landscapes was fully tested in this work. In 1923, he returned to Edinburgh, to follow G. G. Chisholm, the economic geographer, and there he remained to his death in 1954. The work at Edinburgh was begun in his middle thirties with a rich and varied experience marred by intermittent ill-health dating from his war service. He came to a city he knew well and where he was known, and one with an established geographical tradition centred on its map firms (especially Bartholomew's), the work of Chisholm in the university and the successful career of the Royal Scottish Geographical Society with its distinguished editor, Dr Marion I. Newbigin. As the years went on he was drawn into a wide range of public activities, too many for his strength and certainly too many to permit the enjoyment of long clear periods of study and writing. Like many other unselfish people, he was almost oblivious of the social contribution he made to his day and age through his work for so many societies and organizations; and he was always advising others to save some time for recreation and necessary rest. But though he regarded his published output as slight, his work shows some interesting features and, it will be noted, an outlook quite different from that of his near-contemporary, P. M. Roxby.

At all times, Ogilvie insisted that geographical study is incomplete without an adequate study of the physical basis, and this was most clearly stated in a paper given as the Herbertson Memorial Lecture in 1937 at Newcastle-on-Tyne. Referring to the work of Herbertson, he notes that the major 'world regions' which he and later geographers defined were climatic and suggested that these large units could be conveniently subdivided on a land forms basis. If one agrees that 'the character and distributions of all phenomena studied by geographers are intimately bound up with the relief of the land' then to give a satisfactory regional view 'the thoroughness of the geographer's study of the land forms ought to be in direct proportion to the degree of detail in which he views and discusses the other phenomena rooted in a region'. Though physical geography is the last chapter of the geographical story, few geologists in Britain have shown much interest in geomorphology and most geomorphologists have worked in schools of geography and have been concerned with the evolutionary and explanatory description of land forms rather than with a merely empirical approach. Ogilvie in fact was much concerned with the evidences of peneplanes or surfaces of erosion in the landscape and wished students to know how such features had evolved. Yet he agreed wholeheartedly with W. M. Davis in his view that the geographer, as such, should begin with the results of geomorphological work rewritten for his own purposes, for 'the geographer is concerned with the present, which he describes with the main verbs in the present tense'. In fact the 'geographer may well find real use for calculation from the map of such things as stream density, areas of undissected remnants of a given erosional or constructional slope, average degree of slope, stream length compared to valley length, proportion of slopes of given exposure'.

We should note Ogilvie's exemplary interpretation of the physical units of central Scotland, which is anchored to the various surfaces of erosion—a remarkable interpretation of existing land forms in the light of their geochronological development. He extended this study in a portion of the Alps to the mapping of the altitudinal zones of vegetation and cultivation. He also actively encouraged field research into the regional variations of the population composition, seasonal work rhythms, etc., in central Africa. Finally, while employed at the American Geographical Society in New York, he compiled a full-length monograph on the Andes in southern Peru. This was based entirely on maps and records. Ogilvie never put foot in the area. This demonstrates the value of composition in geographic description, as opposed to the minutiae of fieldwork, in which, however, Ogilvie was also skilfully versed.

There is no doubt in my mind in retrospect that Alan Ogilvie was the geographer of his day, and probably also of ours, who had the clearest conceptual picture of the field of geography as a regional science and the proper place of geomorphology. The training of his undergraduates embraced the necessary goals and skills of this geographic approach. It is particularly notable, that while geomorphology and economic history have their own goals, he recognized that they are essential underpinnings to the distinctive field of geographical enquiry.

II CAMBRIDGE[6]

The first lecturer was appointed in 1888 with the aid of the Royal Geographical Society (as at Oxford). The lecturers were successively F. H. H. Guillemard, J. Y. Buchanan (1889) and H. Y. Oldham (1893). Lectures were given, but there was no examination in the subject towards a degree. In 1903 the board of geographical studies was set up with the object, amongst others, of organizing examinations for a diploma in geography and for geography as a subject for the ordinary B.A. degree. The first examination took place in 1907. Lectures and examinations continued, and, in 1919, the geographical tripos (for an honours degree) was established.

A second phase, therefore, started in 1919 with the establishment of the honours degree in geography and with the appointment as reader of Philip Lake, who was designated head of department. The first honours examination was held in June 1920. Lake was succeeded in 1928 by Frank Debenham, an Australian who had served under Captain Scott's Antarctic expedition (1910–13) and who had been appointed lecturer in 1919. With the appointment of Debenham the department moved in 1928 from its cramped quarters in the department of geology to a building of its own. The first open scholarship in geography at either Oxford or Cambridge was awarded by St Catherine's College in 1929. The first Ph.D. research student was H. C. Darby who took his Ph.D. in 1931.

A third phase began in 1931 when Debenham was appointed first Professor of Geography. The academic staff included H. C. Darby and J. A. Steers as lecturers.

In 1932 the faculty of geography (which had replaced the old board in 1926) became part of a new university faculty of geography and geology. A few years later (in 1936) the department moved to a larger and well equipped building, which it still occupies. Debenham retired in 1949 and was succeeded by J. A. Steers, who was followed in 1966 by H. C. Darby.

The department has grown to its present (July 1971) size of about 300 full-time undergraduates and thirty-five graduate students. Over the years, the department has produced a continuous stream of geographers, many of whom have gone into university posts. Graduates of the department occupy over ninety university posts in Britain and over fifty university posts overseas. These include the following who are not on the staff at Cambridge: J. T. Coppock, C. A. Fisher, P. Haggett, P. G. Hall, M. Chisholm, J. B. Sissons, J. N. Jennings, R. F. Peel, O. H. K. Spate.

The Scott Polar Research Institute was founded in 1925 with Debenham as its first director. This became a subdepartment of the department of geography in 1957. Also attached to the department was the aerial photography unit with its own aeroplane.

The important contributions of the Cambridge school of geography need special note. It has a long tradition of specialization on the geography of land forms. This tradition was maintained and strengthened in the interwar years, and critical comments will be offered on a later page (Chapter 10). This field of study has been still further advanced in the post-war years in various ways, notably under the leadership of R. J. Chorley. The geography of man, however, also received constant attention in teaching, though little was published in the way of research in the interwar period. However, the direction of the teaching under Debenham's régime is indicated by a series of four volumes entitled *Teach Yourself Geography* edited by Debenham, with an introductory volume by himself entitled *The Use of Geography*. These were published in the early 1950s and include not only Debenham's ideas of the field of geography, but also, in a volume on *Historical Geography* by Jean Mitchell, what is probably the finest exposition of the scope of historical geography in print. The other volumes are on physical geography, the geography of living things (biogeography) and economic geography. Debenham characterizes geography in one felicitous phrase as 'the philosophy of place'.

The field of human geography has been sharpened and advanced since the war. I merely point to the substantial published works on Ceylon by B. H. Farmer, to *The Historical Geography of Western Europe before 1800* by C. T. Smith, with a specific acknowledgment to Jean Mitchell in its preface, and finally, to the massive researches on the geography of medieval England by H. C. Darby and his collaborators. It is also fitting to note here the conspicuous leadership of O. H. K. Spate, who hails from Cambridge but for the best part of the post-war years has been ensconced in Canberra, Australia. There is also a long succession of graduates who are today among the leaders of research in human geography—P. Haggett, P. G. Hall, G. Manners, M. Chisholm and C. A. Fisher.

FRANK DEBENHAM, 1883–1965,
by J. A. Steers[7]

Professor Frank Debenham died at Cambridge on 23 November 1965, about a month before his eighty-second birthday. He was an Australian who, after leaving the King's School, Paramatta, first read for an arts degree at the University of Sydney and later, after teaching for a few years, returned to read for honours in science, and made geology his main subject. Edgworth David was his professor, and at that time the department was working up the material of the Shackleton expedition of 1907–9. At this time also Captain Scott and Dr Wilson visited Sydney. Scott wished to emphasize the scientific value of his expedition, and also to have Australia represented. Debenham was the man who was selected for these purposes, and so joined Griffith Taylor who had been chosen in England.

In the Antarctic Debenham did a considerable amount of geological and survey work; on account of injury he did not go on the polar journey, but worked mainly round the base camp. Later, in the summer of 1911–12, he made extensive investigations in the region of Granite Harbour, and to do this he found he had to use plane-tabling as well as more precise methods of survey. It was undoubtedly then that he familiarized himself not only with 'textbook' techniques of survey, but also with the many ways in which unconventional means could be adopted. In his later teaching at Cambridge, and particularly in the many cadet courses which took place in the department during the Second World War, his originality of approach, especially in mapping land forms, was derived largely from his Antarctic experience. Similarly, his great interest in measuring physical phenomena dated back to his work on Antarctic glaciers.

At the end of the expedition he was able to go to Cambridge where he began to work up his field notes, and in 1914 he revisited Australia with the British Association. War had begun before his return, and he was drafted into the Oxfordshire and Buckinghamshire Light Infantry and saw service as a major in Salonika, where he was badly shell-shocked and wounded.

After the war he returned to Cambridge, and in 1919 became a lecturer in surveying. Since the cartographer of the Scott expedition had been killed in the war, Debenham had to cope with all the survey material as well as his own geological work. Philip Lake was at that time reader in geography and he and Debenham worked closely together. Debenham's friendly manner soon made him at home with the students, and from the start he played a great part in building the department, not only as an institution, but perhaps even more as an enterprise in which friendship and human relations played a significant and constructive role. From 1923–8 he was a tutor of his college, and this helped him to appreciate the problems he later met when he succeeded Lake as reader in 1928. In 1931 the readership was suppressed, and Debenham became the first Professor of Geography at Cambridge.

Debenham, who had played an important part in its foundation, became the first director of The Scott Polar Research Institute in 1925 and held the post until 1946. During this time, with Priestley and Wordie, he was largely responsible for the growth of, and interest in, polar and other expeditions of various types which were such a marked feature of Cambridge between the two wars.

When Debenham joined the department of geography in 1919, it occupied two rooms in the Sedgwick Museum and shared the lecture rooms. The Polar Research Institute was first established in a private house at the corner of Lensfield Road and Panton Street; this has now disappeared. When in 1928 the department of geography made its first major move to premises in Downing Place, Debenham's ability to organize became apparent. The present building of the Polar Research Institute was erected in 1934, and there, too, his ingenuity was manifest. But his major achievement was in taking over the old forestry school, and adding to it a building considerably larger—to make the present department of geography.

He was president of the Geographical Association in 1952 and gave an address entitled 'Travel'. He received the Murchison Grant (1926) and the Victoria Medal (1948) from the Royal Geographical Society, of which he was for a time a vice-president; in 1965 he was elected an honorary fellow. In 1928 he was secretary to the executive committee of the International Geographical Congress which met at Cambridge and in 1935 he presided over Section E (Norwich meeting) of the British Association.

During the Second World War a great deal of his energy was devoted to the numerous cadet courses organized in the department. Since surveying methods played a large part in their curricula, Debenham was most apt in devising methods and apparatus for their use. Immediately after the war the department passed through a busy and rewarding period, and Debenham understood very well the difficulties and problems of the older men who came to take, or complete, their courses.

After his retirement in 1949 he remained remarkably active. He visited Africa both before and after 1949, and became interested in, and an authority on, water problems in central Africa. He not only published some valuable reports, but also wrote several books on this part of the world. With increasing age he became very deaf and suffered much from his heart; hence in later years he kept almost entirely to his home, but still continued to write.

III LONDON

The University of London, beginning in 1836, has grown to be a mammoth administrative organization of many separate institutions, seven of which are comparable in size with a single provincial university. University College and King's College were founded in the 1820s and are the oldest, but were closely followed at mid-century by Bedford College for women. Birkbeck College began as an institution for extension work for adults, primarily with night-time classes in the 1890s. The School of Economics was established in 1895 through the efforts of the great liberal leaders of the day. A fully equipped geography department has been established since 1960 in the School of Oriental and African Studies, with C. A. Fisher at its helm.

Geography was taught through the 1890s in the extension work of Birkbeck College and was put into the hands of George Chisholm, who came down from Edinburgh, in 1895. H. J. Mackinder was appointed at the new School of Economics in 1895. L. W. Lyde was appointed to a chair in economic geography in 1903. Physical geography was taught in association with geology right through the last quarter of the nineteenth century at King's College, though a lecturer was not appointed until 1925. Bedford College began its department in 1919. The joint school of King's College and the London School of Economics began in 1922. Queen Mary College received a reader in 1947, although before that date geography and geology were combined, and honours courses were instituted in 1919. A stimulus was brought about by the introduction of honours degrees in the subject around 1920. Since this time all the colleges named have had departments of geography with full equipment and staff and ever increasing numbers of students.

The sequence of the most distinguished professors is as follows: University College: Lyde, Fawcett, Darby, Mead; School of Economics: Mackinder, Jones, Stamp, Wise; King's College: Wooldridge; Birkbeck College: Chisholm, Unstead, Taylor, East, Campbell. London also produced one of the most influential and respected teachers of geography in London, and indeed in the nation, James Fairgrieve, and special emphasis should be given to his contributions.

LIONEL W. LYDE, 1883–1948,
by C. Daryll Forde and Alice Garnett[8]

Lionel William Lyde was born in 1863. After a classical education at Sedbergh and Queen's College, Oxford, he became a specialist teacher in English, and later a headmaster. During this period his interest turned to geography. His profound understanding of the subject, together with the remarkable breadth of his scholarship in other fields, distinguished his work from the outset and remained throughout his life one of its outstanding characteristics.

During the first decade of this century, when geographical education was beginning to take shape, his was probably the most profound influence on the teaching of geography in schools. His early textbooks virtually revolutionized the teaching of that time. His connection with university work dates from 1903, when he was appointed to the newly created chair of geography at University College, London, a post which he held until 1928.

When, after the First World War, honours degrees in geography were established by the university, Professor Lyde founded the honours school at University College.

Lyde was a brilliant lecturer. His fine voice, the flash of his brilliant eyes and his unfailing dignity will be recalled and appreciated by all who heard him. In those early days when there was a lack of textbooks and monographs, his gift of 'gutting' (his own phrase) the essential principles and subject matter of special studies and of adapting them to geographical description, was particularly valuable. With highly personal turns of phrase, and striking what he called 'the geographical note', he could evoke both an imaginative picture of a particular scene and a vivid sense of the reality of the factors, climatic, economic and political, at work within it.

The tiny slips of paper on which in his fine handwriting the few headings of his lectures were inscribed—slips which he characteristically carried into the lecture room in his hat or tucked into the back pocket of his cut-away coat—served to recall him from amusing, but often penetrating, digressions on the geographical ignorance of 'politicians', one of his favourite Aunt Sallies. Students in those early days were privileged to spend a long weekend with him towards the end of their course in an intensive reading party before the examination. In his study they could select for themselves from the mass of cuttings and offprints which filled so many envelopes neatly arranged in cabinet drawers, and glimpse from their arrangement and his frequent marginal notes both commendatory and caustic, something of the way in which he assimilated material from all sources as grist to the mill from which his highly individual approach was developed.

Lyde was eclectic in his methods and valued a telling phrase or striking incident as a means of driving home his points. He was not fundamentally deterministic in his approach. He was too much of an individualist himself and too little of a systematizer for that. But striking associations were always in the forefront of his mind so that it was sometimes difficult for the unwary to avoid the impression that continentality, roundheadedness and political tyranny, for example, were linked in the nature of things. He sought above all to develop what he called the capacity for accurate imagination and gave his students vivid, unforgettable impressions of areas which he often knew himself only at second-hand—be it the Tarim Basin or the Andean Puna. He did not stress the importance of scholarship in the strict sense, leaving students to read what they could find and paying little attention to rigorous criticism of assumptions or evidence concerning environmental effects on human life. At its most extreme, his teaching verged on the dogmatic, but this could be corrected by other contacts and experience. What he could and did communicate with brilliant success was a sense of the actuality of other places and peoples. His outlook was at the same time charged with a sense of the importance of accurate geographical knowledge in judging and planning human affairs.

Lyde's tenure of the chair of economic geography at University College came at the end of a long and varied career in which as a schoolmaster, coach and writer he had developed the art of stimulating the imagination of young people and making facts memorable from their intrinsic interest. He was a born teacher and although he wrote many introductory textbooks and larger studies on Europe and Asia, it was in the spoken word that his genius revealed itself.

JOHN FREDERICK UNSTEAD, 1876–1965,
by E. W. Gilbert[9]

J. F. Unstead ('J.F.U.' to his many friends) was prominent among those who, under the influence of H. J. Mackinder and A. J. Herbertson in the early years of this century, laid the foundations of geography as an academic study, and indeed of the Geographical Association.

J. F. Unstead was born in London in 1876, attended an elementary school, and became a pupil teacher at the age of sixteen. Through sheer hard work he obtained a grant from the Board of Education and in 1895 entered the recently formed Day Training College at Cambridge, where he gained a teacher's certificate and the university degree. At that time his interests were largely in social and economic history.

Then, as a teacher in a London elementary school, he attended evening lectures at the London School of Economics where, in 1900, he heard Mackinder give a lecture on the 'New Geography'. Unstead was immediately converted to Mackinder's ideas, and attended his lectures throughout that session. For Unstead 'they shed new light on the evolution of States', then his main economic interest; and they also opened up another possibility in his teaching work—to introduce 'a *reasonable* type of geography in an elementary school'.

Between 1901 and 1904, as a postgraduate evening student, Unstead received much guidance from Mackinder, including an introduction to A. J. Herbertson whose vacation course at Oxford he attended as an observer, and there met W. M. Davis. In Oxford, Unstead found 'the greatest stimulus in a lecture by Herbertson

on Natural Regions'. This lecture planted in his mind the seed
from which grew the idea of using regional units in geographical
thinking and writing, and which, in the following years, occupied
much of his study and teaching. In 1905 Unstead was appointed
lecturer in geography at Goldsmith's College; and in 1906 he
helped Herbertson with his Oxford vacation course. He was asked
by Herbertson to become the correspondence secretary of the
Geographical Association, 'quite a missionary job' which involved
much travelling and which lasted until after Herbertson's death in
1915. At the same time he was engaged in research, and in writing
textbooks and articles. One of the latter was 'The climatic limits
of wheat cultivation', which appeared in the *Geographical Journal*
in 1912, and for which he was awarded the D.Sc.

While still a lecturer at Goldsmith's College, Unstead helped
Mackinder to get geography admitted as a subject for examinations
in faculties other than that of economics. This task continued
when Unstead, following his friend Chisholm, was appointed to
Birkbeck College, where he established a department of geography,
and, in 1921, filled the first professional appointment in the college.

He held the chair of geography at Birkbeck College until 1930,
but found that administrative work took up an increasing amount
of his time and energy, so that it was almost impossible to prepare
his own lectures adequately and to supervise the research of
postgraduate students. He therefore relinquished his post at
the early age of fifty-five 'in order to read and think, to travel and
write'.

EVA G. R. TAYLOR, 1879–1966,
by G. R. Crone[10]

Professor Eva Taylor, who died on 5 July 1966 at the age of
eighty-seven, was one of the last links with the early days of the
Oxford school of geography under Sir Halford Mackinder and A. J.
Herbertson. Her early training was in the natural sciences and she
spent two years teaching in schools. In 1907 she obtained the
Oxford diploma in geography and was an assistant to Herbertson.
Eventually she was appointed lecturer in geography at Birkbeck
College under J. F. Unstead, with whom she collaborated in a
number of textbooks. On his retirement she was appointed in open
competition to the chair of geography following upon her D.Sc.
two years earlier. During the Second World War she was a keen
advocate of a national atlas of Britain as the basis of planning,

E

and contributed to the discussion of regional organization and the location of industry, being appointed to the consultative panel of the Ministry of Town and Country Planning in 1941. She served on the council of the Royal Geographical Society for two periods, 1931–5 and 1937–41. Her work was recognized by the award of the Victoria Medal in 1947, and honorary fellowship in 1965. She was an honorary member of the Institute of Navigation, which published several of her works. She was for many years an active member of the Hakluyt Society and a vice-president.

Professor Taylor's contribution to geography rested on two foundations, her early training in the natural sciences and her connection with A. J. Herbertson and the Oxford school of geography. These later fused into an absorbing interest in the history of ideas, particularly as exemplified in the development of geographical thought, including cartography, and the science of navigation. Her early work included contributions to textbooks by Herbertson and Unstead. Later she wrote a number of volumes on human and economic geography, editions of which appeared down to the 1930s.

In 1937, she stated her belief that geography was 'an exploration of human response' to the environment, and its final objective the examination of 'what have been the most successful or desirable adjustments between man and the earth'. She approached the study of the relation of contemporary economic and social thought to the achievement of Tudor explorers, the European settlers of the Americas, or the planners in wartime Britain with the same comprehensive outlook.

From her interest in maps as research tools sprung her work on the history of cartography, which led on to the evolution of ideas regarding the Earth, the natural environment and men's attitude towards them. The first-fruit of this interest was *Tudor Geography, 1485–1583* (1930), which dealt with 'that fateful century or so during which Englishmen of all ranks were forced gradually by circumstances to think geographically as they had never done before'. It was based largely on research among the manuscripts of the British Museum and the Public Record Office. Arising from this research was her edition for the Hakluyt Society of Roger Barlow's *Briefe Summe of Geographie* (1932), a work of considerable value based on Enciso's *Suma* of 1519. A sequel four years later carried on the story—*Late Tudor and Early Stuart Geography, 1583–1650*. As John Dee had been the central figure of the earlier volume, so Richard Hakluyt the younger and Samuel Purchas were the protagonists in this. These two volumes reconstructed 'the geography of the sixteenth and seventeenth centuries, not as it was, but as it was believed to be'. From this it was a logical step to her next work, *The Writings and Correspondence of the Two Richard Hakluyts* (1935). With Brunner Park's biography of eight years earlier, it forms the basis of all Hakluyt studies. She continued to prepare a third volume on early Georgian geography, and published several papers, but the advent of war and her growing interest in the practical application of mathematics to navigation resulted in its being put aside.

The mathematical practitioners of Tudor and Stuart England did for navigation what her earlier work had done for geography. It is in effect a bio-bibliographical dictionary of those who endeavoured to meet the needs of seafarers—that is, the cartographers, instrument-makers, the compilers of sailing directions, and the authors of navigational guides. A second volume, *Early Hanoverian Mathematical Practitioners,* appeared in 1966, but without the benefit of the author's proof-reading. For the general reader her most popular book is undoubtedly *The Haven-Finding Art* (1956), a history of navigation to Captain Cook unique in its comprehensiveness and clarity of exposition.

LL. RODWELL JONES, 1880–1947,
by S. W. Wooldridge[11]

Ll. Rodwell Jones, M.C., B.Sc., Ph.D., died in August 1947 after a short illness. He had retired in 1945 after holding the chair of geography at the London School of Economics for twenty years. Like many of the geographers of this generation he came to the subject late, after an early training in science. After some years as a schoolmaster, he joined Professor Kendall at Leeds in 1913 as lecturer in railway geography. After the First World War he returned from a distinguished period of army service to Sir Halford Mackinder's staff at the London School of Economics and succeeded him as head of department in 1925.

Rodwell Jones published well-known textbooks on northern England and North America (with P. W. Bryan). He travelled in North America and East Africa and made original contributions to the study of both areas. He had a fundamental interest in the geography of ports, as witness his study of Hull and his important book on the *Geography of London River* (1931).

Such facts may be simply recorded; it is more difficult adequately to express the debt of gratitude owed to him by his colleagues and students as a man, a teacher and a chief. He made small claims for himself, being modest almost to a fault, and at first meeting shy and a little unapproachable. The fine quality of his mind and character and the kindness and charity of his outlook became quickly apparent to those with whom he worked. Into his teaching were put great labour and the whole of his mind and personality. He possessed high intellectual standards and a strong sense of duty and both found expression in his function as the head of a large department. He contributed much to the reshaping of the London honours degree in geography.

C. B. FAWCETT, 1883–1952,
by R. O. Buchanan[12]

C. B. Fawcett, Emeritus Professor of Geography in the University of London, was another of the band of pioneers, who, directly or indirectly influenced by the great Mackinder, carried the new geography to the schools, to the universities and to the wider world of affairs. From school in County Durham Fawcett went as a science student to University College, Nottingham, graduating as an external student in the University of London. A short period of schoolteaching was followed by his entry into the Oxford University school of geography, where he qualified for the diploma in geography and for the B.Litt. degree. It would indeed be difficult to exaggerate the influence at this critical period of his career of Mackinder's brilliantly imaginative treatment of the subject and Herbertson's meticulously thorough methods of training—they gave him an impetus, a direction and a concern for standards in scholarship that lasted throughout his life. His first university post, as independent lecturer, was at University College, Southampton, where he passed the strenuous years of the First World War, supplementing his single-handed teaching by a virtually full-time responsible post at the Ordnance Survey, a war contribution of no small national value. From Southampton he went to Leeds as head of the new, independent department of geography, and there, freed at last from London requirements for its external degrees, he faced the responsibility of developing an honours school *ab initio,* a development that was being paralleled elsewhere in Britain only in London and Liverpool. Nine fruitful years in Leeds were followed by an unsolicited invitation to the chair of geography at University College, London, as successor to L. W. Lyde. The department was reorganized and stamped with the die of his own personality and his philosophy of the subject for twenty-one years. On retirement in 1949 he proceeded to a visiting professorship at Clark University, Massachusetts, which he continued to hold until the summer of 1951. His last appointment was as visiting professor and head of the department of geography in the University of Ceylon and Colombo, an appointment he was never to complete.

As researcher and writer Fawcett will be remembered chiefly for his studies in two distinct though related fields, political geography and population. His major works were all in political geography: *Frontiers* (1918), a dispassionate examination of the character and effects of different kinds of political frontier; *Provinces of England* (1919; new ed. 1960), a persuasive case for a rational reform of the existing chaos of the politico-administrative units of this country; *A Political Geography of the British Empire* (1933), a general treatment that gave scope for shrewd assessment of diverse problems and opportunities, but hardly for the close-knit texture of the two earlier books; and finally, published during the recent war, *The Bases of a World Commonwealth* (1941), which was in effect a summary and application of his whole politico-geographical faith. His population studies, on the other hand, are to be found as shorter articles scattered through various geographical and demographic journals.

Perhaps his outstanding characteristic was his detestation of guess-work. Whatever his problem, his procedure was by way of a patient and unremitting search for the relevant facts and a cool and deliberate appraisal of the facts so garnered. Abhorring alike the slip-shod and the dramatic, he expounded his methods and his conclusions in simple, direct, lucid English. If he had a weakness, as researcher and teacher, it was that he was so concerned to eliminate emotional elements that he kept his constructive imagination in overstrict subjection: he succeeded in avoiding the errors of rash generalization to which the visionary is prone, but he possibly missed also some of the heights he might otherwise have reached.

Fawcett's energies were never confined within the framework of his teaching and his research. In each of his three successive university institutions he gave himself unsparingly to the wider administrative responsibilities inseparable from the successful conduct of university affairs. He was the first president of the Institute of British Geographers, a fitting recognition not only of his eminence in British geography, but also of the effective help he had given in establishing it.

JAMES FAIRGRIEVE, 1870–1952,
by H. J. Fleure[13]

Born in 1870, the son of the United Presbyterian minister of Saltcoats, he was a pupil at Glasgow High School. In 1886 he entered the University College of Wales, Aberystwyth, which at that time drew from all over the country thoughtful students especially of languages and mathematics. Fairgrieve took his London B.A. degree and in 1891 entered as an exhibitioner at Jesus College, Oxford. He took a second class in finals in mathematics in 1895. This was followed by teaching experience at Kelso and at Campbelltown grammar schools and then, having married a fellow student at Aberystwyth, he opened a private school in North London which husband and wife conducted for some years. In 1907, Fairgrieve became a master at the William Ellis endowed grammar school, and the private school was handed over to Mrs Fairgrieve's sister. He had at that time recently joined the Geographical Association and was destined to give it forty-seven years of devoted service.

The years that followed were full of enterprise in geography teaching. Published work included *Geography in School* (1926) and *Geography and World Power* (1915). The latter book derived more than a little of its force from the fact that it was written 'for the fun of the thing' and not for publication. It has been widely appreciated and has been translated into several languages. It is one of those books that, like Mackinder's *Democratic Ideals and Reality* (1919), was too forward-looking to be properly appreciated in pre-war Britain, though both books could have helped Cabinet ministers to avoid mistakes from which our country is unlikely to recover.

Fairgrieve was one of the earliest students of local climates. Still another pioneer effort at this time was the mapping of land utilization on the northern boundary of London.

Fairgrieve believed fiercely in trying new things, but always focused his efforts on the teaching of his subject; and he has often criticized those who merely teach without putting a personal initiative into their work. Until the First World War, geography was the Cinderella subject in schools, but Fairgrieve's work at the William Ellis school made a stir in educational circles and strengthened Herbertson's hand in his hard struggle. The best geography was, for Fairgrieve, 'geography learned through the soles of our feet', and the mapping of land utilization was just one of many lines of the study of the country surrounding our schools, homes, and work-places that Sir Patrick Geddes was to christen 'Regional Survey'. Even the many-sided pioneering that radiated from the William Ellis school was by no means all that Fairgrieve did in those years of hard work.

1912 saw his appointment as 'Lecturer in Education with special reference to Geography' in what was then the London Day Training College, and after became the University of London's Institute of Education. He held this post, developed into a readership in 1931, until his retirement. In this new position he felt more than ever bound to concentrate on improving teaching of the subject and his subsequent publications are in this field. His school books had a very wide circulation but it was the direct influence of his personality that counted for still more. Year after year at the annual conference of the Geographical Association former students would crowd around him. It was in dealing with adolescents and young adults that he was at his happiest and best. His old students are a considerable proportion of the teachers of geography in schools and colleges in Britain, and he extended his influence to the USA during a year's appointment at the University of Chicago.

IV THE COMMONWEALTH LEADER: THOMAS GRIFFITH TAYLOR, 1880–1963

There are today about 100 departments of geography in the new universities throughout the Commonwealth. Before the Second World War there was one department in the University of Sydney in Australia, and another in the University of Toronto in Canada. In the Union of South Africa chairs were founded at Witwatersrand and Pretoria in the mid-1920s, and a third appeared at the University of Cape Town in 1936. The first professor at Sydney was T. Griffith Taylor. He transferred for a few years to the University of Chicago but soon moved to establish a new department of geography in the University of Toronto. This man was a vigorous and productive pioneer of geography. Two appraisals of this remarkable man follow below.

There has been a quite remarkable growth of university departments of geography with distinguished leaders since the war. The main points should be noted.

Canada soon acquired new seats at Montreal (McGill and the French university) and Laval (Quebec), while other departments have since sprouted across the nation, both English and French. R. Blanchard from France gave great prestige to the new department in Laval, and G. H. T. Kimble nurtured the new department at McGill. Today there are over thirty departments in the country.

Australia and New Zealand have also a remarkable record. In terms of personalities, there are some half-dozen men who have contributed strong threads of growth, with or without connection with Griffith Taylor. I refer in particular to G. Jobbyns at the University of Canterbury, a native New Zealander; O. H. K. Spate (Cambridge) at the National University of Australia, K. B. Cumberland (Nottingham) at Auckland, and K. Buchanan (Birmingham) at the Victoria University of Wellington.

THOMAS GRIFFITH TAYLOR, 1880–1963,
by J. K. Rose[14]

Griffith Taylor was perhaps the most widely travelled and experienced geographer of his generation, and possibly the most controversial person the field of geography has produced. Born at Walthamstow, England, the son of a mining engineer, the family early moved to Serbia, then in 1893 moved to Australia. Although he worked for considerable periods in four of the continents, and although his travels, studies and writings included all the continents, he was perhaps most widely known for his many authoritative studies of Australian problems.

Publications of the earlier period, extending roughly through the First World War, in keeping with his initial training in engineering and geology, were mostly on problems of Australian physical geography, such as the coral reefs of the Great Barrier, the physiography of eastern Australia and of New South Wales, and the climatic and meteorological divisions of the continent. Other publications dealt with aspects of Australian paleontology and geology. Between postgraduate training in England and assignment in Antarctica he made an intensive field survey of the proposed Federal Territory in 1910, prepared a relief model, and even suggested the name Canberra (of aboriginal significance), which was adopted in 1913. He later participated in the geological survey of that territory.

His Antarctic opportunity derived largely from his interest in glaciation. He first studied glaciated country on Kosciusko in 1907. Having received the B.Sc. and the B.M.E.[15] degrees from

Sydney, he journeyed to Cambridge via North America in order to visit the glacial district of the Yosemite. While at Cambridge (B.A. 1910) his vacation periods were largely devoted to studies of glacial topography in Europe, in part under the guidance of W. M. Davis. He was selected from among 7,000 applicants to accompany the second and ill-fated Scott expedition to Antarctica, for which he was senior geologist and leader of the Western Parties (1910–13). Meanwhile, he continued as physiographer for the Commonwealth Weather Service (1910–20). En route to the Antarctic, he examined New Zealand's glaciers. His glaciological and Antarctic interests did not end with the Scott expedition but continued active through life. Later expeditions consulted with him; he followed closely and sometimes commented on later work. Six books resulted from these activities. Later he surveyed and published on other glaciated areas. In 1922 he led a party to make the first contour map of Kosciusko (7,316 feet), with its relics of the ice ages in Australia; there he requested that his ashes be laid.[16]

Sydney awarded him the Sc.D. for a thesis on Antarctic geology in 1916. An appointment to the science faculty at the University of Melbourne in that year was followed two years later by appointment as external lecturer in geography. He had given the first lectures in geography at Sydney as early as 1907; in 1920 the McCaughey chair of geography was established, and Taylor was appointed Australia's first professor of geography and head of its first department.

Beginning perhaps with his *Climatic Control of Australian Production* (1915),[17] but reaching a crescendo in the 1920s, a major share of his attention was directed to the diverse and complex problems of Australian settlement, with particular attention to the relation of climate and weather to potential agricultural development and to the problems of white settlement in tropical Australia. His studies indicated that the resources of large parts of the continent were less conducive to effective human habitation than the boosters proclaimed. Whereas the journalists and politicians anticipated population expansion to 100,000,000 or even 200,000,000, he held that the resource potential suggested more nearly 20,000,000 to 30,000,000 at a high standard of living. This early venture of the academician into nation-planning became a public affair, loud and harsh. Some of his books were banned. Because Taylor courageously expressed his convictions frequently and articulately, he became distinctly unpopular in some powerful Australian circles, where he was called unpatriotic and much

E*

worse, as he sought to introduce some realism into planning of
railways and settlements. As his Sydney chair became increasingly
uncomfortable, in 1928 he accepted a professorship at the University
of Chicago.

At Chicago he was able to develop further his interests in race,
early migrations, settlement, environment and history. As early
as 1921 he had published on the evolution and distribution of race,
culture and language. Studies of racial mixtures in Australia,
of migration zones around the Pacific, and of race and nation in
Europe, in a degree culminated in his monumental *Environment
and Race: A Study of Evolution, Migration, Settlement and
Status of the Races of Man* (1927). This developed in a comprehensive way his most original contribution to the study of
geographic distributions, the Zones and Strata concept, a technique
for deducing order of development or evolution.

Attracted by the opportunity to pursue geographic studies in
yet another 'marginal' environment and to build the first Canadian
department of geography, he accepted appointment at Toronto in
1935. There, until 1951, he studied, traveled, and wrote on
Canadian problems without, meanwhile, neglecting his broader
interests which involved problems arising as men associate in ever-
increasing numbers with their fellow creatures. Ten major books
were one result of this period.

Another point of continuing controversy was his geographic
philosophy. He had, it will be recalled, worked intensively in three
areas of strikingly marginal environments. Even as late as 1959
he was described as a 'determined environmentalist'.

In a busy life which included much teaching and very wide
field study, with facile pen and diligent and long-continued effort,
he authored or co-authored some forty-three books, some of
which went into many editions and were translated into other
languages. Fortunately, the total included but did not end with an
autobiography, *Journeyman Taylor—The Education of a Scientist*
(1958).

Even his retirement was active. In 1948 he had returned to
Australia for some months as the official guest of the government,
lecturing widely and visiting each state university in an advisory
capacity regarding its curricula. Upon retirement from Canada
to a pleasant suburb of Sydney in 1952, he was welcomed as the
First Geographer, a tribe which had grown from two in 1928 to
nearly 100. Characteristically he proceeded to produce an
explanatory volume, with drawings from his own pen: *Sydneyside
Scenery and How It Came About* (1958). It sold well as a guidebook.

In 1961 he collated some 20,000 of his letters for the Commonwealth
Archives, and found much pleasure in reliving arguments with
many of the leading scientists of the USA, Britain, and Canada
in most branches of geography, climatology, anthropology and
glaciology. There were many memories and satisfactions for this
final survivor of the Scott group, of family, students, and friends;
of places and features of the landscape named for him; of
portraits hung and eight medals received; of departments and
professional groups established; of presidencies of geographical
associations held in Australia, Britain, the USA (1941), and
Canada, and, near the end, a fine new Griffith Taylor Building for
Geography at the University of Sydney.

A PERSONAL APPRECIATION,
by R. E. Priestley[18]

Sir Raymond Priestley, Griffith Taylor's brother-in-law and friend
of many years' standing, contributed the following note on
Griffith Taylor's up-bringing and on his experiences in the
Antarctic.

Through the death in Australia of Thomas Griffith Taylor, at the
age of eighty-two, the field and world of geography has lost one of
its outstanding and most colourful personalities. After his
return from Scott's last expedition 'Griff' married my youngest
sister, so I knew him more than ordinarily well. When, in 1910,
I arrived at Sydney University to work on the geological results
of the *Nimrod* expedition of Ernest Shackleton, Griff's energy and
self-confidence were already a legend in the school of geology there.
He was one of a large family brought up by strong-minded
parents on spartan lines. I remember him telling me how, in his
schooldays, each of the children was given a bowl of porridge
for breakfast and expected to eat it while tramping down the long
home drive, leaving the bowls on a gatepost from which their
mother would retrieve them later in the day. David himself told
me how 'Griff' on return journeys from geological excursions would
get out of the horse-drawn brake and run behind to let off steam.
His mental activity was of the same order and he was one of
those rather infuriating persons who is always certain he is right
and, unfortunately for his neighbour's peace of mind, usually is.
  It followed that his whole mental climate was decisively
influenced by the fact that, when he became head of the first

The United Kingdom

department of geography in Australia, he formed and, characteristically, preached vehemently, the opinion that Australia was incapable of supporting at any high standard many more than 20 million inhabitants at a time when sanguine politicians were advocating a target of 100 millions and more. The discussion was heated, as any discussion in which 'Griff' took part was found to be, and he left Australia, rather disgruntled, for a professorship in Chicago University from which after several fruitful years he moved to become the first Professor of Geography in Canada, where he served until he retired. Throughout his academic career he wrote freely and his series of geographical textbooks are still bestsellers in many parts of the English-speaking world.

Like all of us who were privileged to share that great experience, the other dominating factor of Taylor's life was his membership of Scott's last expedition. His commitments at home—at that time he was physiographer to the Australian Meteorological Bureau— only allowed him to spend one winter in the Antarctic, but he led two first class scientific summer sledge journeys, was perhaps the chief contributor to the *South Polar Times* in the winter and was considered by Scott one of his most valuable acquisitions. He never lost his interest in Antarctic exploration and Antarctic science, wrote much on the subject, and the experience provided another major strand of interest throughout the whole of a long life. Indeed his last scientific note was one entitled 'The probable disintegration of Antarctica' that appeared in the *Geographical Journal* in June 1963.

9

The Royal Geographical Society

The development of geography—exploration and research and university status—owes much to the leadership and stimulus of the Royal Geographical Society. This record must pay special tribute, therefore, to the Society and its long list of distinguished fellows and officials. This chapter begins with Dr Hugh Robert Mill's record of the Society from 1830 to 1930, followed by a summary of progress since 1930, based on G. R. Crone's published record for 1931–55 and a personal letter from the present Director, L. P. Kirwan, for current activities. The chapter concludes by paying tribute to two of the Society's (and geography's) strongest and longest supporters—Douglas Freshfield and Hugh Robert Mill.

RETROSPECT, 1830–1930, *by H. R. Mill*[1]

The growth of the Royal Geographical Society from 460 noblemen and gentlemen in 1830 to 6,400 men and women in 1930 falls into eight phases.

First, in the first decade of its foundation, 1830–1840, the membership grew to 700. It included the whole tenancy of the Horticultural Society's rooms.

Second, the eleven years from 1840 to 1851, when the Society occupied its second home in Waterloo Place, was served by distinguished but ineffective bi-annual presidents, until the last term when an interval of stationary membership and disordered finances ensued.

Third, a period of nineteen years from 1851 to 1870, when Sir Roderick Murchison was supreme. Under him, the membership grew from 700 to 2,500, exploration was vigorously pursued, and the society occupied its third house in Whitehall Place.

Fourth, a period of twenty-one years, 1871–92, under the rule of strong honorary secretaries, Francis Galton, Clements Markham and Douglas Freshfield, who managed affairs under bi-annual presidents. The whole period was passed in the famous house, No. 1 Savile Row, under the assistant-secretaryship of H. W. Bates. Membership again grew by 1,000, and the Society led the world in exploration.

Fifth, Markham was master of the society as president from 1893 to 1905. The membership increased by a further 1,000, reaching 4,500 by the end of the thirteen years. These years, too, were passed at Savile Row, with Keltie as assistant secretary.

Sixth, triennial presidents led the society from 1905 to 1914. These nine years brought the membership to over 5,000. A guiding power was the quiet influence of John Scott Keltie. The presidency of Lord Curzon in the last three years reorganized the society and settled it in splendid new quarters at Kensington Gore.

Seventh, the years 1914–20 were marked by a falling off in numbers due to the war and its after-effects, the membership for a time being less than 5,000. The period included the presidency of Douglas Freshfield, the retirement of Sir John Scott Keltie, and the diversion of the whole power of the society to war service. It forms a trench, cutting off the older from the present phase of the society's activity.

Eighth, the tenth decade (1920–30) of the society was under triennial presidents and the strong secretaryship of A. R. Hinks. The rate of growth was the most rapid in its whole history, 1,000 new fellows being added in six years.

The bulk of the Society's income has always come from subscriptions for the current year, and grants to explorers had to be scrutinized rigorously. The policy of the society was to spend its whole income in the advancement of geographical science by providing for the preservation of the knowledge acquired as well as for the promotion of exploration and research. In the next 100 years a totally new set of conditions will have to be met. The character of such exploration as remains to be done has entirely changed. The training of geographers must take the place of the encouragement of travellers and the accumulation of a substantial reserve will have to be considered.

The library soon became important as an essential part of the society. A subject catalogue was published in 1870. When the new system of bibliographical entries in the *Geographical Journal* was devised in 1892, a complete account of the monthly accessions to the library was prepared. A subject catalogue of the accessions to the library from 1892 is always available for reference. The library, which was placed in the splendid quarters afforded by the new buildings at Kensington Gore, contains the finest collection of geographical literature in the world.

At the beginning it was found necessary to illustrate the travels of explorers by maps of the country traversed on which the new discoveries could be shown. Such maps were costly to execute, each original drawing having to be engraved on copper and printed as a special plate. Professional cartographers, such as Arrowsmith, Petermann, Walker, Keith Johnston, Bartholomew and Stanford, were employed for a long time on both branches of the work. Later, however, the society employed its own draughtsmen, acting under the supervision of the map curator, to compile the maps in manuscript from the sketches and notes of the traveller, and the finished map was then reproduced by an engraver or lithographer. More than once a map provided by the society has served to lead important military, diplomatic or commercial expeditions through wild country otherwise uncharted.

The greater part of the expenditure of the society is on the production and distribution of publications. The *Journal* was at first confined to papers read to the society. The first volume appeared in 1855. Clements Markham, then honorary secretary, in 1872 started a monthly, *Ocean Highways–The Geographical Record,* finally adopting the style of the *Geographical Magazine.* It was quite independent of the society, and reached a circulation of about 1,200 copies, proving that such a presentation of geographical facts met a real need.

Douglas Freshfield continued to press for a higher literary standard in the presentation of the facts of geography. John Scott Keltie assumed the editorship of the *Geographical Journal* and in January 1893 there appeared the first number. The *Journal* soon won universal recognition as the premier geographical periodical in the world. The papers read to the society were published as before with the discussions. Shorter articles on geographical matters were also included. Room was found for comprehensive reviews of important books, as well as monthly record of notes, designed to take account of the achievements and speculations of the travellers and geographers of all countries.

The instruction of intending travellers has always been held to be of the utmost importance. A report on methods of surveying was published in 1854 under the title of *Hints to Travellers.* Revised editions were issued at intervals. Mr Freshfield took his place as one of the editors. In 1901 the eighth edition appeared in two volumes, the first devoted to methods of surveying, mapping and practical astronomy, with the requisite tables; the second containing articles by experts on meteorology, photography, geology, natural history, anthropology, industry and commerce, archaeology, medicine, and the like. A ninth edition appeared in 1906 and a tenth in 1921. *Hints to Travellers* is now one of the best-known books in the world.

In 1879 the society took steps to supply efficient instruction in practical astronomy, route-surveying and mapping. In the first year seventeen students received instruction from the map curator, and there has been no lack of candidates ever since. For a time the society was content to give a test of proficiency before lending instruments to a would-be explorer. As the classes got more crowded and were frequented systematically by officers of the services, colonial officials, engineers and surveyors in private practice, a demand arose for a guarantee of efficiency, and examinations for a diploma in surveying were authorized in 1896. The establishment of instruction in surveying at the university schools of geography has since 1926 relieved the pressure on the society's staff in this respect. E. A. Reeves, who became the instructor in 1902, sent out 660 travellers and surveyors trained in the use of instruments, nineteen of whom have received the society's gold medal and thirty-seven other awards.

When the society was founded in 1830 geography was a part of the curriculum of most of the large private schools, 'the use of globes' being one of the many accomplishments taught at young ladies' seminaries. The watchword of the society then, and for many years, was 'Exploration not Education'. But it so fell out that the necessity of improving the geographical education of the country, which had deteriorated sadly since 1830, was brought forward by the lively young explorer Francis Galton, who had made himself a force in the council in the early 1860s. He thought that if the great public schools were encouraged to take the lead in creating the lacking interest in geography, their influence would spread in all directions and even reach to the universities. He succeeded, after much opposition, in establishing a system of examinations conducted by a committee of the council and open to the pupils of certain selected schools, more than sixty of which were induced to participate, though only a few responded. The society set papers both in physical and political geography and awarded a gold medal every year for each. The scheme was put in force in 1869 and continued for sixteen years.

A thorough enquiry into the whole question of the teaching of geography at home and abroad was resolved on. In response to an advertisement for an inspector of geographical education, John

Scott Keltie was appointed in 1884. Keltie had the power of mastering complicated problems and expressing the essential facts concisely. He was known as the editor of the *Statesman's Year Book* and sub-editor of *Nature,* while his contributions on geographical subjects to *The Times* were appreciated by many. Keltie was instructed to visit Germany, Austria, France, Switzerland, Italy, Belgium, Holland and Sweden and to make enquiries by correspondence as to the state of geography in America. He was authorized to collect from every country textbooks, maps, and appliances of every kind for the teaching of geography.

In 1886 the council, taking into account the high respect paid to geography in Continental universities and the absence of such recognition in Great Britain, resolved to resume its efforts to advance geographical teaching, this time from the old universities. The vice-chancellors of Oxford and Cambridge were accordingly approached with proposals for recognizing geography as a science and a valuable mental discipline. In 1887 a joint committee of the society and the University of Oxford nominated Halford J. Mackinder for a post as instructor, and he was duly appointed reader in geography, the University of Oxford and the society contributing each one-half of the modest salary offered. Mackinder attracted large audiences and gradually brought geography into respect at Oxford, though the response was quicker on the part of students than of the university, which long continued to exclude geography from degree examination.

Many schemes for improving conditions were framed and discussed. For nearly ten years the ultimate success of the society's efforts hung in the balance, but in 1899 an Oxford school of geography was founded in the university, the initial expense of £800 per annum being borne in equal shares by the university and the society, with practically equal representation on the committee of management. The reader, with three lecturers, including Dr A. J. Herbertson and Dr H. N. Dickson, formed the teaching staff, and the university provided the school with rooms in the old Ashmolean Museum which were later superseded by a special geography building. On Mr Mackinder's retirement from the readership in 1905 Dr A. J. Herbertson was appointed reader, and in 1910 received the personal title of Professor of Geography. The Oxford school established a diploma in geography, which was taken by many students, most of whom were ladies entering the teaching profession. In 1927 a group of young graduates and undergraduates founded the Oxford University Exploration Club, and the society may claim a paternal share in the research in polar regions and elsewhere which they have carried out.

Oxford, despite its good start, allowed itself to be anticipated in the granting of honours degrees in geography by the sister university. At Cambridge a geographical tripos was established in 1919, though the course of development had hardly been so smooth as at Oxford. This may have been due, in part, to the society's subsidy being smaller and the earlier lecturers holding their post for only a short time and so failing to attract a large number of students at first. H. Yule Oldham, who had been lecturer in geography at Owens College, Manchester, for six years, was appointed to Cambridge in 1898 and carried on the work single-handed for six years. Then a board of geographical studies on which the society was represented was set up in 1903 and a school of geography established. In 1908 circumstances required the reorganization of the school, the readership was for the time abolished, and Yule Oldham, A. R. Hinks, and P. Lake were appointed lecturers on an equal footing. The work of Hinks as teacher of surveying and practical astronomy proved of the greatest value to the school. Later, in 1919, the school was again reorganized under the direction of Lake, with the title of reader. The university provided excellent accommodation for the Cambridge school of geography under F. Debenham. The students, mostly men, have responded to the stimulus and run a very spirited geographical club of their own, while the Cambridge explorers in the long vacation are worthy rivals to their brethren at Oxford.

The Royal Geographical Society worked long and hard to secure the full recognition of the dignity and value of geography as a branch of university education, and its reward has been considerable. To its courage in tackling at the outset the most difficult task of securing a lodgment in the ancient seats of learning and backing its appeal by an annual grant, is due the widespread acceptance of geography as a university subject. There is now a geographical department in every British university where forty years ago there was none. For this we have to thank Francis Galton and Douglas Freshfield, supported, often after hard-fought battles, by their colleagues on the council of the Royal Geographical Society. Down to 1924 when, their object accomplished, the grants to the universities ceased, the society had paid out of its own income a total of £11,000 to Oxford and £7,500 to Cambridge, or, taking into account various small grants or donations to the universities of Manchester, Edinburgh and Wales, not less than £20,000. The sum

is substantial when viewed from the standpoint of the society's
resources and the large claims upon them, but ludicrously small
to have achieved so much. It has established in all our universities
a subject not previously thought worthy of attention, and has
supplied to our schools teachers adequately trained in geographical
studies.

TRENDS SINCE 1930

The society has continued its traditional activities in exploration and
geographical education with vigour and distinction since 1930. Its
future policy was heralded in the first annual address of its president
in the immediate post-war years; 'Geography, perhaps least of all
branches of science, can, or should, be, isolated', and, 'As the
horizon expands and specialization inevitably and rightly sets in,
so is the need for sympathetic co-ordination more than ever required'. This philosophy framed the task of the council in forming an active policy in the fields of exploration, education, and
social service.

Notable in the 1930s was the substantial support given to expeditions of exploration, especially the climbing of Mount Everest.
A great enterprise that has been particularly successful, in both
quality and public circulation, was the launching of the *Geographical Magazine* on the initiative of Michael Huxley, grandson of
T. H. Huxley, in 1935. Its purpose is to present 'to the general
reader the geography of the modern world and its relations to
history, politics, and economics'. The *Magazine* assigns one half of
all profits to a fund 'for advancing exploration and promoting
geographical knowledge'. This excellently illustrated and well-
written journal, issued monthly and available on every bookstand,
is almost entirely supported by articles from professional geographers, who deserve the highest praise for the excellent quality
and clarity of their written and photographic exposition. It is also
a tribute to the reading public in Britain, for it is doubtful whether
a journal of this standard of excellence would be able to pay its
way in America.

The activities of the society since the war are summarized by
its current director, L. P. Kirwan (in a personal letter, October,
1971) in these words:

For the later history of the society, you could not do better
than refer to *Royal Geographical Society: A Record, 1931-55* by

G. R. Crone, published by the society in 1955. The principal trend of recent years has been a much closer association with the work of the university departments of geography, which are now fully represented on our research committee, and a much more intensive and scientific emphasis on exploration. You will no doubt have noticed this from my article in the *Geographical Journal* for 1964, and subsequent numbers, especially the articles referring to the South Turkana Expedition.

DOUGLAS FRESHFIELD, 1845–1934, *by T. G. Longstaff*[2]

Douglas William Freshfield went to Eton and University College, Oxford, taking honours in law and history in 1868. He was called to the Chancery Bar, but did not practise, having had the command of ample means all his life.

While yet at Eton, Freshfield ascended Mont Blanc. During the 1860s and 1870s he made at least twenty first ascents, mostly in the Italian Alps.

Going down from Oxford in 1868 he began his career as a traveller by visiting the Nearer East—Egypt and Palestine, Armenia to Mount Ararat and Tabriz in Persia. The character of the [Caucasus] chain was at that date (1868) misrepresented on maps and textbooks. Even the existence of glaciers was doubted and its peaks were all unclimbed and many of the highest unmapped and unmeasured. In 1887, and again in 1889, Freshfield returned to the Caucasus. One result of these journeys was a map indicating its peaks, passes and glaciers. This map was included in two important volumes.

In 1899 he visited India, Burma and Ceylon, accomplishing his second greatest journey of exploration by the first circuit of Kangehenjunga. He was accompanied by Professor Garwood, who produced a map which is still the best for the whole district.

His last great journey was made at sixty years of age. Returning from the meeting of the British Association in South Africa in 1905, he landed at Mombasa and made an abortive attempt on Ruwenzori, at that date the still mysterious Mountains of the Moon.

In 1913 he made a tour of the world, including visits to the Japanese Alps and the USA. He also paid two visits to British Columbia. At different times he visited little-known parts of Dalmatia, Spain, the Pyrenees, Algeria, and all parts of Italy, where he indulged his hobby of collecting works of art. He also revisited the Alps frequently, made tours in Sweden, Norway, Denmark, Russia, Greece, Corsica, Bosnia and Portugal. Many of these excursions are narrated in *Below the Snowline* (1923), one of the gems of mountain literature. Had it not been for the First World War he would have undertaken an ambitious and formidable journey to Chinese Turkistan—in his seventieth year!

Travel was only one side of his geographical work. Freshfield was really responsible for persuading the Geographical Society to detach the late Sir John Keltie from journalism and to send him to study geographical teaching on the Continent. Keltie's report formed the basis of the modern English outlook on geographical teaching. Freshfield saw that recognition of geography by the universities was essential to secure a supply of competent teachers. It was his advocacy which led the society to subsidize geographical teaching at Oxford in 1888 and at Cambridge in 1903.

Freshfield was admitted a fellow of the society by Sir Roderick Murchison in 1869. From 1881 to 1894 he was one of its honorary secretaries. He founded the collection of photographs. He was revolutionary enough to introduce the use of the lantern to illustrate lectures, in opposition to the views of those who feared we should degenerate into a merely 'popular' institution. He was the godfather of the *Geographical Journal*, which replaced the more stolid *Proceedings*. To him is due the recognition of the place of mountaineering in exploration, and he was the mover in the award by the council of gold medals to Hooker, Whymper, the Duke of the Abruzzi and Lord Conway. His early interest in the Mount Everest problem and his contributions to the *Journal* directly led to those expeditions. He was still an extra member of the Mount Everest Committee at the time of his death. He received the Livingstone Medal of the Royal Scottish Geographical Society, and was awarded the society's Founder's Medal in 1903. He was the president of the society from 1914 to 1917. He placed the whole resources of the society at the disposal of the War Office, and amongst other work it was more particularly responsible for the production of many sheets of the 1:1,000,000 map which were invaluable both during the war and at the peace conference.

This by no means disposes of his record of service to geography. In 1883 he was joint editor of three editions of the Royal Geographical Society's *Hints to Travellers,* and editor of two editions of Murray's *Switzerland.* For sixty years he contributed to society publications. Besides papers on his principal explorations he wrote articles on 'The conservative action of glaciers', on 'The Alpine frontiers of Italy', on the 'Mountains of Dante' and on many other matters connected with mountaineering or geography, while an address on 'Men and mountains', given as president of the Geographical section of the British Association at Cambridge in 1904, has been more than once reprinted in Great Britain and in the USA. For thirteen years he was chairman of the Geographical Association which was instituted to carry on that improvement in education set on foot by the action of the Royal Geographical Society's council.

His services to the Alpine Club were no less remarkable and generous. Elected in 1864 he was its oldest member at the time of his death. He edited the *Alpine Journal* from 1872 to 1880. He was elected vice-president in 1878 and president in 1893. He was an honorary member of most of the foreign alpine clubs. His great *Life of de Saussure* (1920) was rewarded with a doctorate by the University of Geneva, and a French edition was called for in 1924. He also published an essay on Hannibal's passage of the Alps, *Hannibal Once More* (1914), and a short volume of verse, *Unto the Hills* (1914). Freshfield was never a great climber in the technical sense. He was essentially a mountain explorer. His reputation as a mountaineer will rest on the pre-eminent quality of his 'mountain sense', on his pathfinding power, on his unrivalled ability for disentangling mountain topography and giving a clear and objective account of it.

HUGH ROBERT MILL, 1861–1950, *by R. N. Rudmose Brown*[3]

When Hugh Robert Mill's long life came to an end on 5 April 1950, in his eighty-ninth year, geography lost one of its oldest and foremost exponents. He was born at Thurso, Caithness, on 28 May 1861, the tenth child of Dr James Mill, a medical man who combined his practice with a successful interest in farming. Mill's early school years were followed by seven years during which he was too ill to have regular schooling, but, educated at home, he became a voracious reader, with a strong bias towards physical science. By 1879 he had decided to go to the University of Edinburgh, where he came under the influence of Crum Brown, P. G. Tait, G. Crystal, James Geikie and other giants of the day. His enthusiasm for chemistry grew and the accuracy of physical science enchanted him. But other influences also left their lasting marks: Patrick Geddes, the most inspiring influence

in Edinburgh in the early 1880s, Sir John Murray and J. Y.
Buchanan with all the scientific wealth of the *Challenger*. The sea
had always appealed to him and in the *Challenger* office in
Granton, he fostered these interests. From 1884 for some years
he worked in the Scottish Marine Station at Granton, which
was later moved to the Clyde, and became the Millport Marine
Station. He worked also on Fishery Board vessels. Mill's genius
for friendship gave him lifelong friends in those days, when the
name of the *Challenger* brought the world's leading geographers
and oceanographers to Scotland. The Scottish lochs, strangely
unsurveyed, attracted him also and in those years he began his
survey of them and of the English Lakes, in association with Sir
John Murray, E. Heawood, H. N. Dickson and others, a work
eventually to be published by the Royal Geographical Society.
Mill also gave lectures at the Heriot-Watt College and at
university extension courses in many towns. These were chiefly
on physical geography, and showed a rarely-equalled faculty
for lucid exposition. The founding of the Royal Scottish
Geographical Society in Edinburgh in 1885 brought Mill, who
was an active participant, into contact with many travellers
from all over the world and, most important of all, it began a
lifelong friendship with that great cartographer, John Bartholomew.
In 1892, Mill moved to London on his appointment as librarian
of the Royal Geographical Society. In some eight years he left
a lasting mark on the society in the new catalogues for which he
arranged. He resigned in 1900, on taking over the private venture
known as the British Rainfall Organization. This was to be his
life work, and he was responsible for it and its great expansion
until 1919, when the Royal Meteorological Society took charge
and past records went to the Air Ministry.

Mill considered himself primarily a geographer and he sought
to find a basis for formulating the principles of geography as a
comprehensive science. His *Realm of Nature* brought him near
to this ambition, and nearer still, perhaps, his presidential
address to the Geographical Association in 1933. But he never
lost his interest in oceanography, even in the stress of his British
rainfall work, and from 1901 to 1909 he was British
representative on the International Council for the Study of the
Sea. 'If I were called upon', wrote Mill, 'to sum up the main purpose
of my scientific work in a single sentence, I should say that it
was the study of the part played by water in the economy of
the world through the action of solar heat and terrestrial

gravitation, raising vapour from the sea and carrying the condensed moisture back over the land.'

Mill succeeded in writing geography without the need of a new jargon and he did not share the narrow limitations of those geographers who would, on account of their lack of population, exclude the polar regions and the sea from their studies. Although governed largely by the discipline of the physical sciences, he was not negligent of the importance of the less precise human and social considerations in a complete geographical synthesis. It is a pity that two of his suggestions never materialized. One was a glossary of geographical terminology; the other, more ambitious, a geographical description of the British Isles, using all existing surveys and statistical records. Mill's writings were too numerous to be listed here, but all his books have lasting value, for to each he brought carefully weighed statements and balanced criticism. Among the best-known are the *Realm of Nature* (1892) which he regarded as his best work, *The International Geography* (1899), of which he was editor, *Record of the Royal Geographical Society* (1930), a survey of a century of British geography, *The Siege of the South Pole* (1905), of which to his annoyance the publisher would not risk a revised edition with later events, and *The Life of Sir E. Shackleton* (1923), in which he showed a rare understanding of that amazing man. But Mill's most interesting book was produced only for private circulation among his friends. It is *Life Interests of a Geographer: An Experimental Autobiography*, privately issued in 1945, a frank and full confession of his aims and achievements and an analysis of his own work, written throughout with unusual intimacy and candour. But all his writings were clear and vivid. He was never boring and never ambiguous.

In his full life, Mill always had time to help others. It is not easy for one who owes much to his help and guidance for nearly half a century not to seem to overrate Mill's influence on modern geography, but there are many others who will gladly acknowledge his generous readiness to help. He was never too busy to read manuscripts and proofs, especially of any polar work, and he never failed to make valuable suggestions. Many works of Antarctic travel are prefaced by words of his for Mill's hobby and latterly almost his chief interest was the study of the Antarctic regions and the friendship of Antarctic explorers. He was never in polar regions, north or south, but so intimate was his study of them that he was recognized as one of the highest authorities on Antarctic geography and history. He sped the departure of nearly every Antarctic ship during his active years. Perhaps this interest had its origin in his task early in his career at the Royal Geographical Society of finding naturalists to serve in the *Balaena* and the *Active* to South Polar regions in 1892. To this interest he put all his habitual care and balanced judgment. He found also a naturalist to serve with the Jackson Harmsworth expedition to Franz Josef Land in 1896, and one to serve in the *Blancatha* to the Barents Sea 1898, in place of himself who had been invited by Major A. Coats to accompany him. On all these occasions he showed his sound understanding in choosing W. S. Bruce. Mill's library of Antarctic works includes every book on Antarctic exploration in all languages, and is certainly the most complete Antarctic library in existence. Two years ago he presented this priceless collection of some 500 volumes to the Scott Polar Research Institute at Cambridge. Several Antarctic features have been named for Mill, including Mill Glacier, tributary of the Beardmore Glacier; Mill Rise in the Southern Ocean, in about Lat. 47° S., Long. 148° E.; Mill Peak in MacRobertson Land, and Mill Cove in the South Orkneys. Well do I recall our decision to pay tribute to Mill's oceanographical interest, as we laboriously sounded the ice-covered bay, drilling holes for wire-sounding in ice of from 12 to 20 inches thick, and at the end of the day the three of us returning to our tent and penguin steaks. An honour which Mill highly appreciated was his election as the sole honorary member of the exclusive Antarctic Club. For many years, until he was well over seventy, he attended its annual dinner. When his failing eyesight made London after dark too dangerous an adventure, I went to his club to fetch him. But at length he had to give in and miss his annual gathering, where he readily distinguished most members by voice and not by eye, and was rarely at fault in recalling details of any particular ship or expedition. Likewise did the Arctic Club make an exception in electing him an honorary member.

Mill's work brought him a number of honours in addition to the recognition by his fellow geographers of his leadership in many aspects of thought. In 1900, he was made an honorary LL.D. of St Andrews; in 1901 he was president of Section E of the British Association; he was a Victoria Medallist of the Royal Geographical Society in 1915; a medallist of the Royal Scottish Geographical Society, and a Commander of the Norwegian Order of St Olav. In 1907 he was elected president of the Royal Meteorological Society, and from 1927 to 1932 he was vice-president of the Royal Geographical Society, the presidency of which society he declined in 1933. He was a member of most other geographical and allied societies in Europe and America.

The views of geography expounded by H. R. Mill were so widespread and influential—even in my young days in the 1920s—that I reproduce here several quotations from his published papers and addresses . He said that throughout his life he sought to formulate an acceptable definition of geography. Let us then look at his viewpoint through forty years.

In 1892 in *Realm of Nature* (written when a university teacher at Edinburgh at the Heriot–Watt College) he wrote: 'Geography takes account of the relations between region and races. Physiography is concerned with the study of man in relation to the earth, while geography treats the earth in its relation to man.' The final chapter of this same book is entitled 'Man in Nature' and is subheaded: 'Civilization and environment; races of mankind; geography: Man's power in nature'.

This eclectic approach is obviously today open to trenchant criticism, but it must be recalled that it reflected the attitude of the social Darwinism and natural philosophy of the late Victorian days. Even so, it must be pointed out that the surprising definition of physiography is very different from that of T. H. Huxley who rigorously confined his interpretation to the processes of nature and excluded man from his framework. Mill, however, like many of his British and American successors, sought to bring in man at the grand finale—races, civilization and all, in their relationships to the physical earth as derivatives from it.

In 1933 he wrote in *Geography*: 'Geography is the description of the earth's surface with special regard to the forms of vertical relief and to the influence which these forms exercise on all mobile distributions.'

His view is put forward forty years before in the introduction to *The International Geography,* a large compendium of geographical essays on nations of the world by foremost authorities, the whole being organized and edited by Mill and first published in 1899. He wrote:

At the meeting place of the physical and human sciences, it [geography] is the focus at which the rays of natural science, history, and economics converge to illuminate the earth in its relation to man.

Geography is akin to physics in its organization inasmuch as it is a generalization, or rather a synthesis, each unit of which may be viewed as a highly specialized branch in itself . . . the unity of geography results from viewing nature in the limited but still general aspect of the phenomena which affect the surface of the earth.

The theory of geography which gives life and unity to the details of topography, and the various facts borrowed from cognate sciences . . . is the far-reaching theory of evolution. Writing in the twentieth century, it is scarcely necessary to point out that this theory is not antagonistic to the doctrine of creation. Evolution exhibits a succession of changes in a definite direction— from lower to higher, from simple to complex—inevitably suggesting some external guidance, and not touching the question of ultimate origin.

Broad based on the smooth hewn blocks of mathematics, rising through tiers of firmly laid stones from the quarries of the physical sciences (physical followed by biological geography), and the less sure products of biology and anthropology (anthropogeography), to the regular courses of political geography and the rubble heap of commercial geography which caps, if it does not crown, the edifice.

The 'incoherent and shifting cap' of economic interests percolates downwards through the whole structure of the pyramid, binding it together:

Commercial motives consolidate national life, accentuate racial differences, redistribute animals and plants, modify physical conditions, start investigations into the nature of the earth, and even invade the solid ground work of mathematics with practical suggestions.

The object of anthropogeography is to study the distribution of the varieties of mankind, their degree of culture, and the manner of their groupings and movements.

Commercial geography has to do mainly with the discovery, production, transport and exchange of useful and desirable things.

The lack of coherence of geography as a single or distinctive body of knowledge at this time is evident in the first chapters of the book on general, worldwide aspects. The 'plan of the earth' is

discussed by a geologist, J. W. Gregory; land forms (their nature
and origin) by Mill himself; the oceans by an oceanographer, Sir
John Murray; climate by a 'physical geographer', H. N. Dickson;
the distribution of 'living creatures' (animals and plants) by a
biologist, J. A. Thomson (using Sclater's six formal regions of
1858 and phytogeographical regions); and the distribution of mankind by an ethnographer, A. H. Keane. The last portrayed the
growth of man through the ages—his migrations, varieties and
cultures, concluding with the 'primary divisions of mankind'—a
treatment that is obviously far removed from the contemporary
geographer's approach to the study of man on the earth.

Mill was a man of vision and ideas, but he was, in fact, expressing a personal philosophy as a natural scientist. He adumbrated, like
many of his contemporaries a field that was far too great and
vague to serve as a single, effective discipline. Above all, the idea of
man's role on earth was singularly different from the ideas of his contemporaries. On the Continent, Ratzel, von Richthofen, Penck
and Vidal de la Blache, who laid the foundations of a much more
clearly formulated framework for geography, focused on the areal
differences of the earth's surface as the expression of nature's en-
dowment and man's domain.

10

Inter-War Trends

THE GENERAL TREND

Since its foundation in the late 1880s professional geography in Britain continued to be dominated by the concept of the interactions between man and nature, and especially the influence of the natural environment on man and his works. In general, the natural environment was the measure of concern with man. Study was anchored to a 'physical base' that long remained in the conceptual vocabulary. In 1933 Mill wrote: 'Geography is the description of the earth's surface with particular reference to the forms of relief and the influence of these forms on all mobile phenomena in their geographical distribution' (*Geography*, 1933). Mackinder in 1931 claimed that the hydrosphere was the *leitmotif* in the study of the human habitat (*Scot. Geog. Mag.*, 1931). He again spoke of 'geographical momentum' as the continuance of human activities in a place even where the original natural factors that determined its location had long since ceased to operate. He repeated his ideas of dynamic and genetic forces that operate in physical geography and human geography alike.

These pioneers considered the natural region as the physical stage upon which the drama of life is played and the patterns of human occupance are interpreted. They sought to emphasize how human adjustments to the natural environment were dependent on racial, social and economic factors as well as upon spatial contacts with surrounding areas. Particular distributions were studied, rather than regional entities. The 'regional synthesis', such as was being repeatedly demonstrated in exhaustive studies in France, was regarded as a well-nigh unachievable goal. This was due to the diversity of problems that arise from the study of relationships.

Very little attention was given to the 'cultural landscape', and there was very little understanding of what was going on in this connection across the Channel. P. R. Crowe of Glasgow urged in

1938 (*Scot. Geog. Mag.*) the study of the regional associations of human phenomena through the medium of urban centres and routes. C. Daryll Forde, with an ethnographic approach, argued in a brilliant essay in reply (*Scot. Geog. Mag.*, 1939) that human geography had its goal in 'the study of human groups as spatial entities in their natural settings'. He clung, however, to the nature v. man theme when he spoke of primitive societies being dependent on their natural milieu through 'fractional responses' rather than direct spontaneous connections with the 'natural environment'. In similar vein P. E. James was saying at this time in the USA that land-man relations are dependent upon the attitudes, objectives and technical abilities of the human groups in occupance. There is a great gap in this conceptual framework between the older and the younger practitioners, the latter in 1939 being in a small minority. In the discussion by Crowe and Forde I sought in the same journal (1939) to focus geographical study on the regional variations of landscape or habitat as the expression of human societies.

A special feature in this period was the thorough study of pre-historic peoples and cultures as functional entities in their environmental settings. Historians, anthropologists and archaeologists participated in these distributional and environmental studies. The work of the Fleure school was outstanding. Daryll Forde's work on primitive societies (*Habitat, Economy and Society*, 1934) was also a major contribution. He placed emphasis on culture groups in their areal patterns, that are dependent upon culture and culture contacts rather than on the direct impact of the physical environment. The approach of 'environmental determinism' as a central theme of selection and interpretation is flatly rejected in these studies.

The distribution of races as breeds of men demands a knowledge of genetics before one can evaluate the exact relations of the environment and the human. The Fleure school worked on both anthropological and place problems. Its contributions mainly appeared in the journal of the Anthropological Society. These include racial surveys in Wales and the Isle of Man, and cover the relations between disease, religion and social attitudes and race types in distinct geographical areas.

Historical geography, as defined by Roxby, evaluates through time the changing interconnections of man and nature. Many such studies examined the distribution of particular human characteristics. Archaeologists also contributed to this field. Sir Cyril Fox's *Personality of Britain* (1932) contained a series of maps of pre-historic distributions. This was rigorously prescribed by both Fleure and Roxby. The symposium edited by H. C. Darby on the *Historical Geography of England before 1800* claimed to be inspired by the work of Jean Brunhes. One would expect its focus, therefore, to be on the visible landscape, but the work, in fact, contains not a single essay with such a morphological objective. In no sense do the problems of its contributions fit into the pattern so clearly set by Brunhes. They are essentially scholarly studies in geographical history. This is still essentially true of the new generation of historical geographies as revealed in the new and modified version of the same work, with the same title, noted on p. 78.

Political geography was weakly developed owing to the lack of a disciplined conceptual focus. C. B. Fawcett wrote an early pioneer book on frontiers in 1918. His *Political Geography of the British Empire* (1934) sought to evaluate the influence of 'geographical factors' in the development and organization of the British Empire and its parts. Fawcett's work on the *Provinces of England*, published in 1919, was without question the most significant work in this field, for it was based on measures of regionalization (especially on the orbits of cities), rather than on the physical determinants of human associations.

Economic geography was a favoured field, but few of its contributions were of lasting significance. This was again due to the lack of a clear theoretical framework, and thus the absence of provocative and repercussive questions of regional investigation. Most of these studies sought to evaluate the 'influence' of natural factors of site and location and resources (usually described as 'the geographical environment') on the localization of economic activities; or the mode of segregation of industries in particular areas in relation to both natural and cultural factors. R. O. Buchanan's *Pastoral Industries of New Zealand* (1935), for example, sought to investigate 'the *interaction* of geographical [meaning physical] and economic conditions in the area and for the products concerned'. This can be applied to agricultural production, but breaks down in the study of manufacturing industries, for the so-called 'geographical conditions' are historically remote and currently often quite insignificant. The question so posed loses significance and must be reformulated, though few (including Buchanan) attempted to do so at that time in clear theoretical terms.

The most important contribution to this field in Britain between the wars, though it did not appear as a book until 1949, was W. Smith's study of the *Economic Geography of Britain*. This was a thorough, logical and systematic investigation of the regional variants of the economics of production in the country. It is in concept and substance an ecological approach far ahead of its contemporaries. It was based entirely on the analysis of statistical data, and showed no concern with field observation. This was the contribution of L. D. Stamp, and is considered below. Smith was a student and colleague of Roxby and later succeeded him for a brief period in the chair of geography at Liverpool before his untimely death.

The regional concept came in for considerable discussion in the 1930s and needs consideration at this point. A collection of essays by leading geographers on the 'regional geography' of Britain— *Great Britain: Essays in Regional Geography,* edited by A. G. Ogilvie— appeared in 1928. It revealed a bewildering variety of points of view and a consistent, but almost routine, portrayal of the natural environment as a basis for human appraisal. There is now a completely new volume, all written by new authors (1962). The diversity of viewpoint may be justified as the pragmatic approach peculiar to British scholarship. It may also be criticized as revealing a weakness of diversity without effective conceptual unity. This was certainly true between the wars. There are many signs of change in the last two decades as we shall see in the next chapter.

I raise here exactly the same question, arising from Roxby's discourse on human geography forty years ago, that confronted me as a young member of his audience. If I choose—as I must—to study a particular area—say eastern England (as was in fact the case)—how do I set about it? Roxby's four fields studied on the basis of 'natural regions' present a procedure of compilation and exposition, certainly not a springboard for research. There are numerous possible points of take-off. Roxby's answer is apparent in his essay on East Anglia in the 1928 volume noted above. It is a conventional presentation of solid geology, glacial deposits, drainage, coastline, climate, vegetation, all these being put together finally at 'natural regions'. This is followed by the 'evolution of man's relation to his physical environment'. This covers the historical sequence of phases of human history in the area, beginning with prehistory and concluding with the modern phase of the 'agricultural revolution' and the historical emergence of 'modern industries'. Stimulating as this sequential round may be, I could not find a 'slot' in my doctorate work on the functions and distribution of clustered settlements in eastern England that make up the pattern of present-day occupance. Roxby's conventional and respected exposition opened no doors in 1930. It has long since been surpassed (even in 1930, especially on the Continent) by the search for problems in the study of human occupance of land. This new approach, as developed at this time fifty years ago, in France, by P. Deffontaines and R. Dion, is neither an environmental sequence nor a systematic study of one of the many aspects of the natural environment or human activity within it. It is ecological in the sense of being directed to the modes of spatial organization and use of the human habitat.

Rural settlements and towns received little attention, for here again objectives were blurred by forcing such studies into the mould (positively or negatively) of the interrelations between the settlement and the land. The search for correlations between settlement and site is significant indeed, but as a research guide it did not go far into the understanding of the arrangement of settlements and field patterns. Such work lingered far behind that of French and German scholars in this period. The Fleure school remained pre-eminent on rural study. Significant contributions were also made by archaeologists. But they were few and *avant-garde*.

The geography of urbanism likewise made little progress. It lacked a clearly defined conceptual framework on the springboard of which meaningful questions could be asked. Some workers turned to provocative questions, such as the concept of the zones of influence of the city; the characterization and distribution of urban settlements; and the relation of settlements and their orbits to the establishment of new administrative areas. But such studies were few in number. Training and research and refereeing were in the realm of economic history. Virtually no attention was paid to the spatial structure of the city, though the way had been indicated a generation earlier by R. Blanchard in France in his book on Grenoble (first published in 1910), and in other later French and German urban studies.

Agricultural geography received a big stimulus from the survey of the uses of land that was initiated in the 1920s by L. Dudley Stamp. The use of the land of Britain was mapped on a scale of one inch to one mile, and a series of monographic studies was produced, mainly on a county basis, for the whole country. It is indicative of the persistence of old ideas, however, that these monographs were initially prepared under a *pro forma* that began with an appraisal of physical (natural) factors of the area in question and that this was described as the 'geographical background'. Some of the younger contributors later changed this conceptual frame. These monographs and other such studies pursued four problems, mainly by the younger contributors: (1) the distribution of individual crops and livestock by parishes on the land-use maps of the survey;

(2) the areal association of these distributions to form 'land-use regions'; (3) the extent and causes of distinctive systems of agriculture; and (4) the functions and distribution of market centres and the movements of the agricultural products to them.

Historico-geographical methods were occasionally used to interpret the changing distributions of industrial production. But, in general, the geographical study of manufacturing made little progress. L. D. Stamp and S. Beaver wrote a major work on *The British Isles: A Geographical and Economic Survey* (1933). In this, they use the term 'geographical' in reference to the physical factors and to location, which leads to confusion of objectives and exposition. The study of the location of industry goes, as it must, far beyond the interrelations of human enterprise and natural conditions, but there is a repeated return to this allegedly central theme. In fact, their pragmatic treatment covers the location and spatial grouping of economic activities, but the theoretical notion of land-man relationships does not fit this need, though it apparently caused them no concern. A sounder theoretical approach is evident in Smith's *Economic Geography of Britain.*

The landscape and its areal variants received very little interest and was, in effect, superciliously discarded as not worthy of intellectual pursuit. P. W. Bryan's *Man's Adaptation of Nature* (1931), handled the landscape. But Bryan drew his sources from Chicago, and he revealed no awareness whatever of Continental work being done during these years. The superficiality of this Anglo-American approach was rightly attacked by P. R. Crowe in 1938, but his strictures did injustice to the scholarly work of Continental colleagues. He urged geographers to pay more attention to the *processes* whereby human groups are spatially associated, a field to which the present writer dedicated a number of studies of city-regional relations in both Europe and America in this period. Further developments on these lines had to await the post-war years. Such study was advanced in Germany in the 1930s by W. Christaller and A. Lösch (both essentially economists), but these writers made a negligible impact in Britain, presumably because they were not read in German. Indeed their works were scarcely known before the Second World War. My own work (1924–34) on English cities and towns was undertaken before I was able to read a word of German.

The study of individual elements of the cultural landscape also received no serious attention. I refer to such matters as the classification, distribution, origins and areal spread of field systems, farmsteads, house forms and their groupings in 'rural' and 'urban' settlements. Studies of this kind were regarded as *avant-garde*. In fact, they were approached by many Continental geographers as a major and acknowledged part of their subject's accepted field of enquiry. This attitude in Britain (as in the USA) is not surprising since researches were still primarily motivated by the search for man-land relationships rather than by the study of the landscape as Sauer (California) had so clearly urged in 1925. Fleure expressed an interest in the layout and build of cities as expressions of regional differences of origin and growth but did no substantive research in this area. The only comparative study of the English cultural landscape on these lines was a study of pre-industrial towns by an Austrian professor of geography, J. Sölch, in the *Geographische Zeitschrift* (1937, pp. 254–72 and 1938, pp. 41–56). After the war, Sölch produced a monumental work, based on work done in the interwar years, on the geography of Great Britain, in which the landscape enjoys a central position (*Die Landschaften der Britischen Inseln*, 1951).

British geography concerned itself little with theory, except for the overdone pseudo-philosophical discourses on possibilism *v.* determinism. Moreover, in spite of the pleadings of Unstead, geographers persisted in breaking down areas according to the distribution of geological outcrops, contours, static settlement patterns, individual crops, etc., instead of grappling with the regional association of these phenomena as distinctive landscape units of different orders or with Mackinder's concept of spatial nodality.

The idea of the natural region received a critical evaluation in an important article by A. Stevens of Glasgow in 1939 (*Scot. Geog. Mag.*). Adopting the peculiarly redundant phrase 'natural geographical region', he writes: 'We are concerned with physical and biological nature only in so far as it may be regarded as human environment, and only with man in so far as he has demonstrable relationships with the environment.'

The natural geographical region, he continued, is a synthetic product with an environmental aspect and a human (functional) aspect. These are then aspects of the same thing. One is environmental space, the other is community, and the natural geographical region must be defined by references to both. The physical region *per se* is 'an irrelevance' in geography. The environment must be defined and evaluated in terms of human occupance. Thus, the natural geographical region is an organized area and the organizing agent is the human community. Its traits are therefore organization, cohesion and intercourse. Quite outside the subject lie those studies such as geology, geomorphology and climatology, which deal purely with the environment and have proper dynamic problems of evolution and change.

These views were quite unorthodox among his contemporaries, especially the so-called 'physical geographers' (see below). They met with a cool reception, but, in terms of the ecological orientation of the regional concept, are valid and unequivocal.

While the old concept of the natural region as a physical entity held the field in terms of general exposition—and more so in Britain than in either Germany or France—between the wars, it began to be displaced by a new interpretation trend in the 1920s and 1930s of which Stevens's statement is clear evidence. For clearly what was needed was not declarations of faith from an evolutionary or teleological viewpoint, but a scientific method of analysis and synthesis of the areal associations of natural, biotic and human environments. Little new work was forthcoming in Britain in the field of the regional concept. The main contributions came from Siegfried Passarge in Germany in the early 1920s and Granö of Finland. These new ideas reached America through Carl Sauer (1925), and in the late 1920s and the early 1930s the Americans made their distinctive contribution through the medium of field mapping. Britain stood aloof and essentially stagnant, obsessed by the concept of environmentalism and showing an interest only in the idea of determinism *v.* possibilism, that has long since ceased to have any real significance in the theory and practice of geography. Meantime, the French school moved from strength to strength in the study of particular areas in which the land and process of human occupance took the central position. The advances in geographic thought and work in France and Germany in this period are fully discussed in *The Makers of Modern Geography*.

One of the few British scholars who at this time pursued the regional concept was J. F. Unstead. He presented his idea of 'geographical regions' in an essay on Spain (*Scot. Geog. Mag.*, 1926). It was carried further in his Herbertson Memorial Lecture in a 'System of regional geography' (*Geography*, 1933). He suggested the terms 'stow' for the smallest unit area (e.g., a chalk block of the North Downs); 'tract' for a contiguous group of interrelated stows, consisting of the chalk blocks and the separating transverse valley floors. The larger physiographic unit of south-east England was a group of tracts (scarps and vales), and the major physiographic unit of north-west Europe was of a still higher order of geographical magnitude. Unstead was clearly much influenced by the German S. Passarge of Hamburg. The idea made no impact in Britain, although one must record the fact that in a more recent year (1951)

Linton drew attention to the idea of the 'terrain facet' from a geomorphic angle, and the hierarchy of land units that can be built from it.

The work of Vaughan Cornish should at this point receive special attention. Though never holding a university post, Cornish pursued a remarkable variety of geographical researches, that were quite literally a generation ahead of his time. Born in 1862, he died in 1948. He studied at the Victoria University of Manchester, where he took a doctorate in chemistry. After teaching for a short time and then serving as a county director of technical education, he retired in 1895, at the age of thirty-three—obviously with independent means—to devote his life to travel and research. He served as the president of the geography section of the British Association for the Advancement of Science in 1923 and of the Geographical Association in 1928.

Cornish published studies on a remarkable variety of topics. One of his earliest was a book on *Waves of Sand and Snow and the Eddies which Make Them* (1913). His interest in the aesthetics of scenery (as adumbrated a hundred years before by Humboldt) is evidenced by an address to the Geographical Association in 1918 on 'The harmonics of scenery: an outline of aesthetic geography', and later works entitled *The Poetic Impression of Scenery* (1931), and *Scenery and the Sense of Sight* (1935). These were preceded many years earlier by *The Scenery of England* (1918). In these works he focused attention on landscape, vision and 'space-perception'—and contemporary sophisticates would be well advised to take careful note of the last term. He also turned to 'strategic geography' or what might alternatively be called geostrategy. A study in political geography is contained in *Borderlands of Language in Europe and their Relation to the Historic Frontier of Christendom* (1936).

Cornish's most important book was *Great Capitals: An Historical Geography*, published in 1923. This has received practically no attention in current work, and finds virtually no place in the indexes or text of recent books. The preface indicates its intent: 'For the purpose of this study the natural regions or districts must be considered in relation to the productive areas—the lines of communication—and the natural obstructions which hinder movement.' It examines the geographic location and the rise or fall of the world's great capital cities. The interpretation is anchored to two primary requirements in the location of a capital, that it should be in a forward or eccentric position in relation to the territory it governs, at its most exposed avenue of entry—immigration, trade or invasion;

and yet it should be within reach, by existing means of communication, of the populous area of the state, the 'metropolitan base', or what James has since called the 'effectively settled area'. The location and function of a capital is the changing expression through history of the demands and balance of these two sets of requirements. Cornish sets out to examine the evidence through history as revealed by many of the world's capital cities. The requirements, incidentally, are as valid for the small county town as for the state capital, for the administrative centre needs to be centrally located to its populous area and to the boundaries of the area it governs, and must be in convenient access (by water, rail or road) to the outside world. The last requirement often results historically in the persistence of a historic entry which has become eccentric to its present populous and political areas (e.g., London, Washington, Delhi, Rio de Janeiro). This book is a remarkable precursor of current trends in the study of the location and function of urban centres, but finds very little attention, not even cursory recognition, from contemporary researchers.

CLASSIFICATIONS OF REGIONS OF THE WORLD

The regional concept, and the classifications of regions of the world based upon it, was the substance of a report with the above title published in *Geography* in 1937 by a distinguished committee of the Geographical Association. The members of this committee were P. M. Roxby, L. Dudley Stamp, J. F. Unstead and J. L. Myres. We are now familiar with the first three names. The fourth, Myres, was a distinguished classical historian of Oxford, one of the staunchest supporters of geography in its formative years, and a close friend and colleague of H. J. Fleure. The report is such an important statement for the period that excerpts from it are reproduced below: [1]

The surface of the earth is so complex in its characteristics, and its peoples have such manifold relations to their environments, that geography must be many-sided, and geographers must approach the study from a number of angles, but there is general agreement that important among the methods of approach is the study of regions—particular areas of the earth's surface—as units.

For long, 'countries' were commonly adopted as the units of study, but, with the progress of scientific geography, the conception of 'natural regions' came into being and won wide

144

acceptance. Various systems of natural regions have been proposed, and their variety is indeed both necessary and desirable. Yet the differences between the schemes have caused controversy, and a committee of the Geographical Association was asked to report upon methods of determining and classifying regions.

It would clearly be improper to recommend the adoption of any schemes to the exclusion of others, or even to attempt to assess their relative merits and demerits. In this report, therefore, the committee reviews some representative systems in such a way that their particular aims and methods may be more clearly realized, and hopes that thereby systems of regional divisions may be better judged and more effectively utilized.

The term 'natural region' has been applied to quite different types of unit-areas, and thereby misunderstandings have arisen. The word 'natural' has several usages, two of which have been employed in this connection: (1) as almost synonymous with 'physical' in contradistinction to 'human'; and (2) as indicating something inherent and not arbitrarily imposed. Consequently, the phrase 'natural regions' has been used to cover two distinct types of unit-areas of the earth's surface: (1) those which are marked out as possessing certain common *physical* characteristics —e.g., a certain kind of structure and surface relief, or a particular kind of climate—and (2) those regions which possess a unity based upon *any* significant geographical characteristics, whether physical, biological or human, or any combination of these, as contrasted with areas marked out by boundaries imposed, frequently for political or administrative purposes, without reference to any geographical unity of the areas.

Moreover, those who have proposed schemes of regional division have envisaged different kinds of region, and for their diverse objectives have devised special methods of delimiting areas. Therefore, unless in each case the particular aim and the appropriate method are clearly expressed by the proposer, and, moreover, these are clearly realized by the critic or student so that the resultant map is regarded from the limited point of view which is justified, confusions and difficulties are bound to occur.

With these considerations in mind, the committee think it would be of service to indicate the main kinds of regional divisions which have been attempted, with their respective aims and limitations, and to set out their relationship to one another.

In the first place, it may be pointed out that regional divisions fall into two broad categories:

(1) Regions which fall into types and may, therefore, be said to be of a generic character, all the representatives of a particular type resembling each other in certain essential respects according to the criteria selected—e.g., climate, character of vegetation or human use. In such cases the regions, when marked out over the whole globe, are so distributed as to form some kind of world pattern, for their distribution is in the main due primarily to the shape and movements of the earth as a planet. The classification of five or six widely separated areas of the world as regions with the 'Mediterranean' type of climate is a well-known example of generic regional division.

(2) Single regions, large or small, which possess a well-marked geographical individuality; these may be called specific as distinct from generic regions. The character of such a region is determined not only by the intrinsic conditions of the area in question, but by its location and geographical orientation. Every region of this kind is, from the nature of the case, unique. Peninsular Europe may be cited as an example of a large specific region. The great variety of its structure and topography, the very high ratio of coastline to total area, the ubiquitous penetration of maritime influences are among the intrinsic conditions which characterize it, but the personality and life of the peninsula are inseparable from its location in relation to the Atlantic and the two groups of seas (Mediterranean and 'Northland') which fringe it to south and north. The profound contrast between it and the trunk of Euro-Asia, to the east of it, depends equally upon intrinsic conditions and geographical setting or orientation. The eastern limit of the beech tree, admittedly of much climatic and economic significance, closely follows the zone where the peninsula 'takes off' from the trunk and a new set of space-relationships begins.

The distinctiveness of the stage and of its setting is often reflected in and enhanced by the characteristic activities, culture and outlook of the people, and to lay stress on geographical orientation as one of the chief factors in the individuality of a specific region is to call attention to a dominant influence in its human life. In that sense, specific regions such as peninsular Europe or the Paris basin can often be thought of as distinctive theatres of human activity, although in the first instance it is the make-up and orientation of the stage which give them marked geographical individuality.

It is obvious that large specific regions may often include several regions of a generic type determined on a different set of criteria—e.g., peninsular Europe includes more than one structural, and more than one climatic, region.

Systems of the generic category have as their objectives the determination of regions of various kinds, among which the following may be distinguished—physiographic or structural regions, climatic regions, soil regions, natural vegetation regions, major natural regions [Herbertson], environmental regions [Passarge, Unstead], human regions.

The regions demarcated in these worldwide schemes vary in extent, but in general they are of an order of magnitude broadly comparable with that of A. J. Herbertson's 'major natural regions', and when marked out over the whole world those of each scheme might number anything up to about 100. In most cases the individual regions are gathered into classes according to their main characteristics, such classes being termed 'types', 'groups', 'zones', or 'realms'; e.g., in the 1913 form of Herbertson's scheme, he distinguished 73 major regions classified into 21 types.

At the other extreme, very small regions may be considered according to the various principles specified above in connection with world schemes; these regions would, however, be studied by direct observation instead of being demarcated with the help of descriptions and maps as the major regions must be. Such unit-areas of the smallest order have been named 'chore' by J. Sölch, and 'stows' by J. F. Unstead.

From detailed examination, P. W. Bryan has divided the country around Leicester into eight unit-regions based upon the character of the visible landscape, including both physical and cultural elements; these unit-regions are determined by the characteristic grouping and repetition of the forms, features and phenomena of the landscape, and suggestions are made as to methods of combining these units into those of higher orders. Of a similar degree of magnitude are the land use regions of the counties of Britain, now being distinguished in the final report of the Land Utilization Survey of Britain.

Intermediate in extent are regions into which many writers have divided particular countries; a classic example of such a division was given by Vidal de la Blache in his *Tableau de la géographie de la France*. In some cases, an author has divided a country into main regions, these into smaller ones, and some of these again into sub-divisions; India has been thus divided into regions of different orders by J. N. L. Baker, and, independently, by L. Dudley Stamp. The latter states ... the criteria which he uses

F*

in dividing a country into 'natural regions' for purposes of study. He says:

> In all the larger political units, the environment varies greatly from one part to another. Hence the necessity for the division into regions. I have called my regions 'natural regions' because they are in the main delineated by natural features of topography, structure, climate and vegetation. But each, in the course of the long occupation by man, has been changed, some in small measure, others very greatly. Features, such as the character of agriculture, which are the results of man's activities in many cases, have become the obvious or outstanding ones of the region, but in so far as these secondary characteristics have been made possible by the fundamental or natural ones, the regions remain 'natural'. Others prefer the term 'geographical region'. My regions are, in fact, environmental regions, and I make no apology for the fact that the outstanding characteristics of some of them today are the direct results of human occupance. I contend, however, that they are fundamentally important in helping us to understand the life of man under conditions different from those of our own environment.

Rather more detailed divisions of countries have been made by O. Maull, who has divided Germany and the southern peninsulas of Europe in a system of regions comprising four orders of magnitude.

The continents, too, have been analysed into their constituent regions by many geographers, in some cases taking into account world schemes and in others restricting the survey and methods of division to one continent.

It is, therefore, possible to conceive a system in which a hierarchy of regions, demarcated according to one general aim—e.g., showing climates, or natural environments, or transformed environments, might be constructed, linking up the smallest unit-areas of geographical study with the major regions of the world. Herbertson himself suggested this possibility, and two such systems have been more definitely attempted.

S. Passarge planned a hierarchy of regions of the 'natural environment' type, centring upon the region (*Landschaft*) which may vary in size, but of which the Harz Upland may be taken as an example. Regions of higher order may be formed by grouping these with similar neighbouring regions into regional domains (*Landschaftsgebiete*)—e.g., the North German plain—

and these again may be grouped into the regional zones
(*Landschaftsgürtel*). In the descending direction in the hierarchy,
the region is divided into sub-regions (*Teillandschaften*) and these
are regarded as made up of regional elements (*Landschaftsteile*).

J. F. Unstead independently devised a somewhat similar
hierarchy of regions of the 'transformed environment' type.
In this system there are five main orders: the smallest unit-areas,
the 'stows', are combined into 'tracts', these into 'sub-regions',
these again into 'minor regions', and these into the 'major regions'
of the world. To allow elasticity, variations of the scheme are
introduced where necessary by such modifications as (1) joining
stows or tracts into 'stow-groups' or 'tract-groups' as an
intermediate stage towards the next higher order; or (2) regarding
particular stows or tracts as exceptional in the larger region
which territorially includes them, and therefore treating them
as exclaves of some neighbouring region.

The problem of boundaries presents a difficulty in every
regional method. In some cases attention is focused upon the region
as a whole, and little thought is given to limits; in other cases
the author takes the view that a careful examination of the
limiting conditions aids an appreciation of the essential
characteristics of the region itself. There is common agreement,
however, that nature seldom presents a sharp boundary between
two regions, and that frequently there is either a belt of rather
indefinite character or an area of more definite nature, but
intermediate in type.

The recognition of such transitional areas may be an aid in
reconciling what appear to be conflicting demarcations of regions
made by different authors upon the same general principle.
If each scheme indicated sub-divisions in addition to the main
regions, and characteristics both of main regions and of
sub-divisions were stated, the reader would see that transitional
sub-divisions were differently placed by different authors.

The regional divisions of the world so far considered are all of
a generic character—i.e., a particular type is distinguished
according to the criteria selected (climate, vegetation, etc.),
and all representatives of this type broadly resemble each
other in these particular respects. But apart from these
generic classifications, it is important to think of regions, large
and small, as being unique, having a particular location and
a combination of conditions found nowhere else. We realize, for
example, that while a 'Mediterranean' type of climate is found
in five or six different parts of the world, there is also the

Mediterranean Region, which in the sum total of its conditions and in its geographical setting has no real parallel and is a very distinctive theatre of human life.

So, too, we think of the Far East as a unique part of the earth's surface with special characteristics and a definite personality of its own. But what is this 'personality'? Nature's particular setting of the stage and man's use of it as expressed in the 'humanized landscape' are important elements in it, but it is the special type of civilization or culture associated in our minds with that terrain which is the chief criterion for defining its extent as a major human region.

The boundaries of such human regions can seldom be precisely drawn. As a general rule a nuclear area exhibits the cultural traits in fullest and most characteristic form, and in marginal areas they become weaker and intermixed with other traits. There are regions whose significance from this standpoint lies in their transitional cultural character, or in their blend of traits derived from distinct nuclear regions.

In the case of the Far East the nuclear area certainly embraces China, Korea and Japan. However great the differences between China and Japan, their civilizations have common cultural roots, and we think of them as constituent members of the same cultural province and as the most typical representatives of it. Indo-China, on the other hand, is marginal and in some respects transitional, although its affinities, both cultural and racial, are definitely Far Eastern rather than Indian.

To the north-west of the Chinese region, the line of the Great Wall, from the narrow coastal sill north of the Gulf of Pe-Chih-Li to the north-eastern bastion of the Tibetan plateau, long coincided closely with the real divide between the 'Steppe' and the 'Sown', and may be said to have marked the limits of the culture which had its origins in the classical Chinese civilization of the Yellow River basin, and was itself the nucleus of the Far Eastern type of civilization. But in the course of time the 'barbarian' tribes beyond the wall came within the cultural as well as the political influence of China, and High Asia as far west as the utmost mountain ramparts defined by the Pamirs, Tien Shan and Altai may be regarded as coming within the marginal area of the Far East, regarded as a major human region.

Within the broad and necessarily vaguely defined limits of this major human region of the Far East, minor regions stand out with definite characteristics of their own, and can be described and delimited with much greater precision.

Another illustration of the advantage of regarding the regions of the world from various points of view is given in the study by H. J. Fleure, entitled 'Regions in human geography—with special reference to Europe', (*Geog. Teacher,* spring, 1917), in which he shows how areas differ according to the response they give to human work. From this point of view Europe includes four zones: (1) Zones of Increment, where moderate effort gives assured increment; (2) Zones of Effort, where more work is needed to raise men above the level of poverty; (3) Zones of Difficulty, where even great and prolonged effort does not bring much increment; (4) Zones of Privation, where life is maintained only at best upon a lowly plane. Such regions are not thought of as permanent; a particular area may change its status as its inhabitants or its circumstances change. Each zone contains a number of regions which are not necessarily contiguous, and may have different physical characteristics. The study does not refer specifically to all the European areas, but suggests a line of thought which may very usefully be extended throughout all the continents.

As the purpose of this report is to aid the appreciation of systems of regions which may be regarded as 'natural', political divisions will be considered only in so far as they are related to the other regions here examined. Although a political map may cover the whole land-surface of the world, the extent and distribution of the various states bear no relationship to any of the systems of regions hitherto described as belonging to the generic category. Moreover, the boundaries, and even the existence, of these states change from time to time; a comparative view extending over some centuries is kaleidoscopic.

Indeed, there is frequently a marked tendency for political units to cut across natural divisions in order to include parts of different physical regions within their territories. This tendency is seen in operation when states advance into their neighbours' territory to obtain economic resources of a different kind from those provided by their own natural environments, and, as a result, frontiers are redrawn to include different natural units. The disadvantages of a state possessing only one type of region is shown by the post-war limitation of Hungary to little more than part of the Pannonian basin. A well-known case of man-made units cutting across natural units is that in which the parish boundaries in certain parts of England are arranged almost at right-angles to the geographical trends; the reason is that these administrative areas grew up as economic units which required to be largely self-contained, and therefore obtained pieces of land which differed in character and thereby offered a variety of resources.

As students of geography have to consider all aspects of their subject, a brief reference may be made to the relating of the 'natural' regions to political states. This may be achieved in various ways—e.g., by superimposition of maps of the two types; thus, if a map is drawn to show the various environmental divisions, and the political boundaries are marked upon it in some distinctive way, each state may be examined from the point of view of the different types of country included in its territory; it may then be shown how the political strength or weakness of the nation concerned is associated with the possession or lack of certain kinds of regions with special economic resources or of military value.

A review of the various regional methods considered in the preceding pages will show that they are all attempts to make comprehensible the complexity of the conditions with which the geographer has to deal. To achieve this end, the author of each scheme focuses his attention on certain phenomena, or certain combinations of phenomena, and from this particular viewpoint tries to reduce the complexity to a relative simplicity. In this process, moreover, individual judgments must be made, and hence there cannot be certainty or finality about the results.

It follows that no system can be either of universal utility, or of universal acceptance; each must be regarded in the light of its particular aim and used with discrimination.

It would be a gain to geography if it were always realized that a regional system is a good servant but a bad master; generalities are necessary, but must never be allowed to obscure realities.

THE ROLE OF PHYSICAL GEOGRAPHY: J. A. STEERS AND S. W. WOOLDRIDGE

We must now examine the goals and progress of 'physical geography' in the interwar years and their relevance to the regional concept. This is a major aspect of study in departments of geography in Britain today. About one half of its professional staffs in the universities' published researches are currently in this field, as against one half in 'human geography', which is a strong contrast to the situation in America.

The trends in this period, and indeed through the 1950s, have been summarized by one of the major exponents, Professor J. A. Steers. He was the head of the department of geography at Cambridge, and is therefore responsible for many teachers of geomorphology in the universities of Britain, and for the gist of teaching of geography in schools.

Physiography, says Steers, in an address to the Geographical Association in December 1959,[2] is focused on the study of land forms. This is approached, he says, by both geologists and geographers, the first as 'the end of a story', the latter as 'a beginning'. I have no option but to accept this view of physiography as the same as geomorphology, but, in fact, historically it emphatically is not. The face of the earth embraces land forms, ocean forms, atmospheric forms and vegetation. However, I shall follow Steers's discussion of geomorphology, as expressed in that address. Each field raises precisely the same questions as are discussed below.

In examining the scope and nature of the field he agrees with the American geologist, who was also trained incidentally as a geographer, R. J. Russell of the University of Louisiana, that 'the survival of geography as a field depends on what we do, rather than how we debate'. I disagree at the outset, for this contradicts the very purpose of the present book. He emphasizes the necessity for local studies of land forms upon which to build 'sound generalizations' about the processes involved in their development. He comments on the rarity of 'good detailed and analytical writing' and cites as a classic example the work of G. K. Gilbert on the Henry Mountains in the USA. Above all, he pleads repeatedly for a 'team approach' of various specialists to 'field problems'. He gives several examples in Britain of such enterprises in the Fens, the Weald, the coast of Norfolk. The last involved the skills of the Nature Conservancy and the atomic station at Harwell. He mentions further the outstanding work of the Institute of Coastal Studies, headed by the late R. J. Russell (see above), in its studies of the delta of the Mississippi. He also instances the co-operation of physicists in work on glaciers and 'the features produced by glaciation and the ways in which they are formed'. Hence, the value of 'wide collaboration' in the study of the 'history of the surface features of the earth', which he apparently sets as the central objective of 'physiography'. He asserts that the contribution of such study is of the 'first importance', together with 'other branches of science'. He emphasizes that one of the new techniques in 'the interpretation of landscape' is statistical analysis. All students of geography, he rightly remarks, get a training in physiography (geomorphology) in university departments of geography. The field demands laboratory training as well as 'wide reading, field excursions and personal fieldwork'.

Certain comments are called for by this presentation. I repeat that they are confined to land forms, but apply equally to the study of other categories of the earth's surface features, be it vegetation, the atmosphere, or the oceans. I confine these comments to the field covered by Steers.

First, while recognizing the superlative researches of geomorphologists in Britain, the objectives and expertise of the geographer, of which Steers writes, are implicit, and are not clearly stated in their distinct contribution to the 'team approach'. The 'interpretation of landscape' is very different from the 'origin and processes of particular features'. The extensive surface form, for example, that S. W. Wooldridge (see below) called 'upland plains' is much closer to the geographical objective, as is also the earlier work of Alan Ogilvie on peneplain levels in central Scotland (see p. 99). The extent and characteristics of such surface forms raise questions of far greater concern to the geographer than the origins of one sandy cusp. Geography is concerned, as generations of scholars have demonstrated, with the surface forms, not with the geochronological sequence of natural processes in the formation of individual surface features. Both must be pursued, but they are greatly different in kind, question and expertise. They call for a difference in focus, but it is wrong to neglect one at the expense of the other.

Second, a varied training and competence in several disciplines is needed to evaluate natural processes—chemistry, physics, mathematics, botany and geology. But there are also new fields of expertise —pollen-grain analysis, tree-ring analysis, radio-carbon dating and the like. The study of natural processes requires, at the research level, not only team work but a highly specialized training that is far beyond the competence and time of a young undergraduate, no matter how intelligent he may be. This, of course, is not peculiar to this particular field of enquiry; it is found in many fields of knowledge that extend far beyond the limits of traditional disciplines. It is equally true of the field of 'human geography', which likewise is not concerned with the origin of individual human features or distributions on the earth's surface, but with the spatial expression over the earth's surface of human processes through time.

Third, since it is granted that undergraduate training should include several cognate disciplines, what are the essential ingredients of training in physical geography? How shall the varied disciplinary studies be coherently assembled into a focus? What is the expertise in which the undergraduate should be trained? This is the area where debate is essential, notwithstanding the arguments of many who prefer to do what they like. It is a fact that one of the strengths of the remarkable growth of geography in Britain is its general recognition as a laboratory science (unlike the USA). Clearly such specialization calls for a distinct degree on the science side. It is questionable, however, whether this field can continue to shelter under the umbrella of 'geography'. There are already separate institutes (with various names) for 'human' and 'physical' geography. This is an advancement that is long overdue in both British and American universities.

Fourth, the leading exponents of geography for over 100 years have recognized that their central concern is with the composite areal variations of the earth's surface, not with the processes *per se*, natural or human, that singly or together produce variations in particular features of the face of the earth. Steers's brand of geomorphology increasingly transcends these limits (as Mackinder and even W. M. Davis pointed out), but at the same time physical geographers have not made clear the purpose and expertise of their own contribution to other scholars in the pursuit of common problems. This is also true of atmospheric physics, plant ecology, paleoecology, industrial archaeology, and the like.

Fifth, Steers's reflections call for three conclusions of agreement and each is evident in post-war trends: (1) there is need for two or three different 'concentrations' in geography in undergraduate training, certainly with a distinction between physical and human geography; (2) there is need for application of expertise in research to problems that are concerned not with the processes involved in the development of individual features, but with the processes involved in the assemblages of related features that result in distinct areal variations of the earth's surface; generalization should be sought in the advancement of the regional concept not about natural processes of origin but about characteristics of land forms; and (3) there is, on the other hand, as Steers rightly insists, a need for 'team work' in research. There is need for institutes dedicated to training and enquiry in various fields. Many such institutes exist today, including institutes of environmental studies, geochronology, coastal studies, natural resources, earth sciences, atmospheric physics. It is highly desirable that such institutes pursue their ends unhampered, with the collaboration of colleagues in appropriate disciplines. Such institutes demand skills at the postgraduate level. This is a matter not only of scientific objective, but also of university organization. Different universities will organize these fields according to their own grass roots.

Sixth, there is the question of the content and purpose of undergraduate training in physical (as well as human) geography. There is a fundamental difference between research and tuition which esoteric intellectuals often overlook. There is investigation at the *research level,* that calls for the application of specialized skills. There is training at the *tuition level,* which concerns *all* who study the field in the university and afterwards teach in school, not merely the handful who go on to 'research'. The first demands team work at the postgraduate level. This is effectively demonstrated by Steers and is intellectually impregnable. The argument has its staunchest exponent in the USA in J. B. Leighly, who was naturally (as a geologist) supported by R. J. Russell. The trend has grown in universities on both sides of the Atlantic in the post-war years—it is a trend of the times. The second, however, is the case that is not argued or presented by Steers. This concerns the content of an undergraduate training in geography in terms of its concepts, procedures and expertise. This should be combined, as Steers rather vaguely argues, with cognate sciences. But in such a combination what are the essentials of the distinctively geographical contribution? This question applied, indeed, in the interwar years, as this writer has contended for over thirty years, to the fields, so ill-defined, of both physical and human geography. It is to this very matter of setting their house in order that leading geographers in Britain, in the realms of both tuition and research, particularly at Cambridge (Steers's successors!), have given their attention in the post-war years. They find their focus in the conceptual framework that leads to further understanding of the regional concept. The exposition of two leading exponents will be presented in the next chapter.

Seventh, there is crying need for a new evaluation of the aims of physical geography in terms of social impact and needs.[3] Some call this 'applied geography'. What matters to the student of man's use of the land is not the precise chronology of terrace remnants, the process of rock disintegration, or the mechanics of ice movement, but the characteristics and spatial extent of terrains in terms of human use, misuse or abuse. The case was admirably stated by Stevens in the essay noticed above. The geomorphologist, biogeographer or climatologist has the skills that such appraisal needs. But it calls for an ecological orientation in the study of man's natural environment. These are challenges of the regional concept that Steers's framework scarcely touches upon in either research or teaching.

I give several examples of targets prompted by the regional concept. A series of maps of geomorphic units is needed on a scale of, say, 1 : 250,000. A similar series is needed of plant associations comparable with Gaussen's in France. Maps of local climatic variations on this scale are also needed. These are challenges of the regional concept to physical geographers. They have not been accepted. There is much work to be done, which demands 'team work'.

Several scholars, who held chairs of geography between the wars and for some years thereafter, offered important confirmations of these criticisms and indeed sought to answer my plea. Chief among these was undoubtedly the late S. W. Wooldridge, who was a remarkable student of 'geographical geomorphology' and enjoyed public (and private!) utterances to further the role of geography in teaching and research. A. A. Miller, who, like Wooldridge, trained as a geologist, was also a first class 'geographical geomorphologist' and made also contributions to climatology, especially notable being his presidential address to the Geographical Association in 1960 (*Geography,* 1961) with the title 'Climate and the geomorphic cycle'. D. L. Linton, student and colleague of Wooldridge, in addition to geomorphic studies, tackled the question of the hierarchy of 'morphological units' (1951) and sought thereafter to enlist the services of younger colleagues in the preparation of such a map of Great Britain. Here too should be mentioned the names of F. K. Hare and P. R. Crowe, originally graduates of the Joint School (King's and LSE) of the University of London, who have done work on what may be referred to, for want of a better name (and it is certainly redundant), as 'regional climatology', though their emphasis borders again on 'atmospheric physics' or meteorology. As far as biogeography is concerned, very little was achieved worthy of note between the wars. There was nothing to compare with the labours of Gaussen in France (*Géographie des plantes,* 1933) and his series of maps of plant ecology, beginning with Toulouse, on a scale of 1 : 250,000, in 1947. In the post-war years one turns for advance in this field to Pierre Dansereau in America (*Biogeography: An Ecological Perspective,* 1957) and to the promising beginnings of Sauer's son, Jonathan, and A. W. Küchler (of German origin) in the USA. Ecological work in Britain between the wars was the special field of the botanist A. G. Tansley (*The British Islands and their Vegetation,* 1939; *Introduction to Plant Ecology,* 1946), and the forestry institute in the University of Oxford, which pursued study of 'site' as an area with homogeneous physical conditions relevant to the establishment of plant communities.

Since the views of Steers have been summarized in the foregoing paragraphs, it is necessary to turn to an evaluation of the contribution of S. W. Wooldridge, who had a far-reaching impact on teachers and researchers between the wars and through the 1940s and 1950s, whereas the Cambridge group worked in scholastic seclusion. The reader can turn to the views of Wooldridge in a collection of his papers with the title *The Geographer as Scientist* (1956). The following comments relate to the contents of that book, and also draw upon personal contact with its author during the interwar period.

Wooldridge died in 1963 at the age of sixty-two. Like Steers, he was a geomorphologist, trained and skilled in geological expertise. But he was unlike Steers in that he became converted in his later years to geography as a discipline, and sought to understand and propagate its distinctive scope and purpose in teaching and research. Wooldridge dedicated his work and teaching to the study of landscape, whereas Steers and his school achieved remarkable results in the processes involved in the development of earth features, and showed a negligible concern in print or in the classroom with the nature and procedures of geography as discipline.

Wooldridge sought persistently and insistently, without mincing words, to advance the study of geography. He declared: 'Geography is a natural science in so far as it concerns itself with the expression of natural phenomena in area.' It is a social science 'in so far as it concerns itself with the expression of man in area' (in which view he repeats the words of Sauer and Leighly).

He early applied his geological skills to investigate what he called 'landscape evolution' in south-east England. In this study, however, he did not remain, as he might well have done, with geochronology. It culminates in a map of the minor 'regional sub-divisions', which are, in fact, geomorphic entities. He later sought in various published papers to trace the modes of spatial adjustments to this base of settlement and land use. In doing so, he turned in particular to the patterns of the Saxon settlement in south-east England. These he determined by mapping (partly adapting the work of other specialists) Saxon burial grounds, place names (suffixes) and Domesday villas. The patterns revealed marked segregations and these were found to be closely related to the detailed variants of his 'physiographic boundaries'.

The purpose and method of definition of these small 'physiographic units' are defined, in his own words:[4]

In the construction of a map of regional sub-divisions for

south-east England, we are primarily concerned with (1) soil, (2) natural vegetation, (3) water supply and (4) texture or pattern of relief and drainage (*not* altitude, as some treatments would seem to imply). Neither a geological map nor a contoured map is fully sufficient for our purpose. The task lies essentially in defining the lines, or narrow zones along which there is a clearly recognizable change in the physical landscape, and probably also in the modern cultural landscape; which reflects some at least of the contrasts effective at an earlier date.

It is highly significant that his final map of what he called physiographic units in south-east England bears the caption 'Soil regions'. This is explicit recognition that the local variants of soil texture are the best overall indicator of the variants of the composite terrain, an approach which was being used on the Continent at that time, as is reflected in my own systematic mapping of the hierarchy of physiographic entities of the whole of western Germany. It is in accordance with the goals of the regional concept and should be warmly heralded as such.

While Wooldridge was very explicit on the concept of a physiographic entity—and sought even more thoroughly than his senior contemporary J. F. Unstead to explore it (see p. 149)—he was always tantalizingly vague as to the scope of the geography of man. Of three things, however, I am certain.

First, he was personally dedicated to the modes of human adjustment to the physiographic background. Wooldridge's unswerving concern was the imprint of man's work and works on the land in relation to the characteristics of the terrain or site. Study of the 'cultural landscape' as an end in itself he was vague about, presumably leaving it to the expertise of others. Alas, his interwar contemporaries took no real interest in such matters, and left this field to certain economic historians (notably W. G. Hoskins) to explore in the post-war years.

Second, he was vehemently opposed to the investigation of where 'bootlaces or Ovaltine' come from (both his examples, cited derisively). In other words, the quantitative analysis of geographical variables, even when cloaked in the scientific nomenclature of 'regional science', was anathema to Wooldridge.

Third, Wooldridge was a dedicated field man. Throughout his career he extolled the virtues of work in the local area on foot, with map in hand, and a keen eye on the landscape, both natural and man-made. On one occasion he declared, 'I need hardly add that it is inherent in the method and point of view I am commending that when in the field one should concentrate on *observable field data*' (italics mine). He sought assiduously to train what Sauer was calling 'the morphological eye'.

It is of further interest to note what Wooldridge had to say about regional geography, for he certainly revealed to his audiences, and commended to them, the works of those he particularly esteemed. Its aim, he said in 1951, is as follows: 'It is to gather up the disparate strands of the systematic studies, the geographical aspects of other disciplines, into a coherent and focused unity, to see nature and nurture, physique and personality as closely related and interdependent elements in specific regions.'[5] 'Where', he asks on the same occasion, 'are the great magistral works on regional geography?' He answers by describing Mackinder's *Britain and the British Seas* (1902) as an 'inspired and germinal book'. He continues: 'the work of Professor Darby has illuminated and will further illumine Mackinder's own distinctive field of historical geography'. and 'Professor Stamp's great work on *The Land of Britain* is rich and ample development of the very few pages devoted to agriculture by Mackinder'. 'More recently Mr Wilfred Smith has repaid some of our debt to the applied economists and provided a real super-structure upon Mackinder's quite small beginnings.'[6]

In spite of this lip-service to his colleagues, I was never convinced of Wooldridge's understanding. I had proof of this in a personal talk with him shortly before his death. After happily agreeing on the rejection of 'bootlaces and Ovaltine', to which I cheerfully added lead pencils at Keswick (the subject of the first undergraduate thesis in my hands on returning to Britain in 1958, which was a study in economic history, with a geological map as a frontispiece), I then raised the critical question: 'What do you do with the facts of human activity and organization of land that have no relation to the physical earth?', to which came the immediate reply, 'Leave 'em out.' Whether this retort was the result of long premeditation, or impulsive belligerence is beside the point. I have never recovered from this final confirmation of my doubt, for thus spoke a neo-environmentalist, not an ecologist. While I have a profound respect for the expertise of Wooldridge as a geomorphologist, he evidently had clearly focused his view of man on the earth on his direct relationships, of adjustment or maladjustment, to the physical environment.

Thus, Wooldridge's contribution to geography lay in insistence on the study of existing land forms; practical illustration of a physiographic entity as a composite localized terrain unit; and persistent endeavour to propagate a discipline he approached after an initial training as a geologist, and sought by exhortation and example to diffuse among teachers and researchers.

Wooldridge, in a controversial rebuttal on the interconnections of geology and geography in the study of landscape, quoted W. M. Davis as follows:[7]

> To look upon a landscape without any recognition of the
> labour expended upon producing it, or of the extraordinary
> adjustment of streams to structure and waste to weather is like
> visiting Rome in the ignorant belief that the Romans of
> today had no ancestors.

This argument applies to the evaluation of natural and human processes in the understanding of the physical (natural) and humanized (man-made) landscapes. It is the heart of the regional concept.

The views and teaching of Wooldridge in London clearly stand in the strongest contrast to Steers and his colleagues in these years in Cambridge. Without presuming to criticize or evaluate the expertise of these men, the fact stands out clearly that the Cambridge school was primarily concerned with the chronology of natural processes and showed not the slightest interest in print or publication in the promotion of their geographical birthright. On the other hand, Wooldridge and his smaller school were concerned with the evolution of landscape with a view to the understanding of physiographic entities of terrain.

The difference in viewpoints of the two schools in the interwar years is evident in the work of their present leaders. Wooldridge has left behind a group of distinguished geographers of the fourth generation who pursue his ends. These include D. L. Linton, who died in 1971, E. H. Brown, F. K. Hare, B. W. Sparks, C. Kidson and R. A. Savigear. The Cambridge descendants include R. F. Peel, J. B. Sissons, Cuchlaine A. M. King and R. J. Chorley, and many able though less well known professionals who hold university posts and effectively propagate the Cambridge tradition.

In conclusion, I recall being disconcerted by a graduate student in a British university, who, in a discussion group of six, remained singularly silent. I was discussing procedures of the regional concept with reference to the clear formulation of objectives for their own studies for a higher degree. I asked the silent one why he had nothing whatever to contribute to the discussion. His reply was that he was not interested in 'that kind of thing'; his concern was with the mode of weathering of rocks at chosen caches in the Lake District in which appropriate instruments were hidden and records regularly kept for about a year. His thesis included a formidable array of formulae and diagrams, for the assessment of which (as a chief examiner for the degree) I had to call in an expert since it was beyond my competence. The man got his degree in geography. Though the thesis may have contained epoch-making material, it was in no way related to the regional concept and quite obviously involved questions, expertise and procedures in a language completely beyond my understanding as a geographer.[8] The regional concept is the purpose of my pursuit. This dichotomy is the problem the profession has to face. A few years ago I pointed out the dilemma of my ignorance of the expertise of 'dynamic geology' to a geomorphologist (now a professor) and have never forgotten his immediate retort—'You'll have to learn it.' There are limits, and one simply cannot operate effectively on both sides of a gulf that increasingly divides.

11

Post-War Trends

There has been a profound change in the goals and methods of geographical study over the past twenty years, both in Britain and in America. This chapter is concerned with the British contribution, which has drawn from and substantially contributed to the change in America. Without further comment I begin with an exposition by two of the leaders, Richard Chorley and Peter Haggett. It is highly significant that both these men hail from Cambridge, and are the principal exponents of the mutation. Two excerpts are taken from the massive symposium on *Models in Geography* (1967), which they edited. A third is taken from a short book written by M. Chisholm for the new Social Science Research Council, London, 1971. The chapter concludes with review of trends in physical geography by Professor E. H. Brown of University College, London.[1] These are extracts to present the new targets and are presented without comment as indicative of current trends in teaching and research.

MODELS AND PARADIGMS, *by R. J. Chorley and P. Haggett*[2]

The term 'model' has been used in such a wide variety of contexts that it is difficult to define even the broad types of usage without ambiguity. One division is between the *descriptive* and the *normative*; the former concerned with some stylistic description of reality and the latter with what might be expected under certain stated conditions. Models can be classed according to the stuff from which they are made into, firstly, *hardware, physical* or *experimental* constructions, and, secondly, *theoretical, symbolic, conceptual* or *mental* models. Another view of models concentrates on *systems* which can be defined on the basis of the relative interest of model builder in the input/output variables, as distinct from the internal status variables.

Paradigms may be regarded as stable patterns of scientific activity. They are in a sense large-scale models, but differ from models in that: (1) they are rarely so specifically formulated; and (2) they refer to patterns of searching the real world rather than to the real world itself. Scientists whose research is based on shared paradigms are committed to the same problems, rules and standards, i.e., they form a continuing community devoted to a particular research tradition. In a sense, then, paradigms may be regarded here as 'super models' within which the smaller-scale models are set.

The importance of the paradigm lies in providing rules that: (1) tell us what both the world—and our science— are like; and (2) allow us to concentrate on the esoteric problems that these rules together with existing knowledge define. Paradigms tend to be, by nature, highly restrictive. They focus attention upon a small range of problems, often enough somewhat esoteric problems, to allow the concentration of investigation on some part of the man-environment system in a detail and depth that might otherwise prove unlikely, if not inconceivable. This concentration appears to have been a necessary part of scientific advance, allowing the solution of puzzles outside the limits of pre-paradigm thinking.

Whatever the range of debate over the purpose and nature of geography, there is considerable communality of practice in the ways in which geographers have tackled their problems. Berry (1964)[3] has analysed this paradigm of practice in terms of alternative approaches to a 'geographical data-matrix'. Here we attempt to diagnose the widespread unease generated by the continued use of this classificatory approach.

Although regional geography, systematic geography and historical geography are regarded as being quite distinct types of geographical study, Berry has deftly illustrated that each may be regarded merely as a different axis of approach to the same basic geographical data-matrix.

If a matrix has only *one* column, it is commonly called a 'column vector', in which may be stored a series of bits of information. Similarly we may store information about elements (i.e. temperatures, elevations, population densities, etc.) in a regional column, to give an inventory of all the available characteristics of a given location. A matrix with only *one* row is termed a 'row vector'. Here we may store a series of bits of information. In this approach, we store information about the same element but we vary the location to give the standard pattern of systematic geography, i.e., the mapping of a single feature (e.g., population densities). By combining both the set of regions and the set of elements we have a rectangular array. This matrix or box is termed by Berry the *geographical data-matrix* in that items containing information about the earth's surface may be stored in terms of their *regional* (or locational) characteristics and their *elemental* (or substantive) characteristics.

By an ingenious series of row and column comparisons and by the addition of a third (time) dimension, Berry is able to reduce the great part of conventional geographical study to ten basic operations on the matrix. For example, areal differentiation is seen as column-vector comparisons and spatial co-variance studies as row-vector comparisons. Comparison of a column over time becomes sequent occupance, while other manipulations give the major modes of historical geography distinguished by Darby.[4] Indeed the major—and apparently fundamental—contrasts between regional, systematic and historical geography are seen by Berry largely as a function of the relative length, breadth and depth of the study in terms of the three axes of the matrix.

The need for the information in the data-matrix to be structured, given coherence, generalized and made intelligible, has long been recognized, and both Humboldt and Ritter scorned the attitude of their predecessors which had reduced geographical studies in the eighteenth century to mere 'pigeon-holing'. There is growing evidence, however, that neither of the two major solutions—the study of column vectors and of row vectors—effectively meet present-day demands.

The exact rate of growth of 'information' that could conceivably be stored in a geographical data-matrix is difficult to assess exactly. We have useful figures on the speed of mapping for selected areas, and are familiar with the rapid accelerations caused by the development of air-photography after the First World War and of satellite scanning and remote sensing since the Second World War. If we add to this the growing volume of statistical material collected by international agencies, national governments, state and local administrators, then the size of the potential world 'data bank' becomes staggering.

What gives added point is the general rate of growth of information. There is evidence of an exponential growth of impressive consistency and regularity—that is, the more information that exists the faster it grows. Depending upon what we measure, it is possible to estimate that the amount of information tends to double within a period of ten to fifteen years— probably slightly shorter. If one accepts the general form of the curve, then the problem facing Humboldt and Ritter was about a thousand times as small as that facing the current generation of geographers. The fact that large areas of the world were still then 'blank on the map' suggests this is in fact a sizable overestimate; that is, the rate of growth of locationally 'storable' information has been *more* rapid than that of scientific information as a whole as the ecumene itself has expanded.

Continuing Berry's matrix algebra analogy, we may trace the problems in columnar analyses to: (1) the expanding number of locational columns as old areas were ever more finely divided and new areas added; and (2) the proven failure of local 'column' factors to explain the juxtaposition of other variables in the same column. For example, the development of general production techniques during the Industrial Revolution tended to destroy unique regional features and to make the geographical characteristics of these regions less explainable in purely local terms. Analysis of row vectors (i.e., systematic distribution studies) has been weakened by the tendency for individual systematic sciences to 'split off' their own rows for separate analyses. It is significant, for example, that systematic sciences are increasingly taking on their own mapping analysis—and in some cases are themselves making substantial contributions to cartographic technique.

It is clear then that technological improvements, largely in computer engineering and programming logic, are at last beginning to restore to the greatly strained geographical data-matrix some of the order that its rapid expansion threatened to destroy. While empirical approaches to the stored material are likely to throw up a good deal of unexpected patterning, we should recall that these programmes are greatly facilitated when preceded by analysis of the problem in terms of some conceptual model—a mental picture—that defines the class of objects or events to be studied, the kinds of measurements to be made, and the properties or attributes of these measurements.

We do not propose to alter the basic definition of geography's prime task, nor challenge the appropriateness of the matrix concept. We suggest, however, that it may be possible to derive a *second* matrix from the first by transforming the two basic vectors in such a way as to throw emphasis away from that of classification towards model-building.

Vector I: locational relativity. The search for greater accuracy along the absolute locational vector (e.g., exact latitude and longitude) and the search for significant 'fixes' in this absolute regional space (e.g., the location of the source of the Nile) is now largely centred in specialized government mapping agencies outside the university research world. However, location in an absolute sense is clearly only one way of viewing space. Although no formal attempts have yet been made to build up a 'general theory of locational relativity', the multivariate analysis of distance (measured in 'real' energy terms rather than 'neutral' *mileage* terms) and their reduction to suitable display maps pose fascinating and complex research problems. A whole new family of atlases might be envisaged showing completely different spatial patterns than the familiar absolute patterns of traditional maps.

Vector II: topological-geometrical form. The successive sub-division of the 'elements' vector has seen the constant departure of newly fledged sciences with their own geographical interpretations. We propose therefore that certain 'abstract properties'—the topological and geometrical form of that object or objects—be substituted for the standard 'element-class' vector. . . . A simple dimensional classification of zero-order (points, cities), first-order (lines, networks), second-order (areas, states) and third-order (surface, terrain) , provides such an appropriate topological vector. In general we feel that geometrical analysis offers a logical, consistent and geographically more relevant alternative to the 'element-oriented' approach, with its inevitable tendency to sub-divide geography and force it outwards towards the relevant external systematic disciplines. It not only offers a chance to weld human and physical geography into a new working partnership, but revives the central role of cartography in relation to the two. Whatever the problems that remain to be solved, particularly problems of system identification and energy monitoring, we may expect that regional systems analysis will emerge as a major theme in geographical work over the next decade.

The period which follows the wholesale adoption of a paradigm is commonly devoted to three main classes of research problem: (1) the determination of significant facts; (2) the matching of facts with theory; and (3) the further articulation of theory. None of these major types of research is designed to produce results entirely outside the paradigm's limits, and the range of acceptable results from the studies is small—certainly small in relation to the results that could be conceived. The internal discipline of the paradigm, its unwritten rules and traditions, guides the pattern of research and ensures by the successive cumulation of small highly-limited advances that the science as a whole will progress. . . .

Geography must measure its progress by the number of puzzles it has effectively solved, not by the magnitude of those that remain unsolved. In welcoming Ackerman's reminder[5] that the philosophical goal of geography is '. . . nothing less than an understanding of the vast, interacting system comprising all humanity and its natural environment on the surface of the earth' we should recall, with Humboldt, that such a goal is utterly unattainable in any complete sense—either now or in the future. Successful application of models in geography ensures no teleological progress towards full understanding, for scientific effort does not reduce the sum total of problems to be solved—it rather increases them.

ORGANISM AND ECOSYSTEM AS GEOGRAPHICAL MODELS *by D. R. Stoddart*[6]

Geography and ecology are concerned with the distribution, organization and morphology of phenomena on the surface of the earth, and both disciplines have developed similar concepts and techniques to handle similar problems. Overt geographical interest in ecological techniques, however, has been largely confined to a small group of biogeographers, whose influence on the rest of the subject has been marginal, and to a group of American sociologists who sought for a time to restate the aims of human geography in terms of human ecology.

The influence of biological concepts in geography, however, has been both deeper and more pervasive than explicit reference might suggest. Thus, in spite of current insistence on the importance of areal differentiation as a methodological framework for geography, derived by Hartshorne from the work of von Richthofen and Hettner, much geographical work in the past 100 years has taken its inspiration directly from Darwin and the biological revolution which he began. Elsewhere I have indicated some of the main strands in the evolutionary impact on geographical thought since 1859: particularly the emphasis on changing form through time, expressed in organic analogies of ageing; the popularity of natural selection and environmental models, particularly in early American human geography; and, latterly, the application of Haeckel's concept of ecology and Tansley's of the ecosystem, which may be traced back to the third chapter of *Origin of Species.*

This essay treats the biological impact on a methodological level. We are concerned with the evolution of geographic *paradigms* of largely biological inspiration: paradigms, or interrelated networks of concepts on a sufficiently general level which serve to define, at least for a time, the nature of geographical goals and the conventional frameworks within which these are pursued. The paradigms examined here are those of organism and ecosystem: they are not the only ones which may have been chosen, nor necessarily the most influential, but both concern fundamental issues in the methodology of geography. The organic paradigm in particular includes several examples of smaller-scale paradigms which can be defined with greater precision: Davis's cyclic and Clements's successional concepts among them. A distinction is thus made between such generalized conceptual models, for which the term paradigm is usefully employed, and their puzzle-solving nature, as in the problem of the definition and statistical treatment of plant and animal communities: and many of these techniques are of direct geographic interest at a comparable level of enquiry. Puzzle-solving procedures of this sort, leading to the development of explanatory or predictive models for particular problems, depend on the acceptance of common standards of procedure and of common scientific aims, but they only become of methodological importance when they require the modification of the prevailing paradigm itself.

Organism and ecosystem are of interest as alternative approaches to a central theme in geographical enquiry: that of the relationship of man and environment in area. Thus Hettner states the classical position, when he writes that 'both nature and man are intrinsic to the particular character of areas, and indeed in such intimate union that they cannot be separated from each other'. It is also in this relationship that geography has faced two of its most difficult methodological problems, of dualism between man and environment, and that between human and physical geography. Both organic and ecosystem concepts have been used to overcome these problems, and to provide coherent frameworks for the organization of geographic data. This essay deals with the nature of these borrowings from the biological sciences, the way in which geographic interpretations have changed with developments in the biological sciences themselves, and the potential paradigmatic value of biological models in geographic methodology.

Organic analogies have been used as 'explanations' of the real world since classical times. In the biological sciences in particular there has been much controversy between mechanists, vitalists and organicists over the reducibility of biological concepts and the scope and significance of organic holistic models. Clements's work in plant ecology may be taken as an example of the use of organic analogy in ecology itself. Clements, following Warming, developed the ideas of climax and succession in vegetation, but went beyond the empirical observation of such changes to assert that[7]

the development study of vegetation necessarily rests upon the assumption that the unit or climax formation is an organic entity. As an organism the formation arises, grows, matures, and dies ... Each climax formation is able to reproduce itself.

The plant community is[8] 'a complex organism, or superorganism, with characteristic development and structure ... It is more than the sum of its individual parts, ... it is indeed an organism of a new order. As with W. M. Davis's scheme of the geographical cycle, to which Clements's successional model bears close resemblance, Clements and his followers regarded the organismic idea as a revealing conceptual framework for understanding the real world: 'this concept is the "open sesame" to a whole new vista of scientific thought, a veritable *magna carta* for future progress.' European ecologists never wholeheartedly accepted Clements's insistence on succession or his metaphysical interpretation of community: while succession may be adequately demonstrated on a small scale (as in marshland, on sand dunes or in pieces of dung) organismic views of community have little practical relevance at such levels; while at larger scales fieldworkers concentrated on empirical descriptive studies in which organismic concepts had no place. Similarly in pedology, earlier organismic views have been rejected by later workers.

For early ecologists, the value of organic analogies lay in their ability to bring large quantities of discrete and often apparently unrelated data into meaningful relationship, to emphasize the organization and functional relationships existing in nature, which, once recognized, served as at least a partial explanation of their complexity. Organic analogies were particularly successful when the problems were most

1   *Patrick Geddes*   2   *Halford J. Mackinder*

3   *Andrew J. Herbertson*   4   *Herbert John Fleure*

5　*Percy Maude Roxby*

6　*L. Dudley Stamp*

7   *Marion I. Newbigin*

8   *Alan G. Ogilvie*

9 *Hugh Robert Mill*

10 *William Morris Davis*

11　*Mark Jefferson*

12　*J. Russell Smith*

13   *Harlan H. Barrows*

14   *Wellington Downing Jones*

15 *Charles C. Colby*   16 *Wallace W. Atwood*

17 *Isaiah Bowman*   18 *Carl Ortwin Sauer*

complex and the analytical techniques too underdeveloped to
produce substantive results. Hence, with the rise of descriptive
ecology, with its diverse body of sophisticated descriptives and
analytical techniques, vague analogy no longer served as a valid
explanation of natural complexity. To take one example, while
Clements emphasized the organic nature of the great vegetational
units of the world, such as the selva and the coniferous forests,
more detailed studies, as in East Asia, have shown that these
do not represent the discrete units of vegetation, but are no
more than the vague patterns joined together by gradual
transition. The overlapping distribution of twenty-four conifer
species along a thermal gradient in Japan, suggests that in this
case vegetation units have no discrete existence. Similar cases
may be cited from animal ecology.

This brief discussion demonstrates the appeal of organic
analogy in ecological problems similar to those faced by geography.
In geography itself, organic analogies are of considerable antiquity,
but received fresh impetus from the Darwinian revolution, and
maintained popularity until the 1930s. Carl Ritter's inspiration
was in no sense biological, but for him and his followers the
organic model not only provided a satisfying explanation of the
relation of man and nature, but provided a religious and moral
justification also. The earth for him was not 'a mere dead,
inorganic plant, but an organism, a living work from the hand of
a living God', in which both animate and inanimate components
form 'in a higher and comprehensive sense a cosmical life, . . .
one great organism'.

The ecosystem is a type of general system, defined as a set of
objects together with relationships between the objects and
between their attributes. Partaking in general system theory, the
ecosystem is potentially capable of precise mathematical
structuring within a theoretical framework, a very different
matter from the tentative and incomplete descriptions of highly
complex relationships which too often pass for geographical
'synthesis'. The limits of the ecosystem may be set at any
desirable areal extent. Within any areal framework the ecosystem
concept will give point to enquiry, and thus highlight both form
and function in a spatial setting. Simplistic ideas of causation
and development, or of geographic dualism, are in this context
clearly irrelevant: ecosystem analysis gives geographers a tool
with which to work.

The value of systems analysis lies not only in its emphasis on
organization, structure and functional dynamics: through its

171

general system properties, it brings geography back into the realm of the natural sciences, and allows us to participate in the scientific revolutions of this century from which the Kantian exceptionalist position excluded us.

RESEARCH IN HUMAN SPATIAL SYSTEMS, *by M. Chisholm*[9]

Geographers in general, including both human and physical geographers, are concerned with space (i.e., physical dimension on the earth's surface) as a basic element in the distribution and interrelationships of phenomena. It is generally true of the social sciences that the implications of space have been ignored, or have been treated at only one or two scales. Perhaps the major contribution made by the human geographer to the social sciences is his concern with the spatial aspects of problems at all scales. Consequently, geography is not distinguished from other subjects either by the class of phenomena studied or by the methods of analysis employed. It *is* distinguished, though, by the class of problems that is examined—namely, the identification, description and measurement of processes operating in a spatial context. Thus, three themes can be seen to run through work in geography, including human geography:

(1) All phenomena occur in a spatial context. Space may be conceived as possessing numerous properties and the way space is conceived and measured has an important bearing on the way in which phenomena are perceived and the significance that attaches to them. It is therefore necessary to examine systematically the effects of space upon human activities of all kinds and hence to examine the properties of space and the logical consequences that follow from these properties.

(2) Economic and social activities require physical facilities such as buildings and means of transport. There is necessarily a close association between the economic and social processes on the one hand and the built forms on the other. As it is often not possible to observe these processes directly, inferences must be drawn about their nature from the effects of their operation, shown in the spatial arrangement of human artefacts of all kinds.[10]

(3) Mankind, in his productive activities, social customs and institutions, cannot be studied in isolation from the environment in which he lives. For over a hundred years, geographers have concerned themselves with the interrelationships of man and his

environment. In recent years, it has become accepted that the relationship is in large measure indirect, operating through man's perception of his surroundings.

In reviewing the position in the USA, Taaffe and his colleagues[11] adopted an essentially inductive approach, in the sense that the starting-point chosen was the substantive work done by acknowledged geographers. An alternative is to develop the logical structure of thinking behind geographical work, more in the deductive than the inductive tradition. It is this that has been attempted here. Consequently [a] chapter begins with the logical difficulties involved in knowing precisely what the spatial dimensions of any problem are, i.e., problems of measurement and pattern identification. [He then] looks at these issues in a static sense and dynamic spatial patterns and their evolution. Together these provide the basis for examining processes operating in space and lead to an examination of theories of spatial organization in Chapter 4. The volume is completed by a chapter on the organization and structure of research and a [conclusion] dealing with research priorities and needs.

Priority Research Areas

(1) Perception studies Geographers have for long been aware of the difference between the 'objective' (or 'real') environment and the environment as perceived. However, it is only in the last decade or two that a systematic attempt has been made to measure space perception and space preferences, to evaluate them and to examine the search procedures that people employ to explore the environment in which they find themselves. The field is a very difficult one in which to operate. Furthermore, it clearly overlaps with psychology in terms of basic techniques and with both sociology and planning in terms of the implications and applications of findings. Consequently, it is an area of study in which especial care must be taken to ensure the adequacy of skills cognate to geography. Despite the difficulties, perception studies are of central importance for the study of geography and its application in the planning process.

(2) Simulation models The comparison is often made that whereas controlled experiments can be undertaken in the natural sciences, this is impossible in the social sciences. Simulation provides an important tool for the social scientist, whereby the

state of the system under investigation can be predicted given specific assumptions. In this way, various developmental or planning strategies can be compared. The simulation of spatial systems is a complex task but nevertheless an important aid in policy-making, especially at the urban level. In addition, a good simulation model allows a good description of actual patterns when the causal processes are not known in full. Simulation models have only come into vogue with the advent of modern computers and to date the models are still rather crude.

(3) Forecasting Any conscious attempt to alter the environment (either the built or the natural environment) implies exercises in forecasting. While much of the work in forecasting has been done by economists for the national economy as a whole, for many purposes it is necessary to make place-specific forecasts. This is a relatively new and untried field in which there is an urgent need for improved technique.

(4) Regional taxonomy The efficient division of space into operational units for particular purposes is an essential prerequisite to further study and to action. Though geographers have for many decades been concerned with this problem, it is only recently that formal statistical procedures have been applied. There is therefore much work to be done at both the theoretical and the applied levels.

(5) Environmental standards Pollution and conservation are now fashionable preoccupations. However, it is all too easy to lose sight of the enduring need for the determination and measurement of environmental standards, a task that requires both the elucidation of theoretical constructs and empirical testing of these constructs, so that positive standards may be specified in respect of identified sectors of the community.

(6) Population and migration Despite the considerable work of geographers on the spatial aspects of population growth and change, the importance of this field warrants a substantially larger investment of effort.

(7) Processes of regional economic and social development All economic and social change implies spatial differentials. There is a vast field to be cultivated, not only to identify the constraints to development but also to seek out the fruitful courses of action.

In this respect, comparative studies have an especial significance.

While it would be idle to pretend that all in the garden is well, it nevertheless does appear that research in geography is not afflicted by problems that differ either in kind or significantly in magnitude from the problems encountered by other subjects. Consequently, there are no obvious, universally accepted conclusions for action that ought to be undertaken immediately, either by the Social Science Research Council or other bodies. Nevertheless, there are two directions for change that may be pointed out as likely to be fruitful.

In terms mainly of postgraduate numbers but also in terms of the subject as a whole, there is no shortage of trained manpower and no lack of research output. While there will undoubtedly be continuing growth in numbers of staff and students, a quantitative increase is not at the present time the first priority. It seems altogether more important to concentrate on improving the already high standards of research work undertaken. This may imply the provision of M.Sc. courses in advanced techniques, etc., and may also imply an increase in the degree of specialization in research undertaken by departments. Such a conclusion is neither very startling nor revolutionary but were it to be acted upon it would make for quite far-reaching changes in the field of human geography in the next decade or so.

The second direction for change reflects the author's own predilection. A long-established habit in the field of geography has been to regard the geographer's role as that of providing background information relevant for solving a problem, the actual solution being left to others. In the context of the present-day world, it is important for the standing of any subject that, within its domain, it press on to the final solution of particular problems. One of the more important changes in human geography in the past decade has been the growing involvement with practical affairs in which decisions must be taken, a concomitant is the growth in the problem-solving attitude among geographers, a trend that is to be supported wholeheartedly. And it is in this context that there is a strong case for the establishment of a research unit concerned with monitoring economic and social changes in their spatial aspects and examining important current problems that are manifest in spatial terms.

175

TRENDS IN PHYSICAL GEOGRAPHY, *by E. H. Brown*[12]

In the late 1940s interest in geomorphology in Britain centred largely on the study of the development of land forms through time. They were studies in denudation chronology, inspired by Wooldridge and Linton's *Structure, Surface and Drainage in South-east England,* published in 1939, which had in its turn received stimulus from the lectures given by Henri Baulig in 1935 at the University of London on 'The changing sea-level'. There was extensive mapping of erosion surfaces, plateau elements deemed to be remnants of pre-existing surfaces of low relief. There was considerable discussion as to the origins of such surfaces and their ages. The majority of workers tended to think of them as being of sub-aerial origin but the traditional British view that such upland plains were former sea floors had its strong adherents.

Allied to the study of planation surfaces were studies of drainage evolution in which two principal schools of thought can be discerned. First, those who regarded the origins of British drainage as dating back to Cretaceous transgression which more or less completely submerged and buried the present site of the British Isles and then those who saw the drainage pattern as having originated more recently, probably in late Tertiary times, by the extension of pre-existing streams from the old land across a series of emergent wave-cut platforms.

In the 1950s emphasis in such chronological studies gradually turned from the Tertiary to the Pleistocene through an increase of interest in glacial drifts and land forms. A number of features came to form the foci of studies. Meltwater channels were examined in a large number of localities and there was considerable discussion as to whether they were produced by glacial meltwater ponded up at the margins of ice sheets or, as some argued, whether many of them had resulted from erosion by sub-glacial meltwater.

Raised beaches have been known around the coast of Britain for over a century but their precise delimitation and their altitudinal relationships were now studied in greater detail. British geomorphologists have contributed their fair share of evidence and discussion concerning the chronology of the Pleistocene but this topic has been mainly the province of geologists and paleobotanists. A substantial number of those actively engaged in Pleistocene studies in Britain are found

among geographer-geomorphologists. More recently, chronological
studies by geomorphologists have extended into the Holocene,
partly as a consequence of the study of the origins of dry valleys,
and partly because of the interest shown by archaeologists in
stratigraphic problems.

Not all British geomorphologists were solely concerned with
denudation chronology. In the early 1950s a number were
inspired by ideas expressed in the University of Sheffield
concerning the necessity for precisely delimiting the form of the
ground on geomorphological maps. From these studies there
developed a considerable interest in the study of slope form
for its own sake, and the British contribution to international
deliberations on the nature and origins of slope form was substantial.
The particular British contribution has been the precise
measurement of slope angles and the analysis of the resultant
data by data-processing methods.

Parallel with this interest in slopes there developed in the
1950s an interest in the detailed measurement of drainage basin
parameters based upon map sources along the lines pioneered
by Horton in the United States. This interest in drainage basins
was to a considerable extent responsible for the introduction of
the so-called quantitative revolution into British physical
geography during the 1950s and 1960s.

As interest in the chronology of geomorphological events
has waned, so under American influence—and especially after
the publication of Leopold Wolman and Miller's *Fluvial
Processes in Geomorphology* in the USA in 1964—there has
blossomed a considerable interest in the measurement of
current geomorphological processes; a large number of
experimental catchments have been established in which
measurements of such phenomena as soil movements and
stream channel form are currently under investigation.
Dissatisfaction with this type of work and particularly the
uncertainties involved in the interpretation of the results and the
difficulties of controlling a multi-variable situation, has led a number
of workers to initiate laboratory studies of some geomorphological
processes in the belief that it will be possible to control
experiments more readily under laboratory conditions than
can ever be the case in the field. The principal work so far carried
out is in the field of weathering.

The great interest shown in climatic geomorphology on the
continent of Europe, particularly in France and Germany, has
hardly been reflected in Britain. After an early stimulus from

the USA following Peltier's paper in the *Annals of the Association of American Geographers* for 1950, British workers have tended to take a somewhat sceptical view of the hypothesis that land form is to any substantial extent a function of climate. On the whole they see the connection between climate and land form as being a very indirect one and hardly worth using as a basis for the study of geomorphology itself.

As the environmental bandwagon started to roll and then to accelerate so the interest of some British geomorphologists turned to studies of the impact of man upon land form and the operation of geomorphological processes, and there are now substantial links between those interested in the nature of current processes as measured in the field and whose major concern is the influence which man has and continues to have upon the natural environment.

Because of the long-standing interest which Britain and thus British academics have in tropical lands, a not inconsiderable number of British geomorphologists have worked in tropical environments and have contributed significantly to the study of weathering and the development of land form in the inter-tropical areas. There have been especially a considerable number of studies in arid land concerned with the nature and origin of pediments and aeolian forms, especially dunes. The extent of deep weathering in humid tropical areas has been a particular interest in western Africa and in Hong Kong.

The occurrence of substantial limestone outcrops in Britain and strong amateur interest in caving have continued to maintain in the post-war years a minority, but powerful, interests in the development of karstic forms. Rigorous quantitative methods were employed at a relatively early stage, especially in the measurement of rates of solution, but only more recently has the surface morphometry of karstic areas come to be analysed in detail.

The numbers of physical geographers interested in climatology were and are substantially less than those concerned with land forms. The major contribution of British physical geographers to climatology has been in the field of local climatology, especially the influence of relief upon temperature and rainfall distributions, and in more recent years the influence of the urban environment upon climatic parameters. A few geographical climatologists have interested themselves in the climatology of agricultural environments and have worked in close co-operation with agricultural climatologists. The study of climatic change has been a minority interest but has produced significant results in co-operation with studies of denudation chronology and paleobotany.

Studies of soils and plant distributions have been a minority interest of British physical geographers in the post-war years. They have normally been of a secondary character and largely linked with the developing concern for the conservation of the natural environment.

While the principal concern of British physical geography was with chronological studies, and especially as it turned its interests to Pleistocene and Holocene developments of landscape, it fitted comfortably into British geography as a whole, the human aspects of which were to a considerable extent committed to an historical approach. The studies of physical geographers could happily be regarded as the basis of later events in the prehistoric and historic developments of the British landscape. With the change of emphasis in human geography from historical to spatial studies, there could have been a divorce between physical and human geography, but the two were held together in part by an increasing mutual interest in quantitative methods, especially statistical analyses and data-processing techniques. But now that the environment is increasingly a focus of popular interest, geographers find themselves in a situation in which the marriage between the physical and human aspects of their subject is regarded as essential and central to a major concern for the quality of the country's life. The physical geographer is perhaps in the process of abandoning some of his concern for physical principles, and prepared to investigate problems of an applied character.

G*

Part Two

AMERICA

12

A Review

THE BEGINNINGS

Courses of lectures on geography—variously described as physical, ancient, political, mathematical and 'the use of globes'—were offered in the colonial institutions in the north-east—Harvard, Dartmouth, William and Mary, Brown, Yale, Columbia, Rutgers, Princeton and Pennsylvania. Indeed, from 1795 to 1799 John Kemp was 'Professor of Geography' at Columbia following on a first appointment as 'Professor of Mathematics and Natural Philosophy' (Kemp came direct from the University of Aberdeen in Scotland).

During the nineteenth century there were two other notable professors of geography. Arnold Guyot was appointed at Princeton in 1854 where he remained until retirement in 1882, when he was followed by a pupil, William Libbey. Daniel Coit Gilman served as Professor of 'Physical and Political Geography' at Yale from 1863 until 1872, when he became president of the University of California at Berkeley. In 1875 he moved to the presidency of Johns Hopkins (as did also a successor, Isaiah Bowman, the director of the Geographical Society some fifty years later).

Harvard had a long tradition of geographical education from its earliest days. But courses in geography dropped from its curriculum in the early nineteenth century. A revival of interest came with the lectures of Guyot, direct from Neuchâtel, Switzerland, delivered in French, at the Lowell Institute in Boston. Guyot's lectures were given with the recommendation of Louis Agassiz, a fellow Swiss and a very distinguished Professor of Zoology and Geology at Harvard. Guyot waited five years before his appointment to Princeton.

Though geography at Harvard was required for admission to the university, it was not introduced into the curriculum until 1870, as 'physical geography' in the department of natural history. In 1877, physical geography was in charge of Josiah D. Whitney and N. S. Shaler. In 1878 W. M. Davis, then an instructor in geology, took over. In 1885 the course was shifted into a newly formed 'department of geography and geology' in which Davis had the rank of assistant professor. This was a revival which ended in 1956 with the dissolution of a short-lived department of geography and the dispersion of tuition between geology and history.

Although the American Geographical Society was established at mid-century (1851) and rapidly became an active seat of interest and promotion in exploration, little headway had been made in 1900 in the advancement of geography as a distinctive discipline worthy of independent status in an institution of higher learning.

Today about 1,000 four-year colleges offer bachelor degrees and nearly all of these embrace courses in geography. In 1900, out of a total of 700 colleges, only a dozen offered courses in geography. The total enrolment in all courses in geography in colleges and universities reached 314,000 in 1960, and 1,185 institutions offered one or more courses. The total number of instructors reached 2,244, nearly 1,000 of whom had a doctor's degree, and 77 institutions offered graduate work. Such has been the pace of growth since 1900.

There have been four tap-roots in this modern growth, each with its beginnings in the 1890s. These tap-roots are associated with founders at four institutions, namely: W. M. Davis in geology at Harvard; Rollin D. Salisbury, together with T. C. Chamberlin, both distinguished geologists in the 1890s at the new University of Chicago; Emory R. Johnson, an economist, at the Wharton School of Commerce and Finance in the University of Pennsylvania; and Mark Jefferson (and his predecessor C. T. McFarlane in the 1890s) at Michigan State Normal College at Ypsilanti, who, though primarily concerned with the training of the teachers, turned out a remarkable number of young men who became leaders in the new geography in both school and college. It should also be noted that already in the late 1890s R. S. Tarr was professor of Geology at Cornell and that he had been trained under Shaler and Davis and taught, wrote and directed postgraduate work in physiography until his premature death in 1912.

The 'disciple record' of each of these four men is evident in the names of those they trained who later achieved national eminence as teachers or researchers, mainly in the first quarter of this century.

Three further remarks are appropriate on these pages. First, the roots are found in schools and colleges for the training of school-teachers. There was considerable concern about the curriculum of teaching in secondary (high) schools in the 1890s. In 1892 the

National Education Association appointed a 'Committee of Ten' to consider the content and purpose of high school education and the conditions of entrance to college institutions. A sub-committee on geography had T. C. Chamberlin, the geologist from Chicago, as its chairman, and its members were all natural scientists. Its report (drafted by Davis) recommended the strengthening of the teaching of natural science, under the heading of 'physiography'. These recommendations stimulated the writing of a number of textbooks on 'physiography' and 'physical geography', such as R. S. Tarr's *Elementary Physical Geography* in 1895. But the definitive scholarly work *Physiography* is an 800-page treatise by Rollin D. Salisbury that appeared in 1907.

The *Journal of Geography* was established for the dissemination of matter and methods of teaching geography for secondary school-teachers. This journal, conceived by W. M. Davis, was founded in 1897 by Richard E. Dodge of Teachers' College, Columbia, who edited it for thirteen years. He was followed by R. H. Whitbeck at the University of Wisconsin, who served for eight years as a school-teacher. It was then turned over to the American Geographical Society and edited by its director, Isaiah Bowman, for two years (1918–20). The National Council of Geography Teachers was established at this time and thereafter it has been responsible for publication of the journal.

The report of the Committee of Ten resulted in what was described by Whitbeck as a 'revolution in geography teaching'. But the content of this teaching was the idea of 'physiography'. Jefferson pointed out ten years later than this that it was, in general, ineffective in schoolteaching. It proved to be 'dry and uninteresting' and gradually receded—an overt confession of ineffective teaching. In 1908, says Whitbeck, there was an active interest among teachers regarding ways and means of 'humanizing physiography' in terms of an acceptable pedagogical series of 'cause-and-effect relations'. Such an approach was logically formulated in the early 1900s by Davis, but resulted in the extension of 'environmental determinism'. Human societies were thought of as constant derivatives from the land, climate and location of their physical environment. This approach, which provides a facile chain of 'cause-and-effect associations', was universally adopted by teachers and professors for a generation. It has taken long to discard it for a more valid approach in the appraisal and teaching of man-land relations.

Second, the universities began to espouse the cause of geography by establishing departments and recruiting staff to organize and teach their discipline, and to promote and direct research in its problems. Progress was slow before the First World War. In 1935, according to Derwent Whittlesey's listing, only 19 doctorates had been awarded in fields that could be described as 'geography': 5 of these were awarded at Pennsylvania (in the faculty of economics); 5 at Chicago (beginning in 1907); 3 at Johns Hopkins (in meteorology and climatology); 2 at Cornell (in physiography); 2 at Yale, and 2 at Harvard. Only 5 of these were directed, examined and awarded by specialists in a department of geography, namely at the University of Chicago. Two of these were studies of big cities, and 3 were 'composite' geographical studies of particular areas— South Dakota, Missouri Ozarks and northern Patagonia. C. C. Colby's *Geography of S.E. Minnesota*, may be added to this group, for it is dated 1917.

Third, the early 'disciple record' of the founders requires clarification. The Davis sequence is outstanding. James reports that in 1891–2 Shaler and Davis at Harvard had the following students who later pursued careers of outstanding eminence: A. P. Brigham (Colgate, 1892–1925); A. H. Brooks (US Geological Survey); R. E. Dodge (Teachers' College, Columbia, 1897–1916); C. F. Marbut (Department of Agriculture, Soil Survey, 1897–1916); R. S. Tarr (Cornell geologist, 1892–1912); R. DeC. Ward (Harvard climatologist, 1890–1930); and L. S. Westgate (US Geological Survey). Later students of Davis included E. Huntington, Mark Jefferson, Isaiah Bowman and D. W. Johnson.

Jefferson 'nursed' a number of young men who continued their studies elsewhere. These included I. Bowman, C. C. Colby, H. H. Barrows, A. E. Parkins, D. H. Davis, G. J. Miller, G. H. Smith, R. S. Platt and R. D. Calkins. Jefferson 'shipped' his best students to Chicago, and, in the 1930s, also to Columbia.

Salisbury, a distinguished geologist, became the head of the new department of geography at Chicago in 1903. He remained at this post till 1919, when he returned to the department of geology, relinquishing the headship in geography to H. H. Barrows. The five doctorates in geography noted above (Emmerson, who became a geologist, Sauer, Jones, Visher and Colby) were all awarded under Salisbury's régime.

Emory Johnson at the Wharton School had a strong interest in what may be called the 'geographic aspects of economics'. His own doctorate at the University of Pennsylvania, dated 1893, was on 'Inland waterways: their relation to transportation'. He directed three of the earliest doctorates in economic geography by men who became professional geographers. J. P. Goode wrote on the influence of physiographic factors on occupations and economic development in the USA (1901). J. Russell Smith wrote on 'The organization of ocean commerce' (1903). W. S. Tower wrote 'A regional and economic geography of Pennsylvania' (1906). A similar study of Virginia was by G. T. Surface (1907). There are few doctorates in the Wharton stream, but it is highly significant in its early growth in the 1890s in economic and regional geography.

CHANGING CONCEPTS

The principal motivator in establishing geography was W. M. Davis at Harvard. He was the prime mover in the recommendations of the Committee of Ten in the teaching of geography, and in establishing the *Journal of Geography* as the organ of the teachers of high school geography.

Ellen C. Semple was a contemporary, and wrote two classic works on the geography of man: *American History and Its Geographic Conditions* in 1903, followed by *Influences of Geographical Environment* in 1911. Both of these works were in the same procedure of environmentalism. Salisbury set out at length the field of physiography in his great work in 1907. J. Russell Smith published his big work on *Industrial and Commercial Geography* in 1913. These were pre-1914 landmarks of growth.

Davis also took the lead in founding the professional Association of American Geographers in 1904. His statement of a 'scheme of geography', delivered as a lecture to the Royal Geographical Society, appeared in 1903, set an essential pattern for the next twenty-five years in school and college. American readers are no doubt familiar with his presidential address to the Association of American Geographers in December 1905 entitled 'An inductive study of the content of geography'. This was published in the *Bulletin of the American Geographical Society* in 1906 (pp. 67–84).

In the mid-1920s, there are again distinct chronological landmarks. Graduate schools and substantial undergraduate programmes were established in Chicago (since 1903), Clark, Berkeley, Pennsylvania, Columbia, Wisconsin and Michigan. At this time, there appeared Barrow's discourse on 'geography as human ecology' and Sauer's monograph on 'the morphology of landscape', which stimulated and directed research and teaching between the wars.

The listing of doctorates awarded down to 1935, according to Whittlesey, gives a measure of the status of departments in the first thirty years, and especially after 1920, when the activity greatly increased. Awards were made in 20 institutions. Over a half came from Clark (46), Chicago (33) and Wisconsin (22). Between 5 and 10 were awarded at California, Berkeley, Yale, Columbia and Nebraska. The total number of doctorates was 174.

A new phase is heralded in 1939 by the publication by the Association of American Geographers of R. Hartshorne's work on *The Nature of Geography*. This had profound repercussions after the war, on both sides of the Atlantic. It marked a decisive break from environmentalism to regionalism. This phase is brought to a peak by *American Geography: Inventory and Prospect* in 1954, edited by P. E. James and C. F. Jones. This work is a summation of the concepts and contributions of three generations of American geographers. It contains some of the most scholarly and informative presentations of the various fields of geography. It aimed at embracing all geographic interests and expertise. There is, however, a conspicuous absence of certain fields of study (for example, cultural geography) and a great diversity of inventory without consistent clarity of focus. Yet it is a thorough and scholarly summation of the work of geographers, especially over the preceding twenty to thirty years, and with it one associates almost all of the senior scholars of today.

Since the mid-1950s a new phase has emerged, mainly in the USA, but also in Britain and on the Continent, notably under Hägerstrand at Lund in Sweden whose views have had a strong attraction for American scholars. This shift is evidenced by the writing of Ackerman, Bunge, Schaefer and Berry. The leaders in Britain over this same period are Haggett and Chorley.

These new trends, besides being quantitative or statistical in approach, concerned with the 'analysis of spatial systems', reveal two other important facets. First, there is a shift of emphasis towards group behaviour in the assessment of the relations between man and environment, currently referred to as 'spatial perception'. Second, there is concern with current social problems and the utility of research in coping with them.

These trends towards the quantitative analysis of spatial systems have had their most recent presentation in a report in 1965 on *The Science of Geography* to the National Academy of Sciences. They are abundantly evident in books and articles over the past ten years. The leaders are men in their forties. They are turning out a generation of men with an entirely new framework and skills. They are not developing a 'new geography', but a new and important field known as 'regional science', which is far removed from the geographical tradition established by their predecessors.

THE MAJOR CONTRIBUTORS

There are four academic generations of American geographers. It is no accident that the landmarks noted above are at twenty to twenty-five-year intervals, which is the normal span of seniority of a distinguished scholar. The wars also make substantial breaks. Without presuming to be comprehensive, I would like to select several leaders from each generation. The reader may add or modify according to where he thinks a particular scholar fits.

The first generation, without question, includes Davis (Harvard), Jefferson (Ypsilanti), Smith (Wharton School), Salisbury (Chicago) and Semple (Clark-Chicago).

The second generation includes as its leaders Sauer, Bowman, Barrows, Colby and Atwood.

The third generation includes Hartshorne, James, Brown, Dicken, Kniffen, Russell, Broek and Leighly.

The fourth generation includes, among the historical geographers, Clark (Wisconsin) and Meinig (Syracuse), and among the quantitative analysts, Berry (Chicago).

A fifth generation covers the many young men who have been awarded masters or doctorates by one of the foregoing professors.

The medals and honorary fellowships awarded by the American Geographical Society to university geographers—excluding all non-Americans, of whom there are many— are as follows:

Cullum Medal (since 1896): W. M. Davis (1908); Ellen C. Semple (1914); Mark Jefferson (1931); D. Johnson (1935); J. Russell Smith (1956); C. W. Thornthwaite (1958); R. J. Russell (1962); J. Leighly 1964).

Daly Medal (since 1902); C. O. Sauer (1940); J. K. Wright (1954); R. Hartshorne (1959).

Livingstone Medal: G. Taylor (1923); I. Bowman (1945); G. M. McBride (1956); P. E. James (1966).

Davidson Medal: G. B. Cressey (1952).

Van Cleef Medal: J. Borchert (1970).

The list of professors who have received the award of honorary membership of the American Geographical Society since 1920 reads as follows (this is a recognition of distinguished scholarship; it does not include the medalists, who automatically become honorary members):

1922	Robert DeCourcy Ward	1962	Samuel Van Valkenburg
1930	Vernor Clifford Finch		Gilbert Fowler White
1935	Charles C. Colby	1964	Arch C. Gerlach

	Nevin M. Fenneman	1965	Peveril Meigs
1956	Stephen B. Jones	1967	William H. Hance
1961	Clarence Fielden Jones	1969	Marvin Mikesell
	John Ewing Orchard	1970	Alexander Melamid

THE MAIN CENTRES

Several semi-official investigations have been made in the USA of the status of graduate work in American universities. The results of Allan M. Carter's report, for the American Council on Education, *An Assessment of Quality in Graduate Education*, 1966, are shown in Table 2.

TABLE 2 *Leading Departments by Quality of Graduate Faculty**

	All respondents	
	Rank	Score
Distinguished		
Wisconsin	1	4·66
Chicago	2	4·41
California, Berkeley	3	4·14
Strong		
Washington, Seattle	4	3·68
Syracuse	5	3·66
Northwestern	6	3·64
Minnesota	7	3·53
UCLA	8	3·49
Michigan	9	3·33
Louisiana State	10	3·17

Good (nine departments, arranged alphabetically)
Clark
Illinois
Indiana
Iowa, Iowa City
Johns Hopkins
Kansas
Michigan State
Ohio State
Pennsylvania State

Adequate plus (four departments, arranged alphabetically)
Columbia
Nebraska
Pittsburgh
Texas

* Based on ratings of thirty institutions that reported the award of one or more doctorates from July 1952 through to June 1962.

In the same report, leading departments are also rated according to what is described as 'the efficiency of graduate programme'. This rating is compared with one on a not dissimilar base in 1925, as shown in Table 3.

TABLE 3   *Leading Departments by Graduate Programmes in 1925 and 1966*

Top 8 departments in 1925*	Top 9 departments in 1966
1 Chicago	'Extremely attractive':
2 Clark	Wisconsin
3 Wisconsin	Chicago
4 Columbia	California, Berkeley
5 Harvard	Washington, Seattle
6 California (rank shared	'Attractive':
with another department)	Minnesota
7 Michigan (also shared	Northwestern
with another department)	Syracuse
8 Yale	California, UCLA
	Michigan

* Listed in order of quality.

The listing in a still more recent survey[1] is shown in Table 4.

TABLE 4   *Leading Departments in 1957, 1964 and 1969*

1957	1964	1969	
2	2	1	Chicago
4	9	2	Michigan
10	7	3	Minnesota
1	1	4	Wisconsin
3	3	5	California
7	4	6	Washington, Seattle
8	16	7	Ohio State
	11	8	Pennsylvania State
	4	8	Syracuse
6	7	10	California, Los Angeles
	13	10	Kansas
5	6	10	Northwestern
	19	13	Clark
13	13	13	Iowa, Iowa City
14	13	15	Johns Hopkins

A report sponsored by the Association of American Geographers, the *Status and Trends of Geography in the United States, 1957-60,* gives the total number of Ph.D. awards for 1952-9 inclusive in 23 institutions. The top 11 are (in order of numbers): Clark (50), Northwestern (35), Michigan (32), Chicago (31), Syracuse (25), Columbia (22), California, Berkeley (21), Illinois (21), Wisconsin (21), Ohio State (18) and Louisiana (15).

The jobs held by trained geographers are in college teaching, business or some branch of government service. The total number of college teachers reached over 2,000 around 1960, in business 200, in planning about 100 and in federal government (mainly clustered in Washington DC, and the most elusive to define) about 500.

Finally, in Table 5 I list all Ph.Ds in the *Orbis Geographicus.*[2] This embraces college teachers, and thus undoubtedly excludes men who are outside the teaching field, such as government and planning. Nevertheless, it gives a measure of the numerical importance of departments as centres of graduate work over the past thirty or forty years. Seven departments are outstanding, and 16 have conferred less than 6 doctorates, nearly all of them only 2 or 3. This gives a total of 23 centres including 7 main centres.

TABLE 5 *Ph.Ds in Geography in the USA, 1964-6*

Total	402
Clark	51
Chicago	45
Wisconsin	38
California, Berkeley	34
Northwestern	28
Michigan	25
Washington	24
Syracuse	16
Harvard	14
Ohio State	13
Nebraska	11
Louisiana State	10
Maryland	9
Illinois	9

13

William Morris Davis, 1850-1934

Geography, in the words of W. M. Davis, remained an 'unorganized subject' until after the middle of the nineteenth century. Arnold Guyot, while Professor of Geography at Princeton from 1855 to 1884—the only professional geographer of his time in the USA—continued the teleological viewpoint of his master, Carl Ritter. Yet, says Davis, he introduced 'the principle of explanatory correlation'.[1] Arnold Guyot explained his approach in the following words in the first pages of his *Earth and Man* (1863); the quotations are from Davis:

> To describe, without rising to the causes or descending to the consequences, is no more science, than merely and simply to relate a fact of which one has been a witness.

> Geography should not only describe, it should compare, it should interpret, it should rise to the how and wherefore of the phenomena which it describes.

> Geography must endeavour to seize those incessant mutual actions of the different portions of physical nature upon the successive development of human societies; in a word, studying the reciprocal action of all these forces, the perpetual plan of which constitutes what may be called the life of the globe.

Guyot's demand for explanatory treatment is basic to the contemporary scientific method. His teleological viewpoint, however, of man's place on the earth took the view that the continents are 'the abode of man' and 'the theatre for the action of human societies'. Guyot's view of the role of man on earth had a great influence on the attitudes of his era through his many school textbooks. Guyot was a student of the physical world as an end in itself. He explored the Appalachians for over thirty years and made some 12,000 barometric observations of altitudes. Together with a director of the Smithsonian Institute he was responsible for the collection of numerous meteorological observations in the USA.

His attempts at empirical description, however, gave scant attention to land or landscape. It is, therefore, not surprising that Guyot's views of the place of man in nature, in spite of the popularity of his writings, had no outstanding scholastic following. He had the same philosophical approach as Ritter. However, he was still farther behind the times than his master, for in his (Guyot's) last years, the evolutionary interpretation of Darwinian thought was well established.

The study of land forms in the modern sense began with the work of geologists in Pennsylvania in the mid-nineteenth century. In this state there is a remarkable correlation between geological structure and the surface forms. These relations were first presented by Lesley, the second director of the Geological Survey, in his *Manual of Coal and its Topography,* published in 1856. In this classic work, Lesley notes the correlation between the zigzag pattern of linear ridges and parallel lowlands with closely folded strata and gently pitching axes. Though he made many observations of the dependence of relief on structure, he still believed in catastrophism, attributing surface features (and notably the Delaware 'wind gap') to the work of an ocean flood from the Arctic. He showed later an appreciation of the slow work of erosion by running water, but by this time he had been out-distanced by Powell and Gilbert.

The work of the two last-named geologists in the western states brought the 'explanatory description of land forms' a big step further. Their field work, on behalf of the United States Geological Survey, took them to the 'Great American Desert', where relief features stand out, often nakedly, and reveal clearly their relations to geological structure. Their work was done at the time that the doctrine of catastrophism was being rapidly displaced by uniformitarianism. The idea of the base level of erosion as developed by these two men provided a key for the further general understanding of land forms. Many other reports on the West by members of the Geological Survey added to geological knowledge of these areas and of genetic processes in the development of the forms of the earth's surface.

All this work was achieved in the last decades of the nineteenth century. Davis wrote in 1924 (ibid., p. 188) in summary:

> One of the most significant signs of this advance was the increase
> in the number of well-defined type forms, of which the
> elements of a landscape might be described; and it thus
> became impossible any longer to hold the new physiographic

wine in the narrow bottles provided by the old textbooks.

The approach of Guyot to the relations between Nature and man persisted until the end of the nineteenth century. This is abundantly evident in the book by Nathaniel Southgate Shaler on *Nature and Man in America,* published in 1893. Shaler was a distinguished geologist at Harvard and was the teacher and senior colleague of the young Davis. He writes in the preface that the book was written in the belief of 'the essential control of a beneficent Providence'. It considers, in the first half, 'the effect of physical conditions of the earth on the development of organic life in general with special emphasis on the origin and character of the relief and climate'. The second half of the book discusses 'geographic influences upon man', and 'how the development of race peculiarities has been in large part due to the conditions of the stage on which the different peoples have played their parts'; and the ways in which 'geographic features' have 'controlled settlement'. This is the presentation of a geologist still seeking to explain human societies in terms of 'controls' of the physical environment, as conceived by Carl Ritter in Germany and through him by Arnold Guyot, by the 'design of divine Providence'. Virtually all thinking at this time still adopted the view that the life of man on the earth was ordained by the offerings of the physical environment. It is from this background that Davis, a geologist, emerges in the first quarter of this century as the main founder of modern geography in America.

In the pages that follow, I want to make it perfectly clear that I am not concerned with Davis's contributions to the geological study of land forms. I am concerned exclusively with his contribution to the founding of geography as a discipline. It is for this reason that I have drawn from five papers. The first of these were: 'A scheme of geography', published in the *Geographical Journal* in 1903, and 'An inductive study of the content of geography' in the *Bulletin of the American Geographical Society,* 1906. Three statements in his later years, a few years after his controversy with the German geographers which is discussed in the latter half of this chapter, reveal a remarkable change of viewpoint on the content of geography, that, in fact, is closely similar to the views of his German opponents. These statements appear in papers entitled. 'The principles of geographic description' (1915), 'The progress of geography in the United States' (1924) and 'A retrospect of geography' (1932). The three papers were all published in the *Annals of the Association of American Geographers,*[2] which was started in 1911.

William Morris Davis graduated from Harvard in 1869 and a year later received a master of engineering degree. He studied geology under N. S. Shaler and L. Agassiz. From 1870 to 1873 he worked at the meteorological observatory in Córdoba, Argentina. In 1875 he returned to Harvard to study with Shaler, and in 1876 he was appointed to an assistantship in geology. During the next year, beginning with observations in Montana, he developed a theory of the cycle of erosion. He presented this concept at the meetings of the International Geographical Congress in Berlin in 1889. He carried on his teaching on land forms and meteorology, but relinquished the latter in 1896 to Robert DeCourcy Ward. He became assistant professor of physical geography in 1885 and professor in 1890, a post which he held with distinction until retirement. He retired in 1912 at the age of sixty-two and died in 1934.

During the 1880s he developed further the unifying scheme of the 'cycle of erosion', which he also defined as the 'geographical cycle' and, in other places, as the 'topographical cycle', both terms being unfortunate in the light of their historical usage. This cycle is briefly defined in Davis's own words (1924, p. 189):

It is a scheme under which a mental counterpart for every land form is developed in terms of its understructure, of the erosional process that has acted upon it, and of the stage reached by such action in terms of the whole sequence of stages from the initiation of a cycle of erosion by upheaval or the deformation of an area of the earth's crust, to its close, when the work of erosion has been completed; and the observed land is then described not in terms of its directly visible features, but in terms of its inferred mental counterpart.

Davis claimed in the same article (1924) that the study of land forms in terms of the cycle of erosion is a 'model', in common parlance, into which an endless variety of forms can be fitted. It directs attention to 'the visible facts of present landscapes, instead of diverting attention to the invisible conditions and processes of past time' which investigations belong properly, as Davis often emphasized, to the field of geology. Davis pleaded repeatedly for the 'explanatory description of existing land forms'. Past geological conditions, he argued, should be telescoped to a minimum of meaningful explanation, in order to reach the geographical goal which, he argued, is an understanding of land forms, and regarded even this, for the geographer, as a means of memorizing the surface varieties of relief.

He goes still further in the distinction between geology and geography (1932, p. 217):

> land forms may, to be sure, be studied from a geological point of view if one desires to trace their historical development; but they may also be studied from a geographical point of view if one wishes to describe their present appearance.

It was in the 1890s that Davis turned to the field of geography (1903, 1907). He sought to integrate the two elements, nature and man, after a period in which a marked dualism had prevailed between geography—regarded exclusively as physical geography, including (for some) plants and animals—and the geography of man which, ill-defined in its potential scope, had been absorbed consciously or unconsciously by ethnographers and historians. Davis found the key at this time in the Darwinian evolutionary approach, that regarded the facts of nature and man as existing in a 'harmonious relationship' in a continuous chain of cause and effect. The approach of Shaler is clearly evident. Davis sought to classify the facts of man in reference to facts of the physical (*qua* geographical) earth. The physical earth was studied by 'physical geographers' with respect to origins and processes. The resultant forms of land, water and air, were to be examined by the geographer in terms of the 'human responses' and 'controls'. The human facts on the earth were called ontography as opposed to the facts of the physical earth (physiography). This was an extension of the evolutionary interpretation of man on the earth in so far as human characteristics show direct results of geographical (physical) influences and controls. Davis believed that such a system would form the framework of an integrated science. This viewpoint very clearly set the pattern for the pursuit of man-land relationships on a deterministic basis that predominated in the first decades of this century. The human geographer, says Davis, must seek constant, repetitive correlations between human facts on the earth and the physical features of the earth's surface. J. K. Wright reports that his mother's diary for 5 February 1903 contains a reference to an informal monthly meeting at different professors' homes at which one professor, in this case W. M. Davis, would open a discussion. The diary reads as follows, according to Wright: 'He gave a new arrangement of the science of geography' in which 'his schedule makes a sort of box: A, B, Natural Phenomena: C, D, Reactions on Man', at which 'all the other men fell foul of him and warned him off their special provinces of religion, history and so on'.[3]

Davis shifted his focus on geography (as revealed in his 1915,

1924 and 1932 papers) in the later years of his life. He was aware
that this study of man on the earth could not be limited to
derivatives from the physical environment. The ecological study of
human groups, as of plants and animals, named ontography,
demands the appraisal of adjustments to the physical earth, as well
as migrations and segregations—a view that was basic to Ratzel's
work.

This change in viewpoint is abundantly evident in Davis's later
writings on the nature of regional geography. He recognized that
the regionalization of phenomena on the earth's surface is the
product of three forces—the site-base, migration and association
(1915):

> If then geography is not defined by the exclusive ownership
> of the things that it studies, or by the exclusive right to the
> methods it employs, it must be, like most other sciences, defined
> by the object that it has in view; and that object is defined,
> by long-established tradition, to be a description of the regions
> of the earth as they today exist.

Regional geography, he writes, seeks to describe 'the geographical
elements of a given area in their totality as they exist together in
their natural combinations and correlations'. There are, however,
other approaches. Similar phenomena from many parts of the earth
or in one area may be assembled, classified and explained. They
may be called topical geography and it, too, can be either empirical
or explanatory. Here again Davis has special reference to the
physical landscape, but he asserts that it is equally applicable to
the living forms of plants, animals and men.

One notes here the remarkable similarity of Davis's concepts
in 1915 with those of von Richthofen in 1883. Davis's viewpoint
has changed as to the content and purpose of geography. He has
turned away from the search for 'responses' and 'controls' of the
physical environment on human phenomena which he adumbrated
in 1903. Like workers elsewhere, and notably A. Hettner in Germany
(with whom he had serious clashes), he envisaged the field of
regional geography as one of elucidating the modes of areal association of phenomena on the surface of the earth. This is expressed
as follows (1915, p. 62):

> The description of existing landscapes, districts and regions of
> the earth's surface is the goal toward which other phases of
> geographical study, whether presented as personal narrative,
> historical review, analytical discussion or systematic arrangement,

all lead. Regional description is not systematic in the sense of describing things of a kind together, for it treats them in their unsystematic natural grouping. It is not analytical, in the sense of striving to find out the origin and meaning of existing facts, for it uses already discovered origins and meanings as an aid in setting forth the facts as they exist. It is not historical, either in the sense of tracing the progress of advancing knowledge regarding an area, though it may use the results of historical study in giving a better account of actual conditions. It is not narrative, for it seeks to present persistent and objective facts rather than temporary and subjective personal experience. Regional geography is, however, synthetic in combining the helpful results of all other modes of presentation in a vivid description of a part of the earth's surface, so that all the geographical elements and activities occurring, inorganic and organic, shall be appreciated in their true spatial relation.

There are, of course, many other methods of geographical presentation, which may be combined in any way that a writer desires; but it still remains true that pure regional geography is the final object of a geographer's efforts. Whatever be the area included in a regional description it can be known only by the summing up of many smaller areas, each of which has been actually seen as a 'landscape'—in the larger sense of the word— by an observer on the ground. In so far as the larger features of an extensive area are treated, they can be described only because their parts have been seen to persist through many contiguous smaller areas. Even the study of a whole continent must begin with the locally visible landscapes; not until they have all been seen, can the continent be fully known.

In the study of land forms Davis says that 'the chief object of physiographic analysis is to increase the number of terms in that part of a geographer's explanatory mental equipment which deal with physical features'. The purpose of each study is 'to provide a safe explanatory theory with respect to the origin of certain observed features'. It does not seek to discover the past action of certain processes (since this belongs to geology), nor to understand the existing forms as the product of past processes, for this may not lead to good description of the actual landscape. This, he declares, is essentially in line with the approach of Passarge's 'physiological morphology' of 1912; and of Hettner's views as expressed in the *Geographische Zeitschrift* of 1911. The scheme of Davis is based on the resultants of 'structure, process and stage', which, he claims, are identical with Hettner's (1) facts of inner structure; (2) processes of transformation; and (3) the effects of these on the resultant land forms and soils. He also cites the geologist Falconer of Glasgow, who classified land forms into sixty types of various orders (*Scot. Geog. Mag.*, 1915). What Davis does not mention here are the criticisms of Passarge and Hettner (see *The Makers of Modern Geography*). These German geographers asserted that Davis's scheme was essentially deductive and did not necessarily provide an adequate basis for the descriptive classification of land forms, or for the operation of processes of erosion and deposition other than the work of rivers. Davis agreed to the addition of two other factors (in the light of Hettner's work), namely, 'relief of surface or local measure of vertical inequality' and 'texture of dissection or spacing of stream lines'. In this way, the Davis 'scheme' becomes five-fold, but structure, process and stage 'suffice as a handy name for it'. This was Davis's attempt to meet the objections of Hettner who sought for a more empirical description of land forms than Davis's chronological scheme allowed.

Davis sought for the geographical description of life forms, which he called 'ontography', on the same lines (1903). He cited as an example the essay of H. C. Cowles, the distinguished botanist of Chicago, on plant formations, one of the first essays published in the *Annals of the Association of American Geographers*.[4] The same treatment is needed, he argued, for 'anthropogeography'. But he could not evade the feeling that 'the forms of the land on which all these human elements are superposed ought to be fairly well understood before the superposed human elements are taken up' (1932, p. 228).

Davis insisted that regional description must be 'homologous', that is, all aspects—land, climate, vegetation, animals and man— should receive equal emphasis. He is of the opinion that the human geographer has less concern with the *chronology* of existing land forms, than with the features of *existing surfaces,* since these are needed to understand the problems of human occupance. He feels that in this concession the human geographers 'fail to become all-round geographers', and that their studies are 'unbalanced' and lack a 'homologous' treatment. It follows that geographers must have a broadly based training in the natural and life sciences.

The purpose of the geographical study of man, he claims, is to arrive at descriptive generalizations on the basis of explanation of geographical qualities. He puts as one of the main questions (1915, p. 98): 'What does it look like?' This is as suitable a question, he says, for cities as for landscapes. He refers to how the city 'lies on the land', the situation and appearance of the city, day and night, summer and winter; and the flows of traffic of people and vehicles. The treatment of this material must be:

> rational, explanatory and even evolutionary, but not historical, that is, that all pertinent features should be treated in view of their present stage in the whole series of stages that they suffer during a city's growth, from its beginning in a village to its most flourishing development and perhaps to its end in vanishing ruins.

The historical development of the city (1915, p. 99) should be avoided as carefully as the:

> presentation of the erosion and development of land forms in geological order; what is needed is a statement of the existing condition and appearance of the city in terms of its historical growth, provided that the general sequence of changes in the growth of cities can be analysed and systematized in some manner as the evolution of land forms has been. Different kinds of villages and cities in different stages of development would then be recognized.

Davis refers to the arrangement of a regional description. Many categories of spatially differentiated phenomena occur simultaneously in natural but unsystematic groupings without any causal connection with each other. They must be selected and described in 'some reasonable sequence, for they cannot all be stated at once'.

In 1924 Davis referred to the divergence of interest between physiographers and human geographers. He suggested that it was high time that they clearly examined their objectives and found agreement on common ground. To this end, he made two suggestions. First, physiographers should separate the analytical study of land forms, which ought to be regarded as a phase of geology, from the 'non-argumentative statement of the results reached, which must be accepted as good geography'. Second, he considered that the economic and historical aspects of geography should have much more clearly defined objectives and set aside the essentially economic and historical as irrelevant to their ends. This, however, is not intended to discourage a worker on either side from making excursions into unknown territory.

To sum up, we shall change the terminology, but keep the concepts strictly within the framework as propounded by Davis in his statements of 1915 and 1924. Geography is the study of the uniqueness of areas of the earth in various orders from localities, through major world areas, to the world. The latter may be referred to as generic regions, in contrast with unique or specific regions. A region is not merely an arbitrary territorial framework for presentation. It is an association of phenomena which one seeks to discover, describe and explain. Finally, geographical description is envisaged by Davis as having two aspects, both of which demand a rigorous, disciplined approach. One is *pure description*; the other, made possible by the advance of ancillary disciplines, becomes *explanatory description*. The distinction between the two—whether Davis was aware of this or not is beside the question—is precisely the same as von Richthofen's distinction between the two modes of areal description, chorographical and chorological. Chorographical description is as old as Strabo. Chorological description is a development of modern knowledge. Both these latter terms appear in the terminology of American geographers, such as James, Trewartha and Finch in the 1930s.

Thus, in brief, Davis's work on the genetic study of land forms is outstanding and is evaluated in many other sources. We are here concerned with his views of the content, purpose and methods of geography. His views around 1900 of the 'scheme of geography' (as delivered to the Royal Geographical Society in 1903) reflected the Darwinian 'evolutionary' philosophy of his time, and were a natural outgrowth from the approach of N. S. Shaler and A. Guyot. His thoughts in his later years after retirement on the scope and purpose of geography, which is our central concern, became markedly ecological. There is no doubt that they continued to exercise a profound influence on the thought and work of his successors. This ecological approach implies that the geographer studies the life forms on the earth's surface in terms of their adaption to the site-base, to the migrations of particular elements or ideas, and to the modes of spatial association or segregation. It is far removed from exclusive concern with land-man relationships in the Darwinian sense. It is abundantly evident, therefore, that Davis's attitude in geography passed through both phases, deterministic and ecological.

We may now turn briefly to the controversy, that came to a head in the 1920s, between Davis and Bowman in America and Hettner and Passarge in Germany.

The so-called Davisian system of 'explanatory description of land forms' was the subject of bitter criticism from certain German geographers in the years following Davis's lectures in Berlin. These lectures were given in 1908 at the invitation of Albrecht Penck, and translated into German by his colleague Alfred Rühl, with the title

Die erklärende Beschreibung der Landformen, published in Leipzig in 1912. The work was never translated into English though the ideas are to be found in many of the articles published both before and after this time by Davis. The views of Davis, as Wellington Jones has reminded us, spread through Germany 'like wildfire', but they met with implacable opposition among several of the senior German geographers, notably Alfred Hettner and Siegfried Passarge.

The attacks on both sides were bitter and were quite clearly based on different ideas of the problems and purpose and methods of geography, as well as being concerned with differences in national temperament.

It must be recalled that in the first two decades of this century, there were a number of mature geographers in Germany, scholars of repute, whose ideas were far in advance of their contemporaries in Britain and America through fieldwork in widely scattered areas of the earth and in the formulation of geography as a distinctive discipline.

All these men were concerned, as geographers, with description and, therefore, classification and association of phenomena on the earth's surface. They were not nearly so fettered by environmental determinism at this time as were Davis in America and Herbertson in Britain, and sought to organize geography as a discipline which they regarded as primarily descriptive and empirical. They considered that the explanation of distinct land forms as well as of man-made forms imprinted on the land are the result of a variety of forces operating in different ways in different areas. The Davisian concept of the geographical cycle (so-called) and its operation on a land surface was envisaged in terms of 'structure, process and stage', and the land surface had features that were theoretically associated with 'youth, maturity and old age'. It was argued by the German geographers that this was an arbitrary scheme, that it neglected, even ignored, other contributory local factors operating in an area, such as weathering, variations in structure and lithology, and climatic factors. These factors were not only factors of climatic change during the cycle of erosion, but also differences in the combination of the processes of erosion and deposition in different climatic milieux of the world. Davis's 'normal' cycle was developed, and primarily applied to, the humid areas in Europe and America. But German scholars had already undertaken extensive scientific observations in arid zones of the earth. It was claimed that the development of land forms through the operation of wind and rain and weathering, and the resultant processes of erosion and deposition, vary in different climates and with changes in climate in one

203

H

and the same area. The vegetation and soil cover have repercussions on surface changes. Davis's scheme was derived inductively from case studies in the USA, by Davis and others, such as his contemporaries, Powell and Gilbert. These case studies, including those of other early workers in Europe, find recognition and praise from both Hettner and Passarge. But they both rejected a generalized system that is deductively applied so as to portray, on this limited explanatory base, the surface features of an area. They argued that the geographical problem is to characterize land forms in their locally repetitive forms and to explain them in terms of *all* the forces operating on them. Davis did not describe the land forms as they occurred in reality. He defined and explained them deductively within the framework of a theoretical system, which, it was argued, itself contained fundamental errors. The system was designed, as Davis very cogently insisted, to 'assist the memory' and to give a single key of cause and effect in understanding land forms.

Hettner insisted that the geographical approach must always be chorological. This, he asserted, cannot be emphasized often enough, since the specialist so often forgets it. He says that Davis does an injustice to German geography when he accuses it of being 'merely descriptive'. Hettner retorts that no science can dispense with explanation and leave this to another science. He claimed that land forms are the result of many forces operating in space in the same area through time. The geographer's chorological approach involves a twofold task: (1) to describe and classify repetitive elements and their spatial groupings into land units; and (2) to analyse the various forces of uplift, erosion, deposition, weathering, rock resistance and geological structure, that explain the existing characteristics of these units. This approach, he continues, is consistent with the tradition of De Margerie, von Richthofen and Penck. One can, therefore, understand, he concludes, the danger of using a deductive model as a master key to the explanation of land forms as Davis's scheme was threatening to do.

Hettner urged that geography must study the individual elements of the land, the *Kleinformen*—the terrain facets as some would say today—and these, he says, are totally ignored by Davis. 'The small forms determine in large measure the face of the landscape, or, as one can say, its physiognomy, the arrangement of its forms, its style of build, and thus its aesthetic character.' A morphological representation without descriptive appraisal of the local forms of landscape is dead and schematic. Also, by this procedure—and here enters still more clearly the geographical approach—'the influence of the landscape on the plant and animal world and upon

man, and thus a great part of its geographic significance, is in large
part lost'. The lesser forms must also be recognized and mapped,
in order to understand the processes of development of the larger
land forms of which they are constituent parts.

The Davisian approach means that a preconceived theory is
formed even before going into the field. One looks first for evidence
of genetic explanation and observations are subsumed to the theory.
The rest is left out:

> Inductive research begins with the description of the facts, and
> steps gradually to a causal explanation. Genetic concepts emerge
> after gradual clarification and sharpening of the original,
> partly empirical, concepts. The observation remains even when
> the theories change. On the other hand, the deductive method
> puts the genetic concept foremost in thought and then steps
> out with them into the realm of nature.

This expresses the essence of the geographical method. It is to
be expected that these arguments of Passarge and Hettner,
reflecting the viewpoint of the geographer, and their objections to
the Davisian system, would meet with rebuttals from the USA.
They received attention in particular from both Davis and Bowman.
Davis searched for compromise in his 1915 paper. He later made
scathing and personal comments in a review of Hettner's work.[5]
This he described as full of 'homilies, truisms, hesitations, obstruc-
tive misunderstandings and disputatious objections'. He claims that
the book was a 'conscientious, but reactionary protest against what
its author regards as the too hasty methods of certain other
geographers', Hettner's book being a 'diatribe against the erosion
cycle'. Davis was evidently and understandably angry, but he really
did not (at that time and on this occasion) understand the point of
view that Hettner was trying to get across, the viewpoint of a
geographer rather than that of a geologist.

Both Davis and Bowman became further involved in trying to
bridge the gap between geography and geology. Bowman concluded
that the difference arose from 'an unwillingness to accept a terminology of foreign origin and in part from an inextricably misunderstanding of *stage* to mean *age,* a failure to see that the word stage
is employed as a measure of development, not of time'.[6] This may
have been correct, but it is not the essential issue of the geographical
argument. Bowman then continues, as did Davis in his review of
Passarge's *Die Grundlagen der Landschaftskunde,* by objecting to
the 'overdoing of empirical description' as opposed to the genetic
approach of the 'geographical cycle' (the term being used, by the

way, as opposed to erosion cycle). This approach undoubtedly still further offended the professional susceptibilities of Hettner as a geographer. For, says Bowman, empirical description, especially in the form of interminable lists of classified landscape phenomena (which make up the bulk of the first volume), offers to the student 'an ideal of complete meaninglessness and deadly monotony'. Bowman further argues, 'Ideas run the world, not outlines or catalogues.' We understand and sympathize with this brilliant aphorism, but we feel now in 1975 that this reaction reveals a lack of real understanding of what Hettner and especially Passarge were driving at *as geographers* fifty years ago. The argument seems to be that empirical classification and mapping *per se* is deadly dull as an end in itself. Such was never the end for either Hettner or Passarge, but an essential means to an end.

All this reflects a historical phase through which geography has passed, although the basic differences of the two approaches are still not generally recognized in the English-speaking world for the reasons expressed by Bowman. The German geographers as far back as the 1900s were riveting their attention on *land* as the product of natural processes of various significance in an area, and on *landscape* as the expression of life forms (including the human imprint) on the land. Two arguments were basic. First, the explanation of the morphology of the earth's surface in terms of a single theoretical system was necessary, but inadequate. Second, they sought for the empirical description and explanation of the associated forces that shape the earth's surface. These ideas had been expressed and developed by Ratzel, von Richthofen and A. Penck in the 1890s and were a part of the German heritage in geography, though it still was not understood in the English-speaking world. The empirical study of landscape elements has been one of the main trends in geographical work in the generation following this discussion.

Two subsequent trends are evident, one geomorphic, the other geographic. The first involves the substantial modification of the Davisian system by appraisal of the other forces that operate together to create the real land forms of an area. Second, we witness the increasing sophistication with which the mosaic of the earth's real, visible landscapes—land forms, soils, surface cover, cultivated land, human settlement—are being analysed on the *basis of the smallest unit areas with distinctive characteristics.*

We may conclude here with the views of two American geographers in more recent years on the validity and usefulness of the Davisian scheme in geography. John Leighly writes:[7]

The system of W. M. Davis pretends to provide a frame into
which all examples of geomorphic development may be fitted.
Any such pretence, in the present state of our knowledge of
the processes involved, is to be viewed with scepticism. . . .
Davis's great mistake was the assumption that we know all
processes involved in the development of land forms. We do not,
and until we do we shall be ignorant of the general course of
their development.

Leighly writes further:

Once on an automobile trip through the local section of the
Coast Ranges, the Berkeley Hills, Davis disposed of the complicated series of forms to be observed by a single phrase 'maturely
dissected'. Penck's reasoning makes 'rounded hilltops, rock
bases, speculate canon heads, and slightly incised stream
channels come alive as forms, in which the structure of the
ranges is gradually becoming more and more evident in their
relief'.

Finally, the experience of one of the finest geographers, the late
Wellington D. Jones of Chicago, should be noted. At the symposium
held at the meetings of the Association of American Geographers
in 1950 to commemorate W. M. Davis, in the midst of the very
proper adulations of the great master, especially from the geomorphologists, Jones made the following sly but meaningful comment: [8]

During the two years in the field in Patagonia [with Bailey
Willis] I had failed miserably at trying to apply Davis's ideas
on geomorphology. With Hettner at Heidelberg and Philippson
from Bonn on a two-weeks' field trip in the Alps, I found
out why I had failed, or at least a part of the reason. Davis's
ideas bore little relation to the facts of life, or, more accurately,
to land forms. While I was in Germany [1913], Davis's ideas
were sweeping over Germany as they had over the USA like
wildfire, but Hettner and Philippson [and Passarge] and their
followers refused to be engulfed in the conflagration. The result
to me thereafter was that I looked at the Davis system with such
a fishy eye that I never used it.

This is the viewpoint of a geographer, not of a geomorphologist,
and certainly not that of an unswerving disciple of a great master.

It is also relevant to point out, in conclusion, that in the late
1920s, certain younger American geographers, in seeking to focus
attention on landscape and its discrete units and associations, turned

to the works of Hettner and especially Passarge. They described
themselves (temporarily) as chorographers (see p. 323). The good
sign was that at the time (around 1930) they were looking to the
work of foreign scholars in their field. They soon tired of the
minutiae of landscape description, however, and moved to the
realm of explanation in terms of natural, biotic and social processes.
Moreover, work on the character and development of land forms
in various climates has revealed the operation of varied processes
and their interaction in the development of land forms, be it in the
study of vegetation and related forms in inner Brazil or the development of periglacial land forms in North America and Europe. (This
was argued and demonstrated long ago in 1912 by the German
Passarge from his studies in the Kalahari desert.) Finally, Davis
himself, in his later years, turned to, and clearly understood and
expressed, the distinctive and essential objective of geographical
work—the characterization of the distinctive areas of the earth's
surface. This in itself is a tribute to the work and attitude of Davis
and his great importance as the dominant figure in the development
of modern geography in America. To sum up Davis's views of
regional geography fifty years ago as 'quaint' in the light of current
trends is nothing short of sheer presumption.

14

Mark Jefferson, 1863-1949

Mark Jefferson began his long career as a student of William Morris Davis. He was for four decades a distinguished and inspiring teacher and researcher at the Michigan State Normal College in Ypsilanti. He awakened a liking for geography in many of the students who attended his courses and nursed a veritable progeny of budding geographers who, in the first half of this century, were placed in teachers' colleges and universities. He advised his students, if they wished to continue their studies at graduate level in geography, to work with Davis at Harvard or Salisbury at Chicago. Harlan H. Barrows and Charles C. Colby who successively became chairmen of the department at Chicago after 1919 were students of Jefferson. Isaiah Bowman, whose work we shall consider in a later chapter, also studied under Jefferson, and became a lifelong friend and professional associate.

Jefferson was a great teacher, linguist and reader. He travelled widely and corresponded frequently and at length. The main library at the college where he spent forty years is named in his honour. It should also be recorded that Jefferson had an immediate predecessor, C. T. McFarlane, who was appointed in 1892 at the age of twenty-one. McFarlane had a keen interest in geography. He studied under Penck at Vienna for one year and recruited students and assistants such as Harlan Barrows, R. D. Calkins and D. H. Davis. Although he left his post in 1901 for the headship of another college, he maintained his work and wrote a series of school books on geography together with A. P. Brigham. The library was already subscribing to several geographical periodicals in 1900, as G. J. Martin tells us in his biography in 1968.[1] A tradition of geographical scholarship was already established when Jefferson took over. In 1902, Jefferson was already offering eight courses in geography, and a similar number with differences in content were offered in the 1890s by McFarlane.

There is full reason, therefore, for the claim that Jefferson was the founder of a real man-oriented geography in America. Although trained by Davis and dedicated (as always) to questions of physiography, he soon turned to the work of man on the earth. The approach of Davis around 1900, growing out of that of Shaler, was directed to accurate generalizations (models) of the relations of man to the physical environment. The approach of Jefferson in exactly the same period sought for generalizations regarding man's imprint on the land. Thus, unlike Davis, he examined the size, extent and functions of cities, and areas of access to railroads under the succinct phrase 'the civilizing rails'. In this way, Jefferson established the foundations of a geography of man, an approach that emphatically was not limited to or even preoccupied with constant correlations between man and land. Jefferson ranks, therefore, as one of the great founders of modern geography and did so in modesty as a dedicated teacher and scholar in a small teacher training college. Indeed, without quibbling about exactitudes, Jefferson headed one of the first undergraduate departments, which became the chief fount of geography in America.

Jefferson rarely committed himself to formalized statements on the field of his enquiries though this is clearly evident in the kinds of questions he sought to answer regarding man's work on the land, especially in cities. However, in searching through the pages of G. J. Martin's biography, one finds the following quotation: [2]

Many people—even educated people—use the word geography in a merely locational or distributional sense. The geography of sardines, they would say, must deal with the distribution of sardines, either before or after catching and canning. The geography of whales would surely tell where to look for whales. What could the geography of wooden shoes mean but their distribution in space? If you could put all the wooden shoes in the world down on a map in the places where they are at the present moment, with some indication of their numbers at every point where they occur, that would certainly show the geography of wooden shoes.

Someone has said that anything that you can put on a map is subject matter for geography. That is what I call locational or distribution geography. Many would prefer to call the study of the features of the moon's visible face lunar geography. Anyone would understand that the geography of my study-furniture meant the placing of the chairs and tables about the room.

But geographers are contemplative persons who cannot be

satisfied with so meagre an account of the subject. We
contemplate the things and their distribution. If asked why, we
can only say that we take pleasure in it. We like to. But no
one can contemplate the distribution of the major features of
the earth and its inhabitants without fancying that he
perceives causes and relations behind and among distributions.
No distribution on earth is fortuitous. One thing is not
independent of another. Some sort of order is usually perceived
in any distribution, even though not understood in all its
details. Wooden shoes are at once seen to be the work of
tool-using men who have risen at least to an iron-using culture.
Also, they occur only in lands with readily worked woods.
Also, they are a response to rainy and muddy weather. The
maps of iron-using men, of forests and of rainy weather enable
us to foretell where we shall find the wooden shoes. Then
come the exceptions, like the USA, where we think we have
found something better in rubber footwear. Their use in parts
of France, and the presence of a compact body of people of
French origin in Quebec province who are known to cling
strongly to old ways, would make it reasonable to look for some
use of wooden shoes among the Canadian French.

Geographers like to think of these contemplations and
reasonings on the facts of distribution of geography. The nature
of geography is the fact that there are discoverable causes of
distributions and relations between distributions. We study
geography when we seek to discover them.

The mere distributed facts are no more geography to us than
a fossil is geology to the geologist. If to the heedless they are
all of geography, geography means nothing much to them
of necessity. The heedless do not even perceive any
distribution or grouping at all. For them a map is as meaningless
as a table of statistics to those who do not understand
statistics. They are folks who see with the eye only and not
with the mind. It appears to us that they do not see at all.
For them there is neither art nor science. But there is an art
of geography—the delineation of the earth's features and
inhabitants on maps—cartography—and a science of geography,
which contemplates the fact delineated and seeks out causes
of the form taken by each distribution and its relationship
to others.

This approach is eminently ecological. It is not content with
individual geographical distributions of wooden shoes, bows and

211

H*

arrows, digging sticks or automobile sales. It seeks to discover causally interrelated associations of various distributions that lead to further understanding of human groups in their environmental settings. This was precisely the purpose of Ratzel's anthropo-geography. It is also, to project a generation ahead, the focus of Carl Sauer's viewpoint. Jefferson was in no sense limited to the rigorous strictures and procedures of environmentalism, which, before the First World War, was adumbrated clearly and logically by none other than the natural scientist and teacher of Jefferson, W. M. Davis. Jefferson was not fettered by the search for 'environ-mental relationships' in the shape of 'influences' or 'controls'. He was concerned with man on land, or, in other words, with society and habitat. It redounds to the credit of Davis, however, that in his later years in the 1920s his own changed view was evident in his challenge to Jefferson to search for the meaning of size and limits of cities.

I can vouch for the truth of these claims from the beginning of my own research in the mid-1920s on the distribution, functions and limits of cities. I found no springboard in the work of most geographers. Guideposts were offered by Jefferson's concepts of 'central places', 'the law of the primate city', the 'civilizing rails', and the hint that the size and functions of some big cities (like Copenhagen) must be due to services rendered beyond the state boundary of Denmark. Similarly, as will be recorded in a later chapter, fecund concepts of the functions and organization of trade centres were offered by J. Russell Smith, who was concerned with the location and structure of trade centres as excrescences produced by man, not as spontaneous eruptions from Mother Earth.

Jefferson published a remarkable series of varied research articles and monographs. The latest of these, on 'the law of the primate city' and 'the great cities of the United States' appeared in the *Geographical Review* for 1939 and 1941, very shortly before his death. In *American Men of Science* in 1906 he declared that his main research interest was 'the geography of tides, river meanders, beach cusps', indicating his attention to 'natural history', the early influence of Davis. But in the 1910 edition of the same source he added 'the distribution of man, distribution of climates and of cultures, population growth, geography of cities'. His studies of urban centres as 'central places' were far ahead of his time, and have had remarkable repercussions. He stated many times that his geographical concern was with men, 'where they are, what they are like, and why they are there'. He was thoroughly familiar with French and German literature (as was McFarlane before him).

Many great contemporaries, by their own admission, developed the notions of Jefferson, including J. R. Smith, E. Huntington (America), J. Brunhes (France), Sten De Geer (Sweden) and G. Chisholm (Britain).[3]

As a pedagogue whose primary job was to train young people to be teachers in school, he early took exception to the recommendations of the sub-committee on geography of the Committee of Ten. It urged in 1894 that observational study be taught by means of 'an elementary course in physical geography in the last year of the high school'. Jefferson claimed in 1909 that virtually none of the high schools of the State of Michigan were doing what had been advised. He sought to focus study on man living on the land, and in this respect reflected what was called at that time a revolution of content and purpose of geography in the high school. This sought 'to humanize physiography'. Unfortunately, it led to the cause-and-effect association of a 'naïve environmentalism' in school and college, that was far removed from the ecological approach of Jefferson's view of man's imprint on the land.

A MEMORIAL, by I. Bowman[4]

Mark Jefferson died in Ypsilanti, Michigan, on 8 August 1949, in his eighty-seventh year. Professor Jefferson was a broadly educated man, with an equally broad cultural background that was visible through all he did. He took the classical course at Boston University and graduated with honours in 1889. His unusual skill in mathematics was indicated by his appointment as assistant at the National Observatory at Córdoba, Argentina. His work there consisted of painstaking observation and recording. Its precision and concreteness delighted him. All his many students will remember how he could bring tables of statistics to life, how he used them to open doors of understanding for men and women who were inclined to think that education consisted of textbook generalities.

After three years Jefferson left the observatory to become superintendent of a sugar hacienda at Tucumán. There he saw Argentina on that moving frontier of settlement in which the sugar central followed hard on the heels of the gaucho in the zone of irrigable piedmont in the north-west. It was this experience that singularly fitted him for the task of interpreting Argentine settlement many years later (1918), and the American Geographical Society made the most of the opportunity for geography by financing a season of fieldwork and persuading him to undertake the task and eventually publishing *Peopling the Argentine Pampa* (Amer. Geog. Soc. Research Series, no. 16, 1926). It is a source book so far as Jefferson's personal comparisons of earlier and later times are concerned, and it is also an acute analysis of Argentine life by one who had lived it.

On his return to the USA, Jefferson served for a time in the Massachusetts public-school system, as teacher, principal, and superintendent. Two years were spent in study at Harvard, then a Mecca for aspiring young geographers because of the pre-eminence of William Morris Davis. In 1901, Jefferson was called to the chair of geography at the Michigan State Normal College, Ypsilanti, a position he held until his retirement in 1939. Here he was somewhat of a phenomenon. To many of the students he was the first broadly cultured man they had met. To some of the faculty members he was a delight; to the loose-minded an annoyance! His keen scythe could mow down a waving field of words at one sweep. He had a dryness and wit that sometimes offended the dull and that were a constant source of amusement to his friends.

In his classes one did not 'learn about map projections' but made them after calculating the elements. One did not 'learn' merely how to read a map on a desk but went into the field and made a map. The diagram in the book was not enough for understanding geysers—the student had to set up a laboratory geyser and make it work. The Foucault pendulum demonstration of the earth's rotation and a dozen other exercises taught the student things and processes first-hand and led him to acquire the habit of using his hands and eyes and brain and creating a substantial part of his knowledge of geography as he went along.

With small facilities Jefferson trained a host to teach geography with spirit and an understanding of basic facts and principles. And he kept his eye always open for the man or woman who had unusual abilities and after a year or two passed along his more talented students to the universities. Whoever their masters might then be, they never forgot Jefferson, the cultured schoolmaster and thinker who considered himself well placed where he was and never sought a university chair. Part of this contentment, it is true, was due to self-deprecation. He often said of himself that he was too sharp and did not get along with people easily. Also, he wanted time and freedom to follow his bent. Emerson's writings meant much to him, for he had lived near Concord and grown up as a New Englander in the environment

of authors and philosophers. For at least half a dozen years
he had a passion for Kipling. He read widely in poetry, biography
and fiction, in French, German, and Spanish as well as in English.
His scientific reading was unsystematic yet sure, with an element
of the venturesome. He cared little for academics as bestowers
of honorifics yet cared greatly for whatever creative work
they did. One of his most charming traits was his desire to tell
the world when he had found a new idea or a new geographer
whose tracks he had discovered in a journal or book. When
Johannes Walther's *Das Gesetz der Wüstenbildung* (1900)
appeared, he lived intellectually in the desert with Walther for a
year or more. He never missed a number of *Petermanns
Mitteilungen,* with its solid stuff. He rarely read a travel article.
He had no taste for the subjective and personal. His choice was
concrete material that one could build into the permanent
structure of science.

About every other year during the active part of his life he
took a journey to a new place. One year it was Norway, and he
learned to speak Norwegian so as to get closer to life there,
only to find that almost everybody he talked with spoke English
very well. A summer in France with Professor Davis and a few
picked companions was a lasting inspiration. The influence
of his enquiring mind ran ahead of his writing. He liked to
talk, and he talked well. Writing was a chore. It took patience
and long persuasion to get him to complete the book on the
Argentine Pampa,[5] after the earlier instalments of the results
of the 'Expedition to the ABC countries' had appeared in 1921—
'Recent colonization in Chile' and 'The rainfall of Chile' (Amer.
Geog. Soc. Research Series, nos 6 and 7).

Jefferson had no use for stock material in teaching and threw
away his own old maps and plates as fast as new ideas arrived.
His *Teachers' Geography* (1911, 10th ed. 1923) went through many
private printings before he could be persuaded to put it in the
hands of a commercial publisher, with 'all its ideas, originality,
and crankiness', as that publisher said when *Principles of
Geography* made its appearance in 1926. It has not been surpassed
as a generator of basic mental activity. *Man in Europe* (1924;
3rd revised ed. 1936), a book that should be in use in every
university, shows him at his best in the use of maps, photographs,
and ideas in the interpretation of a continent. In all his material
for teaching, his skill with the pencil, his sense of line and letter,
was evident. He made maps for his own pleasure as well as
for teaching and publication. If Antarctic exploration was in the

air, for example, he compiled a new map from good sources
and incorporated the new findings to see what they meant.
If a thing was important and mapable, he had to try his hand at
putting it on paper. Colour and form engaged his interest on field
trips. He had learned from Davis the dangers of 'the petrographic
habit' as Davis termed it—kneeling on the ground and looking
at a rock specimen through a microscope to the exclusion of a
broad view of the relations of the field. Beside that phrase he
put another: 'Look up once in a while, man; the sky is also a
part of the picture.'

At the annual meeting of the Association of American
Geographers held at Ypsilanti in 1931, among his friends and
associates, the Cullum Geographical Medal of the Society was
presented to him [*Geog. Rev.*, 1932, p. 305]. The praise he heard
was unexpected, and his remarks in later years showed that
he was deeply moved and grateful for the recognition. It surprised
him, he said, that on the same occasion his old students should
make such a fuss about him. Life presented him with deep personal
as well as professional problems, but his wit and interest were
never dulled, as some of his letters of the past year attest.

Jefferson was appointed chief cartographer to the American
Peace Commission at the peace conference of Paris in 1919,
a job for which he was eminently qualified, though it took much
persuasion to get him to join the team, because, as he said,
'I work better when I'm alone.' He directed the making of about
500 original maps at the conference, and no other delegation
there had such prompt and useful service in laying tentative
or alternative solutions of territorial problems before the various
boundary commissions. A collection of his peace conference
maps is in the library of the society. He served for a time on a
boundary commission designed to bring together cartographers
of the different delegations to decide on symbols, 'finding line'
technique, sources for official maps, and final boundary details.
Although he had no part in substantive territorial decisions, he was
quick to see how they could be graphically represented. Respect
for his work was not confined to the American delegation.
Younger men found him a delightful and informing companion
in rare strolls through the streets of Paris, and he was constantly
being 'discovered' by thoughtful higher-ups. Once, when it
was suggested he could be useful to a government department,
he replied that even the thought of living in the hubbub of
government made him physically ill.

Thoroughness marked all his work. The highest principle he

recognized was that if you are to explain a matter you must know
it through and through. As he kept his own feet on the ground,
so he put the feet of others on the ground. It was the ground first,
then climate, and after that he was ready to interpret while
always on the lookout for the inexplicable and the capricious
in his own culture as well as in another's. Physical geography, as
all his students will remember, had to begin with physical
principles. Never, never, would he let words take the place of
understanding. You had to know why the wind blew and the
rain fell! His writings show that he could grasp and handle
competently the largest concepts and forces of culture and life,
but he approached them through experience, facts, realities. Social
forces detached from the earth he left to other disciplines. For
himself he tried to find out what rooted men. Perhaps this
was partly the result of his old-fashioned classical training;
perhaps it was due to the rigours of mathematics that he loved.
Whatever the cause, it made his work enduring.

15

Albert Perry Brigham, 1889-1929, by *R. E. Dodge*[1]

On a Monday morning early in July 1889 a young minister from a large church in Utica, New York, started his vacation by joining the Harvard summer school of geology at Rochester, New York. Thus began the professional training of Albert Perry Brigham and for the writer an association and a friendship that have deepened in significance and understanding with the years. For Brigham the early portion of the school covered familiar ground inasmuch as his first interest in geology had been aroused in his youth about his old home at Perry in the Genesee valley. We tramped the length of the valley studying the stratigraphic succession and the glacial features, under the leadership of Nathaniel Southgate Shaler of Harvard and Henry Shaler Williams of Cornell. For several members of the group this was their first opportunity to study stratified rocks. For Brigham it was an advanced course, and he, with his greater training and experience, grasped quickly the real significance of features that were to others but illustrative facts. Brigham had already published in 1888 his first scientific paper entitled 'The geology of Oneida County'—the county containing the city of Utica, in which he was then living.

From the study of tilted stratified rocks in the Genesee valley the school moved to Catskill and under the leadership of William Morris Davis studied the simple folds of the Little Helderbergs. Brigham left the school after a week in the lower Connecticut valley where we were skillfully led to work out the faulted structures of the Triassic series which Professor Davis had made his own and later described in one of his most significant geological papers, 'The triassic formation of Connecticut' (1898).

This summer school was a milestone in Brigham's life, for it whetted his interest in geology and caused him to decide on a new life work. He resigned his pastorate in Utica in 1891 and in 1891-2 was a graduate student at Harvard, receiving his master's degree in 1892. Here in a group including, with others, Tarr, Westgate, Marbut, A. H. Brooks, Ward, and Dodge, he continued his training under those master teachers, Shaler and Davis.

Shaler—geologist, humanist, idealist—led his pupils to see, beyond and through the facts of geology or paleontology, the larger problems and relationships of the earth and man. A geologist by training and yet a geographer in instinct—as best illustrated perhaps in his *Nature and Man in America* (1893)—Shaler opened youthful eyes to see beauties in the common features of the landscape so familiar as to be often overlooked, and sent his pupils forth with a vision and an interest in people and in science that formed a perpetual stimulus and inspiration. In Shaler's course in paleontology Brigham caught and absorbed Shaler's philosophy which clarified and perhaps accentuated his own. At least it seems to the writer that in all his popular and some of his semi-technical writings, Brigham has reflected that philosophy, moulded by his own powers of insight and expression. Davis— equally an idealist, trained to accuracy of observation, skilled in exposition, keen in insight, a rigid critic of his own thinking, with a marvellously developed scientific imagination—through his lectures and in his discussion groups, shared with his students the joy of real thinking. . . .

The conditions at Harvard in the early 1890s could not have been more stimulating for those interested in the new science of land physiography. Davis was perfecting his theory of the classification of land forms, and Shaler was combatting the new science, even after he was convinced of its value, as his contribution to putting physiography on a sound and scientific basis. Of the group of graduate students in these years several went forth to teach and promote physiography, carrying into their work the methods of thought, the point of view, and the ideals they had gained at Harvard. Tarr was most active and contributed quickly two text books that for years exerted a large influence in secondary education. His wide field experience gave him an opportunity to make significant contributions to the science, and his untimely death removed in the prime of life not merely an eminent physiographer and geographer but a personality that was beloved by all, and particularly by those who had worked with him in the intimacy of classroom and study. Marbut and Westgate later established new centers for the development of physiography in the Middle West. Brigham, upon leaving Harvard, returned at once to his Alma Mater, Colgate University, where for more than three decades, until his retirement in 1925, he taught youth, not merely geology and physiography, but how to live. A teacher by nature and by training and with an instinctive interest in people, he has never lost sight of the development of the individual while primarily engaged in the development of his chosen subjects.

It is natural therefore that Brigham's reputation as a teacher soon spread abroad and his services were in demand in other institutions. For fourteen summers he taught summer classes at different institutions. Harvard, Cornell, the University of Wisconsin, Oxford, and the University of London have all welcomed him to their summer sessions, Harvard and Cornell each for four years. His last series of summer lectures was at the University of London and forms the basis of his volume *The United States of America* (1927).

Between 1892 and 1904, the year of organizing the Association of American Geographers, Brigham was not only becoming widely known as a geographer but his reputation as a scientific investigator was being enhanced among his colleagues. He was a regular attendant at the winter meetings of the Geological Society of America, which brought together annually many of those interested in physiography and with nebulous tendencies toward geography.

When, therefore, under the leadership of Professor Davis, the Association of American Geographers was organized, it was not only natural but almost inevitable that Brigham should be chosen as the first secretary-treasurer of the small but enthusiastic group that formed the new association. For nine years Brigham was the largest factor in the development of the association. His enthusiasm, his inventiveness, his ability to handle details all contributed to his success in bringing strength to a loosely organized group of co-workers. For three years Brigham acted as treasurer as well as secretary. The minutes of the meetings of the Association and of the council were written in longhand and form valuable historical reference material for the future student of the development of geography in America. These early minutes for many years have been in the safe of the American Geographical Society in New York City.

Brigham not only organized programs for the annual meetings of the association but he contributed a worthwhile series of papers during the period of his secretaryship. The titles of these early contributions indicate the variety of his interests and his early attention to the human phases of geography. These titles were as follows:

1904 'The development of the great roads across the Appalachians'

1906 'Geography for college entrance'
1908 'Three gatherings of geographic interest'
     'The capacity of the United States for population'
1909 'An attempt at a general classification of geography'
     'The organic side of geography; its nature and limits'. . . .

Perhaps the most immediately significant of these first contributions before the Association of American Geographers was his round table discussion of 'The organic side of geography' at the Boston meeting in 1909. For years the interest in human geography had been increasing among the members of the association but the field had largely been approached from the physiographic side. Influence, response, adjustment were common terms in everyday use, each implying certain basal physical factors to which they were related. At the first Chicago meeting of the association in 1907 at a joint session with members of the American Historical Association and of the American Anthropological Association, the discussion waxed warm as to whether the physical environment was a control or an influence or merely, as some protested, like gravity, a factor that was always present and which must be given at least casual attention in any study of the history of man. The common terms of the day were freely and easily used but often without definiteness of connotation, and the leaders were at odds. Geographers with the enthusiasm of youth were claiming perhaps too much and the more conservative workers in older fields were naturally on the defensive. Brigham contributed forcefully to clarifying the situation in two ways—by his round-table discussion at the Boston meeting and in 1914 by his presidential address on the 'Problems of geographic influence'.

In this address he gives many warnings, pricks many iridescent bubbles, and sounds a call for action that has since proved prophetic. Early in this paper he says wisely and truthfully,

> Whether we speak of influence, or response, or adjustment, matters little. Terminology will grow unbidden if we are exact in our thinking. Here lies the weight of our theme. We all have a duty to perform in view of the ill-founded and doubtful conclusions too often set forth, and in view of the vast extent of the unknown in this field. The factors of influence are not carefully isolated. What these forces really do and how they do it are not shown.

After an analysis and a critical interpretation of endeavours in various fields of thought to interpret the interactions of life and its environment, Brigham claims that 'the inclusive bond of world environment belongs to the geographer' but at the same time urges safety through careful investigation and sanity in making generalizations. 'We are to interpret cautiously similar human phenomena in different parts of the world. . . . The same things appear in many places, either through the unity of the human spirit or the likeness of environments, or from both causes.'

With this caution Brigham outlines in this address some of the contrasted types of investigation which await the geographer's attention, in some of which he has since led the way with an unerring touch, and concludes with the following guiding thoughts, which were pertinent then as they are now:

> Our goal is broad generalization. But the formulation of general laws is difficult and the results insecure until we have a body of concrete and detailed observations. . . . Detailed investigations of single problems, in small and seemingly unimportant fields, must for a long time prepare the way for the formulation of richer and more fundamental conclusions and general principles than we have yet been able to achieve. We should not wait for someone to state or demonstrate these laws. This is yet, even for a genius, impossible. We must contribute in a partial, microscopic, sometimes unconscious way to the emergence of such laws. . . . Such then is the mode of advance of our science—the old story of interest, hypothesis, test, correction, publication, criticism, revision; progress by error, by half truth, by zigzag, spiral, and apparent retrograde; by aeroflight, by patient tunneling; some at the salients of progress, and some in the ranks of humble endeavour, the goal in front of all.

Brigham's presidential address, the valedictory of his years of service as an officer of the association, was but a springboard into a wider field of service to the cause of geography. But the association was unwilling to lose his valuable assistance and from 1916 to 1919 he was again in the council and taking an active part in the association meetings. . . .

Again in 1923, the twentieth anniversary meeting, he contributed a paper, this time on the history of the association—and no one knows it as he does. One can say of Brigham and his part in the growth of the association in strength and influence what he said of Professor Davis at the quarter century meeting in 1928, 'All of which I say and part of which I was.'

At this birthday celebration Brigham presented 'An appreciation of William Morris Davis', founder and twice president of the association, whose absence perhaps lent freedom to the tongue of praise but was deeply regretted by all present. Such an appreciation from Brigham was more than appropriate not merely because of his early association with our honored leader but because in 1909 he had by request prepared the biographical sketch of Professor Davis for the *Geographen-Kalender....*

This is in brief the story of Brigham's services to geography through our association, the one to which he is attached by the closest ties. But he gave of himself wherever he could render service to the cause of geography. For years he took an active part in the meetings of the New York State Science Teachers' Association, serving as president in 1905. He has also been president of the National Council of Geography Teachers, an organization of geography teachers that has grown out of the Association of American Geographers much as that association brought together members of the Geological Society of America interested in physiography....

It is safe to say that Brigham's name is probably more widely known to the people of the country than that of any other living geographer. His textbooks for elementary school pupils and for adolescents have carried his name and influence for a better understanding of geography into thousands of homes, and this has continued through several school generations. His college texts have extended that influence widely. His books for laymen dealing with topics or sections of pertinent interest have made him well known as a popular writer in the best sense.

He has addressed large gatherings of teachers and lay audiences in all parts of the country and even abroad. By word and pen he has consistently promoted geography with a skill that few can equal. A clear thinker, firm in his convictions, fearless of criticism, with a knowledge of men and of world affairs, gained by direct contacts, by travel, and not merely through study, Brigham has a unique combination of attributes and skills that in part explains his success in his life-long devotion to geography and related sciences.[2]

16

J. Russell Smith, 1874-1966

The Wharton School of Finance and Commerce was established *circa* 1881 at the University of Pennsylvania. It became the main seat of economic geography under J. Russell Smith in the 1900s, but beginnings of the teaching of geography antedate Smith in the 1890s.

The beginnings are to be traced to Emory R. Johnson, who ended his career as dean of the school. Johnson was an economist and the thesis for which he was awarded a doctorate in 1893 was on the role of inland waterways in transportation. He was appointed lecturer in transportation and commerce in 1896 and offered two courses in geography, one on 'the theory and geography of commerce' and the other on 'physical and economic geography'. Johnson was chosen in 1898 to undertake an investigation on Panama for the Isthmian Canal Commission that preceded the work of construction, and he took J. Russell Smith along as his assistant.

On returning to the school, Johnson's conviction of the value of geography in commerce increased. In 1901 he therefore appointed J. Paul Goode, who had just completed his doctorate (under Johnson) on the economic development of the USA in relation to its physical conditions. Goode left the school in 1903 for Chicago (Salisbury's new department). Johnson then appointed Smith (who, also under Johnson, had just completed his doctorate on the organization of ocean commerce) to lecture on the geography of commerce. In 1906 Smith, as assistant professor, became the head of a separate division of 'geography and industry' in the department of economics and social science. His main course, starting in 1903–4, was 'commercial and economic geography', based on his doctorate work. He also presented a course on 'regional economic geography', beginning in 1906, in the *graduate* division. In 1913 his new course on 'industrial resources and conservation' is first evidence of what was to be a life-long interest.

J. Russell Smith, 1874–1966

W. S. Tower became his assistant in 1906. Tower had undergraduate training under Davis at Harvard, and, apparently leaving Davis with a vote of no-confidence for doctorate work, he transferred to the Wharton School. Here he completed his doctorate in 1906 on the 'Regional economic geography of Pennsylvania'. He gave courses on physical geography, but not for long, for in 1911 he too, was captured by Salisbury at Chicago. There he remained until 1919, when he left an academic life and transferred to the higher echelons of big business. It is interesting, though not surprising, that several of Smith's recruits eventually moved into business administration. It should be recalled here that the two earliest doctorates in regional geography were both undertaken under the guidance of Smith—one by Tower on Pennsylvania in 1906 and the other on Virginia by Surface in 1907.

When Smith had assistants, he was able to offer special courses on one of his main interests—industrial management and business. In this connection he wrote two books, *The Story of Iron and Steel* (1908) and *The Elements of Industrial Management* (1915). Smith was concerned with spatial organization and the location of business and commerce. His roots in geography (in spite of a short stay under Ratzel at Leipzig, when he was more interested in doing first-hand work on the trade of the west European ports) were secondary to his main motivation in economy and, in his later years, in conservation.

The early specialization of Smith in organization of commerce and industry resulted in a book on industrial and commercial geography, first published in 1913. This is a landmark in American geography, serving the same role as Chisholm's *Handbook* in Britain. It was a far more effective and readable exposition of the functions and structure of trade centres and trade routes than the British treatise. To this I can testify, as noted above (p. 212) from my own experience in the early 1920s when embarking on the study of the functions of cities.

The first half of Smith's career was spent at the University of Pennsylvania. For the second half he moved to Columbia University, where he was added to the staff of the university's school of business in 1919 at the request of the president, N. M. Butler. He was to organize economic geography similar to the Wharton School. He had the status of Professor of Economic Geography, the first of its kind. The school of business was founded in 1916. Smith introduced a basic requirement in the new school of economic geography and established a graduate programme in that subject. The M.A. and Ph.D. degrees were inaugurated in the mid-1920s.

This was for economic geography under Smith, alongside the separate department of physiography under Douglas Johnson. Smith early appointed John E. Orchard as his colleague.

Among those who took their doctorates under Smith are Walter Kollmorgen, Hermann Otte, George T. Renner, Otis P. Starkey and Louis A. Wolfanger, all of whom achieved distinguished careers. John Orchard, who for some years had been virtually running the department, became its head on the retirement of Smith in 1944.

In the latter half of his career, when located at Columbia, Smith became concerned with education and conservation. He wrote numerous textbooks in series for use in elementary and high schools, with such titles as *Human Use Geography, Home Folks, Foreign Lands and Peoples, Our Neighbours*. He also dedicated himself to questions of the development and conservation of both natural and human resources. This is evident in such books as *World's Food Resources* (1919), *Men and Resources* (1927) and *Tree Crops* (1929). A regional approach is evident in a large volume on *North America* (1925).

Virginia M. Rowley, in a biography of J. Russell Smith,[1] makes a 'final estimate' as follows:

Smith's work in course development at Columbia, as well as the Wharton School, exhibited, as did his writings, his growing maturity, creativity, and broadening scope of interest. A process of growth can be seen from his initial work in largely commercial areas to that in regional, human-economic geography. By presenting man in relation to his environment, Smith contributed to making geography at Columbia and the University of Pennsylvania a social science with implications for all aspects of man's activities. His work placed him among those pioneering educators who helped give geography status and prestige at the college and graduate levels.

His methodology and his ability to produce students and personnel of high calibre also demonstrated his gifts. Although his specific course work was not as influential in spreading his ideas as were his books, the two were so intimately interlinked that one was indispensable to the other. His work in professional organizations again illustrated the high standards and serious goals he set for American geographers. Thus, Smith's contributions to geography as an academic and professional discipline help to explain Smith, the man, the

author, and the geographer, and to show his specific role in
aiding geography's development as an advanced field of study.

A MEMORIAL, *by Dorothy Orchard*[2]

Throughout his life J. Russell Smith thoroughly enjoyed doing
whatever he did, and there was always something beyond, which
he hoped to get around to doing. He had many projects going
at the same time, many experiments under way, and always new
ideas to explore. His work was his recreation. He had a youthful
enthusiasm and a sense of urgency for the opportunities and
challenges that life offered, and he had the capacity to accomplish
an enormous volume of work. With his death, on 25 February
1966, the geographical profession lost not only a prolific scholar
but a remarkable man.

Dr Smith was born of Quaker parents near Lincoln, Virginia,
on 3 February 1874. As a boy he attended a one-room country
school near his father's farm, and at the age of seventeen he
went to a Friends' school in Pennsylvania to prepare for college.
Working part-time, he completed his college course at the
University of Pennsylvania and in 1898 obtained his B.S. degree.
In June of that year he married Henrietta Stewart. A two-year
assignment followed to carry out economic investigations for
the Isthmian Canal Commission, before he went to Europe
for a year's study at the University of Leipzig. The final weeks
of his European stay were spent in studying trade and shipping
conditions at major European ports. He then returned to the
University of Pennsylvania and in 1903 completed the work for
the Ph.D. degree with a dissertation on the organization of
ocean commerce.

He began his teaching career as an instructor in the Wharton
School of Finance and Commerce of the University of
Pennsylvania, and subsequently became professor and head of
the department of geography and industry. A serious lack of
good geographical texts for college students turned his attention
to writing. In 1913 he published his first major geographical
work, *Industrial and Commercial Geography,* a text of unusually
wide influence, which has endured through many printings and
new editions. The last edition appeared in 1955 when, because
of changing world conditions, the book was drastically rewritten
with the aid of two co-authors, one of whom was his son
Thomas R. Smith.

In 1913, after completing this first major work, he was sent by a committee of the University of Pennsylvania on a field trip to Europe and North Africa to do research in tree-crop agriculture. This study provided the material for a later book and the impetus for his increasing involvement with conservation.

Dr Smith had served sixteen years at the University of Pennsylvania when he was invited to Columbia University to build a curriculum in geography in the newly founded school of business. There he developed regional courses in geography and created his famous research seminar, which his students found highly stimulating. For an economist and a geographer his approach was unorthodox and daring, and he was often a controversial figure among his colleagues in the two disciplines. He remained at Columbia for twenty-five years and in that period published two major works, *North America* (1925) and *Tree Crop* (1929). After the publication of the book on North America he took a year for a journey through Asia to broaden and deepen his geographical comprehension.

In 1921, while at Columbia, he began a vast program of publication of grade-school and high-school geography textbooks, for which he assembled masses of photographs, diagrams, charts and maps. For these books he used the research he had done for his major works. But for him the research process was never-ending. He possessed great intellectual curiosity and was constantly learning from many and unusual sources. His textbooks were provocative, imaginative, and extraordinarily tuned to student response. He had a genius for language. He could take a mass of facts and weld them into a work to excite interest and stimulate creative thinking. He wrote texts for all the grades and for high school, and his books were adopted by State boards of education across the country. Each text had many printings and editions; many had special editions for individual States. It was a massive enterprise, which continued for some thirty-five years.

Dr Smith's work in conservation paralleled and amplified his work in geography. It began as early as 1895, with a practical experiment in which he planted some Persian-walnut seedlings on an acre and a half of mountain land in his native Blue Ridge country. Experiments followed with other trees on more and more acres. The blight wiped out his chestnuts, and there were further discouragements. About 1909 he began writing a continuous stream of articles for scientific and agricultural

journals and for popular magazines, directing attention to the
waste of the nation's resources and the urgent need of
conservation. The articles continued to make frequent appearance
into the 1920s, when the textbooks began to absorb more and
more of his time. He was not deflected from his concern with
conservation, but he moved towards his goal along other ways.
A great deal of energy went into his book on tree crops, a work
close to his heart. He wrote, he said, expecting practically no
financial returns and no results in his time, but in the hope of
firing the imagination of others, who would carry the torch. As
a conservationist he was a crusader. Unofficially, he took his message
to high places in the government, with surprising success. He
had a working ally in the Northern Nut Growers Association,
an organization of dedicated tree breeders. In 1916–17 he was
its president, and until his death he was an active member and
a frequent contributor to its publications.

Dr Smith was not a man who worked alone. Throughout his
career he had many valuable allies. His wife gave him perceptive
counsel and assistance in the 'work-shop' until her death. In
1964 he married Bessie W. Gahn, who had earlier done botanical
research and aided in the preparation of the second edition of
Tree Crop. His three sons also counseled and assisted in the
areas of their specialities: Newlin R. Smith as an economist;
J. Stewart Smith as a scientific farmer, who before he died was
associated with the tree nursery experiments; and Thomas R.
Smith as an economic geographer. The scope and volume of
Dr Smith's works required the participation of many others—
assistants, special experts, scientists, technicians, cartographers,
and colleagues. The number of persons involved in each work
were too great to be adequately mentioned, but the
acknowledgments that are possible were generous and
appreciative and revealed in this man a singular capacity for
enduring friendships.

Beyond the area of his professional career, J. Russell Smith
had a life-long concern for the achievement of world peace. He
wrote and spoke frequently for this cause. Indeed, the imperative
need for outlawing war was the moral lesson in his presidential
address to the Association of American Geographers in 1943.
It was a brilliant, imaginative presentation of the destruction
of ancient civilizations by Eurasian grassland horsemen using
the crossbow as weapon—a weapon he equated in destructive
power with aircraft of modern war.

Among the many honors he received were the degree of doctor of science from Columbia University in 1929, the degree of doctor in economic science from the University of Pennsylvania in 1957, and the Cullum Geographical Medal from the American Geographical Society in 1956.

17

The Chicago Sequence

The first department of geography in a university in the USA was founded in 1903 at the University of Chicago a few years after the university's foundation. It was headed by a geologist, R. D. Salisbury, who transferred from a distinguished department of geology in the same university. For nearly seventy years it has sheltered in its graduate school a succession of outstanding scholars, and it is still esteemed as one of the very top schools in the world. Its members include those who were there virtually throughout their careers, but it also had several who stayed for relatively short periods, either in their early training and experience, or as captures from other centres in the world. It has produced a long series of doctorates, many of whose holders reached distinction in their profession as geographers or geologists and some in business. It is, therefore, to be expected that Chicago illustrates best the sequence of five generations of scholars.

Its succession of chairmen gives an indication of status, but it must be emphasized that the staff has always worked as a community of scholars and that the administrative chairman is *primus inter pares*. The list of chairmen is:

Rollin D. Salisbury, 1903–19
Harlan H. Barrows, 1919–42
Charles C. Colby, 1942–50
Robert S. Platt, 1950–6
Gilbert F. White, 1956–61
Wesley C. Calef, 1961–7
Chauncy D. Harris, 1967–9
Marvin W. Mikesell, 1969–

The first doctorate was awarded in 1907; 6 were awarded under the Salisbury regime and about 50 under Barrows. Just over 100 have been awarded since this date. The list includes the names of many scholars of repute who are scattered at university and other posts throughout the nation, though mainly in the Middle West.

From this long series of contributors I reproduce extracts from memoirs by their senior colleagues. D. Whittlesey and T. G. Taylor (the Commonwealth leader) are in the sequence though they were associated with other universities. The work of Ellen C. Semple is appraised in a separate chapter by an early colleague at Chicago.[1]

As noted in the first chapter of this book, there have been several academic generations of geographers, and we may take the Chicago sequence as a guideline. Salisbury was one of the first-generation founders. His successors were essentially in the same chronological group—Barrows, Colby, Taylor, Whittlesey, Jones and Platt. All belonged to the second generation, as does Carl Sauer, one of its emigrant members. Since the Second World War there have emerged two senior and outstanding scholars, Gilbert White and Chauncy Harris. They belong to the third generation. Their colleagues include Brian J. L. Berry and Marvin Mikesell, who represent the fourth generation. The young doctorates of the post-war years belong to the fifth generation. I shall refer to chronological parallels in other centres in the pages that follow.

ROLLIN D. SALISBURY, 1858–1922, *by S. S. Visher*[2]

Rollin D. Salisbury organized in 1903 the first sizable department of geography in an American university. During the sixteen years of his headship, this department contributed notably to the science of geography, to the training of numerous students who subsequently held prominent positions in geography, and to the firm establishment of geography as a separate department at the University of Chicago, thus hastening the day when geography would be similarly recognized in other universities.

The establishment of the department at Chicago reflected the conviction of leaders there of the need for advanced geographic training. T. C. Chamberlin, very influential there partly because he had been the highly successful president of the University of Wisconsin, 1887–92, was in position to urge effectively the establishment of the department, with his deeply respected associate as its head.

The prominent status that Salisbury's department soon attained reflected several influences in addition to its being for years the only full-fledged university department of geography. There were six influences beneficial to the University of Chicago's department: (1) Salisbury was for most of his students an

exceptionally stimulating teacher; (2) he was a distinguished
administrator, already dean of the graduate school of science;
(3) he selected an able, well-balanced staff (J. Paul Goode, Wallace
W. Atwood, Harlan H. Barrows, Walter S. Tower, Ellen C.
Semple [part-time], Mary J. Lanier, and, later, Wellington D.
Jones, Charles C. Colby, and lastly, Robert S. Platt); (4) the
university's excellent position geographically and in the educational
world was also decidedly advantageous; (5) physiographic
textbooks by Salisbury and geographic texts by Salisbury, Barrows,
and Tower were widely used and helped to attract students; and
(6) the close association of the department with the department
of geology was most advantageous. Geology was then under the
headship of America's most distinguished geologist, T. C.
Chamberlin. To it were attracted many students, some of whom
shifted to geography and several of whom significantly helped the
development of some geography students.

Salisbury's chief contributions to geography may be discussed
under three heads: as a scientist, as a teacher, and as an
administrator.

Salisbury augmented the understanding of physical geography
greatly. This resulted partly from penetrating studies in the field
in several regions, notably, Wisconsin, New Jersey, Wyoming,
and Greenland, with lesser studies in Germany, South America,
the West Indies, and in numerous other areas. He was a keen
observer and an acute, incisive reasoner. The deductions from
his field studies were presented in *The Physical Geography of
New Jersey* (1894) and in several publications of the Wisconsin,
Illinois, and federal Geological Surveys, in numerous articles,
and in several textbooks. Of the three-volume treatise, *Geology*
(with T. C. Chamberlin, 1904–06), Salisbury was author of
most of the first volume, *Physical Geology,* and of considerable
parts of the other volumes. This treatise was condensed into a
widely used *College Geology.* The college text, *Physiography,*
presented to a wider audience his deductions as to physical
geography. It induced a conspicuous increase in the comprehension
of the subjects discussed. This text, first published in 1907, was
substantially revised in 1919, and served long afterwards. An
edition for high school use appeared in 1908. An important
additional way in which Salisbury aided the advancement of
physical geography was that the most widely-used college text
of geography for more than a decade, *Elements of Geography*
(1912),[3] was partly built around his book on physiography.

An adaptation of this was the high school text, *Modern Geography* (1913).

Salisbury's high rating among scientists is revealed partly by his rank in the balloting, secret until recently, done when starring for American Men of Science was inaugurated in 1903. He then rated nineteenth among the 100 starred in geology. (Chamberlin was first, W. M. Davis, sixth). Presumably, Salisbury stood significantly higher a decade later, after the monumental treatise and a lesser one (with Willis) and four texts of which he was author or co-author had appeared, and after five of the eighteen scientists who had topped him in 1903 had died, and five others had largely ceased scholarly work. All except one of the eighteen were older than Salisbury, most of them considerably older. Davis was eight years older.

The significance of Salisbury's scientific contributions is also shown by their influence on the work of later investigators. Apparently all of his researches have proven to be a firm basis on which others have built.

Salisbury was a superb teacher, not only in the classroom and as an author, but also as lecturer and editor. He was so successful as a teacher at Beloit College, where he taught for seven years, that when he was offered a professorship at the University of Wisconsin, a petition signed by practically every Beloit student implored him to remain, which he did for another year. At Chicago, to which he went upon its opening in 1892, many students rated him as their most successful teacher, and scores gave him credit for significantly changing their objectives and methods. As a public lecturer, he spoke frequently, especially to groups of teachers, on the development of the physical features of the earth. These lectures were by no means frivolous or elementary, but they had considerable popularity because of their high educational effectiveness. The present writer attended a series of six on the features of North America in early 1903, while a high school freshman, with considerable consequences on the only lad in the audience.

Salisbury's skill as a concise, direct writer was significant not only to those who read what he wrote and to the students who wrote papers and theses partly under his supervision, but to the many who submitted manuscripts to the *Journal of Geology,* of which he was managing editor for nearly thirty years. He sought to have every sentence so clear that it could not only be understood, but that it 'could not be misunderstood'.

He was adept at pointing out how a given statement might be

misunderstood, and also in showing that certain words therein were unnecessary, and hence undesirable. Another oft-repeated declaration of his was that a given statement was 'perfectly true, perfectly general, perfectly meaningless'. Concerning his editing, Sauer reports:

> He spent days dissecting my Upper Illinois Valley job. I never learned so much about writing as from the queries (as to content) and revisions (as to diction) that he gave me on that paper. Moreover, he did not eviscerate my style or idiosyncrasies—he insisted only on clarity.

A potent part of Salisbury's teaching was his earnest effort to help promising students. He selected from each of his classes a few whom he considered especially promising and devoted much of the class period to increasing their comprehension and effectiveness in presentation. He asked them many questions, sometimes dozens in a single hour. Occasionally he concentrated on one or two of them for several consecutive days. Repeatedly he pointed his finger at them and spoke sharply. The students whom he ignored disliked being neglected, and some resolved to prove that they, too, were 'worthwhile'. When a student whom he had earlier rated as mediocre proved his merit, Salisbury was glad to encourage him further. He was generous, despite considerable gruffness, and many of his students especially remember how he encouraged them. Although characteristically brusque in the classroom, he quickly accepted good suggestions, and displayed generous respect for those who corrected his own inadequacies and mistakes.

In addition to great emphasis on comprehension, clarity, and conciseness, Salisbury stressed the need for careful daily preparation, the significance of small increments of knowledge, and the lasting value of good work. He made special preparation before each class session, spending about fifteen minutes assembling and organizing his notes shortly before each class. This was in addition to time previously spent in preparation— sometimes hours. He strongly encouraged his students to be fully ready. He often started the session with the question: 'Just where were we at the end of the last class period?' He believed firmly that progress of all sorts is made step by step, and hence he welcomed even small contributions to understanding. Highly significant was his conviction, repeatedly expressed, that work well done is not in vain—that its effects extend far beyond the present. As he put it once:

I

One of the great lessons which the world needs most to learn is that progress comes from cumulative achievement. If every individual could be made to realize that even his tiny contribution to the sum of useful work is really moving the world along, it would add grandeur to life and dignity to all human endeavor. This is the frame of mind that should be developed in every young person, and cultivated until it becomes a habit.

In the words of one of his students: 'With an enthusiasm, energy, and intellectual precision of the greatest intensity, he shared his knowledge with students and with the world as if he were the apostle of an exceedingly precious gospel.' Another said: 'He was so concerned with inculcating craftsmanship and critical faculties that he increasingly devoted himself to bringing up the younger generation well.'

That in his later years Salisbury did almost no research contrasted with a few other distinguished geographers, but was usual for scientists, even those who had done much research while relatively young. Salisbury's intense efforts did not decline, but he devoted them to teaching and administration rather than to seeking new truths. As McMurry has expressed it:

Salisbury's concentration on teaching certainly had its productive features. He had an uncanny ability to appraise the quality of teaching being done by his staff. I had my first teaching experience under him and his criticisms, both constructive and destructive, of my procedures were of great value.

Salisbury possessed accurate and thorough knowledge and spent himself unreservedly to share it with his students, who agreed that, though his courses were 'heavy', there was no waste in them, nothing superfluous or academically formal. He used the problem method of teaching. Instead of set lectures or routine recitations, it was his delight to make students think, stand on their own feet and work out in a first-hand grapple with the facts the implications of the facts considered. It was part of his respect for life that he believed that by diligence and zeal men may accomplish much. He sought to make his students not only efficient as scientists, but to have wider vision. He said: 'I believe it to be fundamentally important that young people should be led to see visions and be inspired by the allurements of future developments':

Geography implies great possibilities for better social and international relations over the earth. Viewing the life of different races and communities in relation to the conditions of their environment provides a scientific basis for understanding many of their present limitations and future possibilities, and at least one indispensable condition of genuine sympathy and effective co-operation.

Incidentally, he discouraged note-taking in class, declaring: 'Get this information in your head. You are more likely to have it with you when you need it.' He hated pretense and admired effort and intelligence. He frankly expressed appreciation of others. Although he was a rigid disciplinarian and expected much work from his students, his classes were always filled to the regulation limits. He taught appreciation of nature. For example, he said:

Those who think the landscape of an unrelieved tract like that about Chicago unlovely would have a completely changed attitude if they understood the grand march of events which has made the surface what it is. When men belittle the attractiveness of the level prairie, they advertise their ignorance.

One of the surprising aspects of his teaching was that he, a world-renowned scientist and high dean, regularly taught classes of freshmen, as well as of upper-classmen and of graduate students.

Criteria often used to evaluate teaching include the subsequent achievement of the teacher's students, the judgment of his students as to his success with them, and the number who adopt his methods or become his disciples. On each of these bases, Salisbury ranked high. For example, ten of his students have already been presidents of the Association of American Geographers (Wallace W. Atwood, Harlan H. Barrows, Charles C. Colby, Henry C. Cowles, N. M. Fenneman, Vernor C. Finch, A. E. Parkins, Robert S. Platt, Carl O. Sauer, and Derwent Whittlesey), five have been vice-presidents (Charles C. Adams, William H. Haas, Clarence F. Jones, George J. Miller, and S. S. Visher), and one has been president of the American Association for the Advancement of Science (Kirtley F. Mather). Prominent in other ways have been Charles H. Behre, Mendel E. Branom, Wellington D. Jones, Kenneth C. McMurry, Roderick Peattie, Helen M. Strong, Eugene Van Cleef, William E. Wrather, and a considerable number of others. A recognition of achievement significant in geography is the Distinguished Service to

Geographic Education Award of the National Council of
Geography Teachers. Half of the awards so far made have gone
to students of Salibury's (Allison E. Aicheson, W. W. Atwood,
C. C. Colby, V. C. Finch, Alice Foster, George J. Miller,
Edith Parker, A. E. Parkins, Zoë Thralls, and S. S. Visher).
Of the twenty-eight persons here listed, eighteen received a college
degree at Chicago and nineteen the doctorate. After graduate
work in the department, three received their doctorate elsewhere,
and six others obtained no regular doctorate, but two (Miller and
Wrather) received honorary doctorates.

By contrast, of William Morris Davis's students, seven became
early presidents of the Association of American Geographers,
two became vice-presidents, and five received the Distinguished
Service Award (Isaiah Bowman, Richard E. Dodge, Ellsworth
Huntington, Mark Jefferson, and Ray H. Whitbeck). No other
geographer has yet approached Salisbury in these obviously
highly significant respects.

Two additional evidences of Salisbury's great influence as a
teacher may be given. More members of the Association of
American Geographers reported in a 1939 questionnaire that
Salisbury had 'significantly influenced' them than gave that
testimonial to any other person. Likewise, a 1946 questionnaire
returned by 101 starred geologists revealed that Salisbury was
rated as their 'most stimulating teacher' by a larger number
than was any other teacher. Only T. C. Chamberlin and Charles
Schuchert approached him. Of members of the Association of
American Geographers, W. M. Davis and H. E. Gregory stood
next to Salisbury, but were far behind, each with about a third
as many testimonials.

Many of Salisbury's students have declared that they have
endeavoured to follow his example in their classroom teaching.
More than a dozen have followed his example in extending their
educational influence by writing good textbooks. A considerable
number have followed his example by repeatedly giving public
lectures, and a few have been faithful editors. In addition to
those who studied under Salisbury in the classroom, there are
many who learned from him through his writings, or through
students of his. Moreover, examinations of appropriate parts
of recent textbooks in geography reveals that nearly all of them
have adopted considerable parts of Salisbury's physiography text.
That these adopted parts of Salisbury's text were original is
disclosed by a comparison of his text with those that preceded it,
American, English, German and French.

As an administrator, Salisbury served geography notably. His ideals for the department he headed were high. The staff he selected to teach the courses regularly were all so able and earnest that, with one exception, they became distinguished geographers. Except two who declined the honour and one other, all subsequently became presidents of the Association of American Geographers. Nearly all of those whom he accepted as assistants or fellows subsequently confirmed the soundness of his judgment. As dean of the graduate school of science, he contributed significantly to the establishment of policies which helped it become a world leader, and he helped geography attain parity among the university's departments. He was co-founder and first president of the Chicago Geographical Society. He instigated several state bulletins and Chicago Geographical Society publications. He was president of the Association of American Geographers for 1912.

An administrative accomplishment which merits mention was his relinquishment, after sixteen years, of the headship of the department. The man he recommended as his successor (Barrows) had been partly trained by him, and had been his close associate.

The load of administrative duties that Salisbury carried was large, but he could always be counted upon, it is said, to do all that could reasonably be expected of him, or more. A considerable amount of this administrative work had to do with geology, and with the *Journal of Geology*, from 1892 almost to his death. This gave T. C. Chamberlin much more time for the fundamental research which he did so well and which led to his long being the world's most distinguished geologist. Salisbury's administrative work as dean of the graduate school of science was significant to geography in various ways, including the selection of those to receive fellowships or scholarships. J. Russell Whitaker, not a student of Salisbury's, recalls vividly the penetrating questions Salisbury asked before awarding him a scholarship. Salisbury also gave a succession of graduate students an opportunity to teach sections of elementary courses, and aided them substantially by the suggestions he gave them. Most of the persons so aided subsequently became conspicuously successful teachers. Mary J. Lanier taught thus for some years before going to Wellesley, and Schockel briefly before he became head at Indiana State. Peattie was also helped appreciably, he reports, as were several geologists, one of whom became Professor of Geography at Princeton in 1928. Two bits of advice that Salisbury gave to such young teachers were: 'Make the main story big and strong, don't try to give all the details. Brush aside the non-essentials and hit the essentials hard,' and 'Constantly remember whom you are teaching; every individual has a different background.'

HARLAN H. BARROWS, 1877–1960,
by C. C. Colby and G. F. White[4]

Harlan H. Barrows was born in Armada, Macomb County, Michigan, on 15 April 1877. He was the son of a prominent family in this eastern Michigan village largely settled by families from New England and 'upstate' New York. As a boy, Barrows was a great reader, especially of history and biography. At the age of fourteen, he graduated from high school and at nineteen from the Michigan State Normal College.

After finishing at the State Normal College, Barrows taught geography and history at Ferris Institute, a frontier institution at Big Rapids near the southern border of the Michigan woods. Isaiah Bowman attended the institute and was one of Barrows's students. Here began a life-long friendship of two of the great minds of twentieth-century geography. While he was in Big Rapids, Barrow married Janie E. Gleason on 16 August 1898. They had one son, Robert Harlan, whose accidental death in 1919 was a major blow to Barrows. Mrs Barrows had died on 23 July 1913.

In 1903, Barrows took his BS degree at the University of Chicago, where Chamberlin and Salisbury were making history in the earth sciences. In 1903, the first university department of geography in America was established there. Salisbury became head of the new department and Barrows was one of the early students. The latter's work as student and assistant was so outstanding that in 1907 he was appointed instructor of geography. Thus began a close association with Salisbury in teaching, research, and writing, an association that resulted in many constructive contributions to geography, including their college textbook, *Elements of Geography,* with W. S. Tower as co-author, which provided introductory ideas and materials for use in the many colleges and universities to which geographic teaching spread in the early decades of this century.

In 1906–7, Barrows undertook for the State Geological Survey a study of the Middle Illinois River Valley. The completed study was published in 1910—*The Geography of the Middle Illinois Valley.*

A final chapter ... describes the settlement and development of the Peoria-Hennepin region from the time of the pioneers who emigrated from the South and from New England. The distribution of the early population, its conquest of adverse conditions and final development into a community of great interests, is skilfully traced.

After his first appointment in the department of geography, Barrows moved rapidly up the academic ladder to reach his professorship in 1914.

Probably no American geographer contributed more in the establishment of high geographic standards at the graduate level than did Barrows. This was demonstrated in the winter of 1914, when a graduate seminar was offered as a departmental enterprise. All the staff (Salisbury, Goode, Barrows, and Tower) and all graduate students attended.

From the beginnings of his university work, Barrows maintained an interest in the inter-relations of geography and history. In 1904, he first offered what was to become one of the famous courses of the department and the university. At the outset he called the course 'Influence of geography on American history'. Although this first title represented the thought of the period, in time Barrows became increasingly dissatisfied with the title and the approach it represented. Hence, in 1923, the title became 'Historical geography of the United States'.[5] His change of thought is well stated in his presidential address before the Association of American Geographers (1922). In referring to the trends of geographic thought from 1903 to 1922, he wrote:

Scarcely was physical geography established, or perhaps I should say rejuvenated and re-established, before an insistent demand arose that it be 'humanized'. This demand met with a prompt response, and the center of gravity within the geographic field has shifted steadily from the extreme physical side toward the human side, until geographers in increasing numbers define their subject as dealing solely with the mutual relations between man and his natural environment. By 'natural environment' they of course mean the combined physical and biological environments.

As his work matured, Barrows increasingly sought accuracy in his reasoning and clarity in his expression. He wanted to state a thesis so effectively that he could defend his interpretations and justify his conclusions. He argued that 'a motivating theme,

an organizing concept, is required which shall permeate geography
and give to all its divisions a distinctive point of view'. He
thought that to be truly geographic a discussion must involve
from beginning to end an explanatory treatment in orderly
sequence of 'the mutual relations between men and the natural
environment of the regions or areas in which they live.' At
another point in his definition of geography as human ecology,
he states, 'It is not the human fact which is geography, any more
than it is the environmental fact, but rather the relation which
may exist between the two ... geography is a science of
relationships.' In another place, he states that geographers in the
future will take as the objective of geographic enquiry 'man's
adjustment to environment rather than that of environmental
influence.' Hence, he argues that 'the former approach is more
likely to result in the recognition and proper evaluation of all
the factors involved and especially to minimize the danger of
assigning to the environmental factors a determining influence
which they do not exert.'

Early in his career, Barrows became interested in conservation.
His first major public service came during 1918, when he was
head of the country section of the Bureau of Research, US War
Trade Board.

Barrows became chairman of the department of geography in
1919 and continued in that capacity until he became Professor
Emeritus in 1942. The appointment was occasioned by the
retirement of Professor T. C. Chamberlin, for many years head
of the department of geology. To fill this vacancy, the university
administration asked Salisbury to move to the headship of geology
and Barrows to become chairman of geography. Barrows
inaugurated a policy of inviting some distinguished European
geographers to lecture during the summer quarter. The list
included Ll. Rodwell Jones, from London; Helge Nelson, from
Lund; Baron Sten De Geer, from Stockholm; Raoul Blanchard,
from Grenoble; and Patrick Bryan, from Leicester.

About 1923, Barrows and Edith P. Barker began the preparation
of a series of textbooks for the elementary schools. The finished
series stimulated discussion and produced the hoped-for
invigorating effect on the teaching of geography.

Professor Barrows was appointed a member of the Mississippi
Valley committee of the Public Works Administration in 1933.
With this appointment, he entered a new phase of service; his
interest shifting from academic management to national policy.
By 1934, the preliminary plan had been published as the

committee's report, and the committee entered into a series of transformations under the changing tents of successive national planning agencies. Barrows was on all these groups, resigning from the board in 1941.

Professor Barrows's contributions on the national scene were of three major sorts. While a member of the national water planning committees, he insisted upon exacting standards of writing for the public reports. He also played an influential role in shaping expressions of the emerging national policy of multiple-purpose river development; but the most influential contribution by Professor Barrows was in the design of integrated regional studies. Here, he added a new dimension to federal-state investigations, carrying the broad concepts which Major John Wesley Powell had enunciated fifty years before into concrete and sophisticated study programs. The first of these efforts was the Rio Grande Joint Investigation. With the able collaboration of Frank Adams, Barrows was the architect of the scheme which, in order to obtain the water and land data deemed necessary to successful negotiations of a compact among Colorado, New Mexico, and Texas for the allocation of upper Rio Grande waters, brought together federal agencies and state agencies in a three-year program of investigations, 1935–8. More than $2,000,000 was expended on work which was summarized in the National Resources Committee report, and which led to the conclusion of a compact.

The Pecos Joint Investigation, 1939–41, and the Red River of the North report resulted from application of this method, but the monumental demonstration of it was the Columbia Basin Joint Investigations which Barrows headed up for the bureau of reclamation. He probably had more influence upon thinking about the impacts of water projects in the Columbia basin than in any other area, but his thinking was felt in all phases of irrigation planning. In subsequent years, the report of those investigations shaped technical analysis of water projects over many other areas.

In conclusion, it becomes clear that the vigorous intellectual contributions of Harlan H. Barrows not only helped to define and illuminate the development of geography as a field of learning, but also exercised a constructive impact on the recognition of the principles of water utilization and the design of integrated regional studies.

I*

J. PAUL GOODE, 1862–1933
by W. H. Haas and H. B. Ward[6]

After receiving a bachelor of science degree from Minnesota in 1889, Paul Goode was called to teach natural science in the Minnesota State Normal and stayed in that position until 1898, with periods out for graduate work at Harvard in 1894 and at the University of Chicago as fellow in geology in 1896–7. The born geographer was developing during those first years of teaching, so that he was well prepared to conduct geography classes at the University of Chicago during the summers of 1897–1900 and to accept a position in 1899 at the Eastern Illinois State Normal as Professor of Physical Science and Geography. In 1901 he entered the University of Pennsylvania, where he received his Ph.D. and remained until 1903 as instructor in geography and director of the Geographical Society of Philadelphia.

Because he had already become identified with the University of Chicago by his summer classes, it is not surprising that in 1903 he was called to a permanent position in the geography department of that institution. He became known as an expert in economic geography and, as such, in 1908 was sent by the Chicago Harbor Commission to study the leading ports of Europe. His report was published under the title 'The development of commercial ports'.

Dr Goode first appeared on the program of the Association of American Geographers at the Chicago meeting of 1907. Two addresses were given, one entitled 'An Electrical compensator for the Foucault pendulum', the other 'A college course in ontography'. These topics show his versatility and wide range of interests at that time. In later years one of his favorite avocations was experimenting in dynamics in his home laboratory.

Professor Goode became the leader in the fight against the Mercator Projection for school maps. He deplored the fact that it was used so extensively and started his great work on the problem of producing an equal-area projection that could be used for world maps. . . .

During all the years that Dr Goode was teaching, lecturing and working on the problems of wall maps, his chief ambition was to produce a school atlas that would stand as the finest accomplishment of his life. It was, therefore, a great source of satisfaction to him when his preliminary atlas was published in 1923, and the climax of his life work was reached when the revised and enlarged edition was completed shortly before he died. Professor Goode wrote the introduction 'to the student and teacher' and offered it 'with the sincere hope that it will help toward the better teaching of geography, and toward a greater appreciation of fine maps and a keener pleasure in their use, both during and after schooldays'.

WELLINGTON DOWNING JONES, 1886–1957, by C. C. Colby[7]

In his early years as a geographer (1908–21), Wellington Jones enjoyed such exceptional opportunities for field study that his experience differed in this respect from most other young geographers. In the first term of the summer quarter in 1909 he took a field course in geology and taught the course in the second term. Later in 1909, under the title of 'Scientific Explorer,' he led a field party from the Geographic Society of Chicago in a study of Yellowstone National Park. In 1910 he assisted W. C. Alden in a study of the glacial geology on the Green Bay lobe.

Other field experiences followed. One of major significance in Wellington's career resulted from a course offered by Bailey Willis when he came to the university as a visiting professor in 1910. Wellington took the course and gained much from his association with this distinguished leader in the earth sciences. In his turn, Professor Willis recognized Wellington's potentialities, and in 1911, when the government of Argentina invited Willis to direct a commission to survey the water resources of northern Patagonia, Wellington was hired as a member of the survey staff. Wellington's assignment 'to study possibilities of further economic use of the area' not only provided training in field methods but turned his thoughts to economic geography, a division of geography to which he subsequently made many contributions.

After the two years spent with the Northern Patagonia survey, Wellington returned to the university as an instructor in geography. As he had gathered a wealth of material from the field and from contacts with agencies of the Argentina government, he began active work on his doctoral dissertation under the title 'Studies in the geography of northern Patagonia'.

In 1913, Wellington spent six months at the University of Heidelberg, where he worked with Professor Alfred Hettner. During this period of European study, Jones spent two weeks in the Moselle valley with Professor Hettner and a month in the Swiss Alps with Professor Phillipson from Bonn. These experiences profoundly influenced Wellington's ideas of geography, as did discussions of methods and content while he was a member of Professor Barrows's field party in the southern Appalachians in 1914.

After receiving his doctor's degree in 1914, and with a generous grant from the Swift family, Dr Jones spent many months in the study of eastern Asia. He visited Japan, China, Manchuria, and Mongolia. He traveled overland from the Yangtze to Canton in south China. From this trip through the hills of China came a conviction that, since much of China could not be described as plains, plateaux, or mountains, a new landscape term was needed. Hence he introduced the term 'hill country' into his geographic vocabulary.

Jones's work in eastern Asia was followed in 1920-1 by travel and study in India, again under financial assistance from the Swift family. He made a special study of Kashmir and did considerable field-mapping in that area. Throughout his work in India, he typed a daily record and sent a copy to Chicago, where it went the rounds of the staff and special students.

Jones's experiences in east Asia and India greatly increased his knowledge of world geography. His studies led him to the realization that regions, like men, differ in resources and potentialities. The densely peopled areas of China and India, he noted, stand in sharp contrast with the nearly empty plains of Patagonia or the highly industrialized sections of western Europe. Moreover he was so impressed with the contrasting sections within China and India that subsequently he recognized and mapped their major geographic divisions.

Through the years Dr Jones devoted much time and effort in perfecting the technology of field and regional investigations. Moreover, he was a prime mover in organizing a 'Spring Conference' of Middle Western geographers to experiment with field-mapping. For fifteen years this conference met on the third weekend in May, each year at a different point.[8] Among other things this group developed the 'fractional code' method of field-mapping. This method calls for the use of air photographs as a base, preferably single-lens mosaics. Jones was a leader in this group enterprise, both because of his interest in the method and his enthusiasm for improving geographic field studies.

In discussing field methods and techniques with his students and contemporaries, Dr Jones always emphasized the importance

of detailed field notes. He expressed this approach in some notes
written in 1951 with regard to his fieldwork in northern Patagonia.
In abbreviated form these notes are quoted herewith: [9]

> I well remember Bailey Willis's instructions before my first
> long field trip from Rio Colorado to Valcheta. Willis in effect
> said that I was to travel across the country as rapidly as
> I could on horseback and still see the general aspects of the
> countryside, and that as I traveled I was to stop at a few widely
> separated points, take detailed observations, and make notes
> thereon; each such stop to be located accurately on a map. . . .
> This method is, in my way of thinking, the most valuable
> we know in geography in the field . . . for many years I have
> employed it with identifying digit notations. . . . On this first
> traverse of 150 miles I plotted my observations, and when
> later our topographers determined the latitude and longitude
> of Valcheta my plotted traverse was out only a small fraction
> of an inch, which failure to close I adjusted (spread back over
> the 150 miles). . . . From such records millions of square miles
> on the earth have been mapped and from such maps we learn
> the approximate distribution of vegetation, soils, rocks, land
> forms, population density, and oasis and stream locations.

Following his return from India in 1921, Dr Jones began more
than a decade of effective teaching, writing and research.
His courses in east Asia and India became basic instruments in
training students in regional delimitation and discussion. His
research during the period led him to make intensive use of his
method of isoplethic mapping. Moreover, his wall map of world
agricultural regions with accompanying text led to much fruitful
thinking and discussion of world agriculture. During this period
also the University of Chicago Press published *An Introduction to
Economic Geography* (1925) by Wellington D. Jones and
Derwent S. Whittlesey, a volume that introduced a highly
distinctive method of undergraduate learning
  In the latter part of his university work, Dr Jones became
greatly interested in the study of soil geography. In part this
interest grew out of the 'Spring Conference' on field methods and
partly out of contacts with geographers at the University of
Michigan and soil scientists at Michigan State University. In
studying the distribution of soils, Jones found great satisfaction
in Marbut's insistence that the basic approach to a knowledge
of soils and other natural phenomena was through consideration
of their inherent characteristics.

Professor Jones spent several summers in the Rocky Mountains, more especially in the southern Rockies. As early as 1920, he conducted a graduate field party in the Rocky Mountain Park and later studied the glacial land forms of that area. He was an ardent fisherman and combined this type of recreation with his field studies.

Wellington D. Jones was a highly constructive figure in American geography in the first half of the twentieth century. He was a pioneer in bringing to the USA first-hand knowledge of the economic geography of east Asia and India. By means of his teaching and his creative achievements in regional mapping, he contributed effectively to the development of regional geography and the isoplethic method in the discovery of areal patterns. He possessed a highly original outlook—the outlook of an explorer of many areas of geographic thought. By his teaching, his dynamic personality, and his wide contacts in academic circles he became a colorful and constructive force in the formative period of American geography.

CHARLES C. COLBY, 1884–1965, *by C. D. Harris*[10]

Charles Carlyle Colby was born in Romeo, Michigan, on 13 April 1884. He died in LaCrosse, Wisconsin, on 16 July 1965, at the age of eighty-one, while engaged in fieldwork for the Mississippi Valley investigations, which he headed.

His undergraduate academic career began at Michigan State Normal College under a most stimulating and creative teacher of geography, Mark Jefferson. After receiving his Ph.D. there in 1908 he sought further training at the University of Chicago, where the first department of geography in an American university had been established five years earlier and where some of the great figures of the field at that time were teaching: Rollin D. Salisbury, J. Paul Goode, Harlan H. Barrows, Walter S. Tower, and Ellen Churchill Semple. Among the students with Charles C. Colby in these early days were Wellington D. Jones, Stephen S. Visher, Vernor C. Finch, and Carl O. Sauer. After a B.S. from the University of Chicago he became instructor and head of the department of geography at Minnesota State Normal School in Winona, Minnesota. During his period at Winona his searching eye and inquisitive mind perceived some interesting problems on the historical geography of south-eastern Minnesota and his first paper was on this subject. After this paper William

Morris Davis invited him to discuss the possibilities of the subject. Professor Salisbury at the University of Chicago later suggested that the topic might make a suitable subject for a doctoral dissertation. Thus the young Charles Colby attracted the attention of two leading geographers of the country, even though these two were decidedly cool to one another. At this time George Peabody College was raising standards of teaching in the southern USA and Charles Colby was invited in 1914 to develop work in geography there. In 1916 he returned to the University of Chicago, completed his doctorate, and remained a member of the faculty for the next thirty-three years.

The 1920s were a period of extraordinary energy and productivity. Colby had been brought to the University of Chicago to teach the regional course on North America. He thereafter regarded that continent as his personal domain and promptly embarked on a survey and inventory of the property. In 1921 appeared the first edition of his *Source Book for the Economic Geography of North America.* It was a pathbreaking work, since up to that time no comprehensive professional college-level treatment of the economic geography of this continent had yet appeared. In 1924 appeared his first two lengthy research articles, on the California raisin industry and the apple industry of Nova Scotia, at the two ends of the continent. The first article was organized specifically to illustrate the human ecology approach to geography suggested by Harlan H. Barrows in his presidential address of 1922 to the Association of American Geographers.

The early 1930s were in some ways Colby's most creative period *His Economic Geography for Secondary Schools* in collaboration with Alice Foster was published in 1931. In 1933 four important works appeared. His interest in geographic field techniques was expressed in an article on the railway traverse as an aid in reconnaissance, and in his editing a volume for the Geographic Society of Chicago on geographic surveys with chapters by Robert S. Platt and Vernor C. Finch. He wrote an extensive appraisal of the contributions of Ellen Churchill Semple. His 'Centrifugal and centripetal forces in urban geography' also appeared in the same year. In the field of urban geography this was his only published paper, yet it is undoubtedly the most cited of all his writings. Furthermore, this field was the one in which he occupied the most commanding position in terms of the number of doctoral dissertations supervised and in the contributions of his former students.

The culmination of this early period of major contributions to the field of geography was the presidential address before the association in 1935, entitled 'Changing currents of geographic thought in America'. This was his only published survey of the history of the field to which he devoted his life. Characteristically he traced the antecedents of geography as a discipline in the USA not to Europe, to which there is not a single reference (in contrast to Carl O. Sauer's *The Morphology of Landscape* (1925) which deals almost exclusively with geographical views abroad), but rather to the important American intellectual tradition growing out of the study and conquest of a spacious continent from which there arose much native geographical work before there was an American academic discipline of geography. He devoted himself particularly to the role of the great surveys of the land and its resources in the nineteenth century; to the crucial period at the beginning of the twentieth century with the founding of the association, the creation of university departments of geography, and the appearance of important professional geographical publications; to his view of the current state of various systematic fields of geography; and finally to the future of geography and planning. The last was prophetic since his own interest then turned to the use of geography in planning and in the understanding of international affairs by an informed public.

In 1935 Colby began a series of consulting positions with governmental agencies. He had had earlier experience during the First World War in the United States Shipping Board. Out of this experience grew his course in ocean trade and transportation and his practice of having students write one-page papers rigorously testing their ability to select and summarize effectively and succinctly. With the creation of the Tennessee Valley Authority came a new opportunity for geographers to demonstrate what they could do. With G. Donald Hudson and others he gave long and thoughtful attention to many problems of applied geography and to regional planning. Then in 1938 he became a member of the land committee of the National Resources Planning Board, out of which grew two of his most suggestive publications: *Land Classification in the United States* (1941) and *Area analysis: A Method of Public Works Planning* (1942),[11] in the writing of which he collaborated with scholars in other disciplines. During the Second World War he returned briefly to his old interest as a consultant to the war shipping administration.

In 1946 he served on the planning staff for the United Nations headquarters committee.

In 1942, with the retirement of Harlan H. Barrows, he became chairman of the department of geography of the University of Chicago.

Colby became Professor Emeritus at Chicago in 1949; but that was merely the beginning of a third cycle of interests, with visiting professorships at the University of Illinois in Urbana, the University of California, Los Angeles, and Michigan State University in East Lansing. In each he continued to stress the frontiers of geography and to stimulate graduate students to creative work. In 1951, he began an association with Southern Illinois University which led to his *Pilot Study of Southern Illinois* (1942).[12] He also directed the Kansas Basin Project at the University of Kansas (1955–6). From 1957 to his death in 1965 he directed the Mississippi Valley Investigations at Southern Illinois University. During this period he was closely associated with D. W. Morris, the president, in planning the growth of the university and the development of its regional research program.

Many honors and responsibilities came to Colby. He was an ideas man, whether in the classroom, in the discussion of possible dissertations with students, in professional meetings, or in consultation with governmental agencies or on public issues.

ROBERT S. PLATT, 1891–1964, *by R. Hartshorne*[13]

Robert Swanton Platt, Emeritus Professor of Geography at the University of Chicago, and a former president of the Association of American Geographers died in his home in Chicago on 1 March 1964.

He was born in an established and well-to-do family in Columbus, Ohio, on 4 December 1891, and he attended elementary schools in that city and in New England. He majored in philosophy at Yale, with a minor in history, and graduated in 1914. After a year at Yale-in-China,[14] where he was assigned to teach a variety of subjects, including geography, of which he had not heard since grade schooldays, he arrived at the University of Chicago to enter the department of geography as a student. Here he would continue, as he later said, to 'study geography through almost fifty years'.

The formal record of those years might seem only to indicate a quietly successful career. Appointed instructor in 1919, and

awarded the doctoral degree in 1920, he was advanced through
the ranks to full professor in 1939, and became chairman in
1949, serving until 1957, when he was named Emeritus Professor.

On the return to the USA, a traveling companion, having asked
about Platt's activities as a teacher in China, said: 'My
brother-in-law, Wellington Jones, who is teaching at the
University of Chicago, is interested in much the same sort of
thing. He calls it all Geography.' So the young teacher proceeded
directly to Chicago to investigate geography as a university
discipline and as a possible career.

At that time there was but one large and well-established
department of geography in the country, which was at the
University of Chicago. Rollin D. Salisbury, who was chairman
while Platt was a graduate student and with whom he later lived
in bachelor quarters, had brought together Harlan H. Barrows,
who succeeded him as chairman, J. Paul Goode, Walter Tower,
Wellington Jones, and Charles Colby and, for a part of each
alternate year, Ellen Churchill Semple. When Platt became a
member, in 1919, Tower had left, but Derwent Whittlesey also
had been added. It was a highly stimulating group in its diversity
of training, interests, and personality, but Platt continued to
learn much from each of the others and to become increasingly
attached to each in personal friendship.

In the field course which he conducted nearly every summer,
his wife Harriet joined him in planning and operating the
camp whenever possible; even their children, while still very
young, came camping also. Over the course of years the class
made field studies at a variety of different locations in the upper
Great Lakes region, north to James Bay, east and west along
the international boundary.

During the first half of his career, prior to the Second World
War, he made seven trips to Latin America, each one of from
two to six months' duration. On all but the first of these he
was accompanied by Harriet Platt, who assisted in the fieldwork,
especially in interviewing in Spanish. Traveling by boat and train
and, beginning in 1930 by plane, they made spot studies in rural
areas in most of the major regions of each of the Latin American
countries, including remote trading posts in the Indian area of the
Upper Amazon.

Reciprocally, the Platts made their large house in Chicago into
a veritable second home for a continual stream of students.

During the Second World War, Platt's services were sought by
the geographic sections of a number of federal agencies. In 1943

he served as adviser in the office of the geographer in the Department of State and in 1944–5 as chief of the division of maps of the Library of Congress.

After the war, the Platts had two further field trips to South America, in 1947 and 1948. On the first of these, he was consultant for the Conselho Nacional de Geografia of Brazil, studying proposed sites for the new federal capital. On the second he concentrated on the problems of Tierra del Fuego. In the 1950s, however, Platt shifted his interest to western Europe, particularly West Germany, where he spent a number of terms, intermittently, as a visiting professor at the universities in Frankfurt and at Saarbrücken, engaged in field research on the Dutch-German and Saarland borders, and lectured in other European universities. Then in 1961, at the age of seventy, he and Harriet set out on a second Fulbright research appointment to the University of Dacca, in Pakistan, as part of a worldwide project of comparative study in occupance of tropical lands. . . .

In the decade immediately following Platt's completion of his formal training, American geographers were engaged in vigorous discussion concerning the nature and purpose of their subject and the appropriate methods of study. Platt, who had majored in philosophy as an undergraduate, attended almost every meeting of the group of Midwestern geographers who, beginning in 1923 and continuing for some fifteen years, met each spring for several days in the field primarily to consider and experiment with methods of field study and thereby also to discuss a wide range of methodological questions. Even before, on his first trip to the West Indies, Platt had found the then prevailing concept of environmentalism inadequate to explain the striking contrasts in human geography observed in areas of similar natural conditions. Again, in 1931, in the two papers on the Argentine Pampas, he emphasized the variety of occupance forms found in an area notedly homogeneous in natural environment. The direct methodological attack in the papers on 'Environmentalism' and 'Determinism' of 1948 were the result of many years of consideration.

More commonly, however, his published discussions of points of view and method in geography were positive in tone. When convinced of value for geography, his purpose was to offer them to others, not with intent to challenge the methods others used, or even to suppose that his was more than one of numerous useful methods.

Although recognizing that there was room and need for a wide range of interests among the workers in geography, for himself Platt saw geography as an approach to the overall problem of mutual understanding of the peoples of the world. Human geography was therefore to be viewed, in Mark Jefferson's words, 'not as the study of earth and man but as the study of man using and living on the earth'. His interest therefore was not in any one continent, but rather in all parts of the inhabited lands, perhaps most especially in areas where man lives with maximum difficulties in the nature of the earth.

However they might differ in statement of the purpose of their field, it was the widespread conviction among American geographers of the formative period of the 1920s that one essential method of studying the subject was by direct observation in the field. This conclusion was no doubt automatic for one who had first discovered geography in the countryside of China and who up to his death continued to look forward each year to working somewhere in the field, preferably in foreign areas not previously visited. Like many of his colleagues of the period, but perhaps in greater degree than others, Platt's substantive writings were built upon field studies. Conversely, if he contributed more published discussion of fieldwork than did others, his writings reflect oral discussions in which all were engaged.

In these discussions, he explained the concern for development of field techniques which led to the spring field meetings beginning in 1923. The geographers of that period were familiar with geological and botanical field techniques and with those of military mapping, which Platt as an infantry officer in 1918 had taught in army camps in this country. But these were not directed toward securing data on man's use of his habitat. What field techniques could be developed that were congenitally geographic and sufficiently systematic and precise to lift field study above the level of subjective impressions from casual travel and of inference from postulated theory? In the face of the great multiplicity of elements of interest to the regional geographer, and the resultant complexity of regional geography, and the resultant complexity of regional variations, the field geographer faced two major problems.

The first was the problem of how to determine which data of all that might be observed should be selected for study. In general, Platt concluded, attention must be

focused on a coherent group of things under an organizing theme. The theme chosen concerns the areal pattern of occupance made by human endeavor in the earthly setting, the enterprise of people living and making a living in this place, directed by human will.

Even with this degree of focus of attention, the fieldworker will find a multiplicity of things to observe and about which to enquire, even at any one viewing point. How then can he hope to attain comprehension of large regions while seeing at once only a small area? The discussions and experiments of the spring field group, as developed and published particularly by Carl Sauer, Wellington Jones, and Vernor Finch, had led to a form of regional geography which came to be called, and frequently misunderstood, microgeography. As Platt described this method he would say: 'One must start with the large view, then treat with the small, and then return to the large again.' And he wrote in the introductory statement of his 1933 paper, the method involves

> detailed work in a very small area combined with reconnaissance over a great area. The intensive field work deals with intimate details, the extensive reconnaissance places the small area in the large, and spreads the detailed findings to build up regional generalization.

In the selection and treatment of the small area, however, Platt's principle of focusing on the areal pattern of human occupance led him to the concept of areal units conditioned not by uniformity, or homogeneity of character, but rather by functional organization of human activity. This concept, which represents perhaps his most distinctive contribution to American geography, appeared first in the Ellison Bay study of 1928 and was illustrated in varying form in each of the studies made with his field classes, as published during the period 1928–35. Though explained, if but briefly, in several of these studies, it was largely overlooked during the period when regional geography was dominated by emphasis on the visible landscape. Ultimately, however, the concept as transmitted by his students was recognized, even though with new terminology, in the treatment of the regional concept in *American Geography: Inventory and Prospect*. Platt's fullest presentation of the concept is to be found in the two chapters concerned with the 'geography of areal organization' in his 1959 volume on *Field Study in American Geography*.

In the studies made with his field classes, the level of unit of area was that of a community as defined 'by its trade bounds', to be determined by enquiry in the field. Most of the field studies in

Latin America are focused on units at a still lower level, 'on basic units of human occupance, chiefly on rural units of economic organization'—individual plantations, ranches, farms, or mines. Over ninety such spot studies (of which about half had not previously been published) are included in the volume on Latin America and constitute over two thirds of its contents. Through these the reader is projected directly into the areas under consideration and provided with the local details which elsewhere in the book are woven into regional generalizations. The entire work is therefore to be considered as a contribution to geographic method, demonstrating techniques in field approach to regional understanding.

In subsequent years Platt was repeatedly concerned with testing the utility of his field approach in other areas and situations. In the course of his work in Latin America he had used it in a study of territorial dispute in the wilderness areas of the upper Amazon: in western Europe he applied it in studying political border zones in regions of long established human occupance. The study of the Dutch-German border was based on detailed investigations of twenty-two local units, most of them individual farms; the study of the Saarland border was based on the study of nine villages. The latter also represented a new experiment 'in the possibilities of field investigation in social geography.' Two years later he secured a Fulbright research appointment to Pakistan in order to try the technique in areas similar in climatic conditions to parts of Latin America but notably different in culture.

DERWENT STAINTHORPE WHITTLESEY, 1890–1956, by E. A. Ackerman[15]

The life of Derwent Stainthorpe Whittlesey, Professor of Geography at Harvard University, came to an end on 25 November 1956, as the result of a coronary thrombosis suffered on 20 November. Professor Whittlesey's death at the age of sixty-six seemed peculiarly untimely. His heart attack came when he was enjoying apparently excellent health, in the midst of his last year of teaching before retirement. He was planning a productive retirement, including completion of a major work on Africa that he had in preparation, the publication of results of years of study in the Boston metropolitan area, and graduate geography instruction in the program of regional studies at the Massachusetts

Institute of Technology. And always there would have been further travel.

These plans for well-filled and productive years of retirement were characteristic of Derwent Whittlesey's entire life. Born of Connecticut Yankee stock near Rockford, Illinois, in 1890, he was distinctly a product of the American Midwest. Besides the Midwestern farming community he knew as a boy, it was the Midwest of the historian Ferdinand Schevill, of the novelist Robert Herrick and the poet Carl Sandburg, of the architect Frank Lloyd Wright and the geologist Rollin D. Salisbury, all of whom Whittlesey knew and appreciated. It was also the Midwest of international thinking, found at the University of Chicago from the time of President Harper on.

These marks of the environment of his youth, the days of his university training, and his early professional life set the course for a broad and varied intellectual career and personal life. His first college training was at Beloit College, Wisconsin, whence after two years he went to the University of Chicago. His first professional interest was history, in which he received a master's degree at Chicago in 1915. After a brief career as historian (Denison University, Ohio, 1915–16), courses with Harlan Barrows and Ellen Semple, again at the University of Chicago, aroused an immediate enthusiasm for geography. His pursuit of the subject was interrupted by the First World War, during which he served both as an enlisted man and as a commissioned officer. He returned to Chicago to take his Ph.D. degree in history and geography in 1920 and then was the first staff addition to the Chicago department of geography after Professor Barrows became chairman in 1919. He served in the department from 1920 to 1928, first as instructor and last as associate professor. This was the outstanding department of geography at the time, including Harlan Barrows; J. Paul Goode, Wellington D. Jones, Charles C. Colby, Robert S. Platt, Whittlesey, and Ellen Semple (visiting professor on occasion). A formative experience for Whittlesey during this period was his close association with Wellington Jones, with whom he prepared the well-known text *An Introduction to Economic Geography* (1925).

From Chicago, Professor Whittlesey went to Harvard to undertake the development of a new program in human geography there. In this he accompanied Professor Raoul Blanchard of Grenoble University, France, who went to Harvard at the same time on a half-yearly basis. Whittlesey was soon joined at Harvard by Harold S. Kemp, also of Chicago, who remained with him as colleague and friend.

As a professional geographer Whittlesey will perhaps be best remembered for his contributions to political geography. He was among the first geographers in the United States to develop political geography as an academic subject of teaching and research. With his sound background in the historical method and his fund of historical information, he soon became an outstanding figure in the field. His political geography was the study of the areal differentiation of political structure and events. In it he set guide lines that have influenced the development of the field ever since. The major record of this thought and work is his *The Earth and the State*, first published in 1939. Whittlesey's political geography was a professional reflection not only of his keen sense of the major currents of professional geographers' thought but also of his international viewpoint and a cultured mind well stocked with historical knowledge.

His knowledge of, and respect for, the written record of history were balanced by an avid cultivation of field study. He was an active member of the original and influential Midwestern spring field group, which met annually for many years to discuss and develop methods of improved field observation, recording, and interpretation. Throughout his career, field study on both microgeographic and macrogeographic scales was essential to the standards of professional accomplishment he had set himself. It ranged from his twenty-five years of close study and teaching of changing land use in the Boston metropolitan area, through his many visits to Europe, to his extensive travels on the African continent.

Whittlesey's analyses and interpretations of political geography centered on the cradle of modern history, Europe. As befitted his non-European citizenship and residence, his interest was equally strong in the parts of the world that had been closely connected with Europe in the recent past. This accounted for his thirty-five-year study of Africa, and for a period of extensive travel in Latin America.

Because of this broad but coherent pattern of study, Whittlesey was rapid and sure in his detection of the sound currents of scholarship in political geography as distinguished from the fads and aberrations. He was among the first to appraise *Geopolitik* and its descendants in the setting that history has since accorded them. Some of his more important views, first expressed to students, were recorded in *German Strategy of World*

Conquest (assisted by Charles C. Colby and Richard Hartshorne, 1942) and subsequent secondary works.

Whittlesey's deep and lifelong cultivation of political geography still left him time for significant and lasting contributions in several other phases of geographic study. His introduction and development of the 'sequent occupance' technique of analysing and presenting historical geography will be remembered by geographers, city planners and regional planners. Reflecting knowledge and interests influenced by his youthful environment, he joined Wellington Jones in developing the first regional classification of agriculture that employed consistent agricultural criteria. Throughout his career he was also known as an incisive thinker on the structure of regions. His leadership in this subject was exemplified in the preparation of 'The regional concept and the regional method' (for *American Geography: Inventory and Prospect*), on which he spent a year of his research time. He did much to clarify and to establish the scholarly usefulness of the concepts that are involved in chorography, ecumene, and nodal region.

Whittlesey also served his profession with distinction and devotion as editor of the *Annals of the Association of American Geographers*. For twelve years (1930–42), during a formative period in American geography, his patient reading and perceptive editorial eye guided many a colleague into noteworthy contributions to the field. For him editing was creative effort. The editing of Richard Hartshorne's *The Nature of Geography* was illustrative of his attitude. According to the author, Whittlesey's vision prompted the initial research, his encouragement and suggestion helped the intricate study to take shape, and his planning made the printed publication finally possible.

His service to the Association also included years as councillor and as president (1944). The association recognized him further by selecting him as its first honorary president (1954).

18

Ellen Churchill Semple, 1863-1932, by C. C. Colby[1]

'Man is a product of the earth's surface. This means not merely that he is a child of the earth, dust of her dust; but that the earth has mothered him, fed him, set him tasks, directed his thoughts, confronted him with difficulties that have strengthened his body and sharpened his wits, given him his problems of navigation or irrigation, and at the same time whispered hints for their solution.'

Influences of Geographic Environment, page 1.

'As the Tropics have been the cradle of humanity, the Temperate Zone has been the cradle and school of civilization. Here nature has given much by withholding much. Here man found his birthright, the privilege of the struggle.'

Influences of Geographic Environment, page 635.

In 1897, with a modest article on 'The Influence of the Appalachian Barrier Upon Colonial History.' Ellen Churchill Semple made her initial contribution to American geography. In 1931, in her volume, *The Geography of the Mediterranean Region*, she presented her last and greatest work. Between those years lie three and a half decades of distinguished service to geography. At the beginning of this period she was a young, untried, and unknown student but recently returned from study in a foreign university. At the end of that period she was one of the most widely known and most beloved personalities in American geography, and had become the greatest anthropogeographer in the world.

Ellen Churchill Semple came from a fine family and lived her girlhood in an atmosphere of wealth and refinement. She was born in 1863 in Louisville, Kentucky, during the stirring days of the Civil War. Her father, Andrew Bonner Semple (1805–75), came to Louisville from Pittsburgh in 1835 in order to found a wholesale hardware business under the firm name of A. B. Semple & Bro.—later A. B. Semple & Sons. The business prospered and thus the family was able to give the children good schooling, an abundance of books, and a healthy, well-ordered life. Ellen Churchill was born relatively late in the married life of her parents, her father being fifty-eight and her mother forty-one when she was born. Her mother, Emerin Price (1822–1904), was an exceptionally gifted woman of rare charm. Of her, Miss Semple's brother, Frank J. Semple, writes, 'It was her brilliant mind, her untiring energy and her ambition for her children that was reflected in Ellen's accomplishments.' Ellen Churchill's father died when she was twelve years old and from that time her education was directed by her mother.

To the good health, good breeding, and cultivated bearing assured by her family and her girlhood surroundings, Miss Semple's years at Vassar College added vigorous training and stimulating experiences. By the 1870s Vassar College had attained a widespread reputation for the high quality of its work and its student body was drawn from many parts of the country and even to a small extent from other countries. As a result, Miss Semple came to know a cosmopolitan group of young women. This experience broadened her social horizon, while the training she received in the classics, in English composition, and in history gave her habits of work which subsequently proved invaluable. She took her bachelor's degree in 1882 at the age of nineteen and was the valedictorian as well as the youngest member of her class. After teaching in her sister's private school in Louisville for several years she returned to Vassar for her master's degree in 1891.

Of the period between her degrees at Vassar, not much is recorded in the numerous biographical publications in which Miss Semple is listed. The period is important, however, in its bearing on her subsequent career. It taught her, for example, that social life, while pleasant, did not and could not command her full and continued interest. She tried teaching for a time but soon learned that teaching alone was not sufficiently challenging for a mind as active as hers. During this period she was stimulated by close association with the professional and literary men and women who then were making history at Louisville. Frequent discussions with two widely read and cultivated lawyers and a brilliant Jewish Rabbi gave her an increasing interest in social problems and social distributions. She read sociology, economics and such fragments of geography as came to hand. Either in this reading or during the work for her master's degree at Vassar she came in contact with the writing of Friedrich Ratzel, whose brilliant work at Leipzig was attracting widespread interest. In the summer following the completion of her work for her master's degree, she went abroad with her mother and in England met a young American student who had studied with Ratzel and reported enthusiastically about his work. Instead, therefore, of returning to America with her family she went on to Leipzig to study with Ratzel. Women students at that time were almost unknown in German universities and Ratzel was more or less nonplussed at her presence. She persisted, however, and although she was not permitted to matriculate she heard Ratzel's lectures and attended his seminar.

Her work with Ratzel proved to be the turning point in her career. Contact with his masterly mind first quickened her interest and then brought the conviction that here was the point of view, the discipline, for which she had been seeking. She remained in Leipzig for a year and a half, reading with new interest, studying with a new intensity. She returned to America for a time, but in 1895 again went to Leipzig for further work with Ratzel. This time she was welcomed as a fellow student in a chosen field. Of her high opinion of Ratzel and his work, all her American students are familiar. At the time of his death in 1904 she wrote:

> His great achievement was in anthropogeography, which he was the first to raise to the rank of a science . . . his name will always be associated with the science of anthropogeography, as Adam Smith's is with that of political economy.

If Ratzel raised anthropogeography to a science, Semple illuminated its pages with work which has high artistic values as well as sound scientific qualities. She gave the science, moreover, a needed content and effectively promoted its acceptance as a field of enquiry.

Upon her return to America, Miss Semple began active work in her chosen field. From the time of the appearance of her first article in 1897, her publications of important dimensions averaged more than one a year for the remainder of her life. Three of these were books of major significance. In the early period of her work she confined herself exclusively to articles for the standard geographical publications. The first six, in large measure, were based on secondary source materials and were

notable mainly because they introduced the anthropogeographical
method into the American journals and to American students.
In these early contributions she gained surety in her discipline,
greater facility in her writing, and contact with the American
geographical audience. It remained, however, for her study of
'The Anglo-Saxons of the Kentucky Mountains', published in
the *Geographical Journal* in 1901, to establish her as an
outstanding contributor to geography. In this study she
demonstrated her ability to work effectively in the field. She went
on horseback into the then little-known and inaccessible area of
eastern Kentucky and brought out a study which takes high
rank among the geographical articles in the English language.
Probably this brief article has fired more American students to
interest in geography than any other article ever written. The
appearance of this study forecast in happy fashion the highly
favorable reception accorded her first book upon its publication
in 1903. This volume, *American History and Its Geographic
Conditions,* closed the first distinctive period of her productive
work and established its author in a distinctive place in
American geography. It was widely read and discussed and,
like many other departures from traditional treatment, involved
its author in several interesting and stimulating controversies
with workers in other fields. The book won wide acceptance as
a text in courses in the historical geography of the USA and still
is in active use.

After the appearance of her first book Miss Semple's sphere
of influence broadened notably. She had become a person of
importance and was in demand. In 1906 Professor R. D. Salisbury
invited Miss Semple to act as visiting lecturer for a quarter in
the newly established department of geography at the University
of Chicago. Miss Semple's work was enthusiastically received
and she continued to lecture at Chicago practically every
alternate year until 1924. Her work was particularly helpful in
broadening the horizon and in firing the interest of graduate
students launching into their geographical work. Many men
and women now prominent in American geography recall
Miss Semple's work as a milestone in their training.

During all these years, however, Miss Semple continued her
research and writing and was loath to take much time from these
activities. In the interval from 1904 to 1911 inclusive she
published eleven articles and one book, this interval constituting
the second period of her career. The articles included two
notable studies based on fieldwork in the lower St Lawrence

area and three philosophical studies dealing with the interrelation of geography and history. The period was climaxed by the appearance of *Influences of Geographical Environment* in 1911. This great volume had been undertaken originally at the instigation of Professor Ratzel, who, sometime before his death in 1904, asked Miss Semple to translate into English or to restate in English his great work *Anthropo-Geographie*. Miss Semple found this impracticable, however, because Professor Ratzel's German text does not lend itself to translation, because her work was carrying her beyond the scope of Ratzel's volume, and because she wished to eliminate the organic theory of state and society which permeates the *Anthropo-Geographie*. Following some preliminary study, therefore, Miss Semple decided to write in English a volume along the general lines of Ratzel's book, using the original as much or as little as was found desirable. She set up a new organization, introduced the documentation which had been lacking in the original, added much evidence to support and clarify the original contentions, eliminated some sections and reduced the scale of others, added new chapters and new concepts based on her own research, and, in fact, produced a volume which, although it carries the spirit of the master, is in reality a new, larger and more authoritative work in the same general field. In this volume Miss Semple proved her command of and leadership in the philosophical aspects of anthropogeography, demonstrated the breadth of her scholarship, and produced a volume of enormous value to students of geography and of human affairs.

Following the exacting work on her second book, Miss Semple took a long-contemplated trip around the world. She visited Japan, China, the Philippines, Java and India and reaped great pleasure and profit from her experiences. Through a girlhood friend, Frances Little of *The Lady of the Decoration* fame, and two Japanese women who were her classmates at Vassar, she saw Japan under highly favorable circumstances. Of the latter, one had become the wife of an admiral of the Japanese navy while the other, Princess Oyama, was the widow of a former head of the Japanese army. Through the influence of Princess Oyama, Miss Semple was shown official courtesies which greatly aided her investigation of Japanese conditions. The results of these special studies are embodied in two brilliant articles, the one dealing with Japanese agriculture, and the other with Japanese colonial methods. In the former she utilizes her

amazing power of description in a highly effective portrayal
of both the static and the dynamic aspects of landscape. This
article later was translated into Japanese and published in a
Japanese magazine.

The publication of *Influences of Geographic Environment*
added materially to Miss Semple's reputation both at home and
abroad. Evidence of this is found in an invitation to lecture in
the summer term of Oxford University in England in 1912. Her
work there was so well received that she was asked to return in
the summer of 1914. Following her lectures at Oxford in 1912
she lectured before the Royal Geographical Society in London,
there presenting for the first time the results of her study of
Japanese agriculture. In November and December she appeared
before the Royal Scottish Geographical Society in Edinburgh,
Glasgow, Dundee and Aberdeen.

Following her return from Europe Miss Semple lectured at
Wellesley College in the academic year 1914–15 and at the
University of Colorado in the summer of 1916. She enjoyed these
experiences, for they brought her new contacts and gave her a
necessary change of pace. The year 1915 is notable, for it
witnessed the appearance of her first article dealing with the
Mediterranean. Just when she decided to write her book on the
Mediterranean probably was not known even to herself, but
certainly the appearance of this article shows that she was
actively at work on the great project as early as 1915. Her
interest in the area, however, was displayed much earlier, for in
two of her early magazine articles she deals at some length with
the maritime activities and territorial expansions of the Phoenicians,
Greeks and other peoples of the ancient Mediterranean. From
1915 on, the Mediterranean claimed the major portion of her
time and interest. She traveled widely in the area and worked in
the great libraries of Rome, Paris and London gathering
material for the volume. The work on this book constitutes the
third period in her productive career.

Miss Semple's work, like that of most other scholars, was
interrupted during the period of American participation in the
First World War. In the autumn of 1917 she gave a course of
lectures on the geography of the Italian front to officers at Camp
Zachary Taylor (Louisville, Ky.). From December 1917 to
December 1918 she made special studies of the Mediterranean
region and Mesopotamia for the 'Bureau of Enquiry for the
Peace Terms Commission.' Headquarters for this work were
maintained in the building of the American Geographical

Society on upper Broadway, New York. This close proximity to
Columbia University made it practicable for her to lecture there
during the summer session of the university in 1918. After the
war she returned to her research and writing and in 1920, 1922,
1923, and 1924 again taught at the University of Chicago.

In 1921 Miss Semple became Professor of Anthropogeography
in the school of geography then being established by President
W. W. Atwood at Clark University. She continued as a member
of that faculty until her death. Her professorship gave her a
sense of academic attachment which she had come to prize.
She quickly sensed the opportunities and the responsibilities of
the new school and carried on her part of the programme with
great zest and high skill. She found much stimulation in the work
and in discussions with her colleagues and had high praise for
them and their work. She was given complete freedom as to
what she taught and how much she taught. Commonly she
offered her courses and worked in the seminar during the first
semester and gave her attention to research and writing during
the second half of the year. She taught only in the graduate
school, regularly offering *Anthropogeography, The Geography
of the Mediterranean,* and *The Geography of Europe,* and
occasionally *Southeastern Asia* and *The History of Geography.*
At Clark she came into her full powers as a teacher and as a
director of research. Fortunate indeed were the students who
worked under her effective direction. She was a rigorous
taskmaster but gave freely of her time and energy. She possessed
the ability to bring out the best efforts of her special students
and guided their progress in her own inimitable way.

Although during the last decade of her life, Miss Semple's
thoughts and efforts centred on her Mediterranean work and her
interest and enthusiasm in the subject grew with each passing
year, she found time to accept a limited number of lecture
invitations. She gave a distinguished series of lectures at Vassar
College, a recognition from her Alma Mater which she prized
greatly. She appeared in special series of lectures before the
department of geology and geography at the University of
Michigan and also lectured at the University of Kentucky and
several other colleges and universities. In 1925 she taught during
the second semester at the University of California at Los Angeles
and found the change from the rigors of the New England
winter a gratifying relaxation.

In the late autumn of 1929 Miss Semple was stricken with a
serious heart attack. As a result of this affliction she was in a

hospital in Worcester continuously until the following summer. For weeks running into months her colleagues and friends despaired of her life, and none thought she would be able to finish her book on the Mediterranean. They reckoned, however, without the indomitable spirit of her courageous mind. Bit by bit she fought her way back to activity again. By summer she was working in bed on a schedule of two hours per day at most. In September she was moved to a home facing Clark campus and there, still working in bed, Miss Semple not only continued her work on the Mediterranean manuscript but began a revision of *American History and Its Geographic Conditions.* In this revision she had the active co-operation of her colleague, Clarence F. Jones, and with his aid the project was completed and announced for publication in 1933. Miss Semple remained in Worcester during the winter and spring of 1931 but in early summer was moved to comfortable quarters at Petersham, Massachusetts. There, with the assistance of a former student in the documentation and editorial phases of the work, she endeavored to complete the Mediterranean volume. Progress was slow but finally the task was finished—the great work completed. No more courageous page has been written into the annals of American science or of American letters. In October of 1931 Miss Semple became strong enough to be taken south. She remained at Asheville, North Carolina, for a time and then went to West Palm Beach, Florida, where she died on 11 May 1932.

In spite of a life replete with arduous work and high accomplishment, Miss Semple found time for a wide circle of friends. They were drawn from all walks of life and included senators, governors, lawyers, physicians, businessmen, writers, actors, artists, scientists and many others. She was welcomed in many circles and was much sought after by men and women of affairs. Professionally she knew and corresponded with eminent men and women in practically all centers where geographical science is represented. Everywhere she was honored for her eminent achievements, respected for her honesty of purpose, and welcomed for her facile mind and her attractive personal qualities.

Miss Semple was a charter member of the Association of American Geographers. Her first appearance on the programs of the association was at the Chicago meeting of 1907 where her title read 'Oceans and enclosed seas: a study in anthropogeography'. Subsequently she appeared on seven other programs, her final paper being read for her at the Worcester

K

meeting in 1930. She served a term on the council of the association and was president at the Washington meeting in 1921. She received many honors both at home and abroad. In 1914 the American Geographical Society conferred upon her its Cullum Gold Medal 'for her distinguished contributions to the science of Anthropogeography'. At its June convention in 1923 the University of Kentucky honored Miss Semple with its LL.D. degree—a recognition highly appropriate from her home State. The university, moreover, has established in its new library building an Ellen Churchill Semple Room, where Miss Semple's large private library is housed. One of her final honors was the award by the Geographic Society of Chicago of the Helen Culver gold medal, the inscription on which reads, 'To Ellen Churchill Semple for distinguished leadership and eminent achievement in geography.'

Ellen Churchill Semple played a distinctive role in American geography. She was one of the small but distinguished group whose pioneer work established geography on a firm and lasting foundation in this country. She brought to geography personal qualities which were the outgrowth of a distinguished family, a youth spent in cultivated surroundings, a long period of thorough training and a broad and varied experience. Many a friend and many a student has profited by her possession of these personal qualities. She graced the meetings as well as adorned the programs of the association. She was loyal to her friends, her students, her colleagues, and her science. She introduced anthropogeography to America and by her work enriched the literature of geography enormously. She possessed a distinctive style of writing—a style which gave her work high literary as well as scientific merit. She attained a position of leadership in her chosen field and used her leadership wisely for the advancement of the science which she loved.

19

Ellsworth Huntington, 1876-1947

Ellsworth Huntington was a giant of his era and it is fitting that a full biography should have been recently written by Geoffrey J. Martin (with a foreword by Arnold J. Toynbee) in 1973—after the writing of this chapter. I include in this appraisal a memorial by S. S. Visher; a critical appraisal by O. H. K. Spate (comparing *Mainsprings of Civilization* with Toynbee's *Study of History*); and a brief personal concluding paragraph. The reader is referred both to any one of Huntington's books (preferably *Mainsprings of Civilization*) and to Martin's biography for a fuller appreciation of this great scholar's style and productivity.

A MEMORIAL,
by S. S. Visher[1]

Few geographers or other scientists have left as wide and provocative an impress on the world's thought about the world as has Ellsworth Huntington. The scale of his work was large and bold. His was the 'search for broad interrelationships, for tendencies, for a world view', and a seeking for the 'architectural unity' of the world's structure. Huntington's eagerness to share his findings with others, his indefatigable energy, and a superlative facility for written communication gave him an audience almost as far-reaching as the scope of his work. Several of his volumes have been translated into other languages, and something of his work was known to the intelligentsia of all countries.

Ellsworth Huntington was born in a parsonage in Galesburg, Illinois, on 16 September 1876. He attended high school in Maine and Massachusetts, and college at Beloit, Wisconsin, from where he was graduated in 1897.

His adult life may be roughly divided into four periods. From 1896 to 1905, his work was largely in geology. While attending

Beloit, he spent a summer in the field for the Wisconsin Geological
Survey, and his first paper (1897) was judged a substantial con-
tribution. Upon graduation he became an instructor in Euphrates
College, Harput, Turkey, remaining there until 1901. His summer
vacations were filled with field studies, including the first scientific
exploration of the canyons of the Euphrates River. He left Asia
Minor in 1901 to study two years at Harvard, largely under
William Morris Davis. At Davis's recommendation, Andrew
Carnegie financed Huntington in nearly two years of exploration
in Turkestan and Persia with the Pumpelly expedition.

Early in his professional career Huntington evidenced an interest
in climate. While twenty-three years of age, he wrote two studies
which were published in *The Monthly Weather Review*, and his
observations of the influence of climate in western and central Asia
soon made this his chief interest.

From 1905–22, Huntington concentrated on climate and weather
and their influences. His orderly mind and his concern for
pervading patterns responded to the challenge of the big theme
represented by climate.

At the beginning of this second period of his professional life,
another Asian expedition, about eighteen months long, in 1905–6,
took Huntington to India and Tibet, from where he returned by
way of Siberia and Russia. This trip was financed by a Harvard
classmate, Robert Barrett. *The Pulse of Asia* (1907) resulted, and
aroused widespread interest. It gave rise to the 'Huntington Theory,'
that there have been considerable changes of climate and that
these changes have profoundly influenced the history and nature
of civilization. A chapter of this book was accepted as his Ph.D.
thesis at Yale, and he became a faculty member there, to begin
an association that continued until his death.

In 1909, Huntington returned again to the Middle East, on an
eight-month expedition to the Syrian desert and Palestine—an
expedition partly financed by *Harper's* magazine. *Palestine and Its
Transformation* (1911) embodied results of this work. From
1910–13, he supplemented work initiated in the summer between
his student years at Harvard. This work took him into the south-
western USA, Mexico, and Central America, where his later
researches were concerned chiefly with archeological ruins and with
interpreting the story of past climates through studies of tree rings.
His tree-ring studies supplemented those initiated by the
distinguished astronomer A. E. Douglass of the University of
Arizona. Huntington's writings greatly stimulated interest in tree-
ring studies, and contributed to expanded opportunities in this

field. The south-western studies resulted in *The Climatic Factor as Illustrated in Arid America* (1914). This book was soon followed by the classic, *Civilization and Climate* (1915). Near the close of this period came *Climatic Changes. Their Nature and Causes* (1922), and *Earth and Sun* (1923).

During 1919, shortly before the death of S. W. Cushing, Huntington began his textbook writing with *The Principles of Human Geography*, 1920. Despite the steady volume of Huntington's original work, he wrote and revised a series of textbooks, each of which afforded freshness of approach, educationally valuable contributions and considerable popular interest, as well as pleasure and profit to students.

In the third period of Huntington's work, 1923–8, he emphasized the great influences on civilization of selective migration, selective survival, and intermarriage among culturally homogeneous groups. His presidential address (1923) before the Association of American Geographers (of which he was a charter member) keynoted the theme of selective influences, and in *The Character of Races* (1924), he made it a permanent part of the world's literature.

In 1923, Huntington extended his already extensive first-hand observations of the world. He was appointed an official delegate to the Pan-Pacific Scientific Congress in Australia. He spent weeks en route in Japan, Korea, China and Java, and traveled widely in Australia. His observations were summarized in *West of the Pacific* (1925); this and *Palestine and Its Transformation* are considered by many as gems of descriptive geography. Other observations found their way into *The Human Habitat* (1927), in which are found some of the most fascinating, clearly reasoned, short papers in geography.

Although the last period of Huntington's life (1928–47) was marked by several new interests, it can appropriately be called a period of consolidation. He completed his foreign travels in 1928–30, using textbook royalties for the purpose. He traversed North Africa, going as far south as the equator. He traveled more than 10,000 miles in Europe by automobile, and visited the chief regions and cities of South America.

His interest in eugenics led to two books in this field. Concerning his *Season of Birth* (1938), the editor of the *Journal of the American Medical Association* stated: 'This remarkable book is one of fundamental importance in human biology and should be read by every physician.' Huntington also indicated interests in the

League of Nations and co-operatives in the latter years of this period.

His major effort in consolidating his observations and knowledge was *Mainsprings of Civilization* (1945). Here he brought together and elaborated upon numerous themes in a grand attempt to analyse the role of biological inheritance and physical environment in influencing the course of history. *Time* magazine (27 October 1947) declared it second only to Arnold J. Toynbee's classic in boldness of conception, breadth of scope and erudition, and literary attractiveness. He was at work on a further effort at consolidation, *The Pace of History,* when on the evening of 16 October 1947, he succumbed to a heart attack.

Huntington made a number of contributions to geographical theory, one of these being his theory that past climates have been characterized by significant changes which were irregular in occurrence, not simple cycles or progressive trends. Changes in the sun, he also contended, are a major cause of changes in terrestial climate, and climate profoundly influenced man, his culture, other forms of life, and geologic processes. Even weather in its relative evanescence has, through brief and erratic changes, affected man's energy, health and longevity, and his attitude and achievements. The stimulating influence of weather changes (storms) was first effectively presented by Huntington. The distribution of the various levels of civilization, he suggested, corresponds roughly with the climatic regions. The climate best suited to intellectual activities and progress is characterized by a well-defined seasonal pattern having frequent changes of weather and sufficient warmth and rainfall to permit extensive agricultural production. Civilization has tended to shift into cooler climates as mankind has advanced in his culture—a theory first announced by Herbert Spencer and later supported by S. C. Gilfillan and Huntington. In this movement of civilization toward colder regions, each of the chief crops and types of farm animals has improved in yield and quality (a latitudinal phenomenon apparently first observed by Huntington). Finally, there was his theory that selective migration and selective survival, together with intermarriage of people of relatively homogeneous cultures, have profoundly influenced the course of history.

In his effort to cover this large area of subject matter, Huntington produced an enormous volume of work. He was the author or co-author of 29 volumes, contributed chapters in 27 other books, and wrote more than 180 articles. Of these latter, more than a score were in periodicals of wide circulation, attesting to his interest in reaching a popular audience and his ability to do so. He was for many persons the world's outstanding geographer. His work was known and frequently cited not only by professional geographers of the world, but by many historians, sociologists, economists, agriculturalists, ecologists, climatologists and geologists.

In the course of Huntington's work he received many honors. His textbooks and other educational writings brought him the Distinguished Service to Geography Award of the National Council of Geography Teachers. He served as president of the Association of American Geographers, of the Ecological Society of America, and of the American Eugenics Society. He was a director of the Population Society of America, and an officer in several other organizations. He was associate editor of the *Geographical Review, Ecology, Economic Geography* and *Social Philosophy.* He was starred as a distinguished geologist in 'American Men of Science', 1921. Medals were awarded to him by leading British, French, and American geographical societies, and honorary doctorates by Clark University and Beloit College.

Although Yale University encouraged him to give his full time to research by making him a research associate (with the rank of professor) free from classroom duties, he conducted occasional seminars and supervised the thesis work of a number of students. He taught regular classes during one or two terms at Chicago, Clark, and Harvard, and gave series of lectures at several other universities.

The following excerpts from reviews of some of Huntington's books are of interest here.

Derwent Whittlesey, reviewing *Climatic Changes* in *Journal of Geography,* December, 1923, states: 'The volume forces the reader to extend his spiritual horizon and to orient his personal philosophy afresh.'

Concerning *Season of Birth.* C. E. P. Brooks said in *Meteorological Magazine* (London, 1938): 'Huntington has now proved that climate is of even greater importance with respect to birth than later in life.'

Jan O. M. Broek, reviewing *Principles of Economic Geography* in *Geographical Review,* October, 1941, makes the following observation:

One has to have respect for the breadth of interest, the stimulating ideas, and the interesting maps and cartograms. And, above all, there is a system behind it. Huntington is one of the few geographers who make a genuine attempt to give architectural unity to the world's economic structure. . . . I want to pay homage to an active mind. His work is not another compilation but an eminently readable creation, full of thought, [containing] little dogmatic reasoning but, on the other hand, many stimulating ideas and original maps. [It reveals] a search for broad interrelationships, for tendencies, for a world view.

Reviewing *Mainsprings of Civilization (Journal of Geography,* December, 1946), Ralph H. Brown wrote, 'Huntington is a lucid writer, unsurpassed in the skill of map interpretation. Read the book or any part of it and your intellectual horizon will be very greatly enlarged.' George H. T. Kimble wrote of that book (*Geog. Rev.* January, 1946): 'No other scientist has worked harder to get his opinions corroborated or been at greater pains to see the other side of the question.'

AN APPRAISAL,
by O. H. K. Spate

A critical appraisal of the work of Huntington by O. H. K. Spate appeared in 1952 in the *Geographical Journal*. It is focused on *Mainsprings of Civilization,* in comparison with Arnold Toynbee's *A Study of History,* and carries the subtitle 'A study of determinism'. The assessment may be summarized as follows:

(1) Huntington's avowed determinism is based too much on a part only of the 'immense complex of factors which have gone to the making of history'. He is aware of this, basing his interpretation of the regional variants of civilization on a selective appraisal of the biological and physical environmental determinants.

(2) He consistently follows a quantitative approach in the measurement of civilization, with startling value-judgements. This was evident in his early arrival (on the base of measured criteria) at the remarkable regional coincidence of weather conditions conducive to human physical and mental effort and the levels of assessment of civilization. The selection of criteria is very personal and subjective and the statistical aggregates of doubtful validity. Huntington himself, however, clearly states that the climatic determinant is only one of many others, listing 'heredity, stage of culture, diet, and other factors'. Yet he gives too much weight to

'physical factors', and too little to 'the autonomous development of societies'.

(3) The fundamental historical weakness in Huntington in his interpretation of civilization is his lack of sympathy, due to his insistence on 'scientific detachment'. Huntington writes: 'Unfortunately, no widespread statistics are available for such qualities as idealism, altruism, honesty, self-reliance, originality and artistic appreciation'. Yet he finds quantitative measures of these in literacy, education, the use of libraries, etc. This lack of sympathy is very evident in his 'ranking' of the world's religions, and his discussion at length of the relations between monotheism and the deserts of the Old World, whereas, argues Spate, 'great faiths have their own life and growth'.

(4) Huntington offers many striking correlations between weather cycles and human activity. But his observations contain 'trivialities, misconceptions, injudicious use of statistics, and dubious assumptions. Yet they form important contributions to the direct psycho-physiological influence of climate'.

I conclude this chapter with a personal comment. It is almost customary these days to play down the works of Huntington as 'naïvely deterministic'. This is an overt confession of ignorance of the substance and procedure of a great scholar who made prolific contributions to our knowledge of human societies.

K*

20

The Second Generation

For about twenty years after its birth, the department of geography at Chicago, which was mainly a graduate school, was without a rival. It was virtually the only source of doctorates which could lead and organize the new departments for undergraduate instruction and research that were established across the nation in teachers' colleges and universities in the 1920s. Until that date the membership of the professional Association of American Geographers consisted almost entirely of graduates from Chicago. It is not, therefore, surprising to find that many later leaders in these new centres, from UCLA and Berkeley to Harvard, from Peabody College, Nashville, to University of Washington in Seattle, were alumni of Chicago. Sauer was a student at Chicago. So were Atwood, Whittlesey and Ackerman, who were drawn to Harvard in the 1920s.

It was not until the mid-1920s that doctorates began to be awarded in the new centres. Most notable were Clark, Wisconsin, and Michigan. Berkeley, under Sauer, was a somewhat slower starter, in view of his exacting standards, but it produced outstanding scholars.

Geographically, if the placements of all graduate appointments in colleges and universities be located in the interwar period, it will be found that there were three territorial domains. Chicago spread its seed widely but there was a concentration of Chicago-trained people in the Middle West. Clark graduates were also widely scattered but with a concentration in the eastern institutions. Berkeley, after 1930, spread its graduates across the country, but with a concentration in the western states. These territorial concentrations remain essentially true to this day.

The outstanding contemporaries of this second generation reached their prime, like those leaders we have already discussed, in the 1930s. Their younger disciples who are now in or approaching retirement make up the third generation and will be considered in the next chapter. The former received the first doctorates in the new centres and contributed notably in their younger years to the advancement of their discipline especially in Berkeley, Wisconsin, Michigan, Chicago and Clark.

The senior members of the second generation contributed unevenly to the regional concept. They pursued research on the physical forms of the earth's surface—land forms, both as to process of development (Johnson) and categories, limits and orders in the USA (Bowman and Fenneman); on climates (Ward); and on vegetation and soils (Marbut and Shantz); and the modes of field recording of landscape features and their spatial arrangement, as spurred by Sauer (Finch). In the geographic study of man some sought to break from the search for consistent correlations with the physical environment. Notable were studies of agrarian systems and their distribution (Baker, Jones) and of the regional distribution of manufacturing. But morphological study of the humanized landscape—field patterns, roads, farms, villages, hamlets, towns, architecture—was slow, experimental, and, for the most part, superficial, or as one British critic observed, 'cryptic' (as in Britain), even among the younger members of the third generation. It is for this very reason that the researches of this kind by F. Kniffen on house types in Louisiana and J. Leighly on urban forms in central Sweden and medieval Livonia have been so important as indicators of research trends in Europe and as stimulants to further work in America.

The following are selected as leaders of the second generation, and their work appraised by contemporary colleagues in the following pages: R. DeCourcy Ward, C. F. Marbut, C. W. Thornthwaite, D. W. Johnson, W. W. Atwood, O. E. Baker and V. C. Finch. Each was a specialist in a particular field, but contributed substantially to the advancement of the regional concept.

ROBERT DeCOURCY WARD,
by W. M. Davis[1]

Robert DeCourcy Ward was born in Boston, Massachusetts, on 29 November 1867. His father had spent many years in business in Valparaiso, and had thus become so well known to the Chileans that he was appointed their consul at the court of Saxony at about the time of Robert's birth. Hence, when he was six months old he was taken to Dresden, where four years were spent. A year in Lausanne, Switzerland, followed, and there his father died. After a sojourn in England, his mother then brought him back to Boston, where he was at school for six years. Two more years were next passed at Dresden, and a good command of German was thus secured. Returning once more to Boston, he gave four years, 1881–5, to school before entering Harvard College in the class of 1889. His first summer vacation included a voyage to Madeira and the Azores on a sailing vessel, and he thus gained some practical acquaintance with the ocean and with the art of navigation.

Not until his third year in college did young Ward enter upon subjects of study that he had not sampled in his preparatory school. Davis's course in meteorology was one of his ventures at that time. The following year he extended the beginning he had made in the introductory course on meteorology by taking up special problems, among which were the reduction of observations on thunderstorms and sea breezes. After graduating *summa cum laude,* he spent a year abroad in Germany, Italy and Greece, then returned to Harvard in the autumn of 1890 to assume the position of an assistant, and took two half-year courses on meteorology and physical geography given by Davis.

After taking an MA in 1893 and editing the *American Meteorological Journal* from 1892 to 1896, he was put in charge of the course on meteorology in 1895. It was in 1897 that he married and made a wedding voyage around South America. He visited the southern continent in 1908 and 1910, and made a tour around the world in 1929. All these voyages were faithfully utilized as opportunities for gaining personal acquaintance with the climates of the areas he traversed. He was promoted to an assistant professorship in 1900 and to a professorship of climatology in 1910, a position which he held until his death.

An Appraisal
C. F. Brooks[2]

Professor Ward was an American pioneer in climatology. Others before him had explored American climates, established stations and summarized the observations. None, however, had taken this field for his life's work or sought to develop climatology as a science in the USA.

His early studies of the sea breeze and local thunderstorms are classics. Outstanding was his humanization of climatology, especially his insistence that climates be described not only in terms of temperature, rainfall and the other separate elements, but also in terms of the weather ensemble. It is the weather from day to day, from one storm period to the next, that constitutes climate.

Professor Ward's book, *The Climates of the United States* (1925), is a contribution to climatology which will be standard for many years to come.

Not long after *The Climates of the United States* was published a request came from Europe's veteran climatologist, Dr W. Köppen, and his associate Dr R. Geiger, for Professor Ward's collaboration in a new *Handbuch der Klimatologie* in five volumes. Ward was asked to undertake the preparation of text, tables and maps on the climatology of North America. This he did, and supervised the project during the next four years, finally finishing his last bit of text a month before his death.

It is a noteworthy tribute to Professor Ward's ability and care in writing that all four of his books are still the leaders in their respective portions of the field. And his contribution to the *Handbuch* bids fair to serve as the standard climate for many years to come. His first book, *Practical Exercises in Elementary Meteorology* (1899), led the way and is still the standby for teachers in elementary meteorology who are so fortunate as to have a copy available, since it is out of print. Next, his translations of the first general climatology volume of Hann's *Handbuch der Klimatologie* (1903) not only provided a comprehensive textbook, but collated the best of European climatology. This book greatly stimulated and improved climatology research in the US Weather Bureau.

As a companion volume to the Hann, Ward wrote *Climate, Considered Especially in Relation to Man,* which appeared in 1908.

CURTIS FLETCHER MARBUT, 1863–1935,
by H. L. Shantz[3]

Marbut began his scientific work as a geologist. The science of soils was practically unknown. Many chemists and physicists were interested in the materials from which soil is made, but study dealt with chemical content, physical or mechanical analysis, and with the geological origin of the material. A soil in the modern sense had not yet been recognized. Following the work of Hilgard, Marbut soon began to correlate soils and vegetation. One more step, the correlation of soils with vegetation and climate, completed the modern point of view and enabled soil science to establish itself as a separate field, independent of geology, with which it had been too closely affiliated.

America—with temperature belts running east and west and humidity belts running north and south—presented a very complicated pattern, and the recognition of close correlations with climate, vegetation and soils was extremely difficult. In Russia humidity and temperature run together, an ideal experimental situation. It is not surprising that the Russians first glimpsed the significance of the soil profile. Marbut immediately recognized in the work of Glinka a basic advance in soil science and set to work at once to translate the German's work into English. He knew no Russian at that time but set to work to learn that language, in order better to follow the works of Russian pedologists.

Our soils had been studied from a physical and mechanical and chemical and plant production point of view. Millions of acres had been surveyed and the soil types named. Marbut did not discard the good work already done but started slowly to interpret these types in terms of the new science. Together we pushed over large areas of the high plains, the grassland of the Canadian north-west and the deserts of California, Arizona, New Mexico, Texas, of Colorado, Utah, and Wyoming, planning many a paper on the correlation of vegetation types and soil types. We were both interested in the lack of a direct correlation, in the fact that in the high plains the north and south soil belt swung east of the vegetative belt in the north and west in the south. Desert soils, especially the frothy surface soil in the shad scale area in Utah, interested Marbut immensely. There was no thought of making a town for the night or of getting to a place to eat; the trips were for the purpose of seeing the country, determining the soil profile and collecting samples for studies.

Those who have visited the Ozarks can visualize to some extent the conditions of pioneer families in that region. Dr Marbut lived his early childhood working on the farm, and climbed about the Ozark hills, hunting, and fishing, when leisure permitted. He began his elementary education at the age of five from an itinerant teacher. Until he was seventeen he attended the little school through each short winter term of about four months. A small collection of books which his father had brought with him constituted his library. In 1881 at the age of seventeen he was granted his first certificate to teach in the district school. He entered the University of Missouri, where he was graduated with a bachelor of science degree in 1888. He was appointed a member of the Missouri State Geological Survey in 1890.

In 1893 he entered Harvard University and received a master of arts degree in geology in 1894. At that time he wrote a thesis which was later published in the *Missouri Geological Survey,* but did not receive his Ph.D. from Harvard since he was unable to return for his final examination.

He was instructor in geology and mineralogy in the University of Missouri from 1895 to 1897, assistant professor for the two years 1897–99, and professor and curator of the museum of geology from 1899 until 1910. During the latter part of this period, from 1905–10, he was director of the Soil Survey of Missouri. In 1909–10 he became special agent for the United States Bureau of Soils and from that time to the day of his death he was chief of the Division of Soils Survey.

The years 1899–1900 were spent traveling over much of Europe, chiefly on a bicycle, and in 1919 through central America, studying for the first time tropical soils. In 1923 and 1924 he studied the soils of the Amazon valley on an expedition organized by the department of commerce, which was studying rubber products, and with the aid of the American Geographical Society continued these studies into other parts of Brazil and Argentine. In 1930, aided by the American Geographical Society, he was enabled to study at first hand the soils of Russia. . . .

Dr Marbut served as an inspiration to all students of soils and students of general geography in the discussion and presentation of papers and in his willingness to see and discuss matters with all visitors in his office in Washington, as well as to the many people who at various times had the opportunity to accompany him on fieldwork. For a number of years he lectured for a month each year at the school of geography at Clark University, and in the graduate school of the United States Department of Agriculture, bringing inspiration and encouragement to a very large group of young geographers. While he was chief of the Soil Survey that organization mapped about half of the land area of the USA. This great mass of detailed material enabled Professor Marbut to make a final contribution of the utmost importance, for he combined into a single comprehensive volume on the soils of the USA a distinct picture of the soil resources of the whole nation. This has been published by the Department of Agriculture as Part III of the *Atlas of American Agriculture.* No man in the world was so well qualified to analyse and condense this material.

In the beginning his work extended and amplified the great work of that greatest of all soil scientists prior to his time Dr E. W. Hilgard, who lived from 1833 to 1915. Dr Hilgard's work laid the foundation in America for the further interpretation which has been given by Marbut. Hilgard's work up to the time that Marbut took charge of the Soil Survey had not sufficiently influenced that organization. Marbut, however, recognized that a soil is developed as a result of the interaction of climate and vegetation on the basic rock material and that over great belts soils will be similar notwithstanding the diversity of the basic material from which they have been developed.

At the University of Missouri he had already closely correlated soils and vegetations, for here you find the soils named from the type of vegetation which they support. Immediately recognizing the advance made by the Russians, he was able to take the accumulated materials reported by the then existing Soil Survey and give to this an interpretation in accordance with the new science. This was a matter which could not be accomplished rapidly, for public sentiment cannot easily be influenced and large numbers of men interested in soils and soil problems in the USA had approached the problem from the standpoint largely of physics, chemistry and geology.

Intensive work on Africa resulted in *The Vegetation and Soils of Africa* (1923), published jointly by the National Research Council and the American Geographical Society.

Until the publication in 1935 of the soil atlas of the USA, the material contained in this volume on Africa constituted the best assembled source for an understanding of the new science. As it stands it has served as a tremendous stimulus to younger workers in the field and has enabled them to approach their problem from the standpoint of the whole rather than details of local observation.

Marbut was chairman of the Land Inventories and Land Classification Committee from 1931 until 1933. Defining land used for plant production as 'the sum total of the factors of the geographic environment in which plants grow', the committee undertook the classification of different kinds of land on the basis of differences in capacity to grow plants, and arranged these units in such a way as to express gradation in this capacity.[4]

CHARLES WARREN THORNTHWAITE, 1899–1963, by *J. B. Leighly*[5]

In the first two years after his graduation Thornthwaite taught in a high school in Michigan, to help support his parents and younger siblings. In 1924 he entered the University of California for graduate work in geography. Thus he was one of Carl Sauer's early graduate students at Berkeley, receiving in 1930 the second Ph.D. in geography awarded by the university. At Berkeley he cultivated manual skill in drawing maps and experimented with map projections.

Thornthwaite went to the University of Oklahoma in 1927 as instructor in geography. His years at Oklahoma set the course he followed during the rest of his life. He had an interest in climate, and was familiar with the Köppen classification. But Köppen's definitions, which placed all of Oklahoma except the western Panhandle in the humid climates, did not agree with what Thornthwaite saw. He worked through the whole problem of defining climates, especially with reference to precipitation, from the beginning, and with an immense amount of labor devised his own system of classification in 1931.

In 1934 Thornthwaite left Oklahoma for a year's work with the Study of Population Redistribution at the University of Pennsylvania. His contributions to this study, *Internal Migration in the United States,* with its creative use of census material and its superb maps, and the chapter 'The Great Plains' in *Migration and Economic Opportunity,* in which foreshadowing his *Atlas of Climatic Types in the United States 1900–39* (1941), he emphasized fluctuations of climate, have a permanent value. In 1935, at the instigation of Carl Sauer, a division of climatic and physiographic research, with Thornthwaite as chief, was set up in the new Soil Conservation Service. He formulated many of the investigations carried out in his division in conversations with Sauer at Berkeley or in the field.

The climatic and physiographic division disintegrated in 1942. Thornthwaite spent some time in Mexico, making there the first application of his method of scheduling irrigation according to the water content of the soil. But during most of the war years he was a lonely figure in an office in the South Agriculture Building in Washington, collecting all the observations he could find of loss of water from land surfaces by evaporation and transpiration, and comparing them with climatic records. This prolonged and intense work led to the procedures and conclusions he published fragmentarily, and finally in the article 'An approach toward a rational classification of climate' (1948),[6] by far the most influential of his writings. Already in 1946, however, he had left Washington to become a consultant with Seabrook Farms in south-western New Jersey. Here he rendered invaluable service in synchronizing schedules of planting and harvesting vegetables with the growing season, in applying supplementary irrigation in accordance with his 'simple bookkeeping procedure' for keeping track of the water in the soil, and in disposing of waste water.

He established the Laboratory of Climatology, his crowning achievement, which became a self-supporting enterprise after the termination of his employment with Seabrook Farms. It realized, in part and temporarily, his dream of a research institute of climatology. . . . The laboratory became a Mecca for students of climate from all parts of the earth, and made Thornthwaite's name as widely known. It survives him as the operative agency of the corporation C. W. Thornthwaite Associates.

DOUGLAS W. JOHNSON, 1878–1944,
by J. K. Wright[7]

Douglas Wilson Johnson, for more than thirty years Professor of Geology at Columbia University, died in Sebring, Florida, on 24 February 1944, at the age of sixty-five.

Among the American geomorphologists who found guidance and inspiration in the teachings and writings of William Morris Davis, Professor Johnson was perhaps the closest akin in spirit to that great master. Not only did he devote his life to the study of the kinds of things in which Davis was primarily interested, but in many instances he carried further the investigation of the very problems on which Davis had worked. In 1909 he edited the well-known volume of Davis's studies entitled *Geographical Essays.* His greatest strength, like that of Davis, lay in the application of rigorous analytical procedures to the attempted solution of puzzling physiographic problems. His eight scientific books, his ninety-odd periodical articles and lesser works, and his policy in connection with the *Journal of Geomorphology* (1938–42), of which he was a founder and editor, bear witness to a sustained, conscious and deliberate concern for logical methods of thought and presentation. In his foreword to one of Johnson's books, Davis wrote as follows:

Two essays of historic importance should here be recalled : one is Chamberlin's exposition of the value of multiple working hypotheses; the other is Gilbert's address on the inculcation of scientific method by example; for the principles set forth in both these essays are admirably exemplified in Johnson's discussion.

He has given scrupulous care to the use of all the mental faculties employed in scientific analysis. Observable facts are first gathered in large number, and are critically compared, classed and generalized. Various alternative hypotheses explanatory of Appalachian evolution, each one hopefully representing a set of imagined conditions and processes in the past from which the observed facts of the present may reasonably follow, are then brought forward, and the consequences logically deducible from the assumed premises and the adopted postulates of each hypothesis are deliberately and ingeniously worked out.

These comments, made with reference to *Stream Sculpture on the Atlantic Slope* (1931), apply equally well to many another of Professor Johnson's studies.[8]

Professor Johnson's scientific writings might be grouped in four principal categories. First, and most representative of his essential intellectual qualities and tastes, are those dealing with specific physiographic problems—notably the books and articles on shore-line processes and development, on the evolution of the drainage pattern of the northern Appalachian region, and on the origin of the Carolina 'bays' and of submarine canyons, and the lesser publications on glacial forms, river capture, rock pediments in arid regions, and similar topics. The second category comprises several papers on scientific methods of research as such, particularly methods of analysis. These are directly complementary to the studies of the first type, many of which are drawn upon for examples to illustrate applications of method. The addresses and studies of the third category, which deal with the progress and status of geological or geographical research, are in turn, closely related to those of the second. Among them particular mention may be made of Johnson's address as president of the Association of American Geographers, in 1928, in which he called the geographical profession severely to task for an all too widespread superficiality In his opinion, 'any investigator who would do creative work [in geography] must make himself absolute master of at least one group of physical phenomena and one group of organic phenomena'. The conclusion was reached that, 'rightly conceived, geography is one of the most difficult and exacting of sciences'.

In the fourth category may be grouped Professor Johnson's studies of the relationship between the campaigns of the First World War and the physiographic features of the theatres of operation. These studies, set forth in *Topography and Strategy in the War* (1917), *Battlefields of the World War* (1921), and a number of articles, were in part the outcome of a special assignment when Johnson was a major in the military Intelligence division of the United States army. They are his only works of a scientific character in which anything but incidental attention is given to the correlation of human activities with the facts of the natural environment. Johnson was a geomorphologist first and foremost. Many of his researches, however, had a direct bearing on human problems. To quote from the citation on the occasion of the presentation to Professor Johnson of the American Geographical Society's Cullum Geographical Medal for 1935:

> Keenly conscious of science's obligation to society, he has given freely of his time and technical knowledge to undertakings concerned with the public welfare. The protection of the coast of New Jersey from the attacks of the sea, the continued need for which was again demonstrated only ten days ago; the settlement of the dispute about the boundary between Canada and Labrador; the co-ordination of the mapping services of the federal government with a view to expediting the completion of our topographic map—these are all problems that have had the benefit of his keen analysis and indefatigable search for truth.

Mention must be made of his love for France and his close affiliations with French colleagues. He served as Exchange Professor of Applied Sciences to French universities in 1923-4, and, as De Martonne says in his preface to a book of addresses delivered by Professor Johnson during this period (*Paysages et problèmes géographiques de la terre américaine,* 1927), few exchange professors to France have known such a success.

WALLACE A. ATWOOD, 1872–1949,
by S. Van Valkenburg[9]

Attempting to answer the question what made him choose geography at a time when graduate work in that field was still unknown, my thoughts go back to a talk I had with Atwood a few weeks before his death. He spoke to me at some length about the great men he had known, and before all of them he put Rollin D. Salisbury, his major professor at the University of Chicago. I quote from his notes on Salisbury's first field course in geology:

This was an adventure in education for him and for all the

class. I think it was the first systematic field course in geology in America. . . . The work was fascinating. The students were allowed to discover things themselves. Many days passed without any help in the field. We must discover the problems and go to work to solve them. We were like chemists working a laboratory with 'unknowns'—but what a laboratory! . . .

Several in this little party with Professor Salisbury found in the fieldwork inspiration and joy that guided them into professional careers. Hundreds of youths who worked with that man indoors and in the field were led to choose careers in which his lessons in geology were of basic significance. His training in exact thinking and exact expression was also of basic importance in their lives. He was a great teacher.

Wallace Atwood received his education at the University of Chicago, and it was also at this university that he was given his first important position. He was on the teaching staff from 1901 until 1913, rising from instructor to full professor in the geology department under Thomas C. Chamberlin and Rollin D. Salisbury. During his Chicago years he started his fieldwork in the Rocky Mountains, a work that he continued up to his death. Even in 1948, at the age of seventy-five, he again spent the summer in those mountains, checking and rechecking his results. Although his monograph on the San Juan Mountains was his largest purely scientific publication (1932), he wrote numerous technical articles in the field of physiography. In 1945 he contributed a popular volume on the Rocky Mountains to the American Mountain Series. In this book he tells much about the mountains he knew so well, about field research methods, and about himself that will interest the general reader.

In 1913, Atwood was called to Harvard to occupy the chair vacated by the retirement of William Morris Davis. It was while there that he became interested in the writing of grade-school textbooks, and from 1919 on he was the author and co-author of a long series of textbooks that carried modern geography into all corners of the USA. He consistently promoted and demonstrated the regional approach, both in his books and in the wall-map series prepared under his direction. On his deathbed he was still working at his writing; a new book planned but not completed was intended for use in junior high schools, *An Introduction to World Understanding—a social and economic world geography*. In the college field his chief contribution was the textbook *The Physiographic Provinces of North America* [1940].

In 1920 Atwood accepted an invitation from the board of trustees of Clark University to start a graduate school of geography and at the same time become president of the university. He remained at Clark until his retirement in 1946. This was probably his most productive period. He drew to the faculty many fine scholars both from home and abroad and along with that staff attracted, over his quarter of a century of service, hundreds of graduate students from more than a score of countries. Nor did he neglect to inspire his family, and his two sons, Rollin S. and Wallace W., Jr., followed in his footsteps and are now well-known geographers. The school of geography became his life, and the name of Clark as a center of geographic training will be for ever associated with his name.

OLIVER EDWIN BAKER, 1883–1949,
by S. S. Visher and C. Y. Hu[10]

Dr O. E. Baker, vice-president of the Association [of American Geographers] in 1924 and president in 1932, was a world renowned agricultural geographer and population expert. He achieved this renown as a result of exceptionally earnest effort and persistence, notable initiative, and willingness to accept responsibility. The son of a Cape Cod sea-captain and of a teacher daughter of a Vermont farmer, Dr Baker's earnestness reflected his ancestry.

Dr Baker was born in Tiffin, Ohio, on 10 September 1883. He graduated from Heidelberg College in Tiffin while he was still nineteen, having majored in history and mathematics. He received a master's degree in philosophy and sociology from Heidelberg the next year. In the following year, he was granted a master's degree in political science by Columbia University. The year 1907–8 was spent in the Yale University school of forestry. Graduate work in agriculture at the University of Wisconsin (1908–12) followed. There, he co-authored a substantial Wisconsin Experiment Station bulletin on the climate of Wisconsin and its effects on agriculture (1912). During the summers 1910–12, he worked with the Wisconsin Soil Survey. He joined the United States Department of Agriculture in 1912 and, before long became highly influential, partly because of his active participation in the *Yearbooks,* to which he contributed for twenty-three years (1915–38) and several of which he edited.

He first became very widely known as co-author [with V. C. Finch] of *A Geography of the World's Agriculture,* published in 1917 by the US Department of Agriculture. Not long after it appeared, he returned to Wisconsin for further graduate study, this time in economics, and was awarded the Ph.D. in 1921. An honorary doctorate from the foreign university most widely known for its activity in agriculture, Göttingen, was awarded him in 1937. The success of the *Atlas of World Agriculture* stimulated progress on the ambitious *Atlas of American Agriculture,* of which he was instigator, planner and editor. It was published in parts between 1918 and 1936.

Dr Baker was part-time professor at Clark from 1923 to 1927, and later gave several series of lectures at other universities. When the journal *Economic Geography* first appeared, he was associate editor and later contributed a distinguished series of regional articles on the agricultural geography of North America, based in part on extensive field studies.

Recognizing that few of the world's people live under even half-satisfactory conditions, Dr Baker did what he could to improve the lot of farmers in America.

In 1942 Dr Baker accepted the invitation of the University of Maryland to establish a department of geography. His plans were ambitious. The staff he assembled included several very unusual men—a native of the Netherlands, one of China, one so long and intimately in Latin America as to be almost a native, and an eminent authority on the Soviet Union. When Dr Baker retired in July 1949 from the management of the department, to devote himself so far as possible to completing his researches, the staff consisted of nine men, and the department attracted a sizable share of the university's undergraduate and graduate students. Graduate students came from far and wide, and numbered forty before Dr Baker died. The department which started from scratch in 1942 has already conferred nine masters degrees and five doctorates.

For years, Dr Baker was interested in China. His 1928 article on Chinese agriculture aroused very widespread discussion. The now-famous John Buck's *Study of Land Utilization of China* was first suggested by Dr Baker, and he sponsored it in 1929 before the research committee of the Institute of Pacific Relations. The projected 'China Atlas' was further evidence of his continued interest in China.

Commencing in the 1930s, Dr Baker's interests in regional agricultural geography and land utilization declined relatively. He continued to be recognized as the outstanding expert in these fields, and he taught them at the university, and discussed them helpfully with numerous other people.

His knowledge of American agriculture was profound. No graduate student who attended his seminar on land utilization and agricultural production will ever forget his presentation of his field observations and the results of his analysis of census data concerning the conditions and problems of agricultural land use throughout the United States.

Various population problems were of increasing concern to Dr Baker. These included rural-urban migration, the stability of the family, the desirability of better living conditions on farms, population quality, and the 'outlook for population.' In his later years he no longer cared simply to describe and interpret conditions of the immediate past, as he had done in his earlier years. Instead he endeavoured to predict the future, assuming continuation of various existing trends. Hence he strove earnestly, almost passionately, to reverse undesirable trends. He was especially concerned about the instability of modern urban culture. He sincerely believed that the real strength and enduring greatness of America lay in the preservation of the stable patterns of rural life.

VERNOR CLIFFORD FINCH, 1883–1959,
by R. Hartshorne[11]

Vernor Clifford Finch was born on a farm near Tecumseh, Michigan, on 18 October 1883. He was graduated from Kalamazoo College in June 1908, and received the bachelor's degree also from the University of Chicago after studying there during the summer term of the same year. Following a year of high school teaching in Iowa, he returned to Chicago to do graduate work in geography during the next two years and in 1911 was appointed assistant in geography at the University of Wisconsin. During the remainder of his career he was attached to the University of Wisconsin. When geography was separated from geology in 1938, he was named chairman of the new department and served in that position for seventeen years until relieved at his urgent request in 1945. During the next six years he continued to carry his full share of departmental work, but in 1951 failing health forced him to retire from active teaching, and in 1954 he was named Emeritus Professor.

During his forty years of service at Wisconsin he was on leave for two periods, first for a semester in 1915 to work in the United States Department of Agriculture with Dr O. E. Baker in the production of the *Geography of the World's Agriculture* [1917], and for a year and a half during the First World War, to serve as special expert in the commodity section of the division of planning and statistics of the United States Shipping Board, 1918–19.

Among the leaders of American geography of the past generation, Vernor C. Finch was distinctive in the variety of ways in which he contributed to the development of the profession.

Two of his research publications have been widely recognized as landmarks in the development of American geography. The *Geography of the World's Agriculture,* which he prepared in collaboration with O. E. Baker, was used for decades as a basic work in the study of agricultural geography; in addition it was long recognized as a model in geographic cartography in its use of the dot-map technique to portray distributions on a macroscopic scale. At the opposite end of the scale, his demonstration of the 'fractional' method of representation of landscapes in the 'Montfort study' brought to conclusion a long series of discussions and experiments by a number of American geographers; its definitive demonstration both of the disadvantages and advantages of the technique provided the basis on which later students could determine the feasibility of applying the method to the practical problems of regional planning.

The textbooks on which he collaborated, first with R. H. Whitbeck and later with G. T. Trewartha, were outstanding in college geography in their organization and presentation of challenging material—much of it representing original research. Their wide use in geography did much to raise the level of college courses throughout the country and to establish respect for the subject in the minds of colleagues in other fields. Likewise influential and useful were the several series of wall maps of products and industries which he prepared during the period 1920–30 for publication by Nystrom.

Finch was deeply concerned that geography should have a sound methodological and scientific foundation and was constantly seeking for more effective concepts and methods of work. In the period of turmoil of the 1920s in American geography, originating in concern over the basic purpose of the subject, he was one of the first of his generation to revise his viewpoint and his writings in the light of concepts which have ultimately come to have general acceptance. He presented a vigorous and effective exposition in his presidential address of 1938 on 'Geographic science and social philosophy'.

The value of his services as chairman of the department of geography at the university of Wisconsin from its inception in 1928 until 1945—and as senior advisor during the following years—is reflected in the increase in size and standing of the department in that period. At the same time, Professor Finch was known in the university as a wise adviser and useful citizen; with no desire to assert himself in administration, he was an able and devoted worker on committees to which he was assigned.

21

The American Geographical Society

The American Geographical Society was founded in 1851 as the American Geographical and Statistical Society, a title which it retained until 1871. Its purpose throughout its history has been the advancement of geographical knowledge by means of exploration, mapping, research and teaching. In the first half of this century it was under the direction of two men, Isaiah Bowman from 1915 to 1935, and John Kirtland Wright (previously the librarian) from 1938 to 1949. Under the leadership of these two men, the society played a leading role in the development of American geography. Since this was a formative period in the shaping of geography, it is fitting that their personal contribution to the society and to the profession should be recorded.

I shall begin by quoting the Epilogue of Wright's big volume on the history of the society, 1851–1951:[1]

When we look back over the society's record, we are struck by the vitality and consistency of its growth and guiding policies. From the beginning the institution has experienced a fairly steady increase in strength and influence. While there have been ups and downs—times of financial crisis and times when influence and leadership have lagged—the broader trend has been forward and upward. Individuals—notably Charles P. Daly, Archer Milton Huntington, and Isaiah Bowman—have been powerful factors in restoring the upward course after periods of recession or partial stagnation, but in each case they have had something more solid to build upon than did their predecessors.

The society has adhered to a few simple leading principles. To maintain a library and map collection and to publish works of geographical value have been the cornerstones of its policy from the outset. It has never accepted the doctrine that a sharp line should be drawn between geography and what is not geography or that its interests should be confined within an

academic definition of the subject. This has given its interests
breadth and its activities flexibility. On the other hand, it has
limited the range of its chief activities to enterprises designed to
advance geography along scientific, scholarly, professional and
educational lines, and, except in its lecture courses, has in
general avoided attempts to popularize the field. It has made this
limitation, not because of blindness to the need for disseminating
sound geographical knowledge through popular channels, but
for practical reasons. With the funds, personnel, and facilities
at its disposal, the society has felt it preferable to concentrate
upon what it could do well, rather than to spread its effort too
thinly. Hence, throughout its hundred years it has regarded the
raising of professional standards of achievement in the
advancement of geographical knowledge as its first and most
serious objective. This was true no less before a self-conscious
profession of geography had come into existence in this country
than it has been more recently. Long before the days of the
Association of American Geographers, individuals and
institutions in the USA were engaged in one way or another in
the gathering and interpretation of geographical data. The society
sought to encourage high standards of competence in this work.

  What is the geography that the society has striven to advance?
We have not tried to answer this by adding another definition
to the many that have been proposed, but have seen that geography,
like Proteus, assumes different shapes and natures, which have
something in common. It appears as a Science, to be developed
through accurate observation and logical reasoning; and also
as an Educational Discipline. It takes the form of an Instrument
of practical use to sailor and soldier, merchant, philanthropist
or statesman, and from this it emerges as a Guide pointing
the way toward action. Throughout the ages it has appeared as
Lore that brings delight through its appeal to the imagination
and poetic faculties. More accomplished than Proteus,
geography may take two or more of these forms simultaneously.
It is as difficult to define as Proteus was to grasp and hold.

  In the society's publications geography has assumed all these
forms at every period since the founding of the institution.
Certain forms, however, were especially favored at different
times. Until about 1895 geography appeared more often in the
aspect of Lore than has since been the case. Not necessarily less
respectable in this aspect than in others, it was by later standards
more literary and less 'scientific'. Until 1895 it also frequently
took the shape of an Instrument for practical use. Since 1895 it

has figured as a growing Science. In that year it made its debut
as an Educational Discipline, and it wore this face in many
papers in the *Bulletin* until about 1915. During and since Dr
Bowman's administration, besides manifesting itself as a Science
it has figured largely as a practical Instrument, sometimes as an
Educational Discipline, and sometimes as a potential Guide
toward the understanding and solution of problems of large
human importance. And today it is appearing in these same
forms, but with renewed power as an Educational Discipline.

Only a prophet and a seer could foretell what lies beyond
the gateways to the society's future. Reputed to be blind, the
Fates spin mighty cords out of small and little-noticed threads
and sever the skeins of things that promise greatness. Yet one
cannot but believe that they have an eye with which they have
watched the society for a hundred years and that, when they have
seen things wisely planned and well begun, the shears have been
withheld. The needs for geographical understanding are too
urgent, and the American Geographical Society's record of
achievement in meeting these needs is too impressive, to warrant
doubt that destiny will continue to look with favor on our
institution as its second century unfolds.

ISAIAH BOWMAN, 1878–1950, *by J. K. Wright*[2]

Isaiah Bowman was born at Waterloo, Ontario, on 26 December
1878, died in Baltimore on 6 January 1950, at the age of
seventy-one. He will be remembered for his achievements in the
advancement of geography, the administration of institutions of
higher learning, and the shaping of governmental policies. This
memoir outlines the main events of his life and comments upon
his scientific work and ideas, particularly in the field of geography.
It touches but lightly upon his services as an adviser to the U.S.
government. . . .

Of the total of Bowman's publications, about four-fifths bear
on geography and allied subjects. The remainder consist mainly
of addresses delivered on ceremonial occasions and of reports on
educational and other themes. Of the geographical four-fifths
nearly 95 per cent had appeared before 1935, when Bowman
became president of the Johns Hopkins University. . . .

Isaiah's father was a farmer, but there were also teachers
and preachers among his forebears and kinsmen. Early in 1879
the family moved to a farm in St Clair County, Michigan, where

at a tender age the boy developed a love for reading and, as he put it many years later, found Captain Cook's Voyages 'thrilling and exciting'. Bowman often spoke of being thrilled or excited by an experience, a book, an idea, and his excitement was infectious.

At eighteen he began four years of country schoolteaching, with attendance at summer sessions, and toward the end of this time in 1900 decided to study geography professionally—a bold decision in an era when geography was almost universally regarded as little more than an elementary school subject. Bowman's professional preparation took five years (or nine, until he received his doctorate). The first year he spent at the excellent Ferris Institute at Big Rapids, Michigan, and the next four alternately at the State Normal College of Ypsilanti and at Harvard University. In 1905 Harvard awarded him the degree of B.Sc. and in 1909 Yale made him a Ph.D. His doctoral dissertation was on 'The physiography of the central Andes.'

Jefferson was the attraction at Ypsilanti, Davis at Harvard. Though well grounded in meteorology and physiography, Mark Jefferson was interested primarily in the geography of mankind, whereas William Morris Davis was concerned first and foremost with physical phenomena. Of Davis, Bowman wrote: 'His incessantly enquiring mind, schooled in astronomy, geology, meteorology, and physiography, eventually drove toward a single goal, the analysis of land forms', and since it was already taking this 'set' when Bowman was at Harvard, the chief benefit that the younger man derived from Davis came in the form of rigorous training in logical thought and accurate expression. Jefferson did more to widen Bowman's horizons and encourage his spirit of far-roaming search.

Two currents that sometimes ran separately, but were more often interwoven, appear in Bowman's work. One was of concern with the physical, the other with the human, aspects of geography, and each was due in part to the influence of Davis and of Jefferson, respectively. Until about the beginning of the First World War the 'physical' current was on the whole the stronger, and certain of Bowman's writings up to that time read almost as though Davis himself were the author. In the geographical study of man and in seeking to apply the findings of physiographic and climatological research directly to the solution of practical problems, Bowman made more distinctive contributions. Also in several respects he differed more from his two masters than they did from each other. Davis and Jefferson were teachers to the core. Neither would have given up teaching in mid-career, as Bowman did, and neither had the executive ambition and ability of Bowman, in whom the scholar and the man of action were combined in about equal measure. The scholar in Bowman gave intellectual weight to his action; the urge to action lent a realistic quality to his scholarship.

Bowman began his career as instructor (1905–9) and assistant professor (1909–15) in the division of geology at Yale. Bowman was a stimulating teacher—among other subjects, of physical, political and commercial geography, and of the regional geography of North and South America—and his courses were no 'snaps'. During his early years at Yale he spent several seasons of fieldwork on water-supply problems for the USA and Indiana state geological surveys. One of his earliest publications dealt with the pollution by oil wastes of the water supply of a small Indiana city, a problem for which he offered a solution in the light of a field study of the local drainage pattern. Other works on allied topics followed, including a comprehensive treatise on well-drilling methods in the USA. In 1907, 1911 and 1913 he participated in expeditions into the regions of South America that include southern Peru, northern Chile, north-western Argentina, and the highlands and adjacent lowlands of Bolivia. Bowman himself organized and led the first and last of these, under the sponsorship, respectively, of Yale University and the American Geographical Society. On the second, the Yale Peruvian Expedition of 1911, he served under Hiram Bingham as geographer, geologist and surveyor of the party. With a fire of energy and enthusiasm Bowman studied widely diverse phases of the geography of the areas visited and recorded the results in a spate of articles published while he was at Yale and subsequently in two books: *The Andes of Southern Peru* (1916) and *Desert Trails of Atacama* (1924). These travels took him both to relatively well-known places and into the wilds, where he had the explorer's full share of adventure and hardship.

Probably the clearest, simplest, least pretentious, and therefore, most readable English that Bowman ever wrote describes what he saw and felt in South America. One example, from his account of the canyon of the Urubamba, must suffice:

> It is in such quiet stretches that one also finds the vast colonies of water skippers. They dance continuously in the sun with an incessant darting motion from right to left and back again. Occasionally one dances about in circles, then suddenly darts

through the entire mass, though without colliding against his equally erratic neighbors. An up-and-down motion still further complicates the effect. It is positively bewildering to look intently at the whirling, darting multitude and try to follow their complicated motions. Every slight breath of wind brings a shock to the organization of the dance. For though they dance only in the sun, their favorite places are the sunny spots in the shade near the bank as beneath an over-hanging tree. When the wind shakes the foliage the mottled pattern of shade and sunlight is confused, the dance slows down, and the dancers become bewildered. In a storm they seek shelter in the jungle. The hot, quiet, sunlit days bring out literally millions of these tiny creatures.

'Physiographic interpretations', Bowman wrote in *The Andes* (1916), 'serve the double purpose of supplying a part of the geologic record while at the same time forming a basis for the scientific study of the surface distribution of living forms,' and he used them to both ends in his South American work. When considering such strictly physiographic matters as the uplift of the Central Andes, the origin of Andean cirques, and the asymmetrical crest lines and valley profiles of the mountainous areas, he hewed to the Davisian line, but departed widely from it in his perhaps more congenial investigations of the regional relationships of climate and physiography of the Andean peoples. He had already reached the conviction, as he was to put it many years later, that 'the regional synthesis of life is the geographer's first concern' and 'the heart of the subject is man in relation to the earth.'

'The principles of geographic science', he noted in a paper on his expedition of 1913, 'rest upon the theory that man is to an important degree the product of the earth,' and in the preface to *The Andes* we read: 'The strong climatic and topographic contrasts and the varied human life which the region contains are of geographic interest chiefly because they present so many and such clear cases of environmental control within short distances.' Thus, at this period Bowman was not wholly immune to the doctrine of geographical determinism then prevalent in the minds of American geographers, although he cautioned his readers against oversimplification of the direct influences of the geographical environment upon human affairs. Theodore Roosevelt, reviewing *The Andes,* commented approvingly on Bowman's refusal to follow some of his colleagues, who 'proceed to explain all the immense complexus of the forces of social causation as simply due to geographical causes.' After the First World War, Bowman explicitly repudiated 'geographical determinism' in no uncertain terms.

No less instrumental than his South American travels in adding to Bowman's scholarly reputation during his ten years at Yale were the many hours of library research devoted to the preparation of a 759-page volume entitled *Forest Physiography : Physiography of the United States and Principles of Soils in Relation to Forestry*. It appeared in 1911 as an outgrowth of a course given in the Yale forestry school, and was intended in the first instance for students of forestry. The title, however, is misleading, since nearly six-sevenths of the text consist of a description, region by region, of the land forms of the USA—a description which has proved to be of enduring value to foresters and to geographers, and to many others besides. Although several attempts had previously been made to divide the country into physiographic regions, not until after 1900 did enough information become available through detailed local geological and physiographic studies and through topographic mapping to make possible as systematic and comprehensive a work as Bowman's.

The studies of Andean population groups in their regional settings and the regional chapters in *Forest Physiography* gave expression to the 'regional concept', in the modern development of which Bowman was a pioneer in this country. When answering a questionnaire addressed to American geographers in 1907, he alone specified 'regional geography' as the branch of the subject that interested him the most.

In 1909 Bowman was married to Cora Goldthwait, whose poise, good judgment and literary sensibility were to be of immeasurable help to him through the rest of his life. Also during the Yale period, as one of Professor Davis's right-hand men in the leading of the American Geographical Society's transcontinental excursion across the USA (1912), he made lifelong friends with many of the American and European geographers who went on that memorable tour.

On 1 July 1915, Bowman began work as the director of the American Geographical Society of New York. Founded in 1851, this was the oldest geographical society in the country. Between 1904 and 1915 it had blossomed under the guidance and with the financial aid of Archer Milton Huntington (1870–1955), who recognized the potentialities latent in its library and map

L

collection, its scholarly tradition, and the generally high quality of its council. But there was one serious weakness, the lack of efficient organization and administration, and Mr Huntington probably first suggested Dr Bowman's appointment as a remedy.

While at Yale Bowman made his contributions to geography almost wholly through the books and papers that he wrote and the classes that he taught. While at the society he was no less productive in his own research and writing, but the equivalent of time and energy devoted at Yale to teaching was now turned to the initiation and direction of programs that were actually carried out by the society's staff and others.

His three major achievements here were: (1) to improve the scope and quality of the society's periodical by replacing the old *Bulletin* of the American Geographical Society with a new and better journal, the *Geographical Review*; (2) to launch the publication of several series of monographic books and brochures; and (3) to initiate work on the so-called 'Millionth map of Hispanic America'. In order to defray the additional expenditure for *Geographical Review* Bowman brought about an increase in the society's income through ingenious and successful membership drives. Donations, most of which he secured from Mr Huntington and another councillor of the society, Mr James B. Ford, made the other two programs possible, at a cost of nearly a million dollars. In the period 1916–40 the society published some sixty monographic works as result of arrangements that Bowman made as director. About half of these have more than 400 pages each, and all but three or four are original works first published by the society.

The 'Millionth map' covers in 107 sheets the whole of the American continent south of the USA and also the West Indies and is, essentially if not officially, part of the 'International map of the world on the scale of 1:1,000,000'. Bowman conceived the idea of it when he called at the society before his expedition of 1913 to look over the maps of the regions that he planned to visit, only to find them unsatisfactory. The work began in 1920 and for twenty-five years kept busy a group of seven or eight compilers and draftsmen. The sheets have served officials of governments and corporations in the planning and conduct of numerous enterprises, and diplomats in the settlement of boundary

disputes. From them countless maps in magazines, scientific
works, textbooks and travel books have been copied or
reproduced, but their most genuinely appreciative users have
no doubt been the engineers, army officers, scientists,
explorers, tourists and others who have taken them into
the field. Appropriate, therefore, was the award (1946) of
the society's David Livingstone Centenary Medal to Dr
Bowman 'for outstanding contributions to the geography of
the Southern Hemisphere.'

Soon after the USA entered the First World War, Dr
Bowman placed the facilities of the American Geographical
Society at the government's disposal, and, as a consequence,
the society's building became the headquarters of the 'Enquiry,'
a group of some 150 geographers, historians, economists,
statisticians and experts in government and international
law which Colonel House assembled at President Wilson's
request to gather and organize information for the coming
peace conference. When Wilson and the American delegation
sailed for France in December 1918, they took with them
the leading members of the 'Enquiry' staff and many maps
and books from the society's collections. Bowman played
an influential part in the work of the 'Enquiry' and more
especially in Paris during the following two years, serving
as adviser on geographical matters to the American
Commission and in an executive capacity within the delegation.
This experience brought him a wide circle of acquaintances
among scholars, statesmen and men of affairs, and gave him
the inspiration and background for the writing, in a surprisingly
short time, of a book that was to appear in several editions
both in English and in translations. This was *The New
World: Problems in Political Geography* (1921; new editions,
1924, 1928), a survey of the politico-geographical situation
throughout the world at the time. The improvement of international
relations through the education of politicians and other leaders
thenceforth became one of Bowman's ardent interests—a cause
to which he devoted many an article and address, to the service
of which he came to consider the society's Millionth map a
great contribution, and to which he gave himself unsparingly
during and after the Second World War.

In the 1930s another national emergency, the Depression,
again saw Bowman hard at work for the government. During the
last years of his New York period he spent about half his time
in Washington, serving as chairman of the National Research

Council and as vice chairman of the Science Advisory Board. He reorganized and invigorated the work of the National Research Council and helped establish the Science Advisory Board, which President Roosevelt created in July 1933, upon Bowman's suggestion, to advise the various departments of the government in questions of science. Bowman had first met FDR at the peace conference and had become better acquainted with him while Roosevelt was a councillor of the American Geographical Society (1921–33).

A substantial proportion of the society's publications during Bowman's directorship bear on either Latin America, the polar regions, or pioneer settlements. Bowman wrote two of the thirteen books on Latin American topics, and the other eleven were regarded as a part of a Hispanic American Research Program for which the Millionth map was to provide a foundation. Although Bowman never visited the polar regions, he was on friendly terms with many of the world's leading polar explorers— notably Stefansson, Byrd, Wilkins, Ellsworth, Mawson, and Bartlett—and all these as well as lesser lights sought and benefited by his advice. . . .

Bowman made his most original contribution to science through the development and execution of a comprehensive program for the study of pioneer settlement. In 1925 he presented the plan to the National Research Council, which endorsed it. Supported by the donation of $100,000 from the Social Science Research Council, the society published eight volumes in a collaborative investigation of problems of settlement in pioneer areas of the world.

During the period 1925–37 Bowman wrote a dozen or more papers and addresses on pioneer problems, as well as *The Pioneer Fringe* (1931).

A number of passages in these works are revealing: 'Strong and hopeful and confident, willing to buy their dreams with hard labor', such are the successful pioneers. 'Explorers of more than material realms . . . capable of magnificent moments of decision', such are their leaders. Thus Bowman unconsciously characterized himself. On the pioneer fringe men are engaged upon a mighty 'creative experiment.' So also, 'there is always a fighting border to human experience,' and 'if the border appeals to a man it is because there is a border in his own mind'. Indeed, 'the greatest single fact about humanity—despite its fears and hesitations—is its willingness to advance beyond the borders of experience. . . . There have been pioneers in every generation to question and to venture,' and Bowman visualized himself as one of them. 'Science is like the pioneer in making things happen instead of waiting for them to happen . . . and every scientific truth goes pioneering.'

He advocated and outlined 'a science of settlement', but it was a 'science' only to the extent that any subject may be so regarded when studied scientifically. Though Bowman presented an unimpeachable case for the application of scientific knowledge and techniques to the study of pioneer problems, he developed no distinctive and systematic principles for the guidance of such study, as Darwin did for biology or Davis for geomorphology.

While director of the society, Bowman twice broke away from his desk for a few weeks of fieldwork of the kind that he had done so well in South America. His love of arid lands and pioneers took him westward in the summer of 1930 to Montana, Oregon and the Great Plains of Kansas and Nebraska, and in 1932 to the pioneer fringe north-west of Edmonton. The first journey gave him data for *Jordan Country*,[3] a classic study of an American pioneer community (in Montana). He also made four trips to Europe to attend international geographical congresses. At the Paris Congress (1931) he was elected president of the International Geographical Union, and in this capacity he presided at the Warsaw Congress in 1934. As president of the Association of American Geographers, he read an address on 'Planning in pioneer settlement' at the annual meeting at Ypsilanti in 1931, where he also bestowed a gold medal of the American Geographical Society upon his old teacher, Mark Jefferson. He was closely associated with both the National Research Council and Social Science Research Council, not only in connection with the pioneer belts studies, as we have seen, but in the advancement of many other enterprises. Dr Bowman was elected to the National Academy of Sciences in 1930.

Bowman set forth his views concerning the scope and nature of geography at a conference of the Social Science Research Council and later elaborated and illustrated them in a volume, *Geography in Relation to the Social Sciences* (1934). He developed the themes that the heart of geography is the study of man in relation to the earth and that the regional synthesis of life is the geographer's first concern. He was one of the founders of the Council on Foreign Relations in New York, served long on its board of directors, and went to London in 1929 to represent it at a conference for the study of international affairs. These were but a few of the 'innumerable organizations' that 'sought to avail themselves of his learning, his drive, his passion for exploring the frontiers of knowledge, his practical common sense, his ability to see the forest and the tree'.

Bowman left the American Geographical Society in 1935 to take over the presidency of the Johns Hopkins University that year. Henceforth, in the third and latest phase of his career, he was a top university administrator and a presidential adviser. He died in 1950.

JOHN KIRTLAND WRIGHT, 1891–1969, *by M. J. Bowden*[4]

John Kirtland Wright was a great explorer. In his early childhood he became fascinated by the two large areas then still unknown to the Western world—the polar regions and Arabia—and as a youthful mountaineer he knew well the sheer adventure of traveling in the unmapped wastes of his beloved Goose Eye and the northen Mahoosues. Yet to him the most fascinating terrae incognitae of all were those of men's minds, and it was here that he made his greatest geographical discoveries.

The known world of scientific geography never aroused his research interest; his view of the expanding core of geography was as detached as a Harvard undergraduate as it was in his retirement. He knew the increasingly numerous channels of the mainstream primarily as a disinterested historian of geography, but only became a part of the stream when the quantitative and perception waves that he had done so much to establish in the 1920s and 1930s broke into geography in the 1960s. His scholarly interest was ever following the lures of academic areas on the periphery of geography—into the border zone where history and geography meet and later to the frontier of the behavioral sciences; into the statistical-mathematical world long untraveled by American geographers; and into the realm of bibliographic innovation. Wright's life as a geographer was thus devoted to extending the horizons of academic geography. Few have done more in this cause, and surely none have done it with his impeccable scholarship and literary grace.

Wright was born on 30 November 1891, in Cambridge, Massachusetts, into a family where the literary and the scholarly were taken for granted. His father was appointed Professor of Greek (1887–1908) and dean of the graduate school of arts and sciences (1895–1908) at Harvard University; his mother, Mary

Tappan, was a successful novelist. . . . The Wrights' home was the center of a lively circle of Harvard and Wellesley professors, and some of the most distinguished academics of the period were neighbors and close friends of the family. As a child John paid many calls on William Morris Davis, who lived across the street, and he was enthralled to watch Davis drawing his famous block diagrams. But before his close contact with Davis his geographical sense and love of geography had been revealed in detailed work on his mythical country of Cravay.

It is not surprising, therefore, that as an entering freshman at Harvard in 1909 he had a well-developed philosophy of geography, and was inclined to major in either geology or geography. He studied climatology with R. DeC. Ward and physiography with Douglas W. Johnson, and was soon being groomed by the latter for a career in geography. Wright was selected to be Johnson's field assistant in the Shaler Memorial expedition study of the shoreline of the eastern USA in 1911, and his teaching assistant at the Columbia University summer school in 1912. But close contact with the stodgy and humorless Johnson convinced Wright, in 1912, of what he had felt for a year or more, that there was little of abiding interest and no lifetime challenge in physical geography as practised at Harvard.

In the same summer, in the cold light of reflection, he re-read Miss Semple's *Influences of Geographic Environment*—a book that had excited him greatly on first reading—and agreed with his history tutor, Ephraim Emerton, that such monocausal interpretations of history were untenable, a view unshaken by his extended discussion with Miss Semple at Wellesley two years later. He graduated *cum laude* in 1912, as of 1913, and was elected to Phi Beta Kappa in 1912. As neither of the established geographies—physical geography and anthropogeography—excited his long-term research interest he decided to concentrate on history.

He began graduate study at Harvard in the fall of 1912 in a history department where he was first permitted and later actively encouraged to go his own geographical way. Thoroughly trained in the art of the historian, notably by H. L. Gray and C. H. Haskins, he was nevertheless 'permitted by the history department . . . to offer the history of geographical knowledge as his special field' for the doctorate. Back home from France in 1919 after two years of army service, his search for a doctoral thesis drifted in this field until Haskins 'virtually ordered' him to do a study of Western knowledge of geography in the twelfth

and thirteenth centuries, sending him back to Europe for a year
on a Harvard traveling fellowship, and providing, on his way,
for a first meeting in New York with Isaiah Bowman, director
of the American Geographical Society. . . .

Wright completed most of his research in London, Paris and
Chartres; attended lectures by Brunhes, Gallois, De Martonne, and
Demangeon at the Sorbonne, and was offered (by Bowman) and
accepted the job as librarian of the American Geographical
Society as of September 1920.

As he was to point out eighteen years later: 'Bowman . . .
offered me the one position in the country for which my impractical
preparation and tastes really fitted me.' Bowman had gained
for geography a most prolific and innovative son. . . . Between
1921 and 1928 he completed his Ph.D., wrote five books and
monographs, six articles, 171 geographical record items and
book reviews, and completed the editing of the six volumes of
Alois Musil's *Explorations and Studies in Northern Arabia and
Mesopotamia.*

During the early 1920s Wright made two contributions that
were greatly to facilitate future research in geography. The first
was the book *Aids to Geographical Research* (1923), inspired
by the discovery, soon after he became librarian of the American
Geographical Society, that there was no such book for geographers
in English. When it became necessary to revise *Aids* in the early
1940s . . . Wright set to work to rewrite the book completely. . . .
The result was what Whittlesey praised as 'the outstanding
bibliography of bibliographies' in geography.

The second and more enduring bibliographic contribution
made in this early period was the research catalogue of the
American Geographical Society library, which was devised by
Wright and came into operation in 1923. It gave birth to *Current
Geographical Publications* in 1937, and has been issued in book
form (1962).

He felt emboldened to share his ideas with his fellow
geographers and historians of science in two papers presented
in the winter of 1925–6: 'A plea for the history of geography'
and 'The history of geography: a point of view'. The concern
of the history of geography, he felt, was with geographical
conception and with the many forms in which it had been
expressed through time as geographical knowledge and lore.
Wright advocated the adoption of this view and asked for studies
of the relationship between the environments experienced by
men and their resultant geographical conceptions. The two

articles constitute the earliest plea in American geography for
the study of geographical perception, a plea that found
substantive expression in three books and monographs published
in the mid-1920s.

In the most significant of these works, *Geographical Lore at
the Time of the Crusades* (1925), Wright took a cut through
time and reconstructed the sum total of knowledge concerning
geographical facts available in Europe in AD 1100–260. . . .

Wright realized that there was no more graphic way to grasp
the spirit of an age than through its cartography. He had shown
in *Early Topographical Maps* (1924) that: 'Comparative
examination of maps of different ages gives a remarkably clear
view of varying intellectual qualities and technical abilities.'
And in *Geographical Lore* the maps of crusading times that
Beazley dismissed summarily as 'monstrosities' became to
Wright 'the most convincing possible illustrations of the
geographical ideas that were current'. As Wright showed in his
monograph *The Leardo Map of the Word, 1452 or 1453* (1928),
the history of cartography was more than the antiquarian study
it had generally been considered; it was an important and integral
part of the history of geographical knowledge.

The treatment of false and mistaken beliefs had been carefully
omitted from the histories of geography of Wright's predecessors.
But he accorded Gog and Magog, the Kingdom of Prester
John, St Brandan's Isles, and other lands and peoples coverage
equal to the well-known lands of the inner regions in the
geographical world view of the west: The errors of an age are
'as characteristic as the accurate knowledge which it possesses—
and often more so'. In his extended consideration of geographical
concepts, Wright also differed markedly in orientation from his
predecessors, who had placed special emphasis on regional
knowledge and its acquisition through travel and exploration.

But *Geographical Lore* and Wright's pleas went unheeded.
This was a period when professional geography was renouncing
environmental determinism and finding a new self-respect by
concentrating its research effort in the newly defined core of
the field: regional geography. The call to both a geography of
wider scope and a new look at the environmentalist theme was
simply inopportune for American professional geography. The
concept and method of *Geographical Lore* were equally ignored,
until Ralph Brown put them to a similar purpose in *Mirror for
Americans* (1943). A still later generation of geographers, in the
1960s, began to see the methodological importance of *Geographical*

L*

Lore, which was reprinted as a Dover paperback in 1965.

The lack of any reaction to these writings of the mid 1920s depressed Wright and he experienced flickers of self-doubt that were to affect him for the next decade. In 1925 he had given up the position of librarian in all but name, to become a research editor for the society. His interest in the history of geography was gradually submerged beneath the institutional needs of the American Geographical Society and replaced for a while by his second major interest—statistics and geography. Between 1926 and 1940 he edited well over half the material that appeared in the society's books and pamphlets, producing far more in the research series than any other individual in the society's history. Furthermore, for three years he was more than the editor of the *Atlas of the Historical Geography of the United States* (1932), and *New England's Prospect: 1933* (1933).

The latter was Wright's idea, at the inception. He wanted to do a regional geography of his beloved New England 'à la Vidal de la Blache, Demangeon, etc.', and proposed it to Bowman, who didn't like the idea and urged him instead 'to get a lot of people to write on different aspects and problems of New England'. As a consequence Wright's two chapters on 'Regions and landscapes of New England' and 'The changing geography of New England' give us but a tantalizing view of a classical regional monograph that might have been. Frustrations such as this were indicative of a subtle change in his relationship with Bowman and the American Geographical Society that had taken place since the halcyon years. As a loyal servant of a society suffering from financial difficulty yet planning new emphases, he bore without complaint the increasingly heavy burdens placed on him. By the mid 1930s he had practically suppressed his major research interest in the history of geography.

Wright's fertile imagination was irrepressible, however, and while engaged in editing Paullin's *Atlas* and *New England's Prospect: 1933* he was challenged by the cartographic presentation of statistical data and the devising of summary measures of distributions on statistical maps. In tackling this problem he found a kindred spirit at the American Geographical Society in O. M. Miller, who collaborated with him in a number of articles that went far to establish them as leaders in statistical cartography in America. In 'A method of mapping densities of population' (1936) dasymmetric techniques were introduced to American cartography. Basic equations for the calculation of population densities for parts of administrative divisions were presented, as was a table designed to aid cartographers in solving the equations. In a conference on statistical mapping in the same year, Wright addressed himself to the design problems of statistical cartography, particularly the selection of symbols and the use of isopleths and 'choropleths'—a term coined by him. He began once again to explore, this time in the border zone between statistics and psychophysics, and to plead for the study and measurement of the relationship between the quantitative values of symbols and their visual perception. A prophetic plea was also made for the quantitative analysis of the data presented on statistical maps rather than the qualitative method 'that has been employed almost exclusively up to the present time'.

Some of the means by which such quantitative analysis might be made were outlined in an article that again owed much to O. M. Miller: 'Some measures of distributions' (1937). Statistical data on maps were reduced to Lorenz curves, and locational coefficients measuring the uniformity and association of both areal and linear distributions were derived. These ideas were applied three years later in 'Certain changes in population distribution in the United States' (1941). Wright also devised non-locational coefficients dealing with total populations and ratios, and indexes of concentration and dispersion. It was twenty years before the quantitative revolutionaries began to devise such methods of correlation and areal association apparently independently. Few seem aware of this early and long-neglected thrust to locational analysis. . . .

Following Wright's appointment to the position of director of the American Geographical Society in December 1938, however, the statistical-mathematical theme, as he called it, was increasingly de-emphasized; it was not until the early 1960s that he began in earnest once again. . . . The results of this recent work were in manuscript form at the time of his death and will be published by Dartmouth College in 1970 as a monograph entitled *Distributors and Distributees*.

As director, Wright became charged with a new enthusiasm. He was given the opportunity to return to his first love—the history of geography—and the explorer was once again treading where no other geographer had ventured. Four papers, presented between 1940 and 1946, extended the dimension of geographical enquiry, and revealed that human nature in geography had become his dominant concern.

In the pre-war years Wright had, in his studies of geographical ideas, stressed the influence exerted on them by the environment,

physical and human. After 1939 his search for the origins of
geographical conceptions took him to the study of the grounds
of knowledge, of behavioral tendencies, group and individual
motives, personal qualities, and of the psychological factors
that lay behind the evolution of geography. The world view of
individuals that had been implicit but secondary in his early
conception of geography became explicit and central to his new
vision of 'geosophy'. This field covered: 'the geographical ideas,
both true and false, of all manner of people—not only geographers,
but farmers and fishermen, business executives and poets, novelists
and painters, Bedouins and Hottentots'.

This concept was central to the new and highly distinctive
geographical approach to the history of exploration that he
presented to the eighth American scientific congress—'Where
history and geography meet' (1940). He showed that geographers
could gain deeper insights into the course of exploration and
the acquisition of geographical data by reconstructing the
geographical knowledge and beliefs of the explorer and his
times. Similarly, comparison of the historical geography of the
area explored with the explorer's description would pinpoint
the distortions in his image and shed light on the presuppositions
of the age. Equally fruitful would be the comparison of
geographical world views before and after a particular
exploration as a means of assessing its significance.

'Map makers are human' (1942) showed how the cartography
of a time and region reflected the personal qualities, motives and
objectives of the cartographer and sometimes of his employer. It
was at least in part a cautionary paper intended for military
personnel in Washington, and grew out of the extensive
cartographic services rendered to the military by the American
Geographical Society during the war. Yet it was something
more than this, for in it are blended the statistical theme that
absorbed much of his research time in the 1930s and the human
nature theme that was gradually becoming his principal interest.
It remains as the classic statement on the place and influence of
subjectivity in cartography.

The impact of human nature on science and scholarship as a
whole was elaborated in detail in 'Human nature in science' a
paper Wright presented, as retiring vice-president, to the American
Association for the Advancement of Science (1944). And as
retiring president of the Association of American Geographers,
in 1946, he led those present into a multifaceted world of
aesthetic feeling, imagination and subjectivity in geography.

Geosophy was revealed in its many facets, and a special plea was made for historical geosophy. The history of geography of broad scope for which Wright had pleaded in the 1920s was but the core of this new field conceived as 'embracing all of the geographical knowledge of the past in its various relationships of cause and effect . . . an immense subject indeed'. 'Terrae incognitae: the place of imagination in geography' was the epitome of Wright's conception of geography, a field combining the literary and the imaginative. It was yet another clarion call for research in what is now called geographical perception, and it was made with all the inner fire of one long isolated in a scholarly wilderness.

In 1949 Wright resigned as director of the American Geographical Society. He had taken on the directorship in troubled times and succeeded in steering the society's affairs through the difficult years of the war. He brought the society from a more leisurely past into the modern world of expanded opportunities and challenges, professional and governmental. . . .

The distinctive influence of geographical societies upon the advancement of geographical thought had begun to fascinate him in the mid 1940s, and by 1947 he had already presented a paper on the dissemination of geographical knowledge by geographical institutions. In 'The field of the geographical society' (1951) he showed that geographical societies, compared with other institutions, were free to shape their own policies. Moreover, their motives for geographical investigation were primarily disinterested. This was true of all four types of societies—professional, laymen's, educational and research.

Proof of these claims was afforded in *Geography in the Making: the American Geographical Society, 1851–1951* (1952). Wright showed that the interests of the society had changed markedly through time, reflecting the composition of the governing body and staff, the increasing professionalism of geography, and, above all, the society's fluctuating but lately expanded sphere of influence, as indicated by its membership. As a servant of its members the society had passed through metropolitan, sectional, national and international phases; early group motives for geographical investigation had gradually been replaced by disinterested ones, and as professional geography grew the society, as a servant of mankind, had concentrated its research endeavor in fields and regions neglected by an academic geography that was continually redefining its core and shifting its tastes for approaches. . . .

The remaining five years of the research associateship were
devoted to two 'frightful chores' for the American Geographical
Society, the writing of 'A history of Egypt', and the editing of
A World of Geography of Forest Resources, and a more pleasant
one for the Association of American Geographers, editing as
consultant *American Geography: Inventory and Prospect,* of
which he rewrote large sections and 'blue-pencilled the whole
volume'. His own research focused on the human nature theme
as exemplified in the history of American geography, and
provided the basis for *Human Nature in Geography* (1966). This
book, remarkable for its erudition and literary finesse, maps
out the three new directions in historical geosophy revealed in
Wright's essays of the 1950s and 1960s. One group of contributions
was concerned with the character and careers of individuals as
bearing on the progress of geography: The decisions of Daniel
Coit Gilman and their indirect but powerful influence on
graduate education in American geography; the personal
endowments that lay behind Bowman's creative powers; Jedidiah
Morse's nationalistic motives and his limitations as 'father of
American geography'. Another group focused on the life cycles
of constituent elements of geographical knowledge: 'The open
polar sea' (1953), chronicling the rise and fall of an influential
theory; 'Miss Semple's influences' (1962), outlining the origins
and geographical career in an influential monograph; 'Medievalism
and watersheds in American geography' (1966), stressing the
continuity within American geography as illustrated particularly
by the legacies of the Middle Ages (in content and thought
patterns).

A third and final group explored the border zones between
geography and poetry, religion, and mathematics: 'From Kubla
Khan to Florida' (1956), seeking the links between Coleridge's
symbolism and Bartram's travels; 'Notes on early American
geopiety' (1966), documenting the fundamentalist overtones of
early American geography; and 'The heights of mountains' (1958),
and 'Notes on measuring and counting in early American
geography' (1966), detailing early attempts at accurate measurement
in geography. . . .

Following his retirement to Lyme, New Hampshire, in 1956,
he turned frequently to the reading of his voluminous diaries
and to the happy reminiscences of his childhood and youth in
New England. His delight was to range the Pinnacle and lesser
peaks as he had climbed the White Mountains in his youth,
and to paint and sketch the places, people, and things he held

so dear. But the tranquillity and tender companionship of Lyme were the setting for some sad regrets that he had not followed the Siren's call to be a novelist, artist, or a teacher. He viewed the rapid development of perception and quantitative analysis in geography with deep personal satisfaction, mingled with dismay that his own part in these changes was so little recognized. He seems not to have realized that although the fault lay primarily in the profession, it was also in himself and in his stars.

There is a great difficulty in assessing the importance of a man so far ahead of his times as was Wright. At the time of his death at Hanover, New Hampshire on 24 March 1969, Wright had achieved international renown as an authority on the history of geography, cartography and exploration. But full appreciation of his place in other branches of geography awaits the outcome of current movements in the field and biographical memoirs of Wright and of those he may have influenced.

22

Carl Ortwin Sauer, 1889-1975

Just as William Morris Davis was the main promoter and exponent of geography in the first quarter of this century, so Carl Sauer was the dominant academic figure in the second quarter. Just as the contribution of Davis can only be properly appreciated in the light of thought in his period and the two or three decades preceding it, so appraisal of Sauer's place demands some consideration of the background of thought among his contemporaries. Thus, in this chapter we shall examine the early development of geography as a university study and the views and contributions of its chief contributors, before passing to a more specific discussion of the life and work of Carl Sauer.

ENVIRONMENTALISM

The environmental approach was propounded most lucidly by Davis himself in 1903. It is basic to *Elements of Geography,* a textbook written by Salisbury, Barrows and Tower, all of the University of Chicago, in 1912. This book was still in general use as a college text in 1928. A strong physical base was followed, in each chapter, by the 'human responses', an approach which to this day, no matter how illogical and inadequate in the light of modern concepts, is pursued in some textbooks on 'physical geography'.

A big step forward was J. R. Smith's *Industrial and Commercial Geography,* first published in 1913, which sought 'to interpret the earth in terms of its usefulness to humanity, and deals with human activities as affected by the earth rather than with parts of the earth as they affect human activities'. As already noted, there is much in Russell Smith's treatment that reveals a new kind of appraisal of resources in terms of human needs and technics. It evaluated economic forces as factors in the location of economic phenomena—for example, the location, development and structure of urban centres as markets. Yet the tracing of environmental, still equated with geographical, influences on human history, activities and attitudes, continued to be the goal of others.

Ellen Semple's *Influences of Geographic Environment* (1911) searched for areal associations of human with terrestrial phenomena. It followed a part, but only a part, of the approach of Ratzel. Her *American History and Its Geographic Conditions* (1903) is a work in the same vein, and, in spite of its conceptual defects, stands as a classic in the American literature. The assessment of 'geographic influences' was also strongly supported in these days by Brigham of Colgate, who wrote in 1915 that the problems of 'geographic influences' are the heart of geography, and 'whether we speak of influence, response, or adjustment, matters little' (*Annals of the Assoc. of Amer. Geog.*, 1915).

The environmentalist approach was taken up in the diligent and far-ranging researches of Ellsworth Huntington which have already been discussed. In his early researches (1905–25) he sought to measure with some precision the 'influences' of the 'physical environment' on human activities and historical development. He seems to have changed his stand in later years, for one reads in 1924: 'Geography is primarily the science which describes and maps the phenomena of the earth's surface for the purpose of discovering how the distribution of one set of phenomena is related to that of others' (*Annals of the Assoc. of Amer. Geog.*, 1924).

These views, however, are simplified and often misleading in his college textbooks. He refers throughout his life-time to the 'geographic' as the 'natural' environment, and to human 'adjustment to the geographic environment'. Although many naïve hypotheses and assumptions remained in circulation, Huntington himself, in his later years, undertook to find ways to measure with precision just how the physical environment affects man.

In 1934 Ellsworth Huntington formulated 'principles of human geography' on the basis of 'the nature and distribution of the relationships between geographical environment and human activities'. He examined the influence of climate and climatic change on men and the course of history. He linked, comments a German critic (G. Pfeifer), 'natural phenomena and cultural or historical phenomena in causal relations with breathtaking casualness'. His interpretation of 'geographic' was of the physical or natural environment factors only. Yet, this book sold 85,000 copies in its fourth edition alone.

Still concerned with the fluctuations of human history, Huntington in his *Pulse of Progress* (1926) sought to incorporate biological change as well as environmental influence. He deals here with the relations in time and place of drought and migration, the places of origin of great historical personages, and the history of the growth and spread of the Jewish peoples. His work is rich in stimulating questions, and this was true of his teaching, but it must be criticized for the 'hasty, uncritical assurance with which he answers them' (G. Pfeifer).

A standard book by Huntington first published in 1920 in co-operation with S. W. Cushing was intended as a teaching aid. It set forth to present, in its own introductory words, 'the great principles of geography in its human aspects.' It presents man's relation to location, land forms, bodies of water, soil and minerals, climate, vegetation and animals. Man's relation to man is described as 'political geography', and 'international relations'. Human geography is defined as 'the study of the relations of geographical or physical environment to human activities.' This approach is still found in numerous school and advanced texts. On the one side, are the physical conditions of the 'natural' environment. On the other side are the 'human responses' in the form of 'material needs', occupations, efficiency and higher needs, meaning, by the latter, education, science, religion and art.

Another influential American geographer at this time was R. H. Whitbeck. In 1926 he defined the field of 'geonomics' as the study of 'the environmental activities of man as influenced by his geographical environment', and as the search for laws of unequivocal dependence of economic phenomena on the 'geographic factors' of location, resources and climate. With Olive J. Thomas, he wrote an important work that was published in New York as late as 1932, *The Geographic Factor: Its Role in Life and Civilization*. The 'geographic factor' embraces the facts of the natural environment, including location. These include climate, surface features, soil, minerals, fauna and flora. The environment is variously defined, he continues, as the 'natural' or 'physical' environment and the term 'geographic' is used as the equivalent of each of these. It is recognized that 'both men and the lower forms of life are and must necessarily be dependent in many ways upon their surroundings'. It is, however, 'the well-nigh universal view among geographers that geographical environment is passive or permissive, not mandatory, that man's doings are influenced, not determined by his geographical environment'. In other words, human traditions and heritage condition the way in which groups are influenced by these 'geographical conditions'. To what end, however, are these 'influences' on human groups examined? Apparently in the interpretation of 'human activities and attitudes' of all kinds in which the 'historical' element must be evaluated. This amounts to an evaluation of the 'geographic' factor in the development of nations. Its objectives are closely in line with those of Ritter and Ratzel. Thus, the objective of study is evidently the influence of physical (*qua* geographic) factors on man, and this means on the development of human activities, civilizations, and the development of nations.

THE REACTION: LANDSCAPE AND ECOLOGY

Definite shifts of emphasis took place from the environmental approach in the 1920s and especially in the 1930s. The lead came from men trained in Chicago, notably under Harlan Barrows and Carl Sauer. There was an eager search for an alternative to a so-called 'naïve environmental determinism' that tended to fall into a simple routine of thinking and writing; and a search for more effective methods of geographical analysis, once the goals were clearly set.

The revised approach to land-man relations assumed various expressions—possibilism in France, adjustment in Britain, areal associations for a few in America, and a flat declaration by Barrows of Chicago of an ecological limitation.

Harlan H. Barrows claimed geography to be the 'ecology of man'. He shifted the notion of environmental influence to one of environmental adjustment, meaning thereby that man adjusts himself to and utilizes his environment, according to what James would call the 'attitudes, objectives and technical abilities' of the group. Further, in focusing geography upon the life of man on the earth, the physical aspects of the earth would only be investigated in so far as they were relevant to man's occupance. Thus, the study of physical earth, as an end in itself, must be discarded from geography, and yielded to the ancillary sciences—geomorphology to geology, plant geography to plant ecology, climatology to meteorology, etc. Objections were raised in America to this view on two grounds. First, it allegedly maintained the focus of study on environmental relationships and failed to eradicate environmental determinism. There is little point to this, for Barrows's viewpoint of man-land relationships, with the proviso noted above (which it was Barrows's primary purpose to establish), is identical with that of modern geographers such as P. E. James. Second, Barrows made no mention of the very active pursuit of 'human ecology' in the school of social sciences on his own campus, led by Robert Park and Ernest Burgess. Their studies certainly had a different emphasis, but they were very definitely concerned with the structure of socio-geographic areas and with the hierarchy of urban centres that serve as focal points of human integration.

Geographers in America were singularly and inexplicably silent through these years about the formidable contributions of these 'human ecologists'. It is also peculiar that few were concerned with following up studies of the structure of socio-geographic areas, whether they be 'invisible' social groups, or very definite landscape structures, such as towns. However, Barrows's views expressed those of the Chicago school in the 1920s and many geographers from that school were influenced by them. In 1931 the present writer attended a course on urban geography that was given by Colby at the University of Chicago. Colby's interpretation of man on earth was expressed by three terms: function, form and pattern. The interconnection of these three was interpreted as the keystone to the differentiations of the earth's surface by human impact.

The most active group, however, emerged through contact with Carl Sauer. We recall in 1931 meeting with a group of young geographers in the Middle West, who had derived their philosophy and research objectives directly from Carl Sauer. They rejected the concept of environmental influence as the central purpose of geography, and put in its place the study of landscape. This was to be studied with respect to the forms, functions and patterns of the elements of landscape and their associations in area whether as the expression of adjustments to the physical environment or as the cultural deposit of the group occupying the area. These were the views at the time of the self-styled chorographers (see p. 323). The research energies of W. D. Jones, R. B. Hall, K. C. McMurry, S. D. Dodge, P. E. James, V. C. Finch, C. C. Colby and others, were devoted in the 1930s to reorganizing and directing their work along these lines.

These developments, that reverted to the classical tradition of geography, find their beginnings in the influence of Carl Sauer. The basic work of orientation for which Sauer is best known is his *Morphology of Landscape,* published in 1925. Sauer accepted in this monograph the chorological concept of the German scholars Hettner, Passarge and Krebs but narrowed down the facts it embraces. He considered that geography must find 'its entire expression in the landscape on the basis of the significant reality of chorological relation'.

Morphology [he writes] rests upon three postulates: (1) that there is a unit of organic or quasi-organic quality, that is, a structure to which certain component elements are necessary, these component elements being called forms; (2) that similarity of form in different structures is recognized because of functional equivalence, the forms then being 'homologous', and (3) that the structure units may be placed in a series, especially into developmental sequence.

The facts of geography, he maintains, are place facts, and their association in area gives rise to the concept of landscape. He rejects the terms 'region' and 'area' and adopts the 'landscape' to designate such a terrestrial unit. This is 'an area made up of a distinct association of forms, both physical and cultural'. Its reality is based on 'recognizable constitution, limits and generic relation to other landscape.... Its structure and function are determined by integrant dependent forms.' It is to be understood as to origin, growth and function.

Such an area, Sauer claims, is the equivalent of Penck's and Sölch's 'chore'. It is in origin a 'natural landscape'. He enumerates the forms of the cultural landscape as follows: habitation (type and grouping), production (land use and workshop), communication and population (density and mobility). 'There may be a succession of these landscapes with a succession of cultures.' Hence: 'We cannot form an idea of landscape except in terms of its time relations as well as of its space relations. It is in a continuous process of development or of dissolution and replacement.' It follows from this viewpoint that 'historical geography may be considered as the series of changes which the cultural landscape has undergone and therefore involves the reconstruction of past cultural landscapes'. The natural landscape is the assembly of natural features of area *that are relevant to human occupance.* Geography, he claims, is therefore 'distinctly anthropocentric'. The natural landscape is a 'site' in the sense of the plant ecologist. Study of the natural landscape, however defined, is directed to understanding its significance as habitat. Thus, Sauer concludes, the task of geography is 'to grasp the content, individuality, and relations of areas, in which man comes in for his due attention as part of the area, but only in so far as he is really significant by his presence and works'.

Some comment on these views is called for. The phrase 'content, individuality, and relations of areas' is dead in line with the thinking of nineteenth-century German geographers, more particularly of Carl Ritter, who repeatedly used precisely the same term. Sauer circumvents the problem of 'content' by confining attention to the landscape, as did Schlüter (Germany) and Brunhes (France). Sauer's concept served as a springboard for Whittlesey's concept of 'sequent occupance', that refers to the development of landscape as the expression of the sequence of cultural development. The idea of sequent occupance is developed substantively in Jan Broek's study of the Santa Clara valley, published (in English) by the University of Utrecht in the Netherlands.[1]

It needs to be noted—and from the outset Sauer was well aware of this—that the elements of landscape do not all change simultaneously with a general change of the cultural attitudes and technical abilities of the occupants. A change of people, of new techniques, or socio-economic development, may cause the simultaneous introduction of a number of elements of landscape—fields, farms and towns. Single elements may emerge and add to the sum total. Others may die and become vestigial remnants. The former is illustrated by the covered bridge in the eastern USA. The latter is illustrated by the barrows of prehistoric man in Britain and of pre-urban man in North America, which today stand out in the landscape and fill a function frequently, for example as wooded mounds, in the landscape which is very different from their original purpose. The enclosure movements in England changed the pattern of fields and occasioned the building of many new dispersed farmsteads. The same changes are going on in the transformation of the vast latifundia of southern Italy, where sub-division of the land, irrigation and new crops, and the consequent development of livestock production, is resulting in a transformation of much of the landscape, where vestigial remnants of the 1870s are still occasionally to be found in large areas. These are all refinements of the concept of the 'humanized landscape' and its relation to changes in the techniques and purposes of its inhabitants. The whole of a landscape or of its elements may thus be the subject of investigation. Landscape is studied in terms of the process of human activity in time and in area. Landscape elements are studied in terms of their form, function and pattern. These are interpreted in terms of the way in which they are associated in area as the spatial impact of cultural processes.

Sauer has now been in action for over fifty years. This statement on the morphology of landscape appeared at the beginning of his career and he has long since outgrown it. Most of his published studies, based on arduous and frequent fieldwork, in Mexico in particular, are available in the publications of the University of California. Actually, the *Morphology of Landscape* is today regarded almost with anathema by Sauer himself. It marked a great step forward, however, in American geography. It was written after a thorough reading of the works of European geographers, works in German in particular, that were accessible to very few of his contemporaries.

THE VIEWS OF SAUER

The *Morphology of Landscape* was published at the beginning of Sauer's career, after less than ten years of provocative basic work. Nearly fifty years have elapsed, and Sauer's researches far transcend the prescriptions of his own formula. The following is drawn from an appraisal by his most longstanding and closest colleague, John Leighly.[2]

Carl Sauer was born in Warrenton, Missouri, in 1889, the son of a teacher in a Wesleyan college, now defunct, in that town. He spent his boyhood in a school at Calw in Württemberg and later attended the college in his home town and then moved to the University of Chicago, where he received his doctorate degree in geography in his twenty-sixth year. His first post was at the University of Michigan, where he spent the seven years 1915–23. In 1923 he moved to the University of California at Berkeley and remained there until his retirement in 1957. Throughout this period his personal fieldwork was in Mexico. He died in July 1975.

Sauer was a student and assistant of R. D. Salisbury in Chicago. Salisbury, a geologist, greatly influenced Sauer's initial training. Sauer, however, turned to human geography, although he has always kept contact with the physical earth. He also studied plant ecology at Chicago under the famous scholar H. C. Cowles. From this an ecological approach to human problems in relation to habitat, and an insatiable interest in botany, have always marked his work. Sauer also learned about environmentalism at Chicago from Ellen Churchill Semple, but its traces very soon disappeared from his writings.

Sauer's writings reveal the unfolding of his interests and activities. He has not been directed in this choice by artificial boundaries. The 'morphology of landscape' was an initial part of his general orientation and was needed to give more meaningful guidelines than the land-man environmentalism that was current at that time. It spelled, says Leighly, 'the death blow to the doctrine of environmental determinism' in American geography. Sauer himself soon outgrew this formalistic exposition and his addresses to the Association of American Geographers through the years reveal his changing ideas as a researcher and teacher. He also currently inveighs against 'a more recent mechanistic heresy—the investigation of human beings and their behavior by mechanical processes of organization and computation. This departure from humane philosophy is as repugnant to him as the one he demolished many years earlier'.

Sauer has always had a deep, sympathetic interest in ordinary folk, however humble. This appears in his work on Mexico and in the way in which he tackled prehistoric man's struggle with his habitat. In Leighly's words: 'More than anything else his appreciation of simple people living in close contact with inorganic nature and in symbiosis with plants and animals distinguishes Sauer's writing about man on the earth.'

Sauer, says Leighly, has 'a strong ethical bent'. He avows repeatedly an ethic of responsibility for man's terrestrial inheritance which has suffered such appalling depletion under the impact of technology. This concern is evident in his pioneer work in the establishment of the Michigan Land Economic Survey while he was at the University of Michigan, his participation in the Soil Conservation Service, and again in his leading part in the conference on 'Man's role in changing the face of the earth' in 1955. In this last connection his writings betray his interest in 'pioneer' and 'frontier'. '[Men] burn the grass and trees, plant in newly cleared woodland, break the prairie sod, seek the best places for their houses, adapt as well as they can the local resources to their inherited or newly discovered needs.' In the cumulative process of human occupance in a particular habitat, the earlier stages are the most critical.

Sauer's thinking reflects the wide intellectual influences acquired through his omnivorous reading. The two scholars whose names appear earliest and longest in his books are F. Ratzel and E. Hahn, two Germans. The second volume of Ratzel's anthropogeography interpreted man on the earth, as I have shown in *The Makers of Modern Geography,* as a dynamic rather than a static matter, as 'spread' rather than 'distribution'. Hahn's work drew Sauer's attention to the origins and the domestication of plants and animals.

In the conclusion of his collection of Sauer's writings, Leighly expresses succinctly the philosophy of Sauer in the following words:

There is such a thing as a humane use of the earth; the simpler cultures are less destructive of the terrestrial basis of man's existence than is our present technology; and the possessors of modern technology may find in the past experiences of man over the earth guidance toward a balance of the capacities of the land with the requirement of life that gives some promise of permanence.

To follow the intellectual growth of Sauer, it is necessary to turn to the conceptual statements of his later years, in which he expresses the way in which he has worked as a scholar. These are found in addresses on 'The education of a geographer' (1956) and 'Foreword to historical geography' (1940), both of which were delivered before the Association of American Geographers. In the latter he presents 'a confession of faith that has stood behind one's work'. It is not intended as 'another design for the whole of geography, but a protest against the neglect of historical geography'. He continues: 'A peculiarity of our American geographical tradition has been its lack of interest in historical processes and sequences, even in their outright rejection.' He goes on to state that a second peculiarity of American geography 'has been the attempt to slough off to other disciplines the fields of physical geography'. Barrows sought to do this in the early 1920s and Hartshorne is noted by Sauer as the arch-advocate. A period of forty years (1900–40) is described as the 'Great Retreat', the purpose of which was 'to limit the field in order to secure its domination'. In every direction, the geographer has naturally failed to find virgin land. Community of interest and expertise in the pursuit of common problems seems to be Sauer's message.

An essay on Sauer's work would be woefully incomplete without drawing attention to his remarkable researches in the years of his retirement. The latest is *Sixteenth-Century North America* (1971). This was preceded in the 1960s by *Northern Mists* (1968) and *The Early Spanish Main* (1966). These books are studies of the spread of men over the earth, by both land and sea, and their interpretation and use of the lands they found and the peoples they encountered. It is far, far removed from the methodological framework that Sauer sought to provide for American geography fifty years ago. It reflects his own view a generation later that intellectual curiosity, based on a sound geographical training, should be the guide to scholastic search rather than the strictures of a preconceived conceptual framework.

THE CHOROGRAPHIC SCHOOL OF GEOGRAPHERS
(*c.* 1930)

Back in the 1920s, Sauer left his mark on his young colleagues in the Middle West, notably at Michigan and Wisconsin. They formulated, as we shall see below, a field for geography based on areal characterization, rather than environmental relationship. Their *credo* is expressed in the following statement that fell into my hands in 1932. It is here reproduced directly for the first time. The statement and its later repercussions on the leaders of the third generation reflect the shift in thought, as James personally expresses it, from Semple to Sauer.

We conceive of the earth's surface as composed of a 'mosaic of spaces', differing in their surface impressions as exhibited through both natural and cultural features. To delimit these spaces, to describe and interpret their characteristics is the field of geography. By this definition, geography becomes a comparative study of the earth's regions.

Any area is geographically distinctive and individual by reason of the nature and arrangement of two sets of features which cover its surface: (1) those which are provided by nature (climate, surface features, soils, etc.); and (2) those which man has added (houses, cultivated fields, lines of communication, etc.) in his use of the earth. In this analysis of any portion of the earth's surface, the geographer systematically observes and records both the natural and cultural features, describes them in their associations and patterns, seeks to explain the growth and development of the cultural panorama in its natural setting. He does not limit his study to a search for relationships between man and the natural earth. Rather he shifts the emphasis from a study of relationships to a study of the material features, natural and cultural, within the area. The characteristics, associations, and patterns of these surface forms, together with the bonds of relationship which connect them, are his chief lines of investigation. The region thus studied is viewed as a functioning organism composed of numerous natural and cultural groups. The relationship of the cultural scene to the natural earth is not slighted, but it is far from being the sole objective of the original study.

Since it is the observable material features which give chorographic individuality to any space on our planet, the chorographer does not include man's activities among his primary objects of study. When these activities express themselves in material forms which can be observed and recorded, they [the forms] are then a part of the landscape, and as such open to geographic analysis. If the material features of an area are the primary facts with which a geographer deals, then all of those other facts used to explain and interpret the observable, areal scene may be classed as *secondary*. There are no restrictions as to what these secondary facts may be.

The geographer's study of the natural equipment of an area (natural environment) is chiefly for the purpose of describing it, although simple explanatory statements concerning genesis may profitably accompany the description. It nearly becomes 'explanatory description', which is of a higher quality than that which is solely empirical. Research in the field of plant ecology, geomorphology, generic climatology, may well be relinquished to workers in these fields who are better qualified to undertake these special endeavors. It is unwise to claim for geography a broader field than we can hope to master. Thus the geographer's analysis is both descriptive and explanatory of the man-made landscape.

Finally, it needs to be emphasized that a study giving one set of areal features by itself has somewhat less geographic quality than when all of the features are studied in their regional association. It may be necessary at times for a number of reasons, to study one or more groups of features apart from the others, as for instance, the settlement forms or the climate of a region. Such studies are especially valuable if they are performed with the complete regional synthesis as an eventual goal.

In summary the following are asserted to be some of the major tenets of the chorographer's creed:

(1) Geography is a comparative study of the regions which comprise the earth's surface. This is a different point of view from that which asserts that geography is concerned with the discovery of relationship between man and the natural earth.

(2) Description is an essential part of geography, and is co-equal in importance with interpretation.

(3) Man's activities are not of prime importance to the geographer, but rather those material features resulting from man's activities.

(4) Features of natural environment function in a dual capacity in geography:

    (a) They furnish a set of features in forms which give character to area. As such they are significant even if unrelated to the cultural forms.

    (b) They are one (but only one) of a number of agencies which may help to explain the forms, patterns and functions resultive from human occupation and use of the natural area.

(5) Cultural forms and patterns which are explainable in terms of natural features have no higher geographic quality than those which are explainable in terms of historical antecedents, racial characteristics or any other force or agency.

23

The Third Generation

One academic generation merges into the next, so that the 'juniors' eventually become the 'seniors'. Creative, substantive work is normally undertaken in the first fifteen or twenty years of a career, and the senior half is normally marked by spreading the findings of the earlier years for the benefit of junior colleagues and for the general reading public. This sequence is remarkably illustrated in America in the transition from the second to third generations of geographers, for the latter were very active in the 1930s. The war years from 1940 to 1945 interjects a break between their junior and senior phases.

The labours of the outstanding young leaders of the third generation, and their summation of concepts and trends, are presented in a book entitled *American Geography, Inventory and Practice,* edited by Preston E. James and C. F. Jones, and published in 1954. This large and comprehensive volume contains the thoughts and researches of groups of mature scholars on every major branch of geography over this period. The works of R. Hartshorne on *The Nature of Geography* (1939) and the later commentary, *Perspective on the Nature of Geography* (1966), have provided guiding methodological motifs through three decades.

The leaders sought to advance beyond assumptions and directives of the environmentalism inherited from the first quarter of the century. This indeed was unquestionably their main mission from the beginning of their careers (see the statement of the so-called 'chorographic school of geography, 1931' on p. 323). They sought to clarify and advance geography as the regional science of the earth's surface, and they can be proud of their achievement, in spite of much sideline criticism through the years. They pursued three main goals of enquiry. First, they probed into the purpose and procedures of this study in the field on lines that were first suggested by the two second-generation leaders of Chicago, W. D. Jones and C. O. Sauer.

Second, physical geography, as an eclectic study covering all 'natural history', was on the wane, and more specialized investigations were undertaken. Units and orders of land forms were studied in the USA by Fenneman in a two-volume work (*Physiography of Western United States* (1931) and *Physiography of Eastern United States* (1938)). Climatic regions and their delimitation and related matters were investigated by C. W. Warren Thornthwaite. A. W. Küchler undertook the mapping of vegetation for the USA and on a worldwide scale, on the basis of new criteria of form.[1] Third, several scholars travelled widely and became experts in foreign fields, for which they found international acclaim, notably on China and Japan and Latin America.

The summation of these trends in the 1930s is embodied in several important books that appeared around 1940. These were R. Hartshorne's *Nature of Geography* (1939), P. E. James's *Latin America* (1942), and a major work on Japan by Orchard on its economic development (1930), Ackerman on natural resources (1953) and Trewartha (summing up much research done to date) on geography (1945). These men were subsequently associated in their academic maturity with different activities: Orchard with government service like Bowman before him, Ackerman with the resource development, and Trewartha with studies in the academic field.

It is difficult to select the major contributors and too exacting (for the reader) to attempt a recital of their achievements. But such a list would certainly include the following: R. Hartshorne (Wisconsin), P. E. James (Michigan, Syracuse), J. Leighly (Berkeley), J. R. Whitaker (Wisconsin, Peabody), G. Trewartha (Wisconsin), G. B. Cressey (Syracuse), R. J. Russell (Louisiana), J. Broek (Minnesota) and J. E. Orchard (Columbia). I shall not review the contributions of each of these men, but instead begin with appraisals of four who died prematurely, and conclude with three on the above list, P. E. James, J. B. Leighly and G. Trewartha. These latter reflect different, though interrelated, modes of regional enquiry and, moreover, they have continued to produce creative work throughout their careers in both junior and senior phases. I use their thoughts as mirrors of their time and as a personal appreciation of their value and stimulus.

KIRK BRYAN, 1888–1950,
by D. Whittlesey[2]

Professor Bryan made his career largely in New England, obtaining his doctorate at Yale, teaching there for three years and being a member of the Harvard faculty from 1925 until his untimely death in 1950. His observations of New England, based on numerous excursions into the field, were penetrating and stimulated study and publication by colleagues and students. He himself published relatively little on specific New England subjects, mainly discussions of glacial problems.

As a boy and young man, Bryan had lived mainly in dry western North America, and he became known through studies of that region. Born in New Mexico in 1888, he was introduced to earth science by Professor W. G. Tight at the university of his home state. In 1912 he was appointed to the US geological survey, and an early assignment was a field study in California. Between his return from army service in France at the end of the First World War and his settling at Harvard, he worked full time on the survey, partly in Washington, but chiefly in the western USA. Until the day of his death he continued to devote summers and other leaves to field expeditions, usually in the arid regions of the USA or Mexico.

His publications, beginning with his doctoral dissertation, report continuous observation of the unglaciated country where, as W. M. Davis has pointed out, American geographers first became aware of the normal pattern of stream erosion. His country was landscape-fashioned by wind as well as water, where scant rainfall, unreliably distributed, affected the land forms in distinctive ways.

His studies contributed most immediately to geomorphology, in which he was a constant innovator, moving far beyond the bounds set by his predecessors. Through these successive enlarge-ments of subject matter and viewpoint, he kept constantly in mind the regional aspect of the topics he investigated. The title of his novel and highly valued course, 'Geomorphology of arid regions' accurately states its nature as regional physical geography; his 'Physiography of North America' was no less so, even though the title does not disclose its regional character. Many of his papers likewise reveal the central place in his thinking occupied by distributions of earth features.

Lifelong intimacy with dry country, and professional study of it, brought him into the controversy over the relative potency of man and nature in modifying the landscape. He recognized that human settlement and use of the land might contribute to alternation between erosion and silting in the valleys, to changes in level of the water table, and to destruction of natural vegetation —perhaps by acting as the 'trigger' to release natural forces. At the same time he held that nature plays the dominant role in such changes or oscillations. This view was unpopular in circles where 'soil conservation' had become a shibboleth of vested interests apart from its service as a rationale of applied geography.

His views were based on land use in pre-Columbian times as well as since the advent of Europeans. Interest in early man as part of the geomorphic process brought him into close association with the department of anthropology at Harvard, where, for two score years, physical geography has been an integral part of training for the doctorate. It also led him to investigate the sites where artifacts and skeletons were being unearthed. At intervals from 1923 onward he participated in expeditions to the south-west, demonstrating the value of co-operation between geographers and anthropologists in investigating the remains of early man. In 1948 he extended these field studies to western Europe. In making himself an authority on human beginnings, he became one of the few Americans who combined geography and anthropology. In doing so he prepared the ground for a human geography of a period for which the only evidence is archeological and geomorphic.

From studies of windwork, supplemented by research on pre-Columbian land use and early man, it was a natural although an original step to periglacial conditions. This interest absorbed an increasing portion of his teaching and research, and led to paleobotany, to soils, to Pleistocene climate, and to permafrost. These researches found outlet in another of his novel courses, 'Geography of the Pleistocene.'

Having interests so far-reaching, Bryan inevitably pondered the place of geomorphology in the scientific world. Over many years he subjected rival theories of land formation (such as those of W. M. Davis and Walther Penck) to the criticism of field application. Introducing field observations to his course 'Principles of geomorphology,' he used laboratory practice to test hypothesis.

On the larger field of geography as a whole, he frankly championed environmental determinism, flying gleefully in the face of the trend away from that doctrine. Within the limits of his concentration on arid and glacial lands, his position is readily understood. As an expert in areas of harsh environment, inhabited by retarded peoples or by advanced social groups narrowly restricted by drought or cold, he was working with a world where nature gives humanity little choice of action. In such regions the distinction between determinism and possibilism is shadowy, and perhaps academic.

RALPH HALL BROWN, 1898–1948,
by S. D. Dodge[3]

Ralph Hall Brown was born in 1898, in Massachusetts. He attended Massachusetts State College, 1915–17, and was graduated from the University of Pennsylvania in 1921, with the degree of bachelor of science. In 1925 he was awarded the degree of doctor of philosophy by the University of Wisconsin, at which university he was instructor in geography from 1921 to 1925. From 1925 to 1927, Brown was instructor in geography at the University of Colorado. He was promoted to be assistant professor in 1927, in which capacity he served till 1929, when he was called to the University of Minnesota. There he was assistant professor till 1938, associate professor till 1943, and full Professor till his death on 23 February 1948.

Of the numerous specialties into which geography may be divided for study, Professor Brown chose, as the principal vehicle of his expression, the historical. He found the field practically uncultivated, and left it greatly enriched by his two major works, *Mirror for Americans* (1943) and *Historical Geography of the United States* (1948).

To appreciate the significance of the two major works, it is necessary to view them in the context of American historical geography. In 1903 a pattern for writings in the field was set by Ellen Churchill Semple and Albert Perry Brigham, who then published *American History and Its Geographic Conditions* and *Geographic Influences in American History,* respectively. The titles indicate the underlying concepts. 'Influences' was the current vogue. The two works may be described, then, as rather more historical than geographical, and were in a field which historians, without geographic preconceptions, were better qualified to treat of. In 1907, Brigham continued the work in historical geography by publishing *From Trail to Railway.* In it he moved from an historical toward a geographical bias, and the quality of the work is consequently better than that of his earlier work. Though Miss Semple's book was revised in 1933, there was but little change in its point of view, and so little in its quality. It was, however, the latest word when *Mirror for Americans*[4] appeared. The latter showed what could be done in the field of historical geography, when geography, and not history, was the guide.

Geographers have often lamented the incompleteness of the data given by writers of the past, who, like Morse, wrote the geographies of their time. More information to build on is wanted by them.

M

Ralph Brown supplied the lack by writing *Mirror for Americans*. To summarize the geography of a period fully and to make the map as it was alive in the present took genius of high order. It took imagination to see the possibility of 'doing it that way'; it took fine art to make the map live in works; it took patience, diligence, and acumen to complete the datum of early nineteenth-century geography. This was the contribution of Ralph Hall Brown to American geography. His last work, *Historical Geography of the United States* [1948], completes the picture of historical geography by bringing it up to date. It will be long before that contribution is surpassed, for it will be long before genius and talent are again combined in one person.

GEORGE BABCOCK CRESSEY, 1896–1963,
by T. Herman[5]

George B. Cressey, 1896–1963, took for his field of study the world's largest land mass: Asia and the USSR. Within that tremendous area his special contribution was the first modern geographical work on China in English, published thirty years ago. In addition, he constantly used his knowledge of east Asia and Siberia to help shape opinion and government policy during the Second World War and after. He labored to broaden the International Geographical Union from a small Atlantic-based honorary society into a world-wide working organization.

Born in Ohio, in 1896, he graduated from Denison University in 1919 with a B.S. in geology. In 1923 he received the Ph.D. in geology under Rollin D. Salisbury at the University of Chicago, his dissertation being 'A study of Indiana sand dunes'.

Fresh from Chicago he joined the faculty at Shanghai College, an American Baptist college just north of the old International Settlement on the Huang-p'u River. As was customary, the first year was spent in the College of Chinese Studies in Peking where he met Miss Marion H. Chatfield, another young American mission worker; they were married in 1925.

Professor and Mrs Cressey were at Shanghai College until 1929. He taught both geology and geography, taking his students on numerous field trips around the lower Yangtze delta, and creating a large collection of geological specimens and maps for his department. Whenever time permitted, he traveled to all parts of China, but especially to the Ordos desert and Mongolia to study the evidences of climatic change.

Cressey returned to the USA in 1929 for a year of study at Harvard followed by teaching at Clark, where he earned a Ph.D. in geography with a dissertation on 'The Ordos desert'. In 1931, at the age of thirty-five, he became head of the new department of geology and geography at Syracuse. Although China seemed far away, his first year was full of speeches and articles on east Asia, since that was the year of Japan's march into Manchuria. When the fighting spread to Shanghai in 1932, the maps, photographs, and type for his text, *China's Geographic Foundations,* were destroyed in the bombing of the Commercial Press. From notes and other materials in Syracuse he rewrote the whole book. It appeared in 1934.

The main theme was the adjustment of man to the physical environment, an emphasis that does not seem nearly as heretical in agrarian Asia as in the USA. The physical environment was presented systematically. Here were his fifteen 'natural' regions (physiographic-climatic-agricultural) which were also used by Professor J. Lossing Buck of the University of Nanking in his monumental *Land Utilization of China,* published in 1937. Here was his reminder of the lack of sizable mineral resources needed to make China a great industrial power. For this judgment, based on estimates of the early 1930s and an assumed population of 485 million, he was strongly criticized in Peking after 1949. It was regarded, however, both in China and abroad, as the work of an informed and systematic observer who had studied much of China at first-hand.

At Syracuse he busied himself and his combined department in fieldwork around New York state, and in advanced degree programs in geography. In 1937, Cressey visited Moscow for the International Geological Congress, was invited to consult on the *Great Soviet World Atlas* and then traveled for three-and-a-half months in Siberia and the Arctic. His first trip to the USSR had been in 1923 to Peking via Siberia, Mongolia and the Gobi, so the second trip provided a strong impression of the tremendous economic growth and potential east of the Urals, a concept that he spread widely on his return to the USA.

Such reporting about the Soviet Union was as unusual in the USA in 1937 as similar reporting about mainland China in the 1960s.

America's involvement in the Second World War brought him to Washington as a consultant to the Department of State, the Board of Economic Warfare, and army intelligence, and took him to Chungking in 1943–4 for the National Academy of Sciences in order to help the transplanted Chinese universities. During the war he was also busy teaching in the accelerated army training program at Syracuse and lecturing about the Far East. At the same time, he wrote his second book, *Asia's Lands and Peoples* [1951], where for the first time American students were able to study in English something of the geography of the USSR.[6]

In 1945, he became chairman of the new department of geography at Syracuse.

His retirement from the chairmanship of the department at Syracuse in 1951 at the age of fifty-five, and his election as the first Maxwell Distinguished Professor, gave time over the next decade for constant travel, writing and lecturing. Two years were spent in the Middle East teaching and preparing his text on South-west Asia. Two trips to the USSR, a short stay in Mongolia, a swing through the Asian rimland and a visit to the Antarctic, added to his rounds.

JOHN EWING ORCHARD, 1893–1962,
by O. P. Starkey[7]

John Orchard was born in Nebraska in 1893. At Swarthmore College, he received his B.A. in 1916, majoring in economics. He taught English and history for a year at George School, then started graduate work at the University of Pennsylvania, serving at the same time as assistant instructor in geography and industry while studying economic geography under J. Russell Smith. In 1918 he became assistant mine economist with the US Bureau of Mines, where his reports on the political and commercial control of world mineral resources were added to the materials assembled for the American delegation to the Versailles peace conference.

Orchard resumed graduate work in 1919 and at Harvard pursued studies in economics, political science, history, international law and economic geography—all focusing on his special subject, economic resources. He was awarded the M.A. in 1920.

About the same time J. Russell Smith asked him to help build the new geography department in the Columbia school of business. To prepare for this, he attended the 1920 Chicago summer session. He continued his graduate program at Harvard, completing his Ph.D. in economics in 1923 with a dissertation on 'The world's coal resources and some of their influences on national economy', prepared under Professor F. W. Taussig.

When in 1923 he turned his full energies to building a geography curriculum at Columbia, he became concerned about the lack of courses and materials on Asia. Thus he chose Asia as his regional field. As J. Russell Smith continued to live in Swarthmore and devoted much of his professional time to textbooks, Orchard had much of the responsibility for administration at Columbia. He rose to a full professorship in 1938 and became chairman of the Committee on Advanced Instruction and Degrees in Geography.

In May 1941, Orchard was called to Washington to serve in the office of production management with special responsibility for strategic metals. Six months later, he was asked to shift to the Lend Lease administration. From 1942 to 1944, as senior assistant administrator, he was in charge of its foreign liaison division, which dealt with foreign representatives applying for Lend Lease aid. In 1944 the organization became the Foreign Economic Administration with Orchard as director-general of its areas branch.

Later in 1944 Edward Stettinius. Lend Lease administrator, became under-secretary of state and, at his request, Orchard became special assistant to the under-secretary and special assistant to the assistant secretary for economic affairs. His duties dealt with international economic problems including the problems of liberated areas.

He returned to Columbia in 1945–6. In 1947–8 (and again in 1953–4) he served Columbia as acting dean of the school of business. All of this had played havoc with his Asiatic research, which had started auspiciously with a distinguished book on *Japan's Economic Position* [1930]. Before the Second World War, he had started a parallel book on China, but much of his field data had been made obsolete by the war. For this reason he welcomed an opportunity in 1949 to serve as chief officer of a China mission of the Economic Co-operation Administration (ECA). Before he could leave for Shanghai, China fell to the Communists and new problems had arisen in Paris where ECA was working on the Marshall Plan. There, serving as special adviser to Ambassador Averell Harriman, he specialized in area problems, organizing and heading up the Overseas Territories Program. His mammoth contribution to post-war reconstruction problems was recognized by France, which decorated him as a Chevalier of the Legion of Honor in 1951. He also served as chairman of the Mutual Security Agency advisory committee on underdeveloped areas, which in 1950 had added south-east Asia to its responsibilities. In this position, Orchard succeeded his fellow geographer, the late Isaiah Bowman.

In 1953, the Columbia school of business needed reorganization. Orchard served as chairman of a committee on the future development of the graduate school of business and wrote its report. After administrative assignments he returned to the research he preferred, and in 1957 spent four months in Japan, bringing his data on *Japan's Economic Position* up to date.

At the 1960 meeting of the Association of American Geographers, as honorary president, he summarized his conclusions on the industrialization of the Orient. In 1961 he was further honored by election as honorary fellow of the American Geographical Society. In June of that year, he retired from Columbia to a small farm near Lincoln, Virginia. He died at Charlottesville on 28 January 1962.

PRESTON E. JAMES, 1899–

Born in Brookline, Massachusetts, in 1899, James graduated from Harvard in 1920. He took his doctorate at Clark University in 1923. This was done with remarkable speed, for he instructed at both Harvard (1919–21) and Clark (1921–3). He moved to the University of Michigan in 1923 and remained there until entering war service in 1940. On returning to academia in 1945, he moved to Syracuse University, where he remained until retirement.

His family took him travelling in Europe in 1910, a motor trip in 1911 from Boston to Utica and many times to Florida. Reading about polar explorers was a hobby. He had a sound training in English at school and intended to continue in English at Harvard, but attracted by Atwood, the physiographer and successor of Davis, he majored in geology and physiography.

He received his M.A. at Harvard under R. DeCourcy Ward in February 1921. He then made a trip of several months around South America, giving a course at Clark on Latin America in the summer of 1921. At Clark, Atwood at once assigned him the task of collecting a list of materials on Latin America with no limits of money. He completed his doctorate on transportation development in South America in April 1923.

When the graduate school of geography was founded in 1921 (Atwood became the president of Clark in 1920) the faculty consisted of W. W. Atwood, Ellen C. Semple, Guy Burnham (cartography), C. F. Brooks (climatology), D. Ridgley (teaching of geography). There were also visiting professors, each of whom came for a few weeks, including O. E. Baker, C. F. Marbut, H. L. Shantz, E. Huntington. C. B. Fawcett came later for a year. Lawrence Martin also gave lectures on the political geography of Europe, for he had been an intelligence officer in Paris for the peace conference.

James writes that his most important geographic training was at Michigan. When he went there in 1923 the department had just been set up in social sciences, separate from geology, immediately after Sauer had left for the University of California at Berkeley. McMurry, with a new doctorate awarded at Chicago, was appointed as the first chairman at the age of twenty-eight, since none of the senior people at Chicago were interested in the post. McMurry passed to James the mimeographed outline of the introductory course that had been prepared by Sauer. Out of this course emerged James's own mimeographed and bulky outline of a freshman course called 'A chorographical study of the world'. This later emerged as a book, *An Outline of Geography* (1935), and in a later form as *A Geography of Man* (1949), which is still selling strong, and is, in my opinion, still the best introductory book on the market.

James writes in a letter as follows:

At Michigan we were all under twenty-eight—K. C. McMurry, R. B. Hall, S. D. Dodge, C. M. Davis, and P. E. J. We had four graduate students, some of whom were older—Guthe, Glendinning, Kendall and Davis. We used to argue about geography, and out of our reading of German and French literature (as well as American and British) we sharpened our ideas and methods. This was an intellectually exciting period, because we were coming out from Semple and joining Sauer. The great emphasis at Michigan was on field methods. From 1925 until 1935 (except when I was in Brazil in 1930) I taught the summer field course in Kentucky. There is a kind of geography one absorbs in the field that one cannot get from books and computers. The staff and students in a sense grew up together. A very important part of this process came from Salisbury's seminar at Chicago. I was the only person in the group who had never been to Chicago. In fact, when I was elected to the Association of American Geographers in 1926, I was the only member who had not been to Chicago.

The works of James fall into several aspects and phases. His first published book was *An Outline of Geography,* which grew out of his freshman course at Michigan, and clearly reveals the legacy set by Sauer. His doctorate on transportation in Latin America, followed by specialized work on Brazil, resulted in a major volume, *Latin America,* in 1942. He has published both before and after this date research studies on Brazil. Since the Second World War he has written (with a collaborator) a series of grade-school geographies (1947–55) and two books for the more general reader, *The Wide World* (1959) and *One World Divided* (1964). His most recent book is *All Possible Worlds: A History of Geographical Ideas* (1972). He has also pursued questions of the regional concept and he put regional ideas to the test in a study of the Blackstone valley of southern Massachusetts.[8]

James was the co-editor of *American Geography* in 1954 and his introduction to this comprehensive work expresses his own philosophy and was also acceptable to his collaborators in writing the essays on their special fields that make up the content of this inventory of geographical scholarship.

JOHN B. LEIGHLY, 1895–

John B. Leighly did his undergraduate work at the University of Michigan. He was discovered there by Carl Sauer and taken with him as a junior colleague to the University of California at Berkeley in 1924. Leighly has been there ever since.

While known primarily as a climatologist and a critical student of the development of geographical thought, Leighly probably did his most important published work in the 1930s in urban morphology, an unknown field to American scholarship at that time. These studies, growing out of time spent at the University of Uppsala, Sweden, are concerned with the site, plan and buildings of the towns of central Sweden (1928) and the towns of medieval Livonia (1939). These are undoubtedly the most important substantive researches that Leighly has published. Yet he regards himself as a physical geographer.

The following comments are drawn from a letter to me from Leighly dated 10 August 1971. The views expressed may be regarded as an appendix to his article 'Whither physical geography' (*Annals of the Assoc. of Amer. Geog.,* 1953) in which he criticizes his colleagues for the neglect of study of the earth's physical surface as an end in itself.

W. M. Davis introduced the term 'physiography' as a designation
for what had earlier (and has since) been called 'physical geography'.
I suppose that Davis knew how T. H. Huxley had used the term
in his excellent little book bearing it as a title, and he undoubtedly
knew its etymology. But I am sure that Davis conceived the word
not in its etymological sense, as Huxley had, but as a telescoping of
'physi(cal) (ge)ography'. The term was adopted readily, both in
departments of geology (for what had been called 'physical
geography') and in the new programs in geography established at
Harvard and at Chicago in the 1890s. But because of Davis's
primary interest and because of his post being located in a
department of geology, the part of the subject that dealt with the
land surface was given incomparably more attention than were the
parts concerned with the atmosphere and the ocean. If one looks
at the textbooks, whether the smaller ones designed for use in
the high schools or the magnificent ones for university use by
R. D. Salisbury and R. S. Tarr (completed after his death by
Lawrence Martin), one finds that they are overwhelmingly devoted
to geomorphology. As a result, by the time I became a student
after the First World War 'physiography' was a synonym for
'geomorphology', the latter term not having yet gained a place in
our scientific literature. This use of the term continued in
departments of geology up to about the time of the Second World
War. One sees it perpetuated, for example, in N. M. Fenneman's
two great books *Physiography of Western United States* (1931) and
Physiography of Eastern United States (1938). When I was a
student both Salisbury's and Tarr's books were used in instruction.

The new tendency in the 1920s, when the self-conscious
'geographers' were struggling to emancipate themselves from
geology, led to a rejection of 'physiography' as a part of the
despised subservience to geology. Both H. H. Barrows in 1922
(in his 'Geography as human ecology' in *Annals of the Assoc. of
Amer. Geog.*) and Carl Sauer in his polemical writings of 1924 and
1925 rejected the 'physiography' on which they both (at Chicago)
had been brought up. Barrows thrust the physical earth outside
geography, and Sauer adopted a descriptive geomorphology that
he found in the German writers, in its most radical form in
Passarge. This rejection of physical geography gained almost
complete dominance in the later 1920s and in the 1930s. One finds
it expressed, for example, in Preston James's writings, with his use
of 'surface configuration' and his attempts to represent it on
maps. The popular and radical anthropocentrism found no use for

339

M*

a contemplation of the earth's surface as the site of the play of physical and chemical forces. The need of students for some knowledge of physical geography was now provided for by the immensely popular *Elements of Geography* by V. C. Finch and G. Trewartha (1936).

It is not generally known, I believe, that this book had its roots in Berkeley. In our early days in Berkeley, Sauer and I prepared what at first was an outline for our introductory course in physical geography. This outline, which we called the 'Syllabus', grew from year to year, the outline being filled out as full text in its early parts, on the geometry of the earth and climate, which I wrote. Sauer was to write the later parts, on land forms, but he never got that work done, and lost interest after he turned over the course to me. Finch had a copy of our 'Syllabus' in its later form, and wrote to Sauer to ask permission to use it as a basis for his and Trewartha's book. Since there was no probability of his completing his part of the work, Sauer readily gave Finch permission to use our text and outline. By the fact that my part on climate was written out in full whereas Sauer's prospective part on land forms was only in outline, climate became the predominant topic in Finch and Trewartha's book. Finch and Trewartha's book marks, I think, the exorcism of 'physiography' as a term from instruction in geography. Courses bearing that name persisted, as I remarked before, in departments of geology; and where the instruction in physical geography was not fully maintained in departments of geography, students were referred to these courses in departments of geology. At the same time the new generation of graduates in geography (my generation) gave up concern with the genesis of land forms, and mapped them only as features of the surface as they were presumed to affect the use of the land. That was the time when, for example, soil erosion became an object of close attention, and soils themselves became an object of interest.

Climate remained as an object of primary concern to those who were carrying the banner of geography. Perhaps this retention resulted from the fact that climate was not associated with the cradle of geology from which geography had escaped. Climate had a respectable nursery at Harvard, where Robert DeCourcy Ward had taken over Davis's concern with meteorology when the latter began to devote himself almost exclusively to geomorphology. Preston James helped carry the torch, too, in his earlier years. Chicago had no climatologist, but had instruction in the subject from the early days, given by J. Paul Goode. Mark Jefferson, a student of Davis and Ward, brought a concern with climate to the Middle East when he came to Ypsilanti in 1903. While Brooks was at Clark from 1921 to 1926 he saw several doctoral candidates through to their degrees with dissertations in climatology. Clark has given more doctoral degrees for dissertations in climatology than any other university: twenty-one from 1901 to 1969, with California (Berkeley) in a remote second place with seven. I think that one can say confidently that between the wars climatology was by far the most prominent field of physical geography cultivated in departments of geography in the USA.

As an undergraduate I was interested in geology and related fields. Sauer offered me an assistantship when he came to Berkeley in 1923, assuring me that I might work on anything I chose. California did not offer deposits of continental glaciers to work on, and I was soon immersed in the teaching Sauer assigned me, principally in climatology and cartography, which I had to learn by myself, having had no instruction in them; or, indeed, in anything except geomorphology that I had to teach. So I am almost completely self-taught in most of what I have worked on, having never been indoctrinated in any geography. I have therefore always been somewhat aloof from many of the concerns that have agitated colleagues of my generation. I have taken 'geography' in its etymological sense, and have been impatient with any effort to narrow it to fit a preconceived notion. I have seen fashions in defining geography come and go, from environmental determinism on; but I see the earth persist. I had to turn my hand to many matters, and had no reason or opportunity to specialize. My writings are scattered widely; and I have no regrets that they are. Perhaps my distaste for the definitions of geography my colleagues have published results from the fact that they always defined me out.

Those who were self-conscious 'geographers' paid little attention to the physical earth, except to its climate. Many of the men active wrote on climate: not only Thornthwaite, but also James, Trewartha, Visher, Van Valkenburg and Jefferson among the older men. Interest in physical geography was maintained here at Berkeley with J. E. Kesseli representing geomorphology. The thread of physical geography, including geomorphology, is unbroken at Berkeley; leaving aside the times before Sauer came here in 1923, Sauer connects us back with Salisbury and Chicago.

Interest in geomorphology was maintained at Clark, too, so long as Atwood, father and son, were there.

Since the Second World War there has been appreciable thawing in the arbitrary limits set to geography by its definers. At present there seems to be no obloquy attached to an interest in the physical earth. One can form some judgment concerning the later (and earlier) history of physical geography in Anglo-America from the list of doctoral dissertations given in the work of Browning.[9] It would appear that I was crying 'Wolf!' in my 'What has happened?' Things were not so bad as I imagined.

GLENN THOMAS TREWARTHA, 1896–

Glenn Trewartha, born in Wisconsin in 1896, was awarded the first doctorate in geography at the University of Wisconsin in 1925, and took his master's at Harvard in 1922, after earning an undergraduate degree at the University of Wisconsin in 1921. He became Assistant Professor at the University of Wisconsin in 1926, and has spent the whole of his career there, serving as chairman of the department from 1945 to 1950. Trewartha was associated with the group of 'chorographers' in the 1920s (Finch, the head of his department, was one of its most ardent devotees), but he pursued his own bent and disclaims any direct connection with the *credo* of the 'chorographers' reported on p. 324 that came into my hands in 1932. He has made outstanding contributions to the advancement of the regional concept, and a review of his works—books and articles—without, however, attempting to be accurately comprehensive, reveals the following areas of interest and substantial researches.

First, Trewartha's researches for the doctorate, began in his native state, Wisconsin. They were concerned with the dairying industry (1925, 1926). They continued with the modes of use and settlement in the 'driftless hill land' of southern Wisconsin (1938, 1940, 1941), and several studies of particular settlements (1932, 1939).

Second, Trewartha visited the Far East for the first time with a Guggenheim Fellowship in 1926–7, returned to Japan in 1932, and again in 1948. Out of these sojourns there emerged a number of research studies of settlement in various sections of Japan (1928–38), followed by a second sequence from 1948 to 1952, which included several Chinese studies, notably an examination of the morphology of Chinese cities. He also wrote two books on Japan: *A Reconnaissance Geography of Japan* (1934) and *Japan: A Physical, Cultural and Regional Geography* (1945). The latter earned an award from the Chicago Geographical Society in 1947 as 'the outstanding geographical publication of the past two years'. The book was revised and completely rewritten in 1965.

Third, Trewartha has long been interested in climate. In fact, his first publication was on *The Climates of the World* (1923). This was followed by *An Introduction to Weather and Climate* (1937, rewritten 1968) and *The Earth's Problem Climates* (1960).

Fourth, Trewartha has made signal contributions to the regional variations of rural settlement in the USA. These include: the unincorporated hamlet (1943) (functional definition and patterns of nationwide distribution); types of farmstead (1948) (repetitive modes of grouping of constituent buildings in the farmstead cluster, and their nationwide regional variants in relation to agricultural systems); and contrasted forms of rural settlement in colonial America (1946) (settlement grouping and field patterns in the different sectors of the Atlantic seaboard, with contrasted conditions of colonial settlement).

Fifth, in the latter part of his career Trewartha has turned to the study of regional variants in the density and patterns of population. This began with a discussion of the conceptual field and procedures in a presidential address to the Association of American Geographers in 1952. Later studies were located in inter-tropical Africa and maps were prepared and the materials assembled with the assistance of W. Zelinsky, who today ranks as one of the outstanding geographers in America (1954, 1957.)

Sixth, Trewartha, in retirement, is still actively working on a three-volume work on population. The first volume is entitled *A Geography of Population: World Patterns* (1969) and the second, *The Less Developed Realm: A Geography of its Population* (1972). The third is in preparation and will cover the rest of the world.

Finally, one finds in Trewartha's work an early interest in student textbooks. In collaboration with V. C. Finch, chairman of the department at Madison, he wrote *The Elements of Geography* (1936) (revised three times and rewritten in 1968); *The Earth and its Resources* (again with Finch, 1941), and *Fundamentals of Physical Geography* (with A. H. Robinson and E. H. Hammond, both colleagues at that time in Wisconsin, 1961). These have continued to be standard texts for many years.

343

This is a remarkably productive record. Trewartha's objectives and achievements in climate, land use, rural settlement, urban morphology, and settlement patterns in the USA, have served as examples and stimulus to subsequent studies in these fields of enquiry.

24

Post-War Trends in the USA

American geographers of the third generation paid much attention to the scope and purpose of the regional concept, partly in order to establish a rough but logical definition of its relations with the natural and social sciences; and (more recently) to re-instate geography, with new objectives and procedures, as an integral part of the high school curriculum, from which it has largely been excluded since the war by the adoption of 'social studies'. The status of the whole field was assessed in the early 1950s by almost all senior professional geographers in a symposium with the title *American Geography: Inventory and Prospect,* edited by P. E. James and C. F. Jones (1954; reprinted 1956). Comments in this chapter emphasize the outstanding developments since that date; that is, over the last twenty-five years. However, reference will also be made to the major contributions of the third generation in the interwar years as a springboard for the assessment of current trends.

GENERAL TRENDS

There has been a tremendous boom since 1945 in the teaching of geography at the college and university levels, but an appalling retreat at the high school level. There are about a dozen outstanding graduate schools of geography, some of which have up to 100 postgraduate students working for masters and doctorate degrees. On the other hand, the teaching of geography in the high schools as understood in the countries of western Europe has virtually disappeared. Geography as a subject of tuition usually occupies one year in the full school programme of so-called 'social studies', that are often manned and taught by teachers trained in history. From the point of view of knowing simply where places are or of observing the local environment, this is a serious national situation. Geographers are now considering the role of geography in high school and methods of teaching it, though the new goals are in large part divorced from the regional concept. There is a current trend in some states to revive 'earth sciences', and in one state at least the lead is being taken by geologists from the state university.

Geography now stands on a footing of equality with other disciplines in American universities. Through the adoption over the past three decades of a man-centred viewpoint, it is currently generally regarded as a social science, though it has normally grown out of geology, and is sometimes still associated—in course combinations, facilities and buildings—with the earth sciences.

There has been a strong shift in emphasis in the conceptual framework of geography since the war and, consequently, in the choice of problems. Out of the experience of the war, it was argued that in order to develop as a research discipline or to obtain recognition as being scientifically respectable among other scientists, georaphers must drop the all-round, synthetic approach of what was usually thought of as 'regional geography'. What is necessary, they argued, is specialization in some 'systematic field' in which one can acquire a competence that can be applied to *any* area. Similarly, the concept of 'areal totality' was rejected as leading to the production of compilations and inventories, whereas true competence and understanding can only be obtained by thorough analysis of some particular phenomena that vary areally. In brief, the regional method and its sequential treatment, often with a physical environmental basis, was discredited. And rightly so. The emphasis has since shifted to 'systematic specialization', which means, in effect, the study of particular phenomena over the earth and the processes that lie behind their spatial arrangement. One does not work in an area, large or small, as an end in itself, with particular problems, but as a 'laboratory' to arrive at generalizations of wider applicability. The intensive study of *small* areas, such as was undertaken in the early 1920s, is no longer favoured. Geographers, junior and senior, sometimes (fortunately) train and work with long dedication as specialists in one major overseas area which they know thoroughly at first hand. Favoured areas are Latin America, south-eastern Asia and the Soviet Union, though there is a shortage of such specialists on India, China and Japan. There are, of course, outstanding leaders of the third generation, notably Cressey, James, Orchard and Trewartha, but they have apparently few successors.

In the training of a geographer attention in general is currently focused upon the study of man on the earth or, in other words, the 'man-environment system'. This has several strong repercussions.

The natural environment, the 'new geographers' assert, is investigated in its relevance to man. Geomorphology, plant ecology and climate are usually not taught as ends in themselves, but in their relevance to human occupance, or, if you will, in terms of man-land relationships. The approach of Davis, Fenneman, Johnson and Atwood, Marbut and Shantz, has been neglected over the past three decades. The processes involved in the development of land forms, climate or vegetation have been subordinated to the areal evaluation of land in terms of its significance for human occupance. This means, for example, a particular concern with the conservation and management of resources and the evaluation of slopes in terms, say, of the erosion of soils or their suitability for cultivation. The problem in each case is circumscribed by the objectives, technical abilities and traditions of the group occupying the area. This has meant a neglect of geomorphological problems over the past generation, to which Sauer, and some of his elder students, such as Russell and Leighly, have raised strong objections. It is now being recognized that the geographer ought to know more geomorphology in order to evaluate more effectively the relevance of land to human occupance, but it is at present difficult indeed to find suitably qualified men in the American market. By way of contrast, the study of the physical earth, as an end in itself, has remained strong on the Continent and in Britain, so strong, indeed, that many believe that geography, as Mackinder predicted over fifty years ago, is becoming involved in processes *per se* rather than their regional expression.

Another trend has become especially marked since the publication of *American Geography*. This is the application of statistical methods to the investigation of geographical distributions and arrangements. This procedure, while it is firmly established in the realm of the physical sciences, has recently been applied to the geographical analysis of human phenomena. Mathematical concepts, even laws of astrophysics, are used to measure and explain the functions, size and spacing of urban centres. Statistical techniques are used to determine the co-variance of spatially distributed phenomena. These quantitative methods, that are pursued with a missionary zeal, are undoubtedly needed and are a major advance in the study of the areal co-variations of terrestrial phenomena. But they must be used as tools or means in pursuit of the regional concept. There is a widespread tendency for the quantitative worker to regard the search for the uniqueness of areas as an inferior form of exercise. This is proof positive of a misinterpretation of the regional concept.

The post-war growth of 'systems analysis' in the human sciences is necessitating a more explicit conceptual framework for geography, a clearer conception of focus, for the new language of ecology expresses concepts that have long been implicit, though vaguely conceived, in geographical work. Barrows wrote in 1923 that regional geography 'is the culminating branch of the science because it involves facts and principles from all divisions and subdivisions of systematic geography'. Yet it is, according to Barrows, centred on man and must therefore relinquish the specialized physical disciplines each with its own ends and concerned with natural processes, such as the independent fields of geology, botany, zoology and physics. This seems to be the same approach as that recently expressed by Ackerman and others. They see geography as concerned with a particular kind of 'systems analysis'. These are spatial systems that are integrated around the complex of land-man relationships. According to this approach, the field of geography is ecological, and the physical earth must be evaluated from this point of view. Geography is thus essentially concerned with the study of 'ecosystems'. It must be brought into meaningful relationship with the 'micro' aspects; that is, with the unit area of ecological association. This viewpoint is basically the same as that of Harlan Barrows, though its terms are different.

FIELD STUDIES

American geographers made major contributions between the wars to the purpose and method of local field study in regional analysis. This means mapping on a topographic scale on which individual man-made objects can be recorded, and demands, first of all, clarity of objectives, since it conditions what data shall be observed and recorded. This is a kind of expertise that used to be developed among graduate students, but is now being neglected in many programmes of advanced study. This neglect, in fact, is one of the major tragedies of current American trends. Field study involves much more than learning a method. I have associated with graduate students who have not the faintest idea how to orient themselves in the field, or, indeed, how to describe the land shown on a topographic sheet of the US Geological Survey.

The method of recording is a technical problem that varies with the scale of operations and of the map. Indeed, the whole problem of field mapping depends entirely on objectives, means of travel, area and distances to be covered.

Two sets of phenomena may be observed and recorded in the field. First, there are the facts of the landscape or townscape that can be seen, generalized and recorded as to occurrence, distribution and limits; and, second, there are the facts that cannot be seen, but are obtained by enquiry. Comments are limited here to the former since this is the primary concern of the fieldworker. The data of landscape include all the features of the land and its surface cover—configuration, vegetation, fields, buildings, roads. Any attempt to record a number of these synthetically raises questions of consistency to the observation of *one* set of phenomena.

Areal generalization is, or emphatically should be, the main purpose of geographical science. The individual item visible in the field is the unit, but one seeks repetitive spatial patterns. The ultimate question is not one of observing and recording every individual item. The whole process is one of mental generalization of the relevant elements that are areally repetitive and that are areally associated and functionally interconnected with other elements forming spatial systems. One cannot recognize such repetitions and interconnections until one is at the end of a first traverse.

The study of the local area has long been a primary basis of geographical study, and, from a pedagogical point of view, we owe much to the *Heimatkunde* of our German colleagues of the nineteenth century. We know much of the methods of observation of the great scientific explorers, and, from the inadequacies of many of their published reports, in books and journals, it is evident that many lacked either consistent objectives, methods of recording, or ways of describing the things they saw. The explorer needs guidance, training and advice in field methods, if his observations are to be of any value to others in understanding the locale, the limits and associations of lands and peoples. This, indeed, historically, has been one of the primary functions of geographical societies. The individual specialist will record atmospheric conditions with his instruments (as did Humboldt), and the botanist will collect plants (as did Humboldt and Bonpland). The geographers (like Humboldt) will observe the repetitive associations of relief, vegetation, land-use, settlement. Normally the observations will be focused on one or two of these sets of phenomena. In many field studies in remote areas one is obliged to concentrate on a preliminary recording of these data, and may eventually produce a contour map or a vegetation map or a crude (though invaluable) delimitation of types of rural economy. The fieldwork of Hettner in Colombia is an example of the last.

Further difficulty in the field arises from the fact that record of the landscape is limited to photographs and sketches. The degree of generalization must be adapted to the area, the problem and the scale of operation. A minute survey on foot is one extreme, the single traverse over long distances of several hundred miles by car per day presents another. In between the two lies the procedure of the detailed inventory of sample areas, and this poses the technique of sampling.

We now turn to some developments in field techniques among geographers in the USA that should be the basis of geographical training, but currently are not.

Much attention was given between the wars to experiment and training in field observation. There is nothing in western Europe comparable to the pioneer work of American geographers. Carl Sauer, together with Wellington Jones, wrote an essay on the role of fieldwork in geography that was published in 1915 in the *Bulletin of the American Geographical Society*.[1] This interest continued with discussions in Michigan about land-use problems on the notorious cut-over land in the northern part of the state. This led to the formation of the Michigan Land Economic Survey. Its directive was to undertake a field inventory and cartographic representation of the data relevant to land use. A wide cross-section of specialists was employed in the project. The procedure of the field inventory was proposed by Carl Sauer who at the time was on the staff of the department of geology and geography of the University of Michigan. The direction of the detailed field inventory was essentially in Sauer's hands. This was, in effect, Sauer's first professional assignment and it had important repercussions. It was a pioneer in land-use survey that clarified and focused the geographical contribution to such a problem. In 1921 Sauer published a paper on the problems of land classification and several years later, in the *Annals of the Association of American Geographers* of 1924, he wrote on the geographical objectives of the survey method. Directly out of this work grew Sauer's 'morphology of landscape' in 1925. Sauer left a group of eager followers in the Middle West in Chicago (led by his contemporary and earliest collaborator, Wellington Jones, who remained at Chicago) and Ann Arbor, Michigan (where K. C. McMurry (with a doctorate from Chicago) was appointed as head of the new department of geography. Meetings of Mid-Western geographers took place in the early 1920s.[2] Out of this there emerged the concepts of the fractional code notation in field mapping (first suggested by C. C. Colby) and of the unit area. From the work of this group there emerged papers on detailed field mapping of agricultural areas by Jones and Finch in the *Annals* in 1925 and by Whittlesey in 1927. The most complete specimen of the method of fractional notation was applied to a rural area in south-western Wisconsin by V. C. Finch (*Montfort, A Study in Landscape Type in S. W. Wisconsin,* Geographical Society of Chicago, Bulletin no. 9, 1933).

The laborious procedure of such study needed to be generalized so as to cover a larger area more expeditiously. This step was taken in Donald Hudson's land-use survey for the Tennessee Valley Authority. This survey was carried out by about a dozen young geographers under the direction of Hudson. The scale of the aerial mosaics used was 1:24,000 and the total area surveyed had a coverage of 550 square miles. For this purpose, using air photographs together with field observations, a method was devised for recognizing 'homogeneous land units' and describing them by an elaborate 'fractional code'. The definition of the unit areas apparently took place in the field and was based on two sets of criteria. The first were the six major types of land: agricultural; forest; recreation; rural settlements and villages; urban; and manufacturing and mining. The last four are indicated by a single arabic numeral (no fractional code, since detail of these was not required in the survey). The main concern was with agricultural land. This is classed by use into five categories: major land use; emphasis; field size; idle land; quality of farmsteads and equipment. Forest blocks were classed as unit areas if they covered over 200 acres. The second group of criteria were the major physical conditions of the land unit. These included slope, drainage, erosion, stoniness, rock exposure and soil fertility. Using digits for each of the two categories and their sub-divisions, the first (land use) appears as a series of digits in the numerator of the long fraction; and the second, the physical conditions of the land, appears as seven digits in the denominator of the fraction. A final appraisal of the unit permitted it to be put into one of five classes, applying to each unit area of over 200 acres. These classes are shown by numerals 1 to 5 in the denominator of the short fraction, preceding the long fraction. The short fraction is a summarized judgment by the field men of all the characteristics of the unit area. Finally, a further judgment is based on a five-fold category of 'the severity or absence of problems and needs for adjustments' ((1) no problems; (2) not critical; (3) moderately critical; (4) very critical; (5) suited for forest use). This appears as a Roman numeral at the beginning of the fraction.[3]

The unit area is defined by looking at the terrain as a whole and assessing it as a homogenous unit. On the field map an area was identified and outlined in which a particular kind of land use and a particular combination of slope, soil and drainage were associated. Wherever any one of the elements of an association changed, a boundary line was drawn and a new association recognized. Theoretically, at least, the several associated features were mapped just as they would have been mapped on separate overlays, the only difference being that they were all plotted on one sheet and identified by a complex fractional code, a technique first suggested by C. C. Colby. The purpose of this technique was to assess the areal associations of phenomena at the smallest topographic level so as to break away completely from the facile assumption of consistent land-man relationships. The unit-area is an area with a common association of phenomena.[4]

James's study of the Blackstone valley was an attempt to recognize the detailed articulation of landscape types in an area.[5] Wellington Jones held seminars in Chicago in the early 1930s (which I attended) on the mapping of residential and industrial areas in Chicago. The most recent survey of this kind was that of Puerto Rico. This mountainous and much divided island had to be mapped on a larger scale of 1 : 10,000 under the direction of C. F. Jones and Rafael Pico.[6] Of more recent studies, special mention may be made of the investigation by Murphy and Vance of the central business district of the American city.[7] Field techniques became an established part of the training of all geographers in the USA.

In recent decades, and notably since the war, air photographs have provided a powerful aid to geographical work, though the work in Britain of O. G. S. Crawford, the archaeologist, goes back to the 1920s and of E. C. Curwen, the economic historian, to the 1930s. Sir Dudley Stamp reported on the aerial survey of the Irrawaddy delta in 1925 in the *Journal of Ecology,* and the classification of land on the basis of aerial photographs was first undertaken in northern Rhodesia in the early 1930s again in the *Journal of Ecology.*[8] Specifically geographical work was sponsored by the American Geographical Society in the 1930s in mapping from the air—*Northernmost Labrador Mapped from the Air* by A. Forbes (1938), *Peru from the Air* by G. R. Johnson and R. R. Platt (1930), *Focus on Africa* by Richard Light (1941), and *The Face of South America: An Aerial Traverse* by J. L. Rich (1942).

The evaluation of aerial photographs for the recognition of terrain facets (as discussed above had a pioneer in Carl Troll in Bonn. Great steps were made during and since the war and some training in the interpretation of aerial photographs now figures in the training of the geographer in most universities.

REGIONAL GEOGRAPHY

Regional geography made little impact in America before the First
World War. In 1907 out of fifty-five selected geographers only one,
Isaiah Bowman, regarded regional geography as his major field of
interest. Geography in Europe was focused mainly on the natural
environment and on the differentiated segment called a natural
region. On the supposition that a natural region tended to have
associated with it a unique set of human conditions, occupance
was confused with environment in the term 'natural region', although
Unstead in Britain in the 1930s tried to make a distinction by
referring to the uniform combination of environment and occupance
as a 'geographical region'. The same thinking and procedure applied
to Passarge's work in Germany in this period, who sought to define
the hierarchy of unique areas in terms of the strictly natural
features of the earth. At the same time there appeared the detailed
studies of areal association in particular small sections of the
European countries, that referred their associations of human
occupance back to the physical base.

The European work of these days seems then to have made very
little impact in the USA, on the worldwide, continental or local
scales. The concept of the synthetic natural region of Herbertson
(Britain), Hettner (Germany), Passarge (Germany) and Vidal
(France) found little understanding. More attention was given to
specific sets of criteria. Several composite studies of particular
areas were produced mainly from Chicago, between 1915 and 1925
(see chapter 17), notably by Sauer and Colby.

A new generation of geographers set to work in the 1920s. It was
led by the Chicago School, mainly by W. D. Jones and Carl O.
Sauer. Detailed work on 'unit' areas using elaborate fractional codes,
and then classified lands and regions on the basis of these data,
continued through the 1920s. The work is one of the most distinctive
contributions to knowledge of American geography.

The geographers soon apparently tired of the detail and labour
involved in micro-studies. They searched in the 1930s for a way
of bringing micro-studies into a more meaningful and wider areal
framework. It was felt that what was needed was expertise in a
particular field. Misguided and incorrect as the writer believes this
view to be—for his own experience during the war on terrain
analysis of land and city, in association with geologists, architects,
botanists, mathematicians, proved to be quite to the contrary—this
was evidently the conclusion of L. Wilson and E. A. Ackerman.
The result has been in the post-war years a belittling of 'regional

geography' and a boosting of 'systematic' or 'topical geography'. This is a false distinction due to a misunderstanding of the term 'regional geography'. In the 1950s the progressive geographers of the 1930s, now matured in years and experience, realized that the key to their study lay in the regional differentiation of the earth's surface, but they had difficulty in finding a common conceptual framework. They did, however, seek to do so and the results are expressed in D. Whittlesey's important essay 'The regional concept and the regional method' in *American Geography*. Though this essay came from Whittlesey's pen, it grew out of much discussion, and represents a large measure of basic agreement among senior American geographers at the time. Its main conclusions, as discussed below, represent an important consensus among senior geographers twenty years ago.

For Whittlesey, the region is 'a device for selecting and studying area groupings of the complex phenomena found on the earth'. 'Any segment or portion of the earth's surface is a region if it is homogeneous in terms of such an areal grouping.' Homogeneity is based upon selected criteria. A region is not an object, but an 'intellectual concept' devised and used for a particular purpose. Further, 'the approach to regional study starts with the homogeneous area, which is accepted as a hypothesis. The area is then examined with a view to discovering its components and connections.'

Whittlesey suggested the term 'compage' for a cohesive spatial entity. This term (as noted in the Preface) is defined in Webster's dictionary as 'compages', a 'functioning whole' in terrestrial area. It is a remarkable fact that the term has not been used by Whittlesey's successors as the essential of the regional concept. The reason is almost certainly due to the rejection of this basic concept by many current geographers.

Whittlesey's statement continues: 'The regional method conceived in these terms is a method common to all phases of geographic study.' The so-called dualism between topical and regional geography does not exist. If systematic geography is not exclusively concerned with the arrangement and grouping of phenomena on the earth's surface, it is no longer geographical; for this reason, geography is a 'monistic discipline'. Whittlesey sought to reconcile on these terms the dualism of the physical earth and the forms of life, both biotic and human, that occupy it. He says that some (like Barrows) would relinquish the former to the several natural sciences. A logical corollary to this would be the scattering of human geography among the social sciences. 'In practice most geographers retain physical geography as natural environment, but not as geophysics. This logic permits the retention of human geography as societal environment, but not as sociology.' In this way geographers (in America), writes Whittlesey, seek to avoid 'this duality of natural and human geography'.

Geography can only have a single purpose if it is centrally concerned with a central set of processes. These are social processes involved in man's occupance of the earth. Thus the earth, as terrain, is evaluated not in terms of its geophysical or biotic processes as ends in themselves, but in terms of the relevance of the earth to human occupance. This means that though a thorough grounding in the physical aspects is absolutely essential, and the more thorough the better, the geographer is interested in those aspects of land, atmosphere and water that are relevant to man. These are big objectives and demand an approach that is different from that of the geomorphologist or meteorologist or oceanographer. The unity of geography as the study of the earth's surface in the light of human occupance demands the cultivation of earth studies different from the objectives of the natural scientist. American geographers consistently take this line and it presents them today with an uncomfortable situation that, in terms of scientific advancement and organization, needs to be boldly resolved. The definition adopted by Barrows in 1923 is a man-oriented interpretation. It relinquishes geomorphology, hydrology, oceanography, meteorology, and probably plant and zoogeography, to the ancillary disciplines. This, in fact, has been the trend in the USA and is a cause of much concern to those who are physical geographers. Moreover, it is a trend in direct opposition to the trend in Europe, where the main fields—physical, biotic and human—are pursuing centrifugal courses, with an ever-increasing concern with process rather than with areal differentiations of the earth.

All this means two things that are essential for the advancement of geography in general and in the USA in particular: The first is that the study of the areal differentiations of the earth's surface, if man-centred, demands the precise evaluation of the physical habitat in its localized and worldwide variants from the standpoint of human occupance. A distinctive field of physical geography needs to be developed. Terrains need to be descriptively evaluated as the sites of human occupance from an ecological standpoint. Resources need to be evaluated in their locale, associations and potential. It was suggested fifty years ago by M. Aurrousseau in the *Geographical Review* that countries need to be broken down into small units from the standpoint of their natural and human resources and measures of potential developed. Water-supply needs to be interpreted and trained hydrologists must apply their knowledge to the problems of human occupance. Soil erosion needs to be examined in its relations to land use, densities of population, etc. A whole range of physical problems is involved. This does not mean relinquishing fields to others. It is a question of developing new fields focused on the evaluation of site, as the plant ecologist evaluates site without his being a geomorphologist.

The second point grows out of the prodigious advance in knowledge over the past fifty, and especially in the last twenty-five years. The individual geographer can no longer attain a mastery of all aspects of earth science. But he does need enough familiarity with earth sciences and special techniques to permit the understanding of ecosystems. The process of establishing separate disciplines will continue, and the geographer must rely more and more on the research studies in these other fields. In Britain and America these new disciplines tend to separate from geography. It is interesting, however, that in the Soviet world they remain among the geographical sciences (see P. E. James *All Possible Worlds*, pp. 281–304).

How do these comments apply to the relation of geography to the social sciences? It is here that the differences are most clearly marked, though in fact less generally recognized. The fact that geography is concerned with place-to-place relations on the earth's surface is now generally recognized by social scientists and historians in America. All of these social fields are concerned with man and various facets of man-to-man relations. Some of the (American) economists and sociologists have publicly relinquished the field of spatial structure to the geographers.

Geographers have to be clear then as to their objectives. It is essential more clearly and rigorously to define objectives in terms of problems. The usual argument (particularly in Britain) is that this is a matter of 'academic freedom' and that 'we do what we like'. This is the view presumably of Sauer and Leighly, and for this we have the greatest respect. But it does not resolve the question, in a rapidly developing world of education and research, as to just what is the core of the regional concept. Economists and sociologists almost despise concern with places. They are concerned with process and abstract generalization. They still need to be convinced that social processes vary from one area to another according to differences in the densities, distribution and cultures of the people and the ways in which they occupy the land. They need to be educated to the fact that their abstractions relate to land and people whose patterns vary so widely as to make many of their generalizations meaningless. Their expertise has to be adapted, in any country, to the regional variations of its spatial systems, and this area of analysis and interpretation is the realm of geographical expertise. One needs to evaluate and understand the unique features of land and people, their associations, their causes and their foreseeable consequences. This is the essence of the regional approach. It needs to be developed actively, at all levels, in order to serve the advancement of knowledge and to serve humanity in a rapidly changing world.

P. E. James makes the following statement: [9]

> The regional concept constitutes the core of geography. This concept holds that the face of the earth can be marked off into areas of distinctive character; and that the complex patterns and associations of phenomena in particular places possess a legible meaning as an ensemble which, added to the meanings derived from a study of all the parts and processes separately, provides additional perspective and additional depth of understanding. This focus of attention on particular places for the purpose of seeking a more complete understanding of the face of the earth has been the continuous, unbroken theme of geographic study through the ages.

I agree with this statement in every word. All paths that lead to such understanding should be encouraged and disciplined in this direction.

REGIONAL SCIENCE OR QUANTITATIVE GEOGRAPHICAL ANALYSIS

During the last twenty years, a new orientation and expertise has made a remarkable impact on geography, namely the use of quantitative analysis in the discovery and interpretation of areal distributions and associations. Its impetus in the mid-1950s was due particularly to F. K. Schaefer (1953) and W. Garrison (1957), and later to the work of W. Bunge and B. J. L. Berry.

Quantitative analysis is an old established technique of investigation in both the natural and social sciences. The term 'social physics' reaches back for a hundred years. Yet statistical techniques have made a big impact in the last ten years, since they obviously fill an important gap and raise many new and unanswered questions. The following is an appraisal written by Richard L. Morrill of the department of geography at the University of Washington in a personal report to me:

> Geography has traditionally been viewed as a classificatory

discipline, describing the way in which varying combinations of characteristics [areal differentiation] give identity to different areas. The goal of geography must inevitably be the discovery of regions of distinctive character. Worthwhile certainly, but such a limited view! We may identify, but there is little to explain. Such a view of geography stems from our preoccupation with facts. Given observations, what do they define? In an areal content—regions: valuable and interesting, but not offering much towards science's goal of understanding human and physical behavior. If we check false pride and look at other sciences, we observe the crucial distinction: they are looking for general principles of behavior that give meaning to the observations, not the reverse. (For example, the classification of species of flora into phyla and genera was an essential step in botany, but the emphasis long since shifted to explanation of the processes that account for the variation in the first place!)

A new geography, logically, has its central core and goal in understanding the structure of space and the role of spatial characteristics—geometry, if you will, applied to human behavior and the physical characteristics of the earth's surface. Our observations, whether of physical or human phenomena, are now enlivened examples of principles of spatial behavior in action. Geography must be redefined, if it wishes to be a modern science, as that discipline which studies the spatial oragnization of society, landscape, and their interrelations, of which the search for distinct regions is but one part of the broader goal. Achieving such a goal requires both the study of space in the abstract, and specific explanations of patterns of location, regional development, movement, etc. Christaller's inestimable contribution was as much in showing us that the pure deduction of ideal geometry could be the source of inspiration as in the specific context of location of central places.

The new concept of geography provides a new unity among all branches of geography, physical and human, regional and systematic, and, if we perform well, could restore geography to a respectable position in the sciences, as well as enable us to make a powerful practical contribution in future world development.

Geography as the collector and comparer is in danger of being automated out of existence by sensing devices and computers. Geography as the plane of the spatial context of experience has both an exciting subject and a crucial contribution within science, if we accept the obvious challenge.

Certain comments are called for on this statement and others like it. First, I accept as a springboard the fact that, since the days of Strabo, geography has been concerned with describing the areal variations of the surface of the earth. The so-called 'new geography' is, in fact, regarded as synonomous with 'regional science'. This is not so, as anyone familiar with the history of modern geography will quickly realize. Second, over the past twenty years the followers of the 'new geography' have not produced a single composite study of a small area. Third, the students they train are groomed in statistical procedures, but are woefully ignorant of maps and field-work, which are the essentials of the regional concept.

Mathematical analysis has been effectively applied to the inherited geographical tradition in both America and Britain by two outstanding younger leaders—Brian Berry (Chicago) and Peter Haggett (Bristol). One also has the impression (based on long personal experience in both countries) that in Britain the new expertise in undergraduate and graduate training is geared to, and adds to, the substance of geographical training. On the other hand, in some American universities geographical training is, indeed, so 'new' that it is completely divorced from what is called the 'traditional geography'.

THE ANALYSIS OF SPATIAL SYSTEMS

This is another shift from the general field adumbrated by Hartshorne's *Nature of Geography* in 1939 and the symposium edited by James and Jones, *American Geography: Inventory and Prospect*, in 1954. It is summarized in 1965 in the report of a committee of the division of earth sciences of the National Academy of Sciences and the National Research Council. Its purpose is to define 'geography's research interests, methods, and opportunities'. The purpose and priorities of study so defined are summarized in the report as follows: [10]

Nearly all branches of science may be related to a few great overriding problems, like the problem of the particulate structure of energy and matter, that of the structure of the cosmos, or the problem of the origin and physiological unity of life forms. Geography's overriding problem, which it shares with other branches of science, is that of a full understanding of the vast system on the earth's surface comprising man and the natural environment.

Of the three great parameters of concern to scientists—space, time and composition of matter—geography is concerned with two. Geography treats the man-environment system primarily from the point of view of space in time. It seeks to explain how the sub-systems of the physical environment are organized on the earth's surface, and how man distributes himself over the earth in his space relation to physical features and to other men. Geography's organizing concept, for which 'spatial distributions and space relations' are a verbal shorthand, is a tri-scalar space. The scales comprise extent, density and succession. Geography's theoretical framework is developed from this basic concept. Settlement (central place) hierarchy, density thresholds and diffusion theory are examples of theoretical constructs serving specific research.

Geographers have long believed that correlations of spatial distributions are among the most ready keys to understanding existing or developing life systems, social systems, or environmental changes. As geographers undertook such studies in the past they favored heavily the empirical-inductive method. More recently, particularly since the end of the last war, theoretical-deductive methods have been applied. The two currents of thought are now achieving a healthy balance within the research 'clusters' that are on the 'growing edge' of the field. The same trend also had occurred in the social sciences and biology, particularly through the introduction of systems theory and study techniques. Similar rigorous analytical approaches now offer a common ground for communication among biology, geography and the traditional social sciences.

The committee believes that geography is on the threshold of an important opportunity that derives from: (1) the now vital need to understand as fully as possible every aspect of the man-natural environment system, including spatial distributions, throughout the world; (2) the development of a common interest among several branches of science in the overriding problem and its spatial aspects; (3) the development of a more or less common language for communication for the first time among all the pertinent branches of science through mathematical statistics and systems analysis; (4) the development of far more powerful techniques than ever before for analysing systems problems, including spatial distributions, and (5) a backlog of spatial experience which geographers have accumulated from their spatial perspective and their past dedication to the study of the man-environment complex.

The central section of the report attempts to analyse the interests and competences among geographers that contribute to interdisciplinary progress in studying the great man-environment system. This analysis is presented in the form of discussions of four different problem areas considered illustrative of the growing edge of geography. The four problem areas are: physical geography, cultural geography, political geography and location theory. Within each problem area one or more research clusters are found. These are groups with common research interests whose members habitually communicate with one another. For each problem area the committee evaluates the significance of present and foreseeable research problems, the connection of current working problems with the great overriding problem of man and environment, the relation of the problem area to growing edges in other sciences, and research opportunities considered to be unfulfilled.

Physical geographers study the physiographic-biotic system as determined by natural and cultural processes, with emphasis on the spatial distribution of the system. Current research in physiography is focused on quantitative observation of land forms and superficial earth processes. These processes involve the movement of water, ice, wind and soil in different climatic and geologic environments. Clusters of research activity center on the study of rivers, glaciers, coasts and hill slopes, and the processes acting upon these earth features. Progress has been notable in the study of marine coasts and the Arctic environment, both of which have been characterized by close association of geographers and research workers from other fields in common study.

Joint study of plant geography and physiography is flourishing at several centers. The most recent work in climatology and climatography has been on the heat and moisture balance of the earth, on synthetic climatology, and historical climatology.

Three major research opportunities are thought to lie open to physical geographers: (1) a reformulation of basic hypotheses; (2) further observation of physiographic processes in a systems context; and (3) co-ordination of studies of the natural environment with cultural geography and other clusters of geographic enquiry.

New approaches to the dynamics of process have been provided by recent concepts of equilibria and cycles. The concept of a 'threshold' of erosion, for example, is an especially interesting one that should be easily applied to study. One present need is to treat physiographic processes as a complex multi-variate system rather than a previously static sum of land forms and averaged climatic data.

Another increasingly urgent need is for evaluating the effects of management and technological changes on the physiographic and biotic environment. Examples of research areas within which the physical geographer's techniques can contribute vital information to an understanding of the man-environment system are: the alteration of drainage basins by several types of water-control structures and by 'polluting' substances; the reshaping of landscapes by modern earth-moving techniques (including the impending use of nuclear energy therefor); and the study of soil and surface water movement in the presence of continued mechanical cultivation. Expanded study is long overdue for the natural environments in which most of the world's people live.

Cultural geographers study the material and non-material phenomena relevant to an understanding of the spatial distribution and space relations of human cultures. Cultural geographers are concerned with the earth as the home of man who, by means of culture, has become the earth's ecological dominant. The usual approach of the cultural geographer is that of studying spatial distributions of the elements or traits of a culture. Two different methods have been used in past cultural geography research: (1) the developmental, which emphasizes study of such relatively long-term processes as cultural evolution, growth, and retrogression; and (2) the functional approach, which focuses on the shorter-term processes of cultural interaction, flow and movement. The two approaches are complementary, and both are now used in recording and analysing the effects of man's changing cultures in modifying the face of the earth.

The closest of the past relations of cultural geography with other disciplines have been those with anthropology. Recent cultural geography studies have reflected the advances made by anthropologists in the study of behavior and of value systems. An especially vigorous growing edge in cultural geography has been the study of diffusion.

Specific problem areas in which the techniques of cultural geography seem promising are: (1) study of the nature and rate of diffusion of culture elements, and delineating the evolving spatial pattern of culture contexts; (2) identifying critical geographical zones for contact of culture complexes and discovering 'hybrids' or 'sensitized' areas; (3) identifying regions of cultural values incompatible with those of major aggressive cultures of today; and (4) identifying regions with cultural values and practices that are causing unstable relations between a society and its natural environment.

The study of political geography is concerned with the interaction of geographical area and political process; it is the study of the spatial distribution and space relations of political process. Its attention centers on the part of the earth occupied by a given political system, sub-system, or systems. Studies may be concerned with territorial phenomena of political systems on (a) supranational, (b) national state, (c) domestic-regional, (d) urban-community, or (e) local special-purpose district basis. Each has a distinctive system or sub-system associated with it.

Two problem areas have been cultivated in the past. One has treated the territorial problems of the national state and sub-national governments and their boundaries, and the other has treated resource management. These interests have polarized two distinct clusters of research workers. The general problem area of the resource management group is the study of the internal spatial organization of the giant state, whether federal or another type. The first, or political area group, has been especially concerned with the study of boundaries during its recent activity.

Three problem areas are considered especially significant at the present time: (1) the interfaces of national political systems, particularly in eastern Europe, the south-east Asian area, and Africa; (2) the internal spatial organization of the giant state; and (3) the territorial viability of small national states. Other interesting problems include the spatial distribution of political ideologies, the space relations of voting behavior, and the geography of demagogic control.

Location theory studies have been especially concerned with the development of theoretical-deductive method in geography. They have identified abstract spatial concepts and principles, and have tested these with emphasis upon the interaction of economic, urban and transportation phenomena in regional systems. Thus the older fields of urban, economic and transportation geography are being synthesized in a new approach that is the first concerted application of systems theory within geography. In these studies the 'dialogue' between the empirical and the theoretical has gone the farthest of any problem area in geography. The cluster of research workers in this area typically has a quantitative bias.

Location theory studies may be classified into four types, each at increasingly higher levels of generalization: (1) study of the static aspects of spatial pattern, like location, spread, density and geometry; (2) flow linkages between places; (3) temporal

363

N

dynamics of spatial structure and spatial systems; and (4) normative models leading to 'efficiency' solutions. Examples of each type of study are given in the text.

The major opportunity lying before the location theory research workers is the application of methods developed within this problem area to the spatial systems considered in the political, cultural and physical geography problem areas. This cluster is in a strategic position to improve the dialogue between the theoretical and the empirical in these other problem areas, as it has already demonstrated effectively in the synthesis achieved for the urban-economic-transportation area. Beyond this there are still many opportunities in the areas which have already been treated by this cluster, particularly in the dynamics of spatial systems, and in further development of efficiency studies.

Another opportunity exists for the development of a machine system in which dynamic models of cities or regions might be stored as aids to planning, management, instruction, or other uses that can benefit from observation of dynamic descriptive patterns.

The committee concludes that the 'bridge' position that geography traditionally has occupied, dividing itself between the natural and social science areas, its firm tradition of field observation, and recent rapid growth of theoretical-deductive work within it, offer an increasingly powerful intellectual combination that should be fostered. The committee proposes a strategy for further research, and catalytic actions for implementation of the strategy.

The committee recommends as a first step that the National Academy of Sciences/National Research Council establish a senior committee charged with continuing study of the man-natural environment system on the earth's surface. It further recommends expanded support for location theory studies, expansion of research in physical geography—especially as cultural parameters are concerned—expanded studies of cultural diffusion, and attention to those cultural elements most closely related to interaction within the climate-vegetation-erosion system. In political geography it calls specific attention to the study of the spatial organization of a giant state as a general problem, and the study of the interfaces between the political systems of the giant states. In all, it is hoped that the dialogue between the empirical and theoretical can be developed as well as it has been for the present location theory studies. Regional and historical geography are considered especially fitted to contribute from the empirical side.

The catalytic actions for further development of the field suggested are: support for dual-doctoral degrees, support for increased numbers of pre-doctoral fellowships, expanded field research at the pre-doctoral level, support for a continuing series of post-doctoral fellowships, and joint planning of research within two or more problem areas. There are also recommended two research institutes, one in political geography and the other in physical geography, to be located at or near universities having strong geography programs as well as a strong supporting program in non-geographic fields directly related to the institute's concern. It is suggested that each of these institutes be interdisciplinary, with a staff chosen from geographers and other physical and social scientists interested in the problem area.

It is believed that if an Institute of Political Geography were in existence for ten years it would have a telling impact on our knowledge of political systems, and of the relation of spatial problems to the foreign policy of this country.

The Institute of Physical Geography would focus on the natural system in regions where cultural processes have had a long history and increasing intensity of impact. It is believed that this institute would make an important contribution to our knowledge of the relation of cultural attitudes to physiographic, biotic and other environmental changes.

Finally, the committee recommends that support be given to a continuous effort toward analysing the needs of geography as data systems change. Being concerned with one of the most complex overriding problems that can be studied, geographers have a vital interest in any improvement in the power of analysing complex systems. One immediate step in this direction would be the establishment of three or four geographic data centers located at major universities with the latest computing facilities and a potentiality for adding special geographical input, output and data storage features. These centers would have a major impact upon equipment development and upon training of persons entering location theory studies.

The committee is certain that, as settlement continues to become more dense in the world and in this nation, the arts of managing space efficiently will be ever more in demand and of ever greater economic importance. Geography seeks the fundamental knowledge that supports the space-managing arts, and contributes to satisfaction of scientific curiosity about the man-natural environment system. The recommended measures would strengthen a field that is on the threshold of some of its most effective work.

In 1970 *The Behavioral and Social Sciences Survey,* edited by Edward J. Taffe, was published, the latest of several recent assessments of the status and trends of geography. The six members of the panel are among the leaders of the fourth generation and pace-makers of geography as a social science.[11] Their recommendations for future priorities in geographical research are as follows (p. 131):

(1) geographers should be encouraged to participate more fully in interdisciplinary work with other behavioural and social scientists and in policy-oriented work;

(2) Efforts should be made to alleviate the man-power shortage;

(3) centres or institutes for cartographic research and training should be established;

(4) efforts should be made to further develop and apply remote sensing technology and associated data and information systems;

(5) support programmes for foreign-area study should be expanded;

(6) special programmes should be undertaken to strengthen the mathematical training of geographers.

These objectives sound very much like wishful thinking (note the frequency of 'should'), since no attention whatever is given to basic training in expertise and especially to the distinctive role and purpose of geography in the whole sequence of education, through high school, college and university.

THE GEOGRAPHICAL TRADITION

The geographical tradition, which is so frequently criticized in America, is very much alive on both sides of the Atlantic. Its purpose and procedures were brilliantly presented by Carl Sauer in his presidential address to the Association of American Geographers ('Foreword to historical geography', *Annals of the Assoc. of Amer. Geog.,* 1941, pp. 1–24). This is a review of the scope and procedures of historical geography. Sauer also recognizes a field of physical geography that examines the areal variations of the earth's physical features, independent of human occupance. Sauer's viewpoint is based on his reinterpretation of the changing tradition handed down by his predecessors.

There are today American scholars who eagerly and productively follow these guidelines—R. Hartshorne, P. E. James, Jan Broek, D. Meinig and A. Clark. Substantive researches that have appeared in the last twenty years include Clark's book on Prince Edward Island,[12] which has received a high award from the Canadian Historical Association; Meinig's articles on the Mormon area and books[13] on the Colombia basin, South Australia, Texas and the South-west; Kniffen on the 'folk cultures' of America; Prunty on the southern plantation; Price on the areal variants of the central square of the county town. To these should be added the remarkable books published by the dean of American geographers, Carl Sauer, during the past ten years (as noted on p. 323).

In the same geographical tradition are several micro-studies of the USA. Such are Hammond's mapping of relief units, ultimately arriving at a nationwide pattern from the meticulous mapping in six-mile squares on sheets on a 1 : 250,000 scale for the whole of the country; Küchler's published map of the natural vegetation in the USA, built up in the same way; Marshner's study of land uses; Colby's study in the 1930s of local unit areas for the federal relief of unemployment; Bogue's more recent grouping of statistical divisions as common economic entities for the purposes of census interpretation; and, most recently, Berry's computer study of commuter flows to cities on the basis of local enumeration districts for the 1960 census.

I herald also the contributions of many other specialists. Above all, two remarkable symposia are focused on the nature of environments: the first of these, *Man's Role in Changing the Face of the Earth* (1956) is a mammoth production of outstanding scholarship by a variety of specialists (including geographers from western Europe) dedicated to the same theme. It was edited for the Werner-Gren Foundation (which convened the conference) by W. L. Thomas (geographer) with the collaboration of Carl O. Sauer, Marston Bates (distinguished Professor of Zoology) and Lewis Mumford. The second symposium was directed to the theme of the *Future Environments of North America.* It was convened as a conference and published in 1966 by the Conservation Foundation, and edited by F. Fraser Darling and J. P. Milton.

The works of biogeographers and soil scientists are of the greatest importance in the field of 'physical geography'. Pierre Dansereau's book on biogeography, *Biogeography: An Ecological Perspective* (1957), lays the foundations of a scientific plant ecology. He states in

the preface that the book is 'a new synthesis of the environmental relationships of living organisms', based on the idea of 'the plant
association—as a truly adaptive unit which bears internal cohesion
structurally and floristically'. He examines 'the dimensions of environment' from the local 'biotope' through orders to the worldwide 'biochore', and shows the relation of vegetation and climate.
Here, too, should be placed the evaluation of local variants of
terrain on which soil scientists are building a geographical hierarchy of soil entities upwards from local building blocks, rather
than accepting the mode of world zones established earlier, primarily
by Russian experts.[14] This approach of Dansereau is illustrated
by the following extracts from his book (text, diagram and
table):[15]

An acceptable definition of habitat implies many orders of
magnitude. The *biosphere* is that part of the earth's crust and
atmosphere which is favorable to at least some form of life. It can
be sub-divided into *biocycles,* of which there are three: salt
water, fresh water and land. The ecologically determining physical
factor which varies here is the density of the environment. Life
in the sea, in ponds and streams, and on land requires radically
different adjustments. For this reason the three biocycles are
somewhat diffuse in space, especially the fresh waters.

In turn, the *biochore* is the *geographical* environment where
certain dominant life forms appear to be adapted to a particular
conjunction of meteorological factors. Their world distribution
is due above all to rainfall, and each biochore is characterized
by a major type of vegetation. Forested regions and grasslands,
for instance, have strongly contrasting distributions of light,
heat and moisture. In response, the structure of the plant cover
is different, as are the habits of the animals (browsing and
grazing, singing from a perch or on the wing, etc.).

Within each biochore there develop one or more *formations*
which extend over an entire province. Thus, the forest biochore
of North America forms a gigantic horseshoe extending from
the tropical rainforest of Florida through temperate rainforest
to a vast expanse of summergreen deciduous forest, and on to
needle-leaf evergreen forest which swings to the north and west
and back again south-westward.

Within each one of these four formations, *climax areas* can be
distinguished that are characterized not only by their structure
but also by their composition. Thus the summergreen deciduous
forest of eastern North America is fairly homogenous in its main

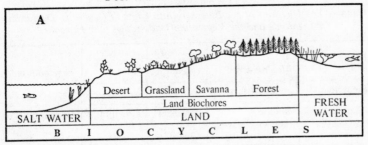

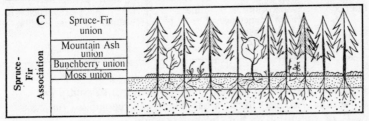

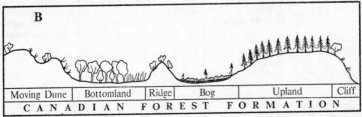

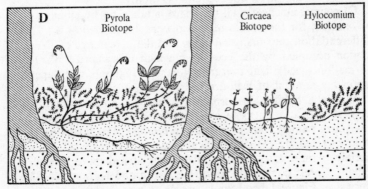

FIGURE 1 *The Dimensions of Environment*

A, the three biocycles in which land is sub-divided into four biochores. B, an example of a formation within the forest biochore and of the several habitats determined by topography. C, a single upland association with its four layers. D, the lowermost layers of the spruce-fir association with their ultimate sub-divisions, the biotopes.

TABLE 6 *The Divisions of the Biosphere into Units of Generally Decreasing Magnitude and the Vegetation Units which they Harbour.*

Environmental unit	Major control	Area covered	Type of response	Vegetation unit
Biocycle	medium (physical)	world	ecological	Various
Biochore	climate (meteorological)	continent or province	structural	Formation-class
Climax area	climate (meteorological)	region	structural and floristic	Climax association and subordinate seres
Habitat	topography and soil (edaphic)	land form	sociological	Association
Synusia	microclimate (micrometeorological)	layer	sociological	Union
Biotope	microclimate (micrometeorological or biological	niche	micro-edaphic	Microsociety or aggregation

structural features from east to west and north to south, but some nine discrete climax areas have been recognized on the basis of quantitative floristic composition.

Of course, not nearly all the space is taken up by climax vegetation, for the nature of the topography will allow a differentiation into many *habitats,* and the percentage of the region occupied by the ecosystem which characterizes the formation (needle-leaf evergreen forest in Figure 1 will depend upon the amount of well-drained upland.

Within a habitat, in turn, which harbors an ecosystem consisting of one or more *communities,* there are other subdivisions, namely, the *layer* and the *biotope.* The layers are characterized by the dominance, presence, or behavior of certain plant species which utilize space at a definite level or height. Forest commonly have tree, shrub and herb strata. The spruce in Figure 1 has four layers. Within each one, several biotopes can develop under conditions even more restricted and of narrower extension in space. Thus, the ground layer has three such distinct biotopes which are named for their most conspicuous plant occupants.

Living beings are limited more or less strictly at each level of integration to the environment, and in a general way they are more and more restricted as the smallest biocenotic unit, the biotope, is approached. Table 6 attempts to draw the line-up of controlling forces and resultant units, whereas Figure 1 illustrates the position of a small plant, the enchanter's nightshade (*Circaea alpina*), in a biotope which is part of a forest-floor layer. This layer is subordinate to the forest stand as a whole, which in turn occurs only on upland topography. Again, the whole evergreen needle-leaf formation, of which the Canadian forest is part, is conditioned by a cold-moist climate. It is the cumulation of all these influences that confines enchanter's nightshade to its niche.

The regional concept is also pursued in the realm of human affairs. Lewis Mumford has emphasized the regional relations of cities, a concept inherited and developed from Patrick Geddes, about which he has been writing for nearly fifty years; his approach has many theoretical and practical ramifications in city and regional planning. Historians and anthropologists also have been concerned with the regional concept. Suffice it to draw attention to the classic work by W. P. Prescott Webb on the history of settlement of *The Great Plains* (1931), and the enormous compilation of the early history and traits of world cultures presented in the late Ralph Linton's *Tree of Culture* (1961), which is about the most fitting basis for the study of man in his environmental milieux in the under-developed world. Linton was building on a long tradition, for it was Clark Wissler who, about 100 years ago, conceived the idea of a 'culture area' as a geographical composite of cultural traits with reference to the Indian peoples of North America. The pioneer efforts of the Chicago school in the 1920s and 1930s in both urban and rural ecology opened rich virgin territory that has long remained untilled by geographers. The tradition continues, however, and is evident in Amos Hawley's *Human Ecology: A Theory of Community Structure* (1950), which, in many ways is a parallel for human associations of Dansereau's treatment of plant associations.

The structure of spatially interconnected ecosystems is broadly discussed by Lee R. Dice, a senior zoologist at the University of Michigan, in *Man's Nature and Nature's Man: The Ecology of Human Communities* (1955). He points to the different categories of human ecosystem—tribal, homestead, village-centred, town-centred, city-centred, national and international. He remarks, however, in the preface:

Few attempts have been made so far to describe human communities from the point of view of their resources, physical habitat, human populations, associated plants and animals, and ecologic interrelations, including community regulatory-mechanisms. Practical methods for describing and measuring the various ecologic features of human communities in quantitative terms are still largely lacking, especially for the complex interrelations within an industrial community.

The field is not such a blank as Dice and his fellow ecologists would have us believe. The work of the Chicago sociologists between the wars blazed new trails—Louis Worth, Robert Park, Ernest Burgess, Roderick Mackenzie. Rural sociologists were also very actively involved fifty years ago in the study of rural spatial groups and their changes in the USA, led by G. J. Galpin and J. H. Kolb, both associated with the University of Wisconsin. Important pioneer works on spatial arrangement of human settlements were published in Germany in the 1930s by W. Christaller and A. Lösch, although their ideas made no direct repercussions in English or American circles until translated into English after the Second World War. During the last twenty years their work has stimulated a new field of spatial enquiry called 'regional science'. The area of interrelated spatial systems from the ecological standpoint has also been actively pursued. This has already been emphasized in the case of Britain. Confining my comments here to the USA, the following leading works may be noted: Trewartha's mapping and definition of hamlets and farmsteads throughout the USA; Brush's study of central places in Wisconsin (following, though he hardly seems to be aware of it, the objectives of the sociologist tradition at his own university); Borchert's exhaustive analysis of the grading and distribution of service centres in the group of states in the upper Middle West, and his wider study of the growth and spread of metropolitan centres throughout the USA since 1790; Thompson's study of the spatial variations (on a county basis) of the level of living in New York state; Berry's work on market centres and retail distribution and on the spatial impact of the urban associations of metropolitan centres; and several studies of the structure and measurement of the range of cultural regions, such as the Mormon complex of Utah and the Ozarks; and the form and spread of human landscape forms, such as the southern plantation and the county-town square. These are all healthy signs of vigorous dedication to problems of an ecological kind, which are far removed from the narrowly conceived and deluding scientific approach of so many workers in the new 'regional science'. The latter seeks to analyse and interpret single geographical variables, and offers modes of analysis that the regional concept could and should use where appropriate to its own ends, rather than to the ends of mathematical sophistication, which is so beguiling to the young student.

Regional planners are today emphasizing the role played by natural site factors as determinants of urban land uses. They refer to these factors as 'physiographic determinants', which is heralded as a virtually new idea. Ian L. McHarg's *Design with Nature* (1969) is acclaimed on the back cover of the paperback edition as 'a permanent landmark for the age', and 'a turning point in man's view and treatment of his environment'. Many so-called geographers today virtually (and in at least one published instance, categorically) reject the study of environment. They thus presumptuously renounce the distinguished contributions by specialists such as Bowman, Fenneman, and Davis to physiography, Marbut to soil science and Shantz to vegetation, all of which added substantially to our knowledge of the variants of the earth's surface. This is a note of responsibilities rejected rather than a record of progress. Environmental study is currently, probably permanently, relinquished to others.

A regional approach is followed in three outstanding introductory texts: R. J. Russell and F. B. Kniffen, *Culture Worlds* (1951); J. E. Spencer and W. L. Thomas, *Cultural Geography* (1969); and J. O. M. Broek and J. W. Webb, *A Geography of Mankind* (1968). All these authors, it should be noted, are followers of Sauer, and reflect a strong ecological orientation. All three works embody the true geographical tradition. Regional science, which has swept the colleges of the USA like wildfire, is an essential part, but only a limited part, of it. In its concern with geographical variables, it involves statistical methods that can be quickly learned and applied. Learning and research in the fields noted above takes concentrated training and years of dedication with the focus on clearly defined objectives.

These are all substantial steps in the direction of the regional challenge. Each has met with widespread acknowledgment and further interpretation. Each demands a very special expertise and training.

GEOGRAPHICAL EDUCATION

To what extent are these general trends reflected in geographical education? Standards of student achievement are low. Courses at all levels frequently lack a co-ordinated sequence through the three or four years of study. Moreover, the geographical illiteracy of the people is not confronted in school. Training at all levels reveals, in comparison with Britain, the almost complete absence of laboratory work in the university, with no attention given to maps or field techniques, which are the essentials of geographical expertise. There is a deplorable lack of reading motivation, which is characteristic of the American people as a result of mass communication, and an almost complete dependence on the spoken word of the professor rather than the vigorous pursuit of independent reading and writing.

A comment for American readers regarding geography in Britain is appropriate in this connection. After ten years at the head of a department at Britain (and twenty in the University of London) I am deeply impressed by the vigour of the professional field, the excellence of its standards and the problems it so fruitfully pursues. There are now two endowed chairs in many universities (usually in physical and human geography), large staffs, and increasing numbers of students for the degrees with honours. Standards are maintained and the reward of a first class honours degree is a rare distinction, its recipient rarely moving to an American university. Buildings in the new and older universities receive high priorities—as evidenced, for example, by the remarkable new hexagonal structure at the University of Sheffield. Geography is generally recognized as a laboratory study and large cartographical laboratories are available, for map collections and exercises, simulation models and quantitative analysis. Not only do the geographers have their own professional institute with its published transactions (including monographs), but also a remarkable illustrated journal, the *Geographical Magazine*. Founded by Michael Huxley (a grandson of T. H. Huxley), this magazine contains articles of high scholarship and remarkable readability, with numerous photographs, designed successfully for a wide reading public. Geography flourishes through the whole course of high school education, and the best entrants to a university possess a better understanding of geography than most graduates of an American university. Students undertake exploratory expeditions to the four corners of the earth, assisted by universities, societies and private companies. The writer has served as chairman of one such 'overseas expedition society'. There are many opportunities for field-work, which is mandatory for all at the undergraduate level.

A comment now for British readers on the post-war American scene. There are certain common research trends between Britain and America, notably dedication to quantitative analysis. But there are wide differences. The deluge of students in the 2,500 colleges of America explains but does not excuse the reduction of standards and the deplorable procedures that are widely prevalent at the undergraduate level today. This is partly due to the virtual elimination of geography in high school (a major contrast with Britain) and the lack of dedication of college teachers to the content and procedures of teaching. The American dream of universal education, of everybody 'going to school', has produced a nation of what Americans call 'functional illiterates'. The main problem of education in America, at all levels, including the doctorate, is to find ways and means simply of persuading people to read.

Geography is widely taught at most colleges, but standards of achievement throughout undergraduate and graduate courses—except in a dozen major universities—are below desirable levels. The thesis is more and more about less and less, with an inadequate foundation of reading and understanding. Many professors (as in Britain) are fortunately aware of this problem of quantity as against quality. They seek to broaden the platform of a general education, without losing the depth and understanding of different disciplines.

In the American universities geography is almost universally regarded as a social science and there is today an exaggerated devotion to 'the quantitative analysis of geographic variables' that masquerades under the banner of 'regional science' and the 'new geography'. Training at all levels in the regional concept is deplorably weak and the confusion among students and colleagues as to what geography is all about is worse than ever. Funds have been readily available for 'field' research in all parts of the world, but there is little evidence in publications of regional study. A particular area is frequently regarded simply as a 'laboratory' to test formulated 'systematic' generalizations.

Fieldwork, which received so much attention from American colleagues between the wars, has fallen into the background. Students at the undergraduate and graduate levels are not even trained to read (as they are in Britain), and still less to interpret, their own topographical maps. Large numbers is no excuse for this neglect. New methods are needed. It is possible in many institutions to graduate or even to reach the doctorate in geography without ever stepping into the field. This is a responsibility in a nation that seethes with agitation about 'environment' and 'ecology' with very little appreciation of what they mean.

Finally, since geography has been established there by choice as a social science, three things are evident. First, the field of 'physical geography', so strong in Britain, has been woefully neglected since the days of Davis and Johnson. Second, departments throughout the nation, including the best, are deficient in all kinds of laboratory and library space. It is a truism, but a major problem of the large university, that ready access to books and periodicals is essential in education. These facilities become ever more remote in the large universities and the problem, if faced as such, has yet to be resolved. Third, there is absent a rigorous disciplinary training at all levels in the fundamentals not only of geographical expertise—maps, map interpretation, fieldwork—but also in the study of the physical aspects. The social sciences are particularly subject to such dilution in America. Learning in a sequence is essential in order to acquire a competence in a discipline and therefore for the handling of social problems, which is a primary motivation in the youth of America. A British colleague once remarked to me that his course on advanced geomorphology (and the same is true of other fields) *at the undergraduate level* was designed to tackle research problems. Students at the graduate level in American universities rarely reach this stage, obviously not through lack of ability, but due to inadequate training. This is the result of 'doing your own thing' and a hedonistic attitude to learning. Such is the challenge. It is expressed currently by the popular concern about 'ecology' and 'environment'. There is also the rude awakening, recently disclosed by various investigations, that as many as half of all students in college simply do not read, not even prescribed textbooks.

Two concluding comments arise from this long journey of appraisal: The record of this book, together with that of its predecessor, *The Makers of Modern Geography,* reveals that there is something radically wrong with the verdict of E. A. Wrigley of Cambridge, England,[16] that 'the study of the region and regional life as the crown and peak of geographic work— is no longer tenable'. This view is out of step with the thought and work of many leading scholars on both sides of the Atlantic. Wrigley takes his springboard in the writings of Vidal de la Blache, which he chooses to call the 'classical' geography. This lip service to Vidal, all too common in Britain, is sadly misguided, since it fails to assess, even to express cognisance of, the works and changes in viewpoint in France in the fifty years since Vidal's death. To trace this growth was the whole purpose of my *The Makers of Modern Geography*. The view that Wrigley rejects lingered through the inter-war years (and still survives) in both Britain and America. It is, however, a generation out of date, as my previous book will reveal to those who cannot read a foreign language with facility. The enthusiastic British and American contemporaries of the fourth generation are flogging a dead horse. They should pay more attention to the contribution of Continental scholars since Vidal's death before expressing a presumptuous denial of their heritage.

Finally, I would remind the leaders of current trends in the USA of the wise words of Preston E. James: [17]

Geography in America is alive and growing. Life and growth, as in any field, produce controversy and dispute. But the future of this field of study requires not the victory of one segment of the profession over the others, but rather the integration of diverse ideas and approaches for the purpose of gaining greater and greater understanding of the complex interplay of elements in the earth's spatial system.

Conclusion

I want to sum up the essentials of the regional concept in the light of its historical development.

The regional concept seeks to characterize and explain the uniqueness of terrestrial areas, viewed as associations of earthbound phenomena, physical, biotic, and human.

Such areal associations occur as interconnected geographic 'orders', from a local through a continental to a worldwide scale.

Its questions and procedures are therefore directed to the analysis, assembling, and explanation of earth entities, as unique associations of groups of interdependent spatially distributed phenomena. Such intensive study may concentrate on any scale or aspect: physical, biotic, or human.

Current trends direct attention, in both tuition and research, to specialized techniques such as statistical analysis, remote sensing, computer analysis, regional science, palynology. These techniques are essential to the equipment of regional enquiry, but they are emphatically not its ends. The area is not a laboratory for abstract generalization. Terrestrial generalizations are valid only for particular associations, natural or human, localized in particular areas.

Geographic expertise, thus defined, studies 'the content of area' (as repeatedly stated by Ritter and Humboldt), that is, of land, people and culture. It is also essential to be fluent in the relevant language(s), for this is the means of access to literature, field enquiry (by interview) and professional contact. Techniques are quickly acquired and beguile the young student (and many professors) into the belief that they are doing worthwhile work: this, of course, may well be the case. The regional concept demands their relevant skills and findings, but does not rest with their goals. Its own goal is the art of regional analysis and description.

Problems and procedures of analysis and description have changed with the advancement of factual knowledge and philosophic modes over the past hundred years or more. It was, however, maintained

378

over fifty years ago that geography is not concerned with the analysis (however sophisticated) of 'geographic variables', ranging from brachiopods to automobile sales. It has come to mean the discovery and evaluation of areal associations of earthbound phenomena.

Geography has been envisaged by many through its historical development, and by many contemporaries, from two vastly different points of view, one as a group of disciplines, the other as a single discipline. On the one hand, the study of spatial phenomena is the broad umbrella. This, in the last analysis, is the meaning of such expressions as 'all possible worlds' and 'I do as I like' (miscalled academic freedom), both statements being asserted by distinguished scholars, past and present. On the other hand, it is regarded as the study of areal composites over the earth's surface, physical, biotic and human, a view that was finally arrived at by one of the most distinguished 'quaternary geologists' in his younger years, who, in his own words, became wiser as a geographer with maturity— Albrecht Penck.[1]

The image of the regional concept is not that of a multi-storeyed mansion with no interconnecting staircase (to use Penck's analogy again), but that of a multi-colored carpet. The patterns of this carpet, often vaguely localised and limited, embrace land, landscape, economy, and culture. Its major ancillary disciplines include, depending on focus, geology, meteorology, and botany; agricultural and urban land economics; cultural history; and demography. Its skills are the specialized interpretation of maps, field observations ('the morphological eye'), and written records and statistics.

A current trend in both Britain and America is to pursue highly specialized technical processes on various floors of the mansion with little creative concern for other segments or floors, the mansion being an arbitrarily selected area, often simply for convenience. There are many such recent exhaustive studies, presented with consummate skill (sometimes even by a number of specialists), which, however, fail entirely to face the question of the changing and present uniqueness of the area handled, be it Wales or New England.

The art of geographic description (so much discussed in Britain) has changed with time. The Hettnerian practice, that dies very hard in Anglo-America (indeed it is on the contrary becoming more and more in vogue), of orderly description of varied spatially distributed phenomena in a more or less arbitrarily defined area has been rejected on the continent for fifty years.[2] Anglo-Americans work in isolation on one of the floors. Systematic specialization deflects from the central question, the unity of the mansion. The so-called 'interconnection of spatially distributed phenomena' leads to

379

o

many false deductions and dead-ends. Nor does the approach of 'environmental adjustment', that has been so widely accepted (superficially) in Britain, lead to worthwhile questions or portrayals. There is ample in the literature to prove this point. The target, in other words, needs to be more sharply focused, as Penck argued in the twenties, and Carl Troll in our own day. Both assert that this focus should lie in the arrangement of phenomena over the earth's surface.

This assertion does *not* mean systematic omniscience, as has so frequently been argued in America, in the sense of an agglomeration of 'areal studies'. Indeed, in such a program, the geographer is challenged (or ought to be) as to his proper scholastic place. This assertion *does* mean the use of skilled methods for the pursuit of clearly envisaged questions of past and present regional relations. There is, in this connection, a great gulf between the early appraisal of the Ozarks by Carl Sauer over fifty years ago (virtually modelled on Hettner), and the fruitful and provocative works of Donald Meinig in our own day.[3] The 'regional scientists' have little to offer, since they reject regionalism as unworthy of their attention.

It is customary to distinguish (particularly in America) between what is called 'systematic' and 'regional' geography. The former refers to a field on a floor of the terrestrial mansion, such as economic geography, political geography, or geomorphology. It has, in recent years, become increasingly fragmented and narrow. The latter simply refers to the composite study of a particular area, essentially still in the outmoded procedure of Hettner. This situation is to be deplored for two reasons. First, systematic and regional are not contrasted in content. They are two facets of the same coin, and their approach should be accordingly disciplined. This was clearly pointed out by De Martonne seventy years ago. Second, divergence into narrow fields leads to the ancillary disciplines, and to questions, situations and processes (whether natural or human), which their experts can (and do) much more expertly handle. These dangers are abundantly evident in the fields of geomorphology in Britain and 'area development' in America. These paths must be followed (one is, of course, free to pursue them and stay with the relevant disciplines, so long as one does not claim to be still under the geographic umbrella).[4] The geographer should, however, always be alert to the regional enquiry, and using the same data pursue independent modes of treatment and pose distinctive questions. This lack of purpose has proved to be my biggest problem in the training of both undergraduates and graduate students.

It would be advisable to be more specific on the above assertions. Recent books on particular areas often contain a series of sophisticated essays on topics (often appearing as research articles) on different storeys of the areal mansion, bearing no relation whatever to each other, and written often by specialists, without any common concern. For what is there in common between 'geochronology' or 'dynamic geology' (which cannot even claim to be geomorphology) and the development and distribution of towns, or the localization of particular agricultural or demographic trends? This, however, is the dominant trend today, rather than regional specialization, since it conforms more respectably to the prevailing scientific attitude.

The study of any area, however defined, from the approach of the regional concept, raises questions that may be selected as follows, which demand skills, dedication, and judgment, equally exacting as any systematic field. Wales and New England may be taken as examples. Each is a man-given name of an area which should be critically examined as an entity. In what respects is it a physical entity, that is, a distinct grouping of similar or associated terrestrial units of land forms, climate and vegetation? What evidences are there, as revealed by old maps and nomenclature, of the unity of the area or of its regional diversity? What may be listed as traits of regional character, and what, in sum, by sample spot findings, is their geographic extent? What facts of the distribution, origin, and attitudes of the people correspond with or break up the area? What are the clusters of similar or interlinked manufactures and land use that are localized within the area, that correspond with it, or extend beyond its boundaries?[5] What elements of spatial cohesion have emerged in time through the orbits of urban centres (large and small), or the network of routes, and relative accessibility.[6] In what measure is the area a unit, or divided in its orientation towards adjacent geographic areas for purposes of government and organization and in popular feeling? Finally, for certain 'fringe' areas there arises the question of differing orientations, past and present, towards major culture spheres (e.g. Viet Nam). These are searching questions. They provide a conceptual framework that may be applied as the goal of study, in whole or in part, in any geographic area, small or large, parish or State. The key question throughout is 'What is a regional entity?'

It will be observed that these two examples are Specific Regions, that are considered in regard to their unique characteristics. There is also, however, a large field of Comparative or Generic Regionalism, in which the emphasis is on analogous regional assemblies, with similar selected characteristics, in different parts of the world. These should be pursued as objects of enquiry and courses of formal instruction in lieu of the narrow, and much favored, specialization on so-called systematic fields, with increasing emphasis on what is called 'process'.

There are three broad modes of approach to such comparative study, in which selection is open to both institution and individual. First, Comparative Natural Regions are analogous regions in terms of landforms, climate, vegetation, and soils, or some preferred combination. Comparative Human Regions are units of similar kind and origins with respect to several fields—demography (population distribution, structure, trends); economies (modes of livelihood, levels of living and stages of development, trade); culture (social structure, ethnic composition, religion, literacy, attitudes); and political organization (political units, their subdivisions, and inter-state organizations). Third, there are major world units which are unique (specific) but cover major world areas and may be treated in depth with respect to the unifying characteristics of their cores, their peripheries, and capitals. Such are, for example, Latin America, the Orient, Black Africa, the Third World. Natural Realms of this major world order include, as examples, The Tropical World, The Middle Latitudes, The Cold Realm. Comparative study may be undertaken of one major climatic or vegetation type, e.g. World Deserts. Still further possibilities are concentration on one continental area, or, in the human field, selection of one major grouping, such as Urban Regions. This comparative approach offers conceptual cohesion, a firm basis for formal instruction, and an intellectual challenge that is every bit as stimulating and demanding as the prevalent systematic approach.

Finally, many scholars adhering to the wider view and ready to shelter under its umbrella, were appointed to the new profession by University authorities fifty or more years ago as recognized practitioners in various fields, especially geology. Many later dabbled in regional presentations in fields in which they were certainly not qualified as researchers (e.g. oceanography and archeology), and remained jacks of all trades, though master of none. Many today are experts and respected as substantial contributors to narrow specialisms, obsessed by scientism and the pursuit of process as an end in itself. Examples lie in the field of geomorphology and regional science, both of which are highly developed and should stand alone as University disciplines, disassociated from the field of geography.

The true geographer is a regionalist, a categorical statement, that will undoubtedly raise a storm of opposition, but this is the main lesson derived from a historical evaluation. He searches for interpretations of regional entities at any scale. He may select at the outset an arbitrary area for his own convenience—of access or assign-

Conclusion

ment. Within this he searches for regional associations as a *terminus ad quem,* not an *origo a qua.* He may examine separate associations, say geomorphology or land use, or urbanism. But his final and guiding question is regional localization. This involves the spatial cohesion of similar forms or functional interconnections, resolved into cores of association, limits, and fluctuations. These find their medium in the network of nodal centers and routes and in uniform surface areas of land cover. This circumscription applies to all of the physical, biotic, and human aspects.

These conclusions are derived from the ideas, procedures and achievements of the makers of modern geography in both western Europe and America.

Notes

Preface
1   C. Troll, 'Die geographische Landschaft und ihre Erforschung', *Stadium Generale*, 1950, *3*, pp. 163–81.

Chapter 2   A Review
1   See J. N. L. Baker, *History of Geography* in *Collected Papers* (1963), p. 123. Baker, who died in 1971, commands high respect for his scholarship. He remained throughout his long career at Oxford essentially a historian of impeccable accuracy, but he made no substantive contribution to the regional concept.
2   This list, compiled for the Geographical Association and first published in *Geography*, 1961, pp. 349–53, brings the record to 1961; it does not list changes since that date. The reader who is not interested in the dates and persons of university appointments may omit this section.
3   The data here are taken from M. Chisholm, *Research in Human Geography* (1971).
4   E. J. Taaffe *et al.*, *Geography* (1970).
5   *Orbis Geographicus 1964-6*, Geographisches Taschenbuchen (1964-6), the world directory of geographers and institutions compiled by E. Meynen (Bad Godesberg) on behalf of the International Geographical Union. A second volume, *Orbis Geographicus 1968-72*, of societies, institutes and agencies, lacks the biographic details of individuals.

Chapter 3   Patrick Geddes, 1854–1932
1   *Town Planning Toward City Development: A Report to the Durbar of Indore* (1918), 2 vols.
2   Quoted (without exact source) by P. Boardman, *Patrick Geddes: Maker of the Future* (1944), p. 188.
3   The cartogram was devised by Geddes in the 1900s in the *Sociological Papers* and was last used in his paper 'The mapping of life', *Sociological Rev.*, vol. XVI, no. 3, July 1924. It was reproduced and discussed by the present writer in a Le Play Society pamphlet entitled *The Leplay Method in Regional Survey* (1932).

Chapter 4 Halford J. Mackinder, 1861–1947
1 See E. W. Gilbert, *Sir Halford Mackinder, 1861–1947: An Appreciation of his Life and Work*, Mackinder Centenary Lecture, London School of Economics and Political Science (1961). See also articles by Gilbert and others in *Geog. J.*, London, and various articles in *Foreign Affairs*, New York.
2 Mackinder, 'The human habitat', *Scot. Geog. Mag.*, 1931, p. 323

Chapter 5 Andrew J. Herbertson, 1865–1915
1 The excerpt quoted here is reproduced, by permission, from Herbertson's *The Higher Units: A Geographical Essay*. This was originally published in 1913 and was reprinted in a memorial issue of *Geography*, 1965, pp. 332–42. Herbertson first presented the concept in an address to the Royal Geographical Society in 1904, entitled 'The major natural regions: an essay in systematic geography', *Geog. J.*, 1905, pp. 300–12.
2 A. J. Herbertson, 'Regional environment, heredity and consciousness', *Geog. Teacher*, 1915, pp. 147–53. See also H. J. Fleure, 'The later developments in Herbertson's thought: a study in the application of Darwin's ideas', *Geography*, 1952, pp. 97–103.
3 For later developments of Herbertson's thought by H. J. Fleure, see Chapter 6.

Chapter 6 The Second Generation
1 'The later developments in Herbertson's thought; a study in the application of Darwin's ideas', *Geography*, 1952, p. 97.
2 P. M. Roxby, 'The agricultural geography of England on a regional basis', *Geog. Teacher* (1913–14), pp. 316–21.
3 H. R. Mill, 'A fragment of the geography of England', *Geog. J.*, 1900, pp. 205–26 and 317–32.
4 P. M. Roxby, 'Theory of natural regions', *Geog. Teacher*, summer 1926.
5 In a personal letter dated 21 February 1972.

Chapter 7 The Third Generation
1 Extracts from the memorial volume to L. D. Stamp, Institute of British Geographers, 1970.
2 Extracts from an article, in English, in *Geographische Zeitschrift*, 1969, pp. 161–76. All footnotes are omitted.
3 Now available, with a second group of authors, *A New Historical Geography of England* (1973), edited by H. C. Darby. See the critical review by an economic historian in *Annals of the Assoc. of Amer. Geog.*, 1974, p. 460. There is no essential change of approach, and the criticisms made later in this chapter still hold.

Chapter 8 Founders of the Main Centres
1 From the Herbertson Memorial Lecture, 'Scotland and some trends in geography', first published in *Geography*, 1948, pp. 107–20.

2 Anonymous obituary article, *Scot. Geog. Mag.*, 1934, pp. 331–3.
3 To this list I would like to add *Frequented Ways* (1922).
4 *Scot. Geog. Mag.*, 1930, pp. 101–4.
5 This authoritative appraisal of the work of Alan Ogilvie comes from *The Geographer's Craft* (1967), pp. 168–86.
6 Based on background material supplied by Professor H. C. Darby in a note to the author dated July 1972.
7 *Geog. J.*, 1966, pp. 1501–1.
8 *Geography*, 1947, pp. 34–6.
9 *Geog. J.*, 1966, pp. 151–3.
10 *Geog. J.*, 1967, pp. 594–6.
11 *Geog. J.*, 1948, p. 258.
12 *Geog. J.*, 1952, pp. 514–16.
13 *Geography*, 1953, pp. 316–20.
14 *Annals of the Assoc. of Amer. Geog.*, 1964, pp. 622–4.
15 Bachelor in Mechanical Engineering.
16 A volume in memory of Griffith Taylor was published in 1966 at Sydney, where he died. Eight scholars contributed essays and the volume was edited by John Andrews, Professor of Geography at the University of Melbourne. The title of the volume is *Frontiers and Men*.
17 *Climatic Control of Australian Production: An Attempt to Gauge the Potential Weather of the Commonwealth* (1915); 'Geographical factors controlling the settlement of tropical Australia', *Proceedings of the Royal Geog. Society of Australasia* (Queensland Branch), 1917; and *The Australian Environment (especially as controlled by rainfall): A Regional Study of the Topography, Drainage, Vegetation and Settlement; and of the Character and Origin of the Rains* (1918).
18 *Geog. J.*, 1964, pp. 189–91. Sir Raymond Priestley accompanied Taylor on Scott's Last Expedition, and, shortly thereafter, Taylor married Priestley's sister.

Chapter 9 The Royal Geographical Society
1 Excerpts from Chapter 15 of H. R. Mill, *Record of the Royal Geographical Society, 1830–1930* (1930).
2 Extracted from a memorial essay, *Geog. J.*, 1934, pp. 257–62.
3 *Geography*, 1950, pp. 124–6.

Chapter 10 Inter-War Trends
1 *Geography*, 1937, pp. 253–82.
2 Published as 'Physiography: some reflections and trends', *Geography*, 1960, pp. 1–15.
3 Special note must here be made of the Russian A. G. Isachenko's *Principles of Landscape Science and Physical-Geographical Regionalization*, translated by R. J. Zatorski and edited by J. S. Massey (1973). This book is precisely on the lines here advocated.
4 His essay 'Some aspects of the Saxon settlement in south-east England', written in 1935, is reproduced in *The Geographer as Scientist* (1956), p. 207.

5 Presidential address to the Institute of British Geographers in 1951, in *The Geographer as Scientist*, p. 53.
6 Ibid., p. 63.
7 *Geog. J.*, 1949, p. 126.
8 Several young British colleagues have refused in discussion to regard geography as a distinct discipline, and certainly pay scant regard to the writings of Hartshorne and others.

Chapter 11 Post-War Trends
1 The reader should also refer to the following: R. J. Chorley and P. Haggett (eds), *Frontiers in Geographical Teaching* (1963); and R. V. Cooke and J. H. Johnson (eds), *Trends in Geography* (1969). Both of these are symposia, the first by a Cambridge group under the same leadership of Chorley and Haggett as the later *Models in Geography*, the second by a London group emanating from University College.
2 Extracts from Chapter 1 of *Models in Geography*, a symposium of seventeen authors, edited by R. J. Chorley and P. Haggett (1967).
3 Reference here is made to the American geographer, B. J. L. Berry's 'Approaches to regional analysis: a synthesis', *Annals of the Assoc. of Amer. Geog.*, 1964, pp. 2–11.
4 See Chapters 7 and 17.
5 Reference is made to the American geographer, the late E. A. Ackerman, 'Where is a research frontier?', *Annals of the Assoc. of Amer. Geog.*, 1963, pp. 429–40.
6 From the essay in R. J. Chorley and P. Haggett, *Models in Geography* (1967).
7 Reference is made to F. E. Clements, *Plant Succession and Indicators* (1928).
8 Reference is made to F. E. Clements and V. E. Shelford, *Bio-ecology* (1939).
9 Extracts from the Introduction (Chapter 1) to *Research in Human Geography* (1971), a Social Science Research Council review.
10 Reference is here made to the writings of D. W. Harvey, notably *Explanation in Geography* (1969).
11 *Geography* (1970), edited by E. J. Taaffe and compiled by a panel of geographers.
12 I am grateful to Dr Eric H. Brown of the Department of Geography, University College, London, for this contribution.

Chapter 12 A Review
1 'Survey of graduate schools', published in *The Chronicle of Higher Education*, vol. 5, no. 13, 4 January 1971, p. 4.
2 From *Orbis Geographicus* (1964–6).

Chapter 13 William Morris Davis, 1850–1934
1 W. M. Davis, 'The progress of geography in the United States', *Annals of the Assoc. of Amer. Geog.*, 1924, pp. 159–215; see also his 'An

inductive study of the content of geography', *Bulletin of the Amer. Geog. Soc.*, 1906, pp. 67–84.

2 'A scheme of geography', *Geog. J.*, 1903, pp. 413–23; 'An inductive study of the content of geography', *Bulletin of the Amer. Geog. Soc.* (1906), pp. 67–84, being the presidential address at the second meeting of the Association of American Geographers in December 1905; 'The principles of geographic description', *Annals of the Assoc. of Amer. Geog.*, 1915, pp. 61–105; 'The progress of geography in the United States', *Annals of the Assoc. of Amer. Geog.*, 1924, pp. 159–215; 'A retrospect of geography', *Annals of the Assoc. of Amer. Geog.*, 1932, pp. 211–30. References in this chapter are to the year of publication.

3 J. K. Wright, 'Wild geographers I have known', *Professional Geographer*, vol. XV, no. 4, 1963, pp. 1–4.

4 H. C. Cowles, 'The causes of vegetational cycles', 1911, pp. 3–20.

5 *Geog. Rev.*, 1923, pp. 318–20.

6 I. Bowman, 'The analysis of land forms: Walter Penck on the topographic cycle', *Geog. Rev.*, 1926, pp. 122–32.

7 O. D. von Engeln, 'Walther Penck's contribution to geomorphology', *Annals of the Assoc. of Amer. Geog.*, 1940, pp. 219–84. From Leighly's contribution to the discussion.

8 L. Martin, 'William Morris Davis: investigator, teacher and leader in geomorphology', *Annals of the Assoc. of Amer. Geog.*, 1950, pp. 172–95. From Jones's contribution to the discussion.

Chapter 14 Mark Jefferson, 1863–1949

1 G. J. Martin, *Mark Jefferson: Geographer* (1968).

2 Ibid., pp. 319–21.

3 Ibid., p. 325.

4 *Geog. Rev.*, 1950, pp. 134–37.

5 The book referred to is *Peopling the Argentine Pampa*, Amer. Geog. Soc. Research Series no. 16 (1926). The term 'Expedition to the ABC countries' was the official title of a field programme sponsored by the Society.

Chapter 15 Albert Perry Brigham, 1889–1929

1 *Annals of the Assoc. of Amer. Geog.*, 1930, pp. 55–62.

2 Brigham wrote the following indicative and influential books in their day that should certainly find recognition in this record. They bear testimony to the development of his varied interests. Beginning under the influence of Davis he wrote a *Textbook of Geology* in 1900 and *An Introduction to Physical Geography* in 1902. *Geographic Influences in American History* appeared in 1903, the year of Ellen Semple's work on the same theme. *From Trail to Railway through the Appalachians* was published in 1907, *Commercial Geography* in 1911, *Essentials of Geography* in 1916, and the *United States of America: Studies in Physical, Regional, Industrial and Human Geography* in 1927. *Cape Cod and the Old Colony* (1920) is a rare example of readable regional literature.

Chapter 16 J. Russell Smith, 1874–1966
1 V. M. Rowley, *J. Russell Smith: Geographer, Educator, Conservationist* (1964).
2 *Geog. Rev.*, 1967, pp. 128–30.

Chapter 17 The Chicago Sequence
1 The extracts are taken from obituary notes and memoirs, reproduced with the permission of the Association of American Geographers and the American Geographical Society.
2 *Annals of the Assoc. of Amer. Geog.*, 1953, pp. 4–11.
3 In collaboration with two colleagues, H. H. Barrows (historical) and W. S. Tower (economic).
4 *Annals of the Assoc. of Amer. Geog.*, 1961, pp. 395–9.
5 In H. H. Barrows, *Lectures on the Historical Geography of the United States as given in 1933* (1962), edited by W. A. Koelach.
6 *Annals of the Assoc. of Amer. Geog.*, 1933, pp. 241–6.
7 *Annals of the Assoc. of Amer. Geog.*, 1958, pp. 51–3.
8 At the outset in 1923 the group included Sauer, McMurry and D. H. Davis from Michigan, Finch and Lobeck from Wisconsin, Haas from Northwestern, Parkins from Peabody College, and Jones, Whittlesey, Platt and Colby from Chicago.
9 These notes were sent to Professor Colby by Professor Charles M. Davis of the University of Michigan.
10 *Annals of the Assoc. of Amer. Geog.*, 1966, pp. 378–81.
11 Both these works were technical papers of the Land Committee of the National Resources Planning Board. Since they appeared during the war, they are not generally known in Great Britain.
12 Here also may be noted *The Kansas Basin: Pilot Study of a Watershed* (1956).
13 *Annals of the Assoc. of Amer. Geog.*, 1966, pp. 630–5.
14 A special programme of study at Yale University. This was followed by a teaching post in China.
15 *Geog. Rev.*, 1957, pp. 443–5.

Chapter 18 Ellen Churchill Semple, 1863–1932
1 *Annals of the Assoc. of Amer. Geog.*, 1933, pp. 229–38.
2 *Annals of the Assoc. of Amer. Geog.*, 1948, pp. 38–50.

Chapter 19 Ellsworth Huntington, 1876–1947
1 *Annals of the Assoc. of Amer. Geog.*, 1948, pp. 38–50.

Chapter 20 The Second Generation
1 *Annals of the Assoc. of Amer. Geog.*, 1932, pp. 29–38.
2 *Annals of the Assoc. of Amer. Geog.*, 1932, pp. 29–38.
3 *Annals of the Assoc. of Amer. Geog.*, 1935, pp. 113–23.
4 It is necessary to add a note here on the distinguished service to the regional concept of the writer of this memorial, Homer Leroy Shantz

(1876–1958), who was a close and longstanding colleague of Marbut.
Trained as a botanist, Shantz undertook extensive travel in Africa.
He was co-author, with Marbut, of *The Vegetation and Soils of Africa*
(1923) and published an important paper on the natural vegetation
of the Great Plains, delivered before the Association of American
Geographers in the same year. He wrote, in co-authorship, the section
on vegetation for the *Atlas of American Agriculture* (1924), as well as
contributing nine articles on the agricultural regions of Africa to
Economic Geography (1940–3). Like Marbut, he was a visiting lecturer
at Clark for a few years, until 1926. He was president of the University
of Arizona from 1928 to 1936, and chief of the division of wildlife
management of the United States Forestry Service. He retired in 1944
and died in 1958. (See C. O. Sauer, *Geog. Rev.*, 1958, pp. 278–80.)

5 Extracts from a memorial, *Annals of the Assoc. of Amer. Geog.*, 1964,
pp. 615–21.
6 *Geog. Rev.*, 1948, pp. 55–94.
7 *Geog. Rev.*, 1944, pp. 317–18.
8 Earlier works in this line were *Shore Processes and Shoreline Development* (1919) and *New England-Acadian Shoreline* (1925).
9 *Geog. Rev.*, 1949, pp. 675–7.
10 Extracts from a memorial, *Annals of the Assoc. of Amer. Geog.*, 1950,
pp. 328–32.
11 *Annals of the Assoc. of Amer. Geog.*, 1961, pp. 339–41.

Chapter 21 The American Geographical Society
1 J. K. Wright, *Geography in the Making* (1952).
2 *Biographical Memoirs*, vol. xxxiii (1959).
3 *Geog. Rev.*, 1931, pp. 22–35.
4 *Annals of the Assoc. of Amer. Geog.*, 1970, pp. 394–403.

Chapter 22 Carl Ortwin Sauer, 1889–1975
1 J. A. M. Broek, *The Santa Clara Valley, California: A Study of Landscape Changes* (1932).
2 John Leighly (ed.), *Land and Life*, a collection of papers by Carl O.
Sauer (1963). I follow closely Leighly's Introduction to this volume.

Chapter 23 The Third Generation
1 These works appeared in various articles and maps. For Thornthwaite
see Chapter 20.
2 *Annals of the Assoc. of Amer. Geog.*, 1951, pp. 89–94.
3 *Annals of the Assoc. of Amer. Geog.*, 1948, pp. 306–7.
4 *Mirror for Americans: Likeness of the Eastern Seaboard* (1943).
5 *Annals of the Assoc. of Amer. Geog.*, 1966, pp. 360–2.
6 His *Land of the 500 Million: A Geography of China* was published in
1955, and *Soviet Potentials: A Geographical Appraisal* in 1962.
7 *Annals of the Assoc. of Amer. Geog.*, 1966, pp. 569–70.
8 *Annals of the Assoc. of Amer. Geog.*, 1929, pp. 67–109. A collection of
the published works of James has been published (1971) since the

above writing, namely *On Geography: Selected Writings of Preston E. James*, edited by D. W. Meinig, with an introduction by Richard Hartshorne.

C. E. Browning, *A Bibliography of Dissertations in Geography, 1901–69* (1970).

Chapter 24 Post-War Trends in the USA

1 'Outline for fieldwork in geography', *Bulletin of the American Geographical Society*, vol. XLVII, 1915, pp. 520–5. This was presented to the seminar in geography in the University of Chicago in the winter term of 1915. The authors used a similar outline to that used by H. H. Barrows and D. W. Johnson. It was checked by Atwood, Bowman, W. H. Hobbs (the geologist at Michigan), Mark Jefferson and Bailey Willis. The whole field of enquiry is covered here. This is an important document in the development of the regional concept. This frame was first used in a field course run from Chicago on Montreal Island in the summer of 1915.

2 The first group of senior men met for the first time in May 1923. The group included: from Chicago, C. C. Colby, W. D. Jones, R. S. Platt, D. S. Whittlesey; from Minnesota, D. H. Davis; from Northwestern, W. H. Haas; from Michigan, C. O. Sauer, K. C. McMurry.

The 'younger boys', as James calls them, who met as a group for the first time in May 1926, included: from Michigan, S. D. Dodge, R. B. Hall, P. E. James; from Minnesota, R. H. Brown, R. Hartshorne; from Wisconsin, L. Durand, G. T. Trewartha, J. R. Whitaker; from Chicago, H. M. Leppard.

3 For further detail see G. D. Hudson, 'The unit area method of land classification', *Annals of the Assoc. of Amer. Geog.*, 1936, pp. 99–112.

4 C. M. Davis, in the chapter on 'Field techniques' in P. E. James and C. F. Jones (eds), *American Geography: Inventory and Prospect* (1954).

5 P. E. James, 'The Blackstone valley: a study in choreography in southern New England', *Annals of the Assoc. of Amer. Geog.*, 1929, pp. 67–109.

6 *The Rural Land Classification of Puerto Rico* (1951).

7 R. E. Murphy and J. E. Vance, 'Delimiting the CBD', *Economic Geography*, 1954, pp. 189–222.

8 James credits K. C. McMurry with one of the earliest experiments in the use of vertical air photographs for mapping land use—in 1929 (reported 1932). *All Possible Worlds* (1972), p. 491.

9 P. E. James, 'Toward a further understanding of the regional concept', *Annals of the Assoc. of Amer. Geog.*, 1952, pp. 195–222.

10 The summary is in *The Science of Geography* (1965), pp. 1–6. Chairman: E. A. Ackerman; members of the committee: B. J. L. Berry, R. H. Bryson, S. B. Cohen, E. J. Taaffe, W. L. Thomas and M. G. Wolman.

11 The panellists were: E. J. Taaffe, I. Burton, N. Ginsburg, P. R. Gould, F. Lukerman and P. L. Wagner, with Taaffe as chairman.

12 A. Clark, *Three Centuries and the Island* (1959).
13 D. W. Meinig, *The Great Columbian Plain, 1805–1910* (1968); *The Margins of the Good Earth: The South Australian Wheat Frontier, 1869–84* (1962); *Imperial Texas: An Interpretive Essay in Cultural Geography* (1969); *The Southwest: Three Peoples in Geographical Change, 1600–1970* (1971).
14 Reference is again made to Isachenko's *Principles of Landscape Science and Physical-Geographic Regionalization*—see p. 386.
15 pp. 125–7.
16 R. J. Chorley and P. Haggett (eds), *Frontiers in Geographical Teaching* (1963), p. 13.
17 S. B. Cohen (ed.), *Problems and Trends in American Geography* (1967), p. 14.

Conclusion
1 See chapter on Penk in *Makers of Modern Geography*.
2 See chapter on Hettner in *Makers of Modern Geography*.
3 See Chapter 24 n. 13.
4 One may choose to become such an expert and bring to bear one's special geographic expertise. The work of Darby is a case in point.
5 This is far removed from course offerings in 'geography' on 'The Localization of Manufactures' or 'Resource Management' that appear in many American University catalogues.
6 Meinig's mode of approach is precisely on these lines and should receive special attention. His works are listed in chapter 24 n. 13 of this book.

Subject Index

Agrarian systems, 277
Agricultural geography, 61, 139, 291
Air photographs, 352, 391
Allgemeine Erdkunde, 40
Anthropogeography, 41–2, 133, 260, 262–3, 264, 266, 268
Anthropology, 59–60, 133
Areas and area development, xvi, xvii, 64–5, 255, 324, 349, 380–1; *Heimatkunde*, 349; nuclear, 150
Atmospheric physics, xiv

Biogeography, 101, 156, 157, 367–71
Botany and botanists, 4
Boundaries, 149

Cartography and cartographers, 2, 108, 109, 121, 341; statistical, 308; *see also* Maps and map work
Catastrophism, 3
Census-takers, 4
Chorography, 40, 202, 208, 318, 323–6
Chorology, xvi, xvii, 1, 3–4, 202, 204, 208, 318
Climate and climatology, 1, 156, 157, 178–9, 277, 283, 340–1, 343, 361; local, 178, 270, 271, 272, 278–9, 283; Mediterranean, 149–50
Commercial geography, 133, 224
Communities, 40
'Compages', xiv, 54, 354
Conservation, 226, 228–9, 242
Conurbations, 33–4
Cross-sectional approach, 82, 83
Cultural geography, 361, 362

Drainage systems, 176–7

'Earth sciences', 346
Ecology and ecological approach, xvii, 1, 5, 7, 168–72, 242; ecosystems, 171–2, 348, 371; of plants, xiv
Economic geography, 63, 94–5, 101, 106, 137, 224–7 *passim*, 247–9 *passim*
Environment and environmentalism, 1, 5, 6, 39–40, 47–54 *passim*, 59, 84, 116, 142, 178, 179, 188, 212, 222, 253, 324; determinism, 7, 26, 185, 203 298, 299, 307, 321, 330; fore casting, 174; heredity and, 48;

'modes of adjustment', 26; standards, 174
Ethnography and ethnographers, 4, 12, 14
Explorers and exploration, 4, 120, 125, 126–7, 310
Expository approach, 62

Field studies, 3, 159–60, 245–6, 252, 253, 258, 287, 337, 348–52, 375–6
Field systems, 140
Fractional code notation, 350–2, 353

Geographical data-matrix, 164–6
Geography and geographers: chairs of, 16–21; in Commonwealth, 23–5; courses in, 13–14; definitions and scope, 1–5, 132–4, 135–6, 168, 193, 210–11, 237, 242, 355; degrees in, 15; statistics, 21–2; status of departments, 22–3; education, 374–7; geographical analysis, 5–7, 357–9; goals and objectives, 163, 356; research in, 172–5, 367; and the social sciences, 346, 356, 375; trends in, 366
Geology and geologists, 4, 11, 14, 26, 39, 89, 117, 218, 231, 233, 239, 287; and geography, 205
Geomorphology, xiv, xvii, 1, 22, 46, 84, 98, 99, 153, 156, 176–7, 206, 284, 286, 329, 330, 339, 342, 376, 380; Mackinder's definition, 41
Geonomics, 316
Geostrategy, 36, 38
Geotechnics, 33
Glaciology, 115, 128

Historical geography, 12–13, 63, 100, 136, 241, 331–2

Human geography, xvi, 62–3, 101, 154, 221, 296; and physical geography, 167, 201
Hydrogeographic surveys, 45

Irrigation, 283–4

Land and land forms, 46, 98, 100, 102, 134, 141, 153, 154, 160–1, 194, 196–203 *passim*, 277, 299, 347; land use, 71–4, 77, 84, 85, 112, 139–40, 290, 350; World Land Use Survey, 74
Länderkunde, 40
Landscape and landscape approach, 5, 6, 85, 140, 143, 158, 161, 206, 320, 362
Location theory, 361, 363–4

Man and environment, 49–51, 54, 57–8, 67, 172–3, 226, 333, 347
Maps and map work, 2, 3, 96, 121, 157, 214, 216, 244, 246, 310, 350–1, 367; Geological Survey, 64; isoplethic, 247, 248; military, 254; 1,000,000 maps, 97, 127, 300; Ordnance Survey, 64, 72, 110; Oxford Wall Maps, 43
Meteorology, 43, 278, 340
Models, 163; simulation, 173–4
Mountaineering and geography, 126–8 *passim*

Navigation, 108, 109
Neighbourhoods, 30

Oceanography, 4, 90, 129
Ontography, 198, 200
Organic concept, 169–71 *passim*

Palynology, xiv, xvii

Paradigms, 164, 167, 169
Physical geography, xvi, 1, 11–12, 22, 39, 77–8, 90–1, 98, 101, 114, 133, 142, 152–62, 176–9, 183–5, 197, 225, 233, 296, 328, 338–42 *passim*, 355, 361, 365, 367, 376; and human geography, 167; proposed Institute of, 365
Physiography, 11, 28, 39, 132, 153–4, 185, 197, 201, 219, 285, 287, 361; physiographic boundaries, 158–9
Planning, 22, 73
Plant geography and ecology, 1, 157, 170, 321, 361, 367
Political geography, 39, 63, 111, 137, 143, 151, 361, 363, 365; proposed Institute of, 365
Pollution, 297
Population, 111, 115, 118, 290, 308–9, 343
'Possibilism', 6, 26, 330

Racial geography, 63, 116, 136
Regional geography and concept, xiii–xvi *passim*, 1, 36, 59, 67, 107, 135, 138, 160, 162, 188, 198, 259, 299, 307, 342, 346, 348, 353–9, 373, 376, 378–83; classification of regions, 144–52; consciousness, 52–4; development, 174–5; 'human regions', 382; microgeography, 255; natural regions', 44–54 *passim*, 63–4, 141–2, 144–5, 148, 152, 382; planning, 73, 373;

regional science, 7; regional surveys, 28–34 *passim*, 243; sub-divisions, 158
Resources and resource development, xvi
Rural studies, 139, 140–1, 343

Scientific approach, 6–7, 26
Social geography, 63
Soils and soil service, xiv, 64, 65, 159, 247, 277, 279–82 *passim*, 356, 362
'Spatial nodality', 141
Spatial systems, 172–6, 188, 277, 358, 359–66, 372; perception and preference, 173
Statistical methods, 347
Surveys and survey approach, 5, 6, 101, 102, 103, 122, 124, 250
Systematic approach, 5–6, 380

Team approach, 153, 155, 156
Town planning, 29, 30
Tree-ring studies, 270

Uniformitarianism, 3
Urban geography, 22, 139, 212, 249, 338; cities, 212, 225, 367

Vegetation, 46, 277

Water utilization, 243

Name Index

Abercrombie, Patrick, 27, 29, 30
Ackerman, E. A., 168, 188, 256–9, 276, 328, 348, 353
Aftermath (Newbigin), 92
Agassiz, Louis, 183, 196
Aids to Geographical Research (Wright), 306
Alden, W. C., 245
All Possible Worlds (James), 338, 356
Alpen in Eiszeitalter (Penck and Bruckner), 56
Alpine Club, 128
Alpine Journal, 128
American Geographical Society, 97, 99, 184, 185, 189, 213, 220, 281, 293–313, 336, 352
American Geography (James and Jones), 54, 188, 327, 338
American Geography: Inventory and Prospect (Platt and Jones), 255, 259, 312, 345, 359
American History and its Geographic Conditions (Semple), 187, 263, 267, 315, 331
Ancient Hunters (Sollas), 61
Andes of Southern Peru (Bowman), 297, 298
Annales de Géographie, 57
Antarctic Club, 131
Anthropo-Geographie (Ratzel), 264

Antlitz der Erde (Suess), 56
Arctic Club, 131
Area Analysis (Colby), 250
Arnold, Thomas, 12
Asia's Lands and Peoples (Cressey), 334
Association of American Geographers, 15, 220, 221, 229, 237, 238, 239, 244, 271, 276
Atlas of American Agriculture (Marbut), 281, 289
Atlas of Climatic Types in the United States (Thornthwaite), 283
Atlas of Meteorology, 43, 88
Atlas of the Historical Geography of the United States (Paullin), 308
Atwood, Wallace W., 8, 189, 233, 266, 276, 286–8, 336, 342, 347; textbooks of, 287
Aurrousseau, M., 355

Baker, J. N. L., 12, 80, 147, 384
Baker, Oliver Edwin, 288–90, 337; and agriculture, 288–9
Barker, Mabel, 30, 34
Barrows, Harlan H., 186, 187, 189, 209, 231, 232, 233, 240–3, 246, 248, 249, 251, 252, 257,

323, 339, 348, 355; and environ-
mentalism, 317; and Public
Works Administration, 242–3
Bartholomew, John, 43, 88, 97,
129
Bases of a World Commonwealth
(Fawcett), 111
Bates, H. W., 11, 120
Bates, Marston, 367
Battlefields of the World War
(Johnson), 286
Baulig, Henri, 176
Beckit, H. O., 15
*Behavioral and Social Sciences
Survey* (Taaffe), 366
Berry, B. J. L., 8, 164–6 *passim*,
188, 189, 232, 357, 359, 367,
372
Biogeography (Dansereau), xvii,
157, 367–71
Blanchard, R., 114, 139, 242, 257
Bonpland, Aimé, 349
Borchert, J., 189, 372
*Borderlands of Language in
Europe* (Cornish), 143
Bowden, M. J., 304–13
Bowen, E. G., 59
Bowman, Isaiah, xvii, 8, 183, 185,
186, 189, 202, 205, 209, 213–17,
240, 293, 295–304, 306, 308,
312, 336, 353, 373; and South
America, 297–8, 300, 302
Branfield, Victor, 28, 29, 30
Briefe Summe of Geographie
(Barlow), 108
Brigham, Albert Perry, 44, 186,
209, 218–23, 388
Britain and the British Seas
(Mackinder), 13, 37, 160
British Islands and their Vegetation
(Tansley), 157
British Isles (Stamp and Beaver),
140
Broek, Jan, 82, 189, 273, 328, 367
Brooks, A. H., 186
Brooks, C. E. P., 273
Brooks, C. F., 337, 341

Brown, Crum, 128
Brown, E. H., 161, 163, 176–9
Brown, Ralph H., 274, 331–2
Brown, Robert, 2
Brown, R. N. Rudmose, 15, 44,
88, 89–91
Bruce, W. S., 131
Brunhes, Jean, xviii, 62, 85, 137,
320
Brush, J. E., 372
Bryan, Kirk, 328–30; and geo-
morphology, 329–30
Bryan, Patrick W., 109, 147, 242
Buchan, Alexander, 43, 88
Buchanan, J. Y., 91, 99, 129
Buchanan, K., 114
Buchanan, R. O., 69–75, 110–11,
137
Bunge, W., 188, 357
Burgess, Ernest, 372
Burnham, Guy, 336

Calef, Wesley C., 231
Calkins, R. D., 186, 209
Campbell, E. M. J., 104
Canada (Newbigin), 92
Carter, Allan M., 190
Central Europe (Partsch), 37
Challenger expedition, 88, 89, 90,
92, 129
Chamberlin, T. C., 184, 185, 232,
233, 234, 238, 240, 242, 284
Character of Races (Huntington),
271
China (von Richthofen), 56
China's Geographic Foundations
(Cressey), 333
Chisholm, George G., 7, 14, 15,
27, 35, 89, 92, 93–5, 103, 104,
107, 213
Chisholm, M., 100, 101, 163; on
spatial systems, 172–5
Chorley, R. J., 100, 161, 163–8,
188
Christaller, W., 140, 358, 372
Cities in Evolution (Geddes), 33

City Development (Geddes), 29

Civilization and Climate (Huntington), 271

Clapham, J. H., 76, 77

Clark, Andrew H., 189

Clark, Sir George, 79

Clements, Frederick E., 169–71 *passim*

Climate (Ward), 279

Climates of the United States (Ward), 279

Climates of the World (Trewartha), 343

Climatic Control of Australian Production (Taylor), 115

Climatic Changes (Huntington), 271, 273

Climatic Factor as illustrated in Arid America (Huntington), 271

Colby, Charles C., 186, 189, 209, 231, 232, 233, 240–3, 245–8, 248–51, 252, 257, 260–8, 318, 350, 352; and historical geography, 248–9; and land surveys, 250

Colour in Nature (Newbigin), 92

Coming Polity (Branford and Geddes), 31

Comment la route crée le type social (Demolins), 61

Coppock, J. T., 100

Commonwealth Weather Service, 115

Cornish, Vaughan, 143–4

Corridors of Time (Peake and Fleure), 57, 60

Cosmos (Humboldt), 11, 14

Cowles, H. C., 200, 321

Crawford, O. G. S., 44, 59, 95, 352

Cressey, George B., 328, 332-4, 346; and Asia, 332–4

Crone, G. R., 119, 126

Crowe, P. R., 135–6, 140, 157

Crystal, G., 128

Cultural Geography (Spencer and Thomas), 373

Cultural Worlds (Russell and Kniffen), 373

Cumberland, K. B., 114

Current Geographical Publications, 306

Curwen, E. C., 352

Cushing, S. W., 271, 316

Daly, Charles P., 293

Darby, Henry Clifford, 69, 75–84, 85, 86, 100, 101, 104, 137, 160, 165, 385; and historical geography, 78–84

Darbyshire, J. W., 66–8

Darling, F. Fraser, 367

Darwin, Charles, 2, 3, 12, 168

David, Edgworth, 101

Davis, C. M., 337

Davis, D. H., 186, 209

Davis, William Morris, 5, 8, 26, 42, 44, 95, 98, 106, 115, 155, 161, 169, 170, 183–4, 185, 187, 189, 193–208, 209, 210, 214, 218, 219, 222–3, 234, 249, 277–8, 284–5, 287, 296, 305, 314, 329, 330, 339, 347, 373, 376; and 'geographical cycle', 203–5; and land forms, 195–7, 202, 207; on regional geography, 198–9, 201

Dawkins, Boyd, 11

Dawn of History (Myres), 61

Debenham, Frank, 76, 77, 99, 100, 101–3, 124; and Antarctic, 101–2; and philosophy of place, 26, 101

Dee, John, 108

Deffontaines, P., 139

De Geer, Sten, 213, 242

De Margerie, Emmanuel, 204

De Martonne, Emmanuel, 95, 286, 380

Democratic Ideals and Reality (Mackinder), 31, 34, 37, 38, 112

Demolins, E., 27, 28

Deniker, Joseph, 12, 61

Desert Trails of Atacama
(Bowman), 297
Design with Nature (McHarg), 373
Deutschland (Ratzel), 37
Dice, Lee R., 371–2
Dicken, S., 8, 189
Dickinson, B. B., 14
Dickinson, Robert E., 27, 136,
162–3, 340, 341
Dickson, H. N., 14, 15, 89, 91, 92,
123, 129, 134
Dion, R., 139
Distributors and Distributees
(Wright), 309
Dodge, Richard E., 185, 186,
218–23
Dodge, S. A., 318, 331–2, 337
Domesday Geography of England
(Darby), 80
Doxiades, Constantin, 33
Draining of the Fens (Darby), 76,
77, 78
Dryer, C. R., 44

Early Spanish Main (Sauer), 323
Early Topographical Maps
(Wright), 307
Earth and its Resources (Finch
and Trewartha), 343
Earth and Sun (Huntington), 271
Earth and the State (Whittlesey),
258
Earth's Problem Climates
(Trewartha), 343
East, W. G., 79, 104
Economic Geography, 289
*Economic Geography for Second-
ary Schools* (Colby and Foster),
249
Economic Geography of Britain
(Smith), 137, 140
*Economic History of Modern
Britain* (Clapham), 76–7
Elementary Physical Geography
(Tarr), 185
Elements of Geography (Barrows,

Salisbury, Tower), 233, 240, 314
Elements of Geography (Finch and
Trewartha), 340, 343
*Elements of Industrial Manage-
ment* (Smith), 225
Environment and Race (Taylor),
116
*Erklärende Beschreibung der
Landformen* (Davis), 203
Evans, E. E., 69
Everest, Mount, 125, 127
*Explorations and Studies in
Northern Arabia and Mesopo-
tamia* (Musil), 306

Fairgrieve, James, 112–13; and
land utilization, 112
Fawcett, C. B., 27, 34, 44, 104,
110–11, 337; and political
geography, 111, 137
Febvre, Lucien, 63
Fenneman, R., 44, 347, 373
*Field Study in American
Geography* (Platt), 255
Finch, Vernor C., 202, 248, 249,
255, 290–2, 318, 343, 351;
textbooks of, 291
Fisher, C. A., 100, 101, 103
Fitzgerald, Walter, 62
Flahault, Charles, 28, 43
Fleure, Herbert John, 7, 15, 16–
21, 27, 28, 30, 31, 44, 55–60, 62,
69, 87, 112–13, 136, 141, 144;
and 'human regions', 57, 151
*Fluvial Processes in Geomor-
phology* (Wolman and Miller),
177
Food and Agriculture Organiza-
tion (FAO), 73
Forbes, Edward, 89
Forde, C. Daryll, 104–6, 136
Forest Physiography (Bowman),
299
Fox, Cyril, 59
Freeman, Thomas W., xv, 69, 95–9

Freshfield, Douglas, 119, 120, 121, 124, 126–8

From Trail to Railway (Brigham), 331

Frontiers (Fawcett), 111

Fundamentals of Physical Geography (Trewartha, Robinson, Hammond), 343

Future Environments of North America (Darling and Milton), 367

Galpin, G. J., 372

Galton, Francis, 119, 122, 124

Garnett, Alice, 15, 104–6

Geddes, Arthur, 28

Geddes, Patrick, 6, 27–34, 37, 43, 57, 71, 89, 113, 128, 371; Outlook Tower, 28–9, 30, 43; Place, Work and Folk concept, 28, 29, 31, 32–3; and town planning, 29, 30; Valley Section, 31–2

Geiger, R., 279

Geikie, Archibald, 11, 88

Geikie, James, 88, 91, 128

Geographer as Scientist (Wooldridge), 158

Geographic Factor (Whitbeck and Thomas), 316

Geographic Influences in American History (Brigham), 331

Geographical Association, 14, 15, 21, 45, 56, 71, 75, 103, 113, 128

Geographical Essays (Davis), 284

Geographical Journal, 62, 118, 120, 121, 126, 127, 263

Geographical Lore at the Time of the Crusades (Wright), 307, 308

Geographical Magazine, 121, 125, 374

Geographical Review, 56, 273, 300

Geographical Teacher, 45, 61, 63

Géographie des Plantes (Gaussen) 157

Geography, 144

Geography and World Power (Fairgrieve), 112

Geography in relation to the Soil Sciences (Bowman), 303

Geography in School (Fairgrieve), 112

Geography in the Making (Wright), 311

Geography of British History (Hughes), 12

Geography of London River (Rodwell Jones), 109

Geography of Man (James), 337

Geography of Mankind (Broek and Webb), 373

Geography of Population (Trewartha), 343

Geography of S.E. Minnesota (Colby), 186

Geography of the Central Andes (Ogilvie), 97

Geography of the Mediterranean Region (Semple), 260, 267

Geography of the Middle-Illinois Valley (Barrows), 240–1

Geography of the World's Agriculture (Baker and Finch), 288, 291

Geology (Salisbury and Chamberlin), 233

German Strategy of World Conquest (Whittlesey, Colby, Hartshorne), 258–9

Gesetz der Wüstenbildung (Walther), 215

Gilbert, G. K., 153

Gilfillan, S. C., 272

Gilman, Daniel Coit, 183, 312

Goode, J. Paul, 186, 224, 233, 244–5, 248, 257, 341; and economic geography, 244; and maps, 244–5

Goodsir, John, 89

Gottmann, Jean, xvii

Granö, J. G., 142

Gray, H. L., 305

Great Britain (Ogilvie), 61, 138

Great Capitals (Cornish), 143–4
Great Plains (Webb), 371
Great Soviet World Atlas, 333
Gregory, J. W., 88, 134
Gregory, S., 21
Grundlagen der Landschaftkunde (Passarge), 205
Grundy, G. B., 14
Guillemard, F. H. H., 99
Guyot, Arnold, 183, 193–4, 195, 202

Haas, W. H., 244–5
Habitat, Economy and Society (Forde), 136
Haddon, A. C., 12
Hägerstrand, T., 188
Haggett, Peter, 8, 100, 101, 163–8, 188, 359
Hahn, E., 322
Hakluyt, Richard, 12, 108, 109
Hakluyt Society, 108
Hall, P. G., 100, 101
Hall, R. B., 318, 337
Handbook of Commercial Geography (Chisholm), 93, 225
Handbuch der Klimatologie (Hann), 279
Hannibal Once More (Freshfield), 128
Hare, F. K., 157, 161
Harris, Chauncy D., 231, 232, 248–51
Hartshorne, Richard, xv, 8, 168, 189, 251–6, 290–2, 328, 367; on regional concept, xv–xvi
Haskins, C. H., 305
Haven-Finding Art (Taylor), 109
Heawood, E., 91, 129
Herbertson, Andrew J., 7, 13, 14, 27, 28, 43–54, 56, 57, 58, 60, 63, 64, 89, 91, 92, 95, 106, 107, 110, 123, 147, 203, 285; and the 'natural region', 44–54, 353
Hettner, Alfred, xvi, 45, 168, 198, 199, 200, 202–8 *passim*, 245–6, 318, 349, 353, 379, 380

Hilgard, E. W., 281–2
Hinks, A. R., 120, 124
Hints to Travellers, 121–2, 127
Historical Geography (Mitchell), 100
Historical Geography of England before 1800 (Darby), 76–82 *passim*, 85, 137
Historical Geography of Europe (Freeman), 12
Historical Geography of the British Colonies (Lucas), 12
Historical Geography of the United States (Brown), 331, 332
Historical Geography of Western Europe before 1800 (Smith), 101
History of Civilization in England (Buckle), 12–13
History of the English People (Green), 12
Hooker, Sir Joseph, 2
Hoskins, W. G., 159
House, J. W., 21
Howard, Ebenezer, 29, 30
Howarth, O. J. R., 44
Hudson, G. Donald, 250, 351
Human Ecology (Hawley), 371
Human Geography in Western Europe (Fleure), 31
Human Habitat (Huntington), 271
Human Nature in Geography (Wright), 312
Humboldt, Alexander von, 2, 4, 5, 165, 166, 168, 349, 378
Huntington, Archer Milton, 293, 299
Huntington, Ellsworth, 186, 213, 269–75, 315, 316, 337; and climate, 270, 271, 272, 275; determinism of, 274, 275; and eugenics, 271; and migration, 272
Huxley, Michael, 125, 374
Huxley, Thomas Henry, 2, 13, 28, 132, 339

Ideas at War (Geddes and Slater), 31

Industrial and Commercial Geography (Smith), 187, 227, 314

Influences of Geographic Environment (Semple), 187, 264, 265, 305, 315

Institute of British Geographers, 15, 21, 75, 111

Institute of Navigation, 108

Internal Migration in the United States (Thornthwaite), 283

International Geographical Union, xiii, 75, 303

International Geography (Mill), 130, 132–4 *passim*

Introduction to Economic Geography (Jones and Whittlesey), 247, 257

Introduction to Physical Geography (Newbigin), 92

Introduction to Plant Ecology (Tansley), 157

Introduction to Weather and Climate (Trewartha), 343

Introduction to World Understanding (Atwood), 287

Isachenko, A. G., xvii, 386

James, Preston E., xv, 6, 8, 136, 189, 202, 317, 318, 328, 336–8, 339, 341, 346, 352, 367, 377; on regional concept, 357

Japan: a Physical, Cultural and Regional Geography (Trewartha), 343

Japan's Economic Position (Orchard), 335, 336

Jefferson, Mark, 8, 184, 186, 189, 209–17, 248, 296, 303, 341; ecological approach of, 210–11, 213

Jennings, J. N., 100

Jobbyns, G., 114

Johnson, Douglas W., 44, 186, 226, 284–6, 305, 347, 376

Johnson, Emory R., 184, 186, 224

Johnston, W. and A. K., 88

Jones, Clarence F., 186, 232, 267, 352

Jones, Ll. Rodwell, 70, 104, 109–10, 242

Jones, Wellington D., 203, 207, 233, 245–8, 252, 255, 257, 259, 318, 327, 350–3 *passim*; and field studies, 245–6

Jordan Country (Bowman), 303

Journal of Geography, 185, 187

Journeyman Taylor (Taylor), 116

Kant, Immanuel, 3

Keltie, Sir John Scott, 13, 27, 35, 120, 122–3, 127

Kemp, Harold S., 258

Kemp, John, 183

Kendrew, W. G., 44

Kesseli, J. E., 341

Kidson, C., 161

Kimble, G. H. T., 114, 274

King, Cuchlaine A. M., 161

Kirwan, L. P., 119, 125–6

Kniffen, F. B., 8, 189, 277, 367

Kolb, J. H., 372

Kollmorgen, Walter, 226

Köppen, W., 279, 283

Krebs, Norbert, 318

Kropotkin, Peter, 27, 28

Küchler, A. W., 157, 328, 367

Lake, Philip, 99, 102, 124

Lanchester, H. V., 29

Land Classification in the United States (Colby), 250

Land for Tomorrow (Stamp), 74

Land of Britain (Stamp), 72–3, 160

Land Utilization of China (Buck), 333

Landschaften der Britischen Inseln (Sölch), 141

Lanier, Mary J., 233, 239

Late Tudor and Early Stuart

Geography (Taylor), 108

Latin America (James), 328, 338

Leardo Map of the World (Wright), 307

Leighly, J. B., 156, 158, 189, 206–7, 277, 282–4, 321, 322, 328, 338–42, 347, 356; on physical geography, 339–42 *passim*

Lend Lease Administration, 335

Lennard, R., 78

Le Play, Frédéric, 27, 29, 43, 44, 57

Le Play Society, 33, 34, 71

Less Developed Realm (Trewartha), 343

Libbey, William, 183

Life by the Sea-Shore (Newbigin), 92

Life Interests of a Geographer (Mill), 130

Life of de Saussure (Freshfield), 128

Linton, D. L., 15, 143, 161

Linton, Ralph, 371

London School of Economics, 35, 36

Longman's Gazetteer of the World (Chisholm), 93

Longstaff, T. G., 126–8

Lösch, A., 140, 372

Lyde, Lionel W., 14, 103–6 *passim*, 110

Macfarlane, C. T., 184, 209

Macfarlane, J., 15, 89, 93

Mackenzie, Roderick, 372

Mackinder, Sir Halford J., 5, 7, 12, 13, 14, 25, 26, 27, 31, 35–42, 44, 56, 64, 103, 104, 106, 107, 109, 123, 135, 141, 155, 347; 'Heartland' concept', 36, 37–8; and 'Metropolitan England', 37; and 'new geography', 38–42

Macmunn, Norah, 44

McMurry, K. C., 318, 337, 350, 391

Mainsprings of Civilization (Huntington), 269, 272, 274

Makers of Modern Geography (Dickinson), xiii, xv, xvi, 7, 42, 63, 142, 200, 322, 376, 377

Making of Geography (Dickinson and Howarth), 44

Man and his Conquest of Nature (Newbigin), 44

Man and his Work (Herbertson), 44

Man in Europe (Jefferson), 215

Man's Adaptation of Nature (Bryan), 140

Man's Nature and Nature's Man (Dice), 371

Man's Role in Changing the Face of the Earth (Thomas, Sauer, Bates, Mumford), 367

Manners, G., 101

Manning, Bernard L., 77, 80

Manual of Coal and its Topography (Lesley), 194

Marbut, Curtis F., 186, 219, 279–82, 337, 347, 373; on soils, 279–82 *passim*

Markham, Clements, 119–21 *passim*

Marshall, William, 61, 63–4

Marthe, F., 4

Martin, Geoffrey J., 209, 210–11, 269

Martin, Lawrence, 337, 339

Maull, O., 148

Mead, W. R., 104

Medieval Fenland (Darby), 76–8 *passim*

Meinig, Donald W., 189, 367, 380

Men and Resources (Smith), 226

Mikesell, Marvin W., 231, 232

Mill, Hugh Robert, 7, 13, 26, 27, 64, 89, 90, 91, 92, 119–25, 128–34, 135; and Antarctic, 130–1; model for small areas, 64; and oceanography, 129–30

Miller, A. A., 157

Miller, G. J., 186

Miller, O. M., 308, 309

Milton, J. P., 367

Mirror for Americans (Brown), 307, 331, 332

Models in Geography (Chorley and Haggett), 163

Modern Geography (Salisbury), 234

Morphology of Landscape (Sauer), 250, 318

Morrill, Richard L., 357–8

Morse, Jedidiah, 312, 331

Mumford, Lewis, 27, 30, 33, 34, 367, 371

Murray, Sir John, 88, 89–91, 129, 134; and Antarctic, 90

Myres, J. L., 44, 81, 144

Nature and Man in America (Shaler), 195, 219

Nature of Geography (Hartshorne), xv, 26, 188, 259, 327, 328, 359

Nelson, Helge, 242

New England's Prospect (Paullin), 308

New Exploration (Mackaye), 30

New World: Problems in Political Geography (Bowman), 301

Newbigin, Marion I., 88, 91–3, 97

North America (Smith), 37, 226, 228

Northern Mists (Sauer), 323

Ogilvie, Alan G., 44, 89, 93–9, 154; and geomorphology, 98–9; and map work, 96–7

Oldham, H. Yule, 99, 124

One World Divided (James), 338

Orbis Geographicus, 23, 192, 384

Orchard, Dorothy, 227–30

Orchard, John E., 226, 328, 334–6, 346; and Asia, 335–6

Ordnance Survey Maps (Newbigin), 92

Origin of Species (Darwin), 11

Ormsby, Hilda, 23

Otte, Hermann, 226

Our Underdeveloped World (Stamp), 74

Outlines of General Biology (Thomson and Geddes), 31

Oxford Survey of the British Empire (Herbertson and Howarth), 44, 45

Oxford University Exploration Club, 123

Palestine and its Transformation (Huntington), 270, 271

Park, Brunner, 109

Park, Robert, 372

Parkins, A. E., 186

Passarge, Siegfried, 142, 147, 199, 202, 203–6 *passim*, 208, 318, 339; and regions, 148–9, 353

Pastoral Industries of New Zealand (Buchanan), 137

Paysages et problèmes géographiques de la terre américaine (Johnson), 286

Peake, H. J. E., 57

Peattie, Roderick, 239

Peel, R. F., 100

Penck, Albrecht, xvii, 95, 134, 202, 204, 206, 207, 379, 380

Penck, Walther, 330

Peopling the Argentine Pampa (Jefferson), 214

Perry, P. J., 75–84

Personality of Britain (Fox), 136

Perspective on the Nature of Geography (Hartshorne), xv, 327

Petermann, A. H., 88

Pfeifer, Gottfried, 315, 316

Phillipson, Alfred, 207, 246

Physical Atlas of Natural Phenomena (Berghaus), 88

Physical Geography (Somerville), 11

Physical Geography of New Jersey (Salisbury), 233
Physiographic Provinces of North America (Atwood), 287
Physiography (Huxley), 11
Physiography (Salisbury), 185, 233
Physiography of Eastern United States (Fenneman), 328, 339
Physiography of Western United States (Fenneman), 328, 339
Pico, Rafael, 352
Pilot Study of Southern Illinois (Colby), 251
Pioneer Fringe (Bowman), 302
Plant and Animal Geography (Newbigin), 92
Platt, Robert S., 186, 231, 232, 233, 249, 251–6, 257; field studies of, 252–6 *passim*
Poetic Impression of Scenery (Cornish), 143
Political Geography of the British Empire (Fawcett), 111, 137
Practical Exercises in Elementary Meteorology (Ward), 279
Priestley, Sir Raymond, 102, 117–18
Principles of Geography (Jefferson), 215
Principles of Human Geography (Huntington), 271
Principles of Landscape Science (Isachenko), xvii, 386
Provinces of England (Fawcett), 31, 34, 111, 137
Pulse of Asia (Huntington), 271
Pulse of Progress (Huntington), 315–6
Purchas, Samuel, 108

Races of Europe (Ripley), 61
Races of Man (Deniker), 61
Ratzel, Friedrich, 5, 134, 198, 206, 212, 225, 262, 264, 317, 322
Realm of Nature (Mill), 11, 12, 14, 129, 130, 132

Reclus, Elysée, 27–9 *passim*
Reclus, Pierre, 28
Reconnaissance Geography of Japan (Trewartha), 343
Record of the Royal Geographical Society (Mill), 130
Reeves, E. A., 122
Regional Ecology (Dickinson), xiii, xv, xvi
Regional Essays (Ogilvie), 60
Regional Survey Association, 30
Relations of Geography and History (George), 12
Renner, George T., 226
Richthofen, Ferdinand von, 4, 5, 42, 134, 168, 198, 202, 204, 206
Ridgley, D., 337
Ripley, W. Z., 11
Rishbeth, O. H. T., 44
Ritter, Carl, xiv, 4, 5, 12, 165, 166, 171, 193, 194, 195, 317, 319, 378
Rose, J. K., 114–17
Rowley, Virginia M., 226–7
Roxby, Percy Maude, 7, 15, 26, 27, 28, 44, 60–8, 69, 87, 96, 98, 136, 138, 144; and human geography, 62–3; and natural regions, 65–6; appraisal of, 66–8
Royal Geographical Society, 13, 15, 25, 35, 39, 56, 75, 89, 96, 103, 119–34, 187
Royal Scottish Geographical Society, 88, 91, 94, 97, 127, 129
Royal Meteorological Society, 129
Rühl, Alfred, 202
Rural Economy of the West of England (Marshall), 63
Russell, R. J., 156, 189, 328, 347

Salisbury, Rollin D., 8, 184, 186, 187, 189, 231, 232–40, 248, 249, 252, 257, 263, 286, 321, 337, 339; and physical geography,

233, 234; teaching and students of, 234–8 *passim*
Sauer, Carl Ortwin, 6, 8, 26, 58, 59, 66, 82, 141, 158, 186, 187, 189, 212, 232, 235, 248, 255, 276, 283, 314–26, 327, 337, 339, 340, 341, 347, 350, 353, 356, 366, 380; and environmentalism, 314–17, 321; and landscape, 66, 318–21
Sauer, Jonathan, 157
Savigear, R. A., 161
Scenery and the Sense of Sight (Cornish), 143
Scenery of England (Cornish), 143
Scenery of Scotland (Geikie), 88
Schaefer, F. K., 188, 357
Schluter, Otto, xviii, 320
Schuchert, Charles, 238
Scott Polar Research Institute, 100, 102, 131
Scott, Robert Falcon, 101, 115, 118
Scottish Geographical Magazine, 57, 91, 93
Season of Birth (Huntington), 271, 273
Semple, Ellen Churchill, 8, 187, 189, 232, 233, 248, 249, 252, 257, 260–8, 321, 336, 337; and anthropogeography, 260–8 *passim*
Senior Geography (Herbertson), 44
Shackleton, Sir Ernest H., 101, 117
Shaler, Nathaniel S., 183, 195, 196, 197, 202, 210, 218, 219
Shantz, Homer Leroy, 279–82, 337, 347, 373, 389–90
Siege of the South Pole (Mill), 130
Simkins, Ethel, 62
Sissons, J. B., 100
Sixteenth-Century North America (Sauer), 323
Slater, Gilbert, 31
Smith, G. H., 186, 189

Smith, J. Russell, 8, 187, 212, 213, 224–30, 314–15, 334, 335; and conservation, 226, 228, 229; textbooks of, 226, 228
Smith, J. Stewart, 229
Smith, Newlin R., 229
Smith, Thomas R., 227, 229
Smith, Wilfred, 62, 69, 160
Societés africaines (de Préville), 61
Sociological Society, 29, 34
Sölch, J., 141, 147
Source Book for the Economic Geography of North America (Colby), 249
Southern Europe (Newbigin), 92
Sparks, B. W., 161
Spate, O. H. K., 100, 101, 114, 269, 274–5
Spencer, Herbert, 12, 272
Stamp, L. Dudley, xvii, 7, 23, 65, 69–75, 84, 85, 86, 104, 138, 139, 144, 147–8, 352; and land use, 71–3, 85, 139
Starkey, Otis P., 226
Status and Trends of Geography in the U.S.A., 1957-60, 192
Seers, J. A., 100, 101–3, 152–62; on physiography, 153–5 *passim*
Stein, Clarence, 30
Stevens, A., 141, 142, 156
Stoddart, D. R., 168–72
Story of Iron and Steel (Smith), 225
Strabo, xvii, 202, 359
Stream Sculpture on the Atlantic Slope (Johnson), 285
Structure, Surface and Drainage in S.E. England (Wooldridge and Linton), 176
Study of History (Toynbee), 269
Study of Land Utilization of China (Buck), 289
Supan, Alexander, 45
Surface, G. T., 187, 225
Switzerland (Murray), 127
Sydneyside Scenery (Taylor), 116

Taaffe, E. J., 173
Tableau de la géographie de la France (Vidal de la Blache), 37, 56, 147
Tait, P. G., 128
Tansley, A. G., 157
Tarr, R. S., 184, 186, 339
Taussig, F. W., 334
Taylor, Eva G. R., 44, 62, 79, 104, 107–9; and cartography, 108
Taylor, Thomas Griffith, 88, 101, 113–18, 232, 386; and Antarctica, 115–16; and Australian physical geography, 115–17
Teach Yourself Geography (Debenham), 100
Teachers' Geography (Jefferson), 215
Tennessee Valley Authority, 250, 351
Thomas, W. L., 367
Thompson, John H., 372
Thomson, J. Arthur, 28, 91, 134
Thomson, Wyville, 89
Thornthwaite, Charles Warren, 282–4, 328; and climate, 283, 341
Tight, W. G., 329
Times Atlas, 88
Topography and Strategy in the War (Johnson), 286
Tower, Walter S., 187, 225, 233, 240, 248, 252
Toynbee, Arnold J., 269, 272
Tree Crops (Smith), 226, 228, 229
Tree of Culture (Linton), 371
Trewartha, Glenn T., 8, 202, 291, 328, 341, 342–4, 346, 372; and climate, 343
Troll, Carl, 352, 380; on regional integration, xiii
Tudor Geography (Taylor), 108

United States of America (Brigham), 220
Unstead, J. F., 15, 44, 104, 106–7,

141, 142, 144, 159, 353; and regional concept, 142, 147, 149
Unwin, Raymond, 27, 29, 31
Use of Geography (Debenham), 100

Vallaux, C., xiv, 66
Van Valkenburg, S., 189, 341
Vegetation and Soils of Africa (Marbut), 282
Vidal de la Blache, Paul, xviii, 3, 5, 43, 60, 62, 95, 134, 353, 376
Visher, Stephen S., 186, 232–43, 248, 269–74, 286–90 *passim*, 341

Wallace, Alfred Russell, 2
Wallas, Graham, 27, 36
Ward, H. B., 244–5
Ward, R. de Courcy, 186, 196, 277–9, 305, 340; and climate, 278–9
Watson, J. Wreford, 89
Waves of Sand and Snow (Cornish), 143
Webb, Sidney and Beatrice, 36
Wells, H. G., 27
West of the Pacific (Huntington), 271
Westgate, L. S., 186, 219
Whitaker, J. Russell, 239, 328
Whitbeck, R. H., 185, 291, 316; and 'geonomics', 316
White, Gilbert F., 231, 232, 240–3
Whitney, Josiah D., 183
Whittlesey, Derwent Stainthorpe, xiv, 54, 186, 187, 232, 252, 256–9, 273, 276, 320, 328–30, 354, 355; and political geography, 258–9
Wide World (James), 338
Williams, Henry Shaler, 218
Willis, Bailey, 245, 247
Wilson, Edward Adrian, 101
Wilson, L., 353

Wise, M. J., 104

Wissler, Clark, 371

Wolfanger, Louis A., 226

Wooldridge, S. W., 23, 69, 79, 104, 109–10, 152–62; on geomorphology, 160–1

Wooster, Catherine Bower, 30

Wordie, J. M., 102

World: a General Geography (Stamp), 70–1

World Geography of Forest Resources (Wright), 312

World's Food Resources (Smith), 226

Worth, Louis, 372

Wright, Henry, 30

Wrigley, E. A., 376

Wrigley, Gladys, 56

Wright, John K., 197, 284–6, 293–313; and history of geography, 305–7, 310–11, 313

Writings and Correspondence of the two Richard Hakluyts (Taylor), 109

Young, Arthur, 64

The Ibo People
and the Europeans

The Ibo People
and the Europeans

The Genesis of a Relationship—to 1906

ELIZABETH ISICHEI, M.A., D.Phil.

Senior Lecturer in History,
University of Nigeria, Nsukka

ST. MARTIN'S PRESS
New York

AFFILIATED PUBLISHERS: Macmillan Limited, London
—also at Bombay, Calcutta, Madras and Melbourne

12-19-78

To my husband, Uche
and to our children
Uche, and Emeka, and Nkem, and Chinye
with all love

Contents

Preface   *page* 13
1 The Beginnings   17
2 Patterns of Internal Migrations and State Formation   27
3 The Slave Trade and Society   44
4 Economic Change in the Nineteenth Century: The Last Phase of the Slave Trade and the Growth of the Palm Oil Trade   61
5 A People in a Landscape: Iboland on the Eve of Alien Rule   71
6 Patterns of Moving Frontiers, 1830–1885   83
7 Moving Frontiers: The Impact on Ibo Society, 1830–1885   101
8 Alien Government: The Niger under Chartered Company Rule, 1886–1899   113
9 Moving Frontiers: The Invasion of Iboland, to 1901   123
10 The Invasion of Iboland, 1902–1906   136
11 The Missionary Presence, 1885–1906   144
12 The Colonial Impact on Society: The Scope of Government   157
13 The Colonial Impact on Society: The Economy   167
14 Colonialism: Some Patterns of Ibo Responses and Initiatives   175

Epilogue: The Colonial Balance Sheet   182

A Note on Archival Sources   187
A List of Books Cited   193
Index   201

MAPS

1 Places and Peoples mentioned in the text						*page* 16

2, 3 Europe's knowledge of Iboland—the late seventeenth
	and early eighteenth centuries (from O. Dapper,
	Description de l'Afrique (French trans., Amsterdam,
	1686), and W. Bosman, *A New and Accurate Descrip-
	tion of the Coast of Guinea* (Eng. trans., London,
	1705))										84–85

4 Europe's knowledge of Iboland—the mid-nineteenth
	century (from W. B. Baikie, *Narrative of an Exploring
	Voyage up the Rivers Kwora and Binue . . . in 1854*
	(London, 1856))								86

5 Patterns of Moving Frontiers: 1878						98

6 Patterns of Moving Frontiers: 1891						122

7 Patterns of Moving Frontiers: 1906						135

Illustrations

1 An Ibo image of Ibo family life. A terracotta sculpture, from Kwale, for the cult of the yam spirit. *British Museum*   *facing page* 24

2 Pottery, from Igbo-Ukwu   *after page* 24

3 Bronze altar stand, from Igbo-Ukwu   24

4 Bronze shell surmounted by an animal, from Igbo-Ukwu
                                                  facing page 25

5 The realities of the eighteenth-century slave trade. From *History of the Rise, Progress and Accomplishment of the Abolition of the Slave Trade*, Thomas Clarkson, London, 1839   48

6 Eighteenth-century Ibo. Olaudah Equiano, autobiographer and merchant seaman. From *The Interesting Narrative of the Life of Olaudah Equiano or Gustavus Vassa, The African, written by Himself* (4th ed. Dublin 1791)   49

7a, b, c Europe's images of Iboland: Life on the Niger in the 1830s. From *Picturesque Views of the River Niger*, William Allen, London 1840   64

8 An Ibo image of the Invader. From an Mbari House, Owerri, 1904. From the *Journal of the African Society*, 1904. Photo by A. A. Whitehouse   65

Plates 2, 3 and 4 are from Thurston Shaw, *Igbo-Ukwu*, London 1970, and are reproduced by courtesy of the author.

Preface

This book is the first volume of a trilogy. A second volume, it is hoped, will continue the story through the period of colonial rule. A final one will deal with the history of a single Ibo community through the period covered by both books.

It is based primarily, though not exclusively, on archival sources in four countries. These have been supplemented by oral traditions collected in Asaba, and, to a lesser extent, in Western Iboland generally. For the rest, I have depended on written versions of oral traditions, such as those preserved in the voluminous Intelligence Reports in the National Archives, Ibadan. It would not be possible for any individual to collect traditions scientifically in even a significant proportion of Iboland's many communities. The book as it stands represents five years' work. To attempt a more extensive collection of oral traditions seemed impracticable.

Because of the nature of the available sources, this book concentrates on the theme of Iboland's changing relationship with a wider world—with the impact of international trade, and of missionary work, and later, with the experience of colonial conquest and rule. It is open to the criticism that too much space is devoted to the Niger area, which was, together with the Delta, the main frontier of alien influence in the nineteenth century. I can only plead in extenuation that this reflects, less the predilections of one who is, at least by marriage, a Niger Ibo, than the historical information at present at our disposal. Our knowledge of history proceeds largely through a dialectic between general syntheses and particular case studies. It is hoped that this book will provoke more local studies, based predominantly on oral traditions, which will, in their turn, provide a groundwork for new and better syntheses.

A Preface is the most pleasant part of a book to write, and compensates, to some extent, for the labours which precede it. I am happy to acknowledge my gratitude for the privilege of five years at Nuffield College, Oxford, first as a Research Student, and later as a postdoctoral Research Fellow. My election to the latter position made the research for this book possible. I am grateful to the Warden and Fellows, not only for my election, but for the generous leaves of absence which enabled me to carry out research in widely scattered archives.

Part of this book was written in intervals snatched from my teaching duties when I was a member of the History Department of the University of Dar es Salaam. I have learnt much from conversations with my former colleagues there, and from their writings, and from the experience of teaching, among other things, West African history to East African students.

I am grateful to the Holy Ghost Fathers, and to the Fathers of the Society of African Missions, for the valuable privilege of access to their archives. In particular, I would like to thank their respective archivists, Father Noël, C.S.Sp., and Father Eerden, S.M.A., for their help. Father Raymond Arazu, C.S.Sp., introduced me to the Holy Ghost Fathers, and generously shared with me his materials on Ihembosi. I would also like to thank the Church Missionary Society archivist, Miss Rosemary Keen, for whom my researches created a great deal of work. I am also grateful to the archivist and staff of the National Archives, Ibadan, for their co-operation. I could not have written this book without the help of the staffs of the following institutions, whom I am unfortunately unable to thank by name: the Public Record Office, the British Museum, the Foreign Office and Colonial Office Library (all in London), Rhodes House and the Bodleian Library, Oxford, and the Staatsbibliothek, Munich.

I am glad of an opportunity to thank a number of scholars who have answered my inquiries on specific points, or, more generally, discussed with me matters treated in this book. My thanks are due to the following: Professor J. F. A. Ajayi, Dr. J. S. Boston, the late Dr. R. E. Bradbury, Professor J. D. Fage, Professor J. E. Flint, Professor D. D. Hartle, Dr. J. Iliffe, Mr. G. I. Jones, Dr. W. Rodney, Professor A. F. C. Ryder, and Professor T. Shaw. None of them, of course, has the slightest responsibility for its contents.

In writing this study I have accumulated many debts to my

extended family. I am particularly grateful to Mr. F. O. Isichei for his invaluable assistance in collecting Western Ibo oral traditions, and for his encouragement. Had he had my opportunities, he would have written more and better books. Father Patrick Isichei shared with me some materials on Asaba, and has encouraged this work throughout. Dr. Veronica Isichei cared for my eldest child, then a baby, while I did research in Paris, at much inconvenience to herself. My dear friend Frau Karola Marchner sacrificed part of her annual leave to do likewise. I am glad of an opportunity to thank Mr. Innocent Isichei, whose help made so much difference to my stay in Rome. Nor must I forget to thank my own dear father and step-mother, Mr. and Mrs. A. V. Allo, for their unfailing moral support, as well as for their material help in my undergraduate days.

My greatest debt is to my beloved husband, Dr. Uche Peter Isichei. It was he who first suggested that I write this book, and his belief in it has given me courage to finish it, in the face of many difficulties, and despite the pressure of other work. He has done far more than cheerfully accept the many trials and inconveniences which research and the writing of books impose on family life. When time for research in London was running out, he interrupted his own work to help me in note taking, in a library which lacks both typing and xerox facilities. As for an earlier book, he has drawn the maps. This book has benefited greatly from his long continued knowledge of those parts of Iboland with which it is mainly concerned. The ideas it expresses are our ideas, and in a very real sense, it is our book. And like everything I do in history, it has benefited greatly from the example of his scholarly dedication and integrity in a completely different field of academic inquiry.

I would like to thank my elder son, Uche, who was born at the time I began this work, and whose happy and loving nature has made its own contribution to its completion. Nor can I refrain from an affectionate mention of Emeka and Nkem, who were born half-way through the final draft, and watched with interest while I finished it.

17 Umuaji King St.,
Umuaji Quarter,
Asaba.
Christmas, 1971.

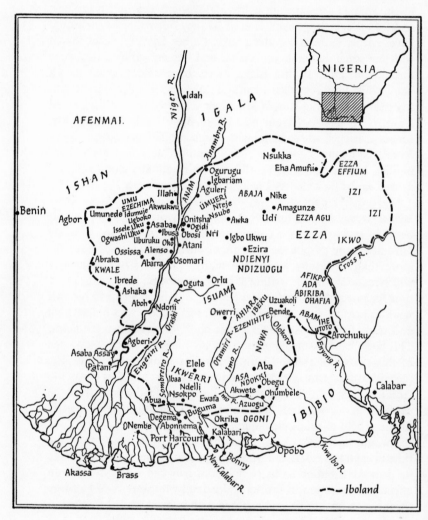

1 Places and Peoples mentioned in the text

1 · The Beginnings

'. . . the groups of the south-east have no history before the
coming of the Europeans . . .'
—Margery Perham, *Lugard, The Years of
Authority, 1898–1945*, p. 459.

The traditional homeland of the Ibo people of south-eastern
Nigeria lies between the Niger and the Cross Rivers, though a
substantial minority lives to the west of the Niger. Like other groups
whose limits are not defined by obvious natural boundaries, they
tend to merge into neighbouring peoples. Some western Ibo communities have much in common with their Ishan neighbours.
Northern Iboland merges into the kingdom of Igala, and a number
of border towns, such as Ogurugu, are equally at home in both
languages. In the south-east, Arochuku, historically one of the most
important of Ibo states, forms a peninsula in Ibibioland. In the
Delta, no simple generalizations are possible. The general pattern is
one of ever increasing Ibo infiltration, a process expanded, though
probably not begun, under the impact of the trans-Atlantic slave
trade. The trading cities of the Delta drew much of their population
from the Ibo hinterland, and one of the most important of them,
Bonny, gradually adopted the Ibo language. The history of the Ibo
people is inextricably entwined with that of the Delta, though
because the Delta has already been the subject of intensive historical
study, its history forms but a subordinate theme of this book.

This study is primarily concerned with those of the Ibo people who
remained in their ancestral homeland. Nevertheless, we must not
forget the Ibos of the Diaspora, the thousands of men and women
who went as involuntary emigrants to the New World in the era of
the slave trade. A few of these victims were recaptured from the slave
ships and resettled in Sierra Leone, where they formed, in the
nineteenth century, a flourishing community with a strong sense of its
Ibo identity. Those who reached the Americas were soon cut off, of

2 17

necessity, from the memory of their origins, and their history becomes one with that of the Afro-Americans.

Like many African peoples, the Ibo lived in a difficult and unpromising natural environment. The Delta is an infertile waste of tortuous creeks and mangrove swamps. Much of the Ibo interior consisted originally of dense tropical rainforest, making both agriculture and communications difficult. Its soils are highly leached and acid—'among the poorest of Nigerian soils'.[1] To the north, the forest merges into orchard bush—a region of rolling hills, grasslands and scattered trees, which homesick Englishmen have sometimes compared with the Downs of southern England. In the long years of their history, the Ibo people were to cultivate the whole of the forest, and, with the other peoples of the Delta, transform a watery and unproductive wilderness into a network of wealthy entrepôt city states.

It was not until 1830 that Europeans discovered the course of the lower Niger, and thus set eyes for the first time on a few of the states of the Ibo interior. From then on, we have a gradually increasing knowledge of Iboland, and an increasing amount of documentation for its history, though it was not until the end of the century that they penetrated beyond the immediate hinterlands of the Delta and the Niger, and in 1906—the concluding date for this study—there were still parts of Iboland which no European had ever seen.

Most of this book deals with less than a hundred years of Ibo history. The history of the Ibo and their forbears goes back four thousand years or more. But unfortunately most of this history is shrouded in obscurity, and is likely to remain so.

We have three main sources of information about the Ibo past before the nineteenth century—the findings of archaeology, the oral traditions of the Ibo people themselves, and the observations of European visitors to the Delta. Each of these deals with a different time scale, and provides different kinds of information, so that it is difficult to combine them in a satisfactory synthesis.

Archaeological findings in Iboland go back as far as four thousand years. But archaeology in the area is still in its infancy, and its flourishing growth was sadly disrupted by the events of recent years, one of the lesser casualties of war. Only a few sites have been

[1] K. M. Buchanan and J. C. Pugh, *Land and People in Nigeria* (London, 1964 reprint), p. 60.

excavated, but these have yielded material of enormous significance, which has, in some respects, transformed our knowledge of the Ibo past. It seems likely that systematic archaeological work in Iboland in the future will add greatly to our understanding of its history, though there are, of course, major limitations to the kind of information which the remains of material cultures can supply.

Europeans began to visit the Delta towards the end of the fifteenth century. Their accounts are invaluable for the history of the Delta, and thus relevant to Ibo history, but they never visited the Ibo interior, and whatever they say about it is generalized hearsay.

The use of oral traditions presents special difficulties in the Ibo context, which are described more fully in the next chapter. These spring largely from the fact that Iboland was not a centralized state, but consisted of a very large number of independent and relatively small polities. Their number makes the scientific study and collation of their traditions difficult, and their complicated and democratic systems of government were not particularly conducive to the systematic preservation of knowledge about the past. Perhaps the key difficulty is the near-impossibility of establishing a reliable chronology for each set of traditions—a necessary prelude to understanding their mutual relationship, and their relationship to external influences, such as the impact of the slave trade. Moreover, like all oral traditions they tend to preserve certain kinds of information only—such as that relating to the town's foundation, and its major wars.

Information based on these three types of source forms the basis of the first three chapters of this book. Inevitably, the evidence is less ample and precise, and there is greater room for hypothesis and conjecture than in the rest of the book. But it is essential to attempt the task, because if we ignore those long and largely hidden centuries, and confine our attention to what is well documented, beginning our study in the nineteenth century, we impose much more serious distortions on our historical perspectives.

The history of many peoples begins with a migration, and a founding father. But the available evidence suggests that the Ibo and their forbears have lived in much their present homes from the dawn of human history. The fact that they and their neighbours speak very different but related languages points to this conclusion. Any attempt to derive absolute time scales from patterns of linguistic change involves us in great methodological difficulties, which were first pointed out by the critics of glottochronology, but the linguistic evidence certainly suggests ancient and continuous settlement. A scholar who has studied it states, 'Rough basic vocabulary counts suggest that Yoruba, Edo, and Ibo may have started to diverge not much less than 4,000 years ago . . . There is no reason to suppose that the divergence of these languages from a parent stock has not taken place side by side more or less *in situ*. Any theory which would derive the carriers of one of them, *en masse*, from far afield, when the others were already established in the area, would raise historico-linguistic difficulties of great magnitude.'[1]

The botanical evidence confirms this picture of long settlement. The Southern Nigeria Conservator of Forests was surprised to discover, some sixty years ago, that the area was not covered with its original rainforest. This survived only on disputed or agriculturally worthless land, or on the verges of paths—this last giving travellers a false impression of its extent. For the rest, the forest was secondary growth: 'The country is literally honeycombed with farms and their overgrown abandoned sites.'[2]

Iboland's high population densities, which have often been re-marked on, point to the same conclusion. The Owerri area has a population density of over four hundred per square mile, rising in places to over a thousand per square mile, one of the greatest densities of a rural population in the world.[3] This again suggests a long period of continuous settlement. Archaeological fieldwork confirms this picture: 'We now have enticing evidence of a cultural continuum from the lithic periods to the present, some employing highly sophisticated techniques.'[4]

The beginnings of the history of what later became Iboland lie, like the pre-history of the rest of West Africa, in an area which is still surrounded by many uncertainties. Scholars have constructed certain hypotheses on the basis of archaeological, linguistic, botanical

[1] R. E. Bradbury, 'The Historical Uses of Comparative Ethnography with special reference to Benin and the Yoruba', in Jan Vansina, Raymond Mauny and L. V. Thomas (eds.), *The Historian in Tropical Africa* (London, 1964), p. 150.

[2] H. N. Thompson, in *Journal of the African Society* (1910–11), X, p. 130.

[3] Buchanan and Pugh, p. 60.

[4] D. Hartle, 'Bronze Objects from Ezira, Eastern Nigeria', *The West African Archaeological Newsletter* (1966), no. 4, p. 28.

and anthro-biological evidence—but it is essentially a period where conjecture still reigns supreme.

It was the great pre-historian Childe who first drew attention to the fundamental importance of the invention of agriculture in the history of human development.[1] Neolithic man—as the man of this revolutionary period is known—advanced from the precarious and wandering life of the hunter and gatherer to the more stable and comfortable life of the farmer. This in its turn made other developments possible, and neolithic man made pottery, and a wide range of wooden and stone tools.

It is thought that agriculture developed in West Africa about five thousand years ago, on the southern fringe of the Sahara—which was, of course, much moister and more fertile than it is today. Scholars disagree as to whether it was invented independently, or spread there from elsewhere, by diffusion.[2]

It seems probable that the first settlement of Iboland was on the northern edge of the rainforest, and the savanna to its north. This would have been easier to cultivate with wooden and stone tools. It was once thought that the rainforests could not be settled until the invention of iron tools and the introduction of a number of Asian food crops,[3] but recent archaeological work has shown the extent of Stone Age forest penetration.[4] Excavations at Nsukka, in the most northerly part of Iboland, and at Afikpo, near the present rain-forest savanna border, show that neolithic men were living there as early as 3000 B.C., and were making stone tools, including ground stone axes, and pottery.[5]

Their subjugation of a forest environment was to be greatly helped by the introduction of iron working. Radio-carbon dates from the Nok complex, further north, suggest that this knowledge may have

[1] Gordon Childe, *What Happened in History* (Harmondsworth, first pub. 1942). His views have been much modified by scholars since.

[2] Cf. J. Desmond Clark, 'The spread of food production in sub-Saharan Africa' and Roland Porteres, 'Primary cradles of agriculture in the African continent', in J. D. Fage and R. A. Oliver (eds.), *Papers in African Prehistory* (Cambridge, 1970).

[3] J. Desmond Clark, 'Prehistoric Origins of African Culture', *ibid.*, p. 21.

[4] Cf. Frank Willet, 'Nigeria', in P. L. Shinnie (ed.), *The African Iron Age* (Oxford, 1971), p. 19.

[5] D. Hartle, 'Archaeology in Eastern Nigeria', *The West African Archaeological Newsletter* (1966), no. 5, pp. 13 ff.; also (1969), no. 11, p. 35.

reached Nigeria by 300 B.C., or even earlier[1]—though scholars
disagree as to whether it came from Meroe, or from the Maghreb, via
the trans-Saharan trade routes.[2]

After more than a thousand years of iron age civilization, in the
ninth century A.D., our knowledge of Ibo history emerges suddenly
from the realm of conjecture and inference to that of positive knowledge.[3] We know that the Ibos of the ninth century were making iron
swords, and bronze and copper vases and ornaments, whose intricate
forms reveal great technical virtuosity. They made pottery which was
to astonish those who found it later by its wealth of form and
vitality. They wore beads imported from as far afield as Venice and
India. They were part of a major complex of international trade,
importing, certainly beads and copper, and probably other metals,
from far afield. No one would have suspected the existence of this Ibo
bronze age, had it not been revealed by sheer chance in 1938.

In that year, a man was digging a hole for a water cistern near his
home in Igbo-Ukwu, a small village twenty-five miles south of
Onitsha, when he came upon a number of bronze objects. These
later found their way into various museums, but it was not until 1959
that systematic excavation of the site began, and not until 1970 that
the results were published in full.

When the first bronzes were discovered, the general reaction was
much the same as it has been to similar finds elsewhere in Africa.
They were thought to be amazing and improbable, and probably
imported from elsewhere, and were assigned a date much later than
the one which has now become accepted. The method of radio-
carbon dating has yielded four ninth-century dates. The other
evidence—such as that based on a study of the beads and pottery
excavated—has been meticulously sifted by Professor Thurstan Shaw,
who excavated the site, and seems compatible with this dating. In the
absence of further evidence, it seems reasonable to assume that the

[1] Willett, p. 14.
[2] *Ibid.*, p. 17.
[3] The account which follows of the Igbo-Ukwu investigations, and of their
significance, is based on Thurstan Shaw, *Igbo-Ukwu, An account of archaeological
discoveries in eastern Nigeria* (2 vols., London, 1970). When this book had reached
page proof stage, an article appeared arguing for the possibility, or likelihood, of
a fifteenth-century date. (B. Lawal, 'Dating Problems at Igbo-Ukwu', *Journal of
African History* (1973), XIV, pp. 1 ff.) At the time of going to press, the question
seems to stand open.

Igbo-Ukwu discoveries are about a thousand years old. What do they tell us about Ibo society at that time?

It is almost certain that the finds are to be linked with the divine kings of Nri, the Eze Nri. Nri is an ancient religious and cultural centre, historically linked with the kingdom of Igala, which is discussed more fully in the next chapter. Igbo-Ukwu is very close to both the towns which have an Eze Nri in modern times. One of the sites excavated was the tomb of a man buried in a sitting position, dressed in ceremonial regalia, with a bronze rod supporting a bronze leopard skull at his side. The chamber was roofed in, and five individuals—perhaps slaves—buried above it. The system of burial has many parallels with the modern burial of an Eze Nri.

The excavations reveal the antiquity of the institution, and the✓ treasures they uncovered, the bronzes and beads, reflect the wealth of the economy, and the great artistic skill of the makers of the bronzes. They show the extent to which the area was part of the network of international trade. Some of the beads may have come from Venice, but most were probably imported from India, via North Africa. The raw materials for the bronzes were certainly imported. Some are made of copper, and some of leaded bronze, but there was no copper in the area that later became Nigeria. The nearest anciently worked copper mines were at Takedda, near the modern borders of Niger and Mali, though there were others further afield in the Sahara. One can only surmise what was exported in return. Ivory was probably a major export. Some of the bronzes depict elephants, and the buried ruler had one foot resting on an elephant's tusk. Perhaps slaves and kola nuts were exported as well—this last important as a stimulant acceptable to the Islamic world.

One obvious question which suggests itself is, who made the bronzes, and what is their relationship to other ancient Nigerian centres of metal working. There is as yet no real agreement about the relationship between the Igbo-Ukwu discoveries and a complex which has been tentatively labelled 'the Lower Niger bronze industry'. Hoards of bronzes have been discovered in many parts of the Delta,[1] and the Nupe people to the north possess a set of bronzes which are supposed to have been brought to Nupe from Idah by their founding father, Tsoede, in the sixteenth century. William Fagg has

[1] Described by Robin Horton, 'A Note on Recent Finds of Brasswork in the Niger Delta', *Odu* (1965), II, pp. 76 ff.

suggested that Idah was an ancient centre of bronze production, but the evidence is tenuous. Horton, in his account of the Delta bronzes, suggests that they were made elsewhere to the specifications of the local people, but there is no evidence to this effect, and the hypothesis, perhaps, raises more problems than it answers. There is no obvious connection between the Igbo-Ukwu bronzes and the more famous works from Ife and Benin, further afield, which are completely different in style and metallic content, and which were made up to five hundred years later.

In the absence of evidence to the contrary, it seems reasonable to assume that the Igbo-Ukwu bronzes were made by Ibos, either in Igbo-Ukwu itself, or elsewhere in Iboland—there are traditions of brass working at Abiriba.[1] Just as the raw materials were imported, it is almost certain that their techniques were learnt from elsewhere. The cire perdue technique of bronze casting used is a complicated one, but was practised in ancient Egypt and Mesopotamia. Its knowledge was widespread in West Africa—bronzes cast by this method were produced by the 'Sao' culture south of Lake Chad, and gold was cast in Ghana by the same techniques.

All who have studied the Igbo-Ukwu bronzes are struck by their technical brilliance. This can be seen from the plates which illustrate this chapter, and, like all visual art, is better seen than described. William Fagg has compared it with the rococo period in Europe, and observes: 'Many of these finely cast works show an extreme addiction to virtuosity, unparalleled in Africa, which reminds us ... of Fabergé.'[2]

Much of the world's art is court art, and that of Igbo-Ukwu, of course, is no exception. It represents the wealth of a great religious leader, and the talents of the artists who worked for him. In that sense the findings are not 'typical', and can tell us relatively little about the ordinary life of the Ibo men and women of the time. Again, there are limits to what we can learn about a society from archaeological findings alone, in the absence of other sources of information. One could not know, for instance, from the objects themselves, that the function of a rosary was purely utilitarian, of a mace, purely

[1] F. Ekejiuba, 'Preliminary notes on Brasswork of Eastern Nigeria', *African Notes* (1967), IV, no. 2, pp. 11–15.
[2] William Fagg and Margaret Plass, *African Sculpture* (revised edn., London, 1966), p. 120.

1. An Ibo image of Ibo family life. A terracotta sculpture, from Kwale,
for the cult of the yam spirit. *British Museum.*

2. Pottery from Igbo-Ukwu

3. Bronze altar stand, from Igbo-Ukwu

4. Bronze shell surmounted by an animal, from Igbo-Ukwu

ceremonial. This is particularly true of religion. The findings, naturally, reveal a situation which was primarily religious in nature. But religion is so much concerned with the immaterial, that we can learn little about its nature from the artefacts used in religious practices.

But if the Igbo-Ukwu findings are atypical, they are not unique in Iboland. Several years ago, similar discoveries were made at Ezira, not far from Igbo-Ukwu. The objects excavated were similar to those found at Igbo-Ukwu—iron gongs and a sword, bronze anklets, bracelets, bells and ceremonial objects, cast by the cire perdue method, and covered with exquisite lace-like designs.[1] It seems likely that further investigations elsewhere in Iboland will reveal comparable artefacts. A government Intelligence Report describes 'various brass objects now ancient with decay' in the western Ibo village of Ibrede, which were brought there six generations before from Aboh[2]—though of course one cannot know the provenance or age of these bronzes in the absence of further information.

In modern times, Ibo metallurgy has been mainly concerned with iron working, though brass working is not unknown.[3] But the technical and artistic achievements of the Igbo-Ukwu bronzes[4] have not been repeated in this medium. The grave site was forgotten, the buried treasures cached nearby were abandoned, in circumstances one can only conjecture, the techniques forgotten, and the very memory of the bronzes entirely lost. We have a parallel in the superb achievements of the apparently short-lived school of brass casting at Ife, in Yorubaland. We can only speculate as to how some unknown catastrophe cut off these traditions in full flower.

But it would be a mistake to look on these discoveries as evidence that Ibo society reached a kind of cultural peak a thousand years ago, and then declined. Bronze was only one of many means of cultural and artistic expression, an especially durable one. But Ibo art was basically directed to transcendental ends, and durability was not the most important consideration. Like other forest peoples, the Ibo chose wood as their most usual sculptural medium—a short-lived

[1] Described in Hartle, 'Bronze Objects'.
[2] N.A.I. C.S.O.26/11 (File 28903), Main Report on Aboh-Sobo Village Groups (1933), p. 9.
[3] Shaw, I, 272.
[4] I have used the word 'bronze' throughout this chapter in its more general sense, to refer to any object made of copper or copper alloy.

one, in a tropical environment. Much outstanding Ibo sculpture is in unbaked clay, the most ephemeral of all sculptural media, for it is in honour of Ala,[1] the divine Earth, and durability is less important than its symbolic meaning. Other equally characteristic Ibo art forms—oral literature, rhetoric, the dance—are of their nature even more subject to time's oblivion. It is only rarely in Africa that a thing of beauty remains a joy forever.

[1] Ala, Ana, or Ani, among different Ibo groups.

2 · Patterns of Internal Migrations
and State Formation

'Toutes les histoires anciens, comme le disait un de nos beaux
esprits, ne son que des fables convenus.'
—Voltaire, *Jeannot et Colin.*

Historians have begun recently to develop a healthy scepticism
about traditions of origin, migrations, and state formation. In the
words of a recent persuasive statement, in the northern Nigeria
context, one must relinquish 'the pursuit of the phantom of the
strange invader, the héros civilisateur from the east . . . Political
institutions, like the other institutions of human culture, are devised
and developed because they offer solutions to the problems which
arise for mankind out of the conditions in which it has to live.'[1]

These caveats apply with redoubled force to Iboland. If one takes
the traditions of her polities at their face value, one must conclude
that many of them were founded within the last three hundred years,
and that the lives of their peoples have been marked by frequent
migrations. Indeed one can discern a general pattern of migrations,
moving anti-clockwise around Iboland. There are a number of
migrations to the south, among which the movements of the Ndokki
and Ngwa are especially well documented. Further east, one has the
northward migrations of the Ada, the Ezza, the Ikwo and their
neighbours, which is followed by the general expansion of the north-
eastern Ibo. A group of the Ezza move westward, until their advance
is blocked by the expansion of the peoples of the densely populated
Udi-Nsukka plateau. A further pattern consists of migrations to the
Niger, from various directions.

But a general pattern such as this—which is distilled from the
copious data in the National Archives, Ibadan—is inherently

[1] Abdullahi Smith, 'Some Considerations relating to the Formation of States
in Hausaland', *Journal of the Historical Society of Nigeria* (December 1970),
pp. 345–6.

unconvincing. The picture of frequent migrations accords ill with the evidence of ancient and continuous settlement. Where migrations did occur, they often affected only a minority, who joined a pre-existing Ibo community—as is often enough attested by the traditions themselves. Stories of migration from elsewhere may, as elsewhere, loom larger in the traditions than the historical reality justifies. Perhaps the myth of migration from elsewhere has a special function in a small face-to-face society—providing a reinforcement for an always precarious unity.

As elsewhere, the constant tendency to elision in oral tradition tends to suggest an inaccurately recent date. This has been interestingly attested by combined archaeological field work and collection of oral traditions in East Africa recently.[1] Not all Ibo traditions in Iboland contain chronological data. Where this exists, whether in family genealogies, in the king lists of her few kingdoms, or in other forms, one must often suspect the workings of some iron law of elision. And where chronological data is so often absent or suspect, it is impossible to be certain of the relationship which different traditions bear to each other, or to external events such as the impact of the trans-Atlantic slave trade. Chronology is the skeleton of all historical inquiry. In its absence, we are in a realm of surmise and conjecture.

Some of these difficulties may be solved through a more extensive and scientific collection of Iboland's historical traditions. No single individual can hope to record the traditions of more than a few of Iboland's many polities in person. At the moment, the written compilations of oral traditions are numerous and full,[2] but not many of them have been recorded by historians trained in modern techniques of historical inquiry. It is likely that in the future, the collection of traditions of origin will need to concentrate on particular themes—such as the movements of the north-eastern Ibo—

---

[1] Researches of Dr. P. Schmidt described by Dr. J. E. G. Sutton at a University of Dar es Salaam History Research Seminar, 16 February 1971.

[2] The largest single collection of traditions is to be found in Intelligence Reports compiled by government officials in the 1930s. Most of these are in the National Archives, Ibadan. There are a number of compilations by anthropologists, whose interest, generally, was not primarily in history, by government officials working on their own initiative, and by missionaries. The traditions of some states, such as Aboh, have been recorded by a number of individuals over a considerable time period.

and that it will add greatly to our knowledge of the Ibo past. But it is likely to remain true that Ibo traditions of origin have intrinsic limitations which reflect the nature of Ibo political life. They lack the plenitude and precision of traditions preserved in large centralized kingdoms, where the society can maintain, for instance, professional remembrancers, and where the records of the past are a dimension of the state's collective identity, and a cherished proof of a dynasty's right to rule.

Having begun with these caveats, we must beware of neglecting important facts about the past in the name of an excessive historical sophistication. Where oral tradition is our main source of knowledge of the past, to reject it is a counsel of despair, and may lead, and sometimes does, to areas of pure conjecture. The rest of this chapter uses Ibo oral traditions to glean at least fragments of the lineaments of those lost centuries which lie between the ninth century, revealed by archaeological researches, and the relatively well-documented nineteenth.

Most fundamentally, these traditions reveal a way of life, a geographical mobility which enabled the Ibo to balance the constantly shifting equation between population pressures and the resources of the environment. When population pressures became too great, or when towns were divided by serious disputes, a section would migrate and establish a new home, preserving the memory of its origins. Other towns would expand to accommodate new quarters of immigrants, who would become part of the town, but preserve the memory of their first identity. This kind of migration was a safety valve, both against overpopulation and against internal wars. The imposition of colonial rule, by freezing settlement permanently in the patterns which existed at that point in time, ended this mobility, and in doing so created pockets of great discontent and hardship.

The traditions contain much information about the formation of states, and relationships between them.

One set of traditions deal with Iboland's relationship to its northern neighbour, the ancient kingdom of Igala, with its capital at Idah. These traditions in their turn have three main themes.

The first set of these relate to Nri, and the group of related towns known collectively as the Umueri clan. There are several versions of the story of their origins. According to one, Idah, Nri, and the other

Umueri towns were all founded by the children of Eri, a sky being.[1] According to another, Eri was an Igala warrior who settled in northern Iboland, and Nri, and the other Umueri towns, were founded by his sons, who married Ibo wives.[2] The traditions by themselves give little indication of how long ago these events took place, but their great antiquity is clearly revealed by the Igbo-Ukwu excavations described in the last chapter. The ancient connection between Igala and the Umueri towns is revealed in other ways. There were many similarities between the sacred kingship of the Igala and that of Nri.[3] It is likely, indeed, that Igala and Nri were the gateways through which a number of important discoveries reached Iboland. It is noteworthy that Nri, alone among Ibo towns, has traditions which describe the invention of agriculture, and of iron working.[4] Awka, whose travelling blacksmiths served much of Iboland with their skills, is situated very close to Nri. Nri was to remain an important religious centre. Its priests attended the ceremonies which conferred major titles in many towns both east and west of the Niger, and specialized in purifying towns from offences against the divine Earth.[5]

A second set of traditions described Igala military expeditions in northern Iboland, especially in the Anambra valley and the Nsukka-Udi plateau. The events to which they refer have probably extended over a very long time period, beginning before the fifteenth century.[6] Some of them refer to the exploits of a semi-legendary Igala hero, Onoja Oboni, who made his capital at Ogurugu, and whose death was as spectacular as the events of his life.[7] Many of the clans north of Enugu preserve memories of Igala raids, which have probably

[1] M. D. W. Jeffreys, 'The Umundri Tradition of Origin,' *African Studies* (1956), XV, pp. 119 ff. This is part of a longer unpublished work, *The Divine Umundri Kings of Igboland* (University of London Ph.D. thesis, 1934).
[2] N.A.I. C.S.O. 26/325 (File 28323), Stone, 'Report on the Umueri Villages' (1932).
[3] Jeffries, *The Divine Umundri Kings*, ch. 2.
[4] Jeffries, 'The Umundri Tradition', p. 126. Cf. Northcote W. Thomas, *Anthropological Report on the Ibo-Speaking Peoples of Nigeria, Part I, Law and Custom of the Ibo of the Awka Neighbourhood, S. Nigeria*, (London, 1913), pp. 50–1.
[5] A. G. Leonard, *The Lower Niger and its Tribes* (London, 1906), pp. 34 ff.
[6] Communication from Dr. J. Boston, 14 October 1970.
[7] N.A.I. C.S.O. 26/240 (File 29380), Milne, 'Report on Ogboli Group of Nsukka Division', p. 7.

extended over a period of at least five hundred years. Similarly, the impact of the Igala is mirrored in their political institutions.[1]

A third set of traditions relate to Igala influence on the lower Niger. In the 1830s—when we have our first eyewitness accounts of the area—the lower Niger was dominated by two naval powers, the Ibo kingdom of Aboh, at the apex of the Delta, and Igala. Igala canoes would travel down-river to trade. Often the Igala would establish a temporary encampment on the river bank or on a sand-bank, for trading purposes. In this way they came to found a number of towns, or quarters of towns. The most important of these was Osomari. According to the earliest version of its traditions, 'It is said to have been peopled by the Igaras originally as a trading station or market.'[2] The Igala immigrants joined with the original Ibo inhabitants to create a new state, the title of whose ruler, the Atamanya, doubtless echoes that of the Atta of Igala (the Atta 'Gala). The people of Osomari have preserved no king list, but believe that they have had nine Atamanya, their reigns separated by long regencies.[3] The data is too fragile to support an estimate of the date of its foundation, but it seems quite likely that Osomari was founded, like other Niger Ibo states, in the sixteenth or early seventeenth century.[4] Other Igala foundations on the lower Niger include the Oko villages, south of Asaba, and two quarters of Illah, the most northerly Niger Ibo town.[5]

Another complex of traditions deals with various movements southwards, and with the foundations of the Delta states. An early southward movement seems to have taken place from the Awka and Orlu area, to what is now the homeland of the eastern Isuama.[6]

As we have already seen, the Ngwa migrated further to the south from an area to the north of their present home, which is now

---

[1] J. S. Boston, 'Notes on Contact between the Igala and the Ibo', *Journal of the Historical Society of Nigeria* (1960), II, no. 1, pp. 56–8.

[2] Bishop Crowther, in *The Church Missionary Intelligencer* (1876), p. 536.

[3] F. Ikenna Nzimiro, 'Chieftaincy and Politics in Four Niger States' (University of Cambridge Ph.D. thesis, 1966), p. 207.

[4] Cf. pp. 38–42 below.

[5] Daryll Forde and G. I. Jones, *The Ibo and Ibibio-speaking Peoples of Southeastern Nigeria* (Ethnographic Survey of Africa, London, first pub. 1950), pp. 48 and 50. There is a discrepancy between Igala and Ibo traditions in a number of cases, the Igala claiming Igala origins for a number of towns (cf. Boston, p. 54), whose own traditions do not confirm this claim.

[6] Cf. G. I. Jones, *The Trading States of the Oil Rivers* (London, first pub. 1963) p. 30.

occupied by the Ezenihite clan. Some of the Ibo peoples whom their migration displaced preserved a separate identity as the Asa clan.[1] The Ndokki Ibo, still further to the south, have the same tradition of origin as the island kingdom of Bonny. Both Bonny and Kalabari— its great economic rival from the sixteenth to the nineteenth centuries —were founded, probably in the fifteenth century, as part of a general movement of Ijaw peoples. The history of Kalabari— founded, according to tradition, a generation earlier than Bonny— lies beyond the scope of this book. But that of Bonny is a major dimension of Ibo history.

Many nineteenth-century visitors to Bonny believed that the town had been founded by Ibos from the interior.[2] The impression shows the extent to which Ibo influences had come to dominate Bonny, as the result of continual importations of Ibo slaves, but traditions collected later, and more carefully, show that Bonny was Ijo in origins, founded after a migration from the west, from 'Otuburu Toro or Abatoro part of Ijo, on the River Niger'.[3] Some of the migrants settled in the Delta, near Akassa. Others went north, to Oguta. Some went as far north as Ndizuogu, and then moved south again. One section settled in what is now the homeland of the Ndokki. Others continued on to found the state of Bonny. At what date did this take place? Talbot and Webber assign it to the fifteenth century, on the basis of Bonny's king lists, which show that Opobo the Great, who ruled from 1790 to *c.* 1830 was either the fifteenth or the sixteenth ruler of Bonny. Jones questions the chronological value of this king list,[4] but a fifteenth-century date fits in well with the evidence that Bonny was already 'a very large village' at the beginning of the sixteenth century,[5] and with the tradition that the Portuguese came to Bonny in the lifetime of its founders.[6]

The first eyewitness account of the area—the oddly entitled *Esmeraldo de Situ Orbis*, written, probably, between 1505 and 1508—

[1] N.A.I. C.S.O. 26/207 (File 29033/II), Allen, 'Report on the Ngwa Clan' (1934).

[2] James Johnson, 'An African Clergyman's Visit to Bonny', *The Church Missionary Intelligencer* (1897), pp. 27–8.

[3] N.A.I. C.S.O. 26/202 (File 29281), Ennals, 'Report on the Ndoki Clan' (1933). Cf. N.A.I. C.S.O. 26/73 (File 27226), Webber, 'Report on Bonny District' (1931), and P. Amaury Talbot, *The Peoples of Southern Nigeria* (London, 1926), I, p. 238.

[4] Jones, *The Trading States*, pp. 24–8.

[5] Duarte Pacheco Pereira, *Esmeraldo de Situ Orbis* (trans. and ed. George H. T. Kimble, Hakluyt Society, 2nd series, LXXIX, 1937), p. 132.

[6] Webber, p. 8.

shows that Bonny had already overcome the problems of economic viability in the Delta environment. She manufactured salt, which she exported to the Ibo hinterland, importing in return the foodstuffs she could not grow for herself. She was already using the vast canoes, holding eighty men or more, which solved the problem of transport, and transformed the Delta's myriad creeks from obstacles into roads.[1]

The advent of the Portuguese, and the subsequent development of the trans-Atlantic slave trade, were to revolutionize the economic and political role of Bonny. These developments form part of the subject-matter of the next chapter.

Like the Delta states, Arochuku grew up at a meeting place between two cultures. The Delta states were a fusion of Ijaw and Ibo elements, which came to create a unique civilization, with its own distinctive political institutions—the *ndi mili nnu* (people of the salt water)—comparable, at least in certain respects, with Swahili civilization in the coastal regions of East Africa. Arochuku grew out of the fusion of Ibo and Ibibio elements, and the present shape of its political institutions dates from a clash between the two peoples. Like the peoples of the Delta, the Aro transformed the crisis of the trans-Atlantic slave trade into an opportunity, a source of economic wealth and political power. By the nineteenth century, Arochuku possessed the greatest of Iboland's oracles, fulfilling both religious and political functions for much of Iboland. The Aro played a unique role on Iboland's inland trade routes, and had established a far-flung network of trading colonies throughout Iboland. We will discuss these aspects of the Aro achievement more fully in later sections of this study. We are here concerned with what tradition tells us about their historical development.

As is so often the case in Ibo tradition, the oral histories of Arochuku[2] give much circumstantial detail about its foundation, but little information about its later history, or the length of time which

---

[1] Pereira, p. 132.
[2] These have been recorded on a number of occasions. Cf. Talbot, I, 182–3; R.H. MSS. Afr. s. 783, Box 3/4 ff., 30 fol., H. F. Matthews, 'Discussion of Aro origins' (Matthews was a government anthropologist in the area in *c.* 1928). N.A.I. C.S.O. 26/51 (File 29017), Shankland, 'Aro Clan' (1933). There are also later accounts of Aro traditions, apparently based on these sources, in G.I. Jones, 'Who are the Aro?', *The Nigerian Field* (1939), espec. pp. 102–3, and an anonymous article, 'Inside Arochuku' in *The Nigeria Magazine* (1957), no. 53, pp. 100ff.

has since elapsed. It was formed after a conflict between the Ibo and the Ibibio. Traditions vary in their account of the causes for this. Some describe it as a revolt of Ibo slaves against Ibibio overlords, others as the result of the pressure of an expanding Ibo population on the original Ibibio settlers. In the war which followed, the Ibo called in 'Akpa' mercenaries, who have not been identified with certainty. The allied Ibo and Akpa were victorious. Shankland records that their victory was due to the use of firearms, and that the Aro still preserved, in the 1930s, two 'blunderbusses of a primitive type' allegedly used by the two Akpa leaders.[1] The nineteen villages of Aro still preserve the memory of their tribal origins. Six claim Akpa, five Ibo and two Ibibio ancestry. The rest were founded through later Ibo accessions.[2]

At what date did these events occur, and when did the Aro establish the prestige of their oracle and their trading network? We have a hint that the latter was of considerable antiquity in the Bonny tradition that the son of the first king of Bonny was called Kamalu. Kamalu is the name used by the Aro and Cross River Ibo for the god of lightning and the sky. This has been taken as an indication of the early development of the trading relationship between the Aro and the Delta states.[3] One version of Bonny tradition, too, states that a Bonny representative was sent to Arochuku at the time of the former's foundation.[4]

We have, however, some less tenuous information about the date when Arochuku was founded. The government anthropologist, Matthews, working in the late 1920s, collected a number of family genealogies going back to that time, which have an average time depth of eight generations. He also collected genealogies from the Ada, further north, who believe that they left their former homeland, near the present Arochuku, at the time the latter was founded.[5] Again, he found a time depth of eight generations. If we allot thirty years to a generation, this suggests that Arochuku was founded some 240 years before Matthews collected his data, that is, in the late seventeenth century.

[1] Shankland, p. 10.
[2] Matthews, fo. 37.
[3] Jones, *The Trading States*, p. 28.
[4] Fombo papers, Ibadan University Library, fo. 4.
[5] Matthews, folios 38–41 and fo. 45v; fo. 65 ff., 'Supplementary Report on the Aro'.

The fact that these genealogies are mutually consistent does not mean that they are complete—they may all be examples of the working of some iron law of elision. The references to the role of firearms would again confirm a fairly late date, for their importation did not become extensive until the eighteenth century.[1] But again, this is not conclusive. A few pieces were imported earlier, and in any case, two separate traditions may have been fused.

Although we cannot be certain, it seems reasonable to assume that Arochuku was founded in the seventeenth century, though the Ibos and Ibibios of the area doubtless traded with the Delta long before. The famous oracle grew out of a local Ibibio shrine, Ibritam. The generation which followed the foundation of the state expanded its influence.[2] The oracle had reached the apogee of its fame and prestige by the nineteenth century—a rise which apparently took place within the short time span of a hundred years. To these years also belong the elaboration of the Aro trading network. Each village of Arochuku had its own sphere of influence in Iboland—or Ibibio-land—an arrangement which drew full advantage from the diversity of their origins.[3] Aro influence was augmented by the practice of establishing Aro colonies at strategic points in Iboland, a process which was still going on at the time of the imposition of colonial rule.[4] The Aro concentrated on trade, and on the manipulation of their oracle, purchasing their food from their neighbours, the Ututo and Ihe,[5] and employing other neighbours, the warlike Ohafia and Abam, as mercenaries.

It is not easy to evaluate the role of the Arochuku oracle in Ibo society. On the one hand, the Aros' manipulation of their oracle to serve their own economic and political ends, and especially to obtain slaves,[6] seems the classic case of the exploitation of religious beliefs

---

[1] Cf. pp. 51–2 below. A few pieces were imported in the seventeenth century.

[2] Shankland, p. 13; 'Inside Arochuku', p. 107.

[3] Matthews, folios 37 and 45; Shankland, pp. 12–14.

[4] Forde and Jones, p. 28, state that the important colonies of Ndienyi and Ndizuogu were founded 'during the last fifty to a hundred years' but give no evidence for this. Cf. Mary Easterfield and E. K. Uku, 'Seeds in the Palm of your Hand', *West African Review* (December 1952), p. 1367; and N.A.E., E.P. 6810, Ross, 'Intelligence Report on Native Administration, Awka Division' (1930), fo. 30.

[5] Shankland, p. 12.

[6] It is well established that the Aro did not believe in their oracle personally, but manipulated it for material purposes. Cf. Shankland, pp. 14–15, and Mbonu Ojike, *My Africa* (New York, 1946), pp. 14–15.

for material ends. On the other hand, the oracle served valuable functions in Iboland, acting as a definitive court of appeal to solve disputes, and prevent their developing into wars. The Aro themselves used the apologia common to slave-owning societies everywhere: '. . . the wealth we derived from slaves gave us leisure to cultivate a less material side of life with institutions and a religion which other tribes were not unwilling to participate in.'[1]

A further complex of traditions deals with the migrations and wars of the north-eastern Ibo, especially the three related clans, the Ezza, the Ikwo and the Izi. Their traditions affirm that their founders were related through a common ancestor, Akumenyi. They migrated from a region to the south, perhaps in the Arochuku area. Chapman, in his report on the Ikwo clan, written in 1930,[2] estimated on the basis of genealogies that this had taken place twelve generations earlier. If we allot thirty years to a generation, the migration would have occurred in the second half of the sixteenth century. North-eastern Iboland, where they settled, was particularly well suited to yam cultivation. Their splendid farms greatly impressed the first European visitors to the region,[3] and continued to export food through the colonial era, and beyond.[4]

An expanding population, and the need for more land for farming, inevitably led to wars. The Ezza, Ikwo and Izi had settled in land which was already sparsely populated by some small tribal groups, whom they assimilated or displaced without difficulty. Further expansion to the north was made impracticable by the decreasing rainfall. The desire for land led to internal disputes, and, in particular, a state of endemic warfare between the Ikwo and the Ezza.[5] The Ezza in their turn attempted to expand to the west. In the nineteenth century, they founded several colonies—including Ezza-Effium and Ezza-Agu—which are separated from the Ezza homeland by the territories of other clans.[6] As the Ezza, and other groups of

[1] Easterfield and Uku, *West African Review* (December 1952), p. 1369.
[2] N.A.I. C.S.O. 26/147 (File 26804), Chapman, 'Report on the Ikwo Clan' (1930).
[3] C.O. 520/31, 'Political Report on the Ezza Patrol', encl. in Egerton to C.O., Confidential, 16 July 1905.
[4] G. I. Jones, 'Ecology and Social Structure among the North Eastern Ibo', *Africa* (1961), XXXI, pp. 119–20.
[5] Chapman, 'Ikwo Clan', p. 9.
[6] N.A.I. C.S.O. 26/116 (File 28179), Chapman, 'Report on the Ezza Clan' (1932), p. 2.

north-eastern Ibo, attempted to expand still further to the west, they came into conflict with another pattern of expansion. The peoples of the densely populated Nsukka-Udi plateau were suffering acutely from land shortage—especially serious in the Abaja area—which led them to expand towards the sparsely populated Anambra valley on the one hand, and in an eastward direction on the other. The traditions of many of the intervening peoples mirror the conflicts which resulted. Thus, a section of the Amagunze clan consists of refugees from Ezza expansion, in the late nineteenth century.[1] The villages of the Eha Amufu clan are not related to each other but were founded by various settlers, some from the Nsukka area and others from north-eastern Iboland.[2] After the imposition of colonial rule, these territorial conflicts were ended, by freezing settlement in the state in which it was thought to be at the time when colonial rule was introduced[3]—a process which involved, in the opinion of one observer, 'an awful injustice on the part of the Government against the Ezza tribes'.[4]

A further complex of historical traditions relates to the foundation of a number of important trading states on the Niger and its tributaries, which probably occurred in the sixteenth or early seventeenth centuries. It seems likely that before this period, the riverain area was very sparsely populated. There were several reasons for this. Below Onitsha and Asaba, the land is low lying, so that riverside towns such as Aboh and Osomari were regularly flooded, as the river rose. Again, the crucial role of water transport, while it gave economic advantages to a riverside town, had a military as well as a commercial significance. Accessibility to war canoes could endanger a town's safety. This is why Onitsha was sited several miles inland. In the nineteenth century, even the oil marketing towns behind the Delta, which relied so heavily on water transport, were often situated

---

[1] N.A.I. C.S.O. 26/45 (File 29457), Beaumont, 'Report on Amagunze Group of Udi Division' (1934), p. 5.
[2] N.A.I. C.S.O. 26/85 (File 29387), Dixon, 'Report on the Eha Amufu and Umualao Village Areas of Nsukka Division' (1933).
[3] C.O. 520/47, 'Annual Report on the Eastern Province for the Year 1906', encl. in Thorburn to Elgin, no. 425, 22 July 1907.
[4] Robert Cudjoe, 'Some Reminiscences of a Senior Interpreter', *The Nigerian Field* (1953), p. 153.

at a distance from the river, for security reasons.[1] Even today, the Niger and Anambra river valleys are less densely populated than adjacent areas.[2]

In the sixteenth or early seventeenth century, an important change occurred. A number of new states were founded, on the banks of the Niger and its tributaries. These have a number of characteristics in common. They were founded through a migration from elsewhere, and, in a number of cases, from outside Iboland. Some, though not all, have kings, and therefore king lists, and a more reliable source of chronological information than is usual in the Ibo interior. They were not founded in uninhabited areas, but in places where small settlements already existed. These earlier inhabitants were usually assimilated in the new state, though occasionally they were expelled from it.

Obviously a change in circumstances had occurred, so that the disadvantages of a riverain situation were now outweighed by its economic advantages. The change was due to the expansion in the volume of trade caused by the trans-Atlantic slave trade. Some, though not all, of these riverain states were destined to rise rapidly to a position of wealth and power. Like the states of the Delta and like Arochuku, they turned the basically destructive situation of the centuries of the slave trade into an opportunity. When the Landers travelled down the lower Niger in 1830, they found that it was a major artery of trade, with the relationships between its wealthy naval states carefully governed by diplomatic and marketing conventions. What does tradition tell us about the origins of these states?

We have already seen the role of the Igala in the area, and the way in which an Igala trading station developed into the state of Osomari. We must now look at Benin, and the traditions of those states which claim that they migrated from a homeland at or near Benin in the sixteenth or early seventeenth centuries.

The Niger was the furthest eastern boundary of the Benin kingdom, and many of the states of western Iboland were at least nominally

---

[1] F.O. 84/1882, 'A Report on the British Protectorate of the Oil Rivers', Section C, 'Towns and Trading Centres', encl. in Johnston to Salisbury, 1 December, 1888.

[2] Cf. Floyd, pp. 51–3, for a discussion of why population density is low in river valleys, and high on infertile uplands where water is scarce.

subject to its Oba. Benin traditions relate that the area was first conquered by Ewuare, in the mid-fifteenth century.[1] Occasionally a warlike Oba fought a compaign in the area, but for most of the time Benin's sovereignty there was nominal, and Obas were content with such ritual tokens of sovereignty as the annual expedition they sent to the Niger, to bring back some of its water to their court.[2] Equiano, the eighteenth-century western Ibo who was sold into slavery, and became the author of a famous autobiography, described matters thus: '. . . our subjection to the king of Benin was little more than nominal; for every transaction of the government, as far as my slender observation extended, was conducted by the chiefs or elders of the place.'[3]

In the sixteenth or early seventeenth century, there was some kind of political upheaval at Benin,[4] which led to a migration, led by Chima, in the course of which a number of Ibo states were founded. Chima and his followers may well have been Ibos, as Chima's own name suggests. Various versions of tradition suggest either that they were Ibos brought as slaves or hostages to the Benin court, or coming from a homeland in western Iboland.[5] This migration moved through western Iboland towards the Niger, founding, *en route*, the towns known collectively as *Umuezechima*. When the Niger was reached, Chima died and the group divided. One section, led by Oreze, crossed the Niger and founded the state of Onitsha, several miles inland from the river, expelling the indigenous people, the Oze, in the process.[6] The other section, led by Esumai,[7] went south.

[1] Jacob U. Egharevba, *A Short History of Benin* (Lagos, 1936), p. 21. Cf. R. E. Bradbury, *The Benin Kingdom and the Edo-speaking Peoples of South-Western Nigeria* (Ethnographic Survey of Africa, London, 1959), p. 22.

[2] Julius Spencer, 'The History of Asaba and its Kings', *Niger and Yoruba Notes* (1901), p. 21.

[3] *The Interesting Narrative of the Life of Olaudah Equiano* (abridged and ed. Paul Edward, London, 1967), p. 1. For the location of Equiano's home, cf. G. I. Jones, in Philip D. Curtin (ed.), *Africa Remembered: Narratives by West Africans from the Era of the Slave Trade* (Wisconsin, 1967), p. 61.

[4] Most versions say that this was caused by Chima's dispute with the Oba's mother, which induced the Oba to send his general, Gbunwala, against him.

[5] Northcote W. Thomas, *Anthropological Report on Ibo-Speaking Peoples of Nigeria, Part IV, Law and Custom of the Ibo of the Asaba District, S. Nigeria* (London, 1914), p. 3; John Waddington Hubbard, *The Sobo of the Niger Delta* (Zaria, 1948), p. 198.

[6] Ben N. Azikiwe, 'Fragments of Onitsha History', *The Journal of Negro History* (1930), XV, p. 476. Cf. also G. T. Basden, *Niger Ibos* (London, 1966, first pub. 1938), pp. 121–2; C. K. Meek, *Law and Authority in a Nigerian Tribe*

Several bands of settlers stopped on the way, founding a number of towns such as Ossissa and Ashaka. The main body continued on to found the state of Aboh. For a time they lived peacefully with the original inhabitants, the Akra, but after a time they were expelled. Some fled north to found Atani and Ogidi; a few returned after a time, to settle in a village near Aboh.[1]

Onitsha and Aboh had many similarities. Both were Ibo states in language and custom, which retained elements of Benin influence—most evident in the institution of Obi, or king. Their fortunes, however, were destined to be very different. Aboh profited by its strategic position at the apex of the Delta, and by the early nineteenth century had reached a position of great wealth and power, with fleets of heavily armed trade canoes. In the nineteenth century it was destined to decline, because neither missionaries nor European traders were prepared to endure the endless inconveniences of periodic flooding. Onitsha, with its inland site, attained neither naval nor commercial power. In the middle of the nineteenth century it was impoverished and surrounded by enemies. Its selection as a missionary and trading centre were destined to transform it—or, more precisely, the new town which sprang up at the waterside—into a major economic and educational centre.

How long ago were these states founded? We have two kinds of evidence—that provided by the names of the Benin obas in the traditions, and that provided by the Onitsha and Aboh king lists.

A number of traditions state that Onitsha was founded in the reign of Esigie.[2] A tradition recorded by Nzimiro states that both Chima and Esumai were sons of the Oba Ozolua, Esigie's father.[3] If this is reliable, it at once solves the problem of dating, for Ozolua is thought

---

(London, 1937), pp. 11–12; R. W. Harding, *Report of the Commission of Inquiry into the Dispute over the Obiship of Onitsha* (Enugu, 1963), pp. 12–13.

[7] There are two versions of the tradition. One is that the migration was led by Esumai, who was later succeeded by his son, Ogwezi. (N.A.O. C.S.O. 26/10 (File 26769), Williams and Miller, 'Aboh-Benin Clans' (1930–1), p. 7; Nzimiro, pp. 9–11). The second is that Ogwezi led the migration. (Hubbard, pp. 199 ff.) Hubbard's information was collected from well-placed local informants from 1929 on, and published many years later.

[1] Hubbard, p. 202; Williams and Miller, pp. 7–8.

[2] Egharevba, p. 34; Talbot, I, p. 158 (but cf. p. 168). A number of other sources which attribute the migration to Esigie's reign, do so on their authority. (Meek, p. 12; Hubbard, p. 198.) Egharevba had also consulted Talbot.

[3] Nzimiro, p. 9.

to have reigned from *c.* 1481 to *c.* 1504, and Esigie, his successor, to have reigned until *c.* 1550.[1] A Government Intelligence Report compiled in 1930-1, states that the migration was led by the sons 'of the Obba Ozenwe'[2]—a name which does not appear in any of the Benin king lists.

If we accept the tradition that these towns were founded in the reign of Esigie, we need look no further for information about the date of their foundation. But the traditions which affirm this are not independent—they may all, indeed, be based on Talbot. If we attempt to ascertain the date when these Niger states were founded by analysing their king lists, we are led to a rather different conclusion. Leonard, who recorded the first version of Onitsha's king list in *c.* 1895, concluded that it had been founded fourteen generations earlier.[3] Subsequent research has shown that he made the mistake of assuming that each successive ruler represented a generation. While the king list was slightly longer than Leonard supposed—Anazonwu, who died in 1899, was the sixteenth Obi—he represented only the eighth generation, for a number of Obis were brothers or cousins.[4] The first of these rulers we can date with certainty was Udogwu, the thirteenth Obi (the sixth generation), who reigned in the 1830s.[5] If we allot thirty years to a generation, it is difficult to avoid the conclusion that Onitsha was founded in the mid-seventeenth century.

The Aboh king list provides a similar picture. Obi Ossai, who was reigning at the time of the expeditions of 1830, 1832 and 1841 was the eleventh Obi, but each succession did not represent a generation, for after the death of each Obi his successor was elected after a contest between the different quarters of the town.[6] It is not clear from the king list how many generations had elapsed—but it seems unlikely that it would support a date earlier than the seventeenth century.

It fairly seems clear, then, that Aboh and Onitsha were founded either in the sixteenth or in the seventeenth centuries. Where the

[1] R. E. Bradbury, 'Chronological Problems in the Study of Benin History', *Journal of the Historical Society of Nigeria* (1959), I, no. 4, pp. 266, 279-80. (Ozolua may have died in 1516, or 1517.)

[2] Williams and Miller, p. 7.

[3] Leonard, pp. 35-6.

[4] Harding, pp. 15-18; Nzimiro, p. 157.

[5] William Balfour Baikie, *Narrative of an Exploring Voyage up the Rivers Kwora and Binue . . . in 1854* (London, 1856), p. 297.

[6] Nzimiro, king list facing p. 192.

evidence conflicts, one cannot hope for a much greater degree of certainty than this. But since there is a large element of conjecture in allocating a number of years to a generation, or a king's reign, it seems reasonable to prefer the dating suggested by the name of Esigie, and conclude that they were founded in the sixteenth century. A possible solution for the difficulty may lie in the time which elapsed between the time the emigrants left Benin, and the time their new states were founded.

Oguta is another state which was founded after a migration from Benin.[1] This is believed to have taken place at the same time—as the result of the same political upheavals. Some traditions identify their leader, Ogwuara, with the war leader, Gbunwala, who is associated with the flight of Chima and his followers.[2] They settled successively at several points on the Niger, but left it after a war with Igala, during which Ogwuara was deposed for betraying his people. His successor, Eroa, led them to the beautiful lake which now bears their name, connected by water both to the Niger and the Delta, a circumstance which was to lead to great prosperity after the development of the palm oil trade in the nineteenth century. Like the founders of Onitsha and Aboh, they did not settle in an unoccupied area. Instead, they united with the original inhabitants.

Oguta's unusual political system makes the compilation of chronological estimates particularly difficult. It is ruled by three Obis, who are replaced only after the death of the last survivor. There are a number of different versions of the Oguta king lists. One informant allocated dates to each reign, suggesting that Eroa led his people to Oguta in 1600.[3] Another version states that Oguta has been ruled by nineteen succession units.[4] The data seems compatible with a sixteenth- or seventeenth-century dating—but it is clear that Oguta traditions are not of a kind to solve these problems of chronology.

As well as these migrations from Idah and Benin, there were others from eastern Iboland, at the time when the Niger was becoming a frontier of economic opportunity. The travels of Awka

[1] The fullest account of Oguta traditions is to be found in H. N. Harcourt, 'Report of the Inquiry into Oguta Chieftaincy Dispute', 1959 (Nigeria, Official Document no. 19 of 1961). Cf. also Nzimiro, pp. 11–12, and 198 ff.

[2] Harcourt, p. 6.

[3] S. B. C. Obiora, in Harcourt, p. 78. For another list, cf. pp. 62–3.

[4] Nzimiro, pp. 198 ff.

blacksmiths and Nri ritual specialists led to the foundation of some new towns, or quarters of towns. The western Ibo towns, Ibusa and Ogwashi-Uku, are among those which claim Nri origins.[1] A number of riverain settlements claim a founder from Nteje, which belongs, like Nri, to the Umueri clan. The Anam people on the eastern bank of the Niger, above Onitsha, claim that their area was uninhabited until a man from Nteje settled there in the eighteenth century.[2] Some sections of Illah claim a founder from Nteje, and Asaba was founded by a man from Nteje, on the site of a small existing settlement, in the sixteenth or early seventeenth century.[3] Nteje traditions confirm these Anam and Asaba histories of their origins.[4]

From all these various traditions, a significant pattern emerges. They describe a process of state formation which went on during the centuries of the trans-Atlantic slave trade. Many of these states—those in the Delta, Arochuku, and Aboh, in particular—rose in these centuries to positions of great wealth and power. Nearly all historical experiences have a destructive and a creative aspect. We shall see, much later in this study, that this was to be true of colonialism. But although the slave trade made it possible for certain states to prosper—in Iboland and the Delta, as elsewhere in Africa—to concentrate on this aspect alone would be to distort the whole significance of its impact. It is the belief of the present writer that the effects of the slave trade, both in Iboland and elsewhere, were overwhelmingly destructive, and retarded and distorted the historical development of African societies. We shall look at the evidence for this in the chapter that follows.

[1] Forde and Jones, pp. 47–8.
[2] N.A.I. C.S.O. 26/48 (File 29576), Stone, 'Report on the Anam Villages', p. 5.
[3] For a detailed attempt to establish the date of the foundation of Asaba, see Isichei, 'Asaba to 1885', pp. 428–32. My calculations were based on the allocation of twenty years to a generation. I now think that a longer estimate of a generation (thirty years) fits the available evidence better, and have used this in all calculations in this book.
[4] Stone, 'Anam Villages', p. 5; Isichei, 'Asaba to 1885', p. 427.

3 · The Slave Trade and Society

'The discerning Natives account it their greatest Unhappiness, that they were ever visited by the *Europeans*. They say, that we Christians introduced the Traffick of Slaves, and that before our coming they lived in Peace.'
—William Smith, *A New Voyage to Guinea* (1744), p. 266.

The Portuguese probably reached the Niger delta soon after 1470. Their arrival was to have revolutionary consequences both for the Delta and for Iboland. These changes were not, however, due to the impact of the Portuguese themselves. Their impact on West Africa was to be short-lived and marginal. Soon they discovered Asia, and the Indies of their dreams, and it was there they established a far-flung commercial empire. In the Delta, they bought ivory, pepper, and slaves—some of these last the western Ibo victims of Benin's wars of expansion.[1] But since the Portuguese economy could not absorb large numbers of slaves, the numbers they purchased were low—destined either to be exchanged for gold on the Gold Coast,[2] or to work on the newly established plantations of San Thomé.[3]

The long-term significance of the advent of the Portuguese was two-fold. West Africa had lived in relative isolation, separated from Asia and Europe by two oceans—an ocean of sand to the north, and the Atlantic to the south. Until the fifteenth century, it was the Sahara which was the easier to cross. West Africa's contacts with the outside world took place across the desert, and it was on the southern fringes of the desert that her splendid empires developed, Ghana, Mali and Songhai. But the arrival of the Portuguese transformed the situation of the coastal peoples. From a subsistence economy,

[1] Pereira, p. 126; Egharevba, p. 21.
[2] *Ibid.*
[3] Curtin estimates San Thomé imported 76,100 slaves between 1450 and 1600, many of whom came from Angola. Philip D. Curtin, *The Atlantic Slave Trade, A Census* (Wisconsin, 1969), p. 116.

remote from the mainstreams of trade, they moved to a position in the forefront of trade. They were offered, and seized, new opportunities for acquiring wealth and power. In the long run, as the importance of the trans-Sahara trade routes dwindled, it was the regions to the north which were to become backwaters.

It was the tragedy of the coastal peoples that this new opportunity was to take the form of a trade in slaves. Although the Portuguese had at first only limited uses for slaves, the situation was soon transformed by developments in the New World. In 1492, Columbus discovered the Americas. In the early sixteenth century, the true nature of his discoveries gradually became apparent. The potential value of the Americas to Europe lay first in their bullion, and later in their tropical crops. Both of these needed an abundant labour force, inured to tropical conditions, for their exploitation. And thus, from about 1530, the infamous triangular trade developed, which sent countless thousands of West Africans into slavery in the New World.

Iboland was one of the areas of West Africa most seriously affected by the slave trade. Ibos were exported as slaves throughout the whole period of the trade, from the first recorded Ibo slave—one Caterina Ybou, sent to San Thomé[1]—until the slave trade came to an end in the middle years of the nineteenth century. To understand its impact on Iboland it is obviously important to know how many people were involved.

It is clear that the number of Ibos puchased by European slavers varied considerably at different periods. In the sixteenth century, it was probably quite low. In the seventeenth century, the total number of West Africans enslaved expanded considerably, especially after 1640, when sugar was introduced to the West Indies.[2] In this period, most slaves from the part of West Africa which became known as the Slave Coast came from Whydah,[3] but a substantial number came from the Delta. The Royal African Company purchased 6,000 slaves from the area between 1673 and 1689[4]—and this was only one trading body in an area where French and Dutch slavers and inter-

---

[1] Communication from Professor A. F. C. Ryder.
[2] K. G. Davies, *The Royal African Company* (London, 1957), pp. 14–15.
[3] *Ibid.*, p. 228; Elizabeth Donnan, *Documents Illustrative of the History of the Slave Trade to America* (Washington, 1930–35), II, 280, 288 and 342.
[4] Curtin, p. 122. This figure includes Benin.

lopers abounded. The Royal African Company's records described it, in 1672, as 'the Bite [i.e. the Bight of Biafra], whither many ships are sent to trade at New and Old Calabar for slaves and teeth [ivory], which are there to be had in great plenty . . .'.[1] The Frenchman, Barbot, who visited the area twice between 1678 and 1682, wrote of 'that vast number of slaves which the *Calabar Blacks* sell to all *European* nations . . .'.[2]

The eighteenth century was the period when the largest number of slaves were exported. During this period, the trade was dominated by the English, who drew the bulk of their slaves from the Bight of Biafra. Probably the years 1730 to 1810 covered the period of the slave trade's most serious impact on Iboland.[3] As for the seventeenth century, we have no adequate statistical data, but only a number of estimates. Captain Adams, who made ten slaving voyages to Africa between 1786 and 1800, stated that 20,000 slaves were sold annually at Bonny, 16,000 of them Ibo. Over a twenty-year period, he estimated that 320,000 Ibos had been sold to European slavers at Bonny, and 50,000 at Old and New Calabar.[4]

We know that in the nineteenth century a certain number of slaves were passed down the Niger trade route from countries further to the north,[5] but it is clear that throughout the period of the slave trade the vast majority of the slaves purchased at the Delta ports were Ibos, though some were Ibibios, and those sold in the western Delta were mainly Urhobos.[6] Adams stated expressly that none of the slaves purchased at Bonny in the late eighteenth century came through Iboland from the north, avowing that he knew nothing about Iboland's northern neighbour, 'but it is certain that there are not any slaves sold at Bonny, that pass from the interior through it'.[7] Indeed, Iboland, with its dense population and many small independent states, was particularly susceptible to exploitation of this kind.

[1] Donnan, I, 192–3.
[2] John Barbot, *A Description of the Coasts of North and South Guinea* (Vol. V in Churchill's Voyages and Travels, London, 1746), p. 381.
[3] Curtin, *The Atlantic Slave Trade*, p. 221.
[4] Captain John Adams, *Remarks on the Country extending from Cape Palmas to the River Congo* (London, 1823), p. 129. For other estimates, cf. Donnan, II, 597 n. 3, 598 n. 6, and 645.
[5] Cf. p. 62 below.
[6] Obaro Ikime, *Niger Delta Rivalry, Itsekiri–Urhobo Relations and the European Presence 1884–1936* (London, 1969), pp. 48 ff.
[7] Adams, p. 116.

It lacked the strong centralized government which enabled some African states to defend their own citizens, and obtain wealth by raiding those of others. The essentially local nature of their loyalties led the little Ibo states to make war on each other, frequently kidnapping each other's members.

Over the centuries of the slave trade, Iboland lost large numbers of its strongest members, in their prime. Their homeland was deprived not only of their labour—which, expended on the plantations, helped Europe accumulate the capital for her subsequent industrialization. It was deprived of the new skills they might have developed, and the children they would have had. Nor was that all, for the centuries of the slave trade had many grave effects on the quality of life for those left behind, and had a corrupting and brutalizing effect both on the Delta and on the Ibo interior.

It is necessary to make an estimate of the numbers involved in the slave trade, but this should not lead us into the error of assuming that the social effects of the trade were always in direct proportion to the number of slaves exported, and that in periods when the numbers enslaved were few, the social consequences were necessarily slight. Brutalities and injustices which affect only a minority can have a profoundly corrupting effect on any human society. The social history of the kingdom of Benin may well be an example of this. Something transformed Benin from the impressive and harmonious society described by the first European visitors in the late fifteenth and early sixteenth centuries, to the 'City of Blood', its streets filled with human sacrifices, which the British conquered in the late nineteenth. It has been claimed that the slave trade cannot have caused this change, because Benin was only marginally involved in it.[1] But perhaps Benin history is only a particularly striking illustration of the way the trade in slaves corrupted every society it touched.

Accounts of the Delta slave trade show that its organization remained much the same over the centuries. When the Barbot brothers visited the Delta in the late seventeenth century, they described how Bonny and Kalabari had become the main centres of the trade. Their people would go to the inland markets in their great trade canoes, exchanging European goods and fish for slaves, and a

[1] Cf. A. F. C. Ryder, *Benin and the Europeans* (London, 1969), pp. 197–8, 232 ff. and 247 ff.

certain amount of ivory.[1] In the second half of the eighteenth century, the basic pattern was much the same.

> The Black Traders of Bonny and Calabar ... come down about once a Fortnight with Slaves; Thursday or Friday is generally their Trading Day. Twenty or Thirty Canoes, sometimes more and sometimes less, come down at a Time. In each Canoe may be Twenty or Thirty Slaves. The Arms of some of them are tied behind their Backs with Twigs, Canes, Grass Rope, or other Ligaments of the Country; and if they happen to be stronger than common, they are pinioned above the Knee also. In this Situation they are thrown into the Bottom of the Canoe, where they lie in great Pain, and often almost covered with Water. On their landing, they are taken to the Traders Houses, where they are oiled, fed, and made up for Sale. ... No sickly Slave is ever purchased; ... When the Bargain is made they are brought away ... They appear to be very dejected when brought on board. The Men are put into Irons, in which Situation they remain during the whole of the Middle Passage, unless when they are sick; ...[2]

The social effects of the slave trade on Iboland depended very largely on the methods by which slaves were obtained. Dike believed that the majority were obtained via the Arochuku oracle.[3] The majority may well have passed through the Aro trade network, but it seems that the oracle, of its nature, was unsuited to supply slaves on the massive scale required by the trans-Atlantic trade, since each individual case required careful prior preparation, and an elaborate ritual.

The evidence suggests that most Ibo slaves were obtained by kidnapping. The Delta traders told an English slaver in the 1760s that 'The great Bulk of them were such as had been taken in piratical Excursions, or by Treachery and Surprise.'[4] Olaudah Equiano was

---

[1] John Barbot, p. 381; James Barbot, *An Abstract of a Voyage to New Calabar River ... in the Year 1699* (Vol. V in Churchill's Voyages and Travels, London, 1746), p. 461.

[2] *Report of the Lords of the Committee of Council concerning the present state of the Trade to Africa, and particularly the Trade in Slaves* (1789), Part I, Evidence of William James.

[3] K. Onwuka Dike, *Trade and Politics in the Niger Delta 1830–1885* (Oxford, 1956), pp. 40–41.

[4] *Report of the Lords of the Council*, Part I, William James' Evidence. Cf. also Falconbridge's Evidence.

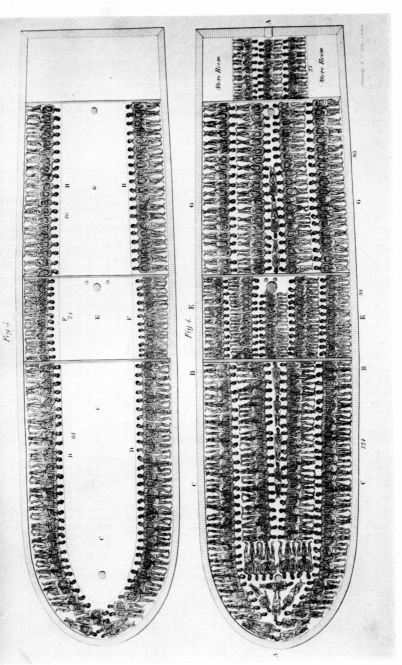

5. The realities of the eighteenth-century slave trade: a contemporary diagram of an English slaver, the *Brookes*.

6. Eighteenth-century Ibo. Olaudah Equiano, autobiographer and merchant seaman

kidnapped at the age of ten, in 1755, and his autobiography gives a vivid account of the prevalence of kidnapping at the time.[1] Another boy, kidnapped elsewhere in Iboland a century later, who was to end life as an Anglican deacon, again bore witness to the prevalence of the practice.[2]

When the linguist, Koelle, was collecting material in Sierra Leone from Africans who had been sold into slavery, rescued by the British naval squadron, and resettled in Sierra Leone, he found that three of his five Ibo informants had been kidnapped.[3] The trader, de Cardi, whose experience of the Delta extended from 1862 to 1896, made a practice of asking slaves how they had fallen into slavery, and was almost always told they had been kidnapped.[4]

Even if we make allowance for the likelihood that some informants who were sold into slavery for their crimes were understandably reluctant to divulge the fact, the overwhelming impression one obtains is of the prevalence of kidnapping. But if this was the most usual means of enslavement, it was not, of course, the only one. Some were captured in war, and others enslaved by their own community as a punishment for their crimes. In this respect, as Africans often pointed out, enslavement filled the role which capital punishment and transportation supplied in the England of the day,[5] and was not, in itself, less humane. A society which lacks prisons has no alternative but to exile, enslave or execute its offenders. But the great weakness of enslavement as a punishment for crime is that any system which makes an economic profit in this way must almost inevitably lead to the multiplication of offences and conviction of the innocent.[6]

Some Ibos became slaves through economic necessity. Debt could force a man to pawn himself or his child. Famine could have the same result—a situation which apparently became endemic among

[1] Equiano, pp. 9, 15–16.

[2] 'Autobiography of David Okparabietoa Pepple', *Niger and Yoruba Notes* (1898), p. 13.

[3] S. W. Koelle, *Polyglotta Africana* (London, 1854), Part V, 'Niger-Delta Languages', A, First Group, 1, Ibo Dialects.

[4] C. N. de Cardi, 'A Short Description of the Natives of the Niger Coast Protectorate', Appendix I in Mary Kingsley, *West African Studies* (London, 1899), p. 480.

[5] Cf. the arguments of King Holiday of Bonny, in *Memoirs of Captain Hugh Crow* (London, 1830), p. 137.

[6] Thomas Clarkson, *The Substance of the Evidence of Sundry Persons on the Slave Trade* (London, 1789), p. 120, Baggs' Evidence.

4

the overpopulated, land-starved Abaja.[1] A missionary wrote in the 1860s, how wars produce famines, and famines produce 'the painful sight of infants and sucklings, children and young men, passing by our gate as slaves, to be sold in order to procure food to support the rest of their family'.[2]

The Europeans came in search of African labour, supplemented by ivory as an insurance policy, 'seeing in that Commodity there's no Mortality to be feared'.[3] What goods did they bring to the Delta and Iboland in return? The records suggest that these remained fairly similar during the seventeenth and eighteenth centuries.

When James Barbot went to the Delta, the price of an adult male slave was thirteen iron bars. Women and children cost much less, and a Bonny ruler apologized for the prevailing high prices. What was an iron bar worth? Barbot tells us that it was equivalent to 'one bunch of beads' or 'one piece of narrow Guinea stuff'.[4]

There could be, of course, no 'just price' in a trade in human beings, but anyone studying the records of what was imported into the Delta and Iboland in return[5] cannot but be struck by the extraordinary inequality of the exchange. When the Europeans first reached the Delta, Iboland was a self-sufficient society. She imported salt and fish from the Delta, and luxury goods, including copper and beads, from further afield. Many of the goods the slave traders brought were already being produced by the Ibo, and the other peoples of southern Nigeria. They brought textiles, at first from India, until the Indian textile industry was undermined by colonial rule, and Manchester became rich by exporting cotton goods to the rest of the world. They imported iron bars, and copper. But Iboland had already met her copper needs from African sources, and had her own textile and iron production. These imports did not increase her productivity, they rivalled her indigenous industries. Salt was another import which rivalled, and ultimately superseded, the local product.

---

[1] W. R. G. Horton, 'The Ohu System of Slavery in a Northern Ibo Village-Group', *Africa* (1954), XXIV, pp. 311–12.

[2] J. C. Taylor, Journal entry for 27 May 1865, in *The Church Missionary Record* (1866), p. 205.

[3] Donnan, II, 327.

[4] James Barbot, pp. 459–60.

[5] For imports to the Delta area in the late seventeenth century, see John Barbot, pp. 361 (Benin), 371 (Warri) and 383 (Old Calabar). He does not give detailed trade lists for Bonny and Kalabari. See also James Barbot, pp. 459 ff. For imports in the eighteenth century see Adams, pp. 243 ff.

A major import took the form of currency. There were a number of currencies already circulating in the area. Pereira, writing at the beginning of the sixteenth century, describes the use of cowries from the Indian ocean,[1] Barbot describes the brass rings, wrought 'with much art' at Old Calabar,[2] and the iron currency, shaped like a sting-ray, made by the southern Ibos of 'Moko'.[3] The Europeans imported large quantities of cowries, and other local currencies. This probably stimulated trade, but had the effect of devaluing them to a point where they became useless for major transactions.[4]

Other goods imported were of no value to their recipients at all. Spirits were imported[5]—and came to be used as a form of currency—but since the Ibo people traditionally extracted palatable palm wine, and later began to manufacture gin, the import again, supplemented or replaced an indigenous product. Many of the goods imported were simply rubbish—trinkets, and items of obsolete or ridiculous finery which were sold to Africans as the emblems of rank and authority in Europe. For centuries, European traders sold these things to the Delta people, and then despised them for wearing them.

In recent years, African historians have given much attention to the role played by firearms in the growth of states, and in their changing relationship to each other. In the seventeenth century, firearms were not imported systematically, though they were given as presents to rulers, and the great trade canoes were armed only with their paddlers' spears.[6] During the eighteenth century, the use of arms became general in the Delta. It was a period of intense warfare between the Delta states.[7] Firearms were used in these wars, but did not in themselves create them. Probably, they were economic in origin. The demand for slaves was expanding more rapidly than the available supplies, and each state fought to maintain and increase its own positions in the trade.

Did their earlier access to firearms give the Delta states a significant

[1] *Op. cit.*, p. 145.

[2] John Barbot, p. 382.

[3] *Ibid.*, p. 380. Moko has not been identified with certainty. Jones suggests Isiokpo, or Okpo-mbu-tolu (*The Trading States*, p. 36).

[4] Marion Johnson, 'The Cowrie Currencies of West Africa, Part II', *The Journal of African History* (1970), XI, no. 3, pp. 331 ff.

[5] A. F. C. Ryder, 'Dutch Trade on the Nigerian Coast during the Seventeenth Century', *Journal of the Historical Society of Nigeria* (1965), III, no. 2, p. 208.

[6] John Barbot, p. 382; James Barbot, p. 460.

[7] Described in Jones, *The Trading States*, pp. 46–8.

advantage over the Ibos of the interior? This may have been so for a time. Köler wrote of Bonny in 1840, that 'The chief weapon is now the flintlock, the use of which has now become so general that even the people of Iboland are beginning to lose their respect for them.'[1] We have seen that the possession of arms may have played a decisive role in the wars which preceded the founding of Arochuku.[2]

But it seems likely that the advantages of the possession of arms have been overestimated, and that their effect may have been largely psychological. The cannon which armed the trade canoes were lashed fast, and could not be trained without manœuvring the whole canoe.[3] The practical effect of the guns imported was reduced by the fact that the Bonnymen had not learnt how to aim them properly, using them like pistols.[4] Their effectiveness was further reduced by the practice—universal in trade with Africa in the eighteenth and nineteenth centuries—of importing only arms of poor quality, and, often enough, those which were already obsolete in Europe. Adams recorded the poor quality of both the muskets and the gunpowder exported to the Delta.[5]

Iboland's most dreaded warriors, the Abams, did not use firearms, preferring to rely on their matchets.[6] Many of the arms purchased by the Ibo interior were valued for their ritual as much as for their practical significance, because they were used ceremonially, at celebrations and funerals.

The inferior quality of the firearms imported was characteristic of the imports to the area generally. The spirits sold at Bonny were adulterated with water and pepper.[7] The textiles were cheap and shoddy, and the poor quality of the goods imported was to be characteristic of the area's trade with Europe long after the abolition of the slave trade.[8]

What was the impact of the slave trade on the societies concerned? Superficially, the Delta states appeared to benefit, for their middleman role gave them a wealth and power they could never have

[1] Hermann Köler, *Einige Notizen über Bonny* (Göttingen, 1848), p. 111.
[2] Cf. p. 34 above.
[3] Köler, p. 111; F.O. 84/1343, Hopkins to Granville, 27 November 1871.
[4] *Ibid.*
[5] Adams, p. 261.
[6] Basden, *Niger Ibos*, p. 385.
[7] Adams, p. 260.
[8] Cf. p. 168 below.

attained by catching fish and making salt. All visitors to the Delta
paid tribute to their traders' brilliant business acumen, which
European traders overlooked at their peril. Frequently, they gained
a working knowledge of several European languages. The Efik of
Old Calabar not only learnt to speak and write English, but perpetuated the knowledge in their own schools.[1]

Yet even in the Delta, the losses were probably greater than the
gains. After centuries of trade, Bonny had nothing to show for it,
even in the basic comforts and decencies of human life. Hutchinson
called it, in words many others echoed, '... the *ne plus ultra* of
abomination and filthiness ... a fitting Pandemonium for that vile
traffic in human flesh.'[2] Like the other Delta states, she could not
maintain her own population, which was replenished by constant
accessions of Ibo slaves.[3] A few of these slaves rose to positions of
wealth and power, but the majority, like slave populations everywhere, were held in subjection only by brutality and terror. Europeans, describing the cruelty of the punishments used, attributed it
to the innate depravity of the African,[4] but the European masters of
slave ships used equally savage punishments, which were an inevitable
concomitant of slavery. Human life was cheapened. The Barbots, at
the end of the seventeenth century, found human skulls displayed in
Andoni, but not in Bonny.[5] By the nineteenth century, a temple constructed entirely of skulls had become Bonny's most prominent
landmark.

The Delta traders often accumulated great wealth, but their wealth
remained unproductive. Duke Ephraim of Calabar imported a house
from Europe. He did not live in it, but filled it with assorted European
objects which were soon in a state of confusion and decay.[6] King
Perekule of Bonny 'accumulated and buried enormous manillas,
silver and brass wares, demijohns of rum, arms and ammunitions,
copper rods for war canoes and numerous coral and glass beads'.[7]
Often their wealth was lost in the fires which periodically ravaged the

[1] Adams, p. 144. Cf. Crow, pp. 285–6.
[2] T. J. Hutchinson, *Impressions of West Africa* (London, 1858), p. 103.
[3] James Johnson, 'An African Clergyman's Visit to Bonny', *The Church Missionary Intelligencer* (1897), p. 28.
[4] [Richard Burton], *Wanderings in West Africa by a F.R.G.S.* (London, 1863), II, pp. 280 ff.
[5] John Barbot, pp. 380–1; James Barbot, pp. 259–462.
[6] Crow, pp. 272–3.
[7] Fombo Papers, Ibadan University Library, fo. 34. Cf. Adams, p. 140.

Delta states. Sometimes it was dispersed in holocausts of hapless slaves at a rich man's funeral, a combination of brutality and waste which recalls the long death agony of the Roman empire.

Why was their accumulated capital put to so little productive use? The answer lies basically in the nature of the slave trade itself. It has become fashionable in recent years to analyse the slave trade in purely economic terms, as a pattern whereby labour was exported, rather than the products which that labour might have produced. This is a monstrous distortion of the historical reality. Neither familiarity nor economic sophistication should dull our minds to one of the major crimes of human history, based entirely on human grief and pain. But even if we analyse it in purely economic terms, it seems that the slave trade hindered the economic growth of the West African societies it influenced.

The only saleable commodity they could produce on a large scale was slaves. The capture and sale of slaves gave no scope for the growth of technical skill and inventiveness. Rather it undermined that social stability which is a commonly accepted precondition for economic growth. The goods they imported were, with the exception of firearms, either useless rubbish, or products they could make or obtain for themselves. What the rulers of the Delta repeatedly asked to buy, Europe was never prepared to sell. This was basically knowledge, which could help them span the ever-widening technological gap between Africa and Europe. They needed knowledge of the means of production, and a market for its products. A letter from an Efik ruler, after the abolition of the slave trade, put the dilemma clearly:

> We can't sell slaves again, we must have too many men for country, and want something for make work and trade. And if we have some seed for cotton and coffee, we could make trade, plenty sugar cane live here; and if some man would come teach way for do it, we get plenty sugar too; and then some man must come teach book proper.[1]

King George Pepple of Bonny made the same point more elegantly, when seeking to import kernel cracking machinery, to obviate the tedious and wasteful labour of cracking them by hand. 'It is . . .

[1] F.O. 84/1001, letter from King Eyamba of Calabar, 1 December 1842, encl. in Hutchinson to Clarendon, 24 June 1856.

incumbent upon all intelligent educated Africans to use every cogent means in their power to develop or devise some means of developing the resources of their country.'[1] But unanswered requests of this kind are a recurrent leitmotif in West African history.[2]

If the slave trade brought more loss than gain to the Delta states, who played the middleman role, this was doubly true of the Ibo interior, which supplied its victims.

As in the Delta, the exchange of the most energetic sections of her population in return for European manufactures was basically disadvantageous, even from a narrowly economic point of view. In return for their energies and skills she gained, in the main, goods which she could have produced for herself. Indeed, the exchange was even less advantageous than in the Delta, for the middlemen took their profit and the goods which finally reached Iboland were often second-hand, or damaged by exposure.[3]

By increasing the amount of currency and goods in circulation, the slave trade probably stimulated the growth of internal trade in Iboland. As against this must be set the general insecurity which the practice of kidnapping engendered, which was both an evil in itself and productive of many others. It discouraged long-distance trade, because long journeys were impossible except for those who travelled in convoy or were protected by special religious sanctions. Basden, in a book published in 1921, bore witness to the dangers of travelling alone, and the prevalence of kidnapping.[4] In the nineteenth century, an Ibo ex-slave bore eloquent witness to the corroding effects of the slave trade on Ibo society:

> Of this he could speak, not merely as an eye-witness, but like one who had felt what it means . . . He commenced by describing the miseries which the slave-trade produced in the Ibo Country; mentioned the continual wars carried on for the purpose of capturing slaves; how many parents became bereaved of their children, and children for ever separated from their parents; how the whole population was continually in a state of excitement and fear, and what an injurious effect this condition had on their own

[1] Fombo Papers, Ibadan University Library, fo. 236, King George Pepple to Lilley and Wheeler, Liverpool 3 April 1875 (transcript).

[2] Cf. Basil Davidson, *Black Mother, Africa the Years of Trial* (London, 1961), pp. 122 ff.; William Smith, *A New Voyage to Guinea* (London, 1744), p. 176.

[3] C.O. 520/15, Moor to C.O., 10 September 1902.

[4] G. T. Basden, *Among the Ibos of Nigeria* (London, 1921), pp. 105–6.

temporal concerns; how their fields were neglected, and their houses left without inhabitants; how every one was afraid of his own neighbour, and none could place confidence in his own brother; . . .[1]

The slave trade of its nature discouraged the arts of peace. We shall never know precisely to how great an extent the economic development of Iboland was hindered by it—by the lost capacities and energies of her exiled sons and their descendants, and by the economic consequences of the insecurity it engendered. But it is clear that even from a purely economic standpoint, Iboland lost greatly by it.

We have seen that the Delta had no productive outlet for its surplus wealth, which was therefore either hoarded or wasted in various forms of conspicuous consumption. What was the effect of the importation of many additional consumer goods into Iboland, which had been, with minor exceptions, a self-sufficient society? Basically, the results were the same—the development of various forms of wasteful consumption. As in the Delta, these sometimes took ritual and ceremonial forms—as in the practice of human sacrifice, which we shall consider soon. Another form was in the political sphere—the development of the practice of acquiring titles by purchase.

The link between economic and political power is found in one form or another in most human societies, and the purchase of political offices and of titles is a familiar spectacle to, for instance, the historian of eighteenth-century England. Ibo communities were in practice ruled by titled men of mature age. These titles were purchased, not inherited—though the recipient of a title had to satisfy other conditions as well, and be of good character.

It seems that many Ibo states went through a political evolution whereby the rule of a single 'natural leader' gave way to a situation where political prestige and authority were shared by those who had acquired it by purchase. These formed societies to protect their rights, and to guarantee a profit from their investment by securing payments from new members. There is a well documented case of this development in the case of Asaba. This was originally ruled by a single Eze, than by half a dozen. By the late nineteenth century, five hundred men held the title, and their number was still growing.[2] The

[1] *Journals of the Rev. James Frederick Schön and Mr Samuel Crowther, who . . . accompanied the Expedition up the Niger in 1841* (London, 1842), p. 68.
[2] Isichei, 'Asaba to 1885', p. 423.

same tendency existed in areas of Iboland which lacked a title system. Areas which had secret societies, tended to stratify them into grades and exact high payments for admission to the upper grades.[1] And those Ibo groups which had neither title systems nor secret societies showed signs of developing in the same direction.[2] One of the ways in which the slave trade affected Iboland, then, was by altering her political institutions.

Political changes of this kind were, in themselves, not necessarily good or bad. Much graver in its implications was the disregard for human life which the slave trade engendered, and which in its turn led to the corruption and distortion of religious custom. This is seen most clearly in the area of human sacrifice. We have seen how the slave trade created Bonny's temple of skulls, and turned Benin into a 'City of Blood'. The same change seems to have taken place in Iboland.

Human sacrifice was, of course, the most serious of religious rituals. Sometimes a victim was sacrificed to expiate the collective trespasses of a community. A missionary called the practice 'fiend-like'[3]—happily oblivious to its strong family resemblance to the central doctrine of the Christian religion. Another, and more frequent form of human sacrifice, was to accompany the death of a great man.

Human sacrifice almost certainly existed in Iboland before the era of the slave trade—as the bodies buried with the Eze Nri in the Igbo-Ukwu excavations bear witness.[4] But in their original form, these practices were not necessarily a matter of horror and dread.[5] The concept of an expiatory sacrifice, while repugnant to modern humanitarianism, would not have been so to the centuries of Christians who found a religious meaning in the story of Abraham's readiness to sacrifice Isaac, and the evidence suggests that even in the nineteenth century, these victims did not always meet their deaths reluctantly. Similarly, when a great man died, the more devoted of

[1] G. I. Jones, *Report on the Status of Chiefs* (Enugu, 1958), par. 75.
[2] *Ibid.*, par. 77.
[3] Bishop Crowther, 'Report of a Visit to the Stations on the Niger in the Year 1870', *The Church Missionary Intelligencer* (April 1871), p. 128. This passage describes an expiatory sacrifice at Onitsha.
[4] Cf. p. 23 above.
[5] Cf. on this whole question the perceptive account in Davidson, *Black Mother*, pp. 196–7.

his wives and slaves were probably not unwilling to accompany him to that world of the dead which, in Ibo religion, mirrors the world we know. Their numbers were probably few—perhaps half a dozen were buried with the Eze Nri at Igbo-Ukwu—and the spirit voluntary. We have no records for Iboland, but can perhaps extrapolate from a Portuguese description of the burial of a Benin king, when 'those who are judged to have been most dear to and favoured by the king (this includes not a few, as all are anxious for the honour) voluntarily go down to keep him company'.[1]

In the centuries of the slave trade, the practice was enormously expanded and distorted. Each of the five hundred Ezes in nineteenth-century Asaba had sacrificed two slaves at his accession, and would have two more sacrificed on his behalf at his funeral. They were kept for the purpose in a separate village, and captured when required for sacrifice, 'greatly against their will'.[2] When Delta rulers died in the first half of the nineteenth century, the numbers of those sacrificed ran into hundreds.[3] The original institution had degenerated into a source of terror and oppression. We have an exact parallel in the degeneration of the institution of suttee—the burning of widows in India—as the original proud and joyful oblation of the heroic age of the Rajputs became, in the late eighteenth and nineteenth centuries a source of horrifying cruelty and oppression, which sacrificed thousands of terrified victims on the altars of family pride.[4]

Another religious institution which was corrupted by the influence of the slave trade was that of osu, or cult slavery. This is found only in certain areas of Iboland, and not at all west of the Niger. By the time when colonial rule was established, the osu—dedicated to a god— were both feared and despised. They were outcasts from the life of the community, and in some areas so numerous that they formed communities of their own. The institution has proved tenacious enough to create problems for their descendants even in present-day Nigeria—a situation movingly depicted in Chinua Achebe's novel,

[1] Extract in Thomas Hodgkin, *Nigerian Perspectives, An Historical Anthology* (London, 1960), pp. 100–1.

[2] Asaba oral tradition. Informant, F.O. Isichei.

[3] Cf., for instance, the account of the death of Duke Ephraim of Old Calabar in 1834, in Hope Masterton Waddell, *Twenty-Nine Years in the West Indies and Central Africa* (London, 1863), p. 497.

[4] Philip Woodruff, *The Men Who Ruled India*, Vol. I, *The Founders* (London, 1953), pp. 253 ff.

No Longer at Ease. Yet traditions recorded by Basden suggest that originally, osu formed a privileged and highly respected group, leading a life of pious dedication, as befitted the servants of a god. 'The "osu" held an honourable position until the slave trade brought it into degradation, and caused it to degenerate to its present unhappy condition.'[1]

The expansion and distortion of ancient customs, the disregard for human life, can be traced in other areas of Ibo life as well as in witchcraft accusations, and trial by ordeal, which reached epidemic proportions at times in the Niger states in the nineteenth century, as they did, at earlier periods, in Europe.

For Iboland, as for the Delta, the total impact of the slave trade was overwhelmingly destructive. Few historical experiences are entirely without positive aspects. Some communities, as we saw in the last chapter, benefited by the expansion in trade, and carved out positions of wealth and power. But the losses were far greater than the gains.

Iboland did not experience the widespread depopulation which the slave trade created in some parts of Africa. Although many of her people were enslaved, her population remained dense. Despite the chronic insecurity which developed, her people retained the capacity to adjust to and profit by new economic opportunities. The first European visitors to the Ibo interior were, as we shall see in a later chapter, impressed by the beauty of their towns, the volume of their internal trade, and the productivity of their farms. This does not mean that in some mysterious ways the effects of the slave trade were more beneficial than all the evidence and all the probabilities lead us to suppose. Rather, they reflect the prior density and continuing fertility of the Ibo population, and that remarkable resilience and adaptability which history has repeatedly required of them. But the losses were evident in the texture of Ibo life.

The picture of Ibo life which one gains from a book such as Basden's *Niger Ibos*, still widely regarded as authoritative, and recently reprinted, is a grim one. This is partly due to the prejudices of the observer, who despite his long acquaintance with Iboland tended always to describe the outward face of institutions while misrepresenting their animating spirit. But the darker element was certainly there—in the human sacrifices, the trials by ordeal, the

---

[1] Basden, *Niger Ibos*, p. 249.

prevalence of kidnapping, and so on. The mistake which is often made—and is often an assumption rather than directly affirmed—is to think that these elements had been there from time immemorial, whereas they were largely, if not wholly, due to the trade in slaves. We have no eyewitness accounts, as in Benin, of Ibo life as it existed previously—only the mute testimony of the findings of archaeologists, of the products of the arts of peace. But the fact that, for all its darker side, traditional Ibo society during and after the slave trade still provided a way of life to which modern Ibo intellectuals, having mastered all the skills of alien worlds, can and do look back to with nostalgia, is an impressive tribute to its quality earlier.

4 · Economic Change in the Nineteenth Century: The Last Phase of the Slave Trade and the Growth of the Palm Oil Trade

Onya na-a apa ya ada ana.
(A wound heals and a scar remains.)
—Ibo proverb.

For much of the nineteenth century, two separate though related economic systems existed in Iboland—a trade in slaves, and a trade in palm oil. Historians have sometimes written as though the slave trade came to an end when the European nations ceased buying slaves, and as if the trade in palm oil was a providentially provided substitute. In fact, the death agony of the slave trade was more complicated and protracted.

There are few episodes of their own history which British historians regard with more complacency than Britain's decision to prohibit her own citizens from trading in slaves, in 1807, and her subsequent efforts to prevent other nations from doing so, through diplomatic means, and through the policing activities of the naval squadron she maintained off the coast of West Africa—one of 'the few totally unselfish international operations'.[1] One may be permitted to question whether the discontinuance of a crime is a matter for self-congratulation—but it is not the purpose of the present work to pass judgment on the corporate moral virtue or obliquity of nations—if, indeed, such a thing exists. Since Eric Williams published his pioneering if controversial study, *Capitalism and Slavery*, historians have become more aware of the economic changes which made it possible, and probably profitable, for Britain to act in this way. This awareness need not make us forget the resolution and dedication of the abolitionists, nor, indeed, is this in danger of being forgotten. Our concern here, however, is not with the background of the abolition movement in England, but with the significance of these

[1] A review of W. E. F. Ward, *The Royal Navy and the Slavers*, in *West Africa*, 15 March 1969.

61

changes for Iboland. We will see that although it was the Europeans who were responsible for the ending of the export of slaves, it was the Africans who paid the price, in economic and social dislocation. The ending of the trans-Atlantic slave trade created a crisis which could only be surmounted by a major adaptation.

The export of slaves from Iboland continued for many years after 1807. It was in the late 1830s, when the British naval blockade became effective, that most Delta ports ceased exporting slaves.[1] The trade lingered longest in Nembe-Brass, for its relatively inaccessible location made it possible for it to continue the trade clandestinely. But by the middle 1850s, the export of slaves had ceased here as well. A visitor reported in 1857 that the last slave ship had called three years earlier, and that the only memorial of the slave trade was an old barracoon, 'so dilapidated as not to afford shelter even for a lizard'.[2]

Unfortunately, the memorials of the slave trade were in reality more enduring. The mechanisms which it had called into existence—the practice of capturing slaves, the slave routes and the slave markets—did not cease to exist when the export of slaves ended. The internal trade in slaves lasted until this century, and in some ways the lot of domestic slaves became worse.

The end of the trans-Atlantic slave trade meant that slaves became cheaper, and sometimes, indeed, super-abundant.[3] This was particularly evident on the slave trade routes, such as the Niger, where in the nineteenth century, an increasing number of slaves were transported from the north.[4] Between five and six hundred slaves a year were sold at Igara Bank, the slave market situated on a sandbank in the Niger, between Asaba and Onitsha.[5] Similarly, slaves were accumulated in large numbers at places on the main overland slave trade routes, such as Nike and Uzuakoli.[6]

[1] Dike, pp. 97–9.

[2] F.O. 84/1030, Hutchinson to Clarendon, 20 February 1857.

[3] Samuel Crowther and John Christopher Taylor, *The Gospel on the Banks of the Niger. Journals and Notices of the Native Missionaries accompanying the Niger Expedition of 1857–1859* (London, 1859), p. 438.

[4] For data re Nupe, Hausa, Kakanda and Igala slaves, cf. C.M.S. F 4/7, Journal of G. Wilmot Brooke, 28 June 1889, fo. 106; C.S.Sp. 191/A/1, Lutz to Assoc. for Propagation of the Faith, 6 February 1889; Schön and Crowther, *Journals, 1841*, p. 232.

[5] J. C. Taylor, Journal, 24 February 1865, in *The Church Missionary Record* (1866), pp. 203–4; C.S.Sp. *Bulletin de la Congregation*, II (March 1890), p. 540.

[6] Cf. Horton, 'The Ohu System of Slavery', *passim*, and A. J. Fox, *Uzuakoli, A Short History* (London, 1964), pp. 22 ff.

The continuation of the internal trade in slaves, at the time when it became no longer possible to export them, had several consequences. It encouraged the sacrifice of unsaleable slaves in religious ceremonies—it appears that the expansion of the practice of human sacrifice, which we noted in the last chapter, became ever more marked in these years. Alternatively, the states of the Ibo interior could employ them in collecting palm oil—the new export industry—or in agriculture.[1] Osomari was estimated to have a population of six to eight thousand—or of twenty thousand, if the slaves on the surrounding farms were included.[2]

In the Delta, the continuing influx of Ibo slaves meant that its population became ever increasingly Ibo in character. The first C.M.S. representative to the Efik state of Old Calabar was told that more than half the population were Ibos.[3] In both Okrika and Bonny, in the nineteenth century, it was Ibo which was commonly spoken, though Ubani and Okrikan retained a certain social cachet, as the language of the freeborn.[4] Most Brass slaves were obtained from Iboland,[5] and Bishop Crowther wrote that 'the Ibo language is more or less spoken . . . in New Calabar, Brass, and Akassa'.[6] Another missionary referred to 'the members of the Ibo tribe, who form the chief inhabitants of the Niger Delta'.[7]

The existence of this large and continually increasing slave population created several problems for the Delta states, when the trans-Atlantic slave trade came to an end. It created a crisis of authority—how could this vast slave population be kept in a state of servitude, in the absence of the sanction of sale abroad? It created an economic crisis, for while in the Ibo interior, slaves were self-supporting, growing their own food on their own farms, in the Delta, most food had to be imported.

The first difficulty was overcome in various ways. We have already noted the effect of the terrifying punishments used against the

[1] Fox, p. 25; Asaba oral tradition (informant, F. O. Isichei).
[2] C.S.Sp. 191/B/II, Lejeune, Report, 1902.
[3] E. Jones, in *The Church Missionary Intelligencer* (1853), p. 258.
[4] Köler, p. 2; C.M.S. G 3/A3/1882/58, Archdeacon D. C. Crowther, 'The 3rd visit to Okrika', February 1882; James Johnson, 'An African Clergyman's Visit to Bonny', *The Church Missionary Intelligencer* (1897), p. 28.
[5] F.O. 403/217, Sir John Kirk's Report after the Brass Inquiry.
[6] C.M.S. CA3/04, Bishop Crowther to Venn, 13 March 1865.
[7] J. Pratt, 'African Town or Village Life in the Niger Delta', *Western Equatorial Africa Diocesan Magazine* (1905), p. 147.

recalcitrant. A number of social mechanisms existed to develop the vertical loyalties of the House system, rather than the horizontal loyalties of class, and to attach the slaves to the various Delta states.[1] For the rest, there was sufficient chance of social mobility for the Delta slave classes to reconcile them to their lot. The occasional slave who rose to power and affluence gave his fellows the hope that they might do likewise—just as so many of the urban poor in nineteenth-century Europe were cheered by the ideology of Self Help, the mirage of ascending the social scale to affluence.

The economic problem was largely solved by the growth of the palm oil trade. The slaves who would have been sold now enriched their masters in other ways, by performingt he laborious tasks involved in collecting the oil from the inland markets. Old Calabar employed its slaves rather differently—in the plantation cultivation of oil palms, which was also undertaken in Dahomey. After Ja Ja established his new state of Opobo, and in doing so cut Bonny off from much of her economic hinterland, the Bonny chiefs in their turn turned increasingly to plantation agriculture.[2]

A few slaves, like Ja Ja, became wealthy and powerful men, but the vast majority—the 'pullaboys' who paddled the great trade canoes, or the plantation labourers, who had no chance of prospering through trade,[3] could look forward to at best, a life of laborious servitude, and at the worst, a terrifying death as a sacrifice to dignify a great man's funeral.

The Ibo slaves of the Delta responded to their predicament in one of two ways. One was the path of individual mobility. This in its turn could take one of two forms. The first was that of rising to traditional goals, the accumulation of wealth, through trade, and the rule of a House. Oko Epelle was an example of this process. Brought as a child from the Ibo interior, he began as a paddler on the trade canoes, and worked his way up until he was the wealthy master of a House.[4]

[1] For a case study, see Robin Horton, 'From Fishing Village to City-State, A Social History of New Calabar', in Mary Douglas and Phyllis M. Kaberry (eds.), *Man in Africa* (London, 1969), pp. 37 ff.

[2] Bishop Crowther, in *The Church Missionary Intelligencer* (1876), p. 473; *Inquiry into the Southern Nigeria Liquor Trade* (1909), Minutes of Evidence, question 13366.

[3] F.O. 84/858, Beecroft to Palmerston, 27 October 1851.

[4] F.O. 84/1343, 'Protest' of Oko Epelle, encl. in Hopkins to Granville, 27 November 1871.

7a, b. Europe's images of Iboland: life on the Niger in the 1830's

7c. Europe's images of Iboland: life on the Niger in the 1830's

8. An Ibo image of the Invader. From an Mbari House, Owerri, 1904

After the establishment of Christian missions in the Delta, in 1866, another possible avenue of mobility presented itself, in mission teaching and western education—a structure of values quite different from that of traditional Delta society. The career of David Okpara-bietoa Pepple, kidnapped into slavery in the Isuama area and brought as a boy to Bonny, who ended life as an Anglican deacon, is a striking example.[1]

The alternative response, as for the urban proletariats of contemporary Europe, lay in collective action. The plantation slaves of Old Calabar acted together with striking success in 1850–51, and obtained the abolition of the practice of human sacrifice.[2] The British traders in the area were hostile to the movement[3]—as the British colonial government was to be, in a similar case, some fifty years later.[4] There was a similar case of successful corporate action at Abarra, on the west bank of the Niger, when the slave community left their masters in a body, and established a new independent town.[5]

Neither of these possible responses did much to ameliorate the condition of the mass of the slave population. In 1904, a missionary wrote of Old Calabar:

> I have visited a number of farms or 'Pindis'. They are full of Ibos. These poor Ibos, so numerous, have furnished all the slaves of Calabar, Bonny, Brass etc. . . . And so all the chiefs have one, two or three storeyed houses, furnished like chateaux in Europe. Port and malaga wine . . . adorn the tables of these *gentlemen*. . . . But on the other hand, how much misery there is among these unfortunate Ibos, who form two thirds of the population of Duketown.[6]

The British recognized their large share of moral responsibility for the slave trade, and undertook to make at least a contribution to the economic cost of its abolition. Between 1836 and 1839, they signed four anti-slavery treaties with the rulers of Bonny. In these, the Bonny rulers undertook to stop exporting slaves in return for an

[1] 'Autobiography of David Okparabietoa Pepple', *Niger and Yoruba Notes* (1898), p. 13.
[2] F.O. 84/858, Beecroft to Palmerston, 27 October 1851; Waddell, pp. 476 ff.
[3] Waddell, p. 477.
[4] Cf. p. 159 below.
[5] N.A.I. C.S.O. 26/10 (File 26769), Williams and Miller, Aboh-Benin Clans (1930–1), pp. 22–3, 'Abarra Clan'.
[6] C.S.Sp. *Bulletin de la Congregation*, IX, Report for May 1902–October 1904, p. 800.

5

annual subsidy—though this was small enough in comparison with the profits of the slave trade. But the British did not ratify or honour any of these treaties.[1] In 1841, the personnel of the Niger Expedition made an agreement with the Obi of Aboh, whereby he undertook to give up trading in slaves, and the British promised to send regular trading vessels for legitimate trade. The years went by, the Obi died, and it was not until 1857 that the first of these trading vessels ascended the Niger. The economic and social costs of the abolition of the slave trade were born by the African peoples concerned.

Some parts of West Africa found that the abolition of the slave trade destroyed the whole basis of their overseas trade, for they had no other commodity which the Europeans required in large quantities. In the Delta, an alternative export commodity was ready to hand in palm oil, which traders had begun purchasing in the late eighteenth century.[2] In the first three decades of the nineteenth century, the export of slaves and of palm oil went on simultaneously—'The staple trade of Eboe [Aboh] consists of slaves and palm oil'[3]—and after the export of slaves came to an end, palm oil became Iboland's staple export commodity.

This change introduced a fundamentally new kind of economic relationship between Europe and Iboland, which was destined to last until the end of the colonial period, and beyond. Iboland became an economic satellite of the European industrial economy—what is sometimes called a dependent monoculture. It provided one of the many raw materials required by Europe's growing industries, and imported manufactured products in return.

Regarded from the viewpoint of the West African historian, it is easy to overemphasize the importance of palm oil to the European economy. Despite its manifold uses, it was essentially only one of a vast number of primary products which Europe imported. The uses to which it was put changed as time went on.[4] In the first half of the nineteenth century, it was used as a lubricant, a fuel, and for the

---

[1] Dike, p. 85.

[2] Adams, pp. 143, 172 and 245; Donnan, II, 651.

[3] MacGregor Laird and R. A. K. Oldfield, *Narrative of an Expedition into the Interior of Africa by the River Niger* (London, 1837), I, 102.

[4] For a contemporary account of the uses of palm oil, cf. 'Palm Oil and Cotton', *The African Times* (23 January 1863), pp. 78–9. See also Charles Wilson, *The History of Unilever. A Study in Economic Growth and Social Change* (London, 1954), I, 10, 72–3 and 117.

manufacture of candles. After the 1860s, mineral oils superseded it in these fields, but new uses were found for palm oil in processing tin plate and in the vast expansion of the soap industry. Yet even in the soap industry, it was only one of a large number of alternative raw materials (the others included tallow, linseed oil, copra and whale oil). From the 1870s on, palm kernels were processed. They were used at first for soap, but later they made an important contribution to European nutrition, for kernel oil was used in margarine manufacture, and the residue for cattle food.

A society whose whole external trade depends on a single primary product is at many disadvantages—this has, indeed, been the central problem of many independent African states in recent times. A primary product may be rendered obsolete by technical change—as African dyewoods were ousted by synthetic dyes. It may be undersold by a cheaper product from elsewhere—a glut of Australian tallow in 1895–6 caused an immediate crisis in the West African palm oil industry.[1] Since most primary producers are only one of a number of alternative sources of a product, they have little if any control over the prices they receive.

The palm oil industry was not as grossly and destructively exploitative as the slave trade. Nevertheless, the new economic relationship it established was basically disadvantageous to Iboland—and was destined to govern her economic life throughout the colonial period. In the nineteenth century, the disadvantageous effects were masked while palm oil prices remained high, while Iboland retained her political independence, and while external trade was valued only as a source of non-essential goods. But from the 1860s onwards, palm oil prices fell, and in the 1880s began the long process of the establishment of colonial rule.

To what extent was the palm oil trade a true substitute for the slave trade? Many of the European firms made a successful transition from the slave trade to the palm oil trade, which utilized their shipping, and their special commercial knowledge of West Africa. But it is important to realize that for much of Iboland it was not an economic substitute, because limitation of transport and geography meant that only a small area of Iboland could participate in it.

Only half of Iboland—the area lying south of a line between

[1] Wilson, I, 63; cf. F.O. 2/180, Niger Coast Protectorate Annual Report, 1897–1898.

Afikpo and Onitsha—lay in the palm oil belt.[1] Even in the palm oil belt, many areas had only sufficient oil palms to supply their domestic needs.[2] Yet the areas which were able to sell palm oil for export were much more narrowly circumscribed by the available transport. Palm oil is a bulky commodity, and in nineteenth-century Iboland, could only be transported by canoe. Whereas slaves, of course, had provided their own transport, and the slave trade routes had been able to develop independently of river transport, the palm oil trade was confined to those parts of Iboland connected with the Delta ports by navigable rivers. In the nineteenth century, apart from the Niger and Cross Rivers, Iboland's waterways were generally navigable only in their lower reaches. It was these areas which served as collecting centres for palm oil, carried to the riverside in calabashes by individual producers, and then purchased in bulk by the Delta traders. Economic rivalry had always been characteristic of the relations between the Delta states, but in the nineteenth century, the need for exclusive access to these limited palm oil markets imbued it with a new bitterness, and led, on occasion, to 'complicated and universal War'.[3]

These limitations had important consequences for Ibo economic history. They gave, for a time, a role of key importance to the southern Ibo towns, such as Ohumbele, which collected oil for the Delta traders. But the problem of transport made it impossible for older economic centres, such as Bende or Uzuakoli, to make this kind of transition. Their continued prosperity depended on the existence of the internal trade in slaves. And the geographic limitations of the palm oil trade inevitably caused discontent in those parts of Iboland which could not participate in it.[4]

To understand the social impact of the palm oil trade on those areas of Iboland which took part in it, it is necessary to look briefly at the way in which the oil was produced. First it was necessary to climb the oil palm and cut down the cluster of nuts. It was a dangerous task: 'Occasionally, the rope breaks or slips, or the climber

---

[1] R.H. MSS. Afr. s. 697, A. F. B. Bridges, 'Report on the Oil Palm Survey, Ibo, Ibibio and Cross River areas', 1938.
[2] E. A. Steel, 'Exploration in Southern Nigeria', *Journal of the Royal United Services Institution* (April 1910), pp. 439 and 446. (This article is to be found in a bound volume of pamphlets, 'Nigeria', I, in the F.O. and C.O. Library, London.)
[3] F.O. 84/1343, New Calabar supercargoes to Hopkins, 20 July 1871.
[4] C.M.S. CA 3/04, Bishop Crowther to Venn, 18 October 1867.

misses his grip, and the result is always horribly painful, if not fatal.'[1]
The methods of extracting the oil from the nuts varied, but all were
laborious. In southern Iboland the nuts were pounded, the pulp
mixed with water and the whole mixed continuously, until the oil
rose to the surface and could be skimmed off. In Onitsha and
western Iboland the nuts were first boiled, then pounded, and then
the oil was squeezed out by hand.[2] A single cask of palm oil represented an enormous expenditure of time and energy, and Iboland's
oil production was measured, not in casks, but in thousands of tons.
In 1855, it was estimated that the Delta exported 22,495 tons of palm
oil annually, over 16,000 of them from Bonny and Kalabari.[3] In
1871, the Delta's annual exports were put at between 25,000 and
30,000 tons.[4]

Once Europe had developed techniques for utilizing the kernel of
the palm nut, the preparation and export of kernels developed rapidly.
The kernel was obtained by cracking the tough outer casing, a skilled,
if tedious task, as the kernel needed to remain intact. It was estimated
that to produce a single pound of kernels, it was necessary to crack
four hundred nuts.

Early in the twentieth century, E. D. Morel reflected on the fact
that in 1910, southern Nigeria had exported 172,998 tons of kernels,
and 76,850 tons of oil. He commented with justice: 'In . . . realizing
. . . the truly enormous sum of African labour which it represents . . .
one cannot but reflect upon the foolish generalities which ascribe
"idleness" to the West African negro . . .'[5]

At the end of the first third of the nineteenth century, the relationship
between Iboland and the Europeans was essentially paradoxical.
Their economic links were centuries old. Iboland had contributed in
the era of the slave trade to the process of capital formation in
Europe, and later, produced both a raw material and a market for
Europe's industrial revolution. In its turn, Ibo society had been

[1] Basden, *Niger Ibos*, p. 403.
[2] *Ibid.*, pp. 404–5.
[3] Hutchinson, p. 252.
[4] F.O. 84/1343, memo. by Livingstone, n.d., received by F.O. 8 December 1871.
[5] E. D. Morel, *Nigeria, Its Peoples and Its Problems* (first pub. 1911, 3rd edn.
London, 1968), pp. 53–4. For another comment to the same effect, cf. John H.
Harris, *Dawn in Darkest Africa* (first pub. 1912, reprinted London, 1968),
pp. 125–6.

profoundly affected by the direct and indirect consequences of this external trade. And yet this long continued trading relationship took place only through intermediaries—the Delta middlemen. No Europeans had set foot in the Ibo interior, and they did not even realize that the many rivers with which they were familiar on the coast formed the Delta of the River Niger.

In the middle years of the nineteenth century, the pattern changes, and we have the beginnings of European penetration of the interior. The process begins in 1830, when the Lander brothers made their gallant canoe journey down the Niger. It continues with the steady development of European—and Sierra Leonian—activity on the Niger, and with the gradual penetration of eastern Iboland, a process which begins in the 1890s, and is still not complete in 1906. The rest of this book is concerned, in the main, with this pattern of moving frontiers, with Iboland's gradual confrontation with various forms of alien culture, and ultimately, with alien rule. But in order to understand the significance of this impact, it is necessary to depict at least the most salient characteristics of the society which experienced it. This forms the theme of the next chapter of this study.

5 · A People in a Landscape:
Iboland on the Eve of Alien Rule

'Our main grievance is that we are not so happy as we were
before . . . Our grievance is that the land is changed.'
— Women rioters in Owerrinta, in 1929.[1]

This chapter seeks to describe Ibo society as it existed in the
middle years of the nineteenth century. Such a survey must be
necessarily brief and impressionistic, and is no substitute for the
patient intuitive understanding and description of particular communities which is the special province of the anthropologist. But if a
social history is not to move on a level of unreal abstraction, it is
necessary to isolate the major characteristics of a given society, at a
particular period in time.

The classic difficulty in reconstructing African social history is that
the observers whose writings mirror a society's characteristics are, at
the same time, changing it. From 1830 on, we have many descriptions
of the Niger Ibo states. From the 1880s on—and, occasionally,
earlier—we have eyewitness descriptions of other areas of eastern
and western Iboland, from missionaries, soldiers and administrators.
But these were, of course, themselves the agents of change. Nevertheless their descriptions, supplemented by studies of Ibo society made
by anthropologists and others in the twentieth century, do show us
the lineaments of Ibo society, before it was subjected to the revolutionary experience of alien conquest and rule.

Since Iboland had no single centralized government, we must look
for unifying institutions in other spheres. It had the broad cultural
unity which came from a common language—albeit with marked
differences of dialect—and similar political and social institutions.
Although the details of government, and of social customs, differed
considerably from place to place, the broad underlying similarities
are ultimately more significant than the differences. The typical Ibo

[1] Quoted in Margery Perham, *Native Administration in Nigeria* (London, 1962
reprint), p. 219.

71

state was, as we have seen, a small, democratic society, with an intricate system of political institutions where the voice of elders generally predominated, and with much scope for individual mobility. It was a French observer who wrote that he had found true liberty in Iboland, although its name was not inscribed on any monument.[1]

Iboland was more, however, than a large collection of independent and unrelated polities. Her states were interrelated in a number of different ways. Many were grouped into clans, or tribes, united by the agnatic charter of a common ancestor. More rarely, groups of un-related towns occasionally united for mutual defence against a common enemy. Thus several leagues, such as the Amakwam confederation, were formed to resist attacks from the Abam.[2]

The economic links created by trade routes and by Iboland's network of markets were much more far-flung. In the last two chapters we saw how the development of trade with Europe led to two successive forms of export trade—in slaves, and in palm oil, and how these forms of trade co-existed throughout the nineteenth century, although the export of slaves ceased, and the slave trade became purely internal. These two forms of trade required two different patterns of trade route.

The palm oil trade routes linked specific Delta ports by water with specific palm oil producing areas. Since the economic life of each Delta state depended on its monopoly of its routes and markets, it was prepared to resort to war if necessary to defend them. It is an occupational vice of the historian to think that whatever is best documented is most important, but in the middle years of the nineteenth century it was the Niger which undoubtedly carried the greatest volume of trade. The trade of the lower Niger was dominated, as we have seen, by the Ibo state of Aboh and the Igala capital, Idah. Their relationship was carefully regulated to avoid destructive rivalries. Occasionally, Igala canoes visited Aboh, or Aboh canoes visited Idah, but usually the trading fleets of the two kingdoms met at the boundary of their respective spheres of influence, at a market which was held, in the dry season, on a sandbank between Asaba and Onitsha.[3] In the middle years of the nineteenth century, the

[1] Ferrieux, in *L'Echo des Missions Africaines de Lyon* (1907), p. 18.

[2] Jeffries, 'The Divine Umundri Kings', ch. 2 (n.p.). For another example, see N.A.I. C.S.O. 26/154 (File 28583), Fox-Strangways, 'Isuochi, Nneato and Umucheze Clans' (1932).

[3] Crowther and Taylor, p. 385.

people of Brass made a determined and successful attempt to challenge Aboh's practical monopoly of trade between the Delta and the lower Niger. In the 1830s, they were paying tribute to Aboh for the privilege of access to the Niger,[1] but in later years the privilege became a right—a change doubtless connected with the decline of Aboh's power in those years. For some years the Brassmen prospered, exporting large quantities of oil from the Niger markets, until their trade was destroyed, first by European competition, and later by a new power, the Royal Niger Company, which successfully defended a monopoly more unqualified than that to which any African power had laid claim, and in doing so reduced the people of Brass to destitution.[2]

The Kalabari markets were on the lower reaches of the Sombreiro River, and to the immediate east of the Niger, on the Engenni River, and in Oguta, which is connected by navigable waterways both to the Niger and to the Delta.[3] In later years, the expansion of European traders to the interior was to shed a vivid light on the bonds of friendship and loyalty which linked the Kalabari middlemen with the Ibo oil producers. The men of the Oguta area told an inquirer 'that they did not wish to trade with the Niger Company but with the Calabar men who were their friends'.[4] The people of Ewafa, when asked if they would welcome direct trade with Europeans, affirmed their loyalty to the Kalabari trader prince, Will Braid. 'Whatever Will Braid says they say, for they would never leave him, but are ready to support him at all times.'[5]

The economic history of Bonny in the nineteenth century shows the steady contraction of her trading empire. In the era of the slave trade, Bonnymen traded as far afield as the lower Niger, and shared the trade of the Engenni and Oguta with the Kalabari.[6] For a time, they

[1] Laird and Oldfield, I, 97.

[2] For the rise of Brass trade in the Niger, and its destruction by European competition, cf. F.O. 84/1498, Letter from King and Chiefs of Brass, 21 February 1877.

[3] F.O. 84/1881, Hewett to Salisbury, 26 December 1888.

[4] F.O. 84/2109, MacDonald, 'Report on the Administration of the Niger Company's Territories', received at F.O. 9 January 1890, ch. 5.

[5] C.M.S. G3/A3/1880, Buck, Journal, 20–26 May 1880 (this journal describes a journey with Consul Hewett to the Kalabari markets in 1880, when Buck acted as interpreter).

[6] F.O. 84/1087, Bonny regents to Hutchinson, 2 December 1858, encl. in Hutchinson to Malmesbury, 24 February 1859. F.O. 84/1881, Hewett to Salisbury, 26 December 1888.

continued to trade for palm oil in these areas—Bonnymen were purchasing palm oil at Aboh in 1841[1]—but they gradually withdrew or were expelled and came to depend entirely on oil from the markets on the lower Imo River. When Ja Ja broke away from Bonny, in 1869, and established a new state at the mouth of the Imo River, he at a stroke cut Bonny off from her main markets. Henceforth Bonny depended on oil from her northern neighbours, the Okrikans, who in their turn obtained it from their Ibo hinterland.[2] But it was no substitute for the trading empire they had lost, and a few years later, Bonny was 'a ruined and impoverished Country'.[3]

Ja Ja in his turn was destined to enjoy less than twenty years of autonomy before he was treacherously kidnapped by a British consul and deported, to die in a distant exile. During his years of power, he developed his trading empire both in the Ibo markets on the Imo River, and in Ibibioland. Far more than a cash nexus linked him to his suppliers. Their bonds were cemented by diplomacy and judicious marriages, and by Ja Ja's skilful use of traditional religious symbolism.[4]

The trading system of the Cross River resembled, in miniature, that of the lower Niger, though it was one in which Ibos were only marginally involved, and trade on the river in the nineteenth century was destined to be frequently disrupted by disputes between the riverain states.

These trade routes were a vehicle, not only for the exchange of goods, but for cultural contacts. This was seen very clearly in the late nineteenth century when a number of Bonny slaves, converts to Christianity, began a work of evangelization in the Ibo oil markets.[5]

In addition to the water routes by which palm oil was transported, there was another system of trade routes, dealing in slaves and luxury goods, for which water transport was not required. Certain of these routes did in fact follow the pattern of the palm oil routes—notably,

[1] William Allen and T. R. H. Thomson, *A Narrative of the Expedition . . . to the River Niger, in 1841* (London, 1848), I, 237.

[2] For descriptions of Okrika's economic role, see C.M.S. G3/A3/1882/58, D. C. Crowther, '. . . the 3rd visit to Okrika', February 1882, and G3/A3/1886, D. C. Crowther, 'Bakana and Ewaffa', 4 December 1885.

[3] F.O. 84/1508, Hopkins to F.O., 23 November 1878.

[4] F.O. 403/73 (F.O.C.P.), Ja Ja to Salisbury, 5 May 1887.

[5] Cf. p. 89 below. For the similar impact of Opobo traders in Ibibioland later on, see *Inquiry into the Southern Nigeria Liquor Trade* (1909), Minutes of Evidence, questions 12421 and 12422.

on the lower Niger—but many of them were overland. Two scholars have mapped some of the major trade routes in nineteenth-century Iboland,[1] but the study of the many references to particular routes in the contemporary archival sources suggests the conclusion that they were both more numerous and individually less important than such depictions might suggest.

The crucial questions are: who travelled along these trade routes and what type and quantity of goods were transported. The type of goods transported is fairly easily established. Both slaves, and cattle and horses were imported from the north, along at least three separate routes,[2] the latter intended not for utilitarian purposes but for sacrifice in religious ceremonies. Slaves and luxury goods were transported along these routes—especially along the central route between Awka and Bende. But the evidence suggests that the crucial economic institution in Iboland was not the trade route, but the market. Many markets served a dual purpose—some of the goods exchanged were luxuries transmitted along the long-distance trade routes, but the vast bulk of goods which changed hands were produced locally. This is evident from almost any contemporary description of a major market, such as the following account of a market in the Ndokki area, in 1866:

> Their market consists of articles of native produce of every sort. Provisions in abundance. It abounds in corn, palm-wine, rum, fish, deer's flesh, dog's flesh, cats, fowls, tobacco, yam, eggs, spices, pine-apple, palm-oil, bananas, and plantains, cassada, cloths, guns, powder, pipes, and things which I could not number.[3]

The people of Ewafa, on the New Calabar River, explained to inquirers the patterns of distant trade routes, along which they themselves did not travel, terminating in north-eastern Iboland, where 'they buy elephants tusks, and some of the people do not know

[1] Simon Ottenberg, 'Ibo Oracles and Intergroup Relations', *Southwestern Journal of Anthropology* (1958), XIV, p. 300; Ukwu I. Ukwu, 'The Development of Trade and Marketing in Iboland', *Journal of the Historical Society of Nigeria* (1967), III, no. 4, p. 652.

[2] For the Ibo-Igala market at Ogurugu, cf. *The Church Missionary Intelligencer* (1867), p. 63; for Ezza imports from the north, cf. C.O. 520/31, 'Political Report on the Ezza Patrol', encl. in Egerton to Lyttelton, Confidential, 16 July 1905; for the Idoma-Afikpo route, cf. N.A.I. C.S.O. 26/240 (File 28298), Helbert, 'Report on Ikem, Eleke and Mbu area' (1932).

[3] Account by W. E. Carew in *The Church Missionary Record* (July 1866), p. 210.

cloth there we are told'.[1] The people of Ndelli, on the Sombreiro River, gave an unmistakable description of Oguta. The Orashi River emerges, they stated, into 'an open river like a sea with large towns on the banks—women are said to be the palm oil traders there, & the rich ones among them wear ivory on their legs & brass bracelets on their arms. They have a King & many district chiefs'.[2]

If one compares Iboland with other parts of Africa, it is the activity of its economic life and the vast number of its markets, carefully timed to avoid clashing with each other, which is perhaps its most striking characteristic. It was, of course, the density of its population which made it possible. But the recognition of the role of both external and internal trade in Iboland should not blind us to the fact that the economy of the states of the Ibo interior was still primarily a subsistence one, and depended on agriculture.

Descriptions of Iboland in the nineteenth century always emphasize how much the landscape had been modified by the human presence, almost covered with orderly and productive farms, where the yam was the central crop. In the extreme south-east of Iboland, near Arochuku, an observer wrote:

> As far as I could see, it had been cleared entirely of the original forest, only a few of the larger trees being left here and there around the villages or in plantations. The absence of forest was compensated for by the numbers of palm trees extending in all directions round the villages . . . The fields seemed to be almost entirely devoted to yam cultivation, although maize was scattered in patches between some of the yams; and in the small gardens around each house and compound in the villages themselves cocos and eddo yams were grown, as well as pumpkins.[3]

One can find this description echoed, almost word for word, throughout eastern Iboland. The sources are full of lyrical accounts of Ibo agriculture—from 'the famous Asaba farms' which extended over thousands of acres, west of the Niger,[4] to the 'thrifty and excellent farmers' of the Ezza clan, in the extreme north-east.[5]

---

[1] C.M.S. G3/A3/1886, D. C. Crowther, 'Bakana and Ewaffa', 4 December 1885.

[2] C.M.S. G3/A3/1890/142, D. C. Crowther, 'Journal of a visit to Abonnema and Ndele', 12 August 1890.

[3] F.O. 2/63, Casement to MacDonald, 10 April 1894.

[4] H. H. Dobinson, 'New Openings on the Niger', *The Church Missionary Intelligencer* (August 1891), p. 573.

[5] C.O. 520/31, 'Political Report on the Ezza Patrol', encl. in Egerton to Lyttelton, Confidential, 16 July 1905.

Observers were equally impressed by the comfort and beauty of Ibo towns. Their layout varied from area to area, but certain factors were universal. The houses had thatched roofs and clay walls—the latter acquired, by dint of daily polishing, the gloss and hardness of marble. 'The houses are kept beautifully rubbed with mud till they shine like stone, patterns being painted in bright red, yellow and black.'[1] It was a type of house construction more adapted to the climate than houses made of imported materials—as the missionaries were to learn by painful experience. Typically, they were surrounded by vegetable gardens, and shaded by ancient trees. The towns of western Iboland were notable for their broad and well-planned streets. Thus Ubulu—'Their streets and roads are well-planned and laid, as if under the supervision of a civilised surveyor . . . There are constructed several porches at the corners of the principal streets, where royal guards, armed with swords and muskets, are kept during the day, to see that order is established in the town.'[2]

Descriptions of nineteenth-century Iboland emphasize the beauty and excellence of her manufactures. The members of Baikie's expedition, in 1854, described the elaborately woven cloths which were made in the eastern Ibo interior, by some groups of the Elugu Ibo, and exported via Onitsha to the north.[3] A later description of cloth manufacture in the small western Ibo town of Idumuje Ugboko shows the way in which Ibo industries were gradually eroded by the importation of foreign products:

> Every woman here weaves cloth from the cotton which grows on the trees in abundance, and they do it beautifully, working patterns in, but foreign cloth is much coveted, and their own cloth despised.[4]

Metallurgy, especially iron working, was another highly skilled industry. The most famous blacksmiths were those of Awka, who worked raw iron from the Abaja towns, and travelled through Iboland plying their trade.[5] Their pride in their ancient craft was

[1] Wilson, 'Village Life in the Ibo Country', *Western Equatorial Africa Diocesan Magazine* (1904), p. 44.

[2] J. Spencer, in *The Church Missionary Intelligencer* (April 1879), p. 242.

[3] William Balfour Baikie, *Narrative of an Exploring Voyage up the Rivers Kwora and Binue . . . in 1854* (London, 1856), pp. 287–8; Samuel Crowther, *Journal of an Expedition up the Niger and Tshadda Rivers . . . in 1854* (London, 1855), p. 179.

[4] F. M. Dennis, 'The "Wild West" ', *Niger and Yoruba Notes* (1903), p. 23.

[5] Jeffries, 'The Divine Umundri Kings', ch. 15; Sidney R. Smith, 'The Ibo People' (Cambridge Ph.D. thesis, 1929), p. 142.

vividly reflected in their first response to missionary teachings: 'Some . . . said they did not wish to learn anything else as they had learnt blacksmithing and that was quite enough for them.'[1] Pottery was made throughout Iboland, often combining utility with great beauty of form and design.[2] This industry again was to be gravely weakened by the importation of less attractive but more durable European substitutes—iron cooking pots, and, later, kerosene cans for water storage—just as the traditional thatch was to give way to the ubiquitous rusting corrugated iron roofs.

We have seen that although Iboland consisted of a large number of small independent states, these states were united in various ways— by language, and similarities of custom and life style, and by internal economic exchanges, which were developed to a degree unusual in Africa. Another major institution, which was superimposed over Iboland's political fragmentation, was the oracle.

Oracles were widespread in West Africa;[3] what was peculiar to Iboland was their number and importance, in a relatively small area. We saw in an earlier chapter how the most famous and influential of these oracles—that of Arochuku—developed. Like another major oracle—that of the Agbala, which spread its influence through Awkas travelling smiths—its success depended largely on the services of Aro's widely scattered sons, who could lead clients to the oracle, and ascertain the true facts of a case. These oracles filled a number of psychological and social needs. Iboland probably gained more than it lost by the possession of a number of final courts of appeal, whose decisions bore the imprint of divine infallibility, and whose reputations depended, in the long run, on the justice of their decisions. Their authority was recognized well beyond the borders of Iboland. Visitors to the Delta were impressed by the readiness of its people to submit disputes to the arbitration of Chukwu's oracle— 'all the tribes of this country beleive [sic] that the truth must come out there, as instant death by an incensed Deity is the fate of the liar in that sacred place'.[4] After the British established their administration in the Delta, and with it a supposedly more efficient system of

[1] E. Warner, 'Onitsha to Oka', *Niger and Yoruba Notes* (1899), p. 95.

[2] Basden, *Niger Ibos*, p. 328. Cf. Plate 2.

[3] Cf. Boniface I. Obichere, 'A Contribution to the Study of West African Oracles', paper presented to a Conference on the History of African Religions, Dar es Salaam, June 1970, p. 5.

[4] F.O. 84/1277, Livingstone to Stanley, 25 April 1867.

justice, the Delta people still showed a 'curious' preference for the decisions of the oracle at Arochuku.[1]

Warfare, between the various Ibo states, was regulated by a number of conventions. In conflicts between related groups, the use of firearms and the killing of women and children were forbidden.[2] Even when unrelated groups fought, the loss of life was usually very small.[3] Different factors could provoke wars. Often a kidnapping would set off a chain reaction of reprisals, part of the evil legacy of the slave trade. Some local skirmishes were essentially a form of dangerous sport, which gave young men a chance to prove their courage to themselves and others. Since yam cultivation requires short periods of intensive labour, interspersed by long slack periods, these conflicts were usually restricted to the agricultural off season.

A more serious form of warfare was occasioned by the attacks of various Ibo warrior groups from near the Cross River—the Abam, Ada and Ohafia. We have seen that these were often hired as mercenaries by the Aro. Frequently, they were hired by other Ibo groups as well[4]—though not infrequently their employers found that they had acquired a two-edged sword. In the second half of the nineteenth century, they made regular raids in north-western Iboland, in the Elugu and Nri-Awka areas, often going as far as the Niger. Unlike local wars, these attacks were accompanied by widespread destruction and bloodshed. The towns affected evolved various forms of defence, such as moats with removable bridges, high earthen walls, or concealed pits filled with stakes.[5] In the Awka area, towers thirty feet high were constructed.[6] In a town near the Niger, missionaries discovered 'in the trees gigantic cradles, which were reached by swinging ladders ... These, they told us, were places of refuge when they were attacked by the Abams.'[7] A more positive form of self-defence lay in the formation of military federations[8]—

[1] C.O. 520/14, Moor, 'Memorandum concerning the Aro Expedition', 24 April 1902, pp. 21–2.

[2] Basden, *Niger Ibos*, pp. 377–81.

[3] *Ibid.* Cf. William Cole, *Life on the Niger, or the Journal of an African Trader* (London, 1862), pp. 10 ff.; *The Gospel on the Banks of the Niger*, III, 27 ff. and 60 ff.

[4] Basden, *Niger Ibos*, p. 382.

[5] *Ibid.*, pp. 386–7.

[6] *Ibid.*, p. 387. Cf. E. Warner, 'Onitsha to Oka', *Niger and Yoruba Notes* (1899), p. 95.

[7] P. A. Bennett, 'A Visit to Opoto', *Niger and Yoruba Notes* (1894), p. 24.

[8] Cf. p. 72 above.

which might, in time, have led to the creation of larger-scale political units, had not colonial rule intervened. When missionaries first visited the area, they were profoundly impressed by the fear these raids created. On occasion, they were forced to flee from them.[1]

In traditional Ibo society there was no clear dividing line between work and recreation, or between art and utility. Attendance at markets, or participation in political meetings had—and have—a marked recreational element. The stories told in the evenings had a serious moral purpose—to instil in the young the values of their society. Many of Iboland's most attractive products, such as pottery, were purely utilitarian in purpose.

This was, however, not always the case. Iboland's recreations included music and dancing. Here as elsewhere in Africa, few Europeans can appreciate, let alone emulate, their intricate complexities. 'Okwe' is an Ibo version of chess. Most present-day adult Ibos look back with nostalgia on their childhood—on the satisfactions of playing in the moonlight, denied to most European children —on its many opportunities both for work and for creative play. Some of the finest Ibo art was purely religious in intention. An outstanding example of this are the mbari houses of the Owerri area, whose wall paintings and unbaked clay sculptures have attracted much well-merited attention from art scholars in recent years.[2]

No aspect of the African past is more difficult to recapture than the history of ideas. How did the Ibo people view the world, in the middle years of the nineteenth century, and how did they interpret the European presence on the coast and on the Niger?

All observers agreed that the Ibo world view was overwhelmingly a religious one. The basic structure of Ibo religion is similar to that of many other African religions. There is a supreme God, known under different names in different parts of Iboland, whose goodness, wisdom and power are described in many Ibo personal names. He is, however, remote. More concerned with the daily affairs of men were a host of lesser divinities and spirits. The Ibo landscape was pervaded with the numinous. It was full of sacred groves, streams, rocks

[1] C.S.Sp. *Bulletin de la Congregation*, XVI (March 1892). (The missionary who fled returned at the risk of his life to baptize a dying woman, and in the following year, the missionaries participated in a successful defence of the town.)

[2] Ulli Beier, *African Mud Sculpture* (London, 1963). Cf. a superbly illustrated article by Herbert M. Cole, '*Mbari* is Life', *African Arts/Arts d'Afrique* (Spring, 1969). See also Plate 8.

and caves. Every village had its shrine, every shrine was honoured with sacrifices. There was no caste of priests, but rather, a number of categories of individual particularly concerned with religion. These included the devotees or priests of particular gods, who reached their status after passing through a succession of ascetic and mystical experiences. There were also *dibia*, who were essentially diviners and specialists in herbal remedies.

The religious quality of life was not, of course, peculiar to Iboland, but has been described in many African societies. Where relatively few natural explanations of the world are known—as in medieval Europe—supernatural explanations become particularly important. Religion was a powerful support of the social order. Many crimes, for instance, were abhorrent abominations, because they were offences against Ala, the Divine Earth. The belief in witchcraft which was found only in limited areas of Iboland, fulfilled both these functions. It explained disaster, by giving it a concrete cause, personified in a particular individual. It served as a mode of reprobating certain forms of anti-social behaviour. But to the present writer, there is more than this in Ibo religion. In at least many of its manifestations, it reflects the *anima naturaliter christiana*, its intimations of the supernatural, its restless search to communicate with divinity.

We have little direct evidence about Ibo attitudes to the European presence, in the period before direct contact with Europe began. In the era of the slave trade, both the Ibo and their neighbours thought that the Europeans bought slaves in order to eat them, and to use their blood for dyeing cloth.[1] The Europeans in their turn regularly attributed cannibalism to unfamiliar peoples, both in Africa and elsewhere—an interesting minor leitmotif in the history of ideas.

We know that some at least of the peoples of the Delta, in the nineteenth century, had a remarkable understanding of the long-term significance of the European presence in Africa. An Efik ruler told the members of a British expedition, rather grimly, in 1841, 'I hear your countryman done spoil West Indies. I think he want come spoil we country all same.'[2] A Bonny chief, with remarkable

[1] Schön and Crowther, p. 42. Cf. Laird and Oldfield, II, 76 and 106 for the same view in regions further north.
[2] J. B. King, 'Details of Explorations of the Old Calabar River, in 1841 and 1842', *Journal of the Royal Geographical Society* (1844), p. 260. Cf. Waddell, pp. 456 and 612.

prescience, expressed his misgivings to a British consul, in 1860. He 'expressed to me his dread of our government doing what he said the French had done at Gaboon—namely induce the Chiefs to sign a treaty whose meaning they did not understand, and then seize upon their country'.[1]

It is difficult to know to what extent the Ibos of the interior shared these apprehensions. Their reactions are recorded only after the penetration of Iboland had begun. Then, indeed, we have a number of intellectual and tactical responses to the various forms of alien presence—to missions, traders, and later, to alien conquest and rule. These will be discussed in later chapters of this book.

This then, in its broadest outlines, was the kind of society which the Ibo people had achieved by the mid-nineteenth century. It had, of course, its darker side. This is seen in the practice of human sacrifice, in the perpetual bondage of the osu or cult slave, in the penalties inflicted on those who infringed, often unwittingly, one of a variety of religious taboos. As we saw in an earlier chapter, these institutions betray the corrupting touch of the trade in slaves. And in order to see these darker elements in perspective, we need to remember that all human societies create, in one way or another, their victims. Victorian England had its victims, in the many individuals judicially murdered for trivial offences,[2] and in the children who laboured and died in the factories and mines on which her prosperity was based. But just as Britain, in time, came to understand and change these abuses, so, one may reasonably expect, would have Iboland. Indeed, in some areas we have hints that such a change of heart was taking place.[3] But these changes had no opportunity to occur by developments within the society. Abruptly, there intervened the revolutionary experience of alien rule. For the rest of this book we shall consider the gradual extension of alien influence in Iboland, which culminated in its incorporation into a British colony.

[1] F.O. 84/1117, Hutchinson to Russell, 12 February 1860.

[2] For the large number of capital offences in Victorian England, and attempts to change this, cf. Elizabeth Isichei, *Victorian Quakers* (London, 1970), pp. 250–1.

[3] C.M.S. CA3/031, Phillips to Bishop Crowther, 30 September 1878.

6 · Patterns of Moving Frontiers, 1830–1885

'. . . the Whiteman was a fish who would die if it left the Niger.'
—The Emir of Kontagora.[1]

One may take 1830—the year of the Landers' journey down the Niger—as a symbolic turning point between two successive phases of historical experience. A period when European trade exercised a great but indirect influence on Iboland is succeeded by one when the frontiers of direct contact with outside influences gradually extend on the borders of Iboland. It is a time of missionary and trading activity, which is most important in the Niger area, which therefore forms the main subject matter of this chapter. It can be said to end in the middle 1880s, with the establishment and subsequent extension of British political authority—in the Royal Niger Company, on the Niger, and the Oil Rivers Protectorate, in the Delta.[2]

One can discern three separate frontiers of alien advance during this half century. Of these, the least important was the Cross River. An expedition travelled up the Cross River in 1841–2,[3] but it was not a prelude to significant advances in this area. The Presbyterian mission established at Old Calabar did not seek to expand to the interior, penetrating no further than some outposts in Ibibioland,[4] and it was not until the twentieth century that British trading firms were reluctantly persuaded to establish factories on the river.[5]

[1] R.H. MS. Afr. r. 81, R. P. Nicholson, 'Northern Nigeria Notes, 1900–1905'.
[2] The Royal Niger Company received a Charter to govern in July 1886. The instruction to establish a Protectorate in the Delta was issued in 1885, but a form of quasi-colonial rule was not established until 1891—the year when the name Oil Rivers Protectorate was first used.
[3] J. B. King, 'Details of Explorations of the Old Calabar River', *Journal of the Royal Geographical Society* (1844), pp. 260 ff.
[4] Cf. J. F. Ade Ajayi, *Christian Missions in Nigeria 1841–1891, The Making of a New Elite* (London, 1965), pp. 94–5.
[5] Cf. pp. 125–6 below.

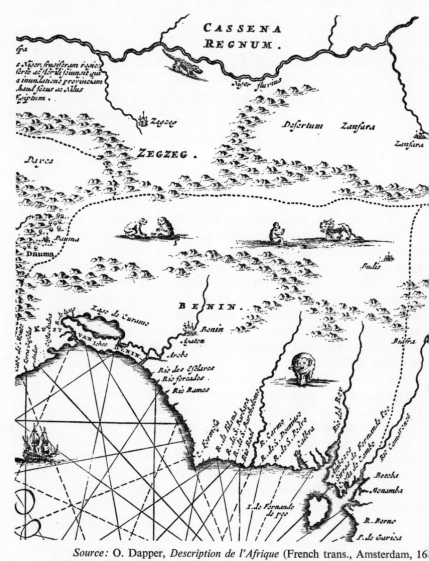

Source: O. Dapper, *Description de l'Afrique* (French trans., Amsterdam, 16

2,3 Europe's knowledge of Iboland—the late seventeenth and
early eighteenth centuries

> 'Geographers in Afric-Maps
> with Savage-Pictures fill their Gaps,
> And o'er inhabitable Downs
> Place Elephants for want of Towns.'
> —Swift, *On Poetry*

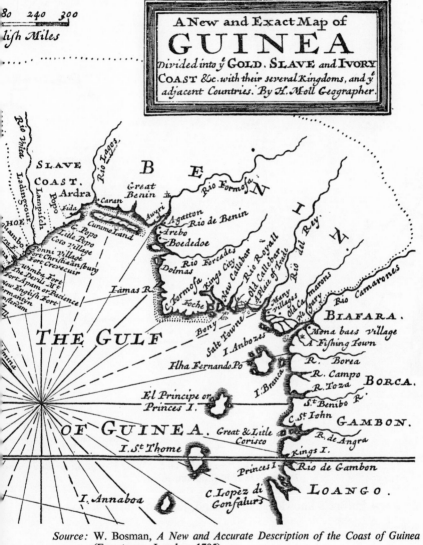

80 240 300

lish Miles

A New and Exact Map of
GUINEA
Divided into y **GOLD, SLAVE** *and* **IVORY**
COAST *&c. with their several Kingdoms, and y*
adjacent Countries. By H. Moll Geographer.

Rio White

SLAVE

COAST.

Ladingcour

Ardra

Ianspuich

Popo

Fida

Caran

B

E

N

I

N

GULE

Great Benin

Awri

Rio Lagos

Rio Formosa

HOE

C. Popo

Litle Popo

Coto village

Bonni village

Fort Christiaanburg

Fort Crevecur

Wimba Fort

The Devils Mt

Fort Apam or Pacience

New English Fort

Amfterdam

Curuma Land

Agatton

Arebo

Boededoe

Rio de Benin

Dolmas

Rio Forcades

C. Formosa

Foche

Kings City

New Calibar

Old Calibar

A Place of Trade

Rio Royall

Rio du Rey

THE GULF

Lamas R.

Bony

Salt Towne

I. Anbozes

Many Villages

Old Calibar

Rio gary

Rio Camarones

mina

BIAFARA.

Mona bae village

A Fishing Town

R. Borea

Ilha Fernando Po

I. Branca

R. Campo

R. Toza

St. Benibo R.

BORCA.

El Principe or Princes I.

Great & Litle Corisco

C. St. Iohn

GAMBON.

OF GUINEA.

I. St. Thome

R. de Angra

Kings I.

Princes I.

Rio de Gambon

I. Annaboa

C. Lopez di Gonfalurs

LOANGO.

Source: W. Bosman, *A New and Accurate Description of the Coast of Guinea*
(Eng. trans., London, 1705)

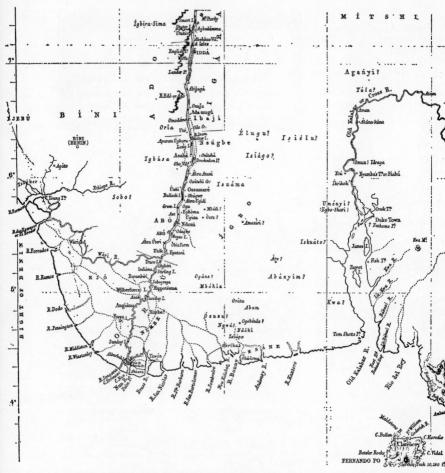

Source: W. B. Baikie, *Narrative of an Exploring Voyage up the Rivers Kwo Binue . . . in 1854* (London, 1856)

4 Europe's knowledge of Iboland, the mid-nineteenth century

The second frontier of advance was the Delta. In 1849, the British appointed a consul to an area which at first extended from the Cameroons to Dahomey,[1] but which was later reduced to the Cameroons and the Delta. This consul was stationed on the island of Fernando Po, separated from the Delta by over sixty miles of sea. He was not, of course, a colonial ruler, but a diplomatic representative among sovereign states. Interestingly enough, in view of later developments, the draft of the letter appointing the first consul contains a clause which is crossed out, stating that the British government 'have no intention to seek to gain Possession, either by purchase or otherwise, of any portion of the African Continent in those parts . . .'.[2] The way in which successive consuls used internal political crises in the Delta states—and the intermittent assistance of a man-of-war—to erode much of their autonomy has been studied by others,[3] and need not detain us here. The Niger was beyond their jurisdiction, though occasionally one of the more energetic consuls paid a visit there.[4] They made no attempt to penetrate beyond the Delta into southern Iboland. As one of them stated frankly to the European trading community, 'I know nothing of the geography or size of the oil markets; you know as little.'[5]

In the 1880s, the climate of political action in the Delta changed. It became a matter for serious debate as to whether Britain should annex the Delta, and if so, what form the annexation should take. These changes, which were full of momentous implications for Iboland, are discussed in a latter chapter of this book. Yet even by the mid 1880s, British consuls had not penetrated beyond the oil markets in the extreme south of Iboland. Hewett visited Ewafa in 1880, and Johnston Ohumbele in 1887.[6] But in the years covered by this chapter, British political influence was effectively confined to the Delta.

The European traders, similarly, had no great desire to visit the interior. In 1850, four of them managed to penetrate as far as

[1] F.O. 84/775, Draft of Beecroft's appointment as Consul, 30 June 1849 (September 1848 erased).

[2] F.O. 84/775, Draft of Beecroft's appointment, 30 June 1849.

[3] Dike, pp. 128 ff.; J. C. Anene, *Southern Nigeria in Transition 1885–1906* (Cambridge, 1966), pp. 26 ff.

[4] F.O. 84/1508, Hopkins to F.O., 18 November 1878.

[5] F.O. 84/1326, Livingstone to Granville, 25 August 1870.

[6] G3/A3/1880, Buck, Journal, 20–26 May 1880.

Ohumbele, and were greatly impressed by it, but on their return to Bonny they were greeted by a total trade stoppage which did not favour a repetition of the experiment.[1] The Delta rulers were careful to protect the middleman role on which the economic life of their states depended, and the colossal profits of the palm oil trade left the Europeans with no pressing incentives to break the established pattern of trade relations. When palm oil profits declined, in the 1880s, they began to think seriously of eliminating the middleman profits of the Delta traders—but they were to have little success in this direction, as we shall see.

The most effective moving frontier of cultural penetration was in the sphere of missionary work—and here the agents of change were neither Europeans, nor the Sierra Leonians who staffed the Niger Mission until the 1880s, but the peoples of southern Nigeria themselves. Missionary work in the Delta began in 1865, when the Niger Mission established a station at Bonny, despite the initial opposition of some European traders, who feared the consequences of literacy among their oil suppliers.[2] Missionary work in the Delta prospered. Soon there were flourishing congregations in Bonny and Brass, though the Brass Christians were destined to be alienated from their new-found faith by their long-continued experience of European injustice.[3] In Bonny, most converts were made among the slave population.

The Sierra Leonian mission agents always hoped to use the Delta as a spring-board to the Ibo interior, but were prevented by the hostility of the Delta rulers, who feared the undermining of their middleman role. In 1866, a Sierra Leonian catechist was able to visit the Ibo oil markets on the lower Imo River,[4] but it did not lead to any permanent results. Missionary work in the interior was to be the result of the initiatives of the local people themselves. In 1878, missionary work was begun in Okrika, a bi-lingual state on the southern fringe of Iboland, through the initiative of an Okrikan.

About the end of 1878, news reached us in Bonny about a very religious man, a convert, in Okrika, by name Atoridibo, who was

[1] Waddell, p. 418.

[2] CA3/04(b), Bishop Crowther, 'The Bonny Mission', April 1865.

[3] F.O. 403/216 (F.O.C.P.), 'Statement made by Chiefs after the Meeting of June 10, 1895.'

[4] *The Church Missionary Record* (July 1866), pp. 210–12.

in the habit of conducting morning and evening prayers for his household. He came to embrace his Christian mode of worship from his intercourse with the people of Bonny. . . . In spite of many difficulties and persecutions, he was able to spread the gospel to many of his people.[1]

With the help of a mission-educated carpenter from Brass, he built up a regular congregation. C.M.S. representatives were invited, and later it was made into a catechist's post.

Mission work in the Ibo oil markets on the lower Imo River, and in the Ndelli area, had a different genesis. In the late 1870s, the slaves who were sent there by their masters to buy palm oil, began an independent work of evangelization. When they found themselves in the oil markets on a Sunday, they held religious services, despite the opposition of their masters—'They never sent their boys to be "Bishops" in Ibo, but to "Trade". . .'[2] At first they erected rough 'preaching sheds', but later these were replaced by chapels.[3] In 1894, two European missionaries visiting Bonny were warned that their sermon would be repeated word for word at six or seven chapels, up to eighty miles in the Ibo interior, by these Bonny trader-evangelists.[4]

It is difficult to know how much this missionary activity affected the societies concerned. In any case, this was the only significant form of cultural impact brought from the Delta to southern Iboland in the period. In other respects, the relationship between the Delta and the Ibo interior was essentially the same in the mid 1830s and the mid 1880s. Southern Iboland had been greatly influenced by trade, but all its contacts with the outside world took place through the medium of the Delta middlemen.

For the Ibo states on the banks of the Niger, however, the same half century was to see more significant changes. For the Niger Ibos, 1830 was the beginning of the *enu oyibo*—the era of the European. More precisely, the years from 1830 to 1880 were the *enu oyibo oji*— the era of the black European, as the Onitsha people perceptively called traders and missionaries from Sierra Leone.[5]

[1] G3/A3/1883/102, 'An Indigenous African Mission. Notes on the Rise and Progress of Christianity at Okrika'.

[2] G3/A3/1884/129, D. C. Crowther to Lang, 30 June 1884.

[3] G3/A3/1890/142, D. C. Crowther, 'Journal of a visit to Abonnema and Ndele', 12 August 1890.

[4] *Letters of Henry Hughes Dobinson* (London, 1899), pp. 183–4.

[5] Crowther and Taylor, p. 262.

In 1830, the brothers Richard and John Lander travelled inland from Badagry until they reached the Niger at Bussa. There they obtained a canoe, and travelled down the great river. On 5 November, they were taken captive at the Asaba market, and brought to the ruler of Aboh. At Aboh they were ransomed by a Brass prince, Ammaikunno, who delivered them to an English ship's captain, but was disappointed in his reasonable expectation that the ransom price would be refunded. This was the unpropitious beginning of European enterprise on the Niger.

Twenty-seven years were to elapse, however, before missions or foreign trading posts were established on the lower Niger. There were a number of expeditions in those years—among them the celebrated and disastrous expedition of 1841—but the high death rates among the Europeans involved had a deterrent effect. In 1854 came the breakthrough in Europe's attempt to establish direct trading relations with the lower Niger, when an expedition was made under the leadership of Baikie, a naval physician, without a single death caused by sickness, thanks to the prophylactic use of quinine. This exploring venture—which like its predecessors, depended largely on the services of African sailors from Liberia[1]—was followed by a further one, again under Baikie's leadership, in 1857. This voyage was to end in disaster, in shipwreck near Rabba, but it achieved the foundation of the first mission and trading posts in the Ibo interior, as well as the establishment of the first form of British political representation on the Niger.

This political representation was destined to be short-lived. Baikie established a consulate at Lokoja on his own initiative, which the British government confirmed, after much initial reluctance, in 1861. Baikie died in late 1864, and the consulate was given up in 1869. During its brief existence, it exercised no real influence on Iboland, for the attention of Baikie and his successors was directed north, to the furthering of the Anglo-Nupe alliance. Nevertheless, Baikie became something of a legend on the lower Niger. His name added a new word to the Ibo language—*beké*, European—and his reputation went much further than his actual influence. He wrote in 1860 that, 'owing to the chiefs at Aboh hearing much of me from above but seldom seeing me, they begin to look on me as a kind of mythical

[1] Baikie's ship's complement consisted of twelve Europeans and fifty-three Africans. Baikie, p. 30.

being, and to regard me with a certain degree of dread'.[1] But effective outside influences on the Niger Ibo polities were to come, not from this distant and short-lived consulate, but from missions, trade, and the conflicts which trade engendered.

In both missionary and trading activity, the Niger Ibo states were but part of a larger enterprise. Since our concern is with Ibo history, our narrative must necessarily concentrate on those aspects which affected Iboland.

Until the middle 1880s, the Church Missionary Society had a monopoly of missionary activity in Iboland. An Anglican body, one of the many fruits of the evangelical revival, it was founded in 1799, and administered by a combination of lay and clerical agency. One of its earliest and most successful missions was established in Sierra Leone, where it found a fruitful field for work among the Liberated Africans, who had been sold into slavery, captured from the slave ships, and resettled there. The way in which these Sierra Leonians not only survived their traumatic experiences, but in a single genera-tion mastered the language and skills of Europe so successfully that they became a prosperous professional and merchant élite, is a major triumph of the human spirit. The Niger Mission was destined to be the spiritual child of that in Sierra Leone—an impressive chapter in the wider story of Sierra Leonian enterprise throughout West Africa and beyond.

Two C.M.S. representatives accompanied the Niger expedition of 1841, one a European, and one a Sierra Leonian, Samuel Ajayi Crowther, who had been enslaved in Yorubaland as a boy, and who was destined to become the first bishop of the Niger Mission. In 1853, as a result of a petition from a hundred Ibos in Sierra Leone, the C.M.S. sent a party to explore the possibility of missionary work and Ibo resettlement in Iboland, but the transport problem defeated them, and they got no further than Calabar.[2] In 1854, Crowther again ascended the Niger, with Baikie's expedition, and in 1857 the first mission post was established in Iboland, at Onitsha.

The distinctive characteristic of this mission was to be the fact that it was run entirely by Africans, under an African bishop. The

---

[1] F.O. 2/34, Baikie to Russell, 29 February 1860, quoted in C. C. Ifemesia, 'British enterprise on the Niger, 1830–1869' (London Ph.D., 1959), p. 489. This study gives a full account of Baikie's expeditions, and of the Lokoja consulate.
[2] *The Church Missionary Intelligencer* (1853), pp. 253 ff.

decision to operate it in this way was originally due to the health problems which confronted European missionaries in the area,[1] but it soon acquired the status of an experiment of momentous symbolic significance, with Crowther himself, 'the symbol of a race of trial'.[2]

The first mission in Iboland was staffed mainly by men of Ibo origin. Crowther went on to Rabba, in the north, and the Onitsha mission was headed by John Christopher Taylor, a clergyman born in Sierra Leone of Ibo parents. His missionary career ended under a cloud,[3] which need not obscure his earlier labours and sacrifices in Onitsha, where he buried two sons. He was accompanied by Simon Jonas, a veteran of the 1841 and 1854 expeditions, whose missionary work at Aboh in 1841 entitles him to be called the first apostle of the Ibo. This former Ibo slave was destined to die in Fernando Po. Taylor described his death and dying message:

> He then told me, 'I call on you, and beg you to say to the *Church Missionary Society* in England, that this is the third time I have gone up the Niger with their agents, and the last was the best I have spent in my fatherland.' As we were going to our family prayers, a messenger came to inform me of his death. I went there to close his eyes, but was broken down with tears.[4]

Thomas Samuel was another former Ibo slave who was at first employed by the new trading post at Onitsha, but later joined the mission, which he served until his death in 1878. It is recorded of him that he had no education but the Bible.[5] Another Ibo Christian Recaptive employed at the trading post was a Baptist deacon, Augustine Radillo, who aided the mission and on one occasion risked his life in an attempt to prevent a human sacrifice. He died soon afterwards at Fernando Po. Like his colleagues, he was the prototype of generations of Ibo Christians who would adopt a meaningless foreign name to replace one with deep religious significance—in his own case, Chukwuma, God knows.

[1] Schön and Crowther, pp. 216 ff. It was originally intended to run the mission by a combination of European and African agency, but no Europeans reached the mission, and by 1864 it was decided to make the mission purely African.

[2] Ajayi, p. 208. For the general history of the Niger Mission, cf. Ajayi, chs. 7 and 8.

[3] He left the mission in 1868, accused of harshness to his fellow missionaries. C.M.S. CA3/04, Crowther's letters of October 1868, and Crowther to Venn, 27 November 1868.

[4] Crowther and Taylor, p. 382.

[5] *Ibid.*, p. 276. C.M.S. CA3/04, Bishop Crowther, Report, 1878.

As in the oil markets behind the Delta, the evangelization of the Ibo was pioneered by the Ibo people themselves.

What sort of men left the settled life of Sierra Leone for the uncertainties and hardships of missionary life on the Niger? Until the 1870s, the mission was staffed by middle-aged men of little education.[1] Crowther always emphasized the value of their work, and the solidity of their Christian life.[2] In the 1870s, some more highly educated missionaries came, who had been to secondary school, and in some cases to Fourah Bay College. They were nearly all of Ibo descent.[3] Some came from a sense of missionary vocation, which often went back to childhood. For others, it was part of a general movement of expansion, in search of opportunities which did not exist in the tiny area round Freetown which then comprised the Colony of Sierra Leone.

There were certain weaknesses in the Niger Mission, which, combined with the rising tide of European racism later in the century, were to lead to its destruction. One of these was an absentee bishop, for Crowther spent most of each year in Lagos. This has been defended in terms of the extent of his titular diocese.[4] It may be defended more plausibly as the natural desire of an ageing man to spend his last years in scholarly pursuits, after a lifetime unusually filled with dangers and hardships. Nevertheless, the habitual absence of the mission's leader was a source of great weakness.

A second weakness was the failure to recruit local personnel. Crowther made efforts in this direction,[5] but was hampered by the lack of a special training institution—which also made recruitment of personnel in Sierra Leone 'Uncertain and unsatisfactory'.[6] The first Niger Ibo agent, the outstanding Isaac Okechukwu Mba, was forced to resign by European prejudice in 1890,[7] and the long-awaited training institution for local youths was to be sold, again by white

---

[1] C.M.S. CA3/04, Bishop Crowther, 'Suggestions for the Parent Committee', 30 March 1870.

[2] *Ibid.*

[3] CA3/04, Bishop Crowther to Hutchinson, 3 November 1876, and Smart to Crowther, 9 October 1876.

[4] Ajayi, pp. 206–7.

[5] G3/A3/1885/111, Bishop Crowther, 'A Brief Review of the Niger Mission since 1857'.

[6] C.M.S. CA3/04, Crowther to Hutchinson, 14 February 1879.

[7] C.M.S. G3/A3/1890/132, memo by Mba.

missionaries, to the Royal Niger Company at a bargain price, for use as an army barracks.[1]

Another source of weakness arose from the parsimony of the C.M.S. towards its servants. The mission agents had to support large families on meagre salaries—as little as £24 a year in some cases. They earned less than they would have done in Sierra Leone, but had additional expenses, such as sending their children away from home for education. For many years, the C.M.S. did not subsidize their children's education, and made no provision for their families if they died, or for their own old age. Help with medical expenses, or a visit to Sierra Leone after many years' service, had to be begged as a favour, not claimed as a right.[2] These conditions discouraged potential recruits, and forced many agents to supplement their income by trading. There is nothing, of course, inherently unspiritual in trading, and missionary self-support has the authority of St. Paul, but this kind of activity tended to deflect their energies, and provided an opening, later, for their critics.

The fourth source of weakness is one which is common to all missionaries, but which was exacerbated in this instance by their isolation, their lack of formal training, of leadership and of encouragement, and by their lack of regular leave. This lies in the difficulty of maintaining the fervent practice of a religion in an alien and unsympathetic environment, lacking the support and stimulus of an established congregational life. It was a European missionary who described the experience most honestly: 'Alone a man soon feels a deadly temptation stealing over him to acquiesce in, or consent to, a low standard of Christian faith and practice.'[3]

This is not, of course, to say that the Niger Mission was a total failure. As we shall see, it was those who were to destroy it who ultimately paid the most unequivocal tribute to its achievements.

The destruction of the Niger Mission in its original form began in 1877, when a European layman was appointed to take charge of the mission's 'temporalities', and was complete by 1891, when Crowther died and was replaced by a white successor. The story of its destruction has been told by others,[4] and need only be mentioned briefly

[1] C.M.S. G3/A3/1893/66, Dobinson to Baylis, 21 June 1893.
[2] C.M.S. G3/A3/1885/57, Johnson to Lang, 22 June 1885.
[3] *Letters of Henry Hughes Dobinson*, p. 121.
[4] Ajayi, pp. 238–55; James Bertin Webster, *The African Churches among the Yoruba, 1888–1922* (Oxford, 1964), pp. 7–41.

here. It is a tragic and bizarre one—the undermining of a whole mission, by missionaries, in the name of religion.

To some extent the conflicts between European and African missionaries was a conflict between two ideals of missionary action. The young English evangelicals clung to an ideal of preaching, and spiritual conversion. To Crowther, with his long years of experience, the best was the enemy of the good, and it was necessary to infiltrate a mission into society, when necessary, by appealing to secular motivations.[1] The English missionaries had a praiseworthy desire to Africanize Christianity. Unfortunately this meant in practice a romantic attachment to the language, dress and customs of Hausaland, and a vitriolic hatred of Christian Africans from Sierra Leone. This is basically a manifestation of that almost pathological dislike of Sierra Leonians and Liberians which recurs repeatedly in European writings on West Africa in the nineteenth and early twentieth centuries. Sometimes, indeed, it had the imprint of hysteria—as when Brooke wrote that Archdeacon Johnson 'was of his father the devil'.[2] They accused the Sierra Leonians of love of money, yet themselves received much larger salaries.[3]

By 1883, the mission was in ruins—'nearly a total clearance of its members . . . by *disconnection, dismissal* and *resignation*'.[4] Too late, its critics discovered that it is more difficult to build than to destroy. Some died, and others left the mission. By the early 'nineties, their sole survivor, Archdeacon Dobinson, a man of rare integrity and humility, was besieging London with requests for more Sierra Leonian missionaries, and lamenting the errors of the past in a touching *retractatio*.

> I greatly long to see an African Diocese formed . . . I do rejoice to think Archn Hy Johnson is again established. I burn with shame & horror now at the awful charges made against him in 1890 . . . May God forgive us the bitter slanderous & lying thoughts we had against him & others in those dark days of 1890 . . . We have suffered, no one knows how much, by those rash & hasty actions.

[1] C.M.S. F4/7, Journal of G. Wilmot Brooke, 28 June 1889, fo. 106; G3/A3/1889/118, Brooke to Lang, 10 July 1889.
[2] G3/A3/1890/93, Brooke to Touch, 5 June 1890.
[3] C.M.S. Precis Book, Niger Mission, 1887–97, 'Extracts from the Minutes of the General Committee', 9 December 1889; G3/A3/1891/209, Dobinson to Lang, 6 August 1891.
[4] C.M.S. G3/A3/1884/20, Bishop Crowther to Lang, 15 December 1883.

We condemned others, & we ourselves have done less than they did.[1]

The painful construction, in the 1890s, of what was in effect a new mission, relying on a combination of English, West Indian and Ibo agency, forms one of the themes of a later chapter of this study.

Iboland was, of course, only part of a wider missionary strategy, to Crowther and his fellow missionaries. By 1880, the Niger Mission had eleven stations, four of them in the Delta, extending from the sea to Egga, far to the north of Iboland. The oldest mission station was Onitsha, worked continuously since 1857. There were also stations at three Niger Ibo towns—Osomari, Asaba and Alenso, all founded in the 1870s. There was no post in the Ibo interior, and none at many important Niger Ibo towns, such as Aboh, Ndoni and Atani. Before we examine the nature of the missionary impact in the few places where it existed, it is necessary to examine the other moving frontier of alien influence, that of trade.

Looked at with the advantage of hindsight, the expansion of trade on the Niger seems inevitable, the obvious way to eliminate the profits of the coastal middlemen. 'To the merchant it offered a boundless field for enterprise; to the manufacturer, an extensive market for his goods; . . .'[2] But in fact, its beginnings were small, and its progress slow and full of difficulties.

The expedition of 1857 established three trading posts, two of which were in Iboland—at Aboh and Onitsha. The station at Aboh was given up after it was plundered by the local people in 1860. The following year, the sponsor of these ventures, the Birkenhead ship-builder, MacGregor Laird, died,[3] and with his death, the subsidy promised by the British government for annual expeditions to the Niger came to an end. The fate of trading enterprise on the Niger lay in the balance—and with it that of the Niger Mission, which depended on traders for transport facilities. Trading ventures on a river which was only navigable by steamer four months a year, which presented many health hazards to Europeans, and which could only be pursued in the teeth of the hostility of the Delta middlemen and their European trading partners, did not seem a particularly

[1] C.M.S. G3/A3/1896/54, Dobinson to Baylis, 30 March 1896.
[2] Laird and Oldfield, I, 3.
[3] For details about Laird's contributions to Niger exploration, see Dike, p. 61 n. 2 and pp. 169 ff.

attractive proposition. What saved it were not the repeated pleas of missionaries, but the American Civil War. British cotton textile manufacturers, cut off from their raw material supplies in the southern states, were forced to look elsewhere. One of the places they looked to was the Niger, where trade promised that combination of economic advantage and humanitarian self-congratulation so beloved of the Victorian middle-class mind. 'The mills of Manchester and Stockport, of Ashton and Preston, will yet shout for joy through the cotton wealth of the Niger districts.'[1]

Two new companies entered the field, only one of which, the Manchester based West African Company, remained in it. It enjoyed the backing of the C.M.S., and at first hoped to export a wide variety of products, including cotton. The missionaries encouraged this, hoping for the development of a Christian peasantry engaged in cash crop agriculture. But the Company's fortunes languished until it was on the verge of bankruptcy, and contemplating withdrawal from the Niger.[2] A good year turned the balance, but when a British government representative visited the Niger in 1871, he stated that in no part of the world had British 'life and treasure' been expended to so little advantage, apart from the Arctic![3]

The failures of the 'sixties had made two facts abundantly clear—the failure of Niger trade under European agents,[4] and the way in which, on the Niger as in the Delta, palm oil was the only really profitable product.[5] In the 1870s, Niger trade began to expand rapidly, but it did so by concentrating on palm oil, and relying on Sierra Leonian agents.[6] The Chief Agent of the West African Company was Bishop Crowther's son, Josiah.

The number of firms engaged in the Niger trade increased rapidly, and they embarked on a competition which benefited the Niger people, but was disastrous from their own point of view.

. . . factories have been established down the banks sometimes within 100 yards of one another, and it is almost impossible to

[1] *The African Times* (23 January 1863), p. 79.
[2] CA3/04/314, Crowther to Venn, 3 July 1869, and 318, Crowther to Venn, 30 October 1869.
[3] F.O. 84/1351, Simpson to Granville, 21 November 1871.
[4] C.M.S. CA3/04, Crowther to Venn, 30 January 1867, and Crowther to Hutchinson, 18 June 1879.
[5] C.M.S. CA3/04, Crowther to Hutchinson, 12 January 1875.
[6] C.M.S. CA3/04, Crowther to Venn, 30 October 1871.

7

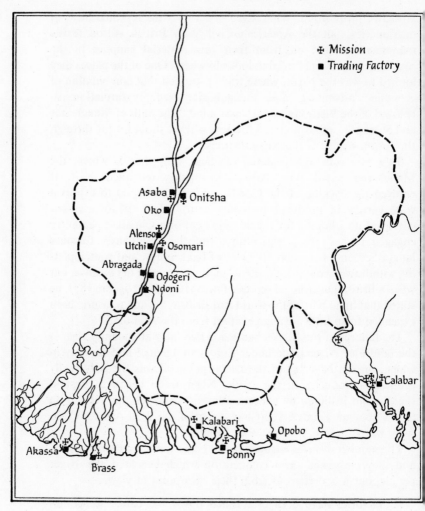

5 Patterns of Moving Frontiers—1878

describe the constant bickerings and heart burnings between these rival factories. Nearly always they are left in charge of Sierra Leonian clerks, . . .[1]

But soon the nature of trading enterprise on the Niger was to change once again. Sierra Leonians, in trade as in the missions, were supplanted by Europeans in the higher echelons. Crowther noted the way the wind was blowing as early as 1875.[2] This tendency was to reach its apotheosis when the Niger came under the rule of a man who disliked and despised all Africans, and educated Africans most of all.[3]

The era of free trade and competition was likewise destined to end abruptly. The man who later became Sir George Goldie entered the Niger trade as a shareholder in the smallest of the companies involved.[4] He had a genius for commercial and political manipulation, and embarked on a series of ambitious amalgamations which ultimately created a single monolithic entity, the United African Company, which enjoyed an effective monopoly on the Niger. In order to protect this monopoly, Goldie then embarked on a quest for political power, a quest which was crowned with success in 1886, when the company was granted a Charter to govern.

What was the impact of the trading companies on life on the Niger in these years? In one sense, it was more extensive than that of the missionaries, if measured by the number of towns affected, and the number of personnel involved. By 1878, there were trading 'factories' in nine Niger Ibo towns, each of which employed over forty-five expatriate personnel, mainly from Sierra Leone.[5] The Niger Mission had fewer stations and a much smaller personnel, but, unlike the trading firms, who simply sought to extract a product for export, they were dedicated to the proposition of change. Indeed, their whole *raison d'être* was to change the lives, both of individuals, and of the societies of which they were members.

Much to missionary displeasure, the Niger peoples persisted in

[1] F.O. 84/1508, Hopkins to F.O., 18 November 1878.

[2] C.M.S. CA3/04, Crowther to Edgar, 3 September 1875.

[3] Goldie's correspondence contains many examples of his negrophobia. Cf. for instance, F.O. 403/71 (F.O.C.P.), Goldie to Salisbury, 8 August 1885.

[4] For the definitive account of Goldie's amalgamations and quest for a Charter, see J. E. Flint, *Sir George Goldie and the Making of Nigeria* (London, 1960).

[5] F.O. 84/1498, Hewett, 'Journal of the Niger Expedition, 1876' and encls. (F.O.C.P.) F.O. 84/1508, Hopkins to F.O., 18 November 1878.

viewing both traders and missionaries as one. 'To them as we are all book people and come from the whitemen's country, we have the same interest one with another.'[1] The most important question for the historian of Iboland remains, what changes did this alien presence actually effect in Ibo societies. It is this question which forms the theme of the next chapter.

[1] C.M.S. G3/A3/1880, Crowther, Annual Report, 1880.

7 · Moving Frontiers: The Impact on Ibo Society, 1830–1885

'We cannot help feeling that you are come to break down rather than to build up.'
—Onitsha Christians to C.M.S. missionaries, 1890.[1]

The advancing frontiers of missionary and trading enterprise created situations of new difficulties and opportunities, both for individuals and for Ibo states. This chapter analyses the way in which the Ibo people responded to these situations, and the way in which the life of their communities was affected.

Initially, the rulers of Ibo states always welcomed the advent of trade and missions. Onitsha, in 1857, was a poor state, surrounded by enemies, and welcomed trade and missions in the hope of increased prosperity, an assured arms supply, and an escape from her dangerous diplomatic isolation.[2] Onitsha's rapid rise to affluence in subsequent years seemed to justify these expectations, and provided an object lesson which was not lost on the rulers of other Ibo states. As a missionary wrote to Bishop Crowther in 1879:

This earnest desire for missionaries which many of the chiefs I visited showed was in a great measure owing to a belief current that missionaries will bring merchants with them, or if they are there already they will not easily remove should missionaries be there also. Onitsha was always brought as an example to prove this.[3]

Even in the late 1850s, other Ibo states were quick to recognize the long-term significance of the new developments on the Niger. The rulers of the great trading state of Aboh were in a particularly difficult position, for they recognized the threat to their middleman

[1] C.M.S. G3/A3/1890/131, Onitsha converts to missionaries, 30 August 1890.
[2] Crowther and Taylor, I, 32–3, 270 and 428 ff.
[3] C.M.S. CA3/04, John to Crowther, 22 March 1879.

role.[1] They had to decide whether to ally with the Europeans—the policy chosen by the statesmanlike Obi Ossai—or to oppose them. In the event, they had little freedom of choice. Their repeated requests for a mission were refused, and trade passed them by, and they experienced a catastrophic decline in their economic and political power. As the Aboh people told a missionary in 1879:

> A long time ago the Abohs were regarded as the most powerful amongst their neighbours, both for riches and strength, and as such were feared by all: but now such places as Onitsha and Alenso—once their slave grounds are lifting up their heads against them: ... they could not describe their feelings to me whenever they saw ships laden with merchandise passing away from them to villages further up; ...[2]

They responded to this situation, at first by an unsuccessful policy of armed resistance, and later by a return to the policy of Obi Ossai—the pursuit of trading and missionary establishments.[3] The people of Asaba and Osomari, similarly, recognized the significance of trading and missionary posts, and sought them.[4]

The rulers of Bonny invited the C.M.S. to establish a mission, and paid half the cost, because their long relationship with European traders had taught them the uses of literacy. They hoped for western education, 'to insure their ability of gauging the oil casks, square up their accounts, read and write their letters, and ... prevent their being made the best of by the merchants and traders of the River ...'[5] The people of Okrika seem to have sought a mission in the hope that this would pave the way to direct trade with the Europeans, bypassing the middleman role of Bonny.[6] The Bonny chiefs opposed the Okrika mission for the same reason.[7]

But if rulers initially welcomed missions and trade—which they saw as inseparable—experience often taught them to distrust the Greeks bearing gifts. Typically, the initial welcome given to a mission

[1] Crowther and Taylor, I, 17.
[2] C.M.S. CA3/04, John to Crowther, 22 March 1879.
[3] Cole, pp. 95 ff.; John Whitford, *Trading Life in Western and Central Africa* (Liverpool, 1877), p. 158.
[4] For Asaba, see Crowther and Taylor, I, 40. For Osomari, see Crowther, *Journal* (1854), pp. 181–2, and Crowther and Taylor I, 22.
[5] C.M.S. G3/A3/1884/166, Pratt to Crowther, 9 September 1884.
[6] D. C. Crowther, in *The Church Missionary Intelligencer* (July 1881), p. 423.
[7] C.M.S. G3/A3/1883/80, D. C. Crowther to C.M.S., 10 May 1883.

was succeeded by a period of persecution, as traditional rulers gradually realized that missionary teachings tended to undermine the customs of their society, and perhaps challenge their own authority. The Bonny chiefs repeatedly persecuted their Christian slaves, in the fear that 'the Christians being numerically superior will declare their freedom temporal'.[1] It was one of these persecutions which led to the cruel death of the martyr, the youthful Joshua Hart.[2] In Okrika, an initial welcome was similarly succeeded by persecution.[3] In Onitsha, after eleven years of mission work, a period of hostility towards it developed. This had a number of causes,[4] but predominant among them seems to have been the sense that Christianity was creating an *imperium in imperio*, and undermining traditional customs and authority. The king requested that converts should avoid gratuitous attacks on traditional religion—such as catching the sacred fish of a local stream—and should eschew European dress. Sierra Leonian settlers should be encouraged to marry local people, 'or else they could not see how we could profess to be their friends without such arrangements'.[5]

Such anxieties were understandable, and, in the long run, well grounded, but the main impression which emerges from a study of mission work in the Niger Ibo towns in the middle decades of the nineteenth century is of the small size of the congregations established, and its limited impact on the society as a whole. By the middle 1880s, after nearly thirty years of mission work in Onitsha, the C.M.S. had gathered a congregation of about four hundred, in a state with a population of perhaps ten to fifteen thousand.[6] And if we except the flourishing congregations of the Delta, Onitsha was where missionary work was most successful. The mission at Obosi, pioneered by Onitsha Christians in the 1880s, attracted 'a mere handful of men and women who are looked upon as the offscourings

[1] *Ibid.*

[2] Bishop Crowther, in *The Church Missionary Intelligencer* (August 1876), p. 474.

[3] James Johnson, 'An African Clergyman's Visit to Bonny', *The Church Missionary Intelligencer* (January 1897), p. 30.

[4] i.e., anxiety about numerous inexplicable deaths in the town, and trade disputes with the West African Company.

[5] C.M.S. CA3/04, Crowther, Journal of a visit to the Niger Mission, 1868, entries for 10 and 12 August 1868.

[6] C.M.S. G3/A3/1885/23, Niger Mission statistics, 1883. The congregation is estimated at 300 in *The Church Missionary Intelligencer* (September 1882), p. 544.

of the land'.[1] The mission at Asaba baptized twenty adults and children in the first six years of its existence.[2] Its tiny Christian congregation consisted of strangers from other places.[3] At Osomari, the first ten years of mission work produced ten adult baptisms.[4] In all the Niger mission stations, Sunday congregations were drawn almost entirely from Sierra Leonian traders and clerks.[5]

Often, though not always, converts were drawn from the lowest strata of society. This was certainly the case at Obosi, and at Asaba, where aliens were despised and excluded from the political life of the community. The composition of the Onitsha congregation was more complex—it was drawn partly from stranger elements, such as the Igala, partly from slaves, and partly from freeborn Onitsha people— plus, of course, the employees of the trading factories.[6] Nearly all Onitsha Christians lived, not in the traditional town, but in the new commercial *entrepôt*, Onitsha Wharf, springing up on the river bank.[7] It was noted that freeborn Onitsha converts showed the greatest tendency to backslide—they were more susceptible to the concomitants of affluence, polygamy, and the taking of traditional titles. This tendency for missions to draw their first converts from the rejects of society has been noted in many parts of Africa. Every human society creates its marginal men, who have little to hope for from existing structures, and can only gain from a new system of values and ideals. Conversely, the well-established member of an Ibo society found his needs satisfied by the world, and the religion, he had inherited, and could only lose by change.

Just as congregations remained small, the missionaries and their flock made little attempt to transform the institutions of traditional society. They recognized that they were aliens, living on sufferance in sovereign states, and behaved accordingly. Thus, in Onitsha, the practice of human sacrifice continued unchecked. Christians were

[1] C.M.S. G3/A3/1889/35, Spencer to Lang, 31 December 1888.
[2] C.M.S. CA3/043, Wood, 'Report of a Visit to the Niger Mission', 1 January– 24 March 1880.
[3] *Ibid.*
[4] Henry Johnson, 'The Mission on the Upper Niger', *The Church Missionary Intelligencer* (September 1882), p. 549.
[5] Cf. CA3/04, John to Crowther, 22 March 1879 (re Ndoni); CA3/043, Wood, 'Report of a Visit' (re Alenso).
[6] CA3/030, Perry to Crowther, 16 September 1872; G3/A3/1897/109, Battersby, 'Report of a Visit to the Niger Mission'.
[7] G3/A3/1890/97, Eden to Lang, 9 July 1890.

divided in their attitude to title taking, but it was observed that those who took titles usually embraced polygamy as well.[1] Similarly, they were divided in their attitude to Onitsha's powerful secret society. The first attempt to attack this was not made until 1892, when English evangelicals did so, to the consternation of some of their flock.[2] Previously, the missions had usually avoided a frontal attack on traditional institutions. In 1879, after a missionary attack on the practice of abandoning twins, Archdeacon Crowther reported:

> This is the [first] year that a direct attack has ever been made against heathenish superstition.[3]

Oral traditions confirm that when practices such as human sacrifice were finally given up, in the various Ibo states, it was due, not to missionary persuasion, but to the coercion of the colonial government.

There is some evidence, indeed, that the hold of traditional religion was actually strengthened in the 1880s and 1890s. The change is mirrored, not only in missionary laments about 'backsliding' but in the spectacular increase in witchcraft scares. The latter phenomenon is a typical manifestation of an era of insecurity and rapid change, a characteristic product of the Age of Anxiety.[4] In 1890, Bishop Crowther, then nearing the end of a long life, summed up the net result of over forty years of missionary work in Onitsha: 'The inhabitants are entirely in the hand and control of the priests of the gods and medicine men, the King not excepted.'[5]

Education has been, characteristically, the missionary's chief means of effecting social transformation, and it was to be so, later among the Ibo, but educational work had made little progress by the 1880s. This was partly due to the lack of trained personnel, but mainly due to the fact that the Ibo people themselves had no incentive, at this time, to welcome European education for their children. Their own society provided amply for the moral and vocational

[1] C.M.S. G3/A3/1888/24, Johnson, 'Report', 1887.
[2] G3/A3/1892/189, Harford Battersby to Wigram, 12 September 1892.
[3] CA3/04, D. C. Crowther to Bishop Crowther, 6 September 1879 (copy).
[4] *The Church Missionary Intelligencer* (September 1885), p. 657; G3/A3/1888/46, Johnson to Lang, 4 April 1888. For the same phenomenon elsewhere, cf. T. O. Ranger, 'The movement of ideas 1850–1939', in I. N. Kimambo and A. J. Temu (eds.), *A History of Tanzania* (Nairobi, 1969), p. 169.
[5] C.M.S. G3/A3/1890/140, Crowther, 'Difficulties in the Way of Missionary Work on the West Coast of Africa', August 1890.

training of the young, and they had no reason for seeking European-type skills until these skills became saleable. This was not the case until the beginning of colonial rule.

By the 1880s, the only viable schools[1] attended by Ibo pupils were those in Bonny and Onitsha. In Bonny, where literacy had a practical value, some forty-nine children were attending school regularly by the early 'eighties.[2] They studied a wide range of subjects, but the standard was low—the wide gap between aspiration and reality was typical of nineteenth-century mission education. In Onitsha there were between eighty and a hundred school children. Foreign observers criticized the use of English as a medium of instruction, and the concentration on English themes—these were the first of generations of Ibo children to establish a literary acquaintance with Autumn, Snow and Daffodils. They achieved, at most, a modicum of literacy. Only Isaac Okechukwu Mba, who received further education in Lagos, before entering the service, first of the C.M.S. and then of the Niger Coast Protectorate, had received an education in any way comparable to that of the élites of Sierra Leone and Lagos.

The advent of European trade and missions affected the balance of power both between separate states, and within them. As we have seen, some states such as Aboh declined, while others, such as Onitsha, attained a new affluence and importance. Within Onitsha, the new settlement on the river bank became increasingly important, while the original town, with its inland site, steadily declined into insignificance.[3] The power and authority of the Obi declined *pari passu* with that of his capital. His ritual seclusion cut him off from participation in the new developments. His essentially religious pre-eminence was undermined by the influx of new ideas. By the 1880s, he had become almost a nonentity.[4]

If some traditional rulers declined, others made use of the new constellation of circumstances to win a power which they could never have attained in traditional society. Rarely, men such as Mba

[1] There were minuscule and short-lived schools at other places, such as Asaba, Osomari and Alenso.

[2] For the state of mission education in the Niger Mission in the 1880s, see C.M.S. G3/A3/1882/76, Pratt, 'Report on St. Stephen's School, Bonny, for the year ending Apr. 1882'; G3/A3/1885/23, Niger Mission Statistics, 1883; CA3/043, Wood, 'Report of a Visit to the Niger Mission', 1 January–24 March 1880.

[3] Whitford, p. 279; C.C.Sp., *Bulletin de la Congregation*, XXI, p. 519.

[4] C.M.S. CA3/04, Bishop Crowther to Hopkins, 22 August 1878; A. F. Mockler-Ferryman, *Up the Niger* (London, 1892), p. 24.

mastered European skills and used them in European-type roles, as mission or trading agents. But more typically, in the early period of the *enu oyibo*, the New Men were those who used their insight into the new patterns of events to win for themselves positions which, although new, were basically traditional in kind. A case in point was Obi Igweli, an Asaba notable who, because of his alien descent—his father came from Ishan—could not have hoped for a position of influence in traditional Asaba society. Both oral traditions and contemporary sources relate how it was Igweli who first realized the importance of missions and trade for the future of the town, and who was responsible for the introduction of a mission there in 1875, though he himself never became a Christian. Igweli built up for himself a position of such wealth and informal influence, that contemporary sources always describe him as Asaba's king.[1] Chief Opia played a very similar role in Aboh at this time—his 'greatest boast was, he is the only one who is bringing back white men into their country—that he had succeeded in bringing trade, and would succeed also to bring again the missionary'.[2] The most successful career of this kind was perhaps that of Idigo, a titled man of Aguleri, who rose to eminence in the 1880s, by welcoming the advent, both of trade, and of Catholic missions. He became a Christian and founded a Christian village—on a well chosen site at the waterside—and succeeded in founding a new royal dynasty.[3]

The impact of trade on Ibo societies had a number of facets. On the one hand, the multiplication of European factories on the Niger led to a great increase in the volume of trade and in consumer goods. The increase in affluence was most dramatic in Onitsha. The missionaries probably exaggerated the initial misery of Onitsha, which in their accounts recalls the Hobbesian state of nature—'very poor, filthy, and rude'[4]—but the town's subsequent increase in prosperity was unmistakable. An observer in 1871 described the trappings of affluence 'in clean, new and decent clothes . . . Some of these were

[1] This account of Igweli's career is based on Asaba oral traditions and scattered references in the C.M.S. archives. See also Adolphe Burdo, *The Niger and the Benueh, Travels in Central Africa* (trans. Mrs. George Sturge, London, 1880), p. 193, and Julius Spencer, 'The History of Asaba and its Kings', *Niger and Yoruba Notes* (September 1901), pp. 20–1.

[2] C.M.S. CA3/04, John to Bishop Crowther, 22 March 1879.

[3] Onuora Nzekwu, 'Gloria Ibo', *Nigeria Magazine* (1960), pp. 75–87.

[4] Bishop Crowther, in *The Church Missionary Intelligencer* (1866), p. 63; cf C.M.S. CA3/04, Bishop Crowther, 'Report of Visit to the Niger Mission', 1877

costly silk velvets and damasks, in addition to which the females wore rows of costly pipe-corals around their necks.'[1]

But trading relationships were marked by a chronic conflict of interest between the foreign firms and the Ibo states. As the price of palm oil fell in Europe, the foreign firms attempted to retain their profit margins by cutting prices. The Ibo states in their turn defended their interests by collective action—especially trade stoppages[2]—the technique which the Delta traders had long used with brilliant success *vis-à-vis* a chronically disunited European trading community. By the late 1870s, the foreign firms on the Niger were forced to adopt the technique of collective action, embarking on the series of amalgamations which ultimately produced the Royal Niger Company.

Increasingly, however, as time went on, differences of economic interest were resolved, not by bargaining, but by violence. Violence had always characterized Ibo–European relations on the lower Niger—as it had so often marred trading relations in the Delta states—from the time of the kidnapping of the Lander brothers. Richard Lander, indeed, was to be killed in a later expedition, several years later, and subsequent vessels sent to the Niger were heavily armed. The first trading factories established at Aboh and Onitsha were sacked by the local people soon after their foundation, and the subsequent development of European trade on the Niger took place in the teeth of the embattled hostility of the Delta peoples whose livelihood it endangered.

In the 1870s, however, these sporadic outbreaks of violence gave way to a deep-seated and endemic hostility between the trading firms and the states they traded with, which sometimes amounted to a state of war. The 'hostile villages' of the Delta continued their vigilance. In 1876, they ambushed a heavily armed steamer, with brilliant success—and were subsequently razed to the ground by a fleet of two gunboats and four steamers.[3] The perils of making war on the British had been made abundantly clear to the lower Niger:

Agberri I have no fear of, they caught it so thoroughly. The villages have not been touched and looked in the rain very

---

[1] Bishop Crowther, in *The Church Missionary Intelligencer* (April 1871), p. 125.
[2] Cf. for instance Bishop Crowther, in *The Church Missionary Intelligencer* (May 1874), p. 156.
[3] C.M.S. CA3/04, Bishop Crowther to Hutchinson, 7 August 1876; F.O. 84/1455, McKellar to F.O., 14 September 1876, and encls.

wretched ... all the houses tumbling down in the rain ... At Ndoni they report our having killed a great number [in] the trenches.[1]

The following year another naval expedition again razed the 'hostile villages' and intervened in the trade relationships of the Niger Ibo states.[2]

But in the late 1870s, relationships between the trading firms and the Ibo states continued to deteriorate. Missionaries complained of the growing insecurity of life on the Niger, and the 'difficulties, trials and oppositions' they met.[3] Trading factories were attacked at Oko, Alenso and Osomari,[4] and the people of Asaba, while not going to these lengths, felt equally dissatisfied with their newly established factory, which they felt treated them unfairly.[5]

In late 1879, the Niger firms amalgamated, and the United African Company which resulted, with David McIntosh as its chief agent, was soon in a state of undeclared war with the states it traded with. As a missionary wrote of McIntosh,

He is at war with the people of Atani ... because they did not like to trade with him—He has also killed a cow belonging to the Asaba people, and ... if they do not take it easily he might also blockade the place as I have heard he *has* threatened ... The violence on the river is awful—and where it will all end I do not know.[6]

Just as it was Onitsha which had profited most from European trade, it was Onitsha which was to suffer most severely by European violence. The sack of Onitsha in 1879, and the blockade which followed it, followed a familiar pattern. The object of the attack was explicitly stated—to coerce the people of the state, and through the spectacle of their coercion, the other peoples on the river. As so often in the history of the conquest of Iboland—and of the rest of Africa— the use of violence affected diplomatic relations in ever widening ripples. It was intended that 'salutary displays of superior force'

[1] F.O. 84/1455, Croft to MacKellar, 24 August 1876 (copied extracts), encl. in McKellar to F.O., 14 September 1876.
[2] F.O. 84/1487, Tait to Derby, 27 August 1877.
[3] C.M.S. CA3/04, Buck to Crowther, 23 December 1878.
[4] *Ibid.*
[5] C.M.S. G3/A3/1881/103, ii. Deposition by Phillips.
[6] C.M.S. G3/A3/1880, Perry to D. C. Crowther, 3 December 1880.

should coerce other states, by showing them the irresistible nature of European military technology, and the uselessness of resistance. And, as before and after on the river, the British government gave its military support to British traders. As a Foreign Office official minuted:

> Where there is money to be made our Merchants will be certain to intrude themselves, and it is all very well to say that they will not be protected, but the fact is that if they establish a lucrative trade Public Opinion in this Country practically compells us to protect them.[1]

Protection being, of course, a euphemism for aggression.

In 1879, in response to traders requests, Acting Consul Easton— 'a very young man'—bombarded Onitsha Wharf from a gunboat, the gunboat standing off safely in mid-stream. Then both the waterside and the inland town were razed, together with the king's palace and its defending walls, by a party armed with a Gatling and with rocket equipment. It destroyed 'property in palm oil, crops, etc to a very large amount'.[2] The sack was only a beginning, for the United African Company manned a blockade, and continued making unofficial attacks on the town—duly concealed from the authorities at home—until the missionaries, who had originally supported both the traders and the sack, were moved to indignant protest.[3] The state of hostility thus created, with its intermittent blockades, was to last until the end of the Royal Niger Company's rule. In the long run, Onitsha was to have a great future as a market centre. In the short run, the gains of the *enu oyibo* had proved illusory.

Aboh, which had waited so long for its trading post, was soon to have the same experience. In 1883, after a trade dispute which led to an attack on a European trader, the town was razed. Again, the intention was to coerce other polities by example: 'The late expedition . . . appears to have had a salutary effect in the river—in plainer English, to have established a funk.'[4]

By 1885, the missionary and trading presence on the Niger was

---

[1] F.O. 84/1455, memo by W. H. W(ylde), 14 November 1876, on McKellar to F.O., 14 September 1876.

[2] The documents relating to the sack of Onitsha can be found in F.O. 403/16 (F.O.C.P.).

[3] C.M.S. CA3/04, Bishop Crowther to Hutchinson, 5 January 1880.

[4] F.O. 403/31 (F.O.C.P.), Rear-Admiral Salmon to Admiralty, 10 March 1884.

nearly thirty years old. As we have seen, the missionary impact had proved negligible, whether judged by the number of converts, or by the impact on Ibo societies in their totality. The advent of traders had brought an increase in consumer goods, but the gains were outweighed by the violence and destruction which so often accompanied them. For the Niger Ibo peoples, the middle years of the nineteenth century were an Age of Anxiety, a time of social malaise reflected in many aspects of life, such as the increase in witchcraft trials, and human sacrifice. Some individuals, and, temporarily, some states, profited by the changes, but taken collectively, the riverain peoples would have echoed the summing up of their northern neighbour, the ruler of Igala:

> He . . . complains bitterly that when he commenced dealings with the white men he had hoped to 'become fat' but now he had 'shrunk up and become dry'.[1]

The last two chapters of this study have dealt with the advance of alien influences on the frontiers of Iboland. How much, if at all, did these developments affect the Ibo peoples of the interior? Members of the northern Ibo groups, such as the Elugu and Abaja, often visited Onitsha for purposes of trade, and carried back reports of the new developments to their inland homes. In the first year of missionary work at Onitsha, a missionary visited Nsube, where he was told that 'They had long *heard* of *Oibo*, but to-day they were satisfied with what they have *seen*.' Here he met people from further in the interior, who were asked to tell their neighbours 'of British love to them'.[2] In the years that followed, people from the Nri-Awka area often visited Onitsha, and, more rarely, so did men from as far afield as Aro and Isuama.[3] But these periodic visits did not influence their way of life. Similarly, craftsmen and specialists from the Nri-Awka area sometimes travelled as far as the Delta.[4] Waddell met one of these itinerant blacksmiths on the Cross River in 1850.[5]

The peoples of the Ibo interior knew, probably with some precision, the nature of the alien presence on their borders. But with the

---

[1] F.O. 84/2109, MacDonald, 'Report on the Administration of the Niger Company's Territories', received at F.O. 9 January 1890, ch. I.
[2] *The Gospel on the Banks of the Niger*, III, 304.
[3] *Ibid.*, 259. C.M.S. CA3/04, Bishop Crowther to Hutchinson, 1 June 1880.
[4] C.M.S. CA3/04, Crowther, 'A charge delivered at Onitsha', 1874.
[5] Waddell, p. 468.

exception of the palm oil trade, and the influx of consumer goods it brought, their lives were unaffected.[1] We can only surmise as to whether they shared the prescience of the northern Emirs who warned the Anglophile ruler of Nupe in 1859 that the British are 'a very dangerous and encroaching nation'.[2] The spread of alien influence, and later, authority, was a slowly moving tide. A few years later, this tide was to engulf them.

[1] Cf. C.M.S. CA3/030, Perry to [Crowther], 16 September 1872.
[2] Quoted in Ifemesia, p. 480.

8 · Alien Government: The Niger under Chartered Company Rule, 1886–1899

'We should naturally fear, at least a temptation to unjust dealing, if a cat were called in as adjudicator and ruler over a community of mice.'
—Anon. pamphlet, *A West African Monopoly* (n.d., but 1888).

From 1886 to the end of 1899, the Niger regions were ruled by a company of merchants, the system which Adam Smith, thinking of the experience of another continent, called 'the worst of all governments for any country whatever'.[1] Chartered Company rule is the type of government which reveals most clearly the economic face of imperialism. Goldie sought and obtained a Charter for his company so that he could exclude commercial rivals, by the manipulation of tariffs, and force the Niger peoples to trade on his own terms, by the exercise of the illegal but highly effective monopoly he obtained in this way. The British government granted the Charter, because it offered a classic solution to its problems in the area in the mid 1880s. It enabled them to exclude other European colonizing powers, by creating at least a façade of effective administration, and did this at the minimum responsibility and cost to the British tax payer. So well did it serve their purposes, that Foreign Office officials defended Goldie's régime, in the face of a rising tide of criticism at home and abroad, so that it survived unscathed for thirteen and a half years.

There is a lack of adequate documentation on the Company's rule in those years. Its servants bound themselves to silence, with a bond of a thousand pounds, a bond which, quite rightly, troubled Lugard by its sinister overtones.[2] Members of the C.M.S. were silenced by a network of common interests and benefits received, though their

---

[1] Adam Smith, *The Wealth of Nations* (5th edn., London, 1930), II, 72.
[2] R. H. Lugard Papers, MSS. Br. Emp. s. 57, fo. 32, Lugard to Goldie, 3 July 1894.

silence became increasingly troubled as the years went by.[1] Of the two Catholic missions which established themselves on the Niger in the 'eighties, one, the Society of African Missions, invited to Asaba by Company officials, was similarly inhibited. The Holy Ghost Fathers, on the other hand, had a history of disagreements with the Company, and described it with a rancour which is equally unconducive to the recovery of historical truth. Much of the other material on the Company comes either from its commercial rivals, both African and European, or from the officials of the neighbouring Oil Rivers Protectorate—the latter exasperated by the squabbles over boundaries and jurisdiction so typical of the early phases of colonial rule. Nevertheless, from these biased and sometimes conflicting sources, it is possible to distil the answers to the key questions—how much authority did the Company really exercise on the lower Niger, and how did this authority affect the lives of the African peoples concerned?

As with any colonial government, the answer lies partly in a consideration of the type of men involved. Goldie himself ruled policies from London with an iron hand. He wrote much later, 'I evidently had no notion how afraid of *me* (G.T.G.) they all were out there.'[2] Goldie always displayed a contempt for Africans, and disregard for their interests or even lives, which were, as the Foreign Office pointed out on one occasion, the worst possible qualification for ruling a region of Africa.[3]

The administration on the Niger combined commercial and political functions in the same individuals. There were two Agents General in the period. The first was McIntosh, whose 'war' on the lower Niger we have noted, who retired in 1888, and the second Flint, 'as *hard* as his name'—who succeeded him.[4] In all, the Company employed about forty Europeans. British soldiers and Protectorate officials tended to despise them for their low social origins and lack

[1] Dobinson, *Letters*, pp. 51 and 68–9; C.M.S. G3/A3/1889/50, Robinson to C.M.S., 17 May 1889 (original missing, summary in Precis Book), and G3/A3/1897/79, Proctor to Baylis, 25 June 1897.

[2] R.H. Royal Niger Company Papers, Vol. 18, MSS. Afr. s. 100*, Goldie to Scarbrough, 3 December 1924.

[3] F.O. 403/122 (F.O.C.P.), F.O. to Royal Niger Company, 26 July 1889.

[4] R.H., Royal Niger Company Papers, Vol. 18, MSS. Afr. s. 100*, Goldie to Scarbrough, 3 December 1924. Cf. G. L. Baker, 'Research Notes on the Royal Niger Company—Its Predecessors and Successors', *Journal of the Historical Society of Nigeria* (December 1960), p. 156.

of formal education.[1] One does not need to subscribe to the nine-teenth-century delusion that a middle-class origin and education were qualifications for ruling whole peoples in other lands, to recognize their peculiar inadequacies. Goldie admitted few criticisms of his Company, but he was always ready to accept the shortcomings of his staff. 'It is difficult to obtain the highest class of men to serve for any length of time in such unhealthy regions.'[2]

Despite Goldie's dislike of Africans, the vast bulk of the Company's work was performed by them. There were only forty Europeans in a total staff of fifteen hundred.[3] The trading operations were carried out by Africans—by men from Sierra Leone in the main—who were forbidden to bring their wives and families with them.[4] The manual labour of loading and unloading casks was performed by men from Brass, Liberia or the Gold Coast.[5] Chartered Company rule offered almost no employment opportunities to the local people themselves, except for a few who worked as domestic servants or gardeners.[6]

The Company's army, which played a vital role in maintaining the authority of an increasingly unpopular régime, depended equally on African agency. Of a total of 421 soldiers in 1889, five were Europeans, and the rest Africans from Hausaland, Yorubaland and the Gold Coast. Asaba oral traditions preserve the memory of their depreda-tions, and a contemporary called them 'quite a scallywag brigade'.[7]

Despite its numerous personnel and its standing army, the main impression one has of the Company's régime is of the limitations of its power. Its influence was confined to the borders of the river. A missionary wrote in 1897:

---

[1] F.O. 403/76 (F.O.C.P.), P. Anderson, 'Notes and Considerations respecting the Present Position of the Royal Niger Company'; *Diary of Captain the Hon. Richard Fitzroy Somerset ... Feb. 5, 1898–Feb. 19, 1899* (privately printed), p. 162.

[2] R.H., MS. Br. Emp. s. 58, Transcript of interview with Goldie by L. Darwin, 15 March 1899. But for exceptions, cf. p. 119 below.

[3] F.O. 403/76 (F.O.C.P.), memo. encl. in Goldie to F.O., 20 August 1888; F.O. 84/1879, Aberdare to Granville, 13 February 1885.

[4] F.O. 403/76 (F.O.C.P.), memo. encl. in Goldie to F.O., 20 August 1888; C.M.S. G3/A3/1893/52, memo. of interview between Goldie and C.M.S. officials, 26 May 1893.

[5] F.O. 403/76 (F.O.C.P.), memo. encl. in Goldie to F.O., 20 August 1888.

[6] Asaba oral tradition. Cf. 'A Remarkable Conversion', *The African Missionary* (1925), p. 13.

[7] F.O. 84/2109, MacDonald Report, ch. XI; C.O. 520/3, Moor to Antrobus (private), 17 November 1900.

It is hardly realised in England how very slight the control of the RNC is over the interior districts. Practically so far as we are concerned, it is nil five miles from the river. The local officials of the RNC do not as a rule attempt any interference with the customs & laws of the people situated on the R. bank.[1]

Even on the lower Niger, some areas, such as Anam, were never visited by Company officials,[2] and most states experienced its influence only in the sphere of trade relations, and in the bouts of periodic violence which these relations engendered. It was probably only in Asaba that the Company's rule made a major impact on daily life.

The Company's practical monopoly had an immediate impact on the balance of trade. Inevitably, Goldie used the power he thus acquired to reduce the price paid to the Niger peoples for their products, and to adulterate the quality of what was imported in exchange. As the Liverpool Chamber of Commerce put it in 1897:

> There is no competition amongst buyers for export on the river. The Company is the only such buyer, and pays its own price for produce, . . . The natives of Nigeria are further subject to the will of the Company in respect of the goods received against produce. The Company import what manufactured goods they choose, and practically impose them upon the native, who has a very limited and inferior class of articles from which to select, . . .[3]

This is the voice of Goldie's rivals, but there is much corroboratory evidence, and Goldie himself admitted the charge. He regarded it, however, as trivial, for those affected were Africans, whose difficulties were unlikely to trouble 'the most earnest negrophile'.[4]

The evidence suggests that the Niger peoples responded to the iron hand of monopoly by producing less for export, and by devoting themselves to agricultural production for their own needs.[5] This

---

[1] C.M.S. G3/A3/1897/82, Bennett to Baylis, 20 July 1897; cf. *Niger and Yoruba Notes* (1900), p. 93, and F.O. 2/122, Moor to Hill (private), 13 June 1897.

[2] N.A.I. C.S.O. 26/48 (File 29576), Stone, 'Report on Anam Villages', 1934.

[3] F.O. 403/249 (F.O.C.P.), Liverpool Chamber of Commerce to Salisbury, 12 August 1897.

[4] F.O. 403/71 (F.O.C.P.), Goldie to Salisbury, 8 August 1885.

[5] Cf. F.O. 403/122, Merchants of Lagos to Moloney, 12 March 1889. F.O. 2/83, MacDonald to Hill, 26 March 1895. But cf. F.O. 84/2109, MacDonald Report, ch. 8, for a different view.

accords well with experience elsewhere in Africa in the colonial period, when the readiness of the people to grow cash crops and produce other goods for export has been always directly proportionate to the profits of the enterprise. A more important question than the total volume of exports, at least to the historian of the Ibo people, however, is the effect which this deteriorating balance of trade had on the African states concerned.

A number of observers claimed that the Niger Ibo states were ruined by the change. MacDonald wrote that their people 'must either take it [the Company's prices] or starve'. A Holy Ghost Father, writing in retrospect in 1902, claimed that the Company had ruined the Niger, drained away its products, and destroyed the first shoots of civilization. Chiefs in the Oguta area are reported to have opposed the establishment of a Company factory there, with the words, 'We have heard you trade in the Niger at Egue [Aboh] and other places, and that those countries are now ruined and so we fear.'[1]

But the extent to which a state could be 'ruined' in this way depended on the extent to which it relied on trade for its livelihood. The people of Brass, surrounded by unproductive swamps, were ruined indeed, and driven by their destitution to a gallant if hopeless war. On the Niger, changes in trade could lead to a relative economic decline. But the Niger Ibo states were still basically self-sufficient. Even Onitsha, where trade was most developed, responded with equanimity to the Company's long blockade. When a missionary was asked if the people had made many complaints, 'he said not from the mass of the people who had quietly gone back to their original occupation viz: Agriculture'.[2]

The changing terms of trade affected the Niger Ibo states much less than the violence by which the Company maintained its rule, and its economic interests. Onitsha suffered less from its blockades—even when these cut her off from trade with other African states[3]—than from violence of this kind.[4] And in the face of the enormous disparity in military resources, no real reprisals were possible—except, for a

[1] F.O. 2/83, MacDonald to Hill, 26 March 1895; C.S.Sp. 191/5/II, account by Lejeune, 1902; F.O. 84/1881, Hewett, 'Substance of statement made by Idu Chiefs', 26 December 1886.
[2] F.O. 84/2109, MacDonald Report, ch. I.
[3] C.M.S. F4/7, Journal of G. Wilmot Brooke, 1 July 1889, fo. 110.
[4] See, for example, C.S.Sp., *Bulletin de la Congregation*, XVIII, p. 416, Report, September 1894–November 1896.

time, the symbolic rejection of all things European.[1] A missionary left a graphic description of the consequences which ensued when the people of Aguleri attacked a factory in the course of a trade dispute—three villages were sacked, and twelve leading citizens taken as hostages.[2] And the Niger peoples were coerced not only in their own persons, but in those of their children. It was standard practice to take the sons of 'obnoxious chiefs' as hostages, the boys concerned being made to work as domestic servants.[3]

When the Company began its second blockade of Onitsha, in 1885, it shifted its installations a little further to the south, creating a commercial headquarters on the banks of the Niger, near the inland town of Obosi. The change brought little profit to its people. In 1889, the town, which had been described by an Englishman several months earlier as 'the most lovely paradise I have ever seen' was sacked, and its farms destroyed. The yams in the ground—necessary for food and seed—were dug up. The Obosi were offered peace, but refused the concessions demanded of them, and continued to resist. They were, said a missionary, 'brave but ignorant savages'.[4]

But it was the little state of Asaba, selected as the site for the Company's administrative headquarters, which experienced the most traumatic changes. In 1882, an observer, enchanted with the beauty of Asaba's urban landscape, had paid tribute to the quality of her life: 'one feels . . . he is in the midst of a free people in a free country'.[5] Suddenly she was invaded by what was in effect an army of occupation. The Company created a town within a town, surrounded by an iron railing nine feet high. 'The whole establishment (not counting "Soldier town") covers an area of 40 acres . . .' Soldiers' town itself comprised three hundred houses.[6] Asaba oral tradition vividly mirrors the trials of life in a garrison town:

> They constituted a great menace to Asaba people, catching goats, fowls and cows at will for their food and pleasure, molesting the

---

[1] C.M.S. G3/A3/1887/101, Bishop Crowther to C.M.S., 5 August 1887.
[2] C.S.Sp., *Bulletin de la Congregation*, XVII, p. 425, Report, March 1892–September 1894.
[3] Mockler-Ferryman, p. 251.
[4] C.M.S. F4/7, Journal of G. Wilmot Brooke, 2 July 1889, fo. 112; G3/A3/1889/170, Johnson to Lang, 16 November 1889; G3/A3/1890/44, Johnson to Lang, 10 February 1890.
[5] *The Church Missionary Intelligencer* (September 1882), p. 547.
[6] F.O. 84/2109, MacDonald Report, ch. 10. Cf. Mockler-Ferryman, pp. 26–7.

inhabitants by invading their farms and stealing their property and sometimes going to the extent of violating by force the chastity of a woman going to the river Niger for water. . . . The people of Asaba were constantly molested and earned no rest both night and day until the soldiers . . . moved away from Asaba.[1]

In 1888, the Company attacked Asaba, destroying half of it. The overt reason for this—as for the attack on Obosi—was to abolish human sacrifice. In Asaba, at least, this may well have been true. The attack was due to the initiative of Sir James Marshall, the Company's Chief Justice, a devout convert to Catholicism, and of Captain Harper, the head of the Constabulary and the son of a Manchester canon— both of whom displayed that religious and humanitarian zeal in which Goldie was so signally lacking.[2] The results, indeed, were good —it abolished a practice which had for some time past been becoming increasingly distasteful to the people of Asaba themselves,[3] and released her large slave community from the shadow under which they had lived for so long.

But the Company's actions elsewhere show little trace of motivation of this kind. The attack on Obosi was clearly designed to protect its commercial installations, and, when some years later, a missionary urged the Company to send an expedition to the town to discourage the practice of abandoning certain babies, whose births infringed taboos, he learnt that 'The R.N.C. are not willing to do anything that might possibly lead to an expedition, on the ground that being a commercial venture, nothing that might prejudice their dividend must be at all attempted.' Consequently, 'Mr. Flint on his arrival felt unable to do anything further than offer the Obosi people good advice.'[4] The wars that the Company fought were designed to strengthen her power, and further her economic interests.

The Company did nothing to develop the areas which it ruled. Its general policy was to leave the existing society unchanged, unless its economic interests were directly involved. It built no schools or hospitals, no railways or roads. It did attempt, by establishing

---

[1] Asaba oral tradition: informant, F. O. Isichei.

[2] C.M.S. G3/A3/1887/117, Johnson to Lang, 20 September 1887, and 1888/77, Johnson to Lang, 5 July 1888.

[3] C.M.S. CA3/031, Phillips to Bishop Crowther, 10 September 1879. *The Church Missionary Intelligencer* (September 1882), p. 547.

[4] C.M.S. G3/A3/1899/52, Bennett to Bayliss, 8 February 1899; and 1899/53, memo. by Bennett on Obosi.

botanical gardens, to extend the range of products available for export. But the attempt failed, partly because the Company's employees lacked the local people's expert knowledge of tropical agriculture, and partly because the latter sabotaged these schemes, because they feared, with considerable insight, that the development of new cash crops would lead to the creation of a plantation economy, where they would be cast for the role of labourers.[1]

The first encounter of the Niger peoples with colonialism was an inauspicious one. It meant the systematic subordination of their interests to the economic interests of a foreign power. It meant the repeated experience of the violence by which this foreign power maintained its authority. And if the Company's total impact was limited, by the nature of its own economic purposes, and by the extent of its power, where it existed, it was a destructive one. Nor was there a positive side, in education, or any other form of 'development'.

At its worst, Company rule displayed a barbaric brutality. Bishop Crowther described its personnel as 'Cruel and overbearing to the Natives; cruel to their native clerks.'[2] When a party of labourers were massacred by two of the Company's European employees, they not only escaped punishment, but continued on in its service. One, at least, went on to a highly successful career.[3] The Brassmen, who unlike the other Niger peoples, speak in the records in their own voice, complained:

> The ill treatments of the Niger Company is very bad . . . Our boys fired, killed, and plundered, and even the innocent provisions sellers were captured and killed likewise . . . They fired, kill and plundered the fishermen, and even the innocent women were caught, stripped naked, and painted with coal tar.[4]

Officials in the nearby Oil Rivers Protectorate claimed that these things were peculiar to the Company, and that there was a difference between 'Queen man' and 'Mackintosh man' of which the Niger

---

[1] Isichei, 'Asaba to 1885', p. 425. Cf. F.O. 84/2109, MacDonald Report, chs. 9 and 10; Mockler-Ferryman, pp. 17 and 26. Cf. Dobinson, *Letters*, pp. 216–17.

[2] C.M.S. CA3/04, Bishop Crowther to Hutchinson, 18 June 1879.

[3] Cf. Flint, pp. 147–9.

[4] F.O. 403/215 (F.O.C.P.), King and Chiefs of Brass to MacDonald, 4 February 1895.

peoples were well aware.[1] The worst of the Company's atrocities have few parallels in neighbouring administrations. Yet its amalgam of violence, economic exploitation and *immobilisme* perhaps reveal, albeit with the exaggerations of caricature, the face of colonial government everywhere.

There is no question as to how the Niger peoples regarded the experience. Their 'unrest' and 'discontent' are constantly recurring leitmotifs in the records of these years. As a missionary noted:

... how fully they believe that the White Traders are untrustworthy and that their country would be richer if all the white men were banished.[2]

[1] F.O. 84/1882, memo. by Johnson on the British Protectorate of the Oil Rivers, 26 July 1888.
[2] C.M.S. G3/A3/1887/109, Robinson to Lang, 14 September 1887.

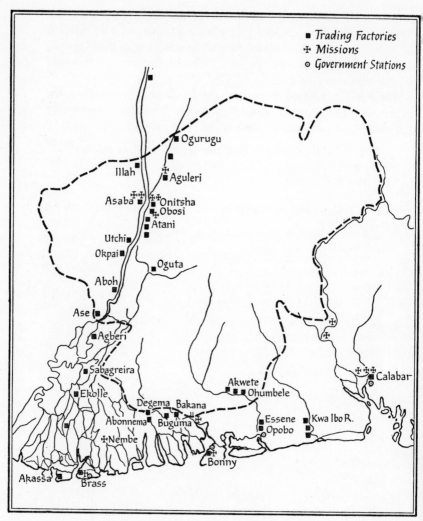

6 Patterns of Moving Frontiers—1891

9 · Moving Frontiers: The Invasion of Iboland, to 1901

Azu kalia, azu oweli, azu nue.
(When a fish is larger than another fish, it swallows it.)
—Ibo proverb.

In the last three chapters we have studied the changes which affected the Niger area of Iboland in the last two-thirds of the nineteenth century. One aspect of these changes—missionary activity in the period of Chartered Company rule—forms a theme of a later chapter. Now we must turn to the process of foreign encroachment on another frontier of Iboland—the spread of British political power from the Delta.

The British established a Protectorate in the Niger Delta for the same reason that they granted a Charter to the Royal Niger Company. They needed to establish some form of government there, to prevent other European powers from doing so. It was, as Granville put it in 1884, '... the scheme ... for keeping the French away from the Niger & Oil Rivers'.[1] This was felt to be necessary, because it was feared that another colonial power would wreck British trading interests in the area by imposing differential tariffs. The unquestioned postulate behind the voluminous Foreign Office and Colonial Office correspondence on the subject is that 'trade is our sole object in West Africa'.[2]

Considerations of this kind conflicted with a reluctance to assume the expense and responsibility of West African colonies—a reluctance well summed up in Kimberley's well-known memorandum on the proposal to annex the Cameroons.[3] The ideal solution might seem to have been, as on the Niger, Chartered Company rule. This proved impossible, because of the dissensions of the merchants concerned,

---

[1] F.O. 84/1682, Draft, G[ranville] to Aberdare, 6 February 1884.
[2] F.O. 2/178, memo. by F.B.[ertie], 25 March 1898.
[3] F.O. 84/1654, memo. by K[imberley], 6 April 1882.

and the Niger Company's growing unpopularity. Instead, the area was declared and for some years remained a Protectorate, under the Foreign Office.

In 1884, the then Consul, Hewett, reached the Delta with quantities of treaty forms. These treaties, signed by the local rulers, were thought to give a legal justification for British power there. This legal justification was constructed on a basis of duplicity and deceit. One example of this must suffice—the assurance given to Ja Ja, two years before he was kidnapped and deported, that

> ... with reference to the word 'Protectorate' as used in the proposed Treaty, the Queen does not want to take your country or your markets; but at the same time she undertakes to extend her gracious power and protection, which will leave your country still under your Government.[1]

Until 1890, however, the nature of the British presence in the Delta remained essentially as it had been before—a Consul, supported from time to time by 'the moral authority of a man of war'. But if the Consul's resources remained the same, his policies changed dramatically. Johnston, who served as Vice Consul and Acting Consul in the area from 1885 to 1888, was a young man, who hoped to advance his career by a dramatic achievement. He found an ally in the trader community, who, faced with the decline of palm oil prices in Europe, hoped to recoup themselves by cutting out the middlemen profits in the Delta. Johnston and the traders soon developed an attitude of embattled hostility to the great middleman king, Ja Ja. The overthrow of Ja Ja seemed to offer Johnston the spectacular achievement he sought, and a gateway to the Ibo interior. To the traders, his fall seemed to presage an era of direct trade with Iboland, and consequently of greater profits.

Ja Ja, like other African kings, placed an excessive confidence in the readiness of the British to abide by their own legal forms. He sent letters and a deputation to London, pointing out the rights guaranteed him by successive treaties. He fell, not in combat, but through treachery. In September, 1887, Johnston lured him on to a gunboat with a promise of safe conduct, then kidnapped and deported him.

[1] F.O. 403/74 (F.O.C.P.), Hewett to Ja Ja, 1 July 1885, encl. in C.O. to F.O., 19 March 1888. For a similar promise to Brass, see F.O. 2/100, Hewett to Furlonger, 17 July 1884 (copy).

The greatest Ibo of his time was to die in a distant exile. It is only just to record that Salisbury recognized the injustice of the action, though he did not remedy it, and that Johnston effectively ruined his own career by it.

The kidnapping of Ja Ja had a profound effect on the British image in the Ibo interior. It seemed a damning demonstration of British perfidy. Nine years later, its psychological effects remained:

> The 'Consul' [wrote a later Commissioner and Consul General] has been so grossly misrepresented in the past by European traders, native middlemen, and others, to serve their own ends, that his coming is greatly feared by the natives of the interior . . . On all the waterways the Consul has been distrusted . . . for the story of King Ja-Ja's capture, as told by the Opobo-men, spread all over the country . . .[1]

One can only surmise the pattern which events would have followed if Ja Ja had retained his freedom. He had already shown his ability to create a state *ex nihilo*, and to unite small disunited polities by the use of religious symbolism—

> We have a very old custom of sending our war canoes up to Eboe for the purpose of making 'Ju Ju', which is simply the celebration of our forefathers' lives and deaths.[2]

At the time of his capture he was in the process of transferring part of his resources to the Ibo interior. Johnston, with justice, feared the role he might have played there, as a focus of opposition to the spread of British rule.[3] He continued to fear his influence when he was a distant prisoner on the Gold Coast.[4] The British presence in the Delta was not thought to be secure from Ja Ja until he was exiled to the West Indies—like so many of his Ibo fellow countrymen in the past.

For the European traders, the dream of enrichment through direct trade with Iboland proved a mirage. In an initial access of optimism, they rushed to Ja Ja's markets,[5] but in the trade war with Opobo

---

[1] F.O. 2/101, Moor to F.O., 14 June 1896.
[2] F.O. 403/73 (F.O.C.P.), Ja Ja to Salisbury, 5 May 1887.
[3] F.O. 84/1828, Johnston to Salisbury, 24 September 1887.
[4] F.O. 403/74 (F.O.C.P.), Johnston to Salisbury, 2 December 1887.
[5] This short-lived advance is marked on the map, 'Patterns of Moving Frontiers 1891'.

which followed, they proved ineffective competitors. Their inexperienced European personnel could not match African traders' accumulated commercial expertise, their knowledge of local customs and languages, and their goodwill. As early as 1890 it was admitted that 'The merchants made a great mistake in going to the markets' and by 1893, the attempt had been given up.[1] They had burnt their fingers severely, and after 1900 we have the curious spectacle of a colonial government exhorting a reluctant trader community to seize the new opportunities created by the extension of colonial rule.[2]

In 1891, the nature of the British presence in the Delta changed. In 1889, Major Claude MacDonald had made two separate trips to Nigeria to report on, respectively, the best form of government for the Delta, and the impact of the Niger Company's rule. In the Delta, the local rulers, offered a Hobson's choice between colonial government and Chartered Company rule, chose the former. MacDonald was selected to implement his own report. He was to be the only nineteenth-century Consul to make service in the Delta a stepping-stone to a successful subsequent career.

In July, 1891, he returned to the Delta as 'Commissioner and Consul General' over a unit called the Oil Rivers Protectorate—rechristened the Niger Coast Protectorate in 1893. It was in fact, though not in name, a colonial administration, possessing the essential elements of government—a regular staff, a regular source of income (derived from customs) and a standing army. The European staff numbered thirteen at first, but expanded rapidly, numbering a hundred by 1897, when permanent African staff numbered two hundred.

The Protectorate staff came from backgrounds euphemistically described as varied. Some, like MacDonald himself, were soldiers, discontented with the slow promotion of a peace-time army. Others came from service in various African campaigns—the end of the Boer War was to mean a large accession. Cattle ranching in Queensland, and tea planting in Ceylon, were other backgrounds thought

---

[1] F.O. 2/51, Armstrong to MacDonald, 10 July 1893, encl. in MacDonald to F.O., 2 September 1893. F.O. 403/149 (F.O.C.P.), Neville to Elder Dempster & Co., 4 January 1891.

[2] C.O. 520/15, Moor to C.O., 25 August 1902. Cf. *The West African Mail* (11 September 1903), p. 648.

suitable for ruling whole peoples, at least in Africa.[1] Some were friends and relatives of MacDonald, or of Jephson, for a time his representative in London. Others were recommended by army friends, or serving members of staff.[2] The idea of selection by examination was entertained and discarded because 'in S. Nigeria . . . the number of *possible* candidates does not greatly exceed the number of vacancies'.[3] Those who joined the service of the Protectorate were attracted by the pay, and the prospect of six months' leave after every year's service, and the hope, seldom realized, of making it a stepping-stone to a career elsewhere.[4] Once there, under MacDonald's leadership, they rapidly developed a sense of enthusiasm and esprit de corps. Unfortunately this was rooted in a sense of infinite superiority to the peoples they sought to rule. As one astute observer wrote, the various groups who came to West Africa 'share little in common, but that of an indefinable dislike and contempt for that black man they come out to govern or exploit'.[5]

Like other colonial governments, they depended heavily on African agency. Their fewness of numbers, and their inability to speak the languages of the local people, gave their African collaborators a position of great importance. We shall discuss their role in a later section of this study. The military spread of British power in Iboland, depended, like the other facets of their rule, on Africans. The Protectorate's armed forces consisted of Hausas, Yorubas, and men from Lagos and the Gold Coast, armed with machine guns, rockets, and specially constructed rifles for bush fighting.[6]

MacDonald left the Protectorate for a diplomatic post in China, in 1896. During his period in Nigeria, the steady erosion of the

[1] C.O. 520/29, folios 107 ff., data on 1907 appointments. F.O. 84/2111, MacDonald to Anderson (private), 15 December 1891. W. R. Crocker, *Nigeria, A Critique of British Colonial Administration* (London, 1936), p. 199. Frank Hives and Gascoigne Lumley, *Ju-Ju and Justice in Nigeria* (Middlesex, 1940), p. 5 and cover.

[2] 'Nemo' [A. C. Douglas], *Niger Memories* (privately printed, n.d.), pp. 1 and 15. F.O. 2/51, MacDonald to F.O., 24 April 1893. C.O. 444/1, Moor to C.O., 23 June 1899.

[3] C.O. 520/45, memo. by C. S[trachey], 28 June 1904.

[4] Douglas, pp. 1–2. F.O. 403/171 (F.O.C.P.), 'Rules and Regulations for leave of absence and pensions'. Cf. C.O. 520/26, Egerton to Antrobus (private), 5 November 1904.

[5] Harris, pp. 122–3.

[6] F.O. 2/64, 'Report on the Administration of the Niger Coast Protectorate', 16 August 1894. Cf. F.O. 84/2194, Moor to MacDonald, 9 August 1892.

autonomy of the Delta peoples, begun under his predecessors, was continued—most spectacularly, in the overthrow of the Itsekiri trader prince Nana, in 1895—but there was little impact on Iboland. His officials made some exploring journeys in the interior, including some exploration of the southern fringes of Iboland. In 1892, Campbell, the Vice Consul at Bonny, went as far as Elele, some twenty-three miles inland from the cluster of villages into which Kalabari had divided.[1] But the ignorance of Iboland remained profound—as he put it, 'The regions north of Okrika, from whence the waters of the Bonny River come are as yet totally unknown . . . The part of this district which can be called *known* to the white man consists almost entirely of mangrove swamp.'[2] The reactions of the inland peoples, insofar as they are recorded, show a mixture of apprehension, and confidence that the British would not move far from the Delta. As the gifted Roger Casement observed of the Ibibio, 'The people . . . fear our coming and dislike it even more than they fear it.'[3]

Ralph Moor succeeded MacDonald, until his retirement in 1903. Moor's career in the Protectorate began and ended in mystery. He joined the Protectorate, from the Royal Irish Constabulary, at his own expense, in 1891,[4] and committed suicide a few years after his retirement. Moor's period of power coincided with a new expansionist military policy. This was only secondarily the result of differences of personality. It was necessary to consolidate the base in the Delta before expansion was possible. But all colonial polities tend to expand, until they reach the boundary of another colonial jurisdiction. In neither Africa nor India were colonial rulers content to retain a common boundary with a free people. Moor stated this explicitly:

> The movement of administration in this country must, to render it effective, be always forward. It is impossible to remain stationary, and any attempt to do so without advance, must . . . result in a gradual drifting back.[5]

[1] F.O. 84/2194, Campbell to MacDonald, 22 February 1892, encl. in MacDonald to Salisbury, 15 March 1892. Cf. the similar journeys made by Gallwey to Benin and in Urhoboland, and by Casement in Ibibioland.
[2] F.O. 2/51, Campbell, 'Report on the Bonny District', 5 July 1892.
[3] F.O. 2/64, Casement to Acting Consul General, 4 July 1894.
[4] F.O. 84/2111, MacDonald to F.O., 22 May 1891.
[5] F.O. 403/267 (F.O.C.P.), Moor to F.O., 30 November 1898.

The foundations for this forward movement were laid towards the end of MacDonald's régime, in 1894, when a government station was established at Akwete, on the Imo River,[1] and when Moor, as Acting Consul General, startled the Foreign Office with a request for five hundred blank treaty forms, for the benefit of 'the large Ibo tribe'.[2]

The expeditions of the mid nineties took place in two main areas—the Cross River, and the Imo River. The Cross River expeditions—not unconnected with the fact that the Consul General headquarters were at Calabar, near the river's mouth—affected the Ibo people only marginally.[3] A Foreign Office official minuted grimly—though official disquiet never led to official action—'It is unfortunate that most of the Expeditions are marked by shelling and burning.'[4]

The other main areas involved were the Ibo oil markets on the lower, navigable stretches of the Imo River. In 1896, a number of small Ibo towns in the area were attacked and sacked. The incident—trivial in the whole context of Ibo history—illustrates several characteristics of the wars of expansion of these years. The towns were raided in conjunction with traders from Opobo and Bonny, who by depicting their trade rivals as 'disaffected' persuaded the British to deal them a crushing blow. This manipulation of the colonial power, by parties in internal African conflicts, which were not understood by colonial officials, has many parallels both in West and East Africa. On this occasion, the Opobo and Bonny men went further—they succeeded in raiding for slaves under the eyes of the British, and with their acquiescence.[5] This attack, too, shows us the gulf in communication which lies at the heart of the colonial situation, and occasions many of its injustices. After their town had been burnt and looted, the people concerned complained: 'The white man, much less the Consul, has never visited us ... We seize for debt like all the other towns. We have never been told that it was wrong to harbour slaves.' And their neighbours made exactly the same point in

[1] It was, however, visited only occasionally. F.O. 403/200 (F.O.C.P.), Report on the Administration of the Niger Coast Protectorate, 16 August 1894. F.O. 2/180, Niger Coast Protectorate Annual Report, 1897–8, 'Civil Establishment'.
[2] F.O. 2/64, Moor to F.O., 20 October 1894, and memo. by C.H.H.[ill], 19 November 1894.
[3] F.O. 2/84, Moor to F.O., 11 September 1895.
[4] F.O. 2/85, memo. by C.H.H.[ill] on MacDonald to F.O., 26 November 1895.
[5] F.O. 2/101, Moor to F.O., 6 May 1896, and encl. 2, Gallwey, 'Report on the Punitory Expedition to Obohia', 25 April 1896.

different words: '. . . the King wished to know what he and his people had done that the Government had made war on them.'[1]

But by the late 1890s, Europeans had still not set eyes on most of the towns of Iboland. Effectively, they were confined to the Delta and the Niger. Their 'punitive expeditions' in the Delta's immediate hinterland, and on the Cross River, did not establish any real control over the lives of the peoples concerned.[2] The weakness of the colonial power was convincingly demonstrated by the continued recalcitrance of Okrika, which was only twenty miles from the Vice Consulate at Bonny, and easily accessible by water.[3] Another case in point was the defiance of the people of Ibaa, who were reported as 'boasting publicly of the fact that they care nought for Government—and . . . say[ing] that if the whiteman goes there they will show him what they think of him'.[4]

In those years, these obscure wars in Iboland were overshadowed by more spectacular campaigns elsewhere—notably, by the overthrow of the ancient kingdom of Benin. But by 1897, it was evident that Moor had a systematic strategy for the conquest of southern Nigeria. He planned a pincer movement, beginning with campaigns on the Cross River, in the east, and in the areas to the west of the Niger Company's jurisdiction, so that Iboland could be invaded from three sides—the south, as before, and the west and the east.[5]

But the conquest of Iboland involved peculiar tactical difficulties. Its small polities could be overthrown with relative ease, but their conquest did not necessarily have significant effects. A town was defeated and sacked. It signed a treaty, paid a fine, rebuilt its houses, replanted its crops—and continued life as before. And there was still another score of similar towns to conquer, within a twenty-mile radius.

And there was another difficulty. The European officers of the Protectorate forces, and its officials—largely drawn from the army—came to Nigeria in search of wars, as a path to honours and

[1] *Ibid.*

[2] F.O. 2/180, Annual Report, Niger Coast Protectorate, 1897–8. Cf. C.O. 520/29, Egerton to C.O., 21 January 1905.

[3] F.O. 2/101, Moor to F.O., 24 June 1896.

[4] C.O. 520/13, Report by Acting District Commissioner, Degema, 12 December 1901.

[5] Cf. F.O. 2/185, Moor to Hill, 19 February 1899, and F.O. 2/179, memo. by Moor, 12 July 1898, on Gallwey to F.O., 2 June 1898.

promotion. Perhaps not all positively enjoyed active service, but it was obligatory to pretend they did—'These military displays naturally added to the interest of service on the Coast in those early days.'[1] But the glory to be obtained in war was naturally dependent on the power and resistance of the enemy, and the burning of villages was more likely to produce anxious memoranda from the Foreign Office than the desired medals and promotions. It was necessary therefore to discover a renowned and powerful enemy. Where none existed, it was necessary to invent one. Such were the origins of the Aro expedition of 1901–2.[2]

Europeans had known of the existence of the Arochuku oracle for at least half a century. As the British came into increasing contact with the states of Ibibioland and southern Iboland, they became increasingly aware of the importance of the Aro network—though they consistently misunderstood it. In the dispatches of the 'nineties, one can see the gradual evolution of an image of the Aro as the collective *eminence grise* of Iboland, as sinister 'jujumen' and slave dealers, indelibly opposed to European advance.[3] A myth developed, which described them as superior to all other Ibo, 'over whom they domineer with an iron hand concealed under the silken meshes of deep diplomacy'.[4] Sometimes we even have the suggestions that the British conquest of Iboland would deliver her people from Aro tyranny![5] By the late 'nineties, every act in Iboland and Ibibioland which was inimical to British interests was confidently ascribed to the nefarious influence of the Aro. They were even blamed for diminished oil production at distant Oguta, and the lack of palm kernels at Atani![6] It is difficult to know how far Moor and his officials believed all this, and how far it was fabricated for the benefit of the Foreign Office, to win approval for an elaborate and expensive expedition, and to enhance the glory of the subsequent victory.

Moor urged such an expedition from 1899 on, but it was not under-

---

[1] H. L. Gallwey, 'West Africa Fifty Years Ago', *Journal of the African Society* (1942), XL, p. 98.

[2] For another account of this expedition, cf. Anene, pp. 222 ff.

[3] Cf., for instance, A. G. Leonard, 'Notes of a Journey to Bende', *Journal of the Manchester Geographical Society* (1898), XIV, pp. 190–207.

[4] *Ibid.*, p. 207.

[5] Cf. F.O. 2/123, Niger Coast Protectorate Annual Report, 1896–7.

[6] C.O. 444/2, Moor to C.O., 9 September 1899. There are other examples in this dispatch.

taken until late 1901. In 1899, the Protectorate was transferred from the Foreign Office to the Colonial Office, and rechristened once more—this time, the Protectorate of Southern Nigeria. At the end of the year, the Niger Company's Charter was revoked, and its territories south of Idah incorporated into the Protectorate. In consequence, this was no longer bisected by another colonial jurisdiction. After the delays these administrative changes imposed, a further one was occasioned by the absence of troops in the Gold Coast, for the Ashanti campaign.[1]

Like other African wars, the campaign against the Aro, which finally took place between November 1901 and March 1902, depended on the assistance of Africans. The invading forces consisted of 74 European officers and 3,464 African soldiers and carriers.[2] In the casualty lists, though some Europeans were wounded, it was only Africans who died[3]—and the much larger numbers of Ibo dead are not, of course, recorded. The invaders were well armed, their equipment including the invariable and invaluable Maxims, which Hilaire Belloc, in an often quoted couplet, correctly diagnosed as the sovereign determinant of African affairs.

The campaign began with an attack on Arochuku itself, by four converging columns, and the oracle was destroyed by early December.[4] The main part of the campaign was still to come—for Arochuku, for all its ritual significance, was of no real strategic importance, and is situated in fact on the edge of Iboland. The main part of the campaign took place in the southern areas of Iboland, and in Ibibioland. Those of the Ibo people who bore its brunt—the southern Ngwa and Ikwerri—were those who had already come into contact with Europe, both indirectly, in their role of oil suppliers, and directly, in earlier campaigns. Some new areas of Iboland were visited—notably Owerri, previously unknown to the Europeans, but destined soon to be transformed in consequence of its selection as an administrative centre. But the original plan of traversing the more

---

[1] C.O. 520/14, Moor, 'Memo. concerning the Aro Expedition . . .', 24 April 1902.

[2] These figures are calculated from C.O. 520/14, Montanaro, 'Military Report on the Aro Expedition', p. 7. But for different figures, cf. p. 14 of this document, and C.O. 520/14, Montanaro to Moor, 5 April 1902.

[3] *Ibid.*, Montanaro, 'Military Report', p. 13.

[4] This brief account of the campaign is distilled from the detailed reports and dispatches in C.O. 520/10 and C.O. 520/14.

northerly areas of Iboland was not followed, and most of Iboland's polities remained unvisited, and, *a fortiori*, unconquered.

An Ibo historian has stated his conviction that the Aro expedition met with little resistance.[1] The Aro themselves were unaware of the role they had assumed in British eyes, and of the intended attack, and what resistance took place was local, and ineffective. This is a view which has some evidence to support it,[2] yet it seems that resistance, although small scale, was more resolute than has hitherto been acknowledged.

It is clear that the resistance which occurred was local and unpremeditated, and inspired not by the destruction of the oracle, or any sense of loyalty to the Aro, but from the threat to the immediate vicinity. Perhaps the southern Ibo were outraged, less by the threat to life, than by the destruction of property, by the destroyed villages and the looted yam barns, and especially by the destruction of guns. Twenty-five thousand rifles and cap guns were collected and destroyed during the campaign. They represented not only a means of self-defence, but one of Iboland's most important forms of capital accumulation. Their destruction showed in concrete and unequivocal terms, the meaning of invasion, and of the loss of sovereignty.[3]

Not all areas, of course, responded to invasion in the same way. Some warned by the fate of their neighbours, surrendered—or postponed their resistance to a more propitious time.[4] The external threat did not succeed in uniting these small states in a common resistance. Apart from the intrinsic difficulties of such an action, it must have seemed impossible to organize a strategy against well armed and fast moving columns, moving rapidly and apparently at random through the country, and imposing their obscurely understood and unreasonable imperatives. Yet resistance occurred, and its pattern illustrates the local nature, in Iboland, of the heart's affections. It seems that resistance was fiercest and most prolonged in the area north of Akwete—with its prior knowledge of the enemy. To preserve the memory of a moment of the campaign:

[1] Anene, pp. 232-3.
[2] Cf. Hives and Lumley, p. 22, and A. C. Douglas, pp. 79 ff.
[3] For gun destruction, cf. C.O. 520/14, Montanaro, 'Military Report', p. 13. The policy followed with regard to property is outlined in C.O. 520/13, Report no. 13 by the Commandant, Aro Field Force, 3 January 1902, encl. in Moor to C.O., 14 January 1902.
[4] Cf. pp. 138–142 below.

The enemy had prepared elaborate entrenchments parallel to the road and stockades across it. These trenches were from three to four feet deep, with head-cover provided by logs. Dense bush grew on either side of the path, but good scouting to the front and flanks discovered the trenches, and the enemy were invariably outflanked. The millimetre gun played on the stockades rendering them untenable. As the column advanced the enemy retired into walled compounds lying off the road, and these had to be assaulted in turn and taken at the point of the bayonet.[1]

And later in the war, in another part of Iboland further west:

The enemy as a rule employed sniping tactics only, but on the 12th February, when the column was marching from Elele to Ubele, the enemy made a determined effort to oppose the column's advance. On approaching the town of Ubele, both the Advance and the Rear Guards were simultaneously engaged, the former in fighting its way into the town whilst the latter was engaged in beating off the enemy pressing on the rear of the column. A large market place was eventually occupied, and the troops formed [a] square . . . The enemy made a determined attack on all sides of the square, advancing with great bravery, but were repulsed with heavy loss, suffering principally from the effect of Maxim and M/m gun fires.[2]

Nor should the fierce resistance of the neighbouring Ibibio—which did much to create the reputation for savagery and ferocity they enjoyed for a time—be forgotten.

But as in other wars at other times, 'great bravery' was unequally matched with a machine gun.

[1] C.O. 520/14, Montanaro, 'Military Report', p. 13.
[2] *Ibid.*, p. 11.

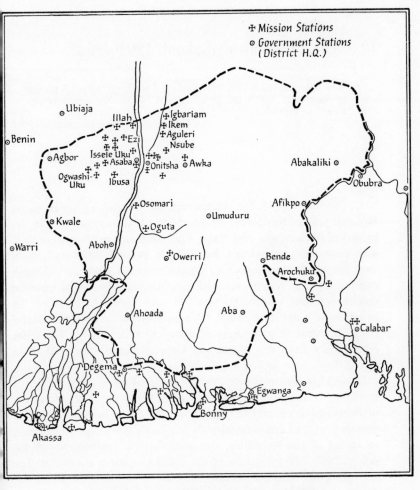

7 Patterns of Moving Frontiers—1906

10 · The Invasion of Iboland, 1902–1906

'The district that has been described . . . is really quite a small portion of Nigeria; . . . but it has been the most troublesome section of any, as well as the richest.'

—Colonel Kemball on Iboland, in 1909.[1]

Neither 1901–2, the years of the Aro expedition, nor 1906, the terminal year of this study, represents any real turning point in the history of the conquest of Iboland. This was a long continued process, which was still incomplete a decade later. In 1906, as in 1901, there were parts of Iboland which no European had ever seen, and British control, even in regions theoretically 'pacified', remained insecure and incomplete. One of the soldiers concerned later recalled the situation as it existed in 1904. 'Our authority only extended inland from the coast to a distance of about 50 miles, and a few miles inland only from the Niger and Cross Rivers (about 100 miles apart).'[2]

It would be wearisome to describe in detail the many patrols and conflicts of these years, and it must suffice to depict the broad pattern of British advance, and Ibo resistance. By far the largest number of patrols took place in areas already 'pacified', sometimes in response to an act of Ibo resistance, and sometimes in consequence of the colonial officials' awareness of the limits of their real control. The two processes were not necessarily distinct, for often an act of Ibo resistance provided an excuse for a campaign which had been decided on anyway—an excuse made the most of for the benefit of the Colonial Office officials in London.[3] A number of wars were fought in the Cross River area—a major field of British military

[1] E. A. Steel, 'Exploration in Southern Nigeria', *Journal of the Royal United Services Institution* (April 1910), p. 446.
[2] *Ibid.*, p. 434.
[3] Cf. C.O. 520/15, Moor to C.O., 22 August 1902, and the campaigns which followed.

expansion in the 1890s—especially against the Ikwo and the Ezza. The Ikwo came into conflict with the British in 1902, and again in 1905. They 'offered stubborn resistance and lost many men', but the experience did not discourage them in their resistance to alien rule. The years from 1905 to 1914 were 'crowded with incidents of individual hostility'. In 1914, the First World War broke out, and the sight of corpses floating down the Cross River, after a battle in the Cameroons, suggested to the Ikwo, as to another colonized people, that England's difficulty was freedom's opportunity. Their resistance was not crushed until 1918, after a gallant and sacrificial struggle.[1]

Their neighbours, the Ezza, offered little resistance in 1905, but, like other colonized peoples, did so later on, when the real significance of colonial rule became more clearly understood.[2]

Another area of obdurate resistance and repeated patrols was south-eastern Iboland—the region, roughly, lying between Owerri, Port Harcourt and Abiriba—and especially, the areas bordering the Owerri–Bende road. Often peoples who had not resisted the Aro expedition, resisted when British forces were weaker, and there was some prospect of success, or when some particular aspect of colonial rule impinged on their lives in a way which seemed intolerable. Thus in 1902, a small town south-east of Owerri attacked a District Commissioner and his escort, and forced them to flee, in a spontaneous protest against 'intrusion into their town' and thefts perpetrated by the Commissioner's party. As a result the town was first burnt, and then systematically sacked.[3] The practice of attacking convoys travelling between Owerri and Bende, punished by repeated patrols from 1902 on, continued, to such good effect that convoys were forced to make a wide detour to the south, and the Ahiara, who were responsible, sent mocking messages 'to ask when the Government intends visiting them again'.[4] In 1905, a doctor, travelling by

[1] C.O. 520/16, Moor to C.O., 18 November 1902; N.A.I. C.S.O. 26/147 (File 26804), Chapman, 'Intelligence Report on the Ikwo Clan' (1930), pp. 11–12. Cudjoe, pp. 154–8.
[2] C.O. 520/31, 'Political Report on the Ezza Patrol', encl. in Egerton to C.O., 16 July 1905. N.A.I. C.S.O. 26/116 (File 28179), Chapman, 'Intelligence Report on the Ezza Clan' (1932), p. 3. Cudjoe, p. 153.
[3] C.O. 520/15, Moor to C.O., 13 August 1902, and encl., H. M. Douglas, 'Report on Operations in Ngor Country'.
[4] C.O. 520/31, 'Extract of Report on the Owerri District for the Quarter ending 30th June, 1905', encl. in Thorburn to C.O. (Confidential), 31 August 1905.

bicycle in the Ahiara area, was put to death, and his death, as always, was expiated in numerous, though uncounted, Ibo lives.[1]

One may pause to comment on the language in which colonial records are written—language from which important areas of the African past must be distilled. The death of a single European, at the hands of those whose country was being conquered by his compatriots, is 'a brutal murder'. The death of scores of Ibos, defending their native land with matchets and muzzle loaders in the face of machine guns, is 'a good bag of the enemy'.

The peoples of western Iboland—also, in theory, 'pacified'—have their own record of heroic resistance in these years. The Kwale people were visited in 1902 by Widenham Fosbery—one of the rare officials who genuinely preferred the methods of peace to the excitements and glories of war. Aided by the moral suasion of a force of seventy men and a machine gun, he negotiated agreements with their many small polities. In 1904, another patrol visited the area, and in the following year, a District Commissioner was established in their midst.

As elsewhere, resistance occurred when colonial rule became an experienced reality, rather than a dimly comprehended possibility. The people of the little town of Ijonnema (Ezionum), with a total estimated population of between two and three thousand, attacked the District Commissioner and his escort, and forced them to flee. The inevitable patrol followed, only to meet with one of the very few reverses suffered by British arms in the conquest of Iboland.

> The patrol attacked Ezionum on 12th October, 1905. The people stoutly defended their town and the patrol suffered a severe reverse. All three Europeans were wounded and of the rank and file one was killed and thirteen severely wounded. The patrol fell back on Abraka and then on Sapele. Two companies of the Lagos Battalion were then sent from Lagos . . . and were joined by one company of the Southern Nigeria Regiment . . . with three maxims and a 'millimetre gun'.

The usual draconian penalties followed, for the town was sacked and fined, and its population deported *en masse* to Urhoboland for some

[1] Steel, *loc. cit.*, pp. 437–8, and C.O. 520/35, Trenchard to Deputy High Commissioner, 22 December 1905, encl. in Thorburn to C.O. (Confidential), 5 January 1906.

years. But when the First World War broke out, the Kwale drew the same conclusions as the Ikwo, and broke into a general insurrection.[1]

The experience of Ezionum showed the futility of resistance by a single Ibo polity. Elsewhere in Africa, the threat of colonial aggression was sometimes sufficient to force hitherto disunited peoples to create new unities, often with the help of religious symbolism. Thus the Shona and Ndebele peoples of Southern Rhodesia united against their invaders in 1896–7, and the peoples of southern Tanzania fought the Maji Maji War against the Germans in 1905. Although both risings were ultimately unsuccessful, they shook the colonial power to its foundations.

Ibo history does not reveal any combinations of this scale and effectiveness, though on occasion former enemies united together to fight the British.[2] But the Ekumeku risings in the hinterland of Asaba, though on a smaller scale, have much in common with them. They show a determined attempt to rise above the particular loyalties of each little independent state, and create a new unity to oppose the colonial enemy. They attempted to do this by adapting traditional institutions.

'Ekumeku' is an archaic Ibo word with the sense of 'breathing' or 'dispersal'.[3] It was the name of a secret society which existed independently in many towns of the western Ibo interior, and among the neighbouring Afenmai.[4] The missionary, Strub, gives us what is probably the best account of it, derived from an informant who was a former member. He describes it as a secret police force-cum-guerilla band, which placed itself at the service of the rulers of a town. 'One cannot deny that the Ekumeku formed the élite of the most capable of the young people.'[5] It was to these secret societies, created to meet

[1] C.O. 520/32, 'Disturbances in Kwale Country', 8 September 1905, encl. in Thorburn to C.O. (Confidential), 7 October 1905, and Thorburn to C.O. (Confidential), 18 November 1905. N.A.I. C.S.O. 26/10 (File 26769), Williams and Miller, 'Intelligence Report on Aboh-Benin Clans of Warri Province' (1930–1), pp. 29–30.

[2] Cf. C.O. 520/15, Moor to C.O., 13 October 1902, and encl., for the way in which the Ibeku and Olokoro people overcame their traditional mutual antipathy to attack Bende-Owerri convoys.

[3] For various interpretations, see G. T. Basden, *Among the Ibos of Nigeria* (London, 1921), pp. 205–6, and S.M.A. 14/80404/15794, Strub, 'Le Vicariat Apostolique de la Nigerie Occidentale depuis sa fondation jusqu'à nos jours' (1928), fo. 13 (henceforward, Strub).

[4] Strub, fo. 13.

[5] *Ibid.* Cf. the more hostile account in Basden, *Among the Ibos*, pp. 205–8.

needs in traditional society, that western Ibo states looked to meet a new challenge—the spread of colonial rule.

In the mid 1890s, the rulers of the states of the western Ibo interior gradually came to a resolve to unite in an effort to expel the Royal Niger Company, using the Ekumeku societies as their instruments. Several years of negotiation were necessary to resolve the problems created by the need for united action, and the jealously guarded autonomy of each little state, and even when agreement was reached, each Ekumeku band fought independently, under its own commander, though side by side.[1] In 1898, they rose in an insurrection 'for the express purpose of . . . driving out of the country all foreigners and everything foreign'.[2] Both missionaries and Company officials fled to the relative safety of Asaba, and soon the Ekumeku controlled the whole Asaba hinterland, except for Asaba itself, the village of Okpanam, some four miles distant, and Issele-Uku, garrisoned by the Company's troops. They used guerilla tactics, attacking, and then disappearing along a maze of forest paths. They sacked the deserted mission stations, and news of their success reached the neighbouring Ishan peoples, who sent reinforcements for the struggle. After suffering several reverses, the forces of the Royal Niger Company succeeded in crushing the rising, with much bloodshed. Strub considered that if it had been united under a single capable leader, the movement could have taken over the whole west bank of the Niger, and threatened the European presence there.[3]

This was not, as was thought at the time, the end of the Ekumeku. Gradually, the societies regrouped, and recouped their strength. In 1900, the Royal Niger Company gave way to the Protectorate of Southern Nigeria. In 1902, in response to the fears of traders and missionaries that another rising was imminent, a patrol was sent against the Ekumeku, capturing many of its leaders and imprisoning them in distant Calabar.[4]

But the Ekumeku survived, and in 1904, despite their memories of the failures of the past, they broke out in another major rising. The

[1] Strub, fo. 13.

[2] E. Dennis, 'The Rising of the Ekwumekwu', *Niger and Yoruba Notes* (1904), p. 83.

[3] This paragraph is based on *ibid.* and on Strub, folios 14–15.

[4] C.O. 520/18, Fosbery to High Commissioner, Southern Nigeria, 2 January 1903.

immediate occasion was dissatisfaction with the workings of the recently established Native Courts, and the abuses and corruption they manifested.[1] Mission property was unharmed, but 'Native Christians and others suspected of foreign sympathies have been made to suffer equally with the foreigners themselves.'[2] None lost their lives, but many lost their property and were forced to flee.

In 1904, the Ekumeku changed their tactics. They abandoned the guerilla warfare, which had enjoyed much success in 1898, and concentrated on the separate defence of each town[3]—a decision which reflected the continuing paramountcy of local loyalties. The change of tactics was disastrous, for it was relatively easy to isolate and conquer the little states, one by one, and their defences—clay walls and ditches—offered no protection against machine guns. The turning point of the rising was the siege of Uburuku, a town which, unlike its allies, had excellent natural defences. After several days of gallant resistance, the town fell. It was the end of the rising, for 'the others in the league understood that they could not resist an enemy who had conquered the bravest of their number, and returned to their homes'.[4]

At least three hundred of those involved in the movement were imprisoned in Calabar, and many died there.[5] A missionary in western Iboland described the consequences of failure in war. 'Result: many towns destroyed, four to five hundred killed; four hundred prisoners. On the British side, one European killed, another wounded, a dozen soldiers killed. All the farms are devastated, and yams, banana groves and cassava, all destroyed.'[6] But it was still not the end of the Ekumeku, and in 1909, resistance broke out again in the Ogwashi area, which was only suppressed after five months of

[1] C.O. 520/24, W. E. B. Copland-Crawford, 'Report on the Rising of the Ekumeku Society in Asaba Hinterland, 1904', 25 April 1904; encl. in Egerton to C.O., 22 May 1904. Cf. E. Dennis, *loc. cit.*, p. 84.

[2] C.M.S. G3/A3/1904/27, Dennis to Baylis, 19 January 1904. Paul O. Emecete, 'Story of My Life', *The African Missionary* (November–December 1919), p. 3.

[3] Strub, fo. 21.

[4] Strub, fo. 22. C.O. 520/24, 'Report on Asaba Hinterland Operations', 14 March 1904, encl. in Egerton to C.O., 7 May 1904.

[5] C.O. 520/24, Copland-Crawford, 'Report on the Rising of the Ekumeku Society in Asaba Hinterland, 1904', encl. in Egerton to C.O., 22 May 1904. Non-official sources put the number higher. Cf. C.S.Sp. 191/A/II, cutting from Depêche Coloniale, 13 June 1905, annotated 'C'est très vrai dit le P. Lejeune'.

[6] C.S.Sp. 192/B/III, Lejeune to Superior General, 17 March 1904.

guerilla warfare.[1] And the western Ibo continue to cherish the memory of the Ekumeku, of those 'select men, brave, courageous, with military prowess', such as Dunkwu Isusu of Onicha-Olona, and Nwadiaju, of Issele Mkpitima.[2]

By 1906, the conquest of Iboland was in no sense completed. A missionary wrote in 1910 that 'Almost continual expeditions, which the newspapers never mention, take place in the interior of the country.'[3] This resistance continued through the period of the First World War and beyond. The Women's Riots of 1929, with their tragic sequel, were not an isolated protest, but were an affirmation of a continuing tradition of resistance.

The conquest of Iboland showed clearly that small states are no match in war for large states. Many responses to colonial invasion were possible. In this chapter we have studied Ibo resistance. In subsequent chapters we shall analyse the gamut of other possible responses.

The Ibo people resisted colonial conquest with courage, and sometimes with temporary success. But the enormous disparity in armaments and in state resources meant that the contest was a hopelessly unequal one, and the colonial presence was first known as a source of fear, bewilderment and despair. A British official analysed the history of a northern Ibo village group in the 1930s. Their history emerged as 'a series of public disasters of the greatest magnitude', beginning with raids by neighbour states, and continuing to 'the coming of Government in the person of a white man nick-named Otikpo, the destroyer'.[4] The officer responsible for the 'pacification' of much of northern Iboland has the doubtful honour of being remembered as 'the Destroyer' in a whole series of Ibo towns.[5]

[1] Ferrieux, letter of 1 October 1910, in *Annals of the Propagation of the Faith* (1911), pp. 72 ff.

[2] Asaba oral tradition.

[3] C.S.Sp. 192/B/VI, Léna to Superior General, 21 December 1910.

[4] N.A.I. C.S.O. 26/211 (File 29180), Clark, Intelligence Report on Nkanu (North) Villages of Udi Division (1933), p. 5.

[5] N.A.I. C.S.O. 26/211 (File 29180), Clark, Report on Nkanu (North) Villages of Udi Division, fo. 5; C.S.O. 26/19 (File 30752), Stone and Milne, Report on Adaba, Nkume, Okpata and Umulokpa Villages of Onitsha Division, fo. 7; C.S.O. 26/42 (File 29881), Barmby, Report on Akwegbe, Ohodo, Ozalla, Lejja Ede and Opi Villages, of Nsukka Division, fo. 5; C.S.O. 26/49 (File 30537), Barmby, Report on Ani, Eror, Nsukka and Ibeagwa Villages of Nsukka Division, fo. 6.

The conquerors of Iboland believed that the end justified the means, and that the sufferings inflicted by the imposition of British rule were outweighed by the blessings that rule would introduce. They believed that they were rescuing the Ibo people from a dark world of cruel barbarism and savagery. It is now obvious that this view rested on a mistaken and distorted stereotype of Ibo society. It remains, however, true, that our final verdict on the process of colonial conquest must depend in large part on our assessment of the colonial experience which followed, and its impact on the lives of the people concerned. This is a theme to which we shall return. Meanwhile we must analyse another dimension of Ibo history—the work of the missionaries, in the era of the Royal Niger Company, and of colonial rule.

11 · The Missionary Presence, 1885–1906

'We came but for souls, that was all our commission.'
—Edmund Campion at his trial, in 1581.

The middle 1880s saw a radical change in the character and context of missionary activity in Iboland. For the past thirty years, it had been the preserve of Sierra Leonian agents of the Church Missionary Society, working within the framework, not of colonialism, but of autonomous African states. Now both the agents of missionary work and the context of their endeavours was to change. Two new missionary societies began work in Iboland, both of them Catholic—the Congregation of the Holy Ghost and the Society of African Missions, while the C.M.S. Niger Mission was so changed by the troubles which afflicted it that it became to all intents and purposes a new mission. Only the C.M.S. churches in the Delta, which responded to these trials by creating an independent Pastorate, carried on the old tradition of Sierra Leonian missionary work. They were to consolidate the pioneering work of Ibo trader-missionaries, establishing catechists and churches in the southern Ibo oil markets.[1]

The history of the C.M.S. Niger Mission in the 'nineties is one of slow and painful reconstruction from a state of utter ruin. We have seen how it was destroyed by Europeans, in the name of a higher missionary ideal. But the critics themselves soon left the mission. Some died or were invalided home, others were dismissed, or resigned in pique or disillusion, and for a time Archdeacon Dobinson was their only survivor on the Niger. More agents were sent from England, many of them women, but their high rate of turnover and frequent home leaves inevitably introduced 'an element of change and instability'.[2] As before, the mission was weakened by the

[1] Cf. pp. 88–9 above.
[2] *Niger and Yoruba Notes* (1900), p. 79.

absence of its bishop, for the European who succeeded Crowther,[1] Bishop Tugwell, was based in Lagos, and his energies were deflected by the twin chimeras of Prohibition and the Conversion of Hausaland.

The tragedies and injustices of the 'eighties have tended to obscure the achievements of those who came afterwards. This should not be so. They included Dobinson himself, 'a marvel of self control, patience, & love' who won the confidence of the Ibo people to a singular degree,[2] and Archdeacon Dennis, who continued the work of translation which Dobinson began, and whose achievements, affectionately embroidered with legend, are well preserved in oral tradition. Sidney Smith and George Basden, who also came at this time, were both destined to crown long years of work in Iboland by writing substantial studies of Ibo life.

But although Europeans had assumed control of the mission, its day-to-day work continued to depend on Africans. Sierra Leonians were now understandably reluctant to join it, though the Reverend Julius Spencer, a solitary survivor of the purges of the 'eighties, survived to give many years of service to Iboland. Several West Indians of African descent also joined the mission—just as they had played a major role in the Presbyterian mission in Calabar. Most African agents were, however, Ibos, who, paradoxically, played a much more important role in the era of European leadership. Typically, they were men of little education, who had worked for the Royal Niger Company as gardeners, carpenters, or servants.[3] But carpenters-turned-evangelists could point to the best of all possible Precedents, and some were men of piety and devotion. Joseph Obimgbo Egbola, a former gardener, may stand for their number. His life's work was the building up of a Christian congregation in Akwukwu, a work he furthered greatly by his knowledge of herbal remedies. When he died, a church holding 600 was necessary to contain his flock. 'He was a spiritually minded man, very unassuming, but exercising a remarkable influence over his people . . . He said, "I did not get much teaching from the C.M.S., all I know I learned

---

[1] After Bishop Hill, who died as soon as he reached Nigeria.

[2] C.M.S. G3/A3/1895, Tugwell to Baylis, 18 November 1894; Basden, *Among the Ibos*, p. 298.

[3] C.M.S. G3/A3/1897/109, Battersby, 'Report of a Visit to the Niger Mission'.

from God's word." '[1] By 1907, there were seventy such Ibo agents in the mission.

The troubles which beset it meant that the extent of C.M.S. missionary work actually shrank in the last two decades of the century. Crowther had been criticized for his failure to evangelize certain large Niger Ibo towns, such as Atani. But now the old stations of Alenso and Osomari were either given up or worked spasmodically, and in the 1890s, C.M.S. work was confined to Asaba, Onitsha, and nearby Obosi—this last, a station pioneered by Onitsha Christians. It was said in 1899, that 'Onitsha and Asaba have been overworked while the rest of the Ibo country has been almost totally neglected except for spasmodic or ill-sustained efforts'.[2]

Within these centres, the success obtained was very limited, as before. Like their predecessors, the missionaries complained of a tendency to eclecticism. Their Catholic rivals claimed, doubtless with some exaggeration, that eight out of ten Protestant converts became polygamists.[3] After a short period of expansion, the Onitsha congregation dwindled in the 1890s—a change doubtless connected with the great unpopularity of the Royal Niger Company.[4] In Asaba, the mission gained accessions from the freed slaves, who gladly attended church 'merely to please the Oyibos . . . who had delivered them from death'.[5] But in Asaba, too, the congregation remained a tiny minority—perhaps two hundred, in 1897, in a town with a population of over ten thousand.[6] And in Obosi, a disillusioned missionary gave a summary which can stand for the whole history of C.M.S. endeavour on the Niger in the nineteenth century:

> In a small district we perhaps touch one percent of the people, the remainder are indifferent or hostile to our work. While it is true that compared with the Mohammedan zone, we have made some progress, yet progress is painfully slow & the great mass of heathenism around is still untouched . . . At first they receive us gladly, but as soon as there are any converts & the inevitable

[1] Julius Spencer and others, 'Joseph Obimgbo Egbola and his Witness for Christ', *Western Equatorial Diocesan Magazine* (1904), pp. 15 ff.

[2] C.M.S. G3/A3/1899/112, T. J. Dennis to Baylis, 17 July 1899.

[3] C.S.Sp. 191/B/IX, Report by Lejeune, Onitsha, 24 November 1901.

[4] Dobinson, *Letters*, p. 52.

[5] C.M.S. G3/A3/1892/52, Spencer, Asaba Annual Report, 1891.

[6] *Niger and Yoruba Notes* (1897), p. 256.

collision between heathen customs and heathen principles takes place, this cordiality is replaced by coldness and suspicion.[1]

1884 brought an end to the C.M.S.'s long monopoly of mission work on the lower Niger. The Society of African Missions decided to establish a station there when the river was still an arena of Anglo-French commercial rivalry. They went there at the invitation of a French company, but when the first band of three reached Lokoja, towards the end of 1884, they found the French on the point of leaving.[2] Years of difficulty and discouragement followed. Naturally, the missionaries lamented the French withdrawal—it was said of the Lokoja mission that it flew the tricolor, and was known as the French, rather than as the Catholic mission.[3] The more fundamental difficulty was the inherent one of obtaining converts to Christianity in a Muslim area. A more promising beginning came in 1888, when Sir James Marshall, the Royal Niger Company's Chief Justice, invited the Fathers to Asaba. A young Milanese priest, Carlo Zappa, accepted, and soon afterwards the Lokoja post was given up. The mission, now centred on Asaba, was destined to be ruled by Zappa until his death in 1917.

The Holy Ghost Fathers, coming to the lower Niger a little later, in 1885, established the first Catholic mission in Iboland. They, too, did so at the invitation of a French trading company. It was originally intended to settle at the Confluence, but transport difficulties, created by the Royal Niger Company's hostility, defeated them, and they went no further than Onitsha.[4] There they obtained land through the good offices of the aged Bishop Crowther, to whom it was already ceded. 'I acquired this land for God's cause, take it.'[5] This pleasantly amicable relationship was to continue, though the C.M.S. might well have resented their settlement at a well-established centre of Protestant mission work, when so many towns lacked missionary

[1] C.M.S. G3/A3/1897, Bennett to Baylis, 27 March 1897.

[2] Holley, 'A travers les pays du Niger', fo. 6 of typed copy in S.M.A. Archives. (Also printed in *Les Missions Catholiques* (1884). S.M.A. 14/80302, Poirier to Superior General, 9 November 1884.)

[3] C.S.Sp. 191/B/I, Folder labelled 'R. P. Lutz, 1889–1896'. Marshall to Barthet, 19 June 1889 (French trans. of English original).

[4] C.S.Sp. 191/A/5, letter from Leroy (C.S.Sp. Superior General) in *Echo de l'Art* (3 April 1904) (cutting); 191/B/II, historical account by Lejeune, based on community journals, 1902.

[5] C.S.Sp. 191/B/II, Lejeune, historical account.

activity altogether. The hostility of the Royal Niger Company, similarly, was to persist and deepen, as the Fathers espoused the grievances of the Onitsha people, which endeared them to the Onitshas, but scarcely to the Company.

Both the Society of African Missions and the Congregation of the Holy Ghost were founded in France in the middle years of the nineteenth century, part of a sudden upsurge of interest in foreign missions, which has often been explained in terms of the growth of interest in colonies abroad, but which was in reality, like the Evangelical revival, a complex social phenomenon deserving more searching analysis from historians. It produced a large number of missionary societies, large and small, supported in part by a number of independent fund-raising organizations, the most important of which was the Association for the Propagation of the Faith. France supplied the lion's share both of finance—collected in small amounts from many humbly circumstanced members—and of personnel.

Both the Catholic missions on the Niger were staffed predominantly by Alsatians—reflecting the long continued importance of Alsace and Brittany as sources of Catholic missionary vocations. They were young—like their equivalents in the C.M.S.—often in their late twenties or early thirties. Many were to die young, either on the Niger or in other mission fields.[1] Both missions grappled with a degree of grinding poverty unknown to the C.M.S. The small sums they received from fund-raising organizations were inadequate to their needs, and were largely dispensed in charity. The Holy Ghost Fathers mission had been established for fifteen years when its two main centres were described in these terms:

> All the *houses* are built in wood & mud. The wood is rotten, the walls are split, and the tatched [*sic*] roofs pierced in thirty or forty places, let in by turn both rain and sunshine. The *Church* is a wreck, its mud walls, likewise split in many places threaten to fall upon us ... The *School Buildings* are mere ruins ... Aguleri is still worse than Onitsha.[2]

The S.M.A. mission was to retain this 'special cachet of poverty' well into the twentieth century.[3]

[1] For details re personnel, see the annual publications, *État de la Société* (S.M.A.) and *État du Personnel* (C.S.Sp.).

[2] C.S.Sp. 191/A/3, General Report on the Lower Niger (anon. but Lejeune, 1900).

[3] S.M.A. 11/200/40542, Chabert to Lacquerie (transcript), 1921–2.

Partly because of this poverty—which government subsidies to Catholic schools and the contributions of Ibo Christians were ultimately to alleviate—the Fathers shared to a large extent the standard of living of their flock. They mastered their language to a degree which few of their successors have been able to emulate and to which Zappa's *Essai de Dictionnaire Français–Ibo* is a permanent memorial.[1] It is a paradox, which is equally true of the C.M.S., that these nineteenth-century missionaries, for all their mastery of Ibo language and customs, had a basically dark view of Ibo society, and believed that the souls of the unconverted were likely to be lost.[2] In a later day, when, largely through the work of anthropologists, the many excellences of Ibo religion and custom had become generally accepted, Ibo congregations took it for granted that they should hear missionary sermons through an interpreter.

The many similarities between the two Catholic missions, included, fortuitously, some parallels in their leadership. The Holy Ghost mission was founded by an Alsatian, Father Lutz, whose career on the Niger was overshadowed by troubles with the Royal Niger Company. After his death, and that of several short-lived successors, Father Léon Lejeune assumed the leadership, in 1900. He was a fiery idealist, whose zeal led to conflicts both with his colleagues and his flock, but in his five years on the Niger he transformed the mission's policies, beginning the wholehearted adoption of education as the primary means of evangelization, which is often credited to his Irish successor, Bishop Shanahan, whose career lies beyond the time limits of this book. After five years, Lejeune was forced by mortal illness to leave the Niger. He died in France of cancer of the throat, displaying not merely equanimity, but gaiety. He had spent twenty of his forty-five years in Africa.[3]

The personality of Father Carlo Zappa moulded the history of the S.M.A. mission until his death in 1917. He was a man cast in a heroic mould, of iron strength and energy, called Ozokpokpo, in reference to his incessant journeys on foot. He showed an equal severity towards his colleagues, his catechumens, and himself. His

---

[1] C. Zappa, *Essai de Dictionnaire Français–Ibo ou Français–Ika* (Lyon, 1904) (written in collaboration with an Ibo catechist, Jacob Nwaokobia).
[2] Cf. Strub, in *L'Echo des Missions Africaines de Lyon* (1922), p. 61. C.S.Sp. 191/A/5, biography of Lutz, by Ebenrecht, folios 34–6.
[3] C.S.Sp., *Bulletin de la Congregation*, XXIII, pp. 491–502.

ideal of missionary action was pastoral, and indeed, paternalist. 'To show authority, to command instead of to ask, seems to the Prefect the only good method for the two districts.'[1] He was a man widely regarded as a saint, and he formed some saintly Ibo converts. Descriptions of the congregations of western Iboland in his time are often more reminiscent of a monastery than of a parish. But he weakened the mission by delaying the adoption of educational work, and it was not, in the long run, the way to form an adult, self-aware and self-perpetuating Christianity.

Both missions depended heavily on the work of Ibo catechists. It was regarded as a special vocation, chosen, in the colonial period, in preference to better paid posts elsewhere—'il restera toujours pauvre'.[2] In 1906, the Holy Ghost mission had ten priests, five lay brothers, and thirty-three African catechists.[3] One of the most outstanding of the S.M.A. catechists was Thaddeus, originally a slave from Afenmai, who ran a number of catechists' posts before working in catechists' formation. He was probably the anonymous catechist of Okpanam, who when living on a salary of 7s. 6d. a month, which he had to supplement by farm work, voluntarily supported several lepers.[4]

Both laid great emphasis on works of charity. The S.M.A., like the C.M.S., found a ready-made congregation in the gratitude and necessities of Asaba's liberated slaves. They assisted them so effectively that it became a proverb, that 'when one is destitute or hopeless of life he goes to Romani'. This kind of work—amateur medical care, the support of lepers, of the aged and of abandoned infants—was carried out largely by nuns. A favourite activity among both missions was baptizing the dying. This work alone was thought to justify a mission's existence, peopling heaven with 'a magnificent phalanx of angels'.[5] The same combination of personal poverty and practical charity was strikingly characteristic of the Holy Ghost Fathers across the Niger. A Protestant missionary paid tribute to

[1] S.M.A. 2E.30, Pellet, Journals (volume re Western Nigeria), fo. 134.
[2] *L'Echo des Missions Africaines de Lyon* (1922), p. 9.
[3] C.S.Sp., *Bulletin de la Congregation*, XXIV, p. 144.
[4] S.M.A., Pellet, Journals (volume re Western Nigeria), folios 154–7. *L'Echo des Missions Africaines de Lyon* (1922), p. 19. Oral tradition adds more details.
[5] *L'Echo des Missions Africaines de Lyon* (1904), p. 27.

their 'active charity, devotions and self abasements' and many traders and officials echoed the theme.[1]

Both sought to effect conversions by the individual visitation of adults. This was a slow and difficult process, largely because of the stipulation that a convert renounce all but one of his wives. As we have seen, congregations gathered in this way showed great fervour. Catholic missionaries, like Protestants, complained of eclecticism among their flock, but as I have tried to show elsewhere, piety and eclecticism are not necessarily irreconcilable.[2] But like the C.M.S., they touched only a tiny part of Ibo society. In 1898, when the S.M.A. had eleven stations, eight of them in Iboland, it had only fifty indigenous adult converts.[3] In the 1920s, a Father reflecting on a long missionary experience concluded:

A large part of the population, sometimes the immense majority, and with it all the youth, is untouched by it ... It has been observed everywhere that in spite of the regularity of house to house visits, the number of catechumens diminishes gradually, even to zero, so that a post is threatened with extinction in the more or less distant future.[4]

And the practice of charity meant inevitably that many, though not all converts were drawn from the poor and needy.[5] Mission congregations acquired a reputation for poverty and helplessness which boded ill for the Christianization of Iboland.

Like the C.M.S., their impact was further limited by the small number of their stations. Both missions tended to cluster round a central station on the Niger. When they moved further afield, it was often in response to Ibo initiatives. The Holy Ghost Fathers' second station, at Aguleri, was founded in response to insistent requests from Idigo, a titled man of the town, who founded a Christian village by the waterside. Hoping that they had found a Constantine, the Fathers actually procured a horse for him to

[1] C.M.S. G3/A3/1887, Annual Report, Onitsha, 1886. Cf. *West Africa* (September 1900); Morel, p. 27; A. C. G. Hastings, *Nigerian Days* (London, 1925), p. 11; Langa Langa, *Up Against it in Nigeria* (London, 1922), p. 16.
[2] Elizabeth Isichei, 'Seven Varieties of Ambiguity: Some Patterns of Igbo Response to Christian Missions', *The Journal of Religion in Africa* (1970), III, 3.
[3] Strub, folios 11–12.
[4] *Ibid.*, fo. 25. It should be noted that mission registers give an exaggerated idea of congregations, for they include many baptized in articulo mortis, who later recovered.
[5] C.S.Sp. 191/A/3, [Lejeune], General Report ... on the Lower Niger.

sacrifice, to obtain the town's highest title.[1] Several other stations in the Anambra Valley followed, with little success. The next advance came when the C.M.S. congregation at Osomari adopted Catholicism *en masse*, under the leadership of Jacob Akubeze.[2] He was also responsible for the next advance—to the wealthy and strategically sited town of Oguta.[3] The work was not confined to Iboland. There was a gallant though unsuccessful venture on the Benue, and a highly successful establishment at Calabar. But the mission's main work was in a small area of Iboland, and complaints were made that Onitsha and Aguleri absorbed the lion's share of finance and personnel.[4]

The history of the S.M.A.'s mission was shaped by the dialectic between Zappa's passionate desire to expand, on the one hand, and the limits of finance and personnel on the other. Half a dozen stations in the western Ibo interior were established. But just as the lack of results at Lokoja had led to the move to Asaba, the slow rate of progress in Iboland led the Fathers to seek a more promising field among the neighbouring Afenmai. But progress here proved equally slow. Gradually the mission expanded, embracing an increasing number of the many peoples and languages of what is now the Mid West State. It was most successful among the Ibo, who by 1911, comprised 1,553 of the 2,086 Catholics on the registers.[5]

By the end of the nineteenth century, missionary activity had made little progress in Iboland. It was confined to a few stations on or near the Niger and its tributaries, and even within these centres affected only a minority of the population. The Catholics, in particular, had succeeded in gathering congregations which were fervent, though small. But even there fervour depended largely on creating and maintaining an artificially protected environment. The missionary ideal was the Christian village of Aguleri, with its members drawn largely from 'poor & castoff creatures',[6] which led a corporate religious life of almost monastic regularity. ('Our Christians follow the holy offices exactly, even during the week, and when night has

[1] C.S.Sp. 191/A/I,3, Lutz, 'Les Agouleris', 2 January 1892.
[2] C.M.S. G3/A3/1899/26, T. J. Dennis, Annual Letter. C.S.Sp. 191/B/II, Lejeune, Historical Account, 1902.
[3] Lejeune, Historical Account, 1902.
[4] C.S.Sp. 192/B/IV, Shanahan to Superior General, 28 August 1907.
[5] Strub, folios 9–10 and 22–3.
[6] C.S.Sp. 191/A/3, [Lejeune], General Report . . . on the Lower Niger.

fallen one hears the voice of men addressing to heaven the beautiful prayer of the rosary.')[1] In the more cosmopolitan environment of Onitsha, where Christians came into contact with men of many religions or none, both Catholics and Protestants lamented a very different state of affairs. 'A thankless task among a thankless people . . . Religion is only wanted for material purposes.'[2] Despite the sacrifices of many missionaries, both black and white, Catholic and Protestant, who had laboured and died in Iboland, the missionary enterprise had on the whole achieved singularly little success.

In 1899, the Royal Niger Company lost its charter, and the area became part of the Protectorate of Southern Nigeria. The development of colonial rule, and its gradual extension over Iboland, were destined to transform the missionary situation.

It helped the spread of mission work by improving communications and creating a context of 'law and order', which, unlike the traditional one, could be relied on to defend missionary interests. The Catholic missions took little advantage of this, in the period covered by this study, for both were temporarily preoccupied with foundations outside Iboland. The C.M.S. profited by developments to open up a large number of small stations on either side of the Niger. But they went no further than Awka—and even that was heralded as a great leap to the interior. But the spread of colonial rule was to lead to missionary penetration of the whole Ibo interior in years to come.

The spread of colonial rule gave missions a new prestige and authority, for now towns invited them in the hope of obtaining friends and advocates *vis-à-vis* their new rulers. A C.M.S. missionary observed of Awka, that 'The motives which prompted such church-building zeal were undoubtedly mixed, and the rumour that British troops were in the vicinity probably helped to induce the chiefs to declare themselves in this way as friends of the Oyibo.'[3]

But the main change in the missionary situation was that under colonial rule the Ibo people had a real incentive to seek Western type education. The Delta peoples had long appreciated the value of education, and some rich men had sought it for their children in

[1] C.S.Sp., *Bulletin de la Congregation*, XVII, p. 430.
[2] C.S.Sp. 191/B/IV, Shanahan, Visite Provinciale, 1912.
[3] Sidney, Smith, 'Oka', *Western Equatorial Africa Diocesan Magazine* (1906), p. 4.

other West African colonies, or even in England.[1] On the Niger, under Company rule, when local people were employed only as servants, there was no such incentive.

The incentive which colonialism brought was twofold. On the one hand, the people needed to communicate with their new masters, especially since the channels of communication tended to fall into the hands of corrupt intermediaries. On the other hand, the government needed Africans who were educated—albeit to a low level—to fill the posts in its lower echelons which had otherwise to be filled by Africans imported from elsewhere. The commercial firms, similarly, needed clerks and artisans, and were prepared, on occasion, to subsidize the schools which would supply them.[2] For the first time, education was seen as the gateway to economic opportunity by the Ibo people themselves. 'They realise as they never did before that knowledge is power, and that it can command a good salary.'[3] A missionary who went to Owerri in 1905 recorded 'that if he had accepted all the lads offered him for training on this journey he could have brought home a small army to Asaba'.[4]

The level of education available was low, but the range of occupations then available to Africans was limited—'they had the choice of becoming policemen, clerks, or teachers'—and it rapidly created a new élite. The question of why the Ibo people responded so eagerly to these opportunities is in itself an interesting historical question. It may perhaps be explained by the substantial mobility and freedom of choice in traditional Ibo society, and the way in which status and rank were achieved, rather than inherited.[5]

The educational system which resulted sprang from a marriage of convenience. The government was eager to use the missions' personnel and expertise in running the schools, and provided subsidies accordingly. To the missions, the new state of affairs offered both a solution to their financial problems, and the opportunity to exercise

[1] F.O. 2/123, Annual Report, Niger Coast Protectorate, 1896–7, 'Education'.
[2] *Niger and Yoruba Notes* (1898), p. 15. C.O. 520/15, Moor to C.O., 29 October 1902.
[3] J. N. Cheetham, 'Work in the Ibo Country', *Niger and Yoruba Notes* (1901), p. 28.
[4] *Western Equatorial Africa Diocesan Magazine* (1906), p. 43.
[5] Cf. Simon Ottenberg, 'Ibo Receptivity to Change', in William R. Bascom and Melville J. Herskovits (eds.), *Continuity and Change in African Cultures* (Chicago, 1959), pp. 130 ff.

a real influence on Iboland, which they had sought in vain for so long.

The Holy Ghost Fathers, under the leadership of Lejeune, and subsequently of Shanahan, seized the opportunity. By 1906, their educational work was well established, with 24 schools and approximately 3,000 pupils.[1] 'All our prestige in this country comes from the fact that we are considered great educators.'[2] By 1910, they had already begun to create a new élite: 'Our children are throughout the Colonies of Northern and Southern Nigeria. They occupy excellent posts, mainly with the Government.'[3] To strengthen this work, Alsatians were gradually replaced by Irishmen, and in the years that followed, the Fathers' school system continued its expansion.

The C.M.S. and the S.M.A. Fathers responded to the new situation more slowly, for basically similar reasons. We have seen Zappa's commitment to a different pattern of missionary action. At first he showed little enthusiasm for schools, believing that children who attended mission schools for material reasons were unlikely to become devout Christians.[4] Some of his colleagues agreed with him; others became increasingly restive as they observed the successes of the Holy Ghost Fathers across the Niger. 'Both Christians and pagans want some schools directed by us, in the absence of which the children will go elsewhere, and since our chapels are frequented by scarcely any but the old, I ask myself what we are going to do.'[5] By 1911, Zappa himself had become convinced of the necessity of an educational programme,[6] but was handicapped by the lack of English-speaking personnel. Then the war intervened, and it was not until after 1918 that the mission, under an Irish bishop, made a serious entry into this field.

The C.M.S. responded equally slowly, for the evangelicals who ran its Niger Mission had a deep emotional commitment to preaching and missionary journeys. In 1900, one of them asked, 'What method of missionary effort is most suited to the type and condition of the Ibo people?' He answered his own question, 'Simple evangelical preaching', claiming that education 'must . . . take a secondary

[1] C.S.Sp., *Bulletin de la Congregation*, XXIV, p. 144.
[2] C.S.Sp. 192/B/III, Shanahan to Superior General, 13 November 1905.
[3] C.S.Sp., *Bulletin de la Congregation*, XXVI, p. 864.
[4] Strub, folios 26–7.
[5] S.M.A. 14/80303/16285, Cermenati to [Pellet], 14 June 1907.
[6] S.M.A. 14/80405/15791, Zappa to Pellet, 12 February 1911.

place'.[1] This was precisely the attitude of Zappa, though probably neither party would have admitted the resemblance.

This is not to say that the C.M.S. neglected education entirely. Its resources were greater, both in finance and in personnel, and it did not, of course, cope with the peculiar difficulty of the Catholic missions, staffed with French-speaking members, in an English-speaking colony. The Delta Pastorate ran eight schools, with a total, at the end of our period, of 764 pupils—not all, of course, in Iboland. An Industrial School was established, first in Brass, and later in Onitsha, and a training centre for catechists led a similarly peripatetic existence. There were several elementary schools on the Niger, and Edith Warner, then near the beginning of a long missionary career, founded a boarding school for girls at Onitsha, which was financed largely by the pupils' manual labour. Archdeacon Dennis, with great foresight, urged the creation of a boys' secondary school, as 'one of the most crying needs of Nigeria'.[2] But the project came to nothing, though it was realized in later years in the school which perpetuates his memory, the Dennis Memorial Grammar School.

In the period covered by this book, the missionaries were probably the only Europeans who came to Iboland with the primary intention of seeking Iboland's good, however narrowly that good was defined. But mission records have their own form of myopia, which easily communicates itself to the historian. Inevitably, they emphasize the progress made, and however great this was, in comparison with the past, one easily forgets how small their impact was, and how few and insufficient their schools, in terms of the whole context and needs of Ibo society. By 1906, there were probably, at the outside, 6,000 Ibo children at school. The numbers are large in comparison with the nineteenth century, but represent only a tiny minority of Iboland's children.

We have examined the pattern of moving frontiers, by which colonial rule was established in Iboland, and the important variable of missionary influence. In the closing chapters of this book we must turn to the crucial question—to what extent did these actually affect the lives of the Ibo people?

[1] A. E. Clayton, 'The Parting of the Ways', *Niger and Yoruba Notes* (1900), pp. 22–3.
[2] C.M.S. G3/A3/1901/9, Dennis to Baylis, 9 January 1901.

12 · The Colonial Impact on Society: The Scope of Government

'The main point in all practical governments is the revenue & taxes.'
—Turner to Moor, 18 May 1897.[1]

The position of the colonial government in the late nineteenth and early twentieth centuries was essentially paradoxical. On the one hand, as we have seen, its military strength was far greater than that of any Ibo polity, a discrepancy due partly to the disparity between their military technologies, but far more to the difference in political scale, a theme to which we shall return. But although the government's resources were sufficient to win any specific conflict, and an 'outrage' was always punished with draconian severity, it was shown repeatedly that although it could punish risings it could not prevent them in the first place, and its resources were insufficient to effect major changes in the lives of the people under its rule. The memoirs of Iboland's early administrators always stress the basically precarious nature of their situation. The man who was District Commissioner at Bende in 1905 wrote, 'To the north and north-east the limits of my District were undefined, and also I could go only about eight miles or so in that direction, unless I had a numerous escort, and that was just then not available.'[2]

The colonial administration was limited in its personnel and in its financial resources. The revenue was raised entirely from customs, and fluctuated from year to year, with the state of trade. Moreover, customs were kept low to avoid protests from traders' pressure groups in England. Economy was a prime virtue in a Governor, and when Egerton succeeded Moor in 1904, and added to his predecessor's passion for military campaigns an equally expensive passion for

[1] N.A.I. Calprof 6/1/3, Turner to Moor, 18 May 1897.
[2] Hives and Lumley, pp. 22–3.

railways and telegraphs, he incurred stringent criticism from the Foreign Office.[1]

The numbers of its European staff were limited. Political Officers (District Commissioners, as distinct from Marine and Forestry Officers, and so on), numbered sixty-nine in 1904–5, and the Colonial Office frowned on Egerton's pleas for an increase.[2] The number was further limited in practice by annual leaves in England and frequent sick leave, and inevitably reduced the Government's real impact on the areas it theoretically controlled. As Egerton complained:

> Past experience has proved that law and order cannot be maintained in territories newly brought under control; unless they are frequently visited by European Officers. The present districts are too large to allow of this being done—especially in the absence of roads; this has been proved over and over again by the necessity of sending military forces time after time into the same district.[3]

Partly because of their limited resources, these early colonial administrators had limited aims. Their primary aim was to expand the area under their jurisdiction until it reached the boundary of another colonial jurisdiction. In areas already conquered, they sought to extend trade, and to maintain 'law and order'. They sought to extend trade—the source of their income, and the fundamental reason for the colony's existence—in many ways, ranging from exhortation to the improving of communications. But the total economic impact of colonialism had many facets, and was different in many ways from administrators' intentions. It forms the theme of a subsequent chapter.

The preservation of 'law and order' had two main aspects. The first of these was the suppression of conflicts between Ibo groups. The nature of colonial apologetic—which suggests that pre-colonial Iboland was in a state of bloody anarchy—need not blind us to the real benefits that were conferred here. Some Ibo groups probably suffered more from Abam raids than they did from British military expeditions. The second facet lay in the suppression of practices which the British considered inhuman—human sacrifice, infanticide, and, more hesitantly, slavery.

---

[1] C.O. 520/43, memo. by C. S[trachey] on Egerton's estimates in Egerton to Elgin, 5 January 1905.

[2] C.O. 520/29, memos. on Egerton to Lyttelton, 21 January 1905.

[3] C.O. 520/29, Egerton to Lyttelton, 21 January 1905.

The abolition of these practices necessarily imposed some temporary injustices—in the sudden change of values which transferred a man offering the highest sacrifice to God he knew, into a murderer. But the results were incontestably good. British rule came as a liberation to whole classes of unfortunates who had long lived in the shadow of death—old women accused of witchcraft, or slaves, waiting for the day when they would be sacrificed. (But to keep our perspectives accurate we need to remember that in the sixteenth century, English Catholics and Protestants calmly butchered each other, that the last trial of an English witch was in 1702, and that even Victorian England, with its many capital offences and its martyred child factory hands and chimney sweeps did not lack its human sacrifices.)

The government's attitude to the institution of domestic slavery was half-hearted and ambiguous. Hesitation over the slavery issue was one of the reasons why the area was declared a Protectorate, rather than a Colony. It was reluctant to abolish slavery, as it existed in the House system, partly because it feared the spectre of social dislocation, and partly because the Delta chiefs were among its most staunch collaborators. Both MacDonald and Moor praised the system, and the joys of slavery, in terms which could scarcely have been bettered by a slave owner. In 1901 a piece of legislation abolished the formal status of slavery, but was notable mainly for the concern it manifested to maintain the reality of the *status quo* and the privileges of chiefs as much as possible.[1] The Government's first act after passing the Proclamation was to suppress a rising among nine hundred slaves at Calabar. Moor rejoiced that the Proclamation gave him the legal power to do so, for otherwise 'no doubt the disease would have spread and thousands upon thousands of boys of all the coast tribes would have run away calling themselves free'.[2] But the love of freedom was a disease too contagious to be suppressed by government action, and the attempt to preserve the fossilized forms of inequality when the social situation which produced them had gone was foredoomed.

The shortage of European staff, and the lack of finance to recruit more, led the Protectorate officials to rely very heavily on African

[1] C.O. 520/14, Moor, 'Memorandum concerning the Aro Expedition', 24 April 1902, folios 371–3.
[2] *Ibid.*, folio 373.

agency. Iboland's new rulers in no instance spoke the language of those they sought to rule. Egerton, whose previous experience was in Asia, was struck by the fact that 'European Government Officers are almost entirely ignorant of the native languages' and by its consequence—'all communication with the natives governed having to be carried on through the medium of Interpreters'.[1]

African agency was employed in a number of different institutional forms. As elsewhere in Africa, a system of Indirect Rule was adopted (to retain the capitals acquired in the decades when the concept became canonical). Indirect Rule did not necessarily mean the retention of traditional institutions of government. All African forms of government were changed to a greater or lesser extent by colonial rule. They had evolved to fulfil needs and purposes which were not those of colonialism. Even those which apparently suited its purposes best—such as the great Emirates of northern Nigeria—were changed by the colonial context, where ultimate authority lay with the colonial master.

The many small polities of Iboland were singularly ill-adapted to the needs of colonialism, or of any modern bureaucratic state, both because of their large number and their small scale, and because of the nature of their political institutions. These were designed to obtain the maximum participation of all citizens in decision-making, while giving due weight to wisdom and experience. This is one of the central preoccupations of the European political tradition, but one remote from the concerns of Iboland's colonial rulers. So Indirect Rule, in Iboland, took the form of new institutions—Native Courts. Their personnel, Warrant Chiefs, had no equivalent in traditional society.

The prototype of the Native Courts can be found in the Governing Councils established by Johnston in 1887.[2] They fell into disuse when he left the Delta, but were revived by MacDonald. MacDonald originally intended that these institutions of colonial rule should apply only to foreigners, and that the local people should continue to govern themselves in traditional ways.[3] His successor, Moor, at first regarded them as a rationalized form of traditional government,

---

[1] C.O. 520/24, Egerton to C.O., 14 April 1904.
[2] F.O. 84/1881, Johnston to Salisbury, 16 March 1888.
[3] F.O. 84/2111, MacDonald to F.O., 21 May 1891.

where the local people could be taught the art of self-government[1]—
as if this was a skill lacking among the Ibo and their neighbours!
But before his term of office came to an end, he had realized that the
Native Court system was in fact a radical departure from traditional
forms of government:

> Practically all the systems of the natives have to be done away
> with. I call them systems for want of another word, but it would
> be more accurate to say that their want of system and method has
> been done away with and native Government organised among
> them.[2]

Often, though not invariably, the Warrant Chiefs were not the
traditional elders of a town. These tended to suspect the Greeks
bearing gifts, and put forward junior members of the community, or
even slaves.[3] Thus the elders of Onicha-Olona politely declined,
when the office of Warrant Chief was offered to them.

Yet their abuse of office, which was to become legendary in the
colonial period, was perhaps due less to their inexperience than to the
novelty of their roles. Positions of responsibility of traditional society
were surrounded by a network of duties, expectations and obliga-
tions. These were known both to the incumbent and to society as a
whole. If he failed to fulfil them, he would feel the weight of popular
disapproval, and the community could apply various sanctions
against him. The Warrant Chief filled a new role, upon which
traditional practices could shed no light. He was responsible, less to
the community he served, than to the colonial master, who alone had
power to dismiss him. It was perhaps inevitable that the Warrant
Chiefs tended to use their positions for personal aggrandizement. In
a world of rapid change, of conflicting values and of manifold
uncertainties, perhaps personal prosperity seemed the one thing
certain.

These abuses were becoming apparent even in the period covered
by this study. In 1899 it was reported that 'The Native Courts are not
in a satisfactory condition. The money is unaccounted for and I have

[1] F.O. 2/85, Moor to F.O., 25 December 1895.
[2] C.O. 520/15, Moor to C.O., 8 August 1902.
[3] There is much evidence of this. Cf., for instance, R.H., MS. Afr. s. 1152, Bain,
note on Warrant Chiefs interleaved after diary entry for 25 February 1924;
MS. Afr. s. 1068, R. A. Stevens, 'Preface', folios 12–13.

strong reasons to suspect that justic is sold to the highest bidder.'[1] The 1904 rising of the Ekumeku was occasioned by the malpractices of these courts.[2]

Because European officials did not speak Ibo, and few Ibo spoke English, those who controlled the channels of communication came to wield great power. The most important agents of communication were the Government Interpreters, whose role was self-explanatory, and the Court Clerks. The power of the Court Clerks arose from the fact that they were usually the only members of a Native Court who spoke and wrote English, and from being the servants of the Courts, and the recorders of their proceedings, they easily became their masters. These and other clerical staff were originally recruited from Lagos, the Gold Coast and Sierra Leone, but the proportion of local personnel increased rapidly. By 1904, 129 out of 409 Africans employed by the Protectorate of Southern Nigeria as Court Clerks, clerks, interpreters and copyists were natives of it.[3]

The rulers of Southern Nigeria were well aware of the power in the hands of these intermediaries, and their often corrupt use of it. Egerton wrote in 1905 'that great injustice frequently occurs owing to the ignorance of European officers of the native languages and the consequent blackmailing of natives by the official Interpreters and Police who are the sole medium of communication between European and native'.[4] But frequent changes of posting, and the intrinsic difficulty of mastering a complex and little studied tonal language, continued to dissuade all Europeans but missionaries from learning Ibo.

The response of the Ibo people to this impasse was to learn English, in the persons of some, at least, of their children. The autobiography of Eke Kalu gives an interesting case study of this process:

> There was in Ohafia one Vincent, a Seirea [*sic*] Leonean, who was the Native Court Clerk. He was extremely wicked in his dealings

[1] C.O. 444/1, Roupell to Moor, 20 May 1899, encl. in Moor to C.O., 14 June 1899.
[2] C.O. 520/24, 'Report on the Rising of the Ekumeku Society', encl. in Egerton to C.O., 22 May 1904.
[3] C.O. 520/16, Moor to C.O., 28 November 1902, and encl.; C.O. 520/24, Minute from H. Bedwell to Egerton, 3 May 1904, encl. in Egerton to C.O. 7 May 1904.
[4] C.O. 520/30, Egerton to C.O., 4 May 1905.

with Ohafia people ... My people wanted a way out of such persecution and my advice to them was to open a school, educate their children who, knowing what the clerk knew, could better challenge him and his successors.[1]

Another group of powerful intermediaries were the police and Court Messengers. The latter had the duty of serving court summonses, but had many of the characteristics of military police. In 1907, there were 222 police in the Central Division, 75 of them Ibo.[2] These groups, too, were accused of corruption and extortion. As one Divisional Commissioner wrote:

I regret to have to state that I fear Police and Court Messengers are themselves the primary cause inmost [*sic*] instances of the mal-treatment they have received on more than one occasion at the hands of the natives ... they demand women and interfere with plays etc. During my journeys through the country constant, I may say incessant complaints are brought to me of the way Police and Court Messengers behave in a town when on Government service.[3]

Those who did not succeed in obtaining these privileged posts, turned, on occasion, to creating them for themselves. In the early years of colonial rule, Iboland was overrun with impostors, who claimed to be government officials, and used their alleged authority as a basis for extortion.[4]

It is only just to note that corruption was not confined to Africans. One of the most senior British officials in the Protectorate, who later became a well-known writer on African affairs, was dismissed in 1902 for his depredations. 'Towns round Asaba now make it a custom, when they hear Major Leonard is coming, to lock up their goats.'[5] But this was exceptional. British officials were usually protected by their substantial salaries and the relative poverty of their subjects

[1] *Autobiography of an Illustrious Son, Chief Eke Kalu of Elu Ohafia*, Owerri Province (Lagos, 1954), p. 8.
[2] C.O. 520/47, Thorburn to Elgin, 15 July 1907.
[3] C.O. 520/24, Annual Report, Cross River Division, year ending 31 March 1904.
[4] Hives and Lumley, p. 111. F.O. 2/179, Lewes to Resident, Benin City, 28 March 1898 (copy). C.O. 520/47, Annual Report on the Eastern Province for the Year 1906, pp. 2–3.
[5] C.O. 520/13, Moor to C.O. (Confidential), 18 March 1902, encls.

from such temptations, and their characteristic failings lay in other directions.[1]

Since no direct taxes were levied, many Ibo first experienced the direct impact of colonialism in the form of a tax levied as labour. No aspect of colonial rule was more resented than forced labour in road-making, or as carriers on military expeditions. Asaba oral traditions relate how men would flee into the bush to escape duty as carriers—often in patrols against their neighbours and allies, and at risk of their lives. An official described how the first coal samples were brought to the Niger from Udi. 'Personally, I cannot imagine anything more inconvenient than a fifty-six pound bag of coal on one's head, on a hundred mile walk.'[2]

The use of forced labour to construct roads was often justified in terms of the Ibo traditional practice of entrusting public works to age groups. But there was a great difference between carrying out projects discussed and approved by the community, in traditional ways, and the often arbitrary and excessive demands of the new régime. H. M. Douglas won praises for his road-making achievements around Owerri—but he also won the name 'Black Douglas' and the reputation of 'a hard man'.[3] A District Officer in western Iboland so exasperated the local people by his excessive exactions of forced labour that he was put to death. A Colonial Office official summed up the incident:

> It is clear that Mr Crewe Read both flogged the Chief of Agbor and other persons ('the flogging,' says Sir W. Egerton, 'is absolutely indefensible') and oppressed the natives of his district by exacting (in the foreman's words) 'a great deal of absolutely unnecessary and even useless work. Thereby he provoked a rebellion —nothing else could be expected—and brought about his own death and the death of a number of those who rebelled and attacked him.[4]

This was doubtless an extreme case—but his superiors had had nothing but praise for the officer concerned until his death provoked an inquiry.

[1] But for British corruption when these conditions were lacking, cf. the plunder of Bengal by the East India Company in the eighteenth century.
[2] R.H. MSS. Afr. s. 375, G. Adams, 'Five Nigerian Tales', fol. 7.
[3] C.O. 520/31, Egerton to C.O., 16 July 1905; Cudjoe, p. 150.
[4] C.O. 520/37, memo. by S.O.[livier], 4 Dec., on Egerton to Elgin (Confidential), 3 November 1906.

The roads built brought much benefit to Iboland—a theme to which we shall return—but the first observable impact of colonialism was often that of forced and hated labour.

We have seen how the combination of government needs, missionary interests, and the demand of the Ibo people themselves led to the rapid growth of a mission-run educational system, but that by 1906 it was still geographically limited, touching only a tiny minority of Iboland's children. The number of schools and scholars was to grow rapidly in the future, but throughout the colonial period it remained true that only a minority of the Ibo children attended school, only a few primary school-leavers won secondary school places, and only exceptionally did secondary school graduates win their way to any further form of education. Nationalist movements sprang in part from the frustrations this engendered—the bitter consciousness of wasted talents and unattainable opportunities. And the characteristics of Nigerian education in the colonial period remained fixed in the pattern they had formed by 1906—the near monopoly of the mission societies, the inadequate involvement of the colonial government, which ran too few schools itself, and gave insufficient subsidies to the mission schools, and the low level of the latter—due largely to inadequate funds.[1]

In some parts of Africa, educators, by concentrating on the sons of chiefs, helped to perpetuate the inequalities of traditional society. This was not the case in the more egalitarian societies of Iboland. Sometimes indeed the reverse was the case—the wealthy were contented with their position in life, and with a similar role for their children, and it was the unfortunate, with little to lose, who embraced Western education most enthusiastically. Even when it was recognized that a town's welfare demanded the education of some of its members, it happened on occasion that 'it at once became important that all places should be filled by the children of those who mattered least'.[2] Sometimes it was the young who recognized the significance of the new developments most clearly, creating something of a conflict of generations.[3]

[1] For the subject matter of this paragraph, cf. Otonti Nduka, *Western Education and the Nigerian Cultural Background* (Ibadan, 1964); James S. Coleman, *Nigeria Background to Nationalism* (Berkeley and Los Angeles, 1965, reprint), ch. 5.

[2] Easterfield and Uku, *West African Review* (January 1953), p. 50.

[3] C.S.Sp. 192/B/VI, Shanahan to Neville, 20 September 1912. Cf. Ojike, pp. 40–44, 62–6.

But although the schools did not perpetuate old inequalities, they laid the foundations of new ones. Within Iboland, as within Nigeria, some towns acquired better schools, and some acquired them earlier. Since education was the main, though not the only[1] highway to wealth, security and influence, it created new and damaging discrepancies both between communities and within them. These inequalities, on a national scale, remain an enduring problem of independent Nigeria—in the persons of the countless individuals and the whole regions which the lack of Western education has condemned to poverty.

A Nigerian historian has said with justice that the most enduring and significant legacy of colonialism in Africa are its boundaries.[2] The small scale of Iboland's face-to-face democracies has many advantages for their members, but it placed them at a hopeless disadvantage *vis-à-vis* a modern bureaucratic state. The threat of foreign invasion was not sufficient to overcome the incorrigible locality of the heart's affections, but the experience of colonial rule, and the spread of education, was to lead to the creation of large-scale political organizations which were in their turn to overthrow it.[3] In a sense, the problem of scale has been the central problem of modern Nigeria, and despite the tragic and devastating conflict it gave rise to, it is true that one dimension of its history in this century is that of emancipation from the limitations of small-scale polities.

[1] Cf. the great wealth of some illiterate women traders.
[2] J. F. Ade Ajayi, 'The Colonial Episode', in L. H. Gann and Peter Duignan, *The History and Politics of Colonialism 1870–1914* (Cambridge, 1969).
[3] The question as to how far nationalist movements were in fact responsible for the overthrow of colonialism is an interesting one which lies beyond the scope of this book.

13 · The Colonial Impact on Society: The Economy

> 'There are few I find who want really to do anything for Africa but many who want poor Africa to do much for them.'
> —Moor, in 1898.[1]

Historians differ greatly in their economic interpretations of colonialism. To some, the colonial era was an Age of Improvement. It increased the volume of a colony's international trade, and established the infrastructure for economic growth. It involved 'A vast transfer of human and physical capital to Africa . . . a host of new economic, medical, social, and administrative techniques.'[2]

Others regard colonialism as primarily a vehicle of economic exploitation. They emphasize the colony's dependence on the metropolis, its powerlessness to alter terms of trade in its own favour, its characteristic and dangerous dependence on one or two major exports—typically raw materials. They point to the continued drain of capital from the underdeveloped world, which is thought to condemn it to a vicious circle of continued poverty and exploitation.[3]

Which of these models is true of the Ibo experience? It is a question which cannot be fully answered in this study. The colonial impact had scarcely begun in 1906, and a full examination of its many ramifications must await a subsequent volume. Nor can it be realistically divorced from the twentieth-century economic history of Nigeria as a whole. But despite these caveats, certain characteristic patterns can be already seen emerging by 1906.

[1] F.O. 2/179, Moor to Farnall, 16 May 1898.
[2] L. H. Gann and Peter Duignan, *Burden of Empire. An Assessment of Western Colonialism South of the Sahara* (London, 1968), p. 371.
[3] For a typical model, cf. A. G. Frank, *Capitalism and Underdevelopment in Latin America* (New York, 1967). For a summary of the theory, with full bibliographical notes, cf. Gavin Williams, 'Social Stratification of a neo-colonial economy: Western Nigeria', in Christopher Allen and R. W. Johnson (eds.), *African Perspectives. Papers . . . Presented to Thomas Hodgkin* (Cambridge, 1970).

The basic pattern of Iboland's economic relationship with Britain had been established, as we have seen, in the nineteenth century. Iboland exported a narrow range of raw materials—mainly palm products—in return for various manufactured consumer goods. This was to remain their characteristic relationship through the colonial period.

Another typical aspect of Nigeria's economic history in the colonial period had nineteenth-century roots—the tendency of European firms to combine in ever larger and more powerful amalgamations which exercised enormous influence over Nigeria's economic life. We have seen the various amalgamations which led to the creation of the Royal Niger Company. In 1889 a number of firms trading in the Delta combined to form the African Association. In 1900, both these giants signed a price-fixing agreement with the two other major companies in the area. The African and Eastern Trade Corporation was formed by the amalgamation of the African Association, Miller Brothers, and other firms, and in the 1920s, both the Niger Company and the African and Eastern were absorbed in the giant Unilever complex.[1]

This process of amalgamation and monopoly meant that the economic life of a colony was effectively controlled, not by officials, whether in Lagos or in London, but by a huge international combine, with financial resources greater than the typical colonial government. By 1907, the basic pattern of Nigeria's economic life was well established, and was described by an astute observer:

> It must be noted that Imports to this part of Africa are not regulated by ordinary laws. There are big 'Combinations' in the trade, and expansion in the accepted sense is hardly admitted. The imports are comprised principally of the same class of goods year after year. If prices rule high for produce in European Markets this does not tend as in most countries to further development of the country that the produce comes from.[2]

Government officials often commented on the poor quality and range of the goods imported[3]—a feature which had always been characteristic of the West African trade. More seriously, these imports tended to undermine traditional manufactures, and inhibit

[1] Wilson, I, 180; '40 Years of UAC', *West Africa* (26 April 1969).
[2] C.O. 520/47, Annual Report on the Eastern Province for the Year 1906.
[3] F.O. 2/180, Niger Coast Protectorate Annual Report, 1897–8.

their development. This was explicitly recognized and sought after. 'Part of the problem . . . is to divert the supply of cotton from the Nigerian hand-looms to the power-looms of Lancashire.'[1] And then as later, observers noted the firms' reluctance to make more than the minimum investment in the country. 'The tendency in the past', wrote Moor in 1902, 'has certainly been to "suck the orange", employing the minimum of capital, putting nothing into the development of the country . . . and taking everything possible out of it.'[2] He pointed out that this tendency was intensified by the way trade was conducted. Agents were appointed for one or two years, and drew their income largely from commission. Inevitably, they showed little interest in the development of the country, or even in the long-term expansion of their own trade.

The peasant collector of palm products had no bargaining power against these economic giants, and little defence against the fluctuations of international trade. Nor did the government intervene to redress the balance. Scholars have often commented on the remarkable degree of economic freedom permitted to these combines. In the Depression years, an Awka palm oil middleman 'enquired whether it would not be possible for the firms to give longer notice to bush producers about [price] fluctuations. He was informed that the control of price fluctuations was scarcely within the province of Government . . .'[3]

But to see these external economic forces in perspective, we must remember that Iboland remained an overwhelmingly subsistence economy. In 1906, one could have removed all European trade and all European products without seriously affecting the people's way of life. This remained true through the colonial period, though the role of the cash economy grew progressively larger. Habit turns luxuries into necessities, and social change created new necessities, such as the payment of school fees. Cash for these purposes was obtained by the sale of palm products, by internal trade, or by migration to the towns in search of work. But even in the 1940s, Iboland remained essentially a self-sufficient agricultural economy.

We have seen that in traditional Ibo society there was a high

[1] Alan McPhee, *The Economic Revolution in British West Africa* (London, 1926), p. 49.

[2] C.O. 520/15, Moor to C.O., 21 September 1902.

[3] N.A.E. Awdist, 2/1/42, Deposition of David Nwume before John Ross, 9 April 1931.

degree of geographic mobility, and that internal migrations had the effect of maintaining the ecological balance between population and resources. The imposition of colonial rule, in Iboland as elsewhere, froze settlement into the patterns which existed at that moment. This created pockets of great discontent and hardship.[1] In some areas, intense population pressures, which could no longer be relieved by internal migration, forced many to leave the land and settle in towns.[2] This is one of the causes of that Ibo Diaspora, both to other parts of Nigeria and to other African countries, which is so striking a feature of their twentieth-century history.

The economic impact of colonialism was never, of course, uniform. In any colonized country, one finds internal patterns of under-development and development. It creates new regional inequalities. The crucial determinants of a particular area's fortunes lay only partly in its natural resources of climate, soil and mineral wealth. They lay also in administrative decisions—especially in the choice of administrative centres and communications routes—and in the pattern of the expansion of European trading firms to the interior. Despite their initial hesitations, this last was an inevitable and irreversible process. It rendered the middleman role of the Delta states obsolete and ruined them, as their peoples had always known they would. The men of Arochuku, similarly, with their oracle destroyed and their trade routes falling into desuetude, faced the same unpalatable alternative—to emigrate in search of work, or to stay home, to face increasing economic stagnation.[3]

For some towns, on the other hand, colonialism led to new economic opportunities. This was especially true of towns such as Owerri and Aba, which were chosen as administrative centres, for commercial firms tended to concentrate near government stations, and they often became nodal points in the communications network.

The sites chosen by the commercial firms for their factories also became the focus for new economic opportunities. The change has been well described by an Ibo historical geographer:

For the inland peoples the European factories represented a new experience. They were permanent centres and offered daily

[1] Cudjoe, p. 153.
[2] Cf., for instance, R.H., MS. Afr. s. 699. Bridges, Intelligence Report on the Uguawkpu Group, Awka Division, 24 March 1934.
[3] Easterfield and Uku, *West African Review* (December 1952), p. 1365.

opportunities for exchange. . . . With their great advantages of opportunity and frequency these centres and their associated markets grew rapidly at the expense of the traditional markets.[1]

The function of bulking oil for these inland factories created a new type of middleman role. These new middlemen acted not as the rivals of the expatriate firms, but as their subsidiaries. On the Niger, the role was typically filled by women until the Depression years.[2]

One of the most truly revolutionary changes lay in the improvement of communications, which did much to rewrite the economic geography of Southern Nigeria. As in other colonies, the key decisions were often made rapidly and arbitrarily, despite their momentous long-term implications.

The Selborne Committee, appointed in 1898 to report on various schemes for the amalgamation of Nigeria, assumed that the Niger would remain the main artery of Nigeria's trade, and recommended that it should be linked by rail to Kaduna in the north.[3] But already the construction of a railway north from Lagos had begun, which, although it was not realized for a time, committed the government to its further extension, to the reconstruction of Lagos harbour, and to the choice of Lagos as the political and commercial capital.[4] Both Moor and Egerton advocated a railway through Iboland, and Egerton went as far as having the route surveyed, but the Colonial Office vetoed the plan on grounds of expense. 'Southern Nigeria simply cannot afford to build this railway as well as the extension to Oshogbo and beyond.'[5] There was truth in the sentiment often expressed by officials working in eastern Nigeria, that its amalgamation with Lagos in 1906 meant its subordination to the latter's economic interests.[6] Finally, during the First World War, the need

[1] Ukwu I. Ukwu, 'The Development of Trade and Marketing in Iboland', *Journal of the Historical Society of Nigeria* (June 1967), pp. 658–9.

[2] Basden, *Among the Ibos*, p. 194; F. Ekejiuba, 'Omu Okwei, The Merchant Queen of Ossomari, A Biographical Sketch', *Journal of the Historical Society of Nigeria* (June 1967), p. 634.

[3] F.O. 403/269 (F.O.C.P.), Selborne, Report of the Niger Committee, 4 August 1898. Alternative southern termini suggested were Lagos, Warri, Sapele and Asaba.

[4] Cf. Antony Gerald Hopkins, 'An Economic History of Lagos 1880–1914' (London Ph.D. thesis, 1964), pp. 374–5.

[5] C.O. 520/7, Moor to C.O., 25 April 1901; C.O. 520/43, Egerton to Elgin, 26 February 1907, and C.O. memos.

[6] C.S.Sp. 192/B/V, Shanahan to Superior General, 21 January 1908.

to exploit the Enugu coal fields gave Iboland its railway. The stations along its route were known locally as 'beaches'—an interesting and significant metaphor.

By 1906, much had been done to clear Iboland's rivers, which were often blocked by snags and fallen trees. The Enyong Creek was cleared, and at once became a flourishing commercial waterway,[1] and similar operations followed on the Imo River, its tributary the Otamiri, and on the Sombreiro River.[2]

Road-making was an activity beloved of Governors and District Officers. To the former it offered a greater measure of political and military control, and an expansion in trade. To the latter it promised more tangible results than their other main responsibility, 'the maintenance of law and order'. By 1905, so much progress had been made that it was possible for Egerton to travel from Lagos to Calabar by bicycle.[3]

These roads brought many advantages to Iboland. They vastly expanded the volume of her internal trade. They helped break down the particularism which divided her polities. As early as 1905 it was noted that improved communications were breaking down the differences in dialect which mirrored this.[4] It emancipated the carriers who had transported goods along the trade routes on their heads, and the pullaboys who had paddled the great trade canoes, with little hope of improvement in the laborious conditions of their lives. On the other hand, as we have seen, they were built by exactions of forced labour which bitterly offended many of the peoples concerned.

The colonial government was anxious to reform Iboland's traditional currencies. The various forms of these—manillas, brass rods and cowries, had the disadvantage of bulk, which made them unsuitable for large-scale transactions. The problem had been greatly exacerbated by the gross inflation caused by unrestricted imports of cowries by European traders in the nineteenth century.[5] Great

[1] C.O. 520/14, 'Political Report in connection with the Aro Field Force Operations'. C.O. 520/24, Annual Report on the Cross River Division for the Year ended 31 March 1904.

[2] C.O. 520/25, Fosbery to Egerton, 27 May 1904, encl. in Egerton to C.O., 27 May 1904.

[3] C.O. 520/31, Egerton to C.O., 16 July 1905.

[4] 'Report of Ibo Language Conference held at Asaba, 14 Aug., 1905', in *Western Equatorial Africa Diocesan Magazine* (1906), p. 75.

[5] Marion Johnson, 'The Cowrie Currencies of West Africa: Part II', *The Journal of African History* (1970), pp. 337 ff.

efforts were made to replace traditional currencies by British coinage, but there was much resistance to the change, and the use of traditional currencies survived in local transactions for many years to come.[1]

The critics of colonialism tend to dislike the word 'infrastructure' because it implies a creative element they are reluctant to recognize in the colonial experience. Yet it seems to the present writer that colonialism had both a creative and destructive face. To neglect either, may facilitate the construction of theories of persuasive brilliance and internal coherence. It does not necessarily facilitate the recovery of historical truth.

> Trusting his images, he assumes their relevance;
> Mistrusting my images, I question their relevance.
> Assuming their relevance, he assumes the fact.[2]

The basic pattern of Iboland's economic relationship with Europe was fixed by 1906. The dependence on a single primary product for export, the excessive power of large commercial combines were already manifest. As usually though not always the case in West Africa, the basis of all production remained the peasant, engaged in subsistence agriculture and collecting and processing palm products for export. Iboland's climate, geography and dense population saved her from the fate of a country like Kenya. Though the occasional European, enchanted by a particularly pleasant upland prospect, sometimes envisaged it covered by European farms, there was no serious threat from potential white settlers. The Ibo suffered in some ways from colonialism. They did not, like the Kikuyu, become trespassers on their own land.

The real danger to Iboland was not white settlement, but the establishment of large-scale commercial plantations, on the southeast Asian model, where the Ibo would have played the role of labourers. This was prevented by the colonial government's refusal to grant these firms freehold or long leases. In 1898, a timber and rubber company sought territorial concessions, and Moor, then on leave, opposed it vehemently, with the words which form the epigraph of this chapter: 'There are few I find who want really to do anything for Africa but many who want poor Africa to do much for

---

[1] Basden, *Niger Ibos*, pp. 336–7.
[2] Robert Graves, *Broken Images*.

them.'[1] Some years later, William Lever, the architect of a gigantic manufacturing empire, tried to obtain territorial concessions to establish palm plantations in Nigeria. He was unsuccessful, and had to turn to the Belgian Congo to obtain the concessions he wanted.[2]

[1] F.O. 2/179, Moor to Farnall, 16 May 1898.
[2] Wilson, I, 165 ff.

14 · Colonialism: Some Patterns of Ibo Responses and Initiatives

'But I tell you my lord fool, out of this nettle, danger, we pluck this flower, safety.'

—Shakespeare, *Henry IV Part One*, II, 3.

It has been one of the major achievements of African historiography in recent years to recognize that colonial conquest and colonial rule were not simply experiences imposed from without, which the African peoples passively accepted. As we have seen in this book, both the conquest and colonial rule of Africa, as well as much missionary and trading activity, were carried out largely by the agency of Africans. Both colonial conquest and colonial rule were experiences to which a great variety of response was possible. The nature of these responses formed a dialectic with the colonial presence, to determine much of its actual impact on the lives of Africans.

Ibo resistance to the spread of colonial rule was never a uniform phenomenon. Different societies—and individuals within societies—made different decisions at different times. Some did not resist when colonial rule was first imposed, but did so after a time, when its true significance was more apparent. Some wished to resist, but were dissuaded by the fate of their neighbours. As the ruler of the small western Ibo state of Issele-Uku put it, if Benin could not resist the British successfully, it would be madness for him to attempt to do so.[1] Others were dissuaded by some spectacular demonstration of British military technology.[2]

Others decided that their interests—as individuals or as communities—were best served, not by resisting the new power, but by

[1] J. Spencer, 'A missionary tour to the towns west of Asaba', *Niger and Yoruba Notes* (1898), p. 97.
[2] Steel, p. 443. Cf. Dilim Okafor-Omali, *A Nigerian Villager in Two Worlds* (London, 1965), pp. 73–4.

co-operating with it. Historians tend to call those who responded in this way 'collaborators', though the term has pejorative overtones which are inappropriate.

Most towns, and most individuals, were at times resisters, and at times collaborators. The full gamut of responses possible within a single town will only become fully documented after the completion of more local case studies. And the attitudes of individuals were not, of course, immutable, but were themselves the product of experience, and modified, sometimes profoundly, by subsequent experience. Time could and did turn the resister into a collaborator, the collaborator into a resister.

The basic postulate of the collaborator was that colonialism was irremovable. In 1904, a missionary made an interesting comparison between the hopeless risings of the western Ibo and the attitude of the neighbouring Afenmai, who were equally hostile to colonial rule, but realized that they could not overthrow it, so 'seek to extract from it all possible profit'.[1] Some years later, an Ezza chief asked an interpreter if there was any way of getting rid of the white man. The reply was, 'Impossible, the white man has come to stay as long as men lived.'[2]

Some scholars have made a fruitful distinction between two types of positive response to the colonial situation.[3] The first may be called that of the manipulators. They did not welcome colonialism as a source of change, and they did not master the skills it brought, such as those inculcated in Western education. They recognized that the colonial government had become incomparably the most important element in the new power equation, and allied themselves with it, either to strengthen their position in their own community, or to strengthen their own town *vis-à-vis* others. 'The use of schools as weapons for the chiefs to fight with among themselves'[4] was a phenomenon colonial officials regularly recognized and deplored.

Often, in the period with which we are concerned, the manipulators came from the frontiers of Iboland. Although colonial rule was to ruin the Delta states, some of their rulers drew a temporary advantage from it. The classic instance was the Efik, Chief Coco Bassey,

[1] Strub, in *L'Echo des Missions Africaines de Lyon* (1905), pp. 42–3.
[2] Cudjoe, p. 159.
[3] Cf. John Iliffe, *Tanganyika under German Rule* (Cambridge, 1969), pp. 146–9.
[4] N.A.E. Aw. 20, D. O. Awka to Bubendorff, 30 June 1917.

who guided British policies on the Cross River so effectively that when he was ill, a British official confessed his astonishment that he could manage without him! When he died, the British paid him unreserved tribute:

> The late Chief Coco Bassey during his lifetime kept these trouble-some tribes in order with a tact and wisdom unusual in an African—to appreciate the work he did one need only glance at the terrible state of disorganisation consequent on his death.[1]

The Warrant Chiefs, too, were essentially manipulators, seeking power and influence in the traditional community, albeit by new means.

Another type of manipulator can be found among men who were either themselves the products of Western education, or who were its strong supporters, but who sought traditional positions and goals. Samuel Okosi, who became Obi of Onitsha in 1900, and reigned until 1931, was a man of this type. In the late nineteenth century, he was one of the few Ibos who were literate in English. He was at first an adherent of the C.M.S., but joined the Catholic Church in 1895 and became a catechist. He then became a candidate for the Obiship, and was elected after a long dispute, as a result of government interven-tion. His reign, though long, was a troubled one. He disappointed the missionaries by adopting polygamy. He antagonized many Onitsha by the irregularity of his election—for another candidate had a much stronger claim. 'The fact of his Catholic religion greatly reduced his traditional prestige. In the later years of his reign he destroyed some of the essential regalia of his cult and his sovereignty.'[2]

By co-operating with the colonial power, the manipulators sought to control and direct its impact. They fulfilled its requirements—supplying labourers for public works and avoiding, at least in public, practices known to offend British susceptibilities. For the rest, they continued much as before. We have studied this response as personi-fied in those of positions of authority. But it was the response of the great majority of the Ibo people throughout the colonial period, though the careers of those who welcomed change have overshadowed their obscure and unrecorded lives.

[1] F.O. 2/180, Gallwey to F.O., 10 October 1898; C.O. 444/1, Roupell to Moor, 20 May 1899, encl. in Moor to C.O., 14 June 1899.

[2] R. W. Harding, 'Report on the Onitsha Obiship Dispute' (Enugu, 1963), p. 24. This report gives the best summary of Okosi's career. There is also much contemporary material in the C.M.S. and C.S.Sp. archives.

12

The other positive response has been called that of the 'improvers' —though the phrase incorporates a good many value judgments. To the improvers, colonialism was a source of new opportunities. They were determined to master the skills which were the basis of the white man's power, and ultimately used these skills to overthrow him. This response 'implies the belief, unquestioned at this time but later to be challenged by radical nationalists, that there was no conflict between personal and social improvement, that the man who won advancement for himself thereby won a victory for his people'.[1]

Later nationalists undervalued the improvers for a time largely because they tended to be divorced from their own cultural heritage. The very process of mastering Western education, with its concomitant of adopting, in various degrees of sincerity and zeal, the Christian religion, inevitably involved some divorce from traditional society. These early pastors, catechists, clerks and teachers often symbolized the divorce by the enthusiastic adoption of European dress and baptismal names. Later when the passage of time made both education and Christianity into a secure inheritance, new possibilities of creative synthesis became possible. But even at the time of greatest cultural estrangement, many traditional African values continued to flourish—especially, perhaps, in that generous and self-sacrificing concern for the welfare of the extended family and of the whole town which financed the education of so many Ibo children, and underpinned the activity of so many community development associations.

By 1906, the age of improvement was still in its infancy in Iboland. There was no equivalent to the educated Yoruba community in Lagos—whose prior access to education was to be evident for several decades more. There were, however, some pioneer Ibo 'improvers'—who usually came from the frontiers of Iboland. The early catechists, studied in a former chapter, belong to this category, as do the C.M.S.' first ordained Ibo clergymen, George Nicholas Anyegbunam and David Okparabietoa Pepple. An outstanding example was Isaac Okechuku Mba, educated in Onitsha and Lagos. He was a loyal and able C.M.S. agent, in charge of the station at Alenso, until they had the folly to dispense with his services. He then joined the service of the Niger Coast Protectorate, where he was

---

[1] Iliffe, p. 166.

criticized only for his zeal in continuing, on a voluntary basis, his missionary work.[1]

We can find a prototype of the later innumerable improvement associations as early as 1905. When Egerton visited Onitsha, he noted:

> Met the Youngmen's Association—they ask for a Government school—they only have a membership of 14 youngmen of Onitsha at present. They have been educated in the various Mission schools. Many of them are small traders . . .[2]

What circumstances led certain Ibo to join the ranks of the improvers? Opportunity was an important factor—Onitsha had had fifty years of missionary and educational work when other Ibo towns had never set eyes on a European. Often the young responded eagerly to change, while the old remained indifferent. But often it was an unpredictable result of an individual's predilections and personality. Uku of Arochuku, whose father died young, observed that 'I have sometimes wondered whether my father would have decided to make use of new opportunities, perhaps becoming a warrant chief, or whether he would have resisted change.'[3]

The reasons that led men to become Christians were similarly complex and various. To the missionaries, there was no problem of explanation—it was simply a case of light shining in darkness. Many early conversions, as we have seen, resulted from the missions' charity to the needy. Later, the missionary monopoly of education gave them an opportunity to influence many of Iboland's children at a crucially impressional age. To many, education and Westernization were aspects of the same phenomenon. This is not to say that their adoption of Christianity was insincere. And the eclecticism which often characterized them—many became polygamists, and consulted diviners in time of trial—marks, less the superficiality of their conversion, than their profoundly religious outlook, suspended as they were between two possible world views.

There were many converts who were neither indigents nor improvers. An outstanding example was Alexander Ubuechi of Issele,

---

[1] For the circumstances of his resignation, see C.M.S. G3/A3/1890/132. Cf. F.O. 2/63, MacDonald to C.M.S., 10 March 1894.
[2] C.O. 520/31, Egerton to C.O., 16 July 1905.
[3] Easterfield and Oku, pp. 1365–6.

a man who has attained most of the leading roles available in traditional society. He was a skilled craftsman, a diviner, and a titled man. One day he attended a Catholic church casually, and was electrified by a sermon on hell. He became a Christian, dismissing three of his four wives, and enduring much petty persecution. He attended church twice daily, succoured the sick and destitute, and held a class for catechumens. When he died in 1903, the missionaries acclaimed him as a saint.[1]

Iboland's confrontation with an alien culture, its conquest, and the experience of alien rule, created a spiritual and intellectual crisis—a phase of that history of thought in Africa which still awaits its historian. The missionary presence—and the success of British arms, with which they were inevitably associated—challenged the inherited certainties of traditional religion—

> Government is teaching now
> Saying that Chukwu
> Is not fixed to a spot;
> That where we go to consult Chukwu
> Is a fake . . .
> And we cannot tell
> Whether they are telling the truth
> Or deceiving us.[2]

In a recent brilliant essay, the spread of Christianity—and, elsewhere, of Islam—has been explained as a dimension of that enlargement of scale we have already had occasion to refer to. The remoteness of the traditional High God, and the active role of lesser spirits, reflected the essentially local nature of traditional life. As the walls protecting the microcosm dissolve, local spirits lose their validity.[3] Only the High God remains

Eterne in mutabilitie.

The presence of mutually antagonistic missionary societies created its own problems. An individual's denominational loyalties were usually decided by chance—the denomination of the school he

---

[1] *L'Echo des Missions Africaines de Lyon* (1905), pp. 21–9.
[2] Reflections of Ezenwadeyi of Ihembosi, recorded by Fr. Raymond Arazu. C.S.Sp., September–October 1966 (MS. in his possession).
[3] Robin Horton, 'African Conversion' *Africa* (April 1971), pp. 85–108.

attended, or the mission established in his area. Some were seriously troubled by their respective claims. We have a record of one village schoolmaster's adventures in comparative religion:

> When I was taking up my scholars in lesson there we read in history about Henry the VIII. How he on account of wife estab-lished a new church on earth which was known to be the C.M.S. After school I call the scholars to my house—that I think we have found out the true Church.[1]

Angst and religious uncertainties were not necessarily resolved by adherence to a Christian denomination. Many concluded that in a time of change it was safest to keep to the traditions of the past. In 1904, we read of a revival of traditional religion in one area, the reconstruction of its long neglected groves and shrines.[2] The most common solution was perhaps that of eclecticism—a personal synthesis of elements of the old and new.

Religion was of course only one dimension of these uncertainties. The overthrow of Iboland's polities, the power of the Oyibo with his different values and irresistible technology, the rapid rise of those with skills which could be utilized in the new system—all these seemed to throw the entire inherited order into question. Traditional society was based on a network of commonly accepted values, duties and expectations. Now the fabric was threatened. The first major novel by an Ibo—Chinua Achebe's *Things Fall Apart*—derived both its title and its epigraph from the imagery of a European poet.

> Things fall apart; the centre cannot hold;
> Mere anarchy is loosed upon the world.

And if these intangibles of inner experience are more readily captured in the poet's or the novelist's imagery, they belong, nevertheless, as much as palm oil exports or road construction, to the realities of the historical past.

[1] *The African Missionary* (November–December 1921), p. 116.
[2] *Niger and Yoruba Notes* (1904), p. 53.

Epilogue:
The Colonial Balance Sheet

'. . . there is nothing either good or bad, but thinking makes it so.'
Hamlet, II, 2.

We have reached the date chosen, arbitrarily enough, as the terminal one for this study. It might well end there, but it seems appropriate to consider briefly the total significance of the story it has related in detail.

It is now unfashionable for historians to construct balance sheets. The historical relativism which is a widespread orthodoxy among non-Marxist historians precludes this. The past, it is claimed, must be understood in terms of the values current at the time. To pass moral judgments on it is thought to show the absence—to the point of naïveté—of historical understanding.

But historical relativism is never uniform or absolute. No one feels precluded from passing moral judgments on Belsen. If we avoid passing moral judgments on the more remote past, we are in danger of becoming unwitting apologists for its vices, follies and crimes. This is seen clearly in some recent studies of the trans-Atlantic slave trade. It is seen, equally, in any study of the industrial growth of Britain or America, which ignores or minimizes the colossal suffering and injustice which accompanied it.

It seems to the present writer that historical relativism leads to a kind of moral and intellectual bankruptcy. The historian must condemn every manifestation of man's inhumanity to man, both as it existed in the past, and as it continues among us in the present.

If we attempt to evaluate the gain and loss of Iboland's relationship with Europe in the period covered by this study we are confronted at once with the colossal debit of the trans-Atlantic slave trade. We must consider the countless Ibos who died during capture, or during the Middle Passage, and the countless others forced into slavery and exile in the New World. We must consider, as well, its corrupting effect on Ibo society, and on the lives of those who remained. No historical experience is totally destructive. Some states, especially in the Delta, rose through the slave trade to wealth and power, though their rise, perhaps, contributed little to the happiness of their inhabitants. But a society which can gain foreign exchange only through enslaving and selling its inhabitants is doomed. Nor, as we have seen, were the goods imported in return of a kind to offer new possibilities of economic growth.

In the middle of the nineteenth century, the picture changes. The external slave trade dies, although parts of its evil heritage continue. Iboland, through her exports of palm products, becomes essentially a dependent monoculture, contributing one of the many commodities needed by industrial Europe. Much has been written on the dangers of this dependence, on the economic insecurity it engenders, on the threat it poses for the state's ultimate political autonomy, on the obstacles it creates for development, and on the basically unfavourable character of the exchange. Having said this it is essential to emphasize that the power of external economic relations to aid or injure Iboland were limited. The export sector remained an enclave in an overwhelmingly subsistence economy.

Many historians have no difficulty in assessing the total significance of the colonial experience. To Marxists, and others on the left, colonialism was purely and simply the vehicle for economic exploitation. Apparently creative aspects—such as education and the construction of communications—are dismissed, either because of their inadequacy, or because of their subordination to the political and economic needs of the colonial power. To others, the benefits brought by colonialism are so evident that to ignore them seems a curious and wilful doctrinaire blindness.

It seems to the present writer that colonialism, as it affected the Ibo people, had both creative and destructive elements. Its total impact on them, in the period under discussion, was limited—both by limitations of personnel and resources, and by administrators' essentially conservative aims. It was mediated largely through the agency of Africans. There is no way in which we can counterbalance the violence with which it was imposed, and the internal violence which it often ended. There is no way to compare the injustices it ended—the fate of slaves and witches—with the new injustices it created. The vast polarity between rich and poor, between the man in a Mercedes, and the man who trudges in the roadside dust, is essentially the artefact of colonial rule. The communications revolution emancipated the pullaboys. But the roads were built by forced labour in an atmosphere of bitter resentment. For some, colonialism proved the pathway to glittering educational and economic opportunities. Some live much as their fathers did, but with a new sense of their poverty, for deprivation, as the sociologists remind us, is a relative concept.

Both for the prosperous and the poor, colonialism undoubtedly meant an Age of Anxiety, a period of *angst*, when values were wrenched and dislocated. The period of witchcraft trials is gone. But belief in witchcraft continues, and perhaps increases.

'I do not know the method of drawing up an indictment against a whole people.' It seems necessary to apply Burke's salutary agnosticism to the whole institution of colonialism.

One must apply it, equally, to the individuals who came to Iboland, whether from Britain or from Sierra Leone. We have lingered over the struggles of the missionaries, whose endeavours loom large in this study. Some condemn them for their undoubted paternalism. I have chosen to emphasize their equally undoubted altruism and self-sacrifice. But in any case, their impact on Iboland was slight—a few small congregations in a handful of centres.

No generalization can be wholly true of the trading companies and the traders. Sometimes—both in the Delta and on the Niger—the main impression is one of corporate rapacity and individual brutality. But the profits of the oil trade were made in England, and the local agents, as a genre, deserve neither praise nor blame, in their efforts to wrest a livelihood from tedious work in an unhealthy country. Most of them are now forgotten, though Charles de Cardi, the author of a celebrated ethnographic monograph, and Captain Boler, who managed to win the esteem both of Mary Kingsley and the missionaries, have escaped, justly enough, from time's oblivion.

Iboland's administrators came to Africa in search of change and adventure, or in pursuit of a career they had been unable to make elsewhere. Their writings mirror their inflexible sense of caste, their incomprehension and disdain for the people they ruled—sometimes, indeed, to the point of Kipling's imagery—'half devil and half child'. But if one speaks to their collaborators from the colonial period—the policemen, clerks and school-teachers, who are now elderly pensioners—one finds, both the recognition of this sense of hierarchy, and generous admiration for their pursuit of justice, and hatred for corruption. Whatever the limitations of their outlook, it is not a bad memorial.

In 1906, the colonial experience was just beginning. It was destined to last less long than a single lifetime. To understand its true significance for Iboland, it is necessary to take the story further, and study the decades which remained until Nigeria regained her independence, in 1960. This, it is hoped, will form the subject matter of another book.

A Note on Archival Sources

London

THE PUBLIC RECORD OFFICE

Until the 1880s, the voluminous material in the relevant volumes of the series F.O. 84 is concerned mainly with the Delta, and to a lesser extent, with the Niger. Thereafter, there is more material on Iboland. From 1899, the series C.O. 444 and C.O. 520 contain much material on Ibo history.

There is much material, especially on the Royal Niger Company, which survives only in Confidential Print. Confidential Prints are cited under their Public Record Office volume numbers (F.O. 403).

The following volumes were consulted:

F.O. 84
Volumes, 775, 816, 858, 920, 950, 975, 1001, 1030, 1061, 1087, 1117, 1161, 1163, 1164, 1249, 1277, 1278, 1290, 1308, 1326, 1343, 1351, 1356, 1377, 1401, 1418, 1455, 1487, 1498, 1508, 1541, 1569, 1593, 1617, 1634, 1654, 1655, 1659, 1660, 1661, 1682, 1683, 1685, 1692, 1697, 1698, 1701, 1702, 1748, 1749, 1828, 1880, 1881, 1882, 1939, 1940, 1941, 2019, 2020, 2110, 2111, 2112, 2193, 2194.

F.O. 2
Volumes 50, 51, 62, 63, 64, 83, 84, 85, 99, 100, 101, 102, 103, 121, 122, 123, 177, 178, 179, 180.

F.O. 403
16, 18, 19, 20, 31, 32, 33, 34, 71, 72, 73, 74, 75, 76, 122, 131, 132, 133,

149, 171, 178, 187, 200, 215, 216, 217, 233, 234, 248, 249, 250, 267, 268, 269.

C.O. 444
Volumes 1, 2.

C.O. 520
Volumes 1, 2, 3, 8, 9, 10, 13, 14, 15, 16, 18, 19, 20, 24, 25, 26, 29, 30, 31, 32, 35, 36, 37, 43, 44, 45, 46, 47, 48, 49, 50.

THE CHURCH MISSIONARY SOCIETY ARCHIVES (C.M.S.)

From the foundation of the Niger Mission until 1881, outgoing letters and journals are filed under the names of individual missionaries, under the general classification CA3. The largest and most valuable series is that filed under the name of Bishop Samuel Crowther, CA3/04. Some of the material is available, with minor emendations, in printed form, in *The Church Missionary Intelligencer* and *The Church Missionary Record*.

From 1881 onwards, the entire outward correspondence of the mission is filed year by year, the letters of each year being numbered consecutively, under the general classification G3/A3. A series of Precis Books provide useful summaries, and, on occasion, the gist of a missing original.

The journal *Niger and Yoruba Notes*, begun in July 1894, and its successor (from July 1904), *Western Equatorial Africa Diocesan Magazine*, contain much valuable additional material.

Oxford

RHODES HOUSE (R.H.)

Material relevant to this study is to be found scattered through a number of manuscript collections.

(1) The archives contains a large collection of letters, memoirs, reports, etc., by colonial administrators in Africa. I consulted the files of all those who worked in Iboland, but have made little use of them in this study, because most date from a much later period.

Their practical value to historians is also lessened by the fact that many documents cannot be quoted without permission. The following are cited in this study:

MS. Afr. s. 783, Box 3, H. F. Mathews, 'Discussion of Aro Origins'.
MS. Afr. s. 697, A. F. B. Bridges, 'Report on the Oil Palm Survey'.
MS. Afr. 87, vols. 4, 10 and 18 (re Royal Niger Company).

(2) *The Lugard Papers*
These refer mainly to northern Nigeria and to East Africa. The following volumes, however, contain valuable data on the Royal Niger Company: MS. Br. Emp. s. 57, 58.

There is a little material on Southern Nigeria in MS. Br. Emp. s. 73–7.

(3) *British and Foreign Anti-Slavery Society and Aborigines Protection Society Papers*
There is some relevant material in MS. Br. Emp. s. 22 G 18.

Paris

THE ARCHIVES OF THE HOLY GHOST FATHERS (C.S.SP.)
(consulted by permission)

There is very full material on Ibo history in the sections 191/A, 191/B and 192/B, each of which comprises numerous files.

The society's own journal, *Bulletin de la Congregation*, written by hand until 1888, also contains much valuable material.

Rome

THE ARCHIVES OF THE SOCIETY OF AFRICAN MISSIONS (S.M.A.)
(consulted by permission)

The following files proved a valuable source for the history of the western Ibo (the Niger Mission was called, rather misleadingly, 'Haut Niger'):

14/80302, Letters, mainly from Head of Mission to the Superior General.

14/80303, Letters and Reports from the missionary holding the office of Visitor in the mission.

14/80404/15794, Strub, 'Le Vicariat Apostolique . . . jusqu'à nos jours' (1928).

14/80306 mainly concerns the mission's finances.

14/80307, Reports to Association de la Propagation de la Foi.

2.E.30, Pellet's journals of visits to S.M.A. missions, 1904–5.

These should be supplemented by *L'Echo des Missions Africaines de Lyon* (1902 on) and *The African Missionary* (1914 on) (Irish province). Further material on Catholic mission work can be found in the general periodicals *Annals of the Propagation of the Faith* and *Les Missions Catholiques* (English version, *Illustrated Catholic Missions*).

Ibadan

THE NATIONAL ARCHIVES (N.A.I.)

(1) *Calprof (Calabar Provincial Office papers)*
Official correspondence to and from Consuls, High Commissioners, District Officers, etc., from the 1840s to 1906. A much less complete collection than the dispatches in the Public Record Office, with their numerous enclosures. Part of the material duplicates that in the Public Record Office, in which case I quote from the Public Record Office document. There is a considerable amount of additional material in the Calprof series—e.g. correspondence with commercial firms, and neighbouring colonial jurisdictions—but it proved of little value for this study.

(2) *C.S.O. (Records of the Nigerian Secretariat, Lagos)*
A very large collection, of great value for the colonial period, but containing little that is relevant to this study. C.S.O. 1/13–16 comprises dispatches to and from the Foreign Office and Colonial Office, from this period, but is much less complete than the material in the Public Record Office. The Intelligence Reports on various Ibo groups, compiled by British District Officers in the 1930s, and filed under C.S.O. 26, proved of the greatest value for this study, both for a group's traditions of origin, and for the events of its later

history. Copies of some of these Reports are also found in the National Archives, Enugu—in which case I quote from the Ibadan version of a document. A few are also to be found elsewhere—e.g. the reports on the Aro in Rhodes House Library, Oxford. They are indexed in L. C. Gwam, 'A Preliminary Index to the Intelligence Reports in the Nigerian Secretarian Record Group' (1961).

IBADAN UNIVERSITY LIBRARY

The Fombo Papers
These comprise a typescript history of Bonny, based on oral tradition, and typed transcripts of a number of valuable documents preserved locally in Bonny and elsewhere, plus several photograph albums. The photographs are largely the work of J. A. Green of Bonny, who died in 1904, and are a most valuable record of social history.

Enugu

THE NATIONAL ARCHIVES (N.A.E.)

These also contain a number of Intelligence Reports, some of which are indexed in Mbah, 'A Preliminary Index to the Intelligence Reports in the Enugu Secretariat Record Group' (1962). Others are listed in the handlist to the Records of the Provincial Office, Onitsha. The other categories of record in these archives are valuable mainly for a later period than that covered by this book. They include the Records of the Secretariat, Enugu (C.S.E.), the Records of the Provincial Office, Onitsha, and papers from the District Offices of Awka, Udi and Okigwe. C.S.E./1/86 contains a few earlier documents.

A List of Books Cited

This is not intended as a full bibliography. It facilitates the identification of works referred to in footnotes, which, after the first reference, as listed under the author's name only (plus a contracted title in the case of several works by the one author). With one exception, it excludes the voluminous material cited from nineteenth-century periodicals and newspapers, to which each reference is given in full.

Books

Adams, John, *Remarks on the Country extending from Cape Palmas to the River Congo* (London, 1823).

Ajayi, J. F. Ade, *Christian Missions in Nigeria, 1841–1891, The Making of a New Elite* (London, 1965).

Allen, Christopher and Johnson, R. W. (eds.), *African Perspectives, Papers . . . presented to Thomas Hodgkin* (Cambridge, 1970).

Allen, William and Thomson, T. R. H., *A Narrative of the Expedition . . . to the River Niger, in 1841* (London, 1848), 2 vols.

Anene, J. C., *Southern Nigeria in Transition 1885–1906* (Cambridge, 1966).

Baikie, William Balfour, *Narrative of an Exploring Voyage up the Rivers Kwora and Binue . . . in 1854* (London, 1856).

Barbot, James, *An Abstract of a Voyage to New Calabar River . . . in the Year 1699*, in Churchill's *Voyages and Travels* (London, 1746), Vol. V.

Barbot, John, *A Description of the Coasts of North and South Guinea*, in Churchill's *Voyages and Travels* (London, 1746), Vol. V.

Bascom, William R. and Herskovits, Melville J. (eds.), *Continuity and Change in African Cultures* (Chicago, 1959).

Basden, G. T., *Among the Ibos of Nigeria* (London, 1921).

Basden, G. T., *Niger Ibos* (London, 1966, first pub. 1938).

Beier, Ulli, *African Mud Sculpture* (London, 1963).

W. Bosman, *A New and Accurate Description of the Coast of Guinea* (Eng. trans., 1705).

Bradbury, R. E., *The Benin Kingdom and the Edo-speaking Peoples of South-Western Nigeria* (Ethnographic Survey of Africa, London, 1959).

Buchanan, K. M. and Pugh, J. C., *Land and People in Nigeria* (London, 1964 reprint).

Burdo, Adolphe, *The Niger and the Benueh, Travels in Central Africa* (trans. Mrs. George Sturge, London, 1880).

[Burton, Richard], *Wanderings in West Africa by a F.R.G.S.* (London, 1853), 2 vols.

Childe, Gordon, *What Happened in History* (Harmondsworth, first pub. 1942).

Cole William, *Life on the Niger, or The Journal of an African Trader* (London, 1862).

Coleman, James, *Nigeria Background to Nationalism* (Berkeley, 1965 reprint).

Clarkson, Thomas, *The Substance of the Evidence of Sundry Persons on the Slave Trade* (London, 1789).

Crocker, W. A., *Nigeria, A Critique of British Colonial Administration* (London, 1936).

Crow, Hugh, *Memoirs of Captain Hugh Crow* (London, 1830).

Crowther, Samuel, *Journal of an Expedition up the Niger and Tshadda Rivers . . . in 1854* (London, 1855).

Crowther, Samuel, and Taylor, John Christopher, *The Gospel on the Banks of the Niger. Journals and Notices of the Native Missionaries accompanying the Niger Expedition of 1857–1859* (London, 1859).

Curtin, Philip D., *Africa Remembered: Narratives by West Africans from the Era of the Slave Trade* (Wisconsin, 1967).

Curtin, Philip D., *The Atlantic Slave Trade, A Census* (Wisconsin, 1969).

O. Dapper, *Description de l'Afrique* (French trans., Amsterdam, 1786).

Davidson, Basil, *Black Mother, Africa the Years of Trial* (London, 1961).

Davies, K. G., *The Royal African Company* (London, 1957).

Davies, Oliver, *West Africa before the Europeans: Archaeology and Prehistory* (London, 1967).

Dike, K. Onwuka, *Trade and Politics in the Niger Delta, 1830–1885* (Oxford, 1956).

Dobinson, H. H., *Letters of Henry Hughes Dobinson* (London, 1899).

Donnan, Elizabeth, *Documents Illustrative of the History of the Slave Trade to America* (Washington, 1930–35), 4 vols.

[Douglas, A. C.], *Niger Memories* (printed privately and anonymously, n.d.).

Egharevba, Jacob O., *A Short History of Benin* (Lagos, 1936).

Equiano, Olaudah, *The Interesting Narrative of the Life of Olaudah Equiano* (abridged and ed. Paul Edwards, London, 1967).

Fage, J. D. and Oliver, R. A. (eds.), *Papers in African Prehistory* (Cambridge, 1970).

Fagg, William, and Plass, Margaret, *African Sculpture* (revised ed., London, 1966).

Flint, J. E., *Sir George Goldie and the Making of Nigeria* (London, 1960).

Floyd, Barry, *Eastern Nigeria, A Geographical Review* (London, 1969).

Forde, Daryll, and Jones, G. I., *The Ibo and Ibibio-speaking Peoples of South-Eastern Nigeria* (Ethnographic Survey of Africa, London, first pub. 1950).

Fox, A. J., *Uzuakoli, A Short History* (London, 1964).

Gann, L. H. and Duignan, Peter, *Burden of Empire, An Assessment of Western Colonialism South of the Sahara* (London, 1967).

The Gospel on the Banks of the Niger, III, Journals and Notices of the Native Missionaries on the River Niger, 1863 (London, 1864).

Harcourt, H. N., *Report of the Inquiry into Oguta Chieftaincy Dispute* (Nigeria, Official Document no. 19 of 1961).

Harding, R. W., *Report of the Commission of Inquiry into the Dispute over the Obiship of Onitsha* (Enugu, 1963).

Harris, John H., *Dawn in Darkest Africa* (first pub. 1912, reprinted London, 1968).

Hastings, A. C. G., *Nigerian Days* (London, 1925).

Hives, Frank, and Lumley, Gascoigne, *Ju Ju and Justice in Nigeria* (Harmondsworth, 1940).

Hodgkin, Thomas, *Nigerian Perspectives, An Historical Anthology* (London, 1960).

Hubbard, John Waddington, *The Sobo of the Niger Delta* (Zaria, 1948).

Hutchinson, T. J., *Impressions of West Africa* (London, 1858).

Ikime, Obaro, *Niger Delta Rivalry, Itsekiri–Urhobo Relations and the European Presence 1884–1936* (London, 1969).

Jones, G. I., *Report on the Status of Chiefs* (Enugu, 1958).

Jones, G. I., *The Trading States of the Oil Rivers* (London, first pub. 1963).

Kalu, Eke, *Autobiography of an Illustrious Son, Chief Eke Kalu of Elu Ohafia, Owerri Province* (Lagos, 1954).

Kingsley, Mary, *West African Studies* (London, 1899).

Koelle, S. W., *Polyglotta Africana* (London, 1854).

Köler, Hermann, *Einige Notizen über Bonny* (Göttingen, 1848).

Laird, MacGregor, and Oldfield, R. A. K., *Narrative of an Expedition into the Interior of Africa by the River Niger* (London, 1837), 2 vols.

'Langa Langa', *Up Against it in Nigeria* (London, 1922).

Leonard, A. G., *The Lower Niger and its Tribes* (London, 1906).

McPhee, Alan, *The Economic Revolution in British West Africa* (London, 1926).

Meek, C. K., *Law and Authority in a Nigerian Tribe* (London, 1937).

Mockler-Ferryman, A. F., *Up the Niger* (London, 1892).

Morel, E. D., *Nigeria, Its Peoples and its Problems* (first pub. 1911, 3rd edn., London, 1968).

Nduka, Otonti, *Western Education and the Nigerian Cultural Background* (Ibadan, 1964).

Ojike, Mbonu, *My Africa* (New York, 1946).

Okafor-Omali, Dilim, *A Nigerian Villager in Two Worlds* (London, 1965).

Pereira, Duarte Pacheco, *Esmeraldo de Situ Orbis* (trans. and ed. George H. T. Kimble, Hakluyt Society, 2nd series, LXXIX, 1937).

Perham, Margery, *Lugard, The Years of Adventure 1858–1898* (London, 1956).

Perham, Margery, *Lugard, The Years of Authority 1898–1945* (London, 1960).

Perham, Margery, *Native Administration in Nigeria* (London, 1962 reprint).

Report of the Lords of the Committe of Council concerning the present state of the Trade to Africa and particularly the Trade in Slaves (1789).

Ryder, A. F. C., *Benin and the Europeans* (London, 1969).

Schön, James Frederick, and Crowther, Samuel, *Journals of the Rev. James Frederick Schön and Mr Samuel Crowther who accompanied the Expedition up the Niger in 1841* (London, 1842).

Shaw, Thurstan, *Igbo Ukwu, An Account of Archaeological Discoveries in Eastern Nigeria* (London, 1970), 2 vols.

Shinnie, P. L. (ed.), *The African Iron Age* (Oxford, 1971).

Smith, William, *A New Voyage to Guinea* (London, 1744).

Somerset, R. F., *Diary of Captain the Hon. Richard Fitzroy Somerset, Feb. 5 1898–Feb. 19 1899* (privately printed).

Talbot, P. Amaury, *The Peoples of Southern Nigeria*, Vol. I (London, 1926).

Thomas, Northcote W., *Anthropological Report on the Ibo-Speaking Peoples of Nigeria, Part I, Law and Custom of the Ibo of the Awka Neighbourhood* (London, 1913).

Thomas, Northcote W., *Ibid.*, *Part IV, Law and Custom of the Ibo of the Asaba District* (London, 1914).

Waddell, Hope Masterton, *Twenty-Nine Years in the West Indies and Central Africa* (London, 1863).

Webster, James Bertin, *The African Churches among the Yoruba 1888–1922* (Oxford, 1964).

Whitford, John, *Trading Life in Western and Central Africa* (Liverpool, 1877).

Wilson, Charles, *The History of Unilever, A Study in Economic Growth and Social Change* (London, 1954), Vol. I.

Articles

Ajayi, J. F. Ade, 'The Colonial Episode', in L. H. Gann and Peter Duignan, *Colonialism in Africa*, Vol. I, *The History and Politics of Colonialism 1870–1914* (Cambridge, 1969).

Anon., 'Inside Arochuku', *The Nigeria Magazine* (1957), no. 53, pp. 100 ff.

Anon., 'Forty Years of UAC', *West Africa* (26 April 1969).

Azikiwe, Ben. N., 'Fragments of Onitsha History', *The Journal of Negro History* (1930), XV.

Boston, J. S., 'Notes on Contact between the Igala and the Ibo', *Journal of the Historical Society of Nigeria* (1960), II, no. 1.

Bradbury, R. E., 'Chronological Problems in the Study of Benin History', *Journal of the Historical Society of Nigeria* (1959), I, no. 4.

Bradbury, R. E., 'The Historical Uses of Comparative Ethnography with special reference to Benin and the Yoruba', in Jan Vansina, Raymond Mauny and L. V. Thomas (eds.), *The Historian in Tropical Africa* (London, 1964).

Cole, Herbert M., 'Mbari is Life', *African Arts/Arts d'Afrique* (Spring 1969).

Cudjoe, Robert, 'Some Reminiscences of a Senior Interpreter', *The Nigerian Field* (1953).

Easterfield, Mary, and Uku, E. K., 'Seeds in the Palm of your Hand', *West African Review* (December 1952–March 1953).

Ekejiuba, F., 'Omu Okwei, The Merchant Queen of Ossomari, A Biographical Sketch', *Journal of the Historical Society of Nigeria* (June 1967).

Ekejiuba, F., 'Preliminary notes on Brasswork of Eastern Nigeria', *African Notes* (1967), IV, no. 2.

Hartle, D., 'Archaeology in Eastern Nigeria', *The West African Archaeological Newsletter* (1966), no. 5.

Hartle, D., 'Bronze Objects from Ezira, Eastern Nigeria', *The West African Archaeological Newsletter* (1966), no. 4.

Horton, Robin, 'African Conversion', *Africa* (April 1971).

Horton, Robin, 'From Fishing Village to City-State, A Social History of New Calabar', in Mary Douglas and Phyllis M. Kaberry (eds.), *Man in Africa* (London, 1969).

Horton, Robin, 'A Note on Recent Finds of Brasswork in the Niger Delta', *Odu* (1965), II.

Horton, W. R. G., 'The Ohu System of Slavery in a Northern Ibo Village-Group', *Africa* (1954), XXIV.

Isichei, Elizabeth, 'Historical Change in an Ibo Polity: Asaba to 1885', *Journal of African History* (1969), X, no. 3.

Isichei, Elizabeth, 'Seven Varieties of Ambiguity: Some Patterns of Ibo Response to Christian Missions', *The Journal of Religion in Africa* (1970), III, no. 3.

Jeffries, M. D. W., 'The Umundri Tradition of Origin', *African Studies* (1956), XV.

Johnson, Marion, 'The Cowrie Currencies of West Africa, Part II', *The Journal of African History* (1970), XI, no. 3.

Jones, G. I., 'Ecology and Social Structure among the North Eastern Ibo', *Africa* (1961), XXXI.

Jones, G. I., 'Who are the Aro?', *The Nigerian Field*, 1939.

Nzekwu, Onuora, 'Gloria Ibo', *Nigeria Magazine* (1960).

Ottenberg, Simon, 'Ibo Oracles and Intergroup Relations', *Southwestern Journal of Anthropology* (1958), XIV.

Ryder, A. F. C., 'Dutch Trade on the Nigerian Coast during the seventeenth century', *Journal of the Historical Society of Nigeria* (1965), III, no. 2.

Shinnie, P. L., 'Meroe and West Africa', *The West Africa Archaeological Newsletter* (1966), no. 5.

Smith, Abdullahi, 'Some considerations relating to the formation of states in Hausaland', *Journal of the Historical Society of Nigeria* (December 1970).

Steel, E. A., 'Exploration in Southern Nigeria', *Journal of the Royal United Services Institution* (April 1910).

Ukwu, Ukwu I., 'The Development of Trade and Marketing in Iboland', *Journal of the Historical Society of Nigeria* (1967), III, no. 4.

Theses

Hopkins, Antony Gerald, 'An Economic History of Lagos 1880–1914' (London Ph.D. thesis, 1964).

Ifemesia, C. C., 'British Enterprise on the Niger 1830–1869' (London Ph.D. thesis, 1959).

Jeffries, M. D. W., 'The Divine Umundri Kings of Igboland' (London Ph.D. thesis, 1934).

Nzimiro, Ikenna, 'Chieftaincy and Politics in Four Niger States' (Cambridge Ph.D. thesis, 1966).

Smith, S. R., 'The Ibo People' (Cambridge Ph.D. thesis, 1929).

Index

Aba, 170
Abaja, 37, 50, 77, 111
Abam, 35, 52, 72, 79, 158
Abarra, 65
Abiriba, 24, 137
Aboh, 28 (n. 2), 73, 74, 96, 108, 117; in 1830s, 31; periodic flooding, 37; traditions of origin, 39–42; 1841 Niger expedition, 66; economic decline, 72, 106; Chief Opia, 107; sacked 1883, 110
Abraka, 138
Achebe, Chinua, 58–9, 181
Ada, 27, 34, 79
Adams, Captain John, 46, 52
Afenmai, 139, 152, 176
Afikpo, 21, 68, 75 (n. 2)
African agency in colonial government, 126–7, 154, 160 ff.; in Niger trade, 97, 99; in Royal Niger Company, 115; in missions, 88–9, 91 ff., 145, 150; in Aro campaign, 132
African Association, the, 168
African Missions, Society of, and Royal Niger Company, 114; established on Niger, 144, 147; organization and recruitment, 148; poverty, 148–9; leadership, 149; catechists, 150; philanthropy, 150; expansion, 151–3; education, 155–6
Afro-Americans, 17
Agbala (Awka oracle), 78
Agberi, 108
Agbor, 164
Agriculture, invention of, 20, 30

agriculture, among Ibo, 18, 76
Aguleri, career of Idigo, 107, 151–2; sacked by Royal Niger Company, 118; Catholic mission in, 148
Ahiara, 137–8
Akassa, 63
'Akpa' (in Aro traditions of origin), 34
Akra (first inhabitants of Aboh), 40
Akubeze, Jacob, 152
Akumenyis (ancestor of Ezza, Ikwo and Izi), 36
Akwete, 129, 133
Ala (divine Earth), 26, 30, 81
Alenso, 102; C.M.S. station and school, 96, 104 (n. 5), 106 (n. 1), 178; attacks trading post, 109
Amagunze, 37
Amakwam confederation, 72
America, 17, 44, 45
Ammaikunno (Brass chief), 90
Anam, 43, 116
Anambra River, and valley, 30, 37, 38, 152
Anazonwu (Obi of Onitsha), 41
Andoni, 53
Anyegbunam, Rev. George Nicholas, 178
archaeology, 18–25
armed forces, Royal Niger Company, 115; Niger Coast Protectorate, 127; Aro campaign, 132
Aro, Arochuku, 17, 48, 52, 76, 111, 170; traditions of origin, 33–5; oracle, 35–6, 78–9; Aro expedition, 131–4, 137
Asaba, 31, 37, 62, 72, 90; foundation,

Asaba—*cont.*
45; political change in, 56; human sacrifice in, 58; farms, 76; missions in, 96, 102, 146, 147, 152, 154; first school in, 106 (n. 1); Obi Igweli, 107; and European traders, 109; and Royal Niger Company, 115, 116, 118, 119; and Ekumeku, 140

Ashaka, 40

Association for the Propagation of the Faith, 148

Atani, 96, 131, 146; foundation, 40; and United African Company, 109

Atoridibo (of Okrika), 88–9

Awka, 31, 75, 79, 169; blacksmiths, 30, 42–3, 77–8, 111; and C.M.S., 153

Badagry, 90

Baikie, Dr. William Balfour, 90

Barbot, James and John, 46, 47, 50, 51, 53

Basden, Rev. George T., 55, 59, 145

Bassey, Coco (Efik chief), 176–7

Bende, 68, 75, 137

Benin, 24, 38–42, 44, 47, 50 (n. 5), 57–8, 175

Boler, Captain (British trader), 184

Bonny, 17, 54, 65, 81, 87–9, 128, 129, 130; traditions of origin, 32–3, 34; and slave trade, 46, 47–8, 50, 53, 57, 63–6; firearms, 52; plantation agriculture, 64; and palm oil trade, 73–4; and C.M.S., 88, 103, 106

Bonny, Christian mission work by Bonny traders, 74, 88–9, 102–3

Brass, 90; slavery and slave trade, 62, 63, 65; and Royal Niger Company, 73, 115, 117, 120; and C.M.S., 88–9, 156

brass, *see* bronzes

bronzes, Igbo-Ukwu, 22 ff.; Lower Niger bronze industry, 23; Nupe, 23; in Delta, 23–4; 'Sao', 24; Ife, 24; Benin, 24; Ezira, 25; Ibrede, 25

Brooke, Graham Wilmot, 95

Buck, Rev. John, 73 (n. 5)

Bussa, 90

Calabar (*see also* Efik), slave trade and slavery, 46, 64–5; seventeenth-century imports, 50; seventeenth-century currency, 51; eighteenth-century schools, 53; requests technical aid, 54; Presbyterian mission in, 83, 145; C.M.S. visits in 1853, 91; Consul-General's headquarters, 129; Ekumeku leaders imprisoned in, 140–1; Holy Ghost Fathers' mission in, 152

Campbell, Kenneth (British official), 128

cannibalism, attributed to unfamiliar peoples, 81

canoes, 33, 37, 40, 47, 51–2

Casement, Roger (British official), 128

Catholic missions, *see* African Missions, Society of, and Holy Ghost, Congregation of

Childe, Gordon, 21

Chima (led migration from Benin), 39

Church Missionary Society, 181; in Delta, 88–9, 102–7, 111; establishment and organization, 91; comes to the Niger, 91; personnel, 93; conditions of service, 94; impact on Niger peoples, 101 ff.; relations with Royal Niger Company, 113–114; in 1890s, 144–7; and education, 105–6, 153–6

colonial government, *see* Protectorate, British

consuls, British, 86, 124–6

copper, 50; *see also* bronzes

cotton growing, on Niger, 97

Court Clerks, 162

Court Messengers, 163

cowries, 51, 172

Crewe Read (British official), 164

Cross River, 17, 111; trade on, 74, 83; Coco Bassey, and, 177; military expeditions on, 129, 136–7

Crowther, Archdeacon Dandeson C., 105

Crowther, Josiah, 97, 101, 105

Crowther, Bishop Samuel Ajayi, 91 ff., 99, 120, 147

currencies, traditional Ibo, 51, 172–3

Curtin, Professor Philip D., 44 (n. 3)

de Cardi, Charles (nineteenth-century trader), 49, 184

Delta, *see* Niger Delta

Dennis, Archdeacon T. J., 145

Dennis Memorial Grammar School, 156

Dike, Professor K. O., 48
Dobinson, Archdeacon Henry Hughes, 95, 144, 145
Duke Ephraim (of Calabar), 53
Dunkwu Isusu (Eknmeku leader), 142

Easton, Acting Consul, 110
education, western, among Ibo, 105–6, 153–6, 162–3, 165–6, 176–81
Efik (*see also* Calabar), 53, 54, 63, 81, 176
Egbola, Joseph O. (C.M.S. agent), 145–6
Egerton, Sir Walter, 157–8, 160, 171–2, 179
Egga, 96
Eha Amufu, 37
Ekumeku, 139–42, 162
Elele, 128, 134
Elugu, 77, 79, 111
Enyong Creek, 172
Equiano, Olaudah, 39, 48–9
Eroa (founder of Oguta), 42
Esigie (Benin Oba), 40
Esmeraldo de Situ Orbis, 32–3
Esumai (led migration to Aboh), 39, 40 (n. 7)
European knowledge of Iboland, 19, 86, 128, 136
Ewafa, 73, 87
Ewuare (Benin Oba), 39
expeditions to the Niger, 90–1
Ezira, 25
Ezza, 176; origins and expansion, 27, 36–7; trade links, 75 (n. 2); yam cultivation, 76; resistance to colonial rule, 137
Ezza-Agu, 36
Ezza-Effium, 36

Fagg, William, 23, 24
Fernando Po, 87, 92
firearms, 34–5, 51–2; destruction of, in Aro campaign, 133
Flint, Joseph (Royal Niger Company Agent General), 114
Fosbery, Widenham (British official), 138
Fourah Bay College, 93

Gbunwala (Benin general), 39 (n. 4), 42
glottochronology, 20

Gold Coast, export of slaves to, 44; workers and soldiers from, 115, 127, 162; Ja Ja exiled to, 125
Goldie, Sir George, 99, 113–16, 119
Granville, Earl, 123

Harper, Captain (head of Royal Niger Company Constabulary), 119
Hart, Joshua, 103
Hausas, Hausaland, 115, 127
Hewett, Edward Hyde (British consul), 87, 124
Holy Ghost, Congregation of the, relations with Royal Niger Company, 114, 117; begins work in Iboland, 144, 147; organization and recruitment, 148; poverty, 148–9; leadership, 149–50; catechists, 150; philanthropy, 150; stations and expansion, 151–3; education, 155
horses, in Iboland, 75
Horton, Robin, 23
house construction, in Iboland, 77
human sacrifice, 47, 54, 56–8, 63, 82, 104, 119, 158–9
Hutchinson, T. J. (British consul), 53

Ibaa, 130
Ibibio, 17, 34–5, 46, 74, 83, 131, 132, 134
Ibo, Iboland, geographical environment, 17–18; diaspora, 17–18; and Delta, 17, 18, 32–3, Chs. 3 and 4 *passim*, 72–4, 78–9, 87–9, 129; prehistory, 18, 19 ff.; oral traditions, 19, 27–43; political institutions, 19, 29, 47, 56–7, 71–2; population density, 20, 59; migrations, geographic mobility, 19–20, 27–43; language, 19–20, 71; religion, 22–5, 80–1, 104–5, 179–81; metal working, 22–5, 30, 77–8; sculpture, 22–6, 80; internal wars, 29, 36–7, 49, 79–80; oracles, 34–6, 78–9; relations with Benin, 38–42, 44; relations with Igala, 23, 29–31, 72–3; relations with Ibibio, 17, 33–5; trade routes and markets, 35, 38, 72–6; and slave trade, 38, 44–60, 61–2; domestic slavery and internal slave trade, 23, 34, 39, 62 ff., 75, 119, 129, 150, 159; and palm oil trade, 66–70, 97–

Ibo, Iboland—*cont.*
100, 107–11, Ch. 8 *passim*, 168–9;
land use and agriculture, 18, 76;
town planning, 77; textile production, 77; pottery production, 22, 78;
attitude to Europeans, 81–2, 100,
111–12, 121; Christian missions
among, 88–9, 90–6, 101–6, 144–56,
179 ff.; spread of European rule
among, 87, 113 ff., 123–43; and
Royal Niger Company, 73, Ch. 8
passim, 140; and western education,
105–6, 153–6, 162–3, 165–6, 176–81;
impact of colonialism on, 157–81;
Warrant Chiefs and Indirect Rule
among, 160–2
Ibrede, 25
Ibusa, 43
Idah, 23, 29, 42, 72
Idigo (king of Aguleri), 107, 151
Idoma, 75 (n. 2)
Idumuje-Ugboko, 77
Ife, 24, 25
Igala, 17, 38, 42; bronzes, 23; and Nri
and Umueri, 29; military expeditions
to northern Iboland, 36; on lower
Niger, 31, 72; trade at Ogurugu, 75
(n. 2); at Onitsha, 104; Attah
comments on European impact on
lower Niger, 111
Igara Bank (near Asaba), 62
Igbo-Ukwu, archaeological discoveries
at, 22–5, 30, 57–8
Igweli (Asaba chief), 107
Ihe, 35
Ijo, 32
Ijonnema, 138
Ikwerri, 132
Ikwo, 27, 36, 137, 139
Illah, 31, 43
Imo River, 74, 89, 129, 172
imports to Iboland, 50–1, 168–9
India, 23, 50
iron, ironworking, 21, 22, 25, 30, 42–3,
50, 77–8, 111
Ishan, 17, 107, 140
Isiokpo, 51 (n. 3)
Issele-Uku, 140, 175
Isuama, 31, 65, 111
Itsekiri, 128
ivory, 23, 44, 48, 50, 75
Izi, 36

Ja Ja, 64, 74, 124–5
Jephson, Sir Alfred, 127
Johnson, Archdeacon Henry, 95
Johnston, H. H. (Acting Consul), 124–125

Kalabari, 32, 46, 47, 48, 73, 128
Kalu, Eke (of Elu Ohafia), 162–3
Kamalu (king of Bonny), 34
Kemball, Colonel (quoted), 137
kidnapping, in Iboland, 48–9, 55
Kimberley, Earl of, 123
Kingsley, Mary, 184
Koelle, Rev. S. W., 49
kola nuts, 23
Köler, Hermann, 52
Kontagora, Emir of (quoted), 83
Kwale, 138, 139

Lagos, 106, 171, 178
Laird, MacGregor, 96
Lander, Richard and John, 38, 83, 90,
108
Lejeune, Rev. Léon, 149, 155
Leonard, Major A. G., 41, 163
Lever, William, 174
Liberia, 115
linguistics, relevance to Ibo history,
19–20
Lokoja, 90, 147, 152
Lugard, Sir Frederick, 113
Lutz, Rev. Joseph, 149

MacDonald, Sir Claude, 126–8
McIntosh, David (United African
Company Chief Agent), 109, 114
Mali, 23
Manchester, 50, 91
markets, in Iboland, 35, 72–6
Marshall, Sir James (Royal Niger
Company Chief Justice), 119, 147
Mba, Isaac Okechukwu, 93, 106, 178
mbari houses, 80
Miller Brothers, 168
Moor, Sir Ralph, 128–31, 157, 167,
169, 171, 173
Morel, E. D., 69

Nana, 128
Native Courts, 141, 160–3
Ndelli, 76, 89   H

Ndienyi, 35 (n. 4)
Ndizuogu, 35 (n. 4)
Ndokki, 27, 32, 75
Ndoni, 96, 109
Nembe, 62, 63 (*see also* Brass)
New Calabar, *see* Kalabari
New Calabar River, 75
Ngwa, 27, 31, 132
Niger Coast Protectorate, *see* Protectorate, British
Niger Delta (*see also* Bonny, Calabar, Kalabari, Brass and Okrika), natural features, 18; European traders and, 19, Chs. 3 and 4 *passim*, 86–8, 125–6; bronzes discovered in, 23–4; traditions of origin, 31–3; and Iboland, 17, 18, 32–3, Chs. 3 and 4 *passim*, 72–4, 78–9, 87–9, 129; impact of slave trade on, 38, 43, Ch. 3 *passim*, especially pp. 52–5, 57; slavery in, 63–5; development of palm oil trade in, 66 ff.; British consuls in, 86; Christian mission work, 88–9, 96, 102–3; British administration in, 123 ff., 176–7; education in, 53, 102, 106, 153–4; twentieth-century decline, 170
Niger Delta Pastorate, 144, 156
Niger Mission, *see* Church Missionary Society
Niger, River, 17, 18, 23, 27, 31, 37 ff., 62, 72–3, 83, 87, 89–111; European traders on, 96–9, 107–11; and Royal Niger Company, 113 ff.
Nike, 62
Nok culture, 21
Nri, Eze Nri, 23, 29–30, 43, 57, 58, 79, 111
Nsube, 111
Nsukka, 21, 27, 30, 37
Nteje, 43
Nupe, 23, 112
Nwadiaju (Ekumeku leader), 142
Nwaokobia, Jacob (Catholic catechist), 149 (n. 1)
Nzimiro, Dr. Ikenna, 40

Obosi, 103–4, 118–19, 146
Ogidi, 40
Ogurugu, 17, 30, 75 (n. 2)
Oguta, origins, 42; relations with Kalabari, 73; a description of, 76;

and Royal Niger Company, 117; and Aro, 131; advent of Catholic mission to, 152
Ogwashi-Oku, 43, 141
Ogwezi (led migration to Aboh), 40 (n. 7)
Ogwuara (founded Oguta), 42
Ohafia, 35, 79, 162–3
Ohumbele, 68, 87–8
Oil Rivers Protectorate, *see* Protectorate, British
Oko, 31, 109
Oko Epelle (of Bonny), 64
Okosi, Samuel (Obi of Onitsha), 177
Okpanam, 140
Okpo-mbu-tolu, 51 (n. 3)
Okrika, 128; and Ibo language, 63; and palm oil trade, 74; establishment of Christianity in, 88–9, 102–3; resists British rule, 130
Old Calabar, *see* Calabar
Onicha Olona, 142, 161
Onitsha, 22, 37, 62, 68, 72, 77, 89, 111; origins, 39–43; and C.M.S., 91–2, 96, 102–3, 146, 152–3; and Holy Ghost Fathers, 147, 148, 152–3; rise of Onitsha Wharf, 106; impact of trade on, 107–8; sack of, in 1879, 109–10; blockaded by Royal Niger Company, 117–18; improvement association, 179
Onoja Oboni (Igala warrior), 30
Opia (Aboh chief), 107
Opobo, 64, 125, 129
Opobo (King of Bonny), 32
oracles, 34–6, 78–9
oral traditions, in Ibo history, 18–19, Ch. 2 *passim*
Oreze (led migration to Onitsha), 39
Orlu, 31
Osomari, 37; origins, 31, 38; slaves around, 63; and C.M.S., 96, 102, 104, 106 (n. 1); attacks trading post, 109; accepts Catholicism, 152
Ossai (Obi of Aboh), 41, 66, 102
Ossissa, 40
osu (cult slavery), 58–9, 82
Otamiri River, 172
Owerri, 137, 154; population density, 20; mbari houses, 80; first visited by British, 132; roadmaking around, 164; colonial impact, 170

Owerrinta, 71
Oze (first inhabitants of Onitsha), 39
Ozolua (Benin Oba), 40

palm oil trade, 37, 61, 88–9, 112; development of, 66; uses of palm oil, 66–7; geographic limitations, 67–8; methods of extraction, 68–9; markets and routes, 72–3; on Niger, 96–9, 108–10, 113 ff.; and giant combines, 168–9; in twentieth century, 170–1
Perekule (King of Bonny), 55
Perham, Dame Margery, quoted, 17
population density, 20, 29, 59
Port Harcourt, 137
Portuguese, in Delta, 44–5
pottery, Ogbo-Ukwu, 22 ff.; in nineteenth-century Iboland, 78
Presbyterian mission, Calabar, 83, 145
Protectorate, British (successively named Oil Rivers Protectorate, 1891–3, Niger Coast Protectorate, 1893–9, Protectorate of Southern Nigeria, 1900–6), 83 (n. 2); protectorate established, 124; treaties, 124; and Ja Ja, 124–5; MacDonald Reports, 126; Oil Rivers Protectorate under MacDonald, 126–7; personnel, 126–7, 158, 159–60; under Moor, 128 ff.; military expansion, 128–43; Aro campaign, 130–4; and Ekumeku, 139–42; limits of power, 130, 136, 157–8; and missions and education, 153–6, 165–166; policy re slavery, 159; Indirect Rule and Warrant Chiefs, 160–3; forced labour, 164; improves communications, 164–5, 171–2; reforms currency, 172–3; refuses land concessions to expatriate firms, 173–4; assessment, 184–5

Rabba, 90, 92
Radillo, Augustine Chukwuma, 92
religion, traditional Ibo, 24, 25, 80–1, 104–5, 179–80, 181
resistance, Ibo, to colonial rule, 108–110, 117–19, 129–43
river transport, 37, 68, 72–4, 172
Royal African Company, 45–6
Royal Niger Company, 123–4; at Oguta, 73; receives Charter, 83, 83 (n. 2); amalgamations, 99, 108; why given Charter, 113; different views of, 114; personnel, 114–15; African agency, 114–15; army, 115; economic effects of monopoly, 116–117; military action, 117–19; failure to develop Niger, 119–20; brutality, 120; and Ekumeku, 140

Sahara, 21, 22, 23, 44–5
Salisbury, Marquis of, 125
salt manufacture, 33, 50
Samuel, Thomas (C.M.S. catechist), 92
San Thomé, 44–5
Sapele, 138
schools, *see* education
sculpture, in wood, 25; in unbaked clay, 25–6; *see also* bronzes
secret societies, 57, 105
Selborne Committee, 171
Shanahan, Bishop Joseph, 149
Sierra Leone, Sierra Leonians, 106; Ibos in, 17; Koelle's informants, 49; and Niger Mission, 88–9, 91–5, 104; trade on Niger, 97–99; at Onitsha, 103; employed by Royal Niger Company, 115; employed by colonial government, 162
Simon Jonas, 92
slave trade, trans-Atlantic, 17; impact on Delta, 38, 45, 52 ff.; impact on Iboland, 38, 43, 44 ff., 55 ff., 82; statistics, 45–6; source of slaves, 48–50; goods imported in return, 50–2; abolition of, 61–2, 65–6
slaves, slavery (*see also* human sacrifice, osu); at Igbo-Ukwu, 23, 57; in Aro tradition, 34; in traditions re migrations from Benin, 39; expansion of, in nineteenth century, 62–3; in Delta, 53, 63–5; at Asaba, 58, 119, 146, 150; at Osomari, 63; slave trading routes, 74; raiding for, in 1890s, 129; and British rule, 159; and missions, 89, 91, 92, 103, 104, 146, 150
slave risings, 65
Smith, Adam, quoted, 113
Smith, Rev. Sidney, 145
Smith, William, quoted, 44
Society of African Missions, *see* African Missions, Society of

Sombreiro River, 76, 172
Southern Nigeria, Protectorate of, *see* Protectorate, British
Spencer, Rev. Julius, 145
spirits, 51–2
stone tools, 21
Strub, Rev. 139, 140

Takkeda, 23
Taylor, Rev. John Christopher, 92
textiles, imported, 50, 52; made in Iboland, 77
Thaddeus (Catholic catechist), 150
title taking, among Ibo, 56–8, 104–5
town planning, in Iboland, 77; military defences, 79
trade routes, in Iboland, 72–6
traders, European, on the Niger, 96 ff., 113 ff.; conflict with Niger states, 108 ff., 117 ff.; in the Delta, 86 ff., 124–6; on the Cross River, 83 ff., 125–6; (*see also* slave trade, palm oil trade)
Tugwell, Bishop Herbert, 145
Turner, Alfred (British official), 157
twins, abandoning of, 105

Ubele, 134
Ubuechi, Alexander (of Issele-Uku), 179–80
Ubulu, 76, 141

Udi, 27, 30, 37, 164
Udogwu (Obi of Onitsha), 41
Uku, E. K. (of Arochuku), 179
Umueri, 29–30, 43
United African Company, 99, 109, 110
Urhobo, 46, 138
Utoto, 35
Uzuakoli, 62, 68

Voltair, François-Marie Arouet de, quoted, 27

Waddell, Rev. Hope Masterton, 111
war, between Ibo and Europeans, 108–110, 117–18, 128–43; between Ibo groups, 29, 36–7, 49, 79–80
Warner, Edith, 156
Warrant Chiefs, 160–2, 177
Warri, 50 (n. 5)
West African Company, 97
Whydah, 45
Will Braid, 73
Williams, Professor Eric, 61
witchcraft, 81, 105, 185
women's riots of 1929, 71, 142

yam cultivation, 75–6
Ybou, Caterina, 45
Yoruba, Yorubaland, 20, 115, 127

Zappa, Rev. Carlo, 147, 149–50, 155